797,885 Books

are available to read at

www.ForgottenBooks.com

Forgotten Books' App
Available for mobile, tablet & eReader

ISBN 978-1-332-88568-8
PIBN 10423539

This book is a reproduction of an important historical work. Forgotten Books uses
state-of-the-art technology to digitally reconstruct the work, preserving the original format
whilst repairing imperfections present in the aged copy. In rare cases, an imperfection in
the original, such as a blemish or missing page, may be replicated in our edition. We do,
however, repair the vast majority of imperfections successfully; any imperfections that
remain are intentionally left to preserve the state of such historical works.

Forgotten Books is a registered trademark of FB &c Ltd.
Copyright © 2015 FB &c Ltd.
FB &c Ltd, Dalton House, 60 Windsor Avenue, London, SW19 2RR.
Company number 08720141. Registered in England and Wales.

For support please visit www.forgottenbooks.com

1 MONTH OF
FREE
READING

at
www.ForgottenBooks.com

By purchasing this book you are eligible for one month membership to ForgottenBooks.com, giving you unlimited access to our entire collection of over 700,000 titles via our web site and mobile apps.

To claim your free month visit:
www.forgottenbooks.com/free423539

* Offer is valid for 45 days from date of purchase. Terms and conditions apply.

English
Français
Deutsche
Italiano
Español
Português

www.forgottenbooks.com

Mythology Photography **Fiction**
Fishing Christianity **Art** Cooking
Essays Buddhism Freemasonry
Medicine **Biology** Music **Ancient
Egypt** Evolution Carpentry Physics
Dance Geology **Mathematics** Fitness
Shakespeare **Folklore** Yoga Marketing
Confidence Immortality Biographies
Poetry **Psychology** Witchcraft
Electronics Chemistry History **Law**
Accounting **Philosophy** Anthropology
Alchemy Drama Quantum Mechanics
Atheism Sexual Health **Ancient History**
Entrepreneurship Languages Sport
Paleontology Needlework Islam
Metaphysics Investment Archaeology
Parenting Statistics Criminology
Motivational

THE

DOCTRINE OF EQUITY.

COMMENTARY ON THE LAW

AS ADMINISTERED BY

The Court of Chancery.

BY

JOHN ADAMS, Jun., Esq.,

BARRISTER AT LAW.

Sixth American Edition.

CONTAINING THE NOTES TO THE PREVIOUS EDITIONS OF

J. R. LUDLOW, J. M. COLLINS, HENRY WHARTON AND
GEO. TUCKER BISPHAM.

WITH

ADDITIONAL NOTES AND REFERENCES TO RECENT ENGLISH AND
AMERICAN DECISIONS,

BY

GEORGE SHARSWOOD, Jr.

———

PHILADELPHIA:

T. & J. W. JOHNSON & CO.,

LAW BOOKSELLERS, PUBLISHERS AND IMPORTERS,

535 CHESTNUT STREET.

1873.

347.8
Ad 6

Entered, according to Act of Congress, in the year 1873,

BY T. & J. W. JOHNSON & CO.,

In the Office of the Librarian of Congress, at Washington.

———————

Entered, according to Act of Congress, in the year 1868,

BY T. & J. W. JOHNSON & CO.,

In the Clerk's Office of the District Court for the Eastern District of Pe

Exchange
12-21-61
MM

HENRY B. ASHMEAD, PRINTER,
Nos 1102 and 1104 Sansom Street, Philadelphia.

PREFACE

TO THE SIXTH AMERICAN EDITION.

WITH the concurrence and approval of the former editors, their notes and references have been combined, and those of the present editor added to them. Their arrangement of notes has been followed, and the present work, has, as far as possible, been confined to references to the recent American and English cases.

GEORGE SHARSWOOD, JR.

PHILADELPHIA, *January,* 1873.

PREFACE

THE task of the present editor has been, in the main, that of supplying notes and references which should embody the more important English and American decisions, upon the topics of which this work treats, since the publication of the last edition. He has, in some instances, however, enlarged and added to his predecessors' notes, though leaving them in general to stand as they were written.

The editor would willingly have made the annotations to the last division of this work, on Pleading and Practice, more systematic and complete than they are; but he found, that in view of the great changes which time and altered circumstances have introduced into the course of Chancery procedure, both in England and the United States, it would not have been possible to do so without adding greatly to the bulk of the book, with no corresponding advantage to the reader. In this country, indeed, between those States in which the distinct equitable jurisdiction is abolished, and those in which the framework of the Court of Chancery still stands, there is to be found a wide range of diversities, chiefly of local origin, and irreducible to any common system; while in none, it is believed, is the older practice, as set forth in the text of this work, in all respects followed. Every State looks in such matters chiefly to its own statutory and judicial regulations; and these it would not have been appropriate or convenient to embody in the notes to so elementary a work, as the present.

In England. the alterations which the last few years have produced, are of the most remarkable character; so that, indeed, the whole structure of Chancery must be considered as remodelled. In the first place, the pleadings have been simplified to an extreme degree. An informal claim is substituted in many cases for a bill; and disputed questions under wills, deeds, contracts, and the like, may be submitted directly to the Court in the form of a case stated. The bill, when used, is only a concise printed narrative of the material parts of the complainant's case, with the prayer for the appropriate relief at the end; for the interrogatories are now filed separately. The answer is substituted in every respect for the old modes of defence; and is a concise statement of the respondent's case. whether in bar or avoidance: and he is, in his turn, authorized, if he choose, to exhibit interrogatories to the complainant, and to compel the production of documents, without recourse to a cross-bill. Exceptions for impertinence on either side are done away with, the only penalty thereon being the costs, if any be occasioned. Objections for the non-joinder or misjoinder of parties, where not abolished altogether, are made as little productive of injury and delay as possible. Bills of revivor and supplement no longer exist; their place being supplied by a greater latitude of amendment, and by the power to make corresponding orders in the cause. The clumsy system of the examination of witnesses on interrogatories is abolished; and testimony is now taken orally, before the examiner, in the presence of the parties, as in suits at law, while objections to the competency of witnesses are

no longer allowed. That *fons malorum*, the office of
Master, is done away, and its duties are transferred to
the Court at chambers, assisted by clerks. The Court
now settles all questions of law, and even a disputed legal
title, itself, without directing an action or a case to a
Court of law. A new tribunal, called the Court of Appeal, with co-ordinate appellate jurisdiction to the Chancellor, has been created. And finally, very judicious
means for the reduction of the expenses of Chancery
proceedings have been adopted, the principal one of which
is the substitution of compensation by salaries to the
officers of the Court, in lieu of the old fee system. Other
ameliorations and improvements are in progress; and before long the English Chancery, once the stronghold of
abuses and delay, will be made one of the simplest, most
effective, and cheapest tribunals in the world. Even
now, the radical, though well-regulated, reforms in this
and other branches of the law, in England, patiently
effected in the face of a thousand obstacles, present a
marked contrast to the slow progress made in this dirco-
tion by most of the United States. It is to be hoped,
indeed, that the subject will soon be taken up by the
profession throughout the whole of our country, with
energy and earnestness, so that we may no longer deserve
the reproach of being left behind in the race of real im-
provement by one of the most conservative of nations.

The references throughout the book have been carefully corrected, and an alphabetical table of all the Reports and Text-books cited in them, has been prefixed,
which will furnish an explanation of the abbreviations
employed.

HENRY WHARTON.

PHILADELPHIA, *April*, 1855.

ADVERTISEMENT.

In preparing this treatise for the press, the chief design of its lamented author was to present to the profession a comprehensive and condensed view of the general Principles of the Doctrine of Equity, as administered in the Court of Chancery, and an outline of the proceedings by which those principles are enforced. It comprises the substance, with additions, of three series of Lectures, delivered before the Incorporated Law Society, in the years 1842–5. The completion of the work in its present form occupied from that period a considerable portion of the time and labor of the author; and, with the exception of the last four chapters of the fourth book, the treatise had received his final corrections, and arrangements were making for its immediate publication, when he was so suddenly called away in the autumn of last year.

The thanks of the author's friends are due to Mr. JAMES WILLIS, of the Equity Bar, for his valuable assistance in the correction of the unfinished chapters of the treatise, and in the general revision of the work during its progress through the press.

J. A.

MICHAELMAS TERM, 1849.

CONTENTS.

CHAPTER III.

Of Mortgages.
>Perfect
>Imperfect

CHAPTER IV

Of Conversion
Of Priorities
Of Tacking

CHAPTER V

Of Re-execution
Of Correction
Of Rescission and Cancellation

CHAPTER VI.

Of Injunction against Proceedings at Law
Of Bills of Peace
Of Bills of Interpleader
Of Injunction against Tort

BOOK III.

OF THE JURISDICTION OF THE COURTS OF EQUITY IN CASES IN
THE COURTS OF ORDINARY JURISDICTION CANNOT ADMINI
RIGHT.

CHAPTER I.

Of Account

CHAPTER II.

Of Partition
Of Assignment of Dower

CHAPTER III.

CHAPTER IV.

CHAPTER V.

CHAPTER VI.

BOOK IV.

OF THE FORMS OF PLEADING AND PROCEDURE BY WHICH THE JURIS-
DICTION OF THE COURTS OF EQUITY IS EXERCISED.

CHAPTER I.

CHAPTER II.

CHAPTER III.

TABLE OF TEXT-BOOKS AND REPORTS.

CITED IN THIS VOLUME.

Abbott's R. (U. S. C. C.).
Adams on Ejectment.
Adolphus and Ellis R. (England).
Alabama Reports.
Allen's R. (Massachusetts).
Ambler's R. (England).
American Law Journal, New Series.
American Law Register.
American Law Register, (New Series).
American Leading Cases (Hare and Wallace).
Arkansas Reports.
Ashmead's R. (Pennsylvania).
Atkyn's R. (England).

Bail Court Cases (England).
Bailey's Equity R. (South Carolina).
Baldwin's R. (Circuit Court, U. S.).
Barbour's Chancery R. (New York).
Barbour's Supreme Court R. (New York).
Barnewall and Alderson's R. (England).
Barnewall and Cresswell R. (England).
Barr's R. (Pennsylvania).
Bay's R. (South Carolina).
Beames on Costs in Equity.
Beasley's R. (New Jersey).
Beatty's R. (Ireland).
Beavan's R. (England).
Bennett's R. (Missouri).
Bibb's R. (Kentucky).
Bingham's New Cases (England).
Bingham's R. (England).
Binney's R. (Pennsylvania).
Blackstone's (Wm.) R. (England)
Bland's Chancery R. (Maryland).
Black's R. (Sup. Ct. U. S.).
Blackford's R. (Indiana).
Blatchford's R. (Circuit Ct. U. S.)
Bligh's R. (England).
Bligh's R. New Series (England).
B. Monroe's R. (Kentucky).
Bosanquet and Puller's R. (England).

Craig and Phillips' R. (England).
Cranch's R. (Sup. Ct. U. S.).
Croke's R. (Elizabeth, James I., Charles I.).
Curtis' R. (Circuit Ct. U. S.).
Cushing's R. (Massachusetts)
Cushman's R. (Mississippi)

Dallas's R. (Pennsylvania).
Dana's R. (Kentucky).
Daniell's Chancery Practice.
Day's R. (Connecticut).
De Gex and Jones' R. (England).
De Gex, Fisher and Jones' R. (England).
De Gex, Jones and Smith's R. (England).
De Gex and Smale's R. (England).
De Gex, Macnaghten and Gordon's R. (England).
Dessaussure's R. (South Carolina).
Devereux's Eq. R. (North Carolina).
Devereux and Battle's Equity R. (North Carolina).
Dickin's R. (England).
Dillon's R. (C. C. of U. S.)
Douglass's R. (Michigan).
Dow's R. (England).
Drewry's R. (England).
Drewry and Smale's R. (England).
Drury's R. (Ireland).
Drury and Warren's R. (Ireland).
Dudley's R. (Georgia).
Duer's R. (New York).

East's R. (England).
Eden's R. (England).
Edwards' Chancery R. (New York).
Edmonds' Select Cases (New York).
Elmer's New Jersey Digest.
English's R. (Arkansas).
English Common Law Reports.
Equity Draftsman.
Equity R. (England).
Equity Cases Abridged (England).
Exchequer R. (England).

Fairfield's R. (Maine).
Finch's R. (England).
Florida Reports.
Foster's R. (New Hampshire).
Freeman's Chancery R. (Mississippi).
Freeman's R. (England).

Gallison's R. (Circuit Ct. U. S.).
Georgia Decisions.
Georgia Reports.
Giffard's R. (England).
Gilbert on Uses, by Sugden.
Gill and Johnson's R. (Maryland).

Jarman on Wills.
Jarman's Powell on Devises.
Johnson's Reports (England).
Johnson and Hemming's R. (England).
Johnson's Chancery R. (New York).
Jones's Equity R. (North Carolina).
Jones and Latouche's R. (Ireland).
Jurist (England).

Kansas Reports.
Kay and Johnson's R. (England).
Keen's R. (England).
Kelly's R. (Georgia).
Kent's Commentaries on American
  Law.
Kernan's R. (New York).
Knapp's Privy Council Cases (England).

M

Lansing's R. (N. Y.).

M

Law Journal R. New Series, Chancery
  (England).
Law Review (England).
Law Reports, Chancery Appeals (England).
Law Reports, Common Pleas (England).
Law Reports, Equity (England).
Leading Cases in Equity, White and
  Tudor, American ed. by Hare and
  Wallace.
Leigh's R. (Virginia).
Lewin on Trusts.
Littell's R. (Kentucky).
Littell's Select Cases, or 6 Litt. (Kentucky).
Lloyd and Goold's R. (Ireland).
Louisiana Annual R.

McCarter's Reports (New Jersey).
McCord's Chancery R. (South Carolina).
McCord's Law R. (South Carolina).
McLean's R. (Circuit Court U. S.).
McMullen's Chancery R. (South Carolina).
Macnaghten and Gordon's R. (England).
Macqueen's Practice.
Macqueen's Scottish Appeal Cases
  (England).
Maddock and Geldart (England).
Maddock's Chancery Practice.
Maddock's R. (England).
Maine Reports.
Manning's R. (Michigan).
Manning and Granger's R. (England).
Marshall's (A. K.) R. (Kentucky).
Marshall's (J. J.) R. (Kentucky).
Martin and Yerger's R. (Tennessee).

Railway Cases (England).
Randolph's R. (Virginia).
Rawle's R. (Pennsylvania).
Reports, Coke's (England).
Rhode Island Reports.
Rice's Equity R. (South Carolina).   S
Richardson's Equity R. (South Caro-
     lina).
Riley's Equity R. (South Carolina).
Robinson's R. (Virginia)
Root's R. (Connecticut). .
Roper, Husband and Wife, by Jacob.
Rotuli Parliamentorum.
Russell's R. (England).
Russell and Mylne's R. (England).

Sanford's Chancery R. (New Yrok).
Sanford's Superior Ct. R. (New York).
Saxton's Chancery R. (New Jersey).
Scammon's R. (Illinois).
Schoales and Lefroy's R. (Ireland).
Scott's New Reports (England).
Selden's R. (New York).
Select Chancery Cases (England).
Selwyn's Nisi Prius.
Sergeant and Rawle's R. (Pennsyl-
     nia).
Seton on Decrees.
Shepley's R. (Maine).
Shower's Parliamentary Cases (Eng-
     land).
Siderfin's R. (England).
Simons' R. (England).
Simons' R., New Series (England).
Simons and Stuart's R. (England).
Smale and Giffard's R. (England).
Smedes and Marshall's Chancery R.
     (Mississippi).
Smedes and Marshall's R.(Mississippi).
Smith's Chancery Practice.
Smith's Leading Cases, by Hare and
     Wallace.
Smith's Mercantile Law.
Sneed's R. (Tennessee).
South Carolina Reports.
Speer's Equity R. (South Carolina).
Stephen's Blackstone's Commentaries.
Stephen on Pleading.
Stewart's R. (Alabama).
Stewart and Porter's R. (Alabama).
Stockton's R. (New Jersey).
Story on Equity Jurisprudence.
Story on Equity Pleading.
Story on Partnership.
Story's R. (Circuit Court U. S.)
Strange's R. (England).
Strobhart's Equity R. (South Caro-
     lina).
Strobhart's Law R. (South Carolina).
Sugden on Powers.

.).
. U. S.).
R. (U. S.)

TABLE OF ENGLISH CASES.

THE PAGES REFERRED TO ARE THOSE BETWEEN BRACKETS [   ].

161,

c

TABLE OF CASES

CITED IN THE AMERICAN NOTES.

3

3

. 302

, 3

D

E

195

F

DOCTRINE OF EQUITY

INTRODUCTION.

THE subject of the present Treatise is the prerogative jurisdiction of the Great Seal for giving effect to certain civil rights, technically called Equities, where the ordinary process of law is inadequate.

By the original system of English jurisprudence as explained by Lord Chief Justice Hale, the whole judicial authority of the Crown was exercised by the King in person, sitting in his Royal Court, called the Aula or Curia Regis. Portions of this authority were afterwards delegated to the courts of law; and where an injury had been committed, which the authority of those courts was adequate to redress, a writ under the Great Seal was issued out of chancery, called an original writ, directed to the sheriff of the county where the injury was alleged to have been committed, containing a summary statement of the cause of complaint, and requiring him to bring the wrongdoer before the proper court of law, there to answer the plaintiff's charge. The use of original writs in personal actions is now abolished. But such a writ was formerly essential to the institution of any action in the superior court of law, and in real and mixed actions it is still necessary. The portion of the royal authority which was not thus delegated to the courts of law appears to have remained in the Sovereign as a branch of the prerogative, and to have been naturally intrusted to the Lord Chancellor as the minister in whose custody the Great Seal was placed.[1] The *manner of its exercise [*xxx] was by another writ, also issuing under the Great Seal, called the writ of subpœna, which was directed to the defendant personally, and commanded him under a penalty to appear to answer such things as were alleged against him, and to abide by the decree which should be made. The principle by which its exercise was regulated appears to have been the one above stated, viz., that of affording an effectual remedy, where the remedy at common law was imperfect, but not, as has been sometimes erroneously supposed, that of creating a right which the common law had denied.

The existence of this prerogative or equitable jurisdiction seems to be in a great decree peculiar to this country, and to pervade the whole system of its judicial polity.[2] The Court of Exchequer, established for enforcing payment of debts and duties to the King, and incidentally administering justice to the debtors and accountants to the Crown, was, until the recent abolition by statute of its equitable jurisdiction, subdivided into a court of equity, and a court of common law; and there are also several inferior courts of equity, which exercise exclusive jurisdiction over matters within their cognisance, having their

[1] Hale's Jurisdiction of H. L.; King v. Hare, 1 Str. 150; 1 Story on Eq., s. 41–49; 3 Steph. Black. 407; Steph. on Plead. 5.

[2] Mitf. 6, 50, 151.

own peculiar courts of appeal, and without any appellate jurisdiction in the Court of Chancery. If, however, a suit be commenced in those courts, where the cause of suit is without their jurisdiction, or where by reason of the limited jurisdiction of the court the defendant cannot have complete justice, the defendant, before decision of the suit, may file a bill in the High Court of Chancery, showing the incompetency of the inferior court, and praying a special writ of certiorari to remove the cause into the Court of Chancery. The principal inferior jurisdictions in England which have cognisance of equitable cases, are those of the counties Palatine of Lancaster and Durham, the Courts of the two Universities of Oxford and Cambridge, the Courts of the City of London, and the Cinque Ports. The County Palatine of Chester, and the Principality of Wales, had also, formerly, courts of equitable jurisdiction, but these courts are now abolished.[1]

The earliest instances which have been hitherto published of the exercise *of the prerogative jurisdiction of the Great Seal, are found in a series [*xxxi] of Chancery records commencing with the reign of Richard 2, and ending with that of Elizabeth, which was published in 1827, 1830, and 1832, by the Record Commissioners.[2]

Some of the petitions contained in this collection appear to have been merely presented to the Chancellor, as the official framer of ordinary writs, to obtain a suitable one for the plaintiff's case; others, especially during the reigns of Edward 4, Henry 6, and Henry 8, are for a writ in the nature of a habeas corpus to have the complainant

---

[1] Mitf. on Pleading 6, 50, 151; 1 Daniel's Chancery Practice 509; 1 Maddock's Chancery Practice 249; 1 Equity Draftsman 131; 5 Vict. c. 5; 11.Geo. 4 & 1 Wm. 4 c. 70, s. 14.

[2] Calendar of Chancery Proceedings, vols. 1, 2 and 3.

released from an illegal imprisonment; but in the majority
of instances they appeal to the prerogative jurisdiction of
the Chancellor, and pray, not that the wrong complained
of may be remedied at law, but that the Chancellor will
examine the parties, and give appropriate redress.

In many cases a special ground is alleged for calling
on the Chancellor to exercise a jurisdiction, which would
naturally fall within the province of the common law
Courts. One of the grounds so alleged, and which strongly
marks the character of the age, is the difficulty of obtaining justice by reason of the wealth and power of the
wrongdoer. Thus in one case, it is said that the plaintiff
cannot have any remedy at law in consequence of the defendant being surrounded by many men of his maintenance. In another, that the defendant is strong and
abounding in riches, and a great maintainer of quarrels,
and the complainant is poor, and hath not the means to
sue for remedy at the common law. In a third, the relief
is prayed, "because your petitioners, John and Catherine,
are so poor, and the said John so ill, that they cannot pursue the common law." Of this sort of jurisdiction there
are many instances, but in one case, towards the end of
Henry the Eighth's reign, the prayer is, that the petitioner, who had been restrained by injunction from proceeding at law, "may be relieved from the prohibition,
because he is a poor man, and unable to sue in the King's
Court of Chancery."[1]

The jurisdiction exercised on the ground of poverty or
overbearing power has necessarily died with the state of
society in which it originated; but it appears, like the

---

[1] Goddard v. Ingepenne, 1 Chan. Cal. viii.; Thomas v. Wyse, Id. xiv.;
Bell v. Savage, Id. xiv.; Royal v. Garter, Id. cxxx.

present jurisdiction of *the Court, to have been based on the principle of giving an efficacious [*xxxii] remedy for a right existing at law, and many instances occur in the records where the ordinary doctrines of modern equity are brought forward as the grounds for relief. The most frequent of these equities, especially in the latter years of Henry 6, and in the subsequent reigns, is for enforcing conveyances by feoffees in trust; but many other ordinary equities occur. Thus, for example, we find a bill seeking to set aside a conveyance which the defendant had obtained by intoxicating the plaintiff;[1] a bill by a tithe-owner to obtain payment for his tithes;[2] a bill stating that the plaintiff had recovered her land at law, but that the defendant continued vexatiously to harass her and seeking to have him restrained;[3] a bill by an executor, stating that the defendant had by a trick obtained from him a general release, when he was ignorant of a debt due from the defendant to his testator, and intended the release to apply to other matters, and praying an injunction against setting it up at law as a discharge of that debt;[4] a bill against an executor for payment of his testator's debt;[5] a bill to perpetuate testimony;[6] a bill for discovery of title deeds;[7] and a bill for specific performance of a contract.[8]

It must not, however, be supposed that in all the petitions to the Chancellor contained in these records the

[1] Stonehouse v. Stanshaw, 1 Ch. Cal. xxix.
[2] Arkenden v. Starkey, Id. xxxv.
[3] Freeman v. Pontrell, Id. xlii.
[4] Cobbethorn v. Williams, Id. li.
[5] Vavasour v. Chadwick, Id. xciii.
[6] Earl of Oxford v. Tyrrell, Id. cxx.
[7] Baker v. Parson, 2 Chan. Cal. 1.
[8] Tyngelden v. Warham, Id. liv.

principles of modern equity were rigorously observed; or even that it was the uniform practice to set out any special ground for interference. In many instances the doctrines of equity may be traced; but there are many others, where the complaints made are merely of violent assaults, or of other wrongs which might apparently have been redressed at law. And we sometimes find the jurisdiction resisted on that ground. Thus, for example, in one of the cases already referred to, the bill, after mentioning the subtraction of the plaintiff's tithes, complains also that the defendant had violently driven away his sheep, and the defendant, after answering to the former charge, says with reference *to the latter, "that [*xxxiii] the same is determined at the common law; Wherefore he understands not, that the King's Court of his Chancery in this case will have knowledge; nevertheless, for declaration of the matter to you, my Lord Chancellor, the defendant saith that he never took nor drove away any sheep of the said complainant." And in a subsequent case we find the defendant alleging that some of the matter contained in the bill is, "matter triable at the common law, by action of trespass or false imprisonment, the which matter ought not by the King's law of this land, to be determined in this Court:" and that other matters in the bill alleged are, in like manner determinable at the common law, by assize of novel disseisin, and by writ of dower: "nevertheless," he goes on to say, "for the truth and plainness of the matter, he denies having done the acts complained of."[1]

Whether this last class of cases were ever properly within the jurisdiction of the Chancellor may admit of some doubt. That they are not so now is unquestionable;

[1] Arkenden v. Starkey, 1 Ch. Cal. xxxv.; Harry v. Lyngeyn, Id. xlix.

and, from the earliest time when such jurisdiction was claimed, down to the time of its final abandonment, we find a perpetual struggle going on against its authority.[1]

The first instance of this opposition occurs in the 13th year of Richard 2 (A. D. 1389), when the Commons petitioned that no man might be brought before the Chancellor or the King's Council for matters remedial at the common law. But the only answer given by the King was, that "he would keep his regality as his predecessors had done before him."[2] In four years afterwards (A. D. 1393–4), on a second petition being presented to the same effect, a partial remedy was granting by a statute, which authorized the Chancellor to give costs to the defendant, where writs of subpœna should have been obtained on untrue suggestions.[3] In the first year of Henry 4 (A.D. 1399), a similar petition was again presented, and the King answered that "the statutes should be kept except where one party was so great and rich, and the other so poor, that he could not otherwise have remedy."[4] In the fourth *year of the same reign (A. D. 1402), the Com- [*xxxiv] mons again made the usual complaint, alleging that, according to the Statutes of Edw. 3, no man ought to be imprisoned or put out of his freehold except by the processes of common law. The King, however, in this instance distinctly asserted his own jurisdiction; and his answer was, that "he would desire his officers to abstain more from sending for his subjects than they had hitherto done; but that it was not his intention that they should refrain from so doing in reasonable causes, as had been

---

[1] Rotuli Parliamentorum ut et Petitiones et Placita in Parliamento, vol. iii. 1377–1411 ; vol. iv. 1413–1436.

[2] Rot. Parl. 266.   [3] Ibid. 323.   [4] Ibid. 446.

done by his good progenitors."[1] This answer, however, was far from giving satisfaction to the Commons; and, in the third and ninth years of his successor (A.D. 1451 and 1421), we find them speaking in very angry terms of the writ of subpœna, and alleging that such writs were never granted or used before the time of the late King Richard, "when John de Waltham, of his subtlety, first found out the novelty, contrary to the form of the common law of the realm."[2] The King still refused to abolish the writ; but, from an inspection of the records already referred to, it is apparent that the instances of interference with the common law were at this time gradually decreasing. The last petitions which we meet with on this subject were presented in the reign of Henry 6, and were couched in the usual terms, praying that the writ of subpœna might not issue for matters determinable at the common law; but the only answer given was a direction that "the statutes which already existed should be observed, and that no writ of subpœna should be granted unless the plaintiff gave proper security for costs."

This is the last time we meet with any petitions hostile to the jurisdiction, and from the tenor of all the remonstrances made, as well as from that of the bills which appeared in the calendar, it seems obvious that the acknowledged jurisdiction of Chancery was in cases where the common law gave or admitted a right, but which were irremediable by its process. We do not find either in the remonstrances or in the bills any trace of a jurisdiction to give relief, on the ground that the strict law had denied a right which, in the Chancellor's view of justice, ought to have been admitted.

If such an authority had ever been claimed, the com-

[1] 3 Rot. Parl. 506.   [2] 4 Ibid. 84, 156

plaints of the Commons would surely have been, not that decisions were made by an *irregular authority, [*xxxv] and under an irregular process, but that when made they were contrary to law. This, however, is not the case; but the only objection made is, that whereas certain matters ought to be decided by a Court of law, they were decided by the Chancellor, and the very pledge which was in one instance given that the Chancery should not interfere in matters of common law, " unless where one party is so rich and the other so poor that justice cannot otherwise be obtained," clearly points to a class of cases in which a right existed according to law, but in which, for some reason or other, the common law remedy was ineffectual.

The same principle still governs the jurisprudence of the Court. It does not create rights which the common law denies; but it gives effectual redress for the infringement of existing rights, where, by reason of the special circumstances of the case, the redress at law would be inadequate.

The manner of redress at law is by a judgment for the plaintiff, entitling him to recover, as the case may be, either possession of his property or damages for its detention or injury, followed by a writ of execution to the sheriff, requiring him to give effect to the judgment obtained. If this redress be sufficient there is no jurisdiction in equity; and, in accordance with this principle, it is held that the Court of Chancery cannot assess damages, or decree possession of land or payment of rent under a legal title; for in the one case the assessment may be made by a jury, in the other the possession may be obtained by ejectment, and the intermediate rent may be recovered either by assumpsit for use and occupation or

by trespass for mesne profits. The manner of redress in
Chancery is by a decree against the wrongdoer, compelling him specifically to make good his default; and therefore if the wrong require specific redress, and such specific
redress is not attainable at law, there is a prerogative
jurisdiction in equity to relieve. And whether specific
redress be requisite or not, the inability of the common
law Courts to examine the defendant creates, in all cases
of civil wrong, a jurisdiction in equity to that extent.

The jurisdiction, however, is confined to civil suits, and
cannot be extended to the trial of crime. It is the right
of every man, when charged as a criminal, to be exempt
from giving evidence against himself, and to have his guilt
or innocence tried by a jury.   And, therefore, in all crimi-
[*xxxvi] nal proceedings, and in those also which *may
be termed quasi-criminal, such as a mandamus,
a quo warranto, or the enforcement of a penalty or forfeiture, there is no jurisdiction in equity (unless conferred
by special enactment), either to compel discovery or to
afford relief.[1]

The jurisdiction over civil rights is founded, as we have
seen, on the writ of subpœna; and, in accordance with the
requirements of that writ, is exerted for a double purpose,
viz.: 1. For discovery, compelling the defendant to answer
the complaint; and 2. For relief, compelling him to perform the decree.

The Court of Chancery, in enforcing discovery, does
not depart from the general policy of the law. It requires
a defendant to discover the truth of the plaintiff's claim,
notwithstanding that he is himself the party sued; but it
does not require him to answer questions which on grounds

---

[1] Story on Plead. 553; Re Hertford, 1 Hare 584; Attorney-General v.
Lucas, 2 Hare 566.

of general policy he is entitled to resist. In accordance with this principle it is held, first, that no man need discover matters tending to criminate himself, or to expose him to a penalty or forfeiture; secondly, no man need discover legal advice which has been given him by his professional advisers, or statements of fact which have passed between himself and them in reference to the dispute in litigation; and thirdly, that official persons must not disclose matters of State, the publication of which may be prejudicial to the community.

Subject to these restrictions, every competent defendant in equity must answer on oath as to all facts material to the plaintiff's case. He must answer to all and not to a portion only. And he must answer distinctly, completely, without needless prolixity, and to the best of his information and belief. He is also bound, if required by the plaintiff, to set forth a list of all documents in his possession or power from which similar discovery can be obtained; and if the possession of such documents and their character as fit subjects of discovery can be shown from this answer, he must permit the plaintiff to inspect and copy them.

The jurisdiction thus exercised for enforcing discovery is available in aid of proceedings of civil relief, whether such relief be asked from the Court of Chancery, or from any other public tribunal which is itself unable to enforce discovery. If the consequent relief *be attainable in equity, a prayer to that effect is intro- [*xxxvii] duced in the bill, which is then termed a bill for relief, or more correctly for discovery and relief. If it be attainable in a different Court, the mere fact that discovery is requisite will not alter the jurisdiction. The Court of Chancery will compel the discovery, but the relief must be sought before the appropriate tribunal, and the bill is for discovery alone.

In addition to the jurisdiction for discovery, there is another substantially similar under which the Court of Chancery interposes; namely, for the procurement of evidence to be used elsewhere, without itself deciding on the result, viz., in suits for a commission to examine witnesses abroad, and in suits for the perpetuation of testimony where the subject-matter cannot be immediately investigated; and for granting, in aid either of its own proceedings or of a proceeding elsewhere, the peculiar remedy termed an examination *de bene esse*.

The jurisdiction of equity to grant relief originates, as we have seen, in the occasional inadequacy of the remedy at law, and the supplemental character which it thus sustains gives rise to two important maxims: the one, that "equity follows the law;" the other, "that he who would have equity must do equity." The former maxim, that "equity follows the law," imports that if a legal claim, *i. e.*, a claim triable at law, be contested in equity, it will be decided in accordance with the legal right, if the contested claim be equitable, *i. e.*, triable in equity alone, the decision will follow the analogy of law. The latter maxim, that "he who would have equity must do equity," imports that where a party, not content with his legal remedy, seeks the supplemental aid of equity, he must give effect to all equitable rights in his adversary respecting the subject-matter of the suit.

The cases of inadequacy at common law, which originate the supplemental jurisdiction of equity, may be conveniently divided under two heads, viz.: 1. Where the Courts of ordinary jurisdiction cannot enforce a right; and 2. Where they cannot administer it.

The equities under the first head of this division, viz.,
where the Courts of ordinary jurisdiction cannot enforce
a right, are those for performance of trusts and contracts;
for election between inconsistent benefits; for completion
of gifts on meritorious consideration in favor of the
donor's intention after his death; for giving effect to
*discharges by matter *in pais* of contracts [*xxxviii]
under seal; for relief against penalties and
forfeited mortgages; for re-execution or correction of
instruments which have been lost or erroneously framed;
for setting aside transactions which are illegal or fraudulent, or which have been carried on in ignorance or mistake of material facts; and for injunction against irrepar-
able torts.

The jurisdiction to enforce performance of trusts arises
where property has been conferred upon, and accepted
by, one person on the terms of using it for the benefit of
another. The former person, or owner at law, is called
the trustee; the latter or owner in equity the *cestui que
trust.* And it is manifest that the trustee, being the admitted owner at law, may deal with the property at law
as his own, and that the equitable ownership, or right to
compel performance of the trust, is only cognisable in the
Court of Chancery.

In order to originate a trust, two things are essential:
first, that the ownership conferred be coupled with a trust,
either declared by the parties or resulting by presumption
of law; and secondly, that it be accepted on those terms
by the trustee. The consequence of its creation and acceptance is, that the property is subjected to a double
ownership, an equitable ownership in the *cestui que trust,*
and a legal ownership in the trustee.

The equitable ownership is in strictness a mere chose

in action, or right to sue a subpœna against the trustee; but it is considered in equity the estate itself, and is generally regulated by principles corresponding with those which apply to an estate at law. The terms in which it is declared are interpreted by the same rules; it is subject to the same restraints of policy, and is governed by the same laws of devolution and transfer. The analogy, however, which exists between the two forms of ownership, is not free from exception. The legal rules of interpretation, though uniformly applicable to an executed trust, *i. e.*, a trust of which the scheme has in the outset been completely declared, are not applied with equal. stringency in determining the limitations of an executory trust, *i. e.*, a trust where the ultimate object has been alone denoted, with a direction to effectuate that object in some convenient way. The legal restraints of policy, though generally binding an equitable estate, admit in that respect of two singular exceptions; the one in what are called the separate use and pin-money trusts, enabling a married woman to hold property independent of her [*xxxix] husband, and allowing *such property to be made inalienable; the other in what is called the wife's equity for a settlement, restraining the husband's rights over her equitable chattels real and choses in action until an adequate settlement has been made. And in respect also to the devolution of trusts, there are two exceptions to the general rule; the one real in their exemption from dower, the other apparent in the attendance of satisfied terms on the inheritance, so that the trust devolves on the real instead of the personal representative.

The means by which an equitable ownership is transferred or charged, where its subject-matter is personal estate, are analogous to those which apply to a legal ownership, rather than strictly identical with them. The distinction originates in the doctrine that personal property passes at law by mere delivery, which, where an equitable interest is transferred, may not be practicable; and, therefore, in order to pursue as nearly as possible the analogy of law, it is required that the assignment of an equitable interest should be perfected by notice to the trustee, so as to deprive the assignor of subsequent control and to effect a constructive delivery to the assignee. It is otherwise with respect to real estate. For real estate passes by title, and not by delivery; and the character of the grantor's interest, whether legal or equitable, does not affect the terms of his deed. The principle of constructive delivery by notice to the trustee is applied also to a debt or other chose in action. The right of recovering such an interest, like that of enforcing a trust, is in strictness merely a right of litigation, and except in the case of negotiable securities, is not capable of transfer at law. But if it be in substance a right of property, it is treated in equity as of that character, and may be transferred by an assignment or agreement to assign, perfected by notice to the party liable.

The legal ownership of the trustee confers on him at law an absolute dominion, but is considered in equity as subservient to the trust; so that the trustee is bound to use it for those purposes, and those only which were contemplated by the grantor; to account for and protect the property whilst the trust continues; to restore it to the parties entitled when the trust is at an end; and not to avail himself of his fiduciary character for any object of personal benefit. If he performs his duties, he may claim indemnity against all personal loss; but if he fail in their performance, he is liable, at the option of the *cestui que*

trust, either to replace the property in its rightful
[*xl] . *state, or to account for any benefit which has
accrued; nor will the mere lapse of time, if unaccompanied by knowledge and acquiescence on the part of
the *cestui que trust*, discharge him from this liability.

Besides the ordinary trusts which we have just considered, there is another class of trusts—those for charitable and public purposes, where the legal ownership is
conferred on a fiduciary holder, but the trust is declared
for general objects, and not for the benefit of a specific
owner. The incidents of a trust of this class are, for
the most part, the same with those of one for ordinary
purposes. But there are two principal distinctions; the
one, that a charitable trust is not affected by lapse of time
in the same manner as a trust for private persons; the
other, that where an apparent charitable intention has
failed, whether by an incomplete disposition at the outset,
or by subsequent inadequacy of the original object, effect
may be given to it by a *cy pres* or approximate application, to the exclusion of a resulting trust for the donor.

The jurisdiction of equity for superintending a charitable trust is called into action by information of the
Attorney-General, suing on behalf of the Crown. It
extends in the case of unincorporated charities, to their
internal administration as well as to the management of
their estates. But in the case of eleemosynary corporations it is confined to the latter object; and the internal
administration of such charities, together with the election and amotion of corporators, is exclusively subject to
the jurisdiction of a visitor. In addition to the jurisdiction of the Court of Chancery over charities, a special
jurisdiction was created by 43 Eliz. c. 4, called the Statute
of Charitable Uses, to be exercised by commissioners ap-

pointed by the Crown. But their jurisdiction has now fallen into disuse. And there is also a summary jurisdiction in equity, to be enforced on petition, instead of information or bill, created by 52 Geo. 3, c. 101, commonly known as Sir Samuel Romilly's Act.

The jurisdiction of compelling performance of a contract involves the consideration, not merely of what is technically termed specific performance, but also of the doctrines of election, of meritorious or imperfect consideration, of the discharge by matter *in pais* of contracts under seal, and of relief against penalties and forfeited mortgages.

The equity to compel specific performance of a contract arises where a contract binding at law has been infringed, and the remedy *at law by damages is inadequate. [*xli] And in order to originate this equity, it is essential that the contract shall have been made for valuable consideration, and that its enforcement in specie be practicable and necessary.

The first requisite is, that the contract be made for valuable consideration. For so long as a promise rest *in fieri*, there is not, in the absence of such consideration, any equity to insist on its performance. It is otherwise if the promise has been already executed, either by the transfer of the legal ownership, or by the creation of a final trust. The exact line of demarcation, where the contract ceases to be an executory agreement and becomes a perfected trust in equity, is often difficult to distinguish. But the principle itself is sufficiently clear. If the donor has perfected his gift in the way which he intended, so that there is nothing left for him to do, and nothing which he has authority to countermand, the donee's right is enforceable as a perfected trust, and the

2

consideration is immaterial. If, on the contrary, the transaction is incomplete, and its final completion is asked in equity, the court will not interpose to perfect the liability without first inquiring into the origin of the claim and nature of the consideration.

The second requisite is, that the enforcement in specie be practicable; and therefore, if the contract is one which the party making it is unable to perform, or which the Court is unable practically to enforce, performance will not be decreed; and the same result will frequently follow where enforcement is sought against the defendant, but a corresponding performance by the other party cannot be secured.

The third requisite is, that the enforcement in specie be necessary as well as practicable; and therefore, if the possession of the specified thing is not essential, but a compensation in damages will redress its loss, the Court will not interpose. And in determining on its necessity, the effect on both parties will be taken into consideration; and specific performance may be refused, if there has been any unfairness on the part of the plaintiff, or if the defendant has entered into the contract by mistake, or even on the mere ground that the contract is a hard one, and that its enforcement in specie would press heavily on him.

In applying this equity to contracts relating to real estate, there are some modifications of legal rules which [*xlii] at first sight appear inconsistent *with them, and repugnant to the maxim, that "equity follows the law." The modifications here referred to are those of enforcing parol contracts relating to land, on the ground that they have been already performed in part; of allowing time to make out a title beyond the day which the contract specifies; and of allowing a conveyance with compensation for defects. The wisdom of permitting any deviation is a subject admitting of much doubt. But the particular doctrines now in question are fully established by the course of precedent, and may perhaps be considered, not so much deviation from the rule of law, as subordinate equities, or developments from the original doctrine, that specific performance of a contract, and not pecuniary compensation for its breach, is the equitable measure of redress.

The first of these subordinate equities is that of enforcing parol contracts relating to land, on the ground that they have been already performed in part. A parol contract in relation to land is made incapable of enforcement by the Statute of Frauds; and, so long as the contract remains *in fieri*, it is alike ineffectual at law and in equity. It sometimes, however, happens that a contract which is still *in fieri* at law, has been already performed by construction of equity; for if it is one of which specific performance would be decreed, it is itself in some sort an equitable title; and if the parties have clothed that title with possession, or have otherwise acted on it as an existing ownership, they are held to have perfected their agreement in equity, and if the terms of their parol contract can be proved, may be decreed to perfect it by a conveyance at law.

The second equity is that of allowing time to make out a title beyond the day which the contract specifies. The rule on this point is expressed by the maxim, that " time is not of the essence of the contract in equity;" and it seems, like that of part performance, to be founded on the principle, that the contract itself is in the nature of a title, so that if a substantial ownership exists, though the title be not fully cleared on the appointed day, specific performance may be properly decreed.

The third equity is that of allowing a conveyance with compensation for defects, where a contract has been made for sale of an estate, which cannot be literally performed *in toto*, whether by reason of an unexpected failure in the title to part, of inaccuracy in the terms of description, or [*xliii] of diminution in value by a liability to a *charge.

The principle of this equity appears to be, that where the property contracted for can be substantially transferred, it is against conscience to take advantage of small circumstances of variation. The equity for performance with compensation may be enforced by either the vendor or purchaser, but is of course more readily granted to the latter. In either case the defect must be one admitting of compensation, and not a mere matter of arbitrary damages, and the compensation given must be really compensation for a present loss, and not indemnity against a future risk.

A corresponding relief to that by specific performance is given, even in the absence of a contract, in the case of title deeds or specific chattels of peculiar value, detained from the legitimate owner, by directing them to be delivered up or secured.

The equities of election and meritorious or imperfect consideration are closely connected with the principle which has been already stated of enforcing those contracts and those only, which are based on valuable consideration.

The first of these equities is that of election. The equity to enforce contracts made for value is extended by parity of reasoning to cases where a benefit has been conferred as the consideration for an act, and knowingly accepted, although the party so accepting it may not be bound by an actual contract, or by a condition of performance annexed to the gift. The equity of election is analogous to this: it applies, not to cases of contract or of conditional gift, but to those in which the donor of an interest by will has tacitly annexed a disposition to his bounty, which can only be effected by the donee's consent; *e. g.*, where a testator leaves a portion of his property to A., and by the same will disposes of property belonging to A. In this case there is no contract by A. to relinquish his own property, nor is there any condition annexed to the testator's gift, which requires him to do so as a term of its acceptance. But the fact that a double disposition has been made, implies that he shall not have both the interests; and he must therefore elect between the two, and must either relinquish his own property or compensate the disappointed donee out of the property bequeathed. A doubt, however, exists on this last point, and it appears to be uncertain whether the consequence of an election to take against the will is confined to a liability to compensate, or is a forfeiture of the property devised.

*The doctrine of meritorious consideration originates in the distinction between the three classes [*xliv] of consideration, on which promises may be based, viz., valuable consideration, the performance of a moral duty, and mere voluntary bounty. The first of these classes alone entitles the promisee to enforce his claim against an unwilling promisor; the third is for all legal purposes a mere nullity until actual performance of the promise. The second or intermediate class is termed meritorious, and is confined to the three duties, of charity, of payment of creditors, and of maintaining a wife and children, or persons towards whom the party promising has placed himself *in loco parentis*. This class of consideration is not distinguished at law from mere voluntary bounty, but is to a modified extent recognised in equity.

The rule of equity on this subject is, that although a promise, made without valuable consideration, cannot be enforced against the promisor or any one in whose favor he has altered his intention, yet, if a gift on meritorious consideration be intended, but imperfectly executed, and the intention remain unaltered at the death of the donor, there is an equity to enforce the intended gift against persons claiming by operation of law, without an equally meritorious claim. The principal applications of this equity are, in supplying surrenders of copyhold against the heir, and in supporting defective executions of powers, when the defect is formal, against the remainderman. Another class of cases to which the doctrine of meritorious consideration applies, are those where a man, subject to a moral duty, does an act which may have reasonably been meant in satisfaction of that duty, and is therefore presumed to have so intended it. In accordance with this principle, acts which, as between strangers, would bear one construction, may be construed differently where meritorious consideration exists ; *e.g.*, a purchase made by one person in the name of another may be construed as an advancement in favor of a child, instead of a resulting trust for the purchaser. A legacy may be construed a provision instead of mere bounty, and may, as such, bear interest from the testator's death.

The equities for giving effect to discharges by matter *in pais* of contracts under seal, and for relief against penalties and forfeited mortgages, are the converse to the equity for specific performance. The first of these equities originates in the rule of law, that an agreement under seal, technically termed an agreement by specialty, can

only *be avoided by another specialty, and that it [*xlv]
is unaffected by matter *in pais* which would operate as a discharge of a simple contract. In equity, the
rule is otherwise; for the form of agreement is immaterial, and if the act done is in substance a discharge, it
will warrant a decree for the execution of a release, or
for delivery up and cancellation of the specialty. The
most ordinary application of this equity is in favor of
sureties, where a guarantee has been given under seal,
and the creditor, without the surety's consent, has discharged or modified the principal's liability.

The second of these equities originated in the rule of
law, that, on breach of a contract secured by penalty, the
full penalty might be enforced without regard to the damage
sustained. The Court of Chancery, in treating contracts
as matter for specific performance, was naturally led to
the conclusion that the annexation of a penalty did not
alter their character; and, in accordance with this view,
restrained proceedings to enforce the penalty on a subsequent performance of the contract itself, viz., in the case
of a debt, on payment of the principal, interest and costs,
or, in that of any other contract, on reimbursement of the
actual damage sustained. A similar authority is now conferred by statute on courts of law, but the equitable jurisdiction is not destroyed. The same relief has been granted
on clauses of re-entry for non-performance of covenants
in a lease; but the soundness of the application is questionable, and it is now strictly confined to cases where the
covenant is for payment of money, so that the damage
may be certainly measured by interest.

The equity for relief against penalties applies most extensively to the case of forfeited mortgages, where a loan
has been secured by the transfer of property, with a con-

dition to redeem on a specified day, and the right of redemption has been forfeited at law by non-payment at the appointed time.

The equity in these cases is, that the real transaction is a loan on security, and the forfeiture by non-payment is a mere penalty, which may be relieved against on subsequent satisfaction of the debt. If it be not in fact a loan, but a *bonâ fide* sale, with power to repurchase, there is no equity to interpose. A clause of redemption, however, is *primâ facie* evidence that a loan was intended; and if that fact be established, no contemporaneous stipulation can clog the right of redemption, or entitle the creditor to more than his principal, interest and costs.

[*xlvi] A partial power to give relief in cases of *mortgage has been also conferred, by 7 Geo. 2, c. 20, on courts of common law.

The right of the mortgagor to redeem is termed his "Equity of Redemption," and is treated in equity as a continuance of his estate, subject to the mortgagee's pledge for repayment. And therefore, whilst he is left in possession by the mortgagee, he is looked upon as holding in respect of his ownership, and is not accountable for his receipts.

The legal ownership of the mortgagee is *e converso* treated as a mere pledge for repayment. He may enter into possession if he think fit; but, if he does so, is accountable for all which he receives, or, without wilful default, might have received; and if he has taken possession when no interest was in arrear, or has continued in possession after both principal and interest were discharged, he is liable for interest.

The remedy of the mortgagee by taking possession is practically very inconvenient, yet if the forfeiture by non-payment had been taken away, and not replaced by any substitute, it would have been the only one attainable under his security. To remedy this objection, he is allowed, after forfeiture, to file a bill praying foreclosure of the equity to redeem. A new day for payment is then fixed by decree; and if default be made, the mortgagor's right is destroyed. The right, however, is merely to foreclose the equity, and does not extend to warrant a sale.

In addition to regular or perfected mortgages, which convey the legal estate to the mortgagee, and specify a day of forfeiture at law, there are other securities of an analogous character, but defective in one or both of these respects. These imperfect securities are seven in number, viz., 1. Mortgages of a trust, or equity of redemption, and equitable mortgages by imperfect conveyance or by contract to convey. In these mortgages the legal ownership is not transferred, and the mortgagee therefore cannot obtain possession at law, but is entitled in equity to a receiver of the rents; 2. Equitable mortgages by deposit of title deeds, unaccompanied by a written contract. Under these mortgages there is the same right to a receiver as in the preceding class; and there is a doubt whether, in addition to the remedy by foreclosure, the mortgagee has not an alternative remedy by sale of the estate; 3. Welsh mortgages, in which there is no specified day of payment, but the contract is for payment out of the *rents : in this case the mortgagee's remedy [*xlvii] is confined to perception of rents, and he has no right to foreclosure or sale; 4. Trust deeds in the nature of mortgage, which are mere conveyances to the creditor on trust to sell and to retain his debt out of the proceeds; 5. The equitable lien of a vendor or purchaser of real estate, where the one has conveyed before payment, or the other has paid before conveyance. In either of these cases the payment or return, as the case may be, of the purchase-money, is secured in equity by an implied charge on the land; 6. Equitable fieri facias and elegit, where a judgment is made available against trusts and equities, either by injunction against setting up an outstanding estate in bar of execution at law, by appointment of a receiver of the accruing profits, or by permiting the judgment creditor to redeem; and, 7. Judgment charges under 1 & 2 Vict. c. 110, ss. 13, 14, by which a judgment is made a charge in equity, on the debtor's interest in real estate and in stock or shares enforceable in like manner with a charge by contract.

In immediate connection with the subjects just considered of trust, contract and mortgage, we have to consider the doctrines of equitable conversion and of priority among conflicting equities : doctrines which, though applicable to all subjects of equitable jurisdiction, are more especially important in regard to these.

The doctrine of equitable conversion is embodied in the maxim, that " what ought to be done, is considered in equity as done;" and its meaning is, that whenever the holder of property is subject to an equity in respect of it, the Court will, as between the parties to the equity, treat the subject-matter as if the equity had been worked out, and as impressed with the character which it would then have borne. The simplest operation of this maxim is found in the rule already noticed, that trusts and equities of redemption are treated as estates; but its effect is most obvious in the constructive change of property from real to personal estate, and vice versa, so as to introduce new laws of devolution and transfer. If, for example, an imperative trust is created, either for employing money in the purchase of land, or for selling land and turning it into money, the money or land, of which a conversion is directed, will be dealt with in equity during the continuance of the trust, and for objects within the scope of the trust, as if the purchase or sale had been actually made. In like manner, if a binding contract be made for *the sale of land, enforceable in equity, [*xlviii] such contract, though in fact unexecuted, is considered as performed, so that the land becomes in equity the property of the vendee, and the purchase-money that of the vendor.

The doctrine of conversion, by changing the character of trusts and contracts, and altering them from mere rights of action into actual, though imperfect titles in equity, gives rise to questions between them and the legal title, and also to questions between conflicting equities, where several have been created in reference to the same thing.

The rule of priority in regard to transfers and charges of the legal estate is, that the order of date prevails, subject, however, to modifications by statute in respect to voluntary or fraudulent grants; and the same rule, subject to the same modifications, governs, in the absence of a special equity, transfers and charges of the equitable interest. But if legal and equitable titles conflict, or if, in the absence of a legal title, there is a perfect equitable title by conveyance on the one hand, and an imperfect one by contract on the other, a new principle is introduced, and priority is given to the legal title, or if there is no legal title, to the perfect equitable one. This doctrine is embodied in the maxim, that " between equal equities the law will prevail."

In order that this maxim may operate, it is essential

that the equities be equal. If they are unequal, the
superior equity will prevail. And such superiority may
be acquired under any of the three following rules: 1.
The equity under a trust or a contract in *rem* is superior
to that under a voluntary gift, or under a lien by judgment at law; 2. The equity of a party who has been
misled, is superior to his who has wilfully misled him; 3.
A party taking with notice of an equity, takes subject to
that equity.

If no superior equity exists, the common course of law
is not interfered with. The equities are equal, and the
law or the analogy of law will prevail. If there be a
legal right in either party, the Court of Chancery remains
neutral, and the matter is left to be decided at law without either relief or discovery in equity. If there be no
legal right it cannot be neutral; and, therefore, acts on
the analogy of law, and gives priority to that title which
most nearly approximates to a legal one, viz., to an executed and perfect title in equity, rather than to one which
is executory and imperfect.

[*xlix]   *The maxim of non-interference between equal
equities is the foundation of the doctrine of tacking in equity. The cases to which this doctrine applies
are those where several encumbrances have been created
on an estate, and two or more of them, not immediately
successive to each other, have become vested in a single
claimant. Under these circumstances the question arises,
whether an intermediate claimant may redeem one of such
encumbrances, and postpone the other to his own charge,
or whether the party holding the two encumbrances may
tack or consolidate them, so that the earlier in date cannot be separately redeemed. The doctrine on this point
is, that if the double encumbrancer is clothed with a legal

or superior equitable right, he may, as against the mesne
claimants, tack to it a claim for any further amount due
to him in the same character, which was advanced expressly or presumptively on the credit of the estate without notice of the mesne equity. A similar equity accrues
where two mortgages of different estates are made to one
person, or, being originally made to two, become vested
in one, whilst the equities of redemption remain united
in a single hand. In such a case neither the mortgagor,
nor any person making title under him, can, after forfeiture, redeem one without redeeming both.

In addition to the equity for performance of a trust or
contract where the original transaction and its evidence
are unimpeached and clear, there is an equity for re-execution, correction, or rescission, where the instrument
evidencing a transaction is destroyed or lost; where,
through mistake or accident it has been incorrectly
framed; or where the transaction is vitiated by illegality
or fraud, or as having been carried on in ignorance or mistake of facts material to its operation. These equities,
like the equity for performance in specie, are incapable
of enforcement by the courts of law, and fall therefore
within the province of the Court of Chancery.

The equity for re-execution and other similar relief
arises, not only on wilful destruction or concealment, but
also on an accidental destruction or loss, where the missing instrument is such that its non-production would perpetuate a defect of title, or would preclude the plaintiff
from recovering at law. Such for instance is a conveyance or bond, which under the old practice must have
been pleaded with profert at law, and a negotiable [*1]
security, which must be produced *at law before verdict, because the court cannot otherwise indemnify the
defendant against its possible reappearance.

The equity to correct written instruments which have been erroneously framed, is appropriate to chancery alone; for a court of law cannot compel an alteration in the instrument, and its entire avoidance would be a nullification, and not an affirmance, of what was meant. It arises, firstly, where an instrument has been executed in order to the performance of a pre-existing trust, but is framed in a manner inconsistent with its terms; secondly, when an instrument purports to carry into effect an agreement which it recites, and exceeds or falls short of. that agreement; and, thirdly, where an instrument is admitted or proved to have been made in pursuance of a prior agreement, by the terms of which both parties meant to abide, but with which it is in fact inconsistent; or where it is admitted or proved that an instrument, intended by both parties to be prepared in one form, has by an undesigned insertion or omission been prepared and executed in another. It is in conformity with this principle that bonds given for payment of a joint and several debt, but drawn up as merely joint, have been reformed in equity, and made joint and several, in conformity with the original liability; and that mortgages by husband and wife of the wife's estate, which have limited the equity of redemption to the husband, have been reformed by restoring it to the wife.

The equity for rescission and cancellation arises where a transaction is vitiated by illegality or fraud, or by reason of its having been carried on in ignorance or mistake of facts material to its operation. And it is exercised for a double purpose; first, for cancelling executory contracts where such contracts are invalid at law, but their invalidity is not apparent on the instrument itself, so that the defence may be nullified by delaying to sue until the evidence is

lost; and secondly, for setting aside executed conveyances or other impeachable transactions, where it is neces
sary to place the parties in *statu quo*. An executed con
veyance, however, cannot generally be set aside on the
ground of its illegal or immoral character, for it is a maxim
that "*in pari delicto melior est conditio defendentis.*" But
it is otherwise where the contract remains executory, for
its illegality would be admissible as a defence at law, and
the decree for cancelling is only an equitable mode of
rendering that defence effectual.

*The ordinary instances of fraud are the procuring [*li]
contracts to be made, or acts to be done, by means
of wilful misrepresentation, either express or implied, and
the procuring them to be made or done by persons under
duress or incapacity. The same principle which vitiates
a contract with an incapacitated person, is extended in
equity to avoid benefits obtained by trustees from their
cestuis que trustent, or by other persons sustaining a fiduciary character from those in regard to whom that character exists. And there is a similar equity, though perhaps less obviously founded on principle, for setting aside
bargains made with expectant heirs and reversioners without the knowledge of the parent or other ancestor, partly
as having been made under the pressure of necessity, but
chiefly as being a fraud on the parent or ancestor, who is
misled in disposing of his estate.

The ignorance or mistake which will authorize relief in
equity must be an ignorance or mistake of material facts;
as, for example, where an instrument is executed, not by
way of releasing or compromising a particular right, but
in ignorance or mistake of the facts which originate the
right. If the facts are known, but the law is mistaken,
the same rule applies in equity as at law, viz., that a mere

mistake of law, where there is no fraud or trust, is immaterial. In addition to the jurisdiction for setting aside contracts on the ground of mistake by the parties, there is a jurisdiction to set aside awards for miscarriage in the arbitrators, where the fact of such miscarriage does not appear on the award.

The equity for rescission which has been just stated, may be effectuated, not only by cancellation of an instrument, or by re-conveyance of property which has been unduly obtained, but also by injunction against suing at law on a vitiated contract, or against taking other steps to complete an incipient wrong. The right, however, to relief by injunction, is not confined to this equity, but extends to all cases where civil proceedings have been commenced before the ordinary tribunals in respect of a dispute which involves an equitable element, or where any act not criminal is commenced or threatened, by which any equity would be infringed. The restraint may be either imposed by a final decree, forbidding the act *in perpetuum* on establishment of the adverse right, or by interlocutory writ, forbidding it *pro tempore* whilst the right is in litigation.

The injunction against proceeding in another Court, where equitable elements are involved in the dispute, is [*lii] commonly issued *in regard to actions at law, and is obtainable as of course within a short period after the commencement of a suit, so as to restrain the proceedings at law until an answer is filed. If the answer show the existence of an equitable question, such question will be preserved intact until the hearing of the cause, by continuing the injunction, either absolutely or in a modified form, until that time. If at the hearing the decision is with the plaintiff in equity, the injunction may be made perpetual. The same jurisdiction exists in regard to proceedings in the Ecclesiastical and Admiralty Courts, and even to proceedings in the courts of foreign and independent countries, when the parties are personally within the jurisdiction of the Court of Chancery. But it does not extend to proceedings in courts which are of equal competency to adjudicate on the equity.

The relief by injunction against proceedings at law is also applied under a distinct equity on bills of peace and bills of interpleader. A bill of peace is a bill filed for securing an established legal title against the vexatious recurrence of litigation, whether by a numerous class of claimants insisting on the same right, or by an individual reiterating an unsuccessful claim; and its equity is, that if the right be established at law, it is entitled to adequate protection. A bill of interpleader is a bill filed for the protection of a person from whom several persons claim legally 'or equitably the same thing, debt or duty, but who has not incurred an independent liability to any of them, and who does not himself claim an interest in the matter. Its equity is, that the conflicting claimants should litigate the matter amongst themselves, without involving the stakeholder in their dispute.

The injunction against an act commenced or threatened, by which an equity may be infringed, is often used as an auxiliary process in respect of ordinary equities. But there is one class of cases in which the necessity for injunctive relief constitutes *per se* an independent equity, viz., that of torts, as a class of civil wrongs, distinct from cases of trust, of contracts, and of fraud. The principle of injunctive relief against a tort is, that wherever damage is caused or threatened to property, admitted or legally adjudged to be the plaintiff's, by an act of the

3

defendant, admitted or legally adjudged to be a civil wrong, and such damage is not adequately remediable at law, the inadequacy of the remedy at law is a sufficient equity and will warrant an injunction against the com- [*liii] missionor continuance of the wrong.   *And though damages cannot be given in equity for the plaintiff's loss, yet if the defendant has made a profit, he will be decreed to account. The equity is not confined in principle to any particular acts; but those in respect of which it is most commonly enforced are waste, destructive trespass, nuisance, infringement of patent right, and infringement of copyright.

The equities under the second head of our division, viz., where the courts of ordinary jurisdiction cannot administer a right, are those for investigation of accounts; for severance of co-tenancies, and other analogous relief; for winding up partnerships and administering testamentary assets; for adjusting liabilities under a common charge; and for protection of the persons and estates of infants, idiots, and lunatics.

The jurisdiction over account is exercised in a two-fold form; first, for compelling an account from an agent or steward, or any person whose duty it is, by reason of his character, position, or office, to render an account, and who has failed to do so; and, secondly, for investigating mutual accounts where items exist on both sides, not constituting mere matters of set-off, but requiring, in order to ascertain the balance, a more complicated account than can practically be taken at law. .

The equity for severance of co-tenancy and other analogous relief. originates in the fact that the co-tenants have a rightful unity of possession, and that its severance cannot be adequately affected at law.   It is most frequently applied, in effecting partition between co-parceners, joint-tenants, or tenants in common. But its principle extends to suits by a widow against the heir for assignment of dower, and to suits by a tithe-owner against the tithe-payer for relief against subtraction or non-payment of tithes; for in the one case the heir is rightfully in possession of the entirety, and ought himself to make the assignment; in the other, the tithe-payer is rightfully in possession of the produce, and ought himself to set apart the tithe. There is also an equity for ascertainment of boundary between the estates of independent proprietors where the confusion has arisen by the defendant's fault, and for compelling payment of rents where by confusion of boundaries or other cause, the remedy by distress is gone without default in the plaintiff.

The equity for winding up the business of a partnership originates in the peculiar character of that relationship, as involving not merely *a community of interest, but the employment of a common stock [*liv] in some common undertaking with a view to a common profit. In order to ascertain this common profit, and the share of each individual partner therein, an account must be taken of the business, the assets, and the liabilities. The incapacity of the Courts of law to take this account, confers a jurisdiction on the Court of Chancery, so that if the partnership has been already dissolved, or if there be misconduct or incompetency in either partner sufficient to warrant its dissolution, a bill will lie to have the assets converted into money, the debts discharged out of their produce, and the surplus distributed among the partners, or the deficiency made good by contribution among them, and a receiver appointed in the meantime to manage the business. If, after a partnership has been dissolved by

death or bankruptcy, the assets are used by the surviving
or solvent partner for the purposes of profit, he is in the
same position as any other fiduciary holder of property,
using it for his own benefit, and is liable to account to
the executors or assignees for the profit which he has
made.   There is also a special equity in the case of mines
and collieries, to deal with them on the footing of a *quasi*
partnership, so that where the co-owner cannot agree on
the management, a receiver may be appointed over the
whole.

The equity for administering the assets of a testator or
intestate, does not authorize the Court of Chancery to try
the validity of a will.   The jurisdiction for that purpose
in regard to wills of personal estate belong to the Ecclesiastical Courts, and in regard to wills of real estate to
the Courts of common law.   If, however, under a will of
real estate, there is a trust to perform or assets to administer, so that the will is drawn within the cognisance of
equity, there is an incidental jurisdiction to declare it
established, after first directing an issue (*devisavit vel non*)
to try its validity at law.

Assuming the title of representative to be established,
whether that of an executor or devisee, or that of an administrator or heir there is an equity for administering
the assets of a testator or intestate originating in the inefficiency of the ordinary tribunals.   In the exercise of
this equity for administration of assets, all such assets as
would be recognised at law are termed legal assets, and
are administered in conformity with legal rules, by giving
priority to debts in order of degree.   There are other
assets, recognised in equity alone, which are termed
[*lv]   equitable assets, and are distributed *among the
creditors *pari passu*, without regard to the quality

of their debts. The principal assets of this class are real estates devised for or charged with payment of debts, and equities of redemption on forfeited mortgages.

The manner of administration in equity is on a bill, filed either by creditors or by legatees, praying to have the accounts taken and the property administered; or if no creditor or legatee is willing to sue, then by the executor himself, who can only obtain complete exoneration by having his accounts passed in chancery. The personalty is secured by payment into court; a receiver of the real estate and of the outstanding personalty is appointed, if the circumstances require it; and a decree is made for taking the accounts; all actions by creditors are stayed; advertisements are issued for claimants to come in; and the funds are ultimately distributed by the court, so as to protect the representative from subsequent **liability.**

The equity for adjusting liabilities under a common charge arises where a charge or claim, affecting several persons, is or may be enforced in a manner, not unjust in the person enforcing it, but unjust or irregular, as between the parties liable. And it is exercised under the three forms of contribution, exoneration, and marshalling. The equities of contribution and exoneration arise where several persons are bound by a common charge, not arising *ex delicto*, and their order of liability has been accidentally deranged. If the liability be joint, he who has paid more than his share is entitled to contribution from the rest. If some are liable in priority to the rest, the parties secondarily liable, if compelled to discharge the claim, are entitled to exoneration. Both these equities are exemplified in the case of suretyship; the one by the rights of sureties as between themselves; the other by

their rights as against the principal. Their enforcement
in equity, instead of at law, is advantageous, because the
machinery of equity is in general best fitted for such enforcement; and more especially in questions of contribution, because all parties can be united in a single suit,
and losses caused by the insolvency of any can be distributed ratably among the rest. The equity of marshalling
arises where the owner of property subject to a charge,
has subjected it (together with another estate or fund)
to a paramount charge, and the property thus doubly
charged is inadequate to satisfy both claims. Under
these circumstances, there is an equity against the debtor
[*lvi] that the *accidental resort of the paramount creditor to the doubly charged estate or fund, and the
consequent exhaustion of that security, shall not enable
him to get back the second property discharged of both
debts. If, therefore, the paramount creditor resort to
the doubly charged estate, the puisne creditor will be substituted to his right, and will be satisfied out of that
other fund to the extent to which his own has been exhausted.

The equities of contribution, exoneration, and marshalling, are applied, as already noticed, in the administration
of assets, to rectify disorders which may incidentally
occur; and the two former are applied where debts or
legacies are charged on several kinds of assets, either
pari passu or successively; the latter, where they are
charged, some on several kinds of assets, and some on one
kind only, and the doubly charged assets have been
applied in discharge of the double secured claims.

The last equity which remains for notice, is the equity
for administering the estates and protecting the persons
of infants, idiots, and lunatics.

.The protection.of an infant's person and estate is to some extent provided for by the right of guardianship, and by the writs of habeas corpus and of account at law. But this protection is of very limited extent, and is far from adequate to secure a proper education of the infant and a prudent management of his estate. For these purposes there is a prerogative in the Crown as *parens patriæ*, exercised by the Court of Chancery, for protection of any infant residing temporarily or permanently within its jurisdiction. The jurisdiction is called into operation by filing a bill, which constitutes the infant a ward of Court; and such wardship is attended by three principal incidents. Firstly, the infant must be educated under the Court's superintendence, which is exercised either by appointment of a guardian where there is none, by a general control of the legal guardian, when there is one within the jurisdiction, or by displacement of the legal guardian, if he has voluntarily relinquished his right, or has forfeited it by misconduct tending to the infant's corruption. Secondly, the estate of the infant must be managed and applied under the like superintendence, to be exercised either by appointment of a receiver when there are no trustees, or by a general control of the trustees where they already exist, and do not misconduct themselves. And in the exercise of such superintendence, an adequate part of the *income will be allowed for maintenance and education, provided such income belong absolutely [*lvii] to the infant, and the allowance be for his benefit; but there is no power to dispose of the estate itself, except in the special cases of partition and election, and of the devolution on an infant of a mortgaged estate, and in the cases where it is expressly conferred by statute. Thirdly, the marriage of the infant must be with the sanction of the Court. And such sanction will only be given on evidence that the marriage is suitable, and, if the infant be a female, on a proper settlement being made.

The jurisdiction to protect persons under mental incapacity, is of an analogous origin with that for protection of infants; and extends in like manner to all persons, whether subjects of the Crown or not, whose persons or property are within the local limits of the jurisdiction. It differs, however, from the jurisdiction in infancy, because the Crown, in the event of idiocy or lunacy, has not a mere authority to protect, but an actual interest in the land of the idiot or lunatic, determinable on his recovery or death. If the owner is an idiot, the profits are applied as a branch of the revenue, subject merely to his requisite maintenance: if he is a lunatic, they are applied on trust for his support, and the surplus is to be accounted for to himself or his representatives. The effect of the interest thus vested in the Crown is twofold; first, that a special grant is required for its administration, and consequently, that such administration does not belong to the Court of Chancery, but is conferred on the Lord Chancellor personally by warrant from the Crown; and secondly, that the mere lunacy does not originate the jurisdiction, but it must be inquired of by a jury under a commission from the Great Seal, and found of record.

When the fact of lunacy has been duly established, the custody of the estate and person of the lunatic is granted by the Chancellor to committees, with a proper allowance for maintenance. On the subsequent recovery of the lunatic, the commission may be superseded; and on his death, the power of administration is at an end, and the property will be delivered up to his representatives.

In addition to the prerogative jurisdiction in equity,

there are other jurisdictions belonging to the Court of Chancery. It is a Court of State, where all public acts of government are sealed and enrolled. It is an *officina justitiæ* for the issuing of writs under the Great Seal, *e. g.*, writs of certiorari, of prohibition, and of habeas corpus, *as well as the original writ which has been already [*lviii] noticed, and the writs of subpœna and injunction, which are appropriated to the equitable jurisdiction of the Court. It has a common law jurisdiction in what is called the Petty Bag Office, the chief objects of which are, to hold plea on scire facias to repeal letters-patent, on petitions of right, *monstrans de droit*, traverses of office, and the like, and in personal actions where any officer or minister of the Court is a party.[1] It has many special jurisdictions by statute, which are generally directed to be exercised by summary orders on petition, instead of the more regular procedure by suit; *e. g.*, for relieving summarily against breaches of charitable trusts, or regulating their administration, for effectuating conveyances and transfers by incapacitated trustees or mortgagees, for managing property belonging to infants, *femes covert*, lunatics, and persons of unsound mind, and for a variety of miscellaneous purposes, depending in each instance for their character and extent on the language of the statute in which they originate.[2] It has a very important jurisdiction, also of statutory origin, under the law of bankruptcy, for administering the property of an insolvent trader in his lifetime, in order to the satisfaction of his creditors *pari passu*, and for discharging the debtor, after full surrender of his property and conformity with the requisitions of the law, from further liability for his

---

[1] 4 Inst. 79; Rex *v.* Hare, 1 Str. 150; 3 Steph. Pl. 408–410; I Madd. C. P. book i.   [2] 2 Dan. C. P. Ch. 40.

antecedent debts.[1]   And lastly, it has a jurisdiction over
the solicitors of the Court for the summary enforcement
of their professional duty, including the delivery of papers
and payment of money in their hands, on satisfaction of
their claims for costs.[2]   The consideration, however, of
these additional jurisdictions is not within the scope of
the present Treatise, which is confined to the prerogative,
or proper equitable jurisdiction.

We have hitherto been considering the jurisdiction in
equity.   But an inquiry still remains as to the forms of
pleading and procedure in accordance with which that
[*lix] jurisdiction is exercised.   It *is obvious that in
every Court some forms must exist; of which
the character will be determined by the nature of the
jurisdiction, and the objects which it is principally exercised to attain.   In accordance with this view, the forms
of pleading and procedure in equity are directed to elicit-
ing discovery on oath from the defendant, and to placing
on the record of the Court a full and clear detail of facts
on which the equities may be adjusted by a decree.

The suit is commenced by filing a bill of complaint, or
if the claim made is on behalf of the Crown, an information by the Attorney-General.   The bill or information
consists of five principal parts, viz.: the statement, the
charges, the interrogatories, the prayer for relief, and the
prayer of process.   The statement is a narrative of the
plaintiff's case; and it is essential that it state a consistent
case on behalf of all the plaintiffs, and that it state such
case in direct terms, with reasonable certainty, and without scandal or impertinence.   The charges are generally

[1] 6 Geo. 4, c. 16, and 1 & 2 Wm. 4, c. 56; 5 & 6 Vict. c. 122; 10 & 11
Vict. c. 102.

[2] 6 & 7 Vict. c. 73 1 Smith's Ch. Pr. c. 3; Beames on Costs, pl. 2; 2
Law Review 317; 3 Id. 155, 319.

used for collateral objects ; such, for example, as meeting an anticipated defence by matter in avoidance, or by inquiries to sift the truth; giving notice of evidence which might otherwise operate as a surprise; and obtaining discovery as to matter of detail, which could not be conveniently introduced in the statement. The interrogatories are an examination of the defendant on oath. The prayer for relief, or statement of the relief required, must state with reasonable clearness what relief is asked, and must not combine distinct claims against the same defendant, or unite in the same suit, several defendants, some of whom are unconnected with a great portion of the case. If the prayer is objectionable on either of these two latter grounds, the bill is termed multifarious. The prayer of process asks that a writ of subpœna may issue, directed to the parties named as defendants, and requiring them to appear and answer the bill, and to abide by the decree when made. In bills for discovery or to perpetuate testimony, the words "to abide by the decree" are omitted, as well as the prayer for relief. If any other writ be required, such as an injunction, a ne exeat, or a certiorari, it should be asked for in the prayer of process, either singly, or, if the defendant be required to appear, together with the writ of subpœna.

The persons against whom process is asked are the defendants to *the bill, and should consist of all persons interested in the suit, who are not already joined as plaintiffs. [*lx]

With respect to the nature of the interest which requires a person to be joined in a suit, there is of course no difficulty as to persons against whom relief is expressly asked; but with respect to those who are incidentally connected with the relief asked against others, the line of demarcation is less easy to draw. The interests, however, which require such joinder seem generally referable to one of the three following heads : first, interests in the subject-matter, which the decree may effect, and for the protection of which the owners are joined; secondly, concurrent claims with the plaintiff, which, if not bound by the decree, may be afterwards litigated; and thirdly, liability to exonerate the defendant, or to contribute with him to the plaintiff's claim. In cases where the persons thus interested are too indefinite or numerous to be individually joined, one or more members of a class may sue or be sued on behalf of the whole, provided the interest of every absent member in the claim made or resisted, is identical with that of the members who are personally before the Court.

After the bill has been filed, it is next requisite that the subpœna should be served, that the defendant should enter his appearance, and that after appearing he should put in his defence. If he be contumacious and refuse to do so, his disobedience may be punished as a contempt; and the plaintiff is enabled, on compliance with certain rules, to enter an appearance for him, and, on continuance of his default, either to take the bill *pro confesso*, or to put in a formal defence in his name and proceed to support the bill by evidence.

Assuming that the defendant is not contumacious, his defence may be made in four forms, those of disclaimer, demurrer, plea, or answer. And any two or more of these forms may be combined, provided they be applied to different parts of the bill and their respective application be distinctly pointed out.

A disclaimer denies that the defendant has any interest

in the matter, and asks that he may be dismissed from the suit.

A demurrer submits that on the plaintiff's own showing his claim is bad. The decision on a demurrer is obtained by setting it down for argument. If the demurrer is allowed on argument the suit is *at an end, unless it be confined to a part of the bill, or the [*lxi] court give permission for the plaintiff to amend. If it is overruled, the defendant must make a fresh defence by answer, unless he obtain permission to avail himself of a plea.

A plea avers some one matter of avoidance, or denies some one allegation in the bill, and rests the defence on that issue. The former class of pleas are termed affirmative, the latter negative, pleas. There is also a third description of plea, which may be termed the anomalous plea, and which is applicable when the plaintiff has anticipated a legitimate plea, and has charged an equity in avoidance of it; e. g., when having stated a release of his original equity, he charges that such release was obtained by fraud. In this case, the release or other original defence may be pleaded with averments, denying the fraud or other equity charged in avoidance; and the term anomalous is used, because it does not tender an independent issue, but sets up anew the impeached defence with averments in denial of the impeaching equity.

The adoption of the negative and anomalous plea has introduced a peculiar form of pleading, called a plea supported by an answer. It often happens, where a negative plea is used, that the bill contains allegations in evidence of the disputed statement. In this case the plea of its untruth will not protect from discovery of matters which would prove it true; and, therefore, these allegations must be excepted from the plea, and must be met by an answer in support. In all instances of the anomalous plea, the same necessity occurs, for such a plea, though good as to the original equity, is clearly ineffectual as to the equity in avoidance; and that equity, therefore, must not only be denied by averments in the plea, so as to render the defence complete, but must in respect of the plaintiff's right of discovery, be the subject of a full answer in support.

The rules of pleading applicable to a plea are, that it must raise a single issue, and that its averments must have the same certainty as in a plea at law. It is also generally requisite to the validity of a plea that it be verified by the defendant's oath.

The decision on a plea is obtained in two ways : first, by setting it down for argument in order to try its validity; and, secondly, by filing a replication and bringing the cause to a hearing on the issue tendered, in order to determine its truth. If the plea is overruled on argument, the defendant must answer; if allowed, its validity [*lxii] is *established, but the plaintiff may still file a replication, and go to a hearing on the question of its truth. If on the hearing it is sustained by the evidence, there will be a decree for the defendant; if disproved, he can set up no further defence, but a decree will be made against him.

The defence by answer is the most usual, and generally, the most advisable course. It puts on the record the whole case of the defendant, and enables him to use all or any of his grounds of defence, subject, only to the necessity of verifying them on oath; and it unites with this statement of the defence a discovery on oath as to the matters alleged in the bill. Its averments, so far as it is a narrative of the defendant's case, are governed by the same rules as those of a bill, viz., they must state a consistent case, and must state it with reasonable certainty, and without scandal or impertinence. In so far as it consists of discovery, it is regulated by the principles which have been already noticed under that head of jurisdiction.

After the answer is put in, the next question which arises regards its sufficiency, viz., whether the defendant has given all due discovery. If he has not done so the plaintiff may except, stating the points on which the answer is defective, and praying that a sufficient one may be enforced. If the defendant does not submit to the exceptions, they are referred to one of the Masters for consideration, and if he reports in their favor, a further answer must be filed. If either party is dissatisfied with the Master's decision, he may bring the question before the Court by exceptions to the report; and it will then be finally decided.

The next step is the amendment of the bill. The object of the amendment may be either to vary or add to the case originally made, or to meet the defence by new matter. If the amendment make fresh discovery requisite, the plaintiff may call for a further answer, or if the defendant considers it material to make a further answer, he may do so, though not required by the bill. The right of amending is not absolutely confined to the plaintiff. The defendant may, under special circumstances, obtain a similar indulgence by getting leave to file a supplemental answer; but as an answer is put in on oath the Court, for obvious reasons, will not readily suffer alterations to be made.

The final result of the pleadings is, that the original or ultimately *amended bill and the answer or successive answers of the defendant constitute the [*lxiii] whole record. The plaintiff may then either set down the cause for hearing on bill and answer, admitting the answer to be true throughout, or if he controverts any part of the answer, or requires additional proof of his case, may file a short general form, called a replication, stating that he joins issue with the defendant.

The answer of the defendant is the chief foundation of interlocutory orders, that is, of orders not made at the hearing of the cause, but obtained during its progress for incidental objects; and such orders, therefore, will naturally fall under our notice at this stage of our inquiry.

The mode of obtaining interlocutory orders is either by a *viva voce* application, called a motion; or by a written one, called a petition. The statements made in the answer have generally a considerable influence on the application, and in some instances they are the only admissible evidence. Where other evidence is admitted it is brought forward, not by the regular examination of witnesses, but by the affidavits of voluntary deponents.

Applications of this kind are made for a variety of objects; but those of most ordinary occurrence, and which alone seem material to be noticed, are six in number, viz., First, production of documents, when documents are admitted to be in the defendant's possession, and to be capable of affording discovery to which the plaintiff is entitled. Secondly, payment into Court, when the defendant admits money to be in his hands, which he does not claim as his own, and in which he admits that the applicant is interested. Thirdly, for a receiver, where no competent person is entitled to hold the property, or the person so entitled is in the position of a defaulting trustee; or even where an adverse title is claimed, if gross fraud or imminent danger be shown. Fourthly, an injunction to restrain a defendant, so long as the litigation continues, from doing acts productive of permanent injury, or from proceeding in an action at law, where an equity is alleged against his legal right. Fifthly, a writ of ne exeat, in the nature of equitable bail, to restrain a defendant from quitting the kingdom; and sixthly, a preliminary reference to the Master, where accounts or inquiries are requisite before the cause can be decided, which cannot be conveniently taken or made by the court.

*The next regular step after replication is that [*lxiv] the parties should prove their cases by evidence.

The general rules of evidence are the same in equity as at law, but the manner of taking it is different. The difference in this respect arises from the difference of the object in view. The object at law is to enable the jury to give their verdict. And for this purpose it is essential that the evidence be taken *viva voce* and publicly, so that conflicting testimony may be compared and sifted. In equity, the object is to elicit a sworn detail of facts on which the court may adjudge the equities, and to preserve it in an accurate record, for the use, if needed, of the appellate court.

For this reason the evidence in equity is taken in writing, by examination or interrogatories previously prepared. And in order to avoid the risk of defects being discovered in the course of taking it, and false evidence procured to remedy them, it is taken secretly by an officer of the court, and no portion is disclosed until the depositions are complete, and the time arrives for publication of the whole.

After the depositions have been published and read, no further evidence is admissible without special leave, except evidence to discredit a witness, either by impeaching

4

his general credibility or by showing him to have sworn falsely in a part of his evidence, not material to the issue in the cause. With respect to the material parts of his evidence, such discretionary evidence is not admissible, lest under the pretence of impeaching his credibility new evidence should be introduced.

The only exceptions to the system of taking evidence on written interrogatories and before publication are, in the case of documents in the custody of a public officer, and of documents, the authenticity of which is not impeached, and which require only the proof of hand-writing or the evidence of an attesting witness. This evidence may be given by affidavit at the hearing.

At the hearing of the cause the pleadings and evidence are stated, and the court either makes a final decree, or, if any questions are involved which the evidence does not satisfactorily determine, it eliminates them from the general statement, and provides for their determination by a preliminary decree.

The causes which create a necessity for a preliminary decree are four in number, viz., 1. That in the course of the suit a dispute has arisen on a matter of law, which the [*lxv] court is unwilling to decide; *2. That a similar dispute has arisen on a matter of fact; 3. That the equity claimed is founded on an alleged legal right, the decision of which the Court of Chancery declines to assume; and 4. That there are matters to be investigated which, although within the province of the court, are such as the presiding Judge can not at the hearing effectually deal with. The machinery for obviating these impediments is that of a preliminary decree, directing, 1. A case for a court of law; 2. An issue for a jury; 3. An action at law, to be determined in the ordinary course;

or 4. A reference to one of the Masters of the Court to acquire and impart to it the necessary information.

Directions for a case, an issue, or an action, are rather transfers to another tribunal than steps of procedure in the Court itself; but a reference to the Master is an ordinary step in the cause, and is directed principally to three objects, viz., 1. To the protection of absent parties against the possible neglect or malfeasance of the litigants; 2. To the more effectual working out of details, which the Judge sitting in Court is unable to investigate; and 3. To the supplying defects or failures in evidence.

The mode of conducting a reference is by written statements and counter-statements, which are supported either by affidavits, by depositions, or by *viva voce* testimony. When the evidence is complete, the Master prepares a draft report, and it is the duty of any dissatisfied party to lay before him written objections, specifying the points . in which he considers it erroneous. If this is not done, he cannot afterwards contest the correctness of the report.

When the Master has disposed of all objections, and come to a conclusion on the matters referred, he settles and signs his report, and such report is then filed.

If any of the persons interested, whether actual or *quasi* parties, are dissatisfied with the report, they may file written exceptions, founded on the objection previously taken, and specifying the alleged errors and the corrections proposed. The exceptions are then heard and determined by the Court.

When the exceptions have been disposed of, and the report confirmed, the cause is heard on further directions, and the costs are generally disposed of, at the same time. If the nature of the case made on the report involves the necessity of new inquiries, a reference is again made, [*lxvi] and further directions are again reserved, *and the same process is from time to time repeated until a final decree is made.

The power to compel obedience to the decree, like that for enforcing appearance or answer, was originally confined to process of contempt; and the party against whom the decree was made was exposed to have his person imprisoued and his goods sequestered as a punishment for disobedience; but if he still continued contumacious, he could not be forced to perform the decree. By the statutes of 1 Wm. 4, c. 36, and 1 & 2 Vict. c. 110, this inconvenience has been to some extent remedied, and the Court is enabled to direct an execution of instruments by another person in the name of the contumacious party, to take possession of documents in his hands which he refuses to deliver up, and to levy moneys out of his property by writ of execution. Where none of these remedies can be adopted, as where the act ordered requires the personal agency of the defendant, the Court is remitted to the process of contempt, and can only enforce its decree by imprisonment and sequestration.

The next subject for consideration after the decree is the jurisdiction for alteration or reversal, and it should be observed that the jurisdiction for this purpose is not confined, as to law, to the final judgment, but extends to interlocutory proceedings in the cause.

A decree, when made, is not perfected until enrolment; and therefore, so long as it continues unenrolled, it may be altered on a rehearing before the same jurisdiction, viz., either before the Judge who originally made it, or before the Lord Chancellor as the head of the court.

After enrolment it is a conclusive decree, and can only be altered on appeal.

For the purpose of such appeal there is a twofold jurisdiction : first, in the King, whose conscience is ill administered, and who may issue a special commission *pro re nata* to reconsider his Chancellor's decree; and, secondly, in the House of Lords, on petition to them as the supreme judicature of the realm. The former of these courses, however, is now disused, and the latter, which at one time was the subject of vehement contention, has practically superseded it.

In the observations which have been hitherto made on procedure in equity, three things have been assumed, viz., first, that a decree on the plaintiff's bill will determine the litigation; secondly, that the bill is properly framed in the outset for obtaining that decree; and *thirdly, that the suit is conducted to its termination [*lxvii] without interruption or defeat. It is obvious that these assumptions cannot always be correct, and it is therefore requisite, before quitting the subject, to consider the means for remedying the imperfections which occur.

The first class of imperfection is where a decree on the plaintiff's bill will not determine the litigation. This may arise either from cross-relief or discovery being required by the defendants, or from the existence of litigation between co-defendants. In either case the imperfection is remedied by one or more cross bills, filed by one or more of the defendants against the plaintiff and against such of their co-defendants, as the cross relief may affect. If this has not been done, and the difficulty appears at the hearing, the cause may be directed to stand over for the purpose. A cross bill may also be filed to answer the purpose of a plea *puis darrein continuance* where a new defence arises after answer, but not for the purpose of indirectly altering the answer itself.

The second class of imperfection is where the bill is framed improperly at the outset. This ought regularly to be rectified by amendment, but if the time for amendment has elapsed, it may be rectified by a supplemental bill, or by a bill in the nature of supplement, the character of which will be considered under the next head.

Imperfections of the third class are those which originate in an interruption or defect subsequent to the institution of the suit, and they are rectified, according to circumstances, by a bill of revivor, or in the nature of revivor, and by bill of supplement, or in the nature of supplement.

Interruptions of a suit are called abatements, and are cured by a bill of revivor, or in nature of revivor. They occur on the death of any litigating party, whose interest or liability does not either determine on death or survive to some other litigant, and on the marriage of a female plaintiff or co-plaintiff. If the interest or liability be transmitted by act of law, viz., to a personal representative or heir, or to the husband of a married plaintiff, the abatement is cured by a bill of revivor, followed by an order on motion to revive. If the transmission is by act of the party, viz., to a devisee, the bill is one in nature of revivor, and requires a decree at the hearing to revive.

Defects in a suit subsequent to its institution may be [*lxviii] caused either *in respect of parties, by the transfer of a former interest, or the rise of a new one, or in respect of issues between the existing parties, by the occurrence of additional facts, and they are cured by bill of supplement, or in the nature of a supplement.

Where an existing interest has been transferred, the transferee is bound by the previous proceedings, and may be introduced into the suit by a supplemental bill, stating the transfer, and praying his substitution for the transferor. Where a new interest has arisen, as on the birth of a tenant in tail, he must be added by a bill in the nature of a supplement, restating the case against him, and praying an independent decree.

With respect to the occurrence of additional facts, it must be observed, that if they intended to establish a new title in the plaintiff, they are not admissible at all, for he must stand or fall by the title which he had at the outset. If they are mere evidence of his original title, it seems that their introduction on the pleadings is not required, but that the proper course is to apply for liberty to examine witnesses, and to have the deposition read at the hearing. But if the new facts are such as, leaving the original equity untouched, vary the form of relief, or create a necessity for additional relief, they are regularly admissible in the suit. And being subsequent to the filing of the bill, and therefore not properly matters of amendment, they are introduced by supplemental bill.

If new matter occurs, or is discovered after the hearing, it is not properly matter of supplement, but may be introduced into the cause, if necessary, by a bill expressly framed for the purpose, and called a bill to execute or to impeach the decree.

A bill to execute a decree is a bill assuming as its basis the principle of the decree, and seeking merely to carry it into effect.

A bill to impeach a decree, is either a bill of review, a supplemental bill in the nature of review, an original bill of the same nature, or an original bill on the ground of fraud.

A bill of review is used to procure the reversal of an enrolled decree, and may be brought either on error of law apparent on the decree, or on the occurrence or discovery of new matter. If it proceed on the latter ground, the leave of the Court must be first obtained.

A supplemental bill in the nature of review is used to procure the reversal of a decree before enrolment, on the [*lxix] occurrence or *discovery of new matter, and must be filed by leave of the Court. The manner of procedure on such a bill is to petition for a rehearing of the cause, and to have it heard at the same time on the new matter. If the ground of complaint be error apparent, it may be corrected on a rehearing alone, and a supplemental bill is unnecessary.

An original bill in the nature of review is applicable when the interest of a party seeking a reversal was not before the Court when the decree was made, and it may be filed without obtaining leave from the Court.

We have now concluded our introductory inquiry into the jurisdiction, the pleadings, and the procedure of the Court of Chancery. The treatise itself will be occupied in filling up the outline which has been drawn, and in presenting a detailed examination of the doctrines which have been already stated in their general effect.

BOOK I.

CHAPTER I.

OF DISCOVERY.

THE jurisdiction of the Courts of equity for the enforcement of civil rights, as distinguished from the jurisdiction,
of the Courts of common law, derives much of its utility
from the power of the Great Seal to compel the defendant
in a suit to discover and set forth upon oath every fact
and circumstance within his knowledge, information, or
belief, material to the plaintiff's case.

This right to enforce *Discovery*, as it is called, does not
exist in the Courts of common law.[1] In those Courts the
plaintiff must make out his case by the evidence of witnesses, or the admissions of the defendant. By this right,
more effectual means of ascertaining the truth are afforded
to plaintiffs in equity than in the Courts of *com- [*2]
mon law; whilst the rights of the defendant are

---

[1] In England, in the United States Courts, and in most of the states, the
common law rule has been altered, and parties are now competent and compellable to testify.

equally provided for, by the privilege, in his turn, of requiring from the plaintiff, by a cross suit (the reconvention of the civil law), the like discovery upon oath of all the circumstances within the plaintiff's knowledge.

The jurisdiction thus enforced in the Courts of equity is, at the same time, carefully guarded, so that it may only elicit the truth, without wrong to the party examined. He is not liable to be examined suddenly and without time for deliberation; he knows from the bill what are the objects aimed at; he has the plaintiff's statement and the whole of the interrogatories before him; he may give a modified or explanatory answer; and he is aided by the advice of counsel, whose duty it is to see that everything really material is stated, as well as that the record of the Court is not encumbered with irrelevant matter.

The Court of Chancery, as has already been observed in the Introduction, does not, in requiring discovery, depart from the general policy of the law.[1] It requires a

---

[1] When the suitor is an individual, although he may be a sovereign of a foreign state suing in his capacity as sovereign, yet he is bound to answer to a cross bill: The King of Spain v. Hallett, 6 Clark & F. 333 ; and to answer upon oath. But, as the right of a plaintiff to sue does not depend upon the effectiveness of the discovery which on a cross bill may be exacted from him, a republic, like the United States, for example, can sue, although no effectual discovery could be had from it on a cross bill: United States v. Wagner, L. R. 2 Ch. Ap. 582. But a suit in the name of " the government of the State of Columbia" is too vaguely brought: Columbian Government v. Rothschild, 1 Sim. 94. Whether the executive of a foreign republic can be made a defendant for the purpose of obtaining discovery on a cross bill seems to be doubtful. See Prioleau v. The United States, L. R. 2 Eq. 659 ; United States v. Wagner (supra). The proper course would seem to be for the defendant to apply to the republic plaintiff to name some person from whom the discovery sought for may be obtained ; and if the information is refused, the Court will be justified in staying proceedings in the suit until the defendant's demand is complied with: United States v. Wagner, per Lord Chelmsford.

defendant to discover the truth of the plaintiff's claim, notwithstanding that he is himself the party sued; but it does not require him to answer questions which, on grounds of general policy, he is entitled to resist.[1] In accordance with this principle it is held, first, that no man need discover matters tending to criminate himself, or to expose him to a penalty or forfeiture; secondly, that no man need discover legal advice which has been given him by his professional advisers, or statements of facts which have passed between himself and them in reference to the dispute in litigation; and thirdly, that official persons cannot be called on to disclose any matter of State, the publication of which may be prejudicial to the community.

The first of these maxims is, that "no man need discover matters tending to criminate himself, or to expose him to a penalty or forfeiture." He has a right to refuse an answer, not merely as to the broad and leading fact, but as to every incidental fact which may form a link in *the chain of evidence, if any person should choose [*3] to indict him.(a)[2]

(a) East India Company v. Campbell, 1 Ves. sen. 246; Claridge v. Hoare, 14 Ves. 59, 65; Litchfield v. Bond, 6 Bea. 88; Short v. Mercier, 3 Macn. & Gord. 205.

---

[1] The defendant may stop at any point in his answer, and defend himself on the ground of privilege, notwithstanding other admissions therein : King of Sicilies v. Willcox, 1 Sim. N. S. 301.

[2] It is well settled in the United States that a defendant in a Bill in Chancery is not bound to make a discovery as to any charge of felony against him, or as to any criminal offence involving moral turpitude: United States v. Saline Bank, 1 Peters 100; Northrop v. Hatch, 6 Conn. 361; Skinner v. Judson, 8 Conn. 528; Hayes v. Caldwell, 5 Gillman 33; Ocean Insurance Company v. Fields, 2 Story 59; The Union Bank v. Barker, 3 Barb. Ch. 358; Marshall v. Riley, 7 Geo. 367; Poindexter v. Davis, 6 Gratt. 481; Stewart v. Drasha, 4 McLean 563; Higdon v. Heard, 14 Geo.

If the objectionable nature of the discovery asked appears on the bill, the protection may be claimed by demurrer; as, for example, if the bill alleges an usurious contract, maintenance, champerty, or simony;[1] or again, if it be filed to discover whether a defendant is married, who would thereby forfeit an estate or legacy, or to discover matter which would subject a defendant, entitled to an office or franchise, to a *quo warranto*.(b)

If the tendency of the question is not apparent on the bill, the defendant may take the objection by a plea setting forth by what means he may be liable to punishment or forfeiture, and may insist he is not bound to answer the bill, or so much thereof as the plea will cover. Thus

(b) Mitford on Pleading, 4th edit. 193–197.

---

255. And it seems an action for slander is in the nature of a penal action, and comes within the general rule: Bailey v. Dean, 5 Barb. S. C. 297. So of a bill to set aside a conveyance on the ground of usury: Masters v. Prentiss, 2 Jones's Eq. 62. But a defendant may be compelled to make a discovery of any act of moral turpitude which does not amount to a public offence or an indictable crime: Watts v. Smith, 24 Miss. 77. A defendant is not privileged against discovery because it will expose him to penalties in a foreign country, of which he is a subject: King of Two Sicilies v. Willcox, 1 Sim. N. S. 301. As a corporation is not in general liable to indictment, it cannot on this ground resist discovery: Id. 334. So of a trustee in a bond for prospective illicit cohabitation, who is not himself exposed to criminal prosecution: Benyon v. Nettlefield, 3 Macn. & Gord. 94. And, in general, that discovery will subject others than the defendant to penalty or forfeiture, is no ground of protection: King of, &c. v. Willcox, 1 Sim. N. S. 301.

An Act of the Legislature which compels a party against whom proceedings have been instituted for the recovery of a fine imposed by the same law, to a discovery under oath, is constitutional: Day v. The State, 7 Gill 322; Higdon v. Heard, 14 Geo. 255. See also Union Bank v. Barker, 3 Barb. Ch. 358.

[1] Atwill v. Ferrett, 2 Blatch. C. C. 39; Higdon v. Heard, 14 Geo. 255; Bank of U. S. v. Biddle, 2 Pars. Eq. 58; Masters v. Prentiss, 2 Jones's Eq. 62. The defendant cannot even waive this protection, for the law is, in this regard, his guardian: Id.

to a bill brought to a discovery of a marriage, the defendant pleaded with success that the person whom she was alleged to have married had previously married her sister, so that the marriage, if real, was incestuous; and to a bill against bankers for obtaining a re-transfer of stock, alleged to have been unduly obtained from the plaintiff for the purpose of making good a deficiency in his son's accounts, the defendants pleaded that the transaction referred to a fraudulent embezzlement by the son as their clerk, and amounted therefore to a composition of felony; and they were held to be exempt from giving discovery. In like manner, where a bill was filed to discover whether the defendant had assigned a lease, he pleaded to the discovery a proviso in the lease, making it void in case of assignment. And to a bill seeking a discovery whether a person under whom the defendant claimed was a papist, the defendant pleaded his title and the statute of 11 & 12 Wm. 3, disabling papists. But such a plea will only bar the discovery of the fact which would occasion a forfeiture. Therefore, where a *tenant for life pleaded [*4] to a bill for discovery whether he was tenant for life or not, that he had made a lease for the life of another, which, if he was tenant for his own life only, might occasion a forfeiture, the plea was overruled. So upon a bill charging the defendant to be tenant for life, and that he had committed waste, it was determined that he might plead to the discovery of the waste, but that he must answer whether he was tenant for life or not.(c)

If the facts are such as to exclude both a demurrer and a plea, the privilege may be claimed by answer, and if the defendant states in his answer that he cannot give

(c) Mitf. 284–287 ; Claridge v. Hoare, 14 Ves. 59.

the information asked without affording evidence of his crime, he will not be compellable to give it.(d)[1]

The protection thus afforded to a defendant against being compelled to prove himself guilty of a criminal act, is subject to modification in respect to frauds.[2] And it seems that an objection will not hold to discovery of a fraud, on the mere ground that it might be indictable as a conspiracy at law, unless there is an indictment actually pending, or at all events a reasonable probability that one will be preferred. The result of an opposite course would be to render the very magnitude of a fraud its protection against redress.(e)[3] It has also been decided that a defendant may have so contracted with the plaintiff as to bind himself to make discovery of the facts relating to that contract, notwithstanding that it may subject him to pecuniary penalties; and therefore a London broker was compelled to give discovery in aid of an action brought against him by his employer for misconduct, although it subjected him to the penalty of a bond given for the

(d) Parkhurst $v.$ Lowten, 1 Meriv. 391; s. c. 2 Swanst. 194, 214; Att.-Gen. $v.$ Lucas, 2 Hare 566.

(e) Dummer $v.$ Corporation of Chippenham, 14 Ves. 245; Lee $v.$ Read, 5 Bea. 381.

---

[1] The defendant should state that he *believes* that the discovery will subject him to penalties: Scott $v.$ Miller, Johns. 328.

[2] A Court of Chancery will generally compel a discovery to detect fraud and imposition, and to set aside a fraudulent conveyance: Skinner $v.$ Judson, 8 Conn. 528; Attwood $v.$ Coe, 4 Sandf. Ch. 412. And see the application of the exception in cases of privileged communications *infra*, note to page 6.

[3] Howell $v.$ Ashmore, 1 Stockton (N. J.) 82. If, in a bill charging fraud, the defendants, without demurring, answer, they must answer fully. An answer that their innocence will appear by the accounts disclosed precludes them from objecting to the order to produce them: O'Connor $v.$ Tack, 2 Brews. (Pa.) 407.

faithful discharge of his official duties. It was his duty to give the account asked, and he was not allowed to set up his own violation *of the law as an excuse for its non-performance. [*5] It was observed by the Court that if such a defence were permitted, it might be difficult to show any reason why an executor or administrator who has made oath duly to administer the assets, and has executed a bond for that purpose, might not allege those matters in answer to a bill, charging him with a fraudulent account. It seems, however, that a mere contract by the defendant to answer, and not to avail himself of the protective privilege, does not *per se* exclude him from the protection of the law.(f)

In addition to the cases just mentioned, there are other cases which have been termed exceptions to the doctrine, but which are in fact instances to which its principle does not apply. Such, for instance, are those where the penalty has ceased by effluxion of time, or where the the plaintiff is alone entitled to the penalty, and expressly waives it by his bill;(g)[1] or where what is called a penalty or forfeiture is in reality mere stipulated damages or cessation of interest. Thus where a lessee covenanted not to dig clay or gravel, except for the purpose of building on the land demised, with a proviso that if he should dig for any other purpose he should pay to the lessor twenty shillings a load, and he afterwards dug great quantities of each article; on a bill for discovery of the quantities, waiving any advantage of a possible forfeiture of the term, a demurrer of the lessee, because the discovery

(f) Mitf. 195; Green *v.* Weaver, 1 Sim. 404; Lee *r.* Read, 5 Bea. 381.
(g) Mitf. 195–197; Trinity House Corporation *v.* Burge, 2 Sim 411.

[1] Skinner *v.* Judson, 8 Conn. 528. But see Northrop *v.* Hatch, 6 Conn. 361; Dwinal *v.* Smith, 25 Maine 379.

might subject him to payment by way of penalty, was overruled. And where a devise over of an estate in case of marriage was considered a conditional limitation, and not a forfeiture, an answer as to a second marriage was compelled. In like manner where the discovery sought is of matter which would show the defendant incapable of having an interest, as, for example, whether a claimant by devise is an alien, and consequently incapable of taking [*6] by purchase, a demurrer will not hold.(h)[1] In *respect also to some transaction made illegal by statute, such as gaming and stockjobbing, it has been expressly enacted, that the parties shall be compellable to give discovery in equity, notwithstanding that by so doing they may expose themselves to penalties.(i)[2]

The second maxim of privilege is, that no man need discover legal advice which has been given him by his professional advisers : or statement of facts which have passed between himself and them in reference to the dispute in litigation.[3]

(h) Mitf. 195, 196, 197.
(i) Mitf. 288 ; 9 Ann. c. 14, s. 3 ; 7 Geo. 2, c. 8, s. 2.

---

[1] See Hambrook v. Smith, 16 Jur. 144.

[2] But it has been recently held that a plea to discovery in a bill for an account, that the party would subject himself by answering to the penalties of the Stockjobbing Act, was good: Short v. Mercier, 3 Macn. & Gord. 205 ; Robinson v. Lamond, 15 Jur. 240.

[3] The application of the rule prohibiting the discovery of legal advice, depends first upon the character of the parties—secondly upon the relations existing between them—and lastly upon the surrounding circumstances. The communication to be protected must, in the first place, be made between the client and his *legal adviser only:* Parker v. Carter, 4 Munf. 273 ; Jackson v. Inabinit, Riley Ch. 9 ; March v. Ludlum, 3 Sandf. Ch. 35 ; Crosby v. Berger, 11 Paige 377 ; Stuyvesant v. Peckham, 3 Ed. Ch. 579 ; The Bank of Utica v. Mersereau, 3 Barb. Ch. 528 ; or some person acting as that adviser's clerk or agent: Parker v. Carter, 4 Munf. 273 ; Russell v. Jackson, 9 Hare 387 ; Goodall v. Little, 1 Sim. N. S. 155 ;

The statement of the above doctrine is thus limited in
its terms, because it seems doubtful whether statements

Jenkyns *v.* Bushby, L. R. 2 Eq. 547; Lafone *v.* Falkland Islands Co., 4 K.
& J. 34; Walsham *v.* Stainton, 2 Hem. & M. 1; Reid *v.* Langlois, 1 Mac.
& G. 627. See, however, Ross *v.* Gibbs, 8 Eq. L. R. 522, where Stuart,
V.-C., *held*, that communications with an unprofessional agent were privileged. Hooper *v.* Gumm, 2 John. & H. 602; but the rule does not apply
to a student in counsel's office: Andrews *v.* Solomon, Pet. C. C. 356; nor
to the son of the attorney, happening to be present in the office, and not
connected professionally with his father: Goddard *v.* Gardner, 28 Conn.
172; nor to a confidential clerk: Corps *v.* Robinson, 2 Wash. C. C. 388;
nor to a stranger casually present: Jackson *v.* French, 3 Wend. 337; nor
to communications between solicitors of opposite parties: Gore *v.* Bowser,
5 De G. & Sm. 30; nor to communications between different defendants
made for the purpose of being laid before their solicitor: Goodall *v.* Little,
1 Sim. N. S. 155; though see Jenkyns *v.* Bushby, L. R. 2 Eq. 547; also
Betts *v.* Menzies, 26 L. J. Ch. 528. In the second place the relation of
solicitor and client must actually exist between the parties; therefore, if
a lawyer acts simply as a friend, communications to him in that capacity
will not be protected: Coon *v.* Swan, 30 Verm. 6; nor communications
made after the relation has ceased to exist: Yordan *v.* Hess, 13 Johns.
492; and the client must not be a merely nominal party, but must have
some interest in or control over the suit: Id. 219; Hamilton *v.* Neel, 7
Watts 517.

Lastly, the circumstances under which the communication is made are
to be taken into consideration. It was at one time thought that the rule
applied only to disclosures made when there was a *cause* pending; see
infra pp. 6 and 7 in the text, and also Whiting *v.* Barney, 30 N. Y. 330,
where the origin of the protection is explained and the old rule in this respect adhered to; but communications made after a dispute has arisen,
though before litigation are now protected: see Warde *v.* Warde, 1 Sim.
N. S. 18 (endorsed on another point in 3 Mac. & Gord. 365); Jenkyns *v.*
Bushby, L. R. 2 Eq. 547; Bluck *v.* Galsworthy, 2 Giff. 453; McLellan *v.*
Longfellow, 32 Maine 494; McMannus *v.* The State, 2 Head 213; and the
privilege has been extended to matters disclosed to an attorney who has
been employed to draw a deed: Parker *v.* Carter, 4 Munf. 273; though see
The Bank of Utica *v.* Mersereau, 3 Barb. Ch. 528; or an affidavit to get an
assessment reduced: Williams *v.* Fitch, 18 N. Y. 546.

This privilege against discovery extends only to those matters "in which
it is lawful for the client to ask and the solicitor to give professional advice;" and therefore not to cases of fraud concerted between counsel and
client: Reynell *v.* Sprye, 10 Beav. 51; 11 Beav. 618; Gartside *v.* Ontram,

5

of fact which have passed between himself and his advisers, if made before the litigated question arose, are entitled to the same privilege.   There is no doubt that the
privilege exists, where the discovery is sought from the
professional adviser; for the rule is in all cases imperative
and express, that wherever an attorney or counsel is professionally employed, any communication with his client
for the purpose of that employment is privileged; and
whether he be examined as a witness, or whether he be
made on some special ground a defendant in the suit, he
cannot divulge what he has so learnt.(k)   There is also

(*k*) Greenough *v.* Gaskell, 1 M. & K. 98; Herring *v.* Clobery, 1 Ph. 91;
Jones *v.* Pugh, 1 Ph. 96.

26 L. J. Ch. 113. The fraud, however, must be concocted between the
solicitor and client, and when the fraud is purely collateral to the communication, and none was charged on the part of the solicitor, the communication was protected: Mornington *v.* Mornington, 2 Johns. & H. 697.
The privilege against discovery is, in general, inapplicable to communications between a testator and his solicitor, with reference to the dispositions contained in his will, notwithstanding that the enforcement of discovery may lead to the disclosure of an illegal purpose entertained by the
testator, as of a secret trust: Russell *v.* Jackson, 9 Hare 387. But in a
case where this question did not arise on the dispositions of the will, but
only collaterally, such communications were held privileged: Chew *v.*
Farmers' Bank of Maryland, 2 Maryl. Ch. Dec. 231. The rule of privilege,
also, is inapplicable to communications between a solicitor and one under
whom both parties to a cause claim: Chant *v.* Browne, 16 Jur. 606; s. c.,
9 Hare 790.

Where husband and wife have distinct interests, and the wife is induced,
in dealing with those interests, to act under the advice of the husband's
solicitor, the latter is to be deemed to act as the solicitor of both, and
either has the right to the production and inspection of the documents relating to such transaction, which have come in the course thereof into the
solicitor's possession : Warde *v.* Warde, 3 Macn. & Gord. 365.

The privilege in question is confined to communications, and does not
apply to the acts of the parties: Kelly *v.* Jackson, 13 Irish Eq. 129.

In some states, as in Georgia and Missouri, these communications between solicitor and client are protected by statute.

no doubt that where discovery is sought from the client, he is not bound to discover the advice•or opinions which have been given. But it has been contended, and generally considered, that he must disclose the statements on which they were given, unless made in contemplation of or pending a suit. The existence, however, of this supposed liability in the client seems open to doubt. The cases which have been considered to establish it, are apparently capable of a different interpretation; and it seems difficult to discover any substantial difference, in point of reason, principle, or convenience, between the liability of the client, and that of his *counsel or solicitor, to [*7] disclose communications made in confidence, or between the communications so made and others which differ from them only in this, that they precede instead of follow the actual arising of a dispute.(*l*) If, before the communications were made, litigation, or a dispute ending in litigation, had commenced, the client is certainly exempt from discovery, at least if they related to the dispute, or matters in dispute. The first point decided on this subject was, that communications made pending litigation, and with reference to such litigation, were privileged. The next, that communications made before litigation, but in contemplation of, and with reference to, litigation which was expected and afterwards arose, were entitled to the same privilege. A third question then arose with regard to communications taking place after a dispute had arisen between the parties, which was afterwards followed by litigation, but not made in contemplation of, or with reference to, that litigation; and these communications were also protected.[1] And it was finally decided that a defend-

(*l*) Pearse *v.* Pearse, 1 De G. & S. 12.

---

[1] Warde *v.* Warde, 1 Sim. N. S. 18, reversed on another point, 3 Macn. & Gord. 365; McLellan *v.* Longfellow, 32 Maine 494. See Jenkyns *v.*

ant might protect from discovery in the suit of one party, cases or statements made after litigation commenced or contemplated on the same subject with other persons, with the view of asserting the same right.(*m*)   The right to protection is not affected by the circumstance that the communications have not been made directly to or by the solicitor or counsel, but have been transmitted through an intermediate agent.(*n*)¹   But it is essential that they should be made in respect of his professional character, and it is not sufficient to allege that they were communications with a solicitor, or that they bore a reference to the legal proceedings.(*o*)²

The third maxim of privilege protects official persons [*8] *from disclosing matters of State, the publication of which might be prejudicial to the community. Such, for example, are official communications between the governor and law officer of a colony, respecting the

(*m*) Walsingham *v.* Goodricke, 3 Hare 122; Holmes *v.* Baddeley, 1 Ph. 476.

(*n*) Bunbury *v.* Bunbury, 2 Bea. 173; Steele *v.* Stewart, 1 Ph. 471.

(*o*) Bunbury *v.* Bunbury, 2 Bea. 173; Greenlaw *v.* King, 1 Bea. 137; Dartmouth *v.* Holdsworth, 10 Sim. 476; [Chew *v.* Farmers' Bank, 2 Maryl. Ch. Dec. 231.]

Bushby, L. R. 2 Eq. 547 (V.-C. Kindersley), where a case stated, prepared by the solicitor of a predecessor in title to the defendant, and the opinion of counsel thereon, was protected—the opinion having been given before litigation was commenced, but after a dispute had arisen.   But communications before any dispute had arisen, are not privileged: Hawkins *v.* Gathercole, 1 Sim. N. S. 150.

¹ Russell *v.* Jackson, 9 Hare 387; Goodall *v.* Little, 1 Sim. N. S. 155; Jenkyns *v.* Bushby, L. R. 2 Eq. 547.

² No presumption of fact is to be made against any one for enforcing the rule against disclosure by his solicitor: Wentworth *v.* Lloyd, 10 H. L. Cas. 589.

state of the colony; orders given by the governor to a military officer; correspondence between an agent of government and a secretary of State; and other communications of the same class. Such communications are privileged from disclosure, because if, at the suit of a particular individual, they were liable to production in a Court of justice, the effect would be to render them less unreserved, and thus to prejudice the public interest. Questions as to the extent of this privilege most usually arise in the examination of witnesses at law. But if discovery of matters within its scope be asked from a defendant in equity, he may successfully refuse to give it. (p)[1]

It will be observed that the exceptions just considered are merely exceptions to the right of discovery. There is no rule that matters falling within their scope cannot be alleged in a bill; or, that, if proved, they may not warrant relief. But the plaintiff must prove them for himself, and has no right to examine the defendant respecting them. (q)

Subject to these exceptions, the rule respecting discovery is that "every competent defendant in equity must answer as to all facts, material to the plaintiff's case, he must answer to all, and not to a portion only, and he must answer distinctly, completely, and without needless prolixity, and to the best of his information and belief."

(p) Phillipps on Evidence, 8th ed. 189 ; Smith v. East India Company, 1 Ph. 50; Rajah of Coorg v. East Ind. Co., 25 L. J. Ch. 365.

(q) Mitf. 196.

___

[1] Although the principle cited in the text is familiar to the profession, yet the American editor has been able to discover only two cases bearing upon the subject, and these decided not in Chancery, but at law : Marbury v. Madison, 1 Cranch 144; 1 Burr's Tr., by Robinson, 186, 187. See this subject fully discussed in Rajah of Coorg v. East Ind. Co., 25 L. J. Ch. 345.

As against an incompetent defendant discovery cannot be enforced, viz., against an infant, or lunatic without committee, or the Attorney-General when made a defendant on behalf of the Crown. (*r*)

The first rule respecting discovery is, that the defendant must answer to all facts material to the plaintiff's case.[1]

[*9] *He is not bound to answer questions of law; for such questions ought to be decided by the Court. He is not bound to answer questions of fact, unless reasonably material; for he is not to be harassed with idle, and perhaps mischievous, inquiries. And it will not be sufficient to show, that, somehow or other, they may be connected with the case; for if such connection be very remote, so that the discovery would be oppressive, it will be refused: as for example, where the bill charged an executor with mixing his testator's moneys with his own, and called on him to set out a monthly account of his banker's balances, with an account of his own property, debts, and liabilities. (*s*) And lastly, he is not bound to answer merely because the question is material to the issue, but it must be also material to the plaintiff's case;[2]

(*r*) Micklethwaite *v.* Atkinson, 1 Coll. 173.

(*s*) Dos Santos *v.* Frietas, Wigr. on Discovery, s. 239 ; Janson *v.* Solarte, 2 Y. & C. 127.

---

[1] Cuyler et al. *v.* Rogert et al., 3 Paige Ch. R. 186 ; Phillips *v.* Prevost, 4 John. Ch. 205 ; Parkinson *v.* Trousdale, 3 Scammon 367 ; Hagthorp *v.* Hook, 1 Gill. & John. 272 ; Salmon *v.* Clagett, 3 Bland Ch. 142 ; Brooks *v.* Ryam, 1 Story 296–301 ; Langdon *v.* Goddard, 3 Story 13 ; Methodist Epis. Church *v.* Jaques, 1 John. Ch. 65 ; Bank of Utica *v.* Messereau, 7 Paige 517 ; King *v.* Ray, 11 Paige 235 ; Kittredge *v.* Claremont Bank, 3 Story 590 ; Champlin *v.* Champlin, 2 Edw. Ch. 362 ; Robertson *v.* Bingley, 1 McC. Ch. 333 ; Wootten *v.* Burch, 2 Maryl. Ch. Dec. 190 ; Rider *v.* Riley, Id. 16 ; Waring *v.* Suydam, 4 Edw. Ch. 426.

[2] The plaintiff is entitled to discovery of the defendant's title, for the purpose of repelling what he anticipates will be the case set up by the defendant, though not of the evidence by which it is to be supported: Atty.-

for although the plaintiff is entitled to know what the defence is, and to have it verified on oath, he is not entitled to cross-examine the defendants as to the precise mode in which he intends to establish it.(t)

Some doubt has been thrown upon the applicability of this last doctrine where the discovery is sought in aid of the defence to an action, or to a suit already pending in equity. The language of the cases which have created the doubt may certainly be taken to imply that, in answer to such a bill, the defendant is bound to set forth his evidence. But it may be doubted whether it was intended to go so far, and whether it must not be limited to the general rule, that he must answer as to the nature of his title, and as to the truth of the assertions by which he sustains it, though not as to the particular evidence on which he relies.(u)[1]

(t) Llewellyn v. Badeley, 1 Hare 527 ; [Atty.-Gen. v. Corp. of London, 2 Macn. & Gord. 247 ; Cullison v. Bossom, 1 Maryl. Ch. Dec. 95.]

(u) Lowndes v. Davies, 6 Sim. 468 ; Bellwood v. Wetherell, 1 Y. & C. 211-218 ; Wigr. on Discovery, s. 378 ; Glascott v. Copperminers' Company, 11 Sim. 305 ; Mitf. 53.

Gen. v. Corp. of London, 2 Macn. & Gord. 247. So, he has a right to the discovery of evidence in support of his title, in proof of any fraud which has been committed to his injury, though the defendant may thereby be compelled to disclose the evidence in support of his own : Stainton v. Chadwick, 3 Macn. & Gord, 575 ; see Young v. Colt, 2 Blatch. C. C. 373.

Where a defendant holds a covenant for the protection of deeds for the maintenance and manifestation of his title, he is not bound to answer to interrogatories to set out such deeds in a suit, the object of which is to show that a disputed piece of land is not comprised in the defendant's title : Bethell v. Casson, 1 Hem. & M. 806.

It seems that in Massachusetts, a more extended right of inquiry is allowed, and that the rule with regard to the title of the defendant is not applied so strictly : Haskell v. Haskell, 3 Cush. 542.

[1] In Swaby v. Sutton, 1 Hem. & M. 514, the bill stated two indentures of settlement, giving dates, and prayed an account, &c., under them. The

This rule is embodied in the maxim that "if a defend-
[*10] ant *answers at all, he must answer fully;" and
its meaning is, that if a defendant, instead of demurring or pleading to the bill, puts in an answer, and
thus professes to take issue on the whole case, and to go
to a hearing on the whole, he cannot deny a portion of
the plaintiff's statement, and than allege that, in couse-
quence of such denial, the rest of the discovery sought
has become immaterial.[1] If he wish to insist on that
point, he must protect himself by demurrer or plea, rest-
ing his defence on the statement in the bill, or on a single
independent issue.   If he does not adopt that course, but
goes to a hearing on the whole controversy, he must give
discovery on all points, so that the plaintiff, if the decision
be in his favor, may obtain a complete decree.(v)[2]   It is
manifest from this explanation of the rule, that it applies
to such matters only as are in themselves proper objects

(v) Lancaster v. Evors, 1 Ph. 340; [Reade v. Woodruffe, 24 Beav. 421.]

---

answer was that there was an indenture of another date, and an appointment exercised under that excluding the plaintiff, and gave no account.
Held insufficient. " If you choose to rest on a short point," said Wood,
V.-C., " you must do so by plea ; or if not, you must answer ; but then you
must meet the way in which the plaintiff puts his case, and must answer
fully everything which, if answered according to his view, would assist
him at the hearing."

[1] See Bains v. Goldey, 35 Penna. St. 51. See also, Chichester v. Marquis of Donegal, 4 Chancery Appeal Cases 416.

[2] Inglessi v. Spartali, 29 Beav. 564. By the interrogatories of a bill
filed by a foreign merchant against his London agent, the defendants were
asked what were the powers and authorities given to them (in relation to
selling currants), and by what documents they made out the same. The
defendants stated that the powers and authorities appeared from written
correspondence, and that various letters had passed between the parties to
which they referred. Held, that the answer was insufficient, and that the
defendants were bound to specify the documents containing their powers
and authorities.

of discovery. It will not, therefore, apply to interrogatories respecting privileged matters, or respecting matters which are immaterial, or which do not concern the plaintiff's case, or which for any other reason are not among the subjects on which the court enforces discovery.(w)

The last rule is that the defendant must answer distinctly, completely, without needless prolixity, and to the best of his information and belief.[1]

His answer must be distinct, as containing a positive allegation of each fact, and not merely implying it by way of argument. And it must distinctly meet each specific question by a specific reply; for the object of specific questions is to sift the defendant; and it might happen that, when he came to answer on individual points, it would recall matters to his memory. An inquiry, for example, whether the defendant did not receive a specified sum at a specified time; is not sufficiently answered by giving a schedule of receipts, which does not include that *sum, and then saying that the schedule contains a list of all moneys received.(x) [*11]

It must be complete, and so framed that the plaintiff can effectually make use of it. For instance, if the plaintiff were to ask for an account, it would not be sufficient to tender him a collection of account-books, saying

(w) Wood v. Hitchings, 3 Bea. 504.

(x) Faulder v. Stuart, 11 Ves. 296 ; Mitf. 309, 210 ; Wharton v. Wharton, 1 S. & S. 235 ; Anon., 2 Y. & C. 310 ; Tipping v. Clarke, 2 Hare 383, 389 ; [Duke of Brunswick v. Duke of Cambridge, 12 Beav. 281.]

---

[1] Taylor v. Luther, 2 Sumner 228 ; Woods v. Morrell, 1 John. Ch. 103 ; Smith v. Lasher, 5 John. Ch. 247 ; Mechanics' Bank v. Levy, 1 Edw. Ch. 316 ; Tradesmen's Bank v. Hyatt, 2 Edw. Ch. 195 ; Wyckloff v. Sniffen, Id. 581 ; Norton v. Warner, 3 Edw. Ch. 106 ; Robinson v. Woodgate, Id. 422 ; Sloan v. Little, 3 Paige Ch. 103 ; Bailey v. Wilson, 1 Dev. & Bat. Ch. 188 ; Pettit v. Candler, 3 Wend. 618.

that he would find the account there. But the defendant must himself examine the books and make out a reasonable account, referring to the books for verification and details.(*y*) The rule, however, will not be enforced to an oppressive extent. And, therefore, where the executors of a deceased partner were called upon for the accounts of a partnership, and answered that they could not state them from their own knowledge; that they had tried to make them out from the books, but found it would occupy a great time, and be a ruinous expense; and that the plaintiff was at liberty to inspect the books himself; the answer was held sufficient, on the ground that they had not been personally concerned in the transaction, and that they had given the plaintiff an opportunity of making out the account as fully as they could do themselves.(*z*)[1]

It must be framed without needless prolixity. The chief cases in which the prolixity of an answer has been discussed, were those where accounts were demanded of receipt and expenditure. And it has been repeatedly decided that, although an interrogatory requiring such accounts would not be satisfied by a mere general statement, yet a statement setting forth the items of a trades-

(*y*) White *v.* Williams, 8 Ves. 193; Attorney-General *v.* East Retford, 2 M. & K. ?5; Wigr. on Discovery, s. 283.

(*z*) Christian *v.* Taylor, 11 Sim. 401.

---

[1] But even if a detailed statement would be too burdensome, the defendant must, nevertheless, do all in his power to facilitate an examination of the accounts by the plaintiff. Thus in Drake *v.* Symes, Johnson 647, where a bill was filed by a shareholder in an insurance company against the directors, asking for an account, and demanding a list of the lives insured, their ages, the bonuses paid, &c., &c., it was held that an answer which merely referred to the books of the company, and set forth those books in a schedule, was not sufficient; for (as Vice-Chancellor Wood remarked) there should have been some reference to the heads of information and some additional facilities should have been afforded the plaintiff.

man's bill, or copying an auctioneer's catalogue of furniture, is impertinent, and will be expunged by the Court. (*a*)
If, however, the matters inquired after be material to the *defence, mere prolixity, such as setting out documents at length which might have been simply [*12] referred to, will not be dealt with as impertinence, although it may be attended with the risk of costs. For in case the answer should ever be used against the defendant in a Court of law, a part of it could not be so used without the whole; and therefore the setting out of such documents may ultimately prove of importance. (*b*)

It must be to the best of the defendant's information and belief. And the information meant is not only that which he actually possesses, but that also which, either by inspecting his books, or by making inquiries of his solicitors or agents, or of others from whom he has a right to information, is fairly within his reach. And a mere allegation that he believes such parties will not give him the information, or even that they have refused to do so, will not be sufficient to excuse its want. Whatever means of information he has a right to possess, the Court will look upon as being in his possession; and he must resort to proper means for enforcing his right. (*c*)[1]

(*a*) Norway *v.* Rowe, 1 Meriv. 346; Byde *v.* Masterman, Cr. & P. 265 · Davis *v.* Cripps, 2 N. C. C. 435.

(*b*) Parker *v.* Fairlie, 1 S. & S. 295; T. & R. 362; Lowe *v.* Williams, 2 S. & S. 574.

(*c*) Taylor *v.* Rundell, Cr. & P. 104; 1 N. C. C. 128; 1 Ph. 222; [Clinch *v.* Financial Corporation, L. R. 2 Eq. 271;] Glengall *v.* Frazer, 2 Hare 99; Stuart *v.* Bute, 11 Sim. 442.

---

[1] Dinsmoor *v.* Hazleton, 2 Fost. (N. H.) 535; Green *v.* Carey, 12 Geo. 601. But a defendant is not compellable to redeem documents relating to matters in question in a suit, which were pledged by him previous to the institution of the suit: Liddell *v.* Norton, 23 L. J. Ch. 169. And he is not bound to produce documents for which he merely holds a covenant for production against a third party: Bethell *v.* Casson, 1 Hem. & M. 806.

A question has sometimes been raised whether a plaintiff having a document in his possession, can by his bill call on the defendant to inspect it, and then to give an answer with respect to its contents. There appears to be some doubt on this point. (d) ·

A defendant is also bound, if required by the plaintiff, to set forth a list of all documents in his possession, from which discovery of the matters in question can be obtained; and if the possession of such documents and their character as fit subjects of discovery, can be shown from the answer, he must permit the plaintiff to inspect and copy them.[1]

In order to obtain this production, an interrogatory is

(d) Shepherd v. Morris, 1 Bea. 175, 179.

---

[1] Roosevelt v. Ellithorp, 10 Paige 415; see also Collom v. Francis, 1 Parsons' Select Eq. Cases 527. A party is not entitled to a discovery of title deeds relating solely to his adversary's title: Thompson v. Engle, 3 Green Ch. 271; Lewis v. Davies, 17 Jur. 253; Cullison v. Bossom, 1 Maryl. Ch. 95; though privity between title of defendant and plaintiff may give the right: Cullison v. Bossom. A defendant is not bound to produce by way of answer, any public documentary evidence of which he is the official keeper: Salmon v. Clagett, 3 Bland. Ch. 145. But land agents will be directed to deliver up maps, plans, &c., made or collected in the course of their employment, though it is alleged that they were made for their own private use: Beresford v. Driver, 14 Beav. 387.

Under the Pennsylvania Statute of the 16th of June, 1836, the Supreme Court has not jurisdiction to compel the discovery of title deeds, unless material to an issue pending in court: Mange v. Guenat, 6 Whart. 141.

An heir at law is not entitled to the production of title deeds; but an heir in tail is, and so also is a devisee: Shaftesbury v. Arrowsmith, 4 Ves., 66; Rumbold v. Forteath, 3 K. & J. 748; Story's Equity, s. 1092. But an heir at law is entitled to the production of such documents or parts of documents as will prove his pedigree: Rumbold v. Forteath, supra.

By the 14 & 15 Vict. c. 99, sect. 6, the Courts of common law of England, are authorized to require the production of documents, as might have been previously done by means of a bill in equity. Similar statutes exist in most of the United States.

*generally included in the bill, asking whether [*13]
the defendant has any documents in his possession
or power relating to any of the matters alleged, and requiring him to enumerate and describe them in the
schedule. If he admits the possession of such documents, a motion is made that he may produce them, that
the plaintiff may have liberty to inspect and copy them,
and that they may be produced before the examiner and
at the hearing of the cause.[1]

The right thus conferred of enforcing the production of
documents, is a substitute for the more troublesome and
expensive method of requiring their contents to be set out
in the answer:[2] and in conformity with this view it is
held, first, that the right exists for the purpose of discovery alone; and secondly, that it must be regulated by
the same principles which regulate the right to discovery
in the answer itself.

It is a right existing for the purpose of discovery alone
and does not depend on, nor will be aided by a title to
possess the documents themselves.

It may happen that a suit is instituted for the purpose
of obtaining possession of documents, alleged to be improperly withheld from the plaintiff; and if that be its
object, and the discovery be not barred by demurrer or
plea, the plaintiff is entitled to have them described in

---

[1] An affidavit in support of a motion for the production of books of account and papers, should specify or refer to some particular entry or paper,
or state some fact or circumstance to show the necessity of an inspection :
Phelps v. Platt, 54 Barb. (N. Y.) 557.

Such affidavit should be made by the plaintiff, or if by the attorney, some
reason therefor should be shown : Ibid.

[2] Carpenter v. Benson, 4 Sandf. Ch. 496. Therefore, where exceptions
would not be sustained, if the bill called for a full statement, production
will not be required, though the custody of the documents is admitted; as
where an answer under oath is waived : Ibid.

the answer, and to be informed whether they are in the defendant's possession, because, without proof on those points, he could not, supposing his claim to be well-founded, obtain a. perfect decree. If the documents on inspection, will or may afford evidence to sustain his claim, he has a further right to their production on the general principles of discovery; but, unless he can require them on that ground, the mere fact that he claims them as his own, will not entitle him to see them, until after the decree.(e)

It is regulated by the same principles which regulate the right to discovery in the answer itself.

[*14]   *An immediate consequence of this doctrine is, that the right to production must be shown from admissions in the answer, and cannot rest on extrinsic evidence. The question is not, whether the allegations in the answer are true or false; for, to try that question, would require a hearing of the cause; but it is whether, in respect of the plaintiff's right to discovery, the documents are necessary to make the discovery complete. If, therefore, the defendant does not admit their possession, or their relevancy to the plaintiff's case, the production cannot be enforced.[1] The same result will follow, if they are uncertainly described, so that the Court cannot ascer-

---

(e) Wigr. on Discovery, s. 295–298; [Snoddy v. Finch, 9 Rich. Eq. 355.]

---

[1] Upon a motion for the production of documents, the court will not receive evidence extraneous to the answer, to show that a particular document had been fraudulently omitted from the schedule, although the defendant does not object to the extraneous evidence, and has adduced evidence to contradict it: Reynell v. Sprye, 1 De G. Macn. & Gord. 656. So, the plaintiff is not, on an allegation that extracts from books, sworn to, embrace everything bearing on the controversy, are garbled, entitled therefore to have inspection of the whole books: Robbins v. Davis, 1 Blatchf. 238.

tain to what its order should apply.(*f*)   If the bill contained interrogatories to elicit the requisite admissions,
and the answer has failed to give them, it may be open to
an exception for insufficiency; or if the interrogatories have
been inadequately framed, their inadequacy may render
an amendment requisite, but in either case the admissions
must be extracted from the defendant before the order for
production can be made.

The admissions necessary to compel production are,
that the documents are in the defendant's possession or
power, and that they are of such a character as to constitute proper matters of discovery within the ordinary
rules.[1]

The documents must be in the defendant's possession
or power.   And for this purpose, it is sufficient that they
are admitted to belong to him, although they may be out
of his actual custody.   The possession therefore of his
solicitor or agent, or of any other person whose possession
he can control, is equivalent to his own.(*g*)[2]   If, however,

(*f*) Inman *v.* Whitley, 4 Bea. 548 ; Tipping *v.* Clark, 2 Hare 383, 389.

(*g*) Ex parte Shaw. Jac. 270; Morrice *v.* Swaby, 2 Bea. 500; [Lady Beresford *v.* Driver, 14 Beav. 387 ; Robbins *v.* Davis, 1 Blatchf. C. C. 238.   See
ante, note to p. 12.]

---

[1] Where the bill charges the possession of documents which relate to
the matters in question, the defendant cannot protect himself from setting
out a list and description of the documents, by merely alleging his belief
that they do not contain evidence of or tend to show the plaintiff's title,
but he is bound distinctly to negative the allegations of the bill: Att.-Gen.
v. Corp. of London, 2 Macn. & Gord. 1.   A denial, under oath, of the relevancy of concealed passages will not be sufficient.   If the court ascertains
that they might possibly refer to the questions at issue, their production
will be enforced: Caton *v.* Lewis, 22 L. J. Ch. 906

[2] Where deeds are in the possession of the solicitor of two tenants in
common, it was held that one of the tenants could not be compelled to
produce them in a suit to which the other tenant was not a party: Edmonds
v. Foley, 30 Beav. 282.

a document be in the joint possession of the defendant and of some other person who is not before the Court, its production will not be compelled: and that for two reasons; one, that a party will not be ordered to do that which he cannot, or may not be able to do; the other, that another [*15] *person not present has an interest in the document, which the Court cannot deal with.(h)[1]   The result is the same if he holds the documents in his sole possession, but on the joint account of himself and of other persons, who are not before the Court.   But, if his possession is on his own account only, and he owes no duty to such other persons, the mere fact that the documents are important to their interests will not prevent their production.(i)[2]

The documents must be of such a character as to constitute proper matters of discovery within the ordinary rules, viz., they must not fall within any of the protected classes; and they must be material to the plaintiff's case. Their character on these points must be learnt from the answer.   If the answer, by its want of distinct allegation, leave the right to protection doubtful, the omission may be supplied by affidavit; or, if part only of the document is entitled to protection, the defendant may seal up such

(h) Taylor v. Rundell, Cr. & P. 104; Murray v. Walter, Cr. & P. 114; [Morrell v. Wooten, 13 Beav. 105; Ford v. Dolphin, 1 Drew. 222; Chant v. Brown, 9 Hare 790; Penny v. Goode, 1 Drew. 474.]

(i) Hercy v. Ferrers, 4 Bea. 97.

----

[1] Where possession of documents is admitted by two defendants, one of whom dies, production cannot be enforced in the absence of his representatives: Robertson v. Shewell, 15 Beav. 277.   See also Warwick v. Queen's College, L. R. 4 Eq. 254.

[2] A defendant cannot refuse to produce private and confidential letters from a stranger, on the ground that the writers forbid their publication; but the plaintiff will be put on an undertaking not to use them for any collateral object: Hopkinson v. Lord Burghley, L. R. 2 Ch. 447.

parts as he shall swear by affidavit to be of a protected character.(k)[1] If, however, the uncertainty be not remedied by affidavit, or if the answer contradict itself or be palpably incredible, production may be enforced, to ascertain the truth.(l)[2]

It will be observed that, in order to entitle the plaintiff to have a document produced, it is sufficient to show that it is material to his own case. His right will not be excluded because it happens to be evidence for the defendant also.(m)[3] But if it be not relevant as affirmative evidence for himself, he will not be entitled to inspect his

(k) Llewellyn v. Badeley, 1 Hare 527; Curd v. Curd, 1 Hare 274; [Robbins v. Davis, 1 Blatch. C. C. 238.]

(l) Bowes v. Fernie, 3 M. & C. 632; Latimer v. Neate, 11 Bligh 112; 4 Cl. & F. 570; Bannatyne v. Leader, 10 Sim. 230.

(m) Burrell v. Nicholson, 1 M. & K. 680.

---

[1] If a plaintiff prays for an order on a defendant to produce books and papers, the Court may, as a condition precedent, require the plaintiff to undertake not to communicate the contents improperly. An injunction will lie to restrain him: O'Connor v. Tack, 2 Brews. (Pa.) 407.

[2] For instances in which the Court refuses to compel the production of privileged documents, the student is referred to Enthoven v. Cobb, 5 De G. & Sm. 595 (affirmed on appeal), in 2 De G., M. & G. 632, and Reynolds v. Godlee, 4 K. & J. 88. In these instances the documents protected were cases stated, and opinions of counsel thereon. And the rule is the same where the defendant claims to resist discovery on the ground of being a purchaser for valuable consideration without notice: Hunt v. Elmes, 27 Beav. 62.

[3] Att.-Gen. v. Corp. of London, 2 Macn. & Gord. 247. The defendant in such case must distinctly negative the ground on which the plaintiff claims inspection of the document, in order to protect himself: Ibid. The defendant may also be compelled to set forth whether he has not made certain allegations of title, though not whether those allegations are true, or of the nature of that title; and may be compelled to set forth a schedule of all documents relating to the matter: Potter v. Waller, 2 De Gex & Sm. 410. It seems that the defendant cannot protect himself from discovery, on the ground of disclosing the evidence of his title, where his only allegation of title is negativing that of the p aintiff: Att.-Gen. v. Corp. of London, 2 Macn. & Gord. 247.

6

adversary's evidence, merely because on inspection it may prove defective.(n)   It is otherwise if the bill alleges [*16] a *specific defect in the defendant's title, and charges that the documents will prove the existence of that defect.   Such a charge will entitle the plaintiff to discovery, to the extent of a positive allegation in the answer that they will not afford such proof.   And if the answer be doubtful, he is entitled to production.(o)   The same principle seems applicable where the bill seeks to impeach a document, and alleges that its invalidity would appear by inspection.   In such a case inspection, before the hearing, would probably be permitted, unless the answer satisfactorily displaced the charge.(p)

If the possession and character of the documents are sufficiently admitted, the next step is to order their production; and unless some ground can be shown for refusing it, an order for that purpose is almost of course.[1] It has indeed been contended to be of absolute right in respect of the maxim that "he who answers at all must answer fully," and it has been argued that, in accordance with the maxim, wherever the possession and character of the documents are admitted, no denial by answer of

(n) Bolton v. Corporation of Liverpool, 3 Sim. 467; 1 M. & K. 88 · Llewellyn v. Badeley, 1 Hare 527.

(o) Smith v. Beaufort, 1 Hare 507; 1 Ph. 209; Coombe v. Corporation of London, 1 N. C. C. 631.

(p) Kennedy v. Green, 6 Sim. 7; Wigr. on Discovery, s. 311.

---

[1] The petition for an order of production must designate, with reasonable certainty, the books and papers called for: Williams v. Williams, 1 Maryl. Ch. Dec. 201; Williams v. Savage Man. Co., 3 Id. 306.   The defendant, though treated as plaintiff's agent, has no right to be present at the inspection of the documents: Bartley v. Bartley, 1 Drewry 233.

The general rule is that the defendant's books in daily use are to be produced at his place of business: Mertens v. Haigh, Johns. 735.

the plaintiff's equity, however full and explicit, will excuse from production. This view, however, seems to be incorrect; for although the fitness of production, so far as it depends on the character of the documents, is determined on the same principles as if the bill had asked that they should be incorporated with the answer, yet it does not follow that an objection to discover their contents must be taken in both cases in the same technical form. The thing demanded is the same in both, but the form of demand is different, and so also may be the form of resisting that demand. In the case which we are now considering the only thing asked is a descriptive schedule; the answer gives the schedule; and is a full answer according to the requirements of the bill. If the contents had been asked *for, the defendant might have been compelled to plead, and might have adopted [*17] that course to avoid the technical rule. But there is no such requisition in the bill; and therefore, if the plaintiff's equity be effectually displaced by the answer, the mere technical rule that an answer must be full, does not apply to the production of documents.(q)[1]

(q) Adams v. Fisher, 3 M. & C. 526; Wigr. on Discovery, s. 148–185; Lancaster v. Evors, 1 Ph. 349.

---

[1] Where discovery is sought in relation to matters in which the plaintiff has no interest, except consequential or resulting from a character or title denied by the answer, and not otherwise appearing on the record, the plaintiff has no equity entitling him to the discovery. But, if the plaintiff's interest in the discovery sought results from a character and a title alleged in the bill, and if the bill properly avers that the discovery will establish that character and title, and also establish a case of fraud by the defendant, in destroying or withholding the plaintiff's remedies, the defendant cannot withhold discovery by generally denying the character and title claimed by the bill: Stainton v. Chadwick, 3 Macn. & Gord. 575. It seems that a defendant cannot protect himself from discovery, on the ground of its disclosing the evidence of his title, where his only allegation of title is a

A defendant may also in some cases bind himself by
the frame of his answer to produce a document, which is
evidence of his own title alone, and which does not contain, nor is alleged to contain, any evidence of the plaintiff's case. A mere reference to the document as existing,
and as constituting a portion of his own evidence, will not
expose him to this liability; but if he professes to set out
its contents, or to give an abstract of it, referring for verification to the document itself, he will be considered to
have made it substantially a part of his answer; and if
he admits possession, will be bound to produce it, in order
that the plaintiff may ascertain that it is correctly stated. (r)

(r) Hardman v. Ellames, 2 M. & K. 732; Latimer v. Neate, 11 Bligh,
112; Adams v. Fisher, 3 M. & C. 526, 548; Att.-Gen. v. Lambe, 3 Y & C.
171; Phillips v. Evans, 3 N. C. C. 647; Wigr. on Discovery, s. 385, 424.

---

negativing that of the plaintiff: Att.-Gen. v. Corp. of London, 2 Macn. &
Gord. 247. But if the plaintiff's title is denied, and the answer states
positively that the documents in the defendant's custody relating to matters
in the bill will not show that title, the Court will not order their production; so, even if he merely states that he is advised and believes that they
will not show the plaintiff's title: Peile v. Stoddart, 1 Macn. & Gord. 192.
In Goodall v. Little, 1 Sim. N. S. 155, however, where there was a denial
of the plaintiff's title in the bill, and the answer, admitting the possession
of certain documents, denied that these documents would show the facts
to be as the plaintiff alleged them, the Court ordered the production of the
documents, on the ground that they might form material links in the chain
of proof. And in Swinborne v. Nelson, 22 L. J. (N. S.) Ch. 331, discovery was enforced, notwithstanding an express denial of the plaintiff's
title in the answer. The general language of Adams v. Fisher, which is
cited as the authority for the doctrine in the text, was said not to be in
accordance with " a long line of authorities before decided in this Court,"
and inconsistent with the principles of equity pleading; and it was supposed that the case in question was intended only to apply to cases where
the discovery would not assist the plaintiff in making out his title to the
relief sought.
    There is no distinction, in the rule to be applied in this matter, between
ordinary discovery and the production of documents: Swinborne v. Nelson,
ut sup.

The right of enforcing discovery on oath is confined to the plaintiff in the cause. If the defendant wishes on his part, to obtain discovery, he must constitute himself a plaintiff by filing a cross-bill, and will be entitled in his turn to an answer on oath, so soon as he has answered the original bill.[1] If, however, the plaintiff's title be made out by documents, the production of which is material for making out the defence, the right of filing a cross-bill would obviously afford no adequate aid to the defendant; because it would not enable him to see the documents, until after his own answer had been filed. It appears that under such circumstances the court cannot compel the plaintiff to produce the documents, but if he states the *alleged document to be in his possession, may ex- [*18] cuse the defendant from answering until it is done.

The leading case on this doctrine is one where a bill was filed against executors, praying payment of two promissory notes given by the testator for securing 15,000l.

---

[1] When defendant seeks the discovery of books and papers in the possession of the plaintiff, he should file a cross-bill: Bogert v. Bogert, 2 Edw. Ch. 399. See also as to cases in which it is proper to file cross-bills: White v. Buloid, 2 Paige Ch. 164; Cloud v. Hamilton, 3 Yerg. 81; Tarleton v. Vietes, 1 Gilm. 470; Josey v. Rogers, 13 Geo. 478. A cross-bill is merely a defence, and cannot be the foundation of a decree concerning matters not embraced in the original writ: Gallatian v. Erwin, Hopk. 48; Draper v. Gordon, 4 Sandf. Ch. 210; Gallatian v. Cunningham, 8 Cowen 361, s. c.; Field v. Schieffelin, 7 John. Ch. 252; May v. Armstrong, 3 J. J. Marsh. 262. See remarks of Kent, Ch., as to cross-bills, in Field v. Schieffelin, 7 John. Ch. 252. Time for answering may be enlarged for the purpose of bringing in a cross-bill: Josey v. Rogers, 13 Geo. 478; Primmer v. Patten, 32 Illinois 528. The Rules of Equity Practice adopted by the Supreme Court of Pennsylvania in 1865 provide that specific interrogatories to the defendants shall not be included in the bill, but shall be filed separately (Rule 39), and that cross-bills for discovery only shall not be allowed, but the defendant shall be at liberty instead thereof to file interrogatories to the plaintiff (Rule 41). A similar rule as to cross-bills had been previously adopted in England by statute 15 & 16 Vic. c. 86, § 19.

One of the executors made an affidavit that he had in-
spected the first note, and had observed on the face of it,
circumstances tending to impeach its authenticity; that
he was informed and believed that the second note had
been produced by the plaintiff for payment in a foreign
country; and that he was advised and believed it was
necessary, in order that his answer might fully meet the
case, that he should, before answer, have inspection of
such second note.   It was ordered that the defendants
should not be compelled to answer, till a fortnight after
the production of the second note.   For the purpose however of obtaining such production, it will not be sufficient
to allege that it may be material to the defence.   But the
circumstances which constitute the materiality must be
so stated by affidavit, that the court may estimate the
alleged necessity, and may be satisfied that it is not needlessly compelling a production.   The validity of the doctrine is still uncertain.   It has been said by a Judge of
great experience, that he never understood the reasoning
on which it proceeded, whilst another has expressed his
conviction that it is founded on principles, which upon
examination would fully support it.(s)[1]

The jurisdiction of the Greal Seal for enforcing discovery is available in aid of proceedings for civil relief,
whether such relief be asked from the Court of Chancery,
or from another public tribunal in this country which is

(s) Princess of Wales v. Lord Liverpool, 1 Sw. 114; Taylor v. Heming,
4 Bea. 235; Milligan v. Mitchell, 6 Sim. 186; Penfold v. Nunn, 5 Sim.
405; Bate v. Bate, 7 Bea. 528.

[1] To entitle a plaintiff in a cross-bill to a stay of proceedings in the
original bill, until the cross-bill has been answered, the cross-bill must be
sworn to positively, either by the plaintiff, or by the person from whom
his information is derived: Talmage v. Pell, 9 Paige Ch. 410; White v.
Buloid, 2 Paige 164.

itself unable to enforce discovery.[1] But discovery will not be enforced to aid a proceeding before arbitrators, or before an inferior court. And it has also been refused in regard *to proceedings in the Ecclesiastical Court. [*19] But the true reason in this latter case is that it is not wanted, for the Ecclesiastical Court itself can compel an answer. Discovery has been enforced in one instance to aid the jurisdiction of a foreign Court; but the propriety of such enforcements seems open to doubt.(t)[2]

In order to entitle himself to such discovery, the plaintiff must show a title to sue the defendant in some other Court, or that he is actually involved in litigation with the defendant, or is liable to be so, and must also show that the discovery prayed is material to support or defend the suit. If he does not show this, he shows no title to the discovery.(u)[3] And therefore, when a bill was filed

(t) Mitf. 53, 186, 225 ; Earl of Derby v. Duke of Athol, 1 Ves. Sen. 202, 205; Bent v. Young, 9 Sim. 185.

(u) Mitf. 191.

---

[1] March v. Davison, 9 Paige 580; Lane v. Stebbins, Id. 622; Atlantic Ins. Co. v. Lunar, 1 Sandf. Ch. 91. But a discovery will not be allowed merely to guard against anticipated perjury in a suit at law : Leggett v. Postley, 2 Paige 599. Whether a court will sustain a bill of discovery merely to procure such admissions as might be used in mitigation of damages, quære? Gelston v. Hoyt, 1 John. Ch. 543.

[2] In New York, it has been decided that a bill of discovery will be sustained to aid the prosecution or defence of a civil suit in a foreign tribunal : Mitchell v. Smith, 1 Paige 287.

[3] Baxter v. Farmer, 7 Ired. Eq. 239 ; Turner v. Dickerson, 1 Stock. Ch. 140. Thus a bill will not lie for the production of title papers, under which the plaintiff claims title, merely on the ground that they may be useful in some future action : Baxter v. Farmer. Where one has an interest in the common law suit of such a kind as makes him in effect a party, though he is not named as a party, a bill for discovery will lie against him : Carter v. Jordan, 15 Geo. 76. Where a demand for a discovery is merely colorable the court will refuse to take jurisdiction : Jones v. Bradshaw, 16 Gratt. (Va.) 355.

for discovery in aid of an action at law, which the plaintiff alleged by his bill that he intended to commence, the Court being of opinion that the case stated would not support an action, allowed a demurrer to the bill.(v)   Where the plaintiff alleges in his bill a sufficient case at law, it has been doubted to what extent discovery can be resisted, by pleading matters which would be a defence at law.[1] In a case of Hindman v. Taylor, before Lord Thurlow, it was said that where the bill was for discovery leading to relief at law, the defendant could not plead matter in bar to the discovery which would be a bar to the relief there. The proposition, however, thus widely expressed, does not seem consistent with later decisions. And the true principle appears to be that, if the legal defence is of a character showing that the discovery would have no bearing on the issue at law, it will be a sufficient answer to the bill. If the legal defence is not of this character, but the trial at law will be of the general merits, the discovery will be enforced.(w)[2]

(v) Mitf. 187.
(w) Hindman v. Taylor, 2 B. C. C. 7; Robertson v. Lubbock, 4 Sim. 161, 172; Scott v. Broadwood, 2 Coll. 447; Hare on Discovery 47–60.

---

[1] As a general rule, when a complainant is entitled to relief, he is also entitled to a discovery of the facts upon which his right to relief is based: Metler v. Metler, 4 Green (N. J.) 457.

[2] Leggett v. Postley, 2 Paige 599; March v. Davison, 9 Paige 580; Lane v. Stebbins, Id. 622; Deas v. Harvie, 2 Barb. Ch. 448; Seymour v. Seymour, 4 Johns. Ch. 409; Lucas v. The Bank of Darien, 2 Stewart 280; Bailey v. Dean, 5 Barb. S. C. 297; Gelston v. Hoyt, 1 John. Ch. 543.

Where a bill seeks for discovery alone, and not for relief also, the defendant will be compelled to make discovery, if the court suppose that it can in any way be material to the plaintiff, in support or defence of any suit: Peck v. Ashley, 12 Met. 478. But see Leggett v. Postley, 2 Paige 569. And a bill of discovery to obtain evidence which might have been useful in a trial at law, must be filed pending the suit at law, unless

*A bill thus filed for enforcing discovery in aid [*20] of proceedings before some other tribunal is called a bill for discovery, in contradistinction to those bills on which the consequent relief is attainable in equity, and which are called bills for relief, or more correctly, for discovery and relief. If the relief be attainable in a different Court, the mere fact that the discovery is requisite will not alter the jurisdiction. The Court of Chancery will enforce the discovery, but the relief must be sought before the appropriate tribunal.[1]

---

some sufficient excuse is shown why it was not filed at that time : Faulkner's Adm'x v. Harwood, 6 Randolph 125 ; and see Foltz v. Pourie & Dawson, 2 Dessau. 40 ; 3 Miss. 433. After a verdict or judgment at law a party comes too late with a bill of discovery : Duncan v. Lyon, 3 John. Ch. 355, 402; Foltz v. Pourie & Dawson, 2 Dessau. 40 ; Cowman v. Kingsland, 4 Edw. Ch. 627. But if equity has concurrent jurisdiction, in such case, and the defendant neglect to interpose the objection by demurrer, and answers on the merits, the jurisdiction will be sustained, notwithstanding a judgment at law : Endicott v. Penny, 14 Sm. & Marsh. 144.

It seems that it is not necessary to state particularly the pleadings at law, so as to show what precise issues are pending : Hinkle v. Currin, 1 Humph. (Tenn.) 74.

The joinder of defendants in separate actions or of separate suits at law in the same bill of discovery, is inadmissible : Broadbent v. State, 7 Maryl. 416 ; MacDougald v. Maddox, 17 Geo. 52.

[1] A bill for discovery alone may be maintained, in a case where, if it had been for relief also, it would have been demurrable; as on a bill in aid of a plea of illegal consideration, in a suit at law on a bond : Benyon v. Nettlefold, 3 Macn. & Gord. 94; Manning v. Drake, 1 Mann. (Mich.) 34. A bill for discovery in aid of an action, must show affirmatively that the plaintiff's right cannot be established at law, without aid of the discovery which he seeks : Stacy v. Pearson & Bobbitt, 3 Rich. Eq. 148 ; Merchants' Bank v. Davis, 3 Kelley 112; Williams v. Harden, 1 Barb. Ch. 298 ; Norwich, &c., R. R. Co. v. Storey, 17 Conn. 364 ; Lindsley v. James, 3 Cold. (Tenn.) 477; though in Peck v. Ashley, 12 Met. 478, it was held that discovery may be enforced notwithstanding the absence of such allegation, where the court can suppose that it would be in any way material in support or defence of an action. But a bill will lie not only where the plaintiff is destitute of other evidence, but also to aid or render it

The discovery obtained by a bill in equity is only available against the answering defendant.[1] It cannot be read as evidence against a co-defendant, unless he refers to it by his answer as correct, or is so connected with the answering party as to be bound, under the ordinary rules

unnecessary : Stacy v. Pearson & Bobbitt, 3 Rich. Eq. 148; though see Bell v. Pomeroy, 4 McLean 57. It is no answer to such bill, to say that the facts can be proved by other witnesses, if they are incompetent by reason of interest: Bell v. Pomeroy.

In England, the modern rule is, that as to matters not originally within the cognisance of equity, and where there is adequate remedy at law, a bill for discovery merely, can alone be sustained; and that if the bill further pray relief, special or general, the whole is demurrable : Story, Eq. Jur. ? 69, 70; Equity Plead. ? 312; Foley v. Hill, 2 H. L. Cas. 37. But in the United States, a more convenient and reasonable doctrine generally obtains in such cases, and where the discovery is effectual, the court will go on and give the adequate relief, if in its power, to prevent a multiplicity of suits; unless where there is a pending action: Story Eq. Jur. ? 71 ; Brooks v. Stolley, 3 McLean 523 ; Warner v. Daniels, 1 Wood. & Min. 90; Traip v. Gould, 15 Maine 82; Lyons v. Miller, 6 Gratt. 438; Sims v. Aughtery, 4 Strob. Eq. 121 ; Holmes v. Holmes, 36 Verm. 525; but in New Jersey this rule has not been adopted. See Little v. Cooper, 2 Stockt. 273. If, however, a jury is necessary to determine the extent of the relief, discovery will be enforced, and the case then sent to law: Lynch v. Sumrall, 1 A. K. Marsh. 468. In a bill for discovery, the general prayer " for such other and further relief as equity and good conscience may require," &c., is referrable only to the main purpose of the bill—discovery : Williams v. Row, 12 P. F. Smith 118.

[1] As a general rule, the answer of one defendant cannot be used as evidence against his co-defendant: Leeds v. Marine Ins. Co. of Alexandria, 2 Wheaton 380; Osborne v. Bank of United States, 9 Id. 738; Van Reimsdyk v. Kane, 1 Gallis. 630; Robinson v. Sampson, 23 Maine 388; Cannon v. Norton, 14 Verm. 178; Conner v. Chase, 15 Id. 764; Grant v. U. S. Bank, 1 C. C. E. 112; Phœnix v. Ingraham, 5 John. 412; Pettit v. Jennings, 2 Rob. (Va.) 676; Holloway v. Moore, 4 S. & M. 594; Felch v. Hooper, 20 Maine 159; Singleton v. Gayle, 8 Porter 270; Webb v. Pell, 3 Paige Ch. 368; Judd v. Seaver, 8 Id. 548; Dykers v. Wilder, 3 Edw. Ch. 496; Hayward v. Carroll, 4 Har. & J. 518; Stewart v. Stone, 3 Gill & J. 510; Calwell v. Boyer, 8 Id. 136; and in numerous other cases.

of law, by his declarations or admissions.(x) If therefore a bill is filed for relief, no person can be made a party who is unaffected by the relief, notwithstanding he might give important discovery, because, as against himself, discovery is needless, and as against the other parties, it would be unavailing. In like manner, if the bill be for discovery alone, no person can be made a defendant who is not a party to the record at law. There is an exception however in the case of suits against corporations; and in such suits it is allowable to join the officers or members personally as defendants, in order that they may give discovery on oath, which the corporate body cannot do.(y)[1]

. As against the defendant himself, if he be not under incapacity, the answer is evidence. If the plaintiff does not reply to it, and thus give him an opportunity of verification by evidence, the whole answer must be taken as true.[2] If a replication be filed, the answer is not evidence in the defendant's favor, but the plaintiff may use *any portion of it, without admitting the remainder [*21] to be read, except so far as it is explanatory of the portion used.(z) The defendant, however, is so far

(x) Mitf. 188 ; Anon., 1 P. W. 301 ; Chervet v. Jones, 6 Mad. 267 ; Crosse v. Bedingfield, 12 Sim. 35 ; Green v. Pledger, 3 Hare 165.

(y) Mitf. 188 ; Kerr v. Rew, 5 M. & C. 154 ; Glasscott v. Copperminers' Company, 11 Sim. 305, 314.

(z) Bartlett v. Gillard, 3 Russ. 149, 156 ; Freeman v. Tatham, 5 Hare 329 ; East v. East, 5 Hare 343 ; [see Glenn v. Randall, 2 Maryl. Ch. 220.]

[1] Lindsey v. James, 3 Cold. (Tenn.) 477.

[2] Fant v. Miller, 17 Gratt. (Va.) 187. This does not apply where an answer under oath is waived: Tomlinson v. Lindley, 2 Carter (Ind.) 569. Where the bill calls for answer not under oath, the *jurat* of the answer will be stricken out, and the answer considered as not sworn to: Sweet v. Parker, 22 N. J. Eq. 453. Where the plaintiff calls on the defendant to answer the allegations of the bill he makes defendant a witness for that purpose and for no other: Eaton's Appeal, 16 P. F. Smith 483 ; see also, Hart v. Freeman, 42 Ala. 567.

entitled to the benefit of his answer, that any material suggestion made by it, though not established by proof may, at the discretion of the Court, be referred for inquiry.(a) And if a positive denial in the answer be met by the evidence of one witness only, the Court will neither make a decree, nor send the question to a trial at law.[1] If there are corroborative circumstances in the plaintiff's favor, the Court will depart from this rule, and will either make an immediate decree, or, if the defendant desire it, will direct an issue, ordering his answer to be read as evidence on the trial, so that it may be contrasted with the testimony given against him.(b)   The defendant's answer may also be read on the question of costs; and the Court, though compelled by the evidence to make a decree against him, may give credit to his statement on oath as to his own conduct, so far as to exempt him from payment of costs.   But it has been held that where a tender is relied on by the defendant, the mere unproved statement

(a) Connop v. Hayward, 1 N. C. C. 33; McMahon v. Burchell, 2 Ph. 127.

(b) East India Company v. Donald, 9 Ves. 275; Savage v. Brocksopp, 18 Ves. 335.

---

[1] When the facts alleged in the complainant's bill are denied in the answer, it is a general principle that they must be proved by two credible witnesses, or one witness and strong corroborating circumstances: Swift v. Dean, 6 Johns. 523; Clason v. Morris, 10 Id. 524; Atkinson v. Manks, 1 Cow. 691; Stafford v. Bryan, 1 Paige Ch. 239; Chance v. Teeple, 3 Green Ch. 173; McDowell v. Bank of Wilmington and Brandywine, 1 Harring. 369; Beatty v. Smith & Thompson, 2 Hen. & M. 395; Raines v. Jones, 4 Humph. 490; Coles v. Raymond, 5 Blackf. 435; Bibb v. Smith, 1 Dana 580; Mason v. Peck, 7 J. J. Marsh. 300; Patterson v. Hobbs, 1 Lit. 275; Littel v. McIver, 1 Bibb. 203; Paulling v. Sturgis, 3 Stewart 95; Neale v. Hagthrop, 3 Bland. 551; Hughes v. Blake, 6 Wheaton 453; Union Bank v. Geary, 5 Pet. 99; Page v. Page, 8 N. H. 187; Daniel v. Mitchell, 1 Story 173; Myers v. Kenzie, 26 Ill. 36; White v. Hampton, 10 Iowa 238; and many other cases.

that such tender has been made is not sufficient to save costs. Nor can the answer of a mortgagor be read against a mortgagee to deprive him, on the ground of misconduct, of his ordinary right to costs.(c)

The rule which allows a plaintiff, who has replied to the answer, to read selected portions only, is necessarily confined to cases where the hearing is in equity. If the bill be for discovery in aid of a procedure at law, the answer is treated at law like any other admission, and must be read throughout, if it be read at all.[1] The costs also of such an answer are subject to a different rule from those of an answer to a bill *for relief. In the one case the costs of discovery are a portion of [*22] the costs in the cause, and are disposed of in that character at the hearing. In the other, the defendant is entitled to costs as a matter of course, immediately on putting in a full answer, for the Court of Chancery never hears the cause; and the Court which does hear it has no jurisdiction over the Chancery costs.

This principle, which applies to bills for discovery in aid of a procedure at law, was, until lately, applied to cross-bills for discovery alone, when filed in aid of a defence in equity; so that in a suit of this class the answer, if read at all, must have been read throughout, and the defendant, on filing it, was entitled to his costs. The practice, however, is now altered, and it is directed that

(c) Howell v. George, 1 Mad. 1; Milnes v. Davidson, 3 Mad. 374; Wright v. Jones, C. P. Coop. 493.

---

[1] Hart v. Freeman, 42 Alab. 567; Fant v. Miller, 17 Gratt. (Va.) 187. This rule also applies where, as in the United States generally, the court goes on to give relief on the ground of discovery, notwithstanding that there is adequate relief at law: Lyons v. Miller, 6 Gratt. 439; Holmes v. Holmes, 36 Verm. 525; Shotwell v. Smith, 20 N. J. Eq. 79.

the answer to a cross-bill for discovery only m
and used in the same manner and under the sa
tions as the answer to a bill praying relief, an
costs of it shall be costs in the original cause
Court otherwise orders.(*d*)

(*d*) 42d Order of August, 1851; 125th Order of Ma

*CHAPTER II. [*23]

ON COMMISSIONS TO EXAMINE WITNESSES ABROAD; OF PER-
PETUATION OF TESTIMONY AND OF EXAMINATIONS DE BENE
ESSE.[1]

In addition to the jurisdiction for discovery, there is
another substantially similar to it, under which the Court
of Chancery interposes for two objects : first, for the procurement of evidence to be used elsewhere, without itself
deciding on the result, viz., in suits for a COMMISSION TO
EXAMINE WITNESSES ABROAD, and in suit to PERPETUATE
TESTIMONY; and secondly, for granting, either in aid of
its own proceedings or of a proceeding elsewhere, an
examination of witnesses *de bene esse.*

---

[1] Courts of Chancery in the United States, and courts of law, exercising
chancery powers, are in the constant practice of entertaining jurisdiction
of bills for the perpetuation of testimony, issuing commissions for the examination of witnesses abroad, and of permitting testimony to be taken *de
bene esse;* and it will be found, that generally the rules of practice are
analogous to those of the English High Court of Chancery. See upon this
subject Clark v. Bundy, 6 Paige 432; Brown v. Southworth et al., 9 Id.
351; Lingan v. Henderson, 1 Bland 236 ; Jerome et al. v. Jerome, 5 Conn.
352; In the matter of Isaac L. Kip, 1 Paige Ch. 601; Fort v. Ragusin,
2 Johns. Ch. 146; Rockwell r. Folsom, 4 Id. 165; Renwick v. Renwick,
10 Paige Ch. 420; Bush v. Vandenbergh, 1 Edw. Ch. 649; Phelps &
Spafford v. Curtis, 1 Green Ch. 387; Stubbs v. Burwell, 2 Hen. & M. 536;
Chapman v. Chapman, 4 Id. 426; Oliver v. Palmer, 11 Gill & J. 426;
Kincheloe v. Kincheloe, 11 Leigh 393; Gordon v. Watkins et al., 1 S. &
M. Ch. 37; Story on Eq. Plead., Ch. VII.; Baxter v. Farmer, 7 Ired. Eq.
239.

The jurisdiction for issuing COMMISSIONS TO EXAMINE WITNESSES ABROAD is sufficiently explained by its name. It originated in the incapacity of the common law courts to issue such commissions without the consent of both parties. That incapacity is removed by a recent statute; but the jurisdiction of equity still continues, though its exercise- is less frequently required.(a)

The jurisdiction in suits to PERPETUATE TESTIMONY arises where the fact, to which the testimony relates, cannot be immediately investigated at law, e. g., where the person filing the bill has merely a future interest, or having an immediate interest, is himself in possession and not actually disturbed, though threatened by the defendant [*24] *with disturbance at a future time.(b) Under a late statute the jurisdiction has been extended; and it has been enacted, that "any person who would, under the circumstances alleged by him to exist, become entitled upon the happening of any future event, to any honor, title, dignity, or office, or to any estate or interest in any property, real or personal, the right or claim to which cannot by him be brought to trial before the happening of such event, shall be entitled to file a bill to perpetuate any testimony which may be material for establishing such claim or right."(c)

The jurisdiction to examine witnesses *de bene esse* is a jurisdiction for permitting evidence to be taken before the cause is regularly at issue, in cases where, from the age or illness of a witness, or from his being the only witness

(a) 1 Wm. 4, c. 22, s. 4 ; Grinnell v. Cobbold, 4 Sim. 546.

(b) Mitf. 51 ; 1 Mad. Ch. Practice 253 ; Dursley v. Fitzhardinge, 6 Ves. 251 ; Angell v. Angell, 1 S. & S. 83.

(c) Earl of Belfast v. Chichester, 2 J. & W. 439 ; Townshend Peerage Case, 10 Cl. & F. 289 ; 5 & 6 Vict. c. 69.

to an important fact, there is reason to apprehend that, before the regular opportunity arrives, material evidence may be lost.   This is called an examination *de bene esse;* and the depositions taken under it can only be read, if the party seeking the benefit of them has used all diligence to examine in the ordinary course, but there has been a moral impossibility of his so doing.(*d*)   The same course may be pursued where a similar danger exists in reference to an action at law; and a bill may be entertained for an auxiliary examination *de bene esse,* provided there be annexed to it an affidavit of the circumstances which render such examination necessary.(*e*)   The principle on which this affidavit is required, where the matter is capable of being immediately the subject of an action at law, seems to be that the bill tends to alter the ordinary course of the administration of justice, which ought not to be permitted on the bare allegation of a plaintiff.   The same principle is applied, as *we shall hereafter [*25] see, where a bill is filed, in respect of an instrument on which an action at law would lie, alleging that it is destroyed or lost, or is in the defendant's custody, to obtain relief which, but for such circumstances, might be had at law.(*f*)

The mode of taking the evidence, either under a commission to Examine Witnesses Abroad, or in a suit to Perpetuate Testimony, or in an examination *de bene esse,* is in all material points similar to that adopted in the ordinary examination in a cause.

In a suit, however, to Perpetuate Testimony, the cause

(*d*) Frere *v.* Green, 19 Ves. 320; Hope *v.* Hope, 3 Bea. 317; McIntosh *v.* Great Western Railway, 1 Hare 328; Cann *v.* Cann, 1 P. W. 567.

(*e*) Mitf. 52, 150; Angell *v.* Angell, 1 S. & S. 83.

(*f*) Post.   Re-execution of Lost Instruments.

does not proceed beyond the examination of the witnesses. When that has been completed it is considered at an énd; and the only remaining step is the publication of the evidence. This is effected by an order of the Court; but such an order cannot be obtained except for the purpose of a suit or action, nor even for that purpose during the lifetime of the witnesses, unless on special grounds, showing that their examination is morally impossible.(*g*)[1]

The same principle applies to depositions taken *de bene esse;* and their publication cannot be obtained, unless the witness dies or is otherwise incapacitated from giving his evidence before issue is joined.

If the evidence is required for the purpose of a trial at law, the order made is that the depositions be published, and that the officer attend with and produce to the Court of law the record of the whole proceedings; and that the parties may make such use of the same as by law they can.(*h*)   It has been determined that it is no objection to the publication of depositions which have been taken in a suit to Perpetuate Testimony, that the proceedings for which they are required are in the Court of a foreign country.(*i*)

(*g*) Morrison *v.* Arnold, 19 Ves. 670; [Barnsdale *v.* Lowe, 2 Russ. & M. 142.]

(*h*) Attorney-General *v.* Ray, 2 Hare 518.

(*i*) Morris *v.* Morris, 2 Ph. 205.

---

[1] A bill to perpetuate testimony, also differs from an ordinary bill, in that it cannot be dismissed for want of prosecution; the only order that can be made is to compel the plaintiff to proceed in a given time or pay the costs: Beavan *v.* Carpenter, 11 Sim. 22; Wright *v.* Tatham, 2 Sim. 459.

BOOK II.

OF THE JURISDICTION OF THE COURTS OF EQUITY, IN CASES
IN WHICH THE COURTS OF ORDINARY JURISDICTION CAN-
NOT ENFORCE A RIGHT.

---

*CHAPTER I. [*26]

OF TRUSTS, BOTH ORDINARY AND CHARITABLE.

THE jurisdiction of equity to grant relief originates as
we have seen, in the occasional inadequacy of the remedy
at law; and the instances in which this inadequacy occurs,
may be conveniently divided under two heads, viz., 1.
Where the Courts of ordinary jurisdiction cannot enforce
a right; and 2. Where they cannot administer it.

It has been already stated in the Introduction, that the
equities under the first head of this division, viz., where
the Courts of ordinary jurisdiction cannot enforce a right,
are those for performance of trusts and contracts, for election between inconsistent benefits, for completion of gifts
on meritorious consideration in favor of the donor's intention after his death, for giving effect to discharges by
matter *in pais* of contracts under seal, for relief against
penalties and forfeited mortgages, for re-execution or correction of instruments which have been lost or erroneously

framed, for rescission of transactions which are illegal or fraudulent, or which have been carried on in ignorance or mistake of material facts, and for injunction against irreparable torts.

The jurisdiction to enforce performance of trusts arises where property has been conferred upon, and accepted by, one person, on the terms of using it for the benefit of [*27] *another. The former person or owner at law, is called the trustee; the latter, or owner in equity, the *cestui que trust.*

The principal advantage of a conveyance on trust is, that it enables the owners of property to effectuate dispositions of a more complex character than is consistent with the machinery of conveyances at law; and that it also affords the means of protecting infants and other incapacitated persons, by vesting their property in trustworthy holders, who manage and apply it for their benefit. It is, on the other hand, attended with some inconvenience and risk, because it makes the *cestui que trust's* security in some degree dependent on a trustee who has no beneficial interest, and may enable a fraudulent trustee, by concealing his fiduciary character, to sell the property to a stranger.

The distinction between a trustee's legal ownership, and the beneficial interest of a *cestui que trust,* is in some instances recognised even at law; and where the trust is created by will, the character of its duties and the nature of the estate required for their performance are allowed to effect the construction of the devise, in reference both to its passing any estate, and also in reference to the extent and duration of the estate passed.(*a*) But, in so far as a legal ownership is conferred, it invests the trustee

(*a*) 2 Jarm. on Wills 196 ; Adams on Ejectment, 4th ed., 60–65.

with absolute dominion at law, and the equitable ownership, or right to compel performance of his trust, is only
cognisable in the Court of Chancery.[1]

In order to originate a trust, two things are essential :
first, that the ownership conferred be coupled with a trust,
either declared by the parties or resulting by presumption
of law; and secondly, that it be accepted on those terms
by the trustee.

The declaration of a trust by the parties is not, independently of the Statute of Frauds, required to be made
or evidenced in any particular way. And therefore, previously *to that statute, a trust, whether of real or
personal property, might be declared either by [*28]
deed, by writing not under seal, or by mere word of
mouth, subject, however, to the ordinary rule of law that,
if an instrument in writing existed, it could not be explained or contradicted by parol evidence.

With respect, however, to real estate, the rule is altered
by the Statute of Frauds, and it is enacted, "that all
declarations or creations of trusts or confidences of any
lands, tenements, or hereditaments, shall be manifested
and proved by some writing, signed by the party who is
by law enabled to declare such trust, or by his last will
in writing; or else they shall be utterly void and of no
effect." And further, that "all grants and assignments
of any trust or confidence shall likewise be in writing,
signed by the party granting or assigning the same, or by
such last will or devise."[2] It will be observed that this

---

[1] The common law rule still exists as to personalty : Martin v. Greer, 1
Geo. Decis. 109; Lord v. Lowry, 1 Bailey's Ch. 510; Rice v. Burnett,
Spear's Ch. 579; Gordon v. Green, 10 Geo. 534.

[2] This provision is in force in most of the United States. See Hill on
Trustees 56, note; Brinnan v. Brinnan, 3 Green (N. J.) 212; Gibson v.
Foote, 40 Miss. 788. When the fact that the trust was created by parol

act does not require that the trust shall be declared in writing, but only that it shall be manifested and proved by writing.[1] And therefore, if the existence of a trust, together with its precise terms and subject-matter, can be proved from any subsequent acknowledgment, written and signed by the trustee, as by a letter, memorandum, or recital in a deed, it will be sufficient.(b)[2]

(b) 29 Car. 2, c. 3, ss. 7 & 9; Gardner v. Rowe, 2 S. & S. 346; 5 Russ. 258.

---

only, appears upon the face of the bill, it may be taken advantage of by demurrer; where it does not so appear the Statute of Frauds must be set up by a plea or in the answer. See Hill on Trustees, 61, note.

[1] The distinction alluded to in the text has this practical importance, viz.: that the commencement of the estate of the *cestui que trust* will not date merely from the execution of the writing by which it is proved, but will relate back to the time of its original creation. Thus where a parol declaration of trust is made in favor of one who afterwards dies, and the trust is after his death declared in writing, the written declaration will be referred back to the date of the parol creation so as to bring the subject of the trust within the scope of the *cestui que trust's* will: Ambrose v. Ambrose, 1 P. Wms. 322. Rights of *bonâ fide* purchasers without notice are of course protected, and the distinction noticed above has been held, after some fluctuation in opinion, not to apply to post-nuptial settlements made in pursuance of ante-nuptial parol agreements. See Hill on Trustees, page 57, note 1. In Maine, Massachusetts, and some other states, trusts must be "created and declared" in writing: Hill on Trustees, page 56, note. See also, Movan v. Hays, 1 Johns. Ch. 339; Johnson v. Ronald, 4 Munf. 77; Jackson v. Moore, 6 Cowen 706; Flagg v. Mann, 2 Sumn. 486; Pinney v. Fellows, 15 Verm. 525; 2 Story's Eq., sec. 972. The instrument creating the trust need not be executed by the *cestui que trust*: Skipwith's Extr. v. Cunningham, 8 Leigh 271.

[2] Any writing, no matter how informal, which *declares what the trust is*, will satisfy the requirements of the statute: Smith v. Matthews, 3 De G. F. & J. 139; Orleans v. Chatham, 2 Pick. 29; Hardin v. Baird, 6 Litt. 346; Graham v. Lambert, 5 Humph. 595; Gomez v. The Tradesman's Bank, 4 Sand. S. C. 106; Wright v. Douglass, 3 Selden 564; Bragg v. Paulk, 42 Maine 502; Maxwell v. Whieldon's Adm'r., 10 Cush. 221; Massey v. Massey, 20 Tex. 134. Where the existence of a trust is shown by writing, parol evidence may, *it seems*, be let in to show its terms: Reid v. Reid, 12 Rich. (S. C.) Eq. 213. See, however, Cook v. Barr, 44 N. Y. 156, and Duffy v. Masterton, Id. 557. See also, Fisher v. Fields, 10 Johns. 495;

With respect to personal estate, including moneys out on mortgage, the original rule continues, and it is sufficient that, either by writing or by word of mouth, there should be a certain declaration of the trust.(c)

The intention thus evidenced, whether by writing or by parol, to impose a trust on the donee, must be declared with certainty; and there must also-be a certain declaration of its terms, viz., of the property on which the trust is to attach, the parties for whom the benefit is meant, and the *interests which they are respectively to take.[1] If there be uncertainty in this latter respect, [*29] but it be sufficiently certain that a trust was meant, and not a gift for the donee's benefit, the case will fall under a different rule, and there will be a resulting trust for the donor by operation of law.

The certainty, however, of a trust is not necessarily

(c) Benbow v. Townsend, 1 M. & K. 506; McFadden v. Jenkyns, 1 Hare 458; 1 Ph. 153.

Orleans v. Chatham, 2 Pick. 29; Dale v. Hamilton, 2 Phil. 266; Maccubbin v. Cromwell, 7 Gill & Johns. 157; Steere v. Steere, 5 Johns. Ch. 1; Unitarian Soc. v. Woodbury, 2 Shepley 281; Walraven v. Lord, 2 Patt. & H. 547; Bankhead's Trust, 2 Kay & John. 560; Ex parte Boyd, 3 Jurist N. S. 897; Pinney v. Fellows, 15 Verm. 525; Menude v. Delaire, 2 Dessaus. 564; Rutledge v. Smith, 1 McC. Ch. 119; Elliott v. Morris, 1 Harp. Eq. 281; Fleming et al. v. Donahoe et al., 5 Hammond 256; Harrison v. Mennomy, 2 Edw. Ch. 251; Slocum v. Marshall, 2 Wash. C. C. 398.

[1] Slocum v. Marshall, 2 Wash. C. C. 398; Steere v. Steere, 5 Johns. Ch. 1; Dorsey v. Clarke, 4 H. & Johns. 551; Mercer v. Stark, 1 Sm. & Marsh. Ch. 479; Knight v. Boughton, 11 Cl. & Fin. 513; Briggs v. Penny, 3 Macn. & Gord. 546; Williams v. Williams, 1 Sim. N. S. 358; Smith v. Matthews, 3 De G., F. & J. 139. Besides the three requisites enumerated in the text, a fourth has been added by recent English authorities; certainty in the manner in which the trust is to be performed: Knight v. Boughton, ut sup.; Reeves v. Baker, 18 Beav. 372; and this, it was said in the latter case, may be referred partly to the subject-matter, and partly to the object of the trust, and reduced to one or other of them. The mere use of the words "trust" or "trustee" will not necessarily create a trust: Brown v. Combs, 5 Dutch. 36; Hill on Trustees 65, note.

affected by the circumstance that it has been declared in
the form of a power, enabling the trustee to give the estate
to the parties interested, instead of an immediate gift to
them : nor by the use of precatory or recommendatory
words, instead of more imperative language.   And on the
other hand, a trust is not necessarily created, because the
formal language of a trust is used, if a contrary intent
appear from the gift.[1]

The creation of trusts in the form of powers occurs
where no positive direction is given that the trustee shall
hold for the parties interested, but he is authorized to
give them an interest, if he see fit.   Such a power as this
does not necessarily constitute a trust; for it may be
absolutely discretionary in the donee, and one which he
cannot be compelled to execute; but on the other hand,
it may be given him in a different character, and as one
which he is intrusted and bound to execute.   If the context of the gift establish this latter construction, he has
not a discretion whether he will execute his power or not,
but if he neglect his duty, the Court will, to a certain
extent, discharge it in his stead.   It will not, however, in
so doing, assume an arbitrary discretion, although such a
discretion may have been given to the trustee, but it will
adopt such general maxim as under the circumstances
appears applicable, e. g., that a fund given for the benefit
of "relations" shall be distributed among those who are
within the Statute of Distributions, although the donee
might have selected out of a wider class.   The leading
case on this subject is one where leaseholds were bequeathed to a man, with a direction to make certain
payments out of the rents : and the testator *em-
[*30]   powered him to employ the residue for such of his

---

[1] Richardson v. Inglesby, 13 Rich. (S. C.) Eq. 59.

nephew's children as he should think proper. On the trustee's failure so to employ the residue, it was decreed to be a trust for all the children.[1] There is another class of cases, apparently similar to these, but based on an entirely distinct principle, where a non-compulsory power of appointment has been conferred, but the context has implied a gift in default of appointment to the persons who in the event of execution would have been objects of the power. Such, for instance, is a gift to children and their issue in such proportions as A. shall appoint, under which it has been held that in default of appointment the children took by implication estates tail. The distinction between the two cases is, that in the one the objects of the power take, notwithstanding the trustee's failure to appoint, because his failure was a neglect of duty; in the other they take, not because he was bound to appoint, but because it is adjudged, on perusal of the gift, that an express trust was by mistake or carelessness omitted.(d)[2]

(d) Brown v. Higgs, 8 Ves. 561; Grant v. Lynman, 4 Russ. 292; Burroughs v. Philcox, 5 M. & C. 73; 2 Sug. on Powers, 7th ed. 157.

---

[1] See accordingly, Withers v. Yeadon, 1 Rich. Eq. 324; Collins v. Carlisle, 7 B. Monr. 13; Gibbs v. Marsh, 2 Metcalf 243; Miller v. Meetch, 8 Penn. St. 417; Whitehurst v. Harker, 2 Ired. Eq. 292; Penny v. Turner, 2 Phillips 493. Where the class is ascertained, the rule of division by the court is, of course, equality.

[2] A good illustration of the rule of distribution which obtains in default of an execution of a power by a donee in trust, will be found in the case of Salusbury v. Denton, 3 K. & J. 529. There a testator gave a fund to his widow, to be disposed of by her as to part to a charity, and as to the remainder among such relations as she should select; and the widow died without making any disposition of the fund. It was held that the charity was entitled to one moiety, and that the other should be divided among the parties entitled under the Statute of Distributions. See, also, White's Trusts, Johnson 656; Fordyce v. Bridges, 2 Phill. 497, and Brook v. Brook, 3 Sm. & Giff. 280. In Smith v. Bowen, 35 New York 83, there was a devise "to my beloved wife, Martha, to be used and disposed of at her discretion, for the benefit of herself and my three daughters;" and it was held that the words gave one-fourth to the wife absolutely, and, as to

The use of precatory or recommendatory words, whether arising from want of due consideration, or from an unwillingness to use language implying distrust, or from an intention to give a control over the suggested disposition, is not unfrequent in-wills; and we often meet with such expressions as "I recommend," "I entreat," or "I desire" that such a thing be done, or "I have no doubt, or well know," that it will be done.[1] In these cases the mere grammatical construction of the words is not sufficient to determine whether a trust exists. It is clear that words simply intimating an expectation, provided their object be expressed with sufficient certainty, may operate as imperative on the person to whom they are addressed. But although they may create a trust, yet they have not necessarily that effect. They are in themselves of a flexible character, and must give way if the [*31] imperative construction *be inconsistent with any positive provision in the will, or if it appear from the general context that the testator meant to depend on the justice or gratitude of the donee. The question, therefore, in each particular case is merely of construction on the terms of the instrument. (e)[2]

(e) Wright v. Atkyns, 17 Ves. 255; 19 Ves. 299; Shaw v. Lawless, 1 Lloyd & Goold, 558; 5 Cl. & F. 129; Knight v. Boughton, 11 Cl. & F. 513; Knott v. Cottee, 2 Ph. 192; 2 Sug. on Pow. 171.

---

the other three-fourths, created a trust in favor of the daughters, which under the statute in New York, was turned into a power in trust. But although a trust will sometimes be created in spite of the failure of the donee of the power to exercise his discretion, yet In re Eddowes, 1 Dr. & Sm. 395, shows that where there is nothing to point out with certainty in whose favor, or in what shares a gift was intended in default of the execution of the power, no trust can be implied.

[1] "Having confidence," Dresser v. Dresser, 46 Maine 48; "Wish and will," McRee's Adm'r. v. Means, 34 Alab. 349.

[2] There has been some fluctuation in the modern English authorities, on

The non-creation of a trust in the donee notwithstanding that a trust is formally declared, occurs principally in conveyances for payment of debts, where the language used, if taken in its literal acceptation, would constitute the creditors *cestuis que trustent*, and would entitle them to enforce an application of the fund. It has been decided, however, that, notwithstanding the similarity of

the subject of precatory trusts, and two classes of cases have consequently arisen, one leaning in favor of affecting the conscience of the donee with a trust by the use of recommendatory words, the other having an opposite tendency. Of the former class, instances will be found in Bernard *v.* Minshull, Johnson 276 ; Shovelton *v.* Shovelton, 32 Beav. 143 ; Gully *v.* Cregoe, 24 Id. 185 ; Ward *v.* Grey, 26 Id. 485 ; Proby *v.* Landor, 28 Id. 504 ; Liddard *v.* Liddard, 28 Id. 266 ; Brook's Will, 34 L. J. Ch. 616 ; and Constable *v.* Bull, 3 De G. & Sm. 411 ; while for examples of the latter class the reader may refer to Briggs *v.* Penny, 3 Macn. & G. 546 ; Johnston *v.* Rowlands, 2 De G. & Sm. 356 ; Webb *v.* Wools, 2 Sim. N. S. 267 ; Reeves *v.* Baker, 18 Beav. 372, and Hood *v.* Oglander, 34 L. J. Ch. 528 ; Eaton *v.* Watts, 5 Eq. L. R. 151. The former class probably includes the more recent and better considered decisions. See, also, the remarks in Hawkins on Wills, page 160.

In the United States, also, it is impossible to reconcile all the authorities. The rule in Pennsylvania is that precatory expressions in a will are not, *primâ facie,* sufficient to create a trust : Pennock's Estate, 20 Penna. St. 268 ; Walker *v.* Hall, 34 Id. 483 ; Kinter *v.* Jenks, 43 Id. 445, and Jauretche *v.* Proctor, 48 Id. 466 ; Second Church *v.* Disbrow, 52 Id. 219 ; Burt *v.* Herron, 66 Id. 400 ; Van Duyne *v.* Van Duyne, 1 McCarter (N. J.) 397 ; and so in Connecticut : Gilbert *v.* Chapin, 19 Conn. 351, where the earlier case of Bull *v.* Bull, 8 Conn. 47, was disapproved ; though even in that state mere discretion in regard to the selection of the objects or the distribution of the subject of a devise is not inconsistent with a trust ; and see Harper *v.* Phelps, 21 Conn. 257. See, also, Ellis *v.* Ellis, 15 Alab. 296. But a more liberal doctrine as to precatory words has been held in Erickson *v.* Willard, 1 N. H. 217 ; Lucas *v.* Lockhart, 10 Sm. & Marsh. 466 ; Collins *v.* Carlisle, 7 B. Mon. 14 ; Harrison *v.* Harrison, 2 Gratt. 1 ; McRee's Adm'r. *v.* Means, 34 Alab. 349, and Dresser *v.* Dresser, 46 Maine 48 ; Warner *v.* Bates, 98 Mass. 274 ; Cook *v.* Ellington, 6 Jones Eq. (N. C.) 371. The student will find this subject discussed in the notes to Harding *v.* Glyn, 2 Lead. Cas. in Eq. 789.

form, the transaction is substantially different from the
creation of a trust; and that a man who, without communication with his creditors, puts property into the
hands of a trustee for the purpose of paying his debts,
proposes only a benefit to himself, and not to his creditors. The nominal trustee, therefore, is merely his agent;
and the nominal trust is only a method of applying his
own property for his own convenience.(f)[1]

(f) Garrard v. Lord Lauderdale, 3 Sim. 1; Bill v. Cureton, 2 M. & K.
503; Hughes v. Stubbs, 1 Hare 476 ; Gibbs v. Glamis, 11 Sim. 584; Wild-
ing v. Richards, 1 Coll. 655; [Simmonds v. Palles, 2 Johnes & Lat. 489;
Smith v. Keating, 6 C. B. (60 E. C. L. R.) 136.]

---

[1] The distinction taken in the text, and for which Garrard v. Lord Lauderdale is the leading authority, between a voluntary assignment for creditors and an ordinary trust, is very important in its results; for, if it be
sound, the assignment before it is acted on constitutes merely a power in
the trustee, revocable at pleasure, invalid against general creditors, and
not enforceable in equity by those who are provided for thereby. Some
of the more recent cases, however, seem to indicate that if the trust be
communicated to the creditors it will cease to be revocable, though not
executed by them ; at any rate, such is the case where the trustee has also
taken possession of the property : Griffiths v. Ricketts, 7 Hare 307 ; Harland v. Binks, 15 Q. B. (69 E. C. L. R.) 713 ; Smith v. Hurst, 10 Hare 30 ;
Acton v. Woodgate, 2 Myl. & K. 495. Where there is an actual execution
by the creditors, the trust becomes irrevocable : Mackinnon v. Stewart, 1
Sim. N. S. 76; see Synnot v. Simpson, 5 H. L. Cas. 121; Montefiori v.
Browne, 7 Ibid. 241 ; Whitmore v. Turquand, 1 Johns. & H. 444
    In the United States, such assignments, before the assent of the benefi-
ciaries, have, in some cases, been treated as mere naked powers : Brooks
v. Marbury, 11 Wheat. 78; Watson v. Bagaley, 12 Penna. St. 164; yet
the general current of authority is clear, that the creditors, on learning of
the existence of the trust deed, may proceed at once to enforce it in equity,
before becoming formally parties thereto ; Moses v. Murgatroyd, 1 Johns.
Ch. 119; Shepherd v. McEvers, 4 Id. 136 ; Weir v. Tannehill, 2 Yerg. 57 ;
Pearson v. Rockhill, 4 B. Monr. 296 ; Robertson v. Sublett, 6 Hump. 313 ;
Ingram v. Kirkpatrick, 6 Ired. Ev. 463 ; Pratt v. Thornton, 28 Maine 355.
See Burrill on Assignments 280, 306, for a discussion of this subject.
    Where a firm made a trust deed for the benefit of its creditors, which
was duly registered, and afterwards made a second deed revoking the

A resulting trust by presumption of law arises where the legal ownership of property has been disposed of, but it is apparent from the language of the disposition itself, or from the attendant circumstances, that the equitable ownership or beneficial interest was intended to go in a different channel, although there is no declaration, or no sufficient declaration, as to what that channel should be. In this case a trust is implied for the real owner, termed a resulting trust, or trust by operation of law.[1] And such a trust, although relating to real estate, is exempted by a proviso in the Statute of Frauds from the necessity of being declared or evidenced in writing.[2] The enactment is, that "where any conveyance shall be made of any lands or *tenements by which a trust or con- [*32] fidence shall or may arise or result by implication or construction of law, or be transferred or extinguished by act or operation of law, then and in every such case such trust or confidence shall be of the like force and effect as the same would have been if this statute had not been made."(g)

(g) 29 Car. 2, c. 3, s. 8.

---

first, it was *held* that the rights of the parties to the first deed became fixed and vested by its execution and registration, subject to the election of the beneficiaries as to whether they would accept or reject its provisions, and that the firm had no power to revoke it: Furman v. Fisher, 4 Cold. (Tenn.) 626.

[1] It must be borne in mind that resulting trusts of this description arise only upon *voluntary* dispositions. Where there is a valuable consideration no trust will result so as to defeat the operation of the deed: Brown v. Jones, 1 Atk. 188. See also Ridout v. Dowding, 1 Atk. 419; Hill on Trustees 179; Dennis v. McCagg, 32 Ill. 429.

[2] Resulting trusts are not within the Statute of Frauds in the different states; nor are they executed by the Statute of Uses. In some states, as in New York, Minnesota and Wisconsin, trusts of this description have been abolished, or confined within narrow limits.

Resulting trusts of the first class, viz., those where the intention to sever the legal and equitable ownership is apparent, either directly or indirectly, from the language of the gift, occur for the most part in dispositions by will. They are not necessarily restricted to such dispositions; for whenever, in any conveyance or disposition of property, it is apparent that any beneficial interest was not intended to accompany the legal ownership, but no other sufficient and effectual gift of it has been made, it will result back to the original owner. But in gifts by deeds, which are generally made with full deliberation and under professional advice, this circumstance does not often occur. In gifts by will it is not unfrequent.

In gifts of this class, the bequest of the beneficial interest is sometimes intentionally deferred; as where property is devised to a trustee "upon trusts to be declared by a subsequent codicil," and no such declaration is made; sometimes a trust is declared, but lapses by the death of the beneficial donee, or is invalidated by its uncertainty, by its illegal character, or by the refusal of the donee to accept the benefit; and sometimes a partial trust is declared, e. g., for payment of debts, which does not exhaust the whole estate, and the surplus is left without any express disposition. In this latter instance, it may appear by the context of the will, or by the aid of parol evidence, that the devisee was intended to take the surplus; but the *primâ facie* inference is, that the creation of the partial trust was the sole object, and that the equitable interest undisposed of is in the nature of a resulting trust.[1]

---

[1] See Flint *v.* Warren, 16 Sim. 124; Onslow *v.* Wallis, 1 H. & Tw. 513; Ralston *v.* Telfair, 2 Dev. Eq. 255; Huston *v.* Hamilton, 2 Binn. 387; King *v.* Mitchell, 8 Pet. 326; Sheaffer's App., 8 Barr 38; Hawley *v.* James, 5 Paige 323; Floyd *v.* Barker, 1 Id. 486; Frazier *v.* Frazier, 2 Leigh 642.

*In all cases of this kind, the rule of law is that [*33] the beneficial interest undisposed of results back to the original owner, or to his representatives, real or personal, according to the nature of the property.

If, for example, a testator devises land for purposes altogether illegal, or which altogether fail, the heir-at-law takes it as undisposed of. If the purposes are partially illegal or partially fail, or if they require the application of a part only of the land devised, the heir takes so much of the land or of its produce as was destined for the ineffective purpose, or so much as is not required for the purpose of the will. And *e converso*, if there be a bequest of personal property for purposes which are altogether or partially illegal, or which altogether or partially fail, the next of kin are entitled to it, or to so much of it as cannot or need not be applied to the purposes of the will.(*h*)

Resulting trusts of the second class, viz., where the intention to sever the legal and equitable ownership is apparent from the attendant circumstances, occur where an estate has been purchased in the name of one person, and the purchase-money or consideration has proceeded

(*h*) Collins *v.* Wakemann, 2 Ves. J. 683 ; Muckleston *v.* Brown, 6 Ves. 52; Fowler *v.* Garlike, 1 R. & M. 232; Ackroyd *v.* Smithson, 1 B. C. C. 503 ; King *v.* Denison, 1 Ves. & B. 260; Clark *v.* Hilton, L. R. 2 Eq. 814 ; Tregonwell *v.* Sydenham, 3 Dow. 194; Sidney *v.* Shelley, 19 Ves. 352 ; Cogan *v.* Stephens, Lewin on Trustees, Appendix vii ; 1 Jarm. on Wills, c. xviii ; Cook *v.* Hutchinson, 1 Keen 42, 50 ; Gordon *v.* Atkinson, 1 De G. & Sm. 478 ; Taylor *v.* Taylor, 3 De G., Macn. & G. 190; see Barrs *v.* Fewkes, 2 Hem. & M. 60; 11 Jur. N. S. 669; Hill on Trustees 119, note ; Craig *v.* Leslie, 3 Wheat. 563 ; Burr *v.* Sim, 1 Whart. 263 ; Sheaffer's App. 8 Penn. St. 42 ; King *v.* Mitchell, 8 Peters 326 ; Lindsay *v.* Pleasants, 4 Ired. Eq. 320; Pratt *v.* Taliaferro, 3 Leigh 419; Wood *v.* Cone, 7 Paige 472; Snowhill *v.* Snowhill, 1 Green Ch. 30; Woodgate *v.* Fleet, 44 N. Y. 1 ; Harrison *v.* Harrison, 36 N. Y. 543. Infra, Conversion.

from another.   In this case the presumption of law is,
that the party paying for the estate intended it for his
own benefit, and that the nominal purchaser is a mere
trustee.[1]

---

[1] It is a general principle, that where on a purchase of property, the
conveyance of the legal estate is taken in the name of one person, but the
purchase-money is paid or secured by another, at the same time or previously, and as part of one transaction, and the parties are strangers, not
in certain relations of blood, a trust results in favor of him who supplies
the purchase-money : Buck v. Pike, 11 Maine 9 ; Boyd v. McLean, 1 John.
Ch. 582 ; Jackman v. Ringland, 4 W. & S. 146 ; Livermore v. Aldrich,
5 Cush. 435 ; Frederick v. Haas, 5 Nevada 389 ; Fleming v. McHall, 47
Ill. 282 ; Dryden v. Hanway, 31 Md. 254 ; Millard v. Hathaway, 27 Cal.
119 ; Mallory v. Mallory, 5 Bush (Ky.) 464, and a great number of other
cases, many of which may be found cited in Hill on Trustees, 4 Am. ed.
147, in note.

It is also held in the United States, by analogy, that a purchase by a
man in his own name, with funds in his hands in a fiduciary capacity,
creates a resulting trust in favor of those whose money is thus employed ;
as in the case of a trustee, a partner, an agent for purchase, an executor,
a guardian, the committee of a lunatic, and the like : Philips v. Crammond,
2 Wash. C. C. 441 ; Kirkpatrick v. McDonald, 11 Penn. St. 393 ; Baldwin
v. Johnson, Saxton 441 ; Smith v. Ramsey, 1 Gilm. 373 ; Pugh v. Currie,
5 Alab. 446 ; Edgar v. Donnelly, 2 Munf. 387 ; Martin v. Creer, 1 Geo.
Dec. 109 ; Freeman v. Kelley, 1 Hoff. Ch. 90 ; Moffitt v. McDonald, 11
Humph. 457 ; Turner v. Petigrew, 6 Id. 438 ; Piatt v. Oliver, 2 McLean
267 ; Smith v. Burnham, 3 Sumn. 435 ; Harrisburg Bank v. Tyler, 3 W.
& S. 373 ; Wilhelm v. Folmer, 6 Barr 296 ; McCrory v. Foster, 1 Clarke
(Ia.) 271 ; Eshleman v. Lewis, 49 Penn. St. 410 ; Day v. Roth, 18 N. Y. 448 ;
Wales v. Bogue, 31 Ill. 464 ; Harper v. Archer, 28 Miss. 212 ; Church v.
Sterling, 16 Conn. 388 ; Hutchinson v. Hutchinson, 4 Dessaus. 77 ; Follansbe
v. Kilbreth, 17 Ill. 522 ; Bridenbecker v. Lowell, 32 Barb. 9 ; Pugh v.
Pugh, 9 Ind. 132 ; Methodist Church v. Wood, 5 Hamm. 283 ; Garrett v.
Garrett, 1 Strob. Eq. 96 ; Wallace v. Duffield, 2 S. & R. 521 ; Claussen
v. La Franz, 1 Clarke (Ia.) 226 ; Schaffner v. Grutzmacher, 6 Id. 137 ;
Reid v. Fitch, 11 Barb. S. C. 399 ; Caplinger v. Stokes, Meigs 175 ; Coder
v. Huling, 27 Penn. St. 84 ; Harper v. Archer, 28 Miss. 212 ; Baumgartner
v. Guessfield, 38 Mo. 36 ; Johnson v. Dougherty, 3 Green (N. J.) 406 ;
Harrold v. Lane, 53 Penn. St. 268 ; Beegle v. Wentz, 55 Penn. St. 369 ; Cecil
Bank v. Snively, 23 Md. 253.   So of a husband purchasing with his wife's
separate property : Methodist Church v. Jaques, 1 John. Ch. 450 ; 3 Id. 77 ;

This presumption exists in all cases where the conveyance of a legal estate is made to one who has not really

---

Brooks v. Dent, 1 Md. Ch. 523 ; Dickinson v. Codwise, 1 Sandf. Ch. 214 ;
Pinney v. Fellows, 15 Verm. 525 ; Barron v. Barron, 24 Id. 375 ; Prichard
v. Wallace, 4 Sneed 405 ; Resor v. Resor, 9 Ind. 347 ; Miller v. Blackburn,
14 Ind. 62 ; Lathrop v. Gilbert, 2 Stockt. 344 ; Filman v. Divers, 31 Penn.
St. 429 ; Kline's Appeal, 39 Id. 463. It is to be observed, however, that
where such employment of fiduciary funds is unauthorized and wrongful
in itself, the parties affected thereby are not confined to the mere enforcement of a resulting trust in the property thus tortiously acquired, but may,
instead thereof, elect to take the money back. See Oliver v. Piatt, 3 How.
U. S. 333 ; Bonsall's Appeal, 1 Rawle 266. Indeed, under such circumstances, where the investment of the money is manifestly hostile to the
original trust, it is even held in some English decisions, approved by Mr.
Justice Gibson, in Wallace v. Duffield, 2 S. & R. 521 ; Harrisburg Bank
v. Tyler, 3 W. & S. 373 ; and in Wallace v. McCullough, 1 Rich. Eq. 426,
that no technical trust is created, and that the beneficiaries can only claim
a lien for their money upon the property acquired, and a consequent decree for a sale. But this is contrary to the uniform current of authority
in this country, as before stated ; and inconsistent in its practical application, with the cardinal rule, that no fiduciary can be permitted to profit by
a violation of his duties. See note to Woollam v. Hearne, 2 Lead. Cas.
in Eq. 404.

The doctrines with regard to the ordinary resulting trust, are applicable
to personal as well as real estate, to choses in action, as stock and annuities,
as well as in possession : Sidmouth v. Sidmouth, 2 Beav. 454 ; Ex parte
Houghton, 17 Ves. 253 ; but not, it has been held, to property perishable
in its nature : Union Bank v. Baker, 8 Humph. 447.

They are also applicable where the purchase-money is paid by several
jointly, and the legal estate taken in the name of one only : Botsford v.
Burr, 2 John. Ch. 405 ; Pierce v. Pierce, 7 B. Monr. 433 ; Stewart v. Brown,
2 S. & R. 461 ; Shoemaker v. Smith, 11 Humph. 81 ; Powell v. Manufacturing Co., 3 Mason 347 ; Purdy v. Purdy, 3 Md. Ch. 547 ; Letcher
v. Letcher, 4 J. J. Marsh. 590 ; Buck v. Swazey, 35 Maine 41 ; but where
it was agreed verbally that any one of three persons should buy in and
hold for the others, and one bought and paid the purchase-money, it was
held that there was no resulting trust : Farnham v. Clements, 51 Maine
426 ; Sheldon v. Sheldon, 3 Wis. 699 ; Morey v. Herrick, 18 Penn. St. 129 ;
see also, Meason v. Kaine, 63 Penn. St. 335. But the part of the purchase-money furnished by one who thus claims a resulting trust must
be a definite one : Baker v. Vining, 30 Maine 121 ; Sayre v. Townsends,

8

advanced the price.   And it is equally applicable whether
such conveyance be in the name of a stranger only, with-

---

15 Wend. 647.   Though it has been held that the presumption was in
the first instance, in such case, that the funds were supplied in equal
proportions by all : Shoemaker v. Smith, 11 Humph. 81.

In order to create a resulting trust, the money must have been actually
paid by the alleged *cestui que trust*, out of his own or borrowed funds, or
secured to be paid at or before the time of the purchase, and cannot be
raised by matter *ex post facto* : Botsford v. Burr, 2 John. Ch. 405 ; Steere
v. Steere, 5 Id. 1 ; Freeman v. Kelly, 1 Hoff. Ch. 90 ; Rogers v. Murray, 3
Paige 390 ; Foster v. Trustees, 3 Ala. 302 ; Mahorner v. Harrison, 13
Smedes & Marsh. 53 ; Graves v. Dugan, 6 Dana 331 ; Magee v. Magee, 1
Penn. St. 405 ; Page v. Page, 8 N. H. 187 ; Brooks v. Fowle, 14 Id. 248 ;
Conner v. Lewis, 16 Maine 268 ; Pinnock v. Clough, 16 Verm. 500 ; Haines
v. O'Conner, 10 Watts 313 ; Gomez v. Tradesman's Bank, 4 Sandf. S. C.
106 ; Buck v. Swazey, 35 Maine 41 ; Lynch v. Cox, 23 Penn. St. 265 ;
Olive v. Dougherty, 3 Green (Iowa) 371 ; Irwin v. Ivers, 7 Indiana 308 ;
Whiting v. Gould, 2 Wis. 552 ; Barnard v. Jewett, 97 Mass. 87 ; Nixon's
Appeal, 63 Penn. St. 279. · Land purchased with borrowed money does
not raise an implied trust in favor of the creditor : Gibson v. Foote, 40 Miss.
788.   The fund may, however, have been supplied by the nominal purchaser
himself on credit : Page v. Page, 8 N. H. 187 ; Runnells v. Jackson, 1
How. (Miss.) 358 ; Rogan v. Walker, 1 Wis. 527 ; Brooks v. Ellis, 3 Iowa
527 ; but in such case the evidence must be very clear : Kendall v. Mann,
11 Allen 15.

The facts from which a resulting trust is to be established, may be
proved by parol, the case being excepted from the Statute of Frauds, though
at the same time the evidence must be clear and positive : Botsford v.
Burr, 2 John. Ch. 405 ; Steere v. Steere, 5 Id. 1 ; Peebles v. Reading, 8
S. & R. 484 ; Elliott v. Armstrong, 2 Blackf. 194 ; Blair v. Bass, 4 Id.
539 ; Pugh v. Bell, 1 J. J. Marsh. 403 ; Depeyster v. Gould, 2 Green Ch.
474 ; Page v. Page, 8 N. H. 187 ; Slocum v. Marshall, 2 Wash. C. C. 397 ;
Enos v. Hunter, 4 Gilman 211 ; Carey v. Cullan, 6 B. Monr. 44, and many
other cases.   In England, it is very doubtful whether such evidence would
be admitted against the answer of the defendant, but it is held in the
United States, generally, that it is so ; though it must be extremely clear,
and is to be received with the greatest caution : Boyd v. McLean, 1 John.
Ch. 582 ; Botsford v. Burr, 2 Id. 405 ; Buck v. Pike, 2 Fairf. 24 ; Baker v.
Vining, 30 Maine 121 ; Page v. Page, 8 N. H. 187 ; Snelling v. Utterback,
1 Bibb 609 ; Letcher v. Letcher, 4 J. J. Marsh. 590 ; Elliott v. Armstrong,
2 Blackf. 198 ; Blair v. Bass, 4 Id. 540 ; Larkins v. Rhodes, 5 Porter 196 ;
Ensley v. Balentine, 4 Humph. 233 ; Faringer v. Ramsay, 2 Md. 365 ;
Fausler v. Jones, 7 Ind. 277 ; Whiting v. Gould, 2 Wis. 552 ; Osborne v.

out mention of the actual purchaser, or in the joint names
of a stranger and the purchaser himself; whether the

Endicott, 6 Cal. 149; Collins *v.* Smith, 18 Ill. 160; Hill on Trustees 96,
note 2. Parol evidence is also admissible, though it may contradict the
recital in the deed, that the consideration was paid by the nominal purchaser, at least during his lifetime: Hill on Trustees 95, note; Livermore
v. Aldrich, 5 Cush. 435, and cases there cited; see also, Wolf *v.* Corby,
30 Md. 356; Colton *v.* Wood, 25 Iowa 43; Groesbeck *v.* Sceley, 13 Mich.
329; Hogan *v.* Jaques, 4 Green (N. J.) 123; and according to decisions in
the United States, the question being unsettled in England, after his death
also, though of course, in such case, the proof should be of the strongest
character, as the protection of an answer is absent: Unitarian Society *v.*
Woodbury, 14 Maine 281; Neill *v.* Keese, 5 Texas 23; Harder *v.* Harder,
2 Sandf. Ch. 17; McCammon *v.* Petit, 3 Sneed 242. See Harrisburg Bank
v. Tyler, 3 W. & S. 373. For the purpose of establishing the fact of
payment by the *cestui que trust*, the declarations or admissions of the
nominal purchaser to that effect are always competent: Malin *v.* Malin, 1
Wend. 626; Pierce *v.* McKeehan, 3 Penn. St. 136; Harder *v.* Harder, 2
Sandf. Ch. 17; Lloyd *v.* Carter, 17 Penn. St. 216; Peabody *v.* Tarbell, 2
Cush. 232; Pinney *v.* Fellows, 15 Verm. 525; Barron *v.* Barron, 24 Id.
375; but parol declarations that he had purchased or was about to purchase for another, without proof of some previous agreement, or advance
of money, are obviously inadmissible, as they would go to establish not a
resulting, but an express trust, in the teeth of the Statute of Frauds: Sidle
v. Walters, 5 Watts 389; Haines *v.* O'Connor, 10 Id. 313; Blyholder *v.*
Gilson, 18 Penn. St. 134; Smith *v.* Smith, 27 Id. 180.

A promise to buy land at sheriff's sale is within the Statute of Frauds:
Smith *v.* Smith, 27 Penn. St. 180; Kellum *v.* Smith, 33 Id. 158; Gilbert *v.*
Carter, 10 Ind. 16. But it must be remembered that where a person at
sheriff's sale makes declaration that he is buying on behalf of the defendant,
and thereby prevents other persons from bidding, he will be held a trustee
for the defendant: Brown *v.* Dysinger, 1 Rawle 448; Bethell *v.* Sharp, 25
Ill. 173; Ryan *v.* Dox, 34 N. Y. 307; for an element of fraud exists in
this last class of cases which does not obtain in the former.

As a resulting trust may be created, so may it be rebutted, by parol evidence, either by way of direct contradiction of the alleged facts, or in proof
of a different intention of the parties at the time, as that the nominal purchaser was designed to be the real beneficiary: Botsford *v.* Burr, 2 John.
Ch. 405; Page *v.* Page, 8 N. H. 189; Baker *v.* Vining, 30 Maine 126;
Elliott *v.* Armstrong, 2 Blackf. 199; McGuire *v.* McGowen, 4 Dessaus. 487;
Sewell *v.* Baxter, 2 Md. Ch. 448. Or that the party advancing the purchase-money, by the original agreement expressly stipulated for himself a

estate be originally conveyed to one purchaser out of
[*34] many, or *become ultimately vested in one as the
survivor, under an assurance which has created a
legal joint tenancy; or whether in the case of several
nominal purchasers, an immediate joint estate be given to
all, or the grant be to take successively one after another.
Whatever be the peculiar form in which the assurance is

---

benefit from the transaction, inconsistent with the creation of a trust: Dow
v. Jewell, 1 Foster 470. And so in general, where a different trust has
been declared at the time in writing: Leggett v. Dubois, 5 Paige 114;
Anstice v. Brown, 6 Id. 448; Clark v. Burnham, 2 Story 1; Mercer v.
Stark, 1 S. & M. Ch. 479.

Resulting trusts of this nature arise from the want of any consideration
between the nominal purchaser and the person who supplies the purchase-
money. Where, therefore, the parties are not strangers, but stand in that
relation of blood, which supplies by itself, in equity, a good consideration
for a conveyance, as in the case of a purchase by a parent in the name of
a child, *primâ facie* no trust results, but the transaction is treated as an
advancement: Page v. Page, 8 N. H. 187; Jackson v. Matsdorf, 11 John.
91; Partridge v. Havens, 10 Paige 618; Knouff v. Thompson, 16 Penn.
St. 357; Dennison v. Goehring, 7 Id. 182, n.; Taylor v. James, 4 Dessaus.
6; Tremper v. Borton, 18 Ohio 418; Stanley v. Brennen, 6 Black. 194;
Dudley v. Bosworth, 10 Humph. 12; Tebbetts v. Tilden, 11 Foster 273;
Rankin v. Harper, 23 Missouri 579. But this is a mere circumstance
creating an adverse presumption, to rebut which, again, parol evidence is
admissible: Jackson v. Matsdorf, 11 John. 91; Dudley v. Bosworth, 10
Humph. 12; Taylor v. Taylor, 4 Gilm. 303; Tremper v. Barton, 18 Ohio
418. And under all circumstances, where the conveyance is in fraud of
creditors, a sufficient interest remains in the parent, to subject it in equity
to the claim of his creditors: Kimmel v. McRight, 2 Penn. St. 38; Guthrie
v. Gardner, 19 Wend. 414; Jencks v. Alexander, 11 Paige 619; Croft v.
Arthur, 3 Dessaus. 223; Rucker v. Abell, 8 B. Monr. 566; Dunnien v. Coy,
24 Missouri 167; Garfield v. Hatmaker, 15 N. Y. 476.

It only remains to state that in some of the United States resulting trusts
have been abolished, or exist only in certain cases and under certain restrictions, specified and imposed by the statutes. Such is the case in New
York, Minnesota, Wisconsin and other states. In regard to trusts of this
description in the first mentioned state, see Lounsbury v. Purdy, 18 N. Y.
515; Swinburn v. Swinburn, 28 Id. 568; Siemon v. Schurck, 29 Id.
598; and Buffalo, &c., Railroad Co. v. Lampson, 47 Barb. 533.

made, it does not affect the presumption that an estate or share of an estate, vested in a man who did not pay its price, was not intended by way of beneficial ownership; and therefore, in all those cases alike, if there be no evidence of an opposite intention, the trust of such legal estate will result to the parties who have advanced the purchase-money, in proportion to the amount of their respective advances. And as trusts of this kind are expressly exempted from the Statute of Frauds, it is competent for the real purchaser to prove his payment of the purchase-money by parol evidence, even though it be otherwise expressed in the deed.

The doctrine, however, is merely one of presumptive evidence. It is not a rule of law that a trust must be intended on such a purchase, but it is a reasonable presumption, as a matter of evidence, in the absence of proof to the contrary. It is therefore open to the nominal purchaser to rebut that presumption by direct or circumstantial evidence to the contrary. He may, for instance, show that it was intended to give him the beneficial interest, either altogether or in part; that the purchase-money was advanced by way of loan to himself, and that the party advancing it intended to become his creditor, and not the equitable owner of the estate; or that the purchase-money, on a conveyance in joint tenancy, was advanced by the several purchasers in equal shares, so that there is no improbability of an estate in joint tenancy having been really contemplated, with equal chance of survivorship to all. In this manner a counter presumption may be raised in opposition to the original one; and this again in its turn may be met by other evidence of an opposite intention. Lastly, the evidence which is thus brought forward on either side may be derived either from con-

[*35] temporaneous declarations[1] *or other direct proof of intention, or from the circumstances under which the transaction took place, or from the subsequent mode of treating the estate, and the length of time during which a particular mode of dealing with it has been adopted on all sides.(*i*)

The most important class of cases in which, as an ordinary rule, this counter presumption arises, are those where a purchase has been made in the name of a child, or of one towards whom the party paying the money has placed himself in *loco parentis*. The general principle on which this counter presumption proceeds is that, inasmuch as it is a father's duty to provide for his child, it is not improbable that he may make the provision by giving the child an estate, or by purchasing one for him in his name. And, therefore, if he does make a purchase in the child's name, the *primâ facie* probability is that he intended it as a provision or advancement. The doctrine on this point will be hereafter separately considered under the head of Meritorious Consideration.

In accordance with the same principle it is held, that if land is acquired as the substratum of a partnership, or is brought into and used by the partnership for partnership purposes, there will be a trust by operation of law for the partnership, as tenants in common, although a trust may not have been declared in writing, and the ownership may not be apparently in all the members of the firm, or if in all, may apparently be in them, not as partners but as joint tenants.(*k*)

(*i*) 3 Sug. V. & P. 275; Lloyd *v.* Spillett, 3 Atk. 150; Dyer *v.* Dyer, 2 Cox 92; Rider *v.* Kidder, 10 Ves. 360; Aveling *v.* Knipe, 19 Id. 441; Wray *v.* Steele, 2 Ves. & B. 388; Vickers *v.* Cowell, 1 Bea. 529.

(*k*) Dale *v.* Hamilton, 5 Hare 369, 382; 2 Ph. 266.

---

[1] But not from subsequent declarations: Sidle *v.* Walters, 5 Watts 389; Hill on Trustees 94, note; Bennett *v.* Fulmer, 49 Penn. St. 155.

Another class of cases, in which the circumstances give rise to the presumption of a resulting trust, is where a man, whose duty it was to create a trust, has done an ambiguous act, and the Court construes such act as having been done in accordance with that duty.

*If therefore a man is a trustee of certain funds [*36] for investment in land, or has bound himself by covenant to lay out money in land, and he purchases an estate at a corresponding price, it will be presumed, independently of positive evidence, that his object in the investment was to effectuate the trust; and a trust may be implied accordingly. But it will be observed that this is not as a hostile or compulsory decree, but on the supposition that such a result was really contemplated; and therefore if the contrary be proved, as by showing that the purchase was made under a mistaken opinion of the trust, the presumption cannot be raised. It is otherwise if the covenant be to settle such land as the covenantor may have on a specified day, or to purchase a specific estate, which he afterwards acquires; for in these cases the trust attaches by virtue of the covenant, independently of any intention in the party bound.(l)[1]

(*l*) Tooke *v.* Hastings, 2 Vern. 97; Deacon *v.* Smith, 3 Atk. 323; Perry *v.* Phelips, 4 Ves. 108; Wellesley *v.* Wellesley, 10 Sim. 256; 4 M. & C. 561.

----

[1] Besides that described in the text, there is another class of trusts "created by operation or implication of law," which are usually denominated *constructive trusts*, and are of much importance and frequency. This class comprehends those cases where the holder of the legal estate in property cannot also enjoy the beneficial interest therein without violating some established principle of equity. The chief instance of this occurs when the property has been acquired by fraud, actual or constructive. As the leading doctrines on this subject will be found discussed in other parts of this volume, particularly under the head of Rescission and Cancellation (post. 174, foll.), it is sufficient to state here that where a party, actively or passively guilty of fraud, has thereby obtained the legal title, he is treated

The second requisite to the creation of a trust is that
the ownership be accepted on the proposed terms. The
effect however of non-acceptance is not to invalidate the
beneficial gift, but merely to free the non-accepting party
from the liability to act. It is a settled principle in equity
that a trust shall not fail for want of a trustee; and,
therefore, whether a trustee has been named, who afterwards refuses the trust; whether, as is often the case in
wills, no trustee be named, or it is doubtful who is the

---

by equity in general as a mere trustee for the parties injured, and subjected
to the consequent liabilities. The agency of constructive trust is also employed, in cases where no fraud has been committed in the acquisition of
the title, for the vindication or enforcement of other equitable principles.
Thus, on an agreement for the sale of land, the vendor is, before actual
conveyance, treated as trustee for the vendee. And, in cases of part performance of parol agreements for the sale of land by payment of purchase-
money, the vendee acquires an equitable interest to the extent of the purchase-money paid: Rose v. Watson, 10 H. L. Ca. 672; Barnes' Appeal, 46
Penn. St. 350. So of an encumbrancer, such as a mortgagee who has obtained a conveyance as security for the payment of money, and the money
has been repaid. So, one to whom property is conveyed by a trustee without notice of the trust, but on no valuable consideration, or with actual or
constructive notice, takes it subject to the original trusts. Many other
similar instances might be put, but they all reduce themselves to the
general principle that, wherever a man cannot hold property beneficially
and for himself, except by fraud or in contravention of equity, he holds it
as trustee for those who, in contemplation of equity, are entitled thereto.

Constructive, like resulting, trusts are excepted out of the Statute of
Frauds, and may therefore be proved by parol. The rules which are applied to them, when established, are in general the same with those which
govern direct trusts, but they are not in every respect identical. For instance, it is a fixed principle with regard to the latter that lapse of time,
by itself, will not bar their enforcement, but in respect to the former the
question of *laches* is a most material one, both with reference to their
establishment and to the consequent relief which is given. Indeed, in
some cases, the Statute of Limitations is directly followed. There are other
distinctions, also, as to the privileges which trustees may claim, as to the
fiduciary relationship of the parties, as to costs, and other matters which
cannot be dwelt upon here, but which are fully considered in the text-
books on the subject.

proper trustee; or whether, from any other cause, there be a failure of a regularly appointed trustee; the Court of Chancery will see to the execution of the trust.[1] it will ascertain in whom the legal ownership is vested, and will declare him a trustee for the purposes of the gift, or will nominate, if required, a trustee of its own, to whom the estate may be conveyed. And it is provided by a late statute that, if a trustee be a lunatic or infant, or if he be out of the jurisdiction of the Court, or if it be uncertain (*where there were several trustees) which [*37] was the survivor, or uncertain whether the trustee last known to have been seised, is living or dead, or, if dead, who is his heir, or if he refuse to convey when required, the Lord Chancellor, in the case of lunacy, and the Court of Chancery, in the other cases, may substitute some person to make the conveyance.(m)[2]

(m) 11 Geo. 4, and 1 Wm. 4, c. 60.

---

[1] After the Court of Chancery has acquired jurisdiction by bill filed, it will not suffer any appointment or substitution of trustees, except with its sanction and control: Hill on Trustees 190, note. Under certain circumstances, as where the fund is very large, the Court will not suffer the property to remain in the charge of one trustee, but will appoint another: Grant v. Grant, 34 L. J. Ch. 641.

[2] Equity never suffers a trust to fail on account of the neglect or refusal of the trustee to act, but if necessary will either appoint a new trustee, or treat the holder of the legal title as such : Shepherd v. McEvers, 4 John. Ch. 136; De Barante v. Gott, 6 Barb. S. C. 492; Crocheron v. Jacques, 3 Edw. Ch. 207 ; King v. Donnelly, 5 Paige 46 ; Cushney v. Henry, 4 Paige 345; McKennan v. Phillips, 6 Whart. 571; Dawson v. Dawson, Rice Eq. 243; Lee v. Randolph, 2 Henn. & Munf. 12; McIntire School v. Zan. Canal & M. C., 9 Hamm. 203; Griffith v. Griffith, 5 B. Monr. 113 ; Field v. Arrowsmith, 3 Humph. 442; Peter v. Beverly, 10 Peters 534; Furman v. Fisher, 4 Cold. (Tenn.) 626. In some cases the appointment is made by a formal suit, in others by a petition simply. The circumstances which justify a resort to the latter method are of course the subject of special statutes in England and the various United States. As to the power of a court of chancery to appoint new trustees, and the occasions when that power is to

If, however, there is not merely a failure of the specific trustee, but the estate derived from the donor is at an end, and there is an owner holding by a paramount or adverse title, the trust ceases to bind. It is binding on the trustee himself if he accept it, and on any person claiming through or under him, except a purchaser for value without notice of the trust. And if he do not

---

be exercised, see Hill on Trustees, p. 190–194, 4th Am. ed., where the American and English statutes are referred to. See, also, Morgan on Statutes and General Orders, pp. 58 to 123. A trustee is at liberty at any time before acceptance to disclaim or refuse the trust: Maccubin v. Cromwell, 7 Gill & John. 157; Trask v. Donoghue, 1 Aik. 370. It is always to be inferred, however, in the first instance, that a gift by deed or will is accepted by the donee: Wilt v. Franklin, 1 Binn. 502; Eyrick v. Hetrick, 13 Penn. St. 494; Read v. Robinson, 6 W. & S. 331; 4 Kent Comm. 500; and after the lapse of a great length of time, as twenty-five years, without disclaimer, the trustee having notice, acceptance of the trust may be presumed: Eyrick v. Hetrick, 13 Penn. St. 493; see Penny v. Davis, 3 B. Monr. 314; Re Uniacke, 1 Jones & Lat. 1 .It is not necessary, in order to the acceptance of the trust, where created by deed, that there should be any execution thereof by the trustee, except so far as regards his legal liability upon the covenants contained therein: Flint v. Clinton Co., 12 N. H. 432; but it will be presumed from any act in the management of the trust estate; and the rule is the same as to trusts created by will: Flint v. Clinton Co. ub sup.; Chaplin v. Givens, Rice Eq. 133; Latimer v. Hanson, 1 Bland 51; Maccubbin v. Cromwell, 7 G. & J. 157. Where the trustee is also executor, probate of the will is an acceptance as to personalty at least: Worth v. McAden, 1 Dev. & Batt. Eq. 207. Although in those states where security is required, he is held to have no power until qualification: Monroe v. James, 4 Munf. 195; Trask v. Donoghue, 1 Aik. (Verm.) 373. Where one of several trustees disclaims, the trust estate devolves on the remainder: King v. Donnelly, 5 Paige 46; Trask v. Donoghue, 1 Aik. 370; Putnam Free School v. Fisher, 30 Maine 523; Jones v. Maffet, 5 S. & R. 523; Taylor v. Galloway, 1 Hamm. 232. Where, however, there has once been acceptance, a trustee cannot afterwards, by any renunciation or disclaimer, rid himself of the duties of his office, except by consent of all parties, or by the intervention of a court of chancery: Shepherd v. McEvers, 4 John. Ch. 136; Cruger v. Halliday, 11 Paige 314; Latimer v. Hanson, 1 Bland 51; Chaplin v. Givens, 1 Rice Eq. 133; Drane v. Gunter, 19 Alab. 731.

accept it, it is in like manner binding on those who take in his stead under the donor.   But it is not binding on an adverse claimant making title by a *bonâ fide* disseisin of the trustee;[1] nor was it, until a late statute, binding on the lord entitled by forfeiture or escheat.   The privilege of the lord by escheat is now excluded by statute; and the Court is enabled to appoint new trustees, and to direct a conveyance by substitution to them, when a trustee dies without an heir, in like manner as when his heir is uncertain.(n)

The acceptance of a trustee may be direct, by execution of the trust deed, or by a statement that he accepts the trust; or it may be implied from any act which shows an intention on his part to deal with the property, and to act in the execution of the duties imposed.(o)[2]   And in like manner his renunciation may be evidenced by his conduct, without an express declaration to that effect. But the more prudent course is to execute a deed of disclaimer.(p)   If, instead of a formal disclaimer, he execute an immediate release to his co-trustees for the mere purpose of disclaiming, *it seems doubtful whether [*38] such a release, although technically a dealing with

(n) Gilbert on Uses, by Sug. 429; Burgess v. Wheate, 1 Eden 177; [Sweeting v. Sweeting, 33 L. J. Ch. 311;] Attorney-General v. Duke of Leeds, 2 M & K. 343; 4 & 5 Wm. 4, c. 23, ss. 2 and 3.   [See Hill on Trustees, 4 Am. ed. 77, and notes.]

(o) Urich v. Walker, 3 M. & C. 702; Kirwan v. Daniel, 5 Hare 493.

(p) Stacey v. Elph, 1 M. & K. 195.   [See Judson v. Gibbons, 5 Wend. 224; Maccubbin v. Cromwell, 7 Gill & Johns. 165.]

---

[1] See Stuyvesant v. Hale, 2 Barb. Ch. 151; Woods v. Farmere, 7 Watts 382.

[2] As a general rule the acceptance of the trustee must be of the entire trust, and he cannot limit his responsibility to a particular portion.   But there may be exceptions to this rule, of which an instance will be found in Malzy v. Edge, 2 Jurist N. S. 80.

the property, would be treated as an acceptance of the trust.(q)   If the legal ownership has become vested in him, so that he cannot get rid of it by mere disclaimer, e. g., on a descent to him as heir, he must convey to a new trustee under. the sanction of the Court, but is not bound to do any further act.[1]

A trustee after acceptance cannot divest himself of his trust except in three ways, viz.: 1. By assent of all his cestuis que trust; 2. By means of some special power in the instrument creating the trust; and 3. By an application to the Court of Chancery.[2]

If all the cestuis que trust are of full age and free from disability, there is no difficulty on the subject; for their sanction will necessarily secure the trustee.   But if there are infants or femes coverte interested, or if there is a trust for children not in esse, or if for any other reason the sanction of all cannot be obtained, then the mere act of transfer would be a breach of trust; and therefore the trustee cannot, by his own act, relinquish his office, but would incur an additional liability for any misconduct on the part of his transferree.   In order to meet this inconve-

(q) Nicloson v. Wordsworth, 2 Swanst. 365; Urch v. Walker, 3 M. & C. 702.

---

[1] In the event of the death of the person nominated as trustee, before his acceptance, it appears doubtful whether the right of disclaimer will fall to the ground, or will pass to the heir or personal representative. The point arose in Goodson v. Ellison, 3 Russ. 583, but was not decided. It would seem most reasonable to hold that the right to disclaim would pass to the heir or personal representative: Hill on Trustees, page 222. See, however, King v. Phillips, 16 Jur. 1080.

[2] Cruger et al. v. Halliday's Adm'x, 11 Paige 314; Jones v. Stockett, 2 Bland 409; Shepherd v. McEvers, 4 John. Ch. 136.

It is proper in this connection to add, that courts of equity, will in cases of fraud, negligence, incapacity to act, and breach of trust, remove the trustee: Chambers et al. v. Mauldin et al., 4 Ala. 477; Thompon v. Thompson, 2 B. Monr. 161. See Hill on Trustees, 4 Am. ed. 298, &c., and notes.

nience, it is usual in all settlements, the trusts of which are likely to last for any length of time, to introduce a clause, authorizing the retirement of existing trustees and the nomination of new ones, with such provisions against misuse of the authority as may be considered expedient. If no such authority be given, or if the trustee is unwilling to exercise it, he can only be denuded of his office by a decree in equity. If he has a sufficient ground for retiring, the costs of a suit for that purpose will be paid out of the estate ; as, for instance, if he becomes involved in complicated questions, which could not have been anticipated when he undertook the trusts; but he cannot burden the estate with costs occasioned by a capricious abandonment *of his charge.(r)[1] After a bill has been filed for the appointment of new trustees, it is [*39] improper, though not absolutely incompetent, for the original trustees, to make an appointment without authority from the Court, notwithstanding there may be a power of appointment in the deed of trust; nor will the existence of such a power induce the Court to appoint new trustees on the nomination of the old ones, without inquiry as to the fitness of the parties nominated.(s) In some decrees appointing new trustees, a power for such new trustees to supply future vacancies without a fresh application to the Court has been inserted, but the admissibility of such a power, except under special circumstances, appears to be doubtful.(t)[2]

(r) Coventry v. Coventry, 1 Keen 758 ; Greenwood v. Wakeford, 1 Bea. 576.

(s) Attorney-General v. Clack, 1 Bea. 467 ; Cafe v. Bent, 3 Hare 245; ——— v. Roberts, 1 J. & W. 251.

(t) White v. White, 5 Bea. 221 ; Bowles v. Weeks, 14 Sim. 591.

[1] Matter of Jones, 4 Sandf. Ch. 615 ; Cruger v. Halliday, 11 Paige 314; Courtney v. Courtney, 3 Jones & Lat. 529.

[2] It is now established that such power cannot be exercised by the

Where a conveyance by substitution under the statute is requisite, an appointment of new trustees may be made summarily on petition without bill. But this authority is confined to cases of substituted conveyance, and does not apply generally to the appointment of new trustees.(*u*)

A trustee of stock or money is now enabled to get rid of his trust by payment or transfer to the Accountant-General, without the necessity of filing a bill. For this purpose, it is enacted that all trustees, executors, administrators or other persons, holding moneys, stock, or government or parliamentary securities, belonging to any trust, or the·major part, may pay, transfer, or deposit them into or in the name of the Accountant-General, on filing an affidavit shortly describing the instrument creating the trust; and that the application of the fund shall be afterwards regulated by the Court on petition.(*v*)

So soon as the creation and acceptance of a trust are perfected, the property which it affects is subjected, as we [*40] *have seen, to a double ownership; an equitable ownership in the *cestui que trust*, and a legal ownership in the trustee.

The equitable ownership or interest of the *cestui que trust* is in strictness a mere chose in action, or right to sue a *subpœna* against the trustee. But it is considered in equity the estate itself; and is generally regulated by principles corresponding with those which apply to an estate at law. The terms in which it is declared are interpreted by the same rules; it is subject to the same

(*u*) 1 Wm. 4, c. 60.
(*v*) 10 & 11 Vict. c. 96.

court: Holdin *v.* Durbin, 11 Beav. 574; Oglander *v.* Oglander, 2 De G. & Sm. 381.

restraints of policy, and is governed by the same laws of devolution and transfer. The analogy, however, is not free from exception ; and the character of the exceptions which exist, together with the general operation of the rule, will now form the subject of consideration.

I. The terms in which a trust is declared are interpreted by the ordinary rules of law.[1]

It was at one time suggested, that the language of a trust might be construed with greater·license than that of a gift at law. But this notion is now at an end. And it is clear that the declaration of an executed trust, *i. e.*, a trust of which the scheme has in the outset been completely declared, will bear exactly the same construction as if it had been a conveyance of the legal estate. If the scheme has been imperfectly declared in the outset, and the creator of the trust has merely denoted his ultimate object, imposing on the trustee or on the Court the duty of effectuating it in the most convenient way, the trust is called executory, and is construed by a less stringent rule.[2]

The reason of this apparent exception is obvious, for

---

[1] Equity subjects trusts to the same construction that a court of law does legal estates; and a donee must have capacity to take whether it is attempted to convey title directly to the party himself, or to another in trust for him : Trotter *v.* Blocker, 6 Porter 269 ; see Cudworth *v.* Hall's Adm'r, 3 Dessaus. 256.

[2] The distinctions between executory and executed trusts, especially with regard to the application of the rule in Shelley's Case, are generally recognised in the United States: Croxall *v.* Shererd, 5 Wall. S. C. 281 ; Dennison *v.* Goehring, 7 Penn. St. 177 ; Wood *v.* Burnham, 6 Paige 518 ; Tallman *v.* Wood, 26 Wend. 19 ; Horne *v.* Lyeth, 4 Harr. & J. 434 ; Garner *v.* Garner, 1 Desaus. 444 ; Porter *v.* Doby, 2 Rich Eq. 49 ; Edmonson *v.* Dyson, 2 Kelly 307 ; Lessee of Findlay *v.* Riddle, 3 Binn. 152 ; Neves *v.* Scott, 9 How. U. S. 211 ; Berry *v.* Williamson, 11 B. Monr. 251 ; Imlay *v.* Huntington, 20 Conn. 162 ; Saunders *v.* Edwards, 2 Jones Eq. 134 ; Wagstaffe *v.* Lowere, 23 Barb. 215 ; Note to Lord Glenorchy *v.* Bosville, 1 Lead. Cas. Eq. 1.

the very existence of a requirement to devise means for effectuating the trust, proves that the language already used is not meant as a conclusive declaration of its terms. And such language is accordingly treated by the Court as indicating the mere heads of an arrangement, the details of which must be ascertained from general usage.

If, for example, an executed trust be declared in favor [*41] *of one for life, with remainder to his issue, subject to a proviso that he shall not bar the entail, the first taker will be tenant in tail, under the rule in Shelley's Case, and the proviso will be void as inconsistent with his estate. But if the trust were executory, a similar direction would be held to signify that the estate should go as nearly as possible in the line of an entail, without giving the first taker a power to alienate, and would be effectuated by directing a strict settlement, *i.e.*, an estate to himself for life, with a limitation to trustees to preserve contingent remainders, with remainder to his sons successively in tail.

In the case of executory marriage articles, there is an indication furnished by the nature of the instrument, independently of any expressed intention leading to this construction of the trust; for it is assumed, in accordance with ordinary practice, and in the absence of reason to conclude the contrary, that the settlement contemplated by such articles is one which will not only provide for the husband and wife, but will also secure a provision for the children of the marriage. If, therefore the articles, strictly interpreted, would have a different result, they will be moulded in conformity with the presumed object. In the case of wills, on the other hand, there is no such *primâ facie* indication of intent. The gifts in a will are mere bounty, and are themselves the only guide in the construction of their terms.   If, therefore, technical words are used, and are not modified or explained by the context, it seems that the trusts, whether executory or not, must be construed in accordance with the technical sense.   But in the case of an executory trust, the intention so to modify them may be collected from slighter indications than would be sufficient in that of an executed one; *e. g.*, in case of an executory trust to make an entail, the Court would be enabled to direct a strict settlement of the estate upon the intention gathered, and from an express limitation to the first taker for life, though followed by a remainder to the heirs of *his body (especially if the gift for life be made in terms unimpeachable of waste); or from a limitation to preserve contingent remainders; or a limitation of the remainder to issue instead of heirs; although clauses of this kind would be ineffectual to vary an executed trust, if its terms would in themselves create an entail.(*w*)[1]   [*42]

In cases where marriage articles, after limiting a freehold estate in strict settlement, have directed that leaseholds shall be settled on analogous trusts, or that pictures or other personal chattels shall be settled to go as heirlooms with the estate, a question has arisen as to the correct frame of the settlement.   The effect of a settle-

(*w*) Austen *v.* Taylor, 1 Eden 361; Blackburn *v.* Stables, 2 Ves. & B. 367; Jervoise *v.* Duke of Northumberland, 1 J. & W. 559; Rochford *v.* Fitzmaurice, 1 Conn. & L. 158; 2 Jarm. on Wills 253–266; Lewin on Trustees 45–61.

[1] See Garner *v.* Garner, 1 Dessaus. 444; Berry *v.* Williamson, 11 B. Monroe 251; Imlay *v.* Huntingdon, 20 Conn. 146; Carrol *v.* Renich, 7 Sm. & Marsh. 799; Neves *v.* Scott, 9 How. U. S. 196; and see a discussion of the subject in Egerton *v.* Brownlow, 4 House Lds. Cas. 1; see also Gevers *v.* Wright's Ex'rs, 3 Green (N. J.) 330; Steinberger's Trustees *v.* Potter, Id. 452.

ment of personal chattels on limitations identical with those of the freehold estate, would be, that the leaseholds or other personalty, being incapable of entail, would vest absolutely in the first tenant in tail, and on his death would go to his executor. This inconvenience, however, may be to some extent obviated during the period within the limits of perpetuity, viz., a life in being, and twenty-one years afterwards, by directing that on the death of a tenant in tail, without issue, the personalty shall go by way of executory gift to the party next entitled under the settlement; and it seems that articles directing such a settlement are to be construed to imply such an executory gift on death, under twenty-one and without issue. $(x)^1$

2. The equitable ownership is subjected to the same restraints of policy as if the legal estate were transferred.

It cannot, for example, in the case of real estate be enjoyed by an alien; $(y)^2$ it cannot be made incapable of alienation by the owner, or be denuded of any other right incidental to ownership; $(z)^3$ nor can it be settled in

---

(x) Duke of Newcastle v. Countess of Lincoln, 3 Ves. 387, 12 Ves. 218; Lord Deerhurst v. Duke of St. Albans, 5 Madd. 232. [See Rowland v. Morgan, 13 Jur. 23; s. c. 2 Phill. 764.]

(y) Du Hourmelin v. Sheldon, 1 Bea. 79; 4 M. & C. 525.

(z) Brandon v. Robinson, 18 Ves. 429; [Rochford v. Hackman, 9 Hare 475.]

[1] A very full discussion of the authorities on the subject of the settlement of personal chattels will be found in Scarsdale v. Curzon, 1 Johns. & H. 40; and see 7 Jur. N. S. pt. 2, 71.

[2] Atkins v. Kron, 5 Ired. Eq. 207; Hubbard v. Goodwin, Leigh 492; Leggett v. Dubois, 5 Paige 114; Taylor v. Benham, 5 How. U. S. 270; Rittson v. Story, 3 Sm. & Giff. 230; though see Barrow v. Wadkin, 24 Beav. 1, when it was held that the crown could claim the benefit of a purchase made in trust for an alien. But it is different as to the proceeds of real estate, directed to be sold by will; an alien being able to hold personalty: Craig v. Leslie, 3 Wheat. 563; Comm. v. Martin, 5 Munf. 117.

[3] In a recent case in the Supreme Court of the United States, Nichols v. Levy, 5 Wallace 441, the law on this subject was thus stated by Mr. Jus-

a *series of limitations extending, or which may [*43]
extend, beyond the limits of perpetuity, viz.. a life
or lives in being, and twenty-one years afterwards;(a) and
in the particular case of trusts for accumulation, the period
of duration is still more narrowly limited; and it is enacted,
that no such accumulation shall be allowed for a longer
term than the life of the grantor, or twenty-one years from
the death of the grantor or testator, or the minority of
some person living or in *ventre sa mere* at his death, or
during the minority only of such persons as would for the
time being, if of full age, be entitled to the rents and
profits. This restriction, however, does not extend to any
provision for payment of debts, or for raising portions for

(a) 1 Jarm. on Wills, c. ix, s. 2.

tice Swayne. "It is a settled rule of law that the beneficial interest of the
cestui que trust, whatever it may be, is liable for the payment of his debts.
It cannot be so fenced about by inhibitions and restrictions as to secure to
it the inconsistent characteristics of right and enjoyment to the beneficiary,
and immunity from his creditors. A condition precedent that the provision
shall not vest until his debts are paid, and a condition subsequent that it
shall be divested and forfeited by his insolvency with a limitation over to
another person are valid, and the law will give them full effect. Beyond
this, protection from the claims of creditors is not allowed to go." In this
case the application of the rule was prevented by reason of a statute in
Tennessee, by the law of which state the trust was governed : see also Hallett *v.* Thompson, 5 Paige 583; Dick *v.* Pitchford, 1 Dev. & Bat. eq. 480.
But in Pennsylvania and Kentucky, such proviso is held good, where the
cestui que trust is himself entirely excluded, by the terms of the trust, from
any control over the property: Vaux *v.* Parke, 7 W. & S. 19; Pope *v* Elliott,
8 B. Monr. 56; see also, Campbell *v.* Foster, 35 N. Y. 361. It is only in
cases where a clear surplus will exist after a reasonable sum has been appropriated to the support of the person for whose benefit a trust was
created, that courts of equity are authorized to interfere in behalf of judgment creditors, and divert a portion of the income or annuity to the payment of the debts of such person : Genet *v.* Beckman, 45 Barb. (N. Y.)
382. Even in Pennsylvania, however, a person sui juris cannot settle property on himself for life, free from debts: Mackason's Appeal, 42 Penn.
St. 330.

children, or to any directions touching the preservation of
woods of timber.(b)[1]

The rule, however, which subjects equitable estates
to the same restraints of policy as if they were legal,
admits of two singular exceptions, both having reference
to married women; the one in what are called the separate use and pin-money trusts, enabling a married woman
to hold property independent of her husband, and allowing such property to be made inalienable; the other in
what is called the wife's equity for a settlement, restraining the husband's right over her equitable chattels real
and choses in action. until an adequate settlement has
been made.

The effect of the separate use trust, is to enable a
married woman, in direct contravention of the principles
of law, to acquire property independently of her husband;
and to enter into contracts, and incur liabilities in reference to such property, and dispose of it as a *feme sole*,
notwithstanding her coverture and disability at law;[2]
When this object had been effected, it was found that the
influence of the husband in inducing his wife to alienate,
rendered the trust in practice nugatory; and to obviate
[*44]   this difficulty, *and secure to her the desired protection against the marital rights, another principle

(*b*) Thelusson *v.* Woodford, 4 Ves. 227; 11 Ves. 112; 39 and 40 Geo. 3,
c. 98; 1 Jarm. on Wills, c. ix, s. 3.

. [1] See ante, note 1 to page 40; and see the subject of perpetuities, discussed in Lorillard *v.* Coster, 5 Paige Ch. 172; Hillyard *v.* Miller, 10
Penn. St. 335. In some of the United States as in Pennsylvania, and
New York, there are legislative provisions against accumulation. See Hill
on Trustees 394, note.

[2] Upon the trusts for separate use in the United States, see 2 Kent's
Comm. 162; notes to Hulme *v.* Tennant, 1 Lead. Cases in Eq. 394; Hill
on Trustees, 4th Am. ed. 625.

was infringed, by deciding that the gift of the separate estate, whether for life, or for an absolute interest, might be fettered and qualified by prohibiting anticipation or alienation. (c) The question then arose, whether the operation of such a clause was confined to an existing coverture, or might be extended to take effect on a future marriage. It was admitted, that during discoverture the clause was void, and that the ownership was absolute up to the moment of marriage; and it might therefore have been expected that, by the act of marriage, the usual interest would be conferred on the husband. A contrary decision, however, was not a greater violation of principle than that which originally gave validity to the trust. The trust is founded on the power of the Court of equity to model and qualify an interest in property which it had itself created, without regard to those rules by which the law regulates the enjoyment of property in other cases. And in accordance with this view, it was decided that, although the prohibitory clause is nugatory whilst the discoverture lasts, yet if the property be not disposed of during that period, the prohibition will attach immediately on the second marriage. (d) [1] At this point, how-

(c) Bagget v. Meux, 1 Coll. 138; 1 Ph. 627; Rennie v. Ritchie, 12 Cl. & Fin. 204; Gaffee's Trust, 1 Macn. & Gord. 541.

(d) Tullet v. Armstrong, 1 Bea. 1; 4 M. & C. 377; [Gaffee's Trust, 1 Macn. & Gord. 541; Hawkes v. Hubback, 11 Eq. L. R. 5.]

---

[1] The latter English doctrine, as stated in the text, has been followed in the United States, in Beaufort v. Collier, 6 Humph. 487; Shirley v. Shirley, 9 Paige 363; Fellows v. Tann, 9 Alab. 1003; Fears v. Brooks, 12 Geo. 197; Waters v. Tazewell, 9 Md. 291. But in Hamersley v. Smith, 4 Whart. 126; Kuhn v. Newman, 26 Penn. St. 227; Lindsay v. Harrison, 3 Eng. (Ark.) 311 (and see Dick v. Pitchford, 1 Dev. & Batt. Eq. 480), the separate use and the clause against anticipation were held to be valid only where there was an existing coverture, and ineffectual as regards a subsequent one: see Dubs v. Dubs, 31 Penn. St. 149. And a similar decision was made in Miller v. Bingham, 1 Ired. Eq. 423, followed in Apple v. Allen,

ever, a line has been drawn; and the separate use trust is so far bound by the policy of the law, that it must contemplate the wife's continuance with her husband. If it be framed with a view to future separation, it violates principle beyond the authorized limit, and is for that reason invalid. A deed, however, which contemplates an immediate separation, and makes a separate provision for the wife, with a view to that object, may be sustained and enforced, notwithstanding that its primary object— the separation itself—is incapable of enforcement by either party. But such a provision is upheld on the ground of its legal validity, and not on the footing of a separate [*45] trust. The consistency of the doctrine *which thus invalidates the primary object of a deed, but gives effect to a collateral one, was doubted by Lord Eldon, but he felt himself bound by the decisions at law. If after a provision has been made for an immediate separation, the parties come together again, its operation is at an end with respect to any future, as well as the past, separation. (e)[1]

(e) Lord St. John v. Lady St. John, 11 Ves. 537; Westmeath v. Salis-

3 Jones Eq. 120; though see Bridges v. Wilkins, Id. 342. Upon Hamersley v. Smith, however it is to be remarked, that it was based upon the English decision of Massey v. Parker, 2 M. & K. 174, which has since been repeatedly overruled; and that in so far, therefore, its authority has been weakened. See Wells v. McCall, 64 Penn. St. 207. And it is difficult, moreover, to assent to the reasoning in that case, without denying the validity of the separate use altogether. For if such a restraint upon ownership be lawful when applied to a state of coverture, the obvious contrivance of giving an unfettered estate to the woman while sole, with express limitations over to a trustee for the separate use, &c., upon the concurrence of the next and succeeding covertures, would obviate any objection which could be urged. If this be so, it would be contrary to every principle of equity, to hold that the mere absence or imperfection of the proper machinery, where the intention to create such a trust was obvious, would interfere with its enforcement.

[1] A contract between husband and wife for immediate separation, and

The language which will create a separate trust, as well as that which will impose a fetter on anticipation, has been the subject of nice distinctions. It is not sufficient that there be a gift for the wife's benefit, or a direction to pay the money into her own hands, for there is nothing in this inconsistent with the marital right. But there

bury, 5 Bligh 339; [Cartwright v. Cartwright. 17 Jur. 584;] Frampton v. Frampton, 4 Bea. 287; Jodrell v. Jodrell, 9 Id. 45; [Webster v. Webster, 22 L. J. Ch. 837.]

---

for a separate allowance to his wife, made through the intervention of a trustee, is valid: Carson v. Murray, 3 Paige Ch. 483; Champlin v. Champlin, 1 Hoff. Ch. 55; Hutton v. Duey, 3 Penn. St. 100; Dillinger's Appeal, 35 Penn. St. 357; Simpson v. Simpson, 4 Dana 140; Rogers v. Rogers, 4 Paige 518; Carter v. Carter, 14 Sm. & M. 59; Barron v. Barron, 24 Verm. 375; McKennan v. Phillips, 6 Wharton 571; Reed v. Beazley, 1 Blackf. 97; and where a reservation of a right to visit each other in case of sickness, was made in the deed, but never acted on, this reservation was held not to invalidate the agreement: Carson v. Murray. But see Rogers v. Rogers, 4 Paige Ch. 516; Wallingsford v. Wallingsford, 6 Har. & J. 485; McKennan v. Phillips, 6 Wharton 571; McCrocklin v. McCrocklin, 2 B. Monr. 370. Although generally the provisions of a separate deed are annulled by reconciliation and re-cohabitation, yet the husband may conduct himself subsequently so as to create new obligations on the footing of those in the separate deed. As where in a deed of separation, the husband covenanted to pay an annuity to the wife for her life, and subsequently, after living apart for a while, he promised her that if she would come and live with him again, the annuity should be continued, it was held that the annuity was not forfeited by re-cohabitation: Webster v. Webster, 22 L. J. Ch. 837; 27 Id. 115.

In England, it is now established, that specific performance of articles of agreement to a separation, so far as they regard an arrangement of property agreed upon, may be decreed: Wilson v. Wilson, 1 H. Lords Cas. 538; see s. c. 5 H. Lords Cas. 40. And a covenant to live separate will be enforced by injunction: Sanders v. Rodway, 16 Jur. 1005; though where the agreement contains provisions for the education of the children, which are contrary to public policy, it cannot be enforced in any part: Vansittart v. Vansittart, 27 L. J. Ch. 295. But a different doctrine from that established in Wilson v. Wilson, is still held in the United States. See cases collected in Hill on Trustees, 4th Am. ed. 668; Calkins v. Lang, 22 Barb. 97.

must be a direction that it shall be for her sole, separate,
or independent use, or in other equivalent terms showing
a manifest intent to exclude the husband.$(f)^1$ In like
manner, in order to create a fetter on anticipation, there
must be positive words, or a manifest intention to restrain
that power of disposal, which is *primâ facie* incidental to
ownership.$(g)^2$

(f) Tyler *v.* Lake, 2 R. & M. 183; Massey *v.* Parker, 2 M. & K. 174;
Blacklow *v.* Laws, 2 Hare 49.

(g) Brown *v.* Bamford, 11 Sim. 127; 1 Ph. 620; Medley *v.* Horton, 14
Sim. 222; Baggett *v.* Meux, 1 Coll. 138; 1 Ph. 627; [Cooke *v.* Husbands,
11 Md. 504; Ross's Trust, 1 Sim. N. S. 196.]

---

[1] It is difficult to lay down any precise rule on this subject, and impossible to reconcile all the decisions. There must be an intention to confer
a separate interest on the wife; and this intention must be properly manifested. The intention must exist; for without it, words which would
otherwise create a separate estate will not have that effect. Thus in Lewis
v. Mathews, L. R. 2 Eq. 177, there was a devise of real and personal estate
to H., a *feme sole* who afterwards married, " her heirs, executors, administrators and assigns, for her and their own sole and absolute use and benefit," and it was held that these words did not create a separate estate in
H., because they were applied equally to her heirs and executors, as to
whom no such intention could exist: see also Rudisell *v.* Watson, 2 Dev.
Eq. 430. The intention must be properly manifested; and this may be
done by the use of expressions which either confer upon the *feme* a dominion over the property inconsistent with her position as coverte, or which
exclude the rights of the husband. Of the first class of expressions instances will be found in Jamison *v.* Brady, 6 S. & R. 466: Gardenhire *v.*
Hinds, 1 Head 402; Ellis *v.* Woods, 9 Rich. Eq. 19; Ozley *v.* Ikelheimer,
26 Alab. 332; Nix *v.* Bradley, 6 Rich. Eq. 48; Bridges *v.* Wood, 4 Dana
610; of the latter, Woodrum *v.* Kirkpatrick, 2 Swan 218; Martin *v.* Bell,
9 Rich. Eq. 42; Young *v.* Young, 3 Jones Eq. 216; Ballard *v.* Taylor, 4
Dessaus. 550; Evans *v.* Knorr, 4 Rawle 66; Perry *v.* Boileau, 10 S. & R.
208, are examples.

In general as to what words will or will not create a separate use, see
the American note to Hulme *v.* Tenant, 1 Lead. Cas. Eq. 539, and Hill on
Trustees 654 to 650 (4th Am. ed.). Particular attention may perhaps be
called to Gilbert *v.* Lewis, 1 De G., J. & Sm. 38, and Tarsay's Trusts, L.
R. 1 Eq. 561. The intervention of a trustee is not necessary: 1 Lead.
Cas. Eq. 641.

[2] But it is now held that express negative words are not necessary to

In the absence of any fetter on anticipation, the wife has the same power over her separate property as if she were unmarried. Her disability to bind herself or her general property is left untouched; but she may pledge or bind her separate property, and the Court may proceed *in rem* against it, though not *in personam* against herself. In order that the separate property may be thus bound, it is not necessary that she should execute an instrument expressly referring to it, or purporting to exercise a power over it. It is sufficient that she professes to act as a *feme sole*. For the Court of Chancery, in giving her the capacity to hold separate property, gives also the capacity incident *to property in general, of incurring debts to be paid out of it; and enforces payment of such debts when contracted, not as personal liabilities, but by laying hold of the separate property, as the only means by which they can be satisfied.(*h*)[1] [*46]

(*h*) Murray *v.* Barlea, 4 Sim. 82; 3 M. & K. 209; Aylett *v.* Ashton, 1 M. & C. 105; Tullett *v.* Armstrong, 4 Bea. 319; Owens *v.* Dickinson, Cr. & P. 48; Lord *v.* Wightwick, 2 Ph. 110; [Wilton *v.* Hill, 25 L. J. Ch. 157; Vaughan *v.* Vanderstegen, 2 Drew 363.]

---

create a restraint upon alienation. Thus in Baker *v.* Bradley, 7 De G., M. & G. 597, there was a provision that the married woman's receipts alone, or those of some person authorized to receive any payments of the said rents and income, after such payment should have become due, should alone be a sufficient discharge, and it was held affirming, Field *v.* Evans, 15 Sim. 375, that this was a valid restraint. To the same effect is Freeman *v.* Flood, 16 Geo. 528; see, however, Cooke *v.* Husbands, 11 Md. 504. The restraint on alienation, though a creature of the Court of Chancery, cannot be dispensed with by the Court, even where the interest of the married woman might require it. Thus, where a testator gave a legacy to a married woman, on condition that she should convey to a third person her interest in certain property of small value, included in an estate which was settled to her separate use, without power of anticipation, it was held that the condition could not be accomplished, and the legacy failed: Robinson *v.* Wheelwright, 6 De G., M. & G. 535.

[1] The English rule is that, in the absence of any restraint on alienation, a *feme covert* has the same power of disposition over personal property

The *pin-money* trust is so far similar to that for separate
use, that in both cases the property subject to the trust

settled to her separate use, as a *feme sole;* and a recent decision has declared
that she has a similar capacity as to her real estate: Taylor *v.* Meads,
34 L. J. Ch. 203 ; 11 Jur. N. S. 166. Her power of disposing of her realty
had formerly been limited to the rents and profits ; but in the case last
mentioned it was said that she could convey the corpus thereof by a will or
by a deed not acknowledged according to the formalities of the statute.
See Hill on Trustees 658, note. In some of the United States the English
doctrine as to personalty and the income of real estate is followed: Ives *v.*
Harris, 7 Rh. Island 413 ; Leaycraft *v.* Hedden, 3 Green Ch. 551 ; Imlay
v. Huntington, 20 Conn. 175; Coleman *v.* Wooley, 10 B. Monr. 320; Vizon-
neau *v.* Pegram, 2 Leigh 183 ; Newlin *v.* Freeman, 4 Ired. Eq. 312; Bradford *v.* Greenway, 17 Alab. 805; Fears *v.* Brooks, 12 Geo. 200; Coats *v.*
Robinson, 10 Miss. 757; Cooke *v.* Husbands, 11 Md. 504.

In others the *feme* has only such power of disposition as is given by the
instrument creating the trust: Lancaster *v.* Dolan, 1 Rawle 231 ; Reid *v.*
Lamar, 1 Strobh. Eq. 27; Porcher *v.* Reid, 12 Rich. Eq. 349; Doty *v.*
Mitchell, 9 Sm. & M. 435 ; Marshall *v.* Stephens, 8 Humph. 159. In New
York the Court of Appeals, in Jacques *v.* The Methodist Church, 17 Johns.
548, overruling a decision of Chancellor Kent, adopted the English rule ;
but now, under the revised statutes, the interest of a married woman is
inalienable, and she cannot charge or affect it in any manner: Noyes *v.*
Blakeman, 3 Sandf. 538 ; 2 Seld. 567 ; Leggett *v.* Perkins, 2 Comstock 297.
See Yale *v.* Dederer, 18 N. Y. 265 ; 22 Id. 450 ; Hill on Trustees 664, note.

In Pennsylvania it was at one time held that the " Married Woman's
Act" in that state had altered the rule: Haines *v.* Ellis, 24 Penn. St.
253. But a more recent and better considered decision has established the
contrary: Wright *v.* Brown, 44 Penn. St. 224. In none of the states has
the doctrine been carried to the extent which it has reached in England
in Taylor *v.* Meads (supra) ; and an express power is necessary to enable
the *feme* to dispose of the corpus of real estate.

The decisions in the United States, as to the liability of the separate
estate to the debts and charges of a *feme covert*, are not uniform. In some
of those states in which she is held to possess an implied power over her
separate property, the decisions establish that, in order to make a debt a
charge on that property, there must be some reference thereto, or the debt
be contracted for the benefit, or on credit thereof: N. A. Coal Co. *v.* Dyett,
7 Paige 14; Dickson *v.* Miller, 11 Sm. & M. 594; Frazier *v.* Brownlow, 3
Ired. Eq. 237. In others the broader English rule is followed: Collins *v.*
Lavenburg, 19 Alab. 685 ; Coats *v.* Robinson, 10 Missouri 757 ; Bell *v.*
Kellar, 13 B. Monr. 381 ; Lillard *v.* Turner, 16 Id. 374 ; Whitesides *v.*

is placed at the wife's sole disposal, independent of her husband's control. But in one respect the two trusts are essentially different : the one places the property at her absolute disposal for any purpose which she may select; the other secures to her an income during the coverture, to be specifically expended in her dress and personal expenses, lest the husband should refuse her an adequate allowance. It is a fund, therefore, which she is not entitled to accumulate, but may be made to spend during the coverture by the intercession and advice, and at the instance, of her husband : it seems probable that, should she refuse to spend it, the husband would be entitled to withhold it from her; and it has been decided that, if it be not in fact paid to her, no claim for arrears beyond a year can be made by herself, and no claim, even for that period, by her personal representatives.(i)

It has been contended that alimony is in the nature of separate estate, so that the wife may bind herself by contracts respecting it, and that a bill may be sustained by her executors for an account. This, however, is not the case. Alimony is not separate estate, but a mere provision for maintenance from day to day, decreed by a competent Court to a wife legally separated from her

(i) Howard v. Digby, 8 Bligh 224, 245, 267, 268 ; Beresford v. Archbishop of Armagh, 13 Sim. 643.

Cannon, 23 Missouri 457. Where, however, no power is attributed to the *feme* except such as is expressly given, as in Pennsylvania, the question cannot arise, except perhaps in the case of necessaries. See Wallace v. Coston, 9 Watts 137. In South Carolina, however, the separate estate is held liable for debts contracted on its account and for its use : Magwood v. Johnston, 1 Hill Eq. 228 ; Adams v. Mackay, 6 Rich. Eq. 75. Under the Revised Statutes, in New York, the trustee alone has the power to subjcet the estate to debts for its necessary expenses, &c. : Noyes v. Blakeman, 3 Sandf. S. C. 531 ; 2 Seld. 567. The equitable doctrines on these subjects are modified in many of the States by the " Married Woman's Acts."

husband, and is subject in respect to its amount, continuance, and mode of payment, to the discretion of the
[*47] *Ecclesiastical Court.[1] The wife has in fact no
property therein; and the Court of Chancery can
give no relief respecting it, except by granting a writ of
ne exeat regno, where the husband is about to leave the
kingdom, on the special ground that the Ecclesiastical
Court cannot compel him to find bail.(*k*)

The wife's equity for a settlement attaches on her
equitable chattels real, and on such of her equitable choses
in action as are capable of being immediately reduced into
possession, and it authorizes a restraint of the husband's
right, until he shall have made an adequate settlement.[2]

The rule at law with respect to chattels real and choses
in action, of which the wife has the legal ownership, is
that in both cases, if the wife survive her husband, and
no act be done by him to bar her right, she is entitled by
survivorship on his decease. But the nature of the husband's title and the means by which he may bar his wife's
right, differ materially in the two cases. With respect to
terms of years and other chattels real, the right of the

(*k*) Vandergucht *v*. De Blaquiere, 8 Sim. 315; 5 M. & C. 229.

---

[1] For these reasons no action can be maintained in another state upon
a decree of alimony: Barber *v*. Barber, 1 Chand. (Wisc.) 280. Though
arrears before a decree of divorce *a vinculis* in another state may be recovered in the latter: Harrison *v*. Harrison, 20 Alab. 629. See Hill on
Trustees 663, note.

[2] It is now the rule in England that the wife's equity to a settlement will
be sustained as well against real as personal estate: Sturgis *v*. Champneys,
5 Myl. & Cr. 97; though this doctrine has been followed reluctantly; Hanson *v*. Keating, 4 Hare 1; and will not (it is said) be extended: Gleaves *v*.
Paine, 1 De G., J. & Sm. 87. See, however, Newenham *v*. Pemberton, 11
Jur. 1071; 1 De G. & Sm. 644. In Virginia this doctrine has been approved: Poindexter *v*. Jeffries, 15 Grat. 363, and see Rees *v*. Waters, 9
Watts 90; Hill on Trustees 626, note.

husband is a right to the profits during coverture, with an absolute right of disposal by act *inter vivos ;* and if he survive his wife, they are absolutely his.   With respect to choses in action his right is more limited; for the mere right of action is not transferable, but remains in the wife notwithstanding her coverture, to be exercised by her and her husband jointly.   If it is so exercised by them, and the chose in action is reduced into possession, it becomes, like her other personalty in possession, the husband's property; but until that time it remains in the wife.   If she survives, she takes it absolutely; and if the husband survives, he takes it as her administrator, and not in his own right.(*l*)[1]

In order therefore to exclude the wife's right of survivorship, the husband must assign her chattel real, and must reduce into possession her chose in action.   And if *he can effectuate this by course of law, there is [*48] no equity to restrain him.   It might therefore be expected that where the wife's interest is equitable, instead of legal, the analogy of law would be pursued in equity, so that the husband's assignee of the chattel real would be entitled wholly to exclude the wife, and the husband himself might proceed of right in equity to reduce into possession the chose in action.   The practice of the Court, however, is otherwise.   The trustee or holder of the property may transfer it without suit to the husband, and will not be responsible for so doing.   But if he refuses to do so, or a bill be filed on the wife's behalf to prevent him, so that the property is brought within the control of the Court, and the assistance of the Court is required to give

(*l*) 2 Steph. Blacks. 300.

---

[1] For authorities in the United States, on this question, see Hill on Trustees, 4th Am. ed. 642, note, and see post 142, note.

any benefit in it to the husband or his assignee, it is an
established equity, founded on long practice, that the husband shall not have it, if it exceeds 200*l.*,[1] unless he makes
or has already made an adequate provision for his wife
and children.   This is termed the wife's equity for a settlement.   It is unaffected by any act or assignment of the
husband; and the only mode by which it can be barred,
is by the wife's personal waiver in Court on examination
apart from her husband.(*m*)   If the chose in action be one
which the husband cannot reduce into present possession, as if it be to take effect after the coverture, or on the
determination of an existing life estate, the wife is entitled to the whole, notwithstanding her marriage, and
there is no interest in the husband on which the equity
can attach.[2]

(*m*) Elibank *v.* Montolieu, 5 Ves. 737 ; Murray *v.* Elibank, 10 Ves. 84 ;
13 Ves. 1 ; Johnson *v.* Johnson, 1 J. & W. 452 ; Sturgis *v.* Champneys, 5
M. & C. 97 ; Hanson *v.* Keating, 4 Hare 1.

---

[1] It is not material now, in England, that the property should exceed
200*l.* : Cutlers' Trust, 14 Beav. 220 ; Kincaid's Trusts, 1 Drewry 326,
where it was said that the rule applied to taking the wife's assent to parting with her interest.

[2] The doctrine stated in the text is sustained by the American authorities : Tevis's Rep. *v.* Richardson's Heirs, 7 Monroe 654 ; Fabre *v.* Colden,
1 Paige 166 ; Smith *v.* Kane, 2 Id. 303 ; McElhatton *v.* Howell, 4 Heywood 19, 24 ; Kenny *v.* Udal, 3 Cowen 590 ; s. c., Kenney *v.* Udall, 5
Johns. Ch. 464 ; Elliott *v.* Waring, 5 Monroe 340 ; Van Duzer *v.* Van
Duzer, 6 Paige 366 ; Whitesides *v.* Darris, 7 Dana 107 ; Andrews & Bro.
v. Jones et al., 10 Ala. 400 ; Rees *v.* Waters, 9 Watts 90 ; Rorer *v.* O'Brien,
10 Penn. St. 212 ; James *v.* Gibbs, 1 Patt. & Head 277 ; Moore *v.* Mooney,
14 B. Monroe 259 ; Bell *v.* Bell, 1 Kelly 637 ; see also, cases in notes to
Murray *v.* Lord Elibank, 1 Lead Cas. Eq. 348, 3d Am. ed. ; Duncombe *v.*
Greenacre, 7 Jur. N. S. 175 ; Hill on Trustees, 4th Am. ed. 632, note. But
not in New Hampshire and North Carolina : Parsons *v.* Parsons, 9 N. H.
309 ; Allen *v.* Allen, 6 Ired. Eq. 293.   And a court of equity will go to a
great length in protecting the wife, and the doctrine has been carried so
far that the court say that the husband and his assignees will be restrained

The equity, though called that of the wife, is effectuated by a settlement on her children also, as being, if the property is settled at all, the most proper mode of doing it; and the wife cannot 'separate their interest from her own, or claim a settlement on herself to their exclusion. Their right, however, though inseparable from hers, is *merely incidental, and does not constitute an independent equity; and therefore, if she die with- [*49] out having asserted her right, or if, after its assertion and while the matter rests in proposal, she come in and waive it, the husband after her death may receive the property, and the children have no equity to compel a settlement.(n)

The provision usually made is one commencing from the husband's decease; for, during his lifetime, he is the proper person to maintain his family. And accordingly, if the wife's interest be a mere life income, the equity does not attach; for the payments during the coverture are properly receivable by the husband; and those to accrue afterwards are reversionary, and not reducible into the husband's possession.(o) If, however, the husband does not in fact maintain his wife, or if he has deserted her, or by ill usage has driven her from him;

(n) Murray v. Elibank, 10 Ves. 84; s. c., 13 Ves. 1; Lloyd v. Williams, 1 Mad. 450; Fenner v. Taylor, 2 R. & M. 190; Hodgens v. Hodgens, 11 Bli. 62, 103; 4 Cl. & F. 323, 371; Lloyd v. Mason, 5 Hare 149.

(o) Wright v. Morley, 11 Ves. 12, 18; Elliott v. Cordell, 5 Mad. 149; Stanton v. Hall, 2 R. & M. 175, 180; Stiffe v. Everitt, 1 M. & C. 37.

---

in obtaining possession of his property by process of law, if she has no other means of supporting herself and children, unless a suitable provision is allowed her out of it: Van Epps v. Van Deusen, 4 Paige 63. The equity to a settlement can only be waived on a privy examination by a commissioner appointed for the purpose. A transfer acknowledged before an ordinary commissioner out of the state, will not be enough: Coppidge v. Threadgill, 3 Sneed 577.

or if he has become incapable of maintaining her, as by his bankruptcy or by an assignment of all his property in trust for creditors, an immediate provision will be directed. In this case it is immaterial whether the wife's interest is for life only, or of a more permanent character;[1] and it is competent for the Court to settle such a proportion on her as the circumstances require, or even to settle the entire income, if the husband has already received other portions of her fortune. If the desertion be on the part of the wife, the Court will give her no benefit from the fund; but it has been held that, as the husband does not in fact maintain her, he cannot be entitled to the whole property, and the dividends therefore should be paid into Court. (p)[2]

3. The equitable ownership is governed by the same laws of devolution and transfer as the legal one.

[*50] *The maxims therefore of the common law as to descent, *possessio fratris,* customs of gavelkind and borough English, and the like, have been always enforced by analogy in equity, subject however to an exception in the case of dower, which we shall presently notice. A trust estate may be entailed or otherwise settled by the owner, and will devolve regularly in the line of entail; it might, until the late statute, be again disentailed by a fine or recovery, and may now be disentailed by a statute deed, in the same manner as a legal estate. But a trust of realty

(p) Ball v. Montgomery, 2 Ves. Jun. 191; Duncan v. Campbell, 12 Sim. 616; Gardner v. Marshall, 14 Sim. 575.

---

[1] This is overruled with regard to a purchaser for value of a life interest of the wife; and no equity to a settlement arises in such case whether the husband maintain her or not: Tidd v. Lister, 3 De G., M. & G. 857; aff'g s. c. 10 Hare 157.

[2] Though see as to adultery, Greedy v. Lavender, 13 Beav. 62; Carter v. Carter, 14 Sm. & Marsh. 59.

is not liable to escheat; for escheat is merely an incident of tenure, arising out of the feudal system, whereby the escheated estate on the death without heirs of the person last seised escheats to the lord as reverting to the original grantor, there being no longer a tenant to perform the services incidental to the tenure. It is therefore inapplicable to estates which do not lie in tenure, such as rents, commons, &c., and is equally inapplicable to an equitable estate. If the line of descent fails by the death of the *cestui que trust* without heirs, the trustee will have the enjoyment as the legal owner, for there is no one who can sue a *subpœna* against him.(q)[1] If the descent fails by attainder, there appears to be some doubt as to the position of the trustee, as to his right of holding against the felon if pardoned, or against his heir if the felon be executed. The forfeiture to the Crown by attaint of treason has been specially extended by statute to trusts.(r) And where a trust of land is declared for an alien, the Crown is entitled, as in the case of a legal estate; for the incapacity *of an alien is not an incident of tenure, but a result of public policy, which disables an alien [*51]

(q) On the subject of the escheat and forfeiture of trust estates and the respective rights of the Crown and trustee on the death of the *cestui que trust* without heirs or his attainder: vide Burgess v. Wheate, 1 Eden Ch. Cas. 177; [Sweeting v. Sweeting, 33 L. J. Ch. 211;] Onslow v. Wallis, 1 Macn. & Gord. 506.

(r) 33 Hen. 8, c. 20, s. 2; 1 Hale P. C. 248; but see King v. Dacombe, Cro. Jac. 512. In case of the death of a trustee or mortgagee without heirs, or his attainder, it is provided by a recent statute, 4 & 5 Wm. 4, c. 23, that no lands, chattels or stock, vested in such person, upon any trust, or by way of mortgage, shall escheat or be forfeited, but shall be conveyed by the Court of Chancery, as the case may require.

[1] It may well be doubted whether this proposition would hold under the statutes of distribution in the United States generally. See Matthews v. Ward, 10 Gill & John. 443; Darrah v. McNair, 1 Ashm. 236; 4 Kent's Com. 425.

from purchasing except for the king's use.[1] In the case of chattels, whether real or personal, the doctrine of escheat has no place, but if the *cestui que trust* die intestate and without leaving next of kin, his interest vests in the Crown as *bona vacantia*, and if he be convicted of treason or felony, it has always been deemed forfeitable to the Crown.(s)

The subjection of equitable estates to the legal rules of devolution and transfer admits of two exceptions : the one real, in their exemption from dower,[2] the other apparent, in the attendance of satisfied terms on the inheritance.

The right of a widow to dower at common law was a right to have a third part of her husband's freehold lands of inheritance assigned to her for her use, on his decease, for her life. And as the right was given as a matter of general policy, it might have been expected that Courts of equity, following the policy of the law, would have annexed the same right to an equitable estate. It was,

(s) 1 Steph. Bl. 401, 443 ; 4 Id. 446 ; Att.-Gen. v. Sands, Freem. 130 ; Lewin on Trustees 556 ; Burgess v. Wheate, 1 Eden 177 ; Williams v. Lonsdale, 3 Ves. 752 ; Taylor v. Hagarth, 14 Sim. 8 ; [Cradock v. Owen, 2 Sm. & Giff. 241.]

---

[1] Barrow v. Wadkin, 24 Beav. 1. See, however, Rittson v. Stordy, 3 Sm. & Giff. 230.

[2] The general principle is, that at common law a wife was not entitled to dower in a trust estate : Stevens v. Smith, 4 J. J. Marsh. 64 ; Danforth v. Lowry, 3 Heywood 61 ; Herron v. Williamson, 6 Litt. Sel. Cas. 250 ; Lenox v. Notrebe, 1 Hempst. 251. Though in some of the states, as in Kentucky and Virginia, special statutes have been enacted, relieving the wife from this disability : Stevens v. Smith, before cited, and Braxton v. Lee, 4 Hen. & Munf. 376.

By the usage and law of Pennsylvania, a woman is entitled to dower in a trust estate : Shoemaker v. Walker, 2 S. & R. 554 ; Dubs v. Dubs, 31 Penn. St. 149.

See Williams on Real Property, 229, note, and post, note to page 233, 234.

however, decided otherwise : and the reason assigned is, that long before the question was raised, a general impression had prevailed that the widow would be barred by trust, and that many estates had been purchased on the faith of this opinion, the titles to which would be shaken and much mischief produced, by a decision to the contrary.   And, on this ground of anticipated inconvenience, whether a judicious one or not, the decision in question was made.(*t*)   The point is worth noticing, as having for many years been an anomaly in the doctrines of equity. But by the passing of the Dower Act,(*u*) which abolishes the distinction in this respect between legal and equitable estates, *and at the same time gives to the husband a control over his wife's dower, which previously he did not possess, it has ceased to be of much practical importance. [*52]

The exception in respect to attendant terms is rather apparent than real.   It frequently happens that long terms of years are created in real estates, for securing moneys lent on mortgage, for raising jointures and portions for children, and for other special trusts; and that after the fulfilment of the trust, the terms continue in existence. It might *primâ facie* be supposed, that so long as the legal term subsists, the trust under it is in the nature of a chattel, and will devolve to the executor and not to the heir.   But the rule is rightly otherwise.   For the trust of the term, under these circumstances, is not for any individual person, but for the owner of the inheritance, whoever he may be.   This would be the effect if a surrender were compelled; and the mere absence of a legal surrender does not change the effect in equity.   In ac-

(*t*) D'Arcy *v.* Blake, 2 Sch. & L. 387.
(*u*) 3 & 4 Wm. 4, c. 105.

cordance with this principle, a term may be made attendant, either by implication of law, where the effect of a
surrender would be immediate merger, or by express declaration of the parties. And the trust of such attendant
term will follow the descent of the inheritance, and the
conveyances, assurances, and charges of the owner. It
may, however, be afterwards disannexed by the owner
and converted into a term in gross; and it will be so disannexed whenever it fails of a freehold to support it, or
is divided from the inheritance by distinct limitations.(v)
The effect of getting in an attendant term, where two purchasers or encumbrancers are contending for priority, will
be hereafter considered under a different head.(w)

The doctrine(ww) of attendant terms will shortly become of little importance; for, by 8 & 9 Vict. c. 112, it is
enacted that every term of years which on the 31st Dec.
1845, *should be attendant on the inheritance,
[*53] should cease and determine on that day, except for
the purpose of any protection which it would have afforded
if it had continued to exist, but had not been assigned or
dealt with after that day; and that every term which after
that day should become attendant, should immediately on
its becoming so attendant cease and determine.

The means by which an equitable ownership is transferred or changed, where its subject-matter is personal
estate, are analogous to those which apply to a legal
ownership, rather than strictly identical with them. The
distinction originates in the doctrine that personal property
passes at law by mere delivery, which where an equitable

(v) Willoughby v. Willoughby, 1 Term Rep. 763; Capel v. Girdler, 9
Ves. 509; 3 Sug. V. & P. 10th edit. c. 15.
(w) Infra, Priorities.
(ww) See the case of Doe d. Clay v. Jones, 13 Q. B. 774.

interest is transferred, may not be practicable; and therefore in order to pursue as nearly as possible the analogy of law, it is required that the assignment of an equitable interest should be perfected by notice to the trustee, so as to deprive the assignor of subsequent control, and to effect a constructive delivery to the assignee.(x)[1] It is otherwise with respect to real estate; for real estate passes by title, and not by delivery, and the character of the grantor's interest, whether legal or equitable, does not affect the terms of his deed. The period at which the transfer of an equity becomes complete is often material to be considered, where such transfer has been made without consideration, or where several purchasers or encumbrancers have acquired conflicting rights; but its effect in these cases will be hereafter separately considered.(y)

The principle of constructive delivery by notice to the trustee is applied also to a debt or other *chose in action*. The right of recovering such an interest, like that of enforcing a trust, is in strictness merely a right of litigation; and except in the case of negotiable securities, is not capable of transfer at law. But if it be in substance a right *of property, it is treated in equity as of that character, and may be transferred by an assign- [*54]

(x) Dearle v. Hall, 3 Russ. 1; Foster v. Cockerell, 3 Cl. & F. 456; Jones v. Jones, 8 Sim. 633; Wilmont v. Pike, 5 Hare 14; [Voyle v. Hughes, 2 Sm. & Giff. 18; see Kekewich v. Manning, 1 De Gex, Macn. & G. 176; Stocks v. Dobson, 4 Id. 11; Hill on Trustees 140 and 698, 4th Am. ed.]

(y) Infra, Priorities.

---

[1] In the United States, however, notice is not generally held necessary to perfect the assignee's title: U. S. v. Vaughan, 3 Binn. 394; Muir v. Schenck, 3 Hill 228; Littlefield v. Smith, 17 Maine 327; Warren v. Copelin, 4 Metc. 594; *contra*, Vanbuskirk v. Ins. Co., 14 Conn. 145. Though a payment without notice is, of course, good.

ment or agreement to assign perfected by notice to the party liable. If the right is not substantially a title to property, but a mere litigious right, as, for instance, the right of action for a personal wrong, or for suing in equity to redress a fraud, it cannot be made the subject of assignment; for the transaction would be directly adverse to the policy of the law, which prohibits the encouragement of litigation, by the introduction of strangers to enforce rights which the owners are not disposed to maintain.(z)

The regular mode of transferring a debt is by an instrument purporting to assign it, accompanied by a power of attorney to sue in the name of the assignor, and followed by notice to the party from whom the assignor is to receive payment. There is not, however, any special form necessary, but any declaration. either by writing or word of mouth, that a transfer is intended, will be effectual, provided that it amount to an appropriation to the assignee; for inasmuch as the fund is not assignable at law nor capable of manual possession, an appropriation is all that the case admits.(a)

Possible and contingent interests are also to a certain extent assignable in equity,[1] on the same principle as

(z) Prosser v. Edmonds, 1 Y. & C. Exch. 481; Wood v. Downes, 18 Ves. 120; Hunter v. Daniel, 4 Hare 420. [See American note to Row v. Dawson, 2 Lead. Cas. Eq. 612.]

(a) Gardner v. Lachlan, 4 M. & C. 129; Thompson v. Speirs, 13 Sim. 469; Burn v. Carvalho, 4 M. & C. 690; Cook v. Black, 1 Hare 390; McFadden v. Jenkyns, Id. 458; 1 Ph. 153; Malcolm v. Scott, 3 Hare 39, 52; Braybrooke v. Meredith, 13 Sim. 271.

---

[1] The student will find a very clear statement of the difference between assignments of future and contingent interests in equity and at law, in the opinion of Lord Chan. Westbury in Holroyd v. Marshal, 10 H. L. Cas. 191; see also, Hart v. The Farmers' Bank, 33 Verm. 252; Stover v. Eycleshimer, 46 Barb. 84; Pennock v. Coe, 23 How. 117; Bayler v. The Commonwealth,

choses in action, although, by reason of their being devoid of any substantive or certain character, they were until 8 & 9 Vict. c. 106, and in the case of personal estate still are, incapable of assignment at law. In this way a contingent legacy or other interest may be made the subject of equitable assignment; and so also may the freight to be earned by a ship on some future voyage, although the earning of such freight *is at the time of assignment a mere expectant possibility.(*b*) There is [*55] however, a distinction between choses in action and possibilities in personalty with respect to the completion of an equitable transfer. In the case of choses in action, the transfer may be completed, as we have already seen, by a constructive delivery; but in the case of possibilities, the interest, though a substantial one, is for the time being non-existent, and there are no means of perfecting the possession by notice or otherwise, but the contract remains *in fieri* until the contingency determines.(*c*)

The next subject for notice is the legal ownership of the trustee, which confers on him at law an absolute dominion, but is considered in equity as subservient to the trust; so that the trustee is bound to use it for those purposes, and those only, which were contemplated by the grantor: to account for and protect the property whilst the trust continues; to restore it to the parties entitled when the trust is at an end; and not to avail himself of his fiduciary character for any object of personal benefit.

(*b*) Langton *v.* Horton, 1 Hare 549.

(*c*) Meek *v.* Kettlewell, 1 Hare 464; 1 Ph. 342. [See, however, *contra*, Kekewich *v.* Manning, 1 De G., M. & Gord. 176.]

40 Penn. St. 37; Hill on Trustees 44; see on this subject, Mitchell *v.* Winslow, 2 Story 630; Letcher *v.* Shrœder, 5 J. J. Marsh. 513; Varick *v.* Edwards, 1 Hoff. Ch. 382; Merriweather *v.* Herran, 8 B. Monr. 162.

A trustee is bound to use his legal dominion for those purposes, and those only, which were contemplated by the grantor.[1] If, for instance, he is trustee for sale of an estate, he must not sell unless there be a legitimate object in view; and, when he does sell, he must take care that the interests of all his *cestuis que trust* are duly consulted, and that all prudent precautions are taken for obtaining the full value.(d)[2] If he is a trustee of renewable lease-holds, he must be careful that the renewals are made in the usual course, and the requisite funds provided for that purpose.(e) If he is a trustee of money secured by cove-
[*56] nant, *or of other outstanding property, he must realize or secure it with all convenient speed.(f) And if he is trustee of moneys for the purpose of invest-ment, he should invest them in three per cent. consols as the fund sanctioned by the Court, or on such other securi-

(d) Ord v. Noel, 5 Mad. 438; Mortlock v. Buller, 10 Ves. 292, 308; Wil-kins v. Fry, 1 Meriv. 244, 268; 2 Sug. on Powers 486. [See for American authorities on powers of sale, notes to Hill on Trustees, 4 Am. ed., 735.]

(e) Lord Montfort v. Lord Cadogan, 17 Ves. 485; Greenwood v. Evans, 4 Bea. 44; Shaftesbury v. Marlborough, 2 M. & K. 111; Bennett v. Col-ley, 2 M. & K. 233.

(f) Maitland v. Bateman, 13 Law Journ. 273.

---

[1] A sale made under a deed of trust, after the debt secured by it has been fully paid, is void, there being no valid subsisting power under the deed: Penny v. Cook, 19 Iowa 538.

[2] The sale must be effected within a reasonable time: Walker v. Shore, 19 Ves. 387; but it must not be hastened to a disadvantage: Hunt v. Bass, 2 Dev. Eq. 297; and the court, on proper cause shown, will give a trustee leave to delay a sale: Morris v. Morris, 4 Jur. N. S. 802–964. As a general rule the sale should be at auction, although it is not absolutely essential, and private sales are now allowed and regulated by statute in England and in some of the United States as in New York and Pennsylvania. Where, however, the trust instrument expressly requires a public sale, that method must be adopted: Greenleaf v. Queen, 1 Peters 145. A power of sale will not authorize an exchange: Ringgold v. Ringgold, 1 H. & G. 11.

ties, if any, as are authorized by his trust;[1] and should at the same time execute a declaration of trust, so that in the event of his bankruptcy or insolvency the fund may be identified. (g)[2] If there be an express power to lend on personal security, it will of course warrant a loan to a responsible person on his mere bond or promissory note; but such a loan would not be warranted by an authority to adopt such security as the trustee shall think safe; (h) nor would a power to lend generally on personal security authorize an advance to a trader by way of accommodation, or a loan to one of the trustees themselves. (i) If the fund is already outstanding on personal security, but no authority is given to leave it so, the trustee is bound

(g) Clough v. Bond, 3 M. & C. 496; Stickney v. Sewell, 1 M. & C. 8; Ames v. Parkinson, 7 Bea. 379.

(h) Bullock v. Wheatley, 1 Coll. 130; Styles v. Guy, 4 Y. & C. 571, in note; Walker v. Symonds, 3 Sw. 1, 62.

(i) Langston v. Ollivant, Coop. 33; —— c. Walker, 5 Russ. 7.

---

[1] Where trust funds are directed by will to be invested in certain securities, and such securities cannot be purchased, the trustee may invest in such a manner as shall seem to him safe and productive: McIntyre v. Zanesville, 17 Ohio 352. Quære, if he can without applying to the court for authority.

[2] Investments by trustees are generally regulated both in England and in this country by statute. See Hill on Trustees 560–561, in notes. The investment of trust funds in personal security is a breach of trust: Nyce's Estate, 5 W. & S. 254; Wills' Appeal, 22 Penn. St. 330; Smith v. Smith, 4 John. Ch. 281; De Jarnette v. De Jarnette, 41 Ala. 708. Massachusetts appearing to be the only state in which this rule does not obtain: Lovell v. Minot, 20 Pick. 119; Clark v. Garfield, 8 Allen 427. Trustees are chargeable with interest if they have made use of the money themselves, or have been negligent in not paying it over, or properly investing it: Bruner's Appeal, 57 Penn. St. 46. If the fund is directed to be invested at a specified time, it is to be considered as invested at that time, and bearing interest from that date: Halsted v. Mecker's Ex'rs, 3 Green (N. J.) 136. And in some cases they are chargeable with compound interest. The authorities on this subject will be found collected in the notes to Hill on Trustees, pp. 570–571, 4th Am. ed.

to call it in and make a proper investment. If, however, it is invested on an actual security, the trustee is not bound to call it in for the mere purpose of reinvestment in consols, unless a direction to that effect is contained in the instrument, or is deducible by implication from the character of the trusts. A question as to what will amount to such an implied direction has frequently arisen where property of a less safe or less permanent character than the regular investment of the Court, and therefore yielding a larger immediate income, such as leasehold estates, or foreign funds, has been bequeathed for life with remainder over. The general principle is, that a gift of the kind implies a [*57] *conversion into three per cent. consols, unless there be something in the language of the will pointing to a continuance in specie.$(k)^1$

A trustee is bound to account for and protect the property whilst his trust continues.[2] It is one of his principal

(k) Howe v. Lord Dartmouth, 7 Ves. 137 ; Pickering v. Pickering, 4 M. & C. 289; Hinves v. Hinves, 3 Hare 609; Pickup v. Atkinson, 4 Hare 624; Mills v. Mills, 7 Sim. 501; 1 Jarm. on Wills, 546.

[1] See a discussion of this question in Hill on Trustees, 4th Am. ed. 597. and American notes, and particularly Scholefield v. Redfern, 32 L. J. Ch. 627. In this country the rule of duty for a trustee in investing funds for the benefit of his *cestui que trust* is, that he is bound to observe the limits prescribed by the terms of the trust, or fairly implied from its nature and objects ; and in selecting an investment within those limits, he is bound to employ such diligence and such prudence in the care and management of the fund, as, in general, prudent men of discretion and intelligence employ in their own affairs. This necessarily excludes all speculation, and every investment for an uncertain and doubtful use in the market. For it does not follow, that because prudent men, in investing their own funds, often take the hazard of adventures with the hope of growing rich ; therefore a trustee may do so : per Woodruff, J., King v. Talbot, 40 N. Y. 76. All that a court of equity requires from a trustee is common skill, common prudence, and common caution : Neff's Appeal. 57 Penn. St. 91.

[2] If trustees either use or mix trust funds with their own, they will be liable for all losses which may arise from their neglect or mismanagement: Case v. Abeel, 1 Paige 393; Brackenridge v. Holland, 2 Blackf. 377;

and most important duties that he should keep regular and accurate accounts, clearly distinguishing the trust property from his own, and showing all his receipts and payments in respect of it; and that he should be always ready to produce those accounts to his *cestui que trust*.(*l*) It is also a most important duty that he should protect the property confided to him whilst the trust continues, and should for that purpose retain the control of it in his own hands. And it has been doubted whether he is even warranted in devising the estate, so as to break the descent to his heir, and whether, by so doing, he may not render his executors responsible for any breach of trust by the devisee.(*m*)[1]

(*l*) Pearse *v.* Green, 1 J. & W. 135; Freeman *v.* Fairlie, 3 Meriv. 24, 42.

(*m*) 1 Jarm. on Wills, 638; 2 Id. Appendix.

Myers *v.* Myers, 2 McC. Ch. 265; Utica Ins. Company *v.* Lynch, 11 Paige 520; Mumford *v.* Murray, 6 John. Ch. 1; Hart *v.* Ten Eyck, 2 Id. 513; Marine Bank *v.* Fulton Bank, 2 Wal. (S. C.) 252; Stanley's App., 8 Penn. St. 431; Jenkins *v.* Walter, 8 Gill & J. 218; Pennell *v.* Deffell, 4 De G., M. & G. 372; Frith *v.* Cartland, 34 L. J. Ch. 301; Hill on Trustees 575, note.

So guardians and trustees may be called to account by infants, and may be required to bring the trust-moneys into court, and to give further security to account when the infants become of age: Monell *v.* Monell, 5 John. Ch. 297. Though if a trustee or an executor be robbed of trust-money, it is a good answer to a bill for an account: Furman *v.* Coe, 1 Cal. Ca. 96.

If a trustee permit a debtor to retain possession of a trust estate, waste, and use it as his own, he will be held responsible for the injury to the trust fund out of his own estate: Harrison *v.* Mock, 10 Ala. Rep. 185.

It has been settled in England, after some fluctuation in authority, that where trustees have a discretion to invest either in stock or real securities, and neglect to make any proper investment, they are chargeable only with the amount of the principal sum and interest, and not with the value of the stock they might have bought. See Robinson *v.* Robinson, 1 De G., M. & G. 256, in which case Watts *v.* Girdlestone, 6 Beav. 188 (where a contrary doctrine had been held) was overruled, and the earlier case of Marsh *v.* Hunter, 6 Mad. 295, approved.

[1] The tendency of authority in England seems now, however, in favor of

The duty of retaining the control in his own hands precludes the trustee, not only from assigning the property altogether to a stranger, but even from conferring on such stranger a joint authority with himself.[1] It is true that in the latter case, he does not actually part with the estate, but he enables a third party to interfere with his discretion, and defeats *pro tanto* the object contemplated by the trust.(*n*)[2] A trustee, however, is not necessarily precluded from acting by the agency of others, where such a mode of acting is according to the ordinary course of business. For instance, he may employ a steward or agent; he may direct moneys to be paid into a bank; he may transmit money by means of bills drawn on respectable parties, and so forth; and if there has been sufficient [*58] *ground for his so doing, and he take care to keep the fund separate from his own property, he will not be answerable for incidental loss.(*o*)[3]

(*n*) Salway *v.* Salway, 4 Russ. 60; 2 R. & M. 215.

(*o*) Wren *v.* Kirton, 11 Ves. 377; Massey *v.* Banner, 1 J. & W. 241; Clough *v.* Bond, 3 M. & C. 490; Drake *v.* Kartyn, 1 Bea. 525; Matthews *v.* Brise, 6 Bea. 239.

---

the validity of such a devise: see Hill on Trustees, 4th Am. ed. 436, note; Fonda *v.* Penfield, 56 Barb. (N. Y.) 503; Schenck *v.* Schenck's Ex'rs., 1 Green (N. J.) 174. Special statutory provisions in some of the United States, obviate the necessity of this discussion.

[1] A trustee who has only delegated discretionary power cannot give a general authority to another to execute such power, unless he is specially authorized to do so by the deed or will creating the trust; and when an estate is devised with power to sell, a general authority to an agent to sell and convey lands belonging to the estate, or to contract absolutely for the sale of such lands, cannot be legally given by the trustees: Hawley *v.* James, 5 Paige 323; Berger *v.* Duff, 4 John. Ch. 368; Black *v.* Erwin, Harper's Law 411; though see Sinclair *v.* Jackson, 8 Cowen 582. In some states the power of trustees to act by attorney has been enlarged by statute; such is the case in Tennessee and Pennsylvania.

[2] Sugden *v.* Crossland, 3 Sm. & Giff. 192.

[3] Sinclair *v.* Jackson, 8 Cowen 532; Hawley *v.* James, 5 Paige 487.

The same principle which prohibits a trustee from giving up the control of the trust estate to a stranger, also prohibits him from supinely leaving it to his co-trustees. For when several trustees are appointed, the property is committed to the charge of all, and the *cestui que trust* is entitled to the vigilance of all.[1]

It is not meant that in every act done under the trust every trustee must actively interfere, for such a course would be practically impossible; and it is therefore the ordinary doctrine of the Court, that trustees are responsible for their own acts only, and not for those of each other. If, for instance, there be a sum of money payable to several trustees, it is sufficient that one should

---

[1] Co-trustees are bound to know the receipts, and watch over the conduct of each other: Ringgold *v.* Ringgold, 1 Har. & Gill. 11.

In matters requiring the exercise of discretion by trustees, and not in mere ministerial acts, co-trustees must all join, and cannot act separately in discharge of their trust: Vandever's Appeal, 8 W. & S. 405.

And it is not sufficient to exempt one of the two joint trustees from liability, that the duties of the trust have been exclusively performed by the co-trustee, with the concurrence and consent of the former. On the contrary, he is responsible for the conduct and management of his co-trustee, to whom he has thought proper to delegate his power, in the same manner and to the same extent as if they had been executed by himself: Maccubbin *v.* Cromwell, 7 Gill & J. 157; Spencer *v.* Spencer, 11 Paige 299; but see 3 Ala. 83; 3 Sandf. Ch. 99.

So when by the act of one trustee, a portion of the trust fund gets into the hands of his co-trustee, they are both responsible therefor: Graham *v.* Davidson, 2 Dev. & Bat. Ch. 155. But a trustee is not liable for money received by his co-trustee, in the regular discharge of the trust, though he join in a receipt; but where he joins in a receipt for money received by his co-trustee, when he had no right to receive it, he will be liable: Wallis *v.* Thornton, 2 Brock. 422; see also Monell *v.* Monell, 5 John. Ch. 296.

The common law made no provision for the execution of a joint trust by one of the trustees, where the co-trustee, by reason of lunacy or other inability, becomes incompetent to execute the trust: In the matter of Wadsworth, 2 Barb. Ch. 381. But by special statute, the court may remove the incompetent trustee, as in the state of New York: Ibid.

actually receive it; and, unless it be afterwards improperly left in his hands, the co-trustees will not be responsible. Nor will their position in this respect be
altered by their being parties to a joint receipt for the
sake of conformity, unless the money be improperly
raised, or there be some other independent act of misconduct; because, as no single trustee has any separate
authority, the receipt would not be valid without the signature of all. It is otherwise in regard to executors;[1]
for the receipt of one is a valid discharge; and, therefore,
if all join, it is treated, in the absence of special circumstances, as an admission that the money was under the
control of all.(p)[2]

(p) Brice $v.$ Stokes, 11 Ves. 319; Walker $v.$ Symonds, 3 Sw. 1, 64; Joy
$v.$ Campbell, 1 Sch. & L. 328, 341 ; Gregory $v.$ Gregory, 2 Y. & C. Exch.
313.

---

[1] In some cases, in the United States, it has been held, that this distinction as to executors had been now broken down : Stell's App., 10 Penn. St.
152; Ochiltree $v.$ Wright, 1 Dev. & Batt. Eq. 336.

[2] The liability of joint trustees for each other's acts has not always been
enforced with as great strictness in the United States as in England. The
rule has been most frequently stated to be that each is responsible only for
his own acts, and not for the acts of the others, unless he has made some
agreement by which he has expressly agreed to be bound for the other, or
has by his voluntary connivance, enabled one or more to accomplish some
known object in violation of the trust. A joinder in receipts, though *primâ
facie,* is not, as in the case of executors, conclusive evidence of an interest
to be jointly bound, but may be explained. Wherever it is necessary and
convenient for the purpose of the trust, that a part or all of the business
should be intrusted to one or more of the co-trustees, the others not cog-
nisant of, or concurring in any way in a misapplication of the funds, will
not be liable therefor; though see Maccubbin $v.$ Cromwell, 7 G. & John.
168. If, however, the acting trustee is known to be unfit for the management of the trust, or is suffering under pecuniary embarrassment, the co-
trustees will be responsible, if they permit money to be received by him or
to remain in his hands. And, if a trustee who has actually received money
or securities, pays or assigns them to his colleagues without necessity, he
will become liable for their misconduct. With regard to the effect of a

The cases, however, in which joint trustees may permit some of their body to act in the management without themselves incurring personal liability, are very different from those where a trustee so conducts himself as to throw the whole *trust fund into the hands of [*59] his colleagues, and to abandon the interests which it is his duty to protect. Any conduct of this latter kind is a dereliction from duty, and will make him responsible for consequent loss. If, for instance, he voluntarily aid his co-trustees to commit a breach of trust; if he neglect to prevent or remedy such breach of trust, when it comes to his knowledge; if he give facilities for it, as by suffering his co-trustee to detain the trust-money for a long period, without security; or even if he unnecessarily incur the risk of it by parting with that control which has been intrusted to him; as by a mutual agreement between himself and his co-trustee, that one shall have the exclusive management of one part of the property, and the other of the other part, he will be chargeable for the result of his misconduct or negligence, to the full extent of any mischief incurred.(q)

(q) Booth v. Booth, 1 Bea. 125; Broadhurst v. Balguy, 1 N. C. C. 16.

joinder in sales, which is of course a necessary act, the authorities are not agreed, though it has been held in most cases, that the trustees are jointly responsible for the collection and investment of the purchase-money. Where, indeed, there is an express direction that the trust-fund, or the proceeds of a sale, shall be invested in a particular manner, all are bound to see such investment made. In any case, however, where a proper investment has been once made, the liability of the non-acting trustees ceases. It is to be remembered, also, that the innocent trustees are not to be made ultimately responsible for the misfeasance or nonfeasance of the others, unless the latter, by reason of insolvency or the like, cannot be reached. The American authorities which justify these conclusions will be found in the note to Townley v. Sherborne, 2 Lead. Cas. Eq. 718; Irwin's Appeal, 35 Penn. St. 294; Hill on Trustees, 2d Am. ed. 470; Story's Eq., sec. 1280, &c. See Chandler v. Fillett, 25 L. J. Ch. 505; Cottam v. Eastern Counties Railroad Co., 1 Johns. & H. 243; Mendes v. Guedalla, 2 John. & H. 259.

If in any case there is a *bonâ fide* doubt as to the course
which, under the circumstances, a trustee should pursue,
he may obtain directions by a suit in equity at the cost
of the estate. And a cautious trustee will generally do
so, whenever a reasonable doubt exists.

When the trust is at an end, the trustee is bound to
restore the estate to the parties entitled, and for that
purpose to make such conveyance as they may require,
receiving from them a release of his trust.(r)[1]

Lastly, a trustee must not avail himself of his fiduciary
character for any object of personal benefit. His fundamental duty is to do his utmost for the *cestui que trust;*
and every advantage which he appropriates to himself,
must be acquired by a dereliction from that duty. If,
therefore, a trustee or executor buy in charges on the
estate for less than their actual amount, the purchase will
inure for the benefit of the trust;(s)[2] if a trustee or executor, *holding renewable leaseholds, renew in his
[*60]   own name, he cannot hold for himself, even though
a renewal on the former trusts may have been refused by
the lessor;(t) and the same result will follow on a renewal
by a mortgagee or partner, or by a tenant for life; for

(r) Goodson v. Ellison, 3 Russ. 583; Holford v. Phipps, 3 Bea. 434;
Whitmarsh v. Robertson, 1 Y. & C. 715; Hampshire v. Bradley, 2 Coll. 34.

(s) Ex parte Lacey, 6 Ves. 625; Hamilton v. Wright, 9 Cl. & F. 111;
Ex parte James, 8 Ves. 337, 345.

(t) Rumford Market Case, Sel. Ch. Ca. 61; James v. Dean, 11 Ves. 383;
Randall v. Russell, 3 Meriv. 190.

---

[1] The trustee, however, has no right to insist on such a release, where a
conveyance is in accordance with the trust; it is only where he is called
upon to depart from the tenor of the trust that he can do so: King v. Mullin, 1 Drewry 300; Hill on Trustees, 4th Am. ed. 897.

[2] Green v. Winter, 1 John. Ch. 26; Van Horne v. Fonda, 5 Id. 409; Butler v. Hicks, 11 Sm. & Marsh. 78; Mathews v. Dradaud, 3 Dessaus. 25;
Irwin v. Harris, 6 Ired. Eq. 221.

although he may not be bound to renew, yet if he does renew behind the back of the other parties interested, he cannot by converting the new acquisition to his own use, derive an unconscientious benefit out of the estate on which it is a graft. (u) In like manner it is a breach of trust if a trustee employ the trust fund in carrying on a trade, or if he deposit it at his bankers, mixed up with his own moneys, so as to obtain the credit of an additional balance. (v)[1]

The most obvious instance of the abuse of a fiduciary character is, where a trustee for sale or purchase, attempts to buy from or sell to himself. The permitting such a transaction to stand however honest it might be in the particular case, would destroy all security for the conduct of the trustee; for if he were permitted to buy or sell in an honest case, he might do so in one having that appearance, but which from the infirmity of human testimony, might be grossly otherwise. It is not therefore necessary to show that the trustee has in fact made an improper advantage; but the *cestui que trust*, if he has not confirmed the transaction with full knowledge of the facts, may at his option set it aside. The rule, however, which imposes this absolute incapacity, applies to those cases only where a trustee attempts to purchase from or sell to himself. There is no positive rule that he cannot deal with his *cestui que trust*. But in order to do so, he must fully

(u) Stone v. Theed, 2 B. C. C. 243; Waters v. Bailey, 2 N. C. C. 219; Featherstonehaugh v. Fenwick, 17 Ves. 298.

(v) Heathcote v. Hulme, 1 J. & W. 122; Moons v. De Bernales, 1 Russ. 301; Melland v. Gray, 2 Coll. 295; [Royer's App., 11 Penn. St. 36; Stanley's App., 8 Id. 431; Jenkins v. Walter, 8 Gill & J. 218.]

---

[1] See Pennell v. Deffell, 4 De G., M. & G. 372; Frith v. Cartland, 34 L. J. Ch. 301; Commonwealth v. McAlister, 28 Penn. St. 480; School v. Kirwin, 25 Ill. 73; Kip v. The Bank of New York, 10 John. 65.

11

divest himself of all advantage which his character as

[*61]   trustee might confer, and *must prove, if the transactions be afterwards impugned, that it was in all
respects fair and honest.$(w)^1$

(w) Ex parte Lacy, 6 Ves. 625 ; Coles v. Trecothick, 9 Ves. 234, 237 ;
Ex parte Bennett, 10 Ves. 381 ; Downes v. Grazebrook, 3 Meriv. 200, 208 ;
2 Sug. V. & P. 10th ed. c. xix, s. 2.

---

[1] Michoud v. Girod, 4 How. U. S. 503 ; Drysdale's Appeal, 14 Penn. St.
531 ; Winter v. Geroe, 1 Hurlst. Ch. 319 ; Hudson v. Hudson, 5 Munf.
180 ; Edmonds v. Crenshaw, 1 McCord's Ch. 252 ; Baines v. McGee, 1 Sm.
& M. 208 ; Baxter v. Costin, 1 Busbee's Eq. (N. C.) 262 ; De Caters v. Le
Ray de Chaumont, 3 Paige Ch. 178 ; Child v. Brace, 4 Id. 309 ;
Campbell v. Johnston et al., 1 Sandf. Ch. 148 ; Boyd v. Hawkins, 2 Ired.
Ch. 304 ; Mathews v. Dragaud, 3 Dessaus. 25 ; 1 Gilm. 614 ; Davis v. Simp-
son, 5 Har. & J. 147 ; Richardson v. Jones, 3 Gill & J. 163 ; In the matter ·
of the petition of Oakley et al., 2 Edw. Ch. 478 ; Hawley v. Mancius, 7
John. Ch. 174 ; Haddix's Heirs v. Haddix's Adm'rs., 5 Lit. 202 ; Dorsey v.
Dorsey, 3 Har. & J. 410 ; Breckenridge v. Holland, 2 Blackf. 377 ; Case v.
Abeel, 1 Paige 393 ; Davoue v. Fanning, 2 John. Ch. 252 ; Churchill's
Heirs v. Akin's Adm'rs., 5 Dana 481 ; Torrey v. Bank of Orleans, 9 Paige
650 ; Remick v. Butterfield, 11 Foster 70 ; Lenox v. Lotrebe, 1 Hempst. 25 ;
Lefevre v. Laraway, 22 Barb. 167 ; Blauvelt v. Ackerman, 20 N. J. Eq. 141 ;
Washington, &c., Railroad Co. v. Alexander Railroad Co., 19 Gratt (Va.)
592 ; Renew v. Butler, 30 Ga. 954 ; Sypher v. McHenry, 18 Iowa 232.   A
trustee incompetent to purchase on his own account, cannot purchase as
agent for a third person : Hawley v. Cramer, 4 Cow. 717 ; North Baltimore, &c., Association v. Caldwell, 25 Md. 420.   Nor can a third person
purchase in trust or as the agent for the trustee : Hunt v. Bass, 2 Dev.
Ch. 292 ; Michoud v. Girod, ut supr. ; Paul v. Squib, 12 Penn. St. 296 ;
Buckles v. Lafferty, 2 Rob. (Va.) 292 ; Lewis v. Hillman, 3 H. Lords
Cases 629.   But in Beeson v. Beeson, 9 Penn St. 280, it was held that a
purchase by a trustee through a secret agent was not absolutely void,
unless there were actual fraud.   And if the trustee purchase a mortgage
or judgment, which is a lien on the trust estate, at a discount, he will not
be allowed to turn the purchase to his own advantage : Green v. Winter,
1 John. Ch. 27 ; see also, Boyd v. Hawkins, 2 Dev. Ch. 195 ; Van Horne
v. Fonda, 5 John. Ch. 409.   And it seems a trustee may not purchase
the trust property for his own benefit, when it is sold under a judicial
decree, which he was not instrumental in procuring, unless by the order
of sale he was specially allowed so to purchase : Chapin v. Weed, 1
Clarke 464 ; Beeson v. Beeson, 9 Penn. St. 279 ; Wallingtons Est., 1

The restraint on any personal benefit to the trustee is not confined to his dealings with the estate, but extends

---

Ashm. 307; Ricketts *v.* Montgomery, 15 Md. 46; Jamison *v.* Glascock, 29 Missouri 191; Bank *v.* Dubuque, 8 Clarke (Ia.) 277; Obert *v.* Obert, 1 Beas. 423; Elliott *v.* Pool, 3 Jones Eq. 17; Hoitt *v.* Webb, 36 N. Hamp. 158; Chandler *v.* Moulton, 33 Verm. 245; Parker *v.* Vose, 45 Maine 54; Freeman *v.* Harwood, 49 Id. 195; Martin *v.* Wyncoop, 12 Ind. 266. But see, *contra*, Fisk *v.* Sarber, 6 W. & S. 18; Chorpennings Appeal, 32 Penn. St. 315; Elrod *v.* Lancaster, 2 Head 571; Mercer *v.* Newcum, 23 Georgia 151; Huger *v.* Huger, 9 Rich. Eq. 217; Earl *v.* Halsey, 1 McCart. 332. A trustee permitted to bid at his own sale, must act within the strictest line of his responsibility: Cadwalader's Appeal, 64 Penn. St. 293.

But a mortgagee of personalty does not fall within the principle which prevents a trustee to sell, from buying at his own sale: Black *v.* Hair et al., 2 Hill Ch. 623. So of a mortgagee generally: Iddings *v.* Bruen, 4 Sand. Ch. 223; Knight *v.* Marjoribanks, 2 Macn. & Gord. 10; Murdock's Case, 2 Bland 461; unless with a power of sale: Waters *v.* Groom, 11 Cl. & Fin. 684; Mapps *v.* Sharpe, 32 Illinois 13; or he buys in without a power and without a foreclosure: Gunn *v.* Brantley, 21 Alab. 633. But a second mortgagee may purchase under a power of sale exercised by the first mortgagee: Shaw *v.* Bunny, 34 L. J. Ch. 257; 11 Jur. N. S. 99, and see Britton *v.* Lewis, 8 Rich. Eq. 271. And where *bonâ fide* creditor afterwards becomes a trustee, he may buy in a judgment against a *cestui que trust*, and may pursue all legal remedies to enforce payment of it; nor has the *cestui que trust* any right to inquire how much the former paid for it: Prevost *v.* Gratz, Peters Ch. 364; but see Irwin *v.* Harris, 6 Ired. Eq. 221. If a trustee for creditors sues out a mortgage belonging to the trust, and purchases the real estate at such sale in his own name it is as trustee for the creditors: Campbell *v.* McLain, 51 Penn. St. 200.

A purchase by the trustee, when perfectly fair, made from the *cestui que trust*, or with his assent, under a full knowledge of the circumstances, or when subsequently confirmed by him directly or by long acquiescence, with such knowledge, will not be set aside by a court of equity: Pennock's App., 14 Penn. St. 446; Bruch *v.* Lantz, 2 Rawle 392; Harrington *v.* Brown, 5 Pick. 519; Dunlap *v.* Mitchell, 10 Ohio 117; Scott *v.* Freeman, 7 Sm. & M. 410; Jenison *v.* Hopgood, 7 Pick. 1; Musselmen *v.* Eshelman, 10 Penn. St. 374; Hawley *v.* Cramer, 4 Cowen 719; Todd *v.* Moore, 1 Leigh 457; Villines *v.* Norflett, 2 Dev. Ch. 167; Roberts *v.* Roberts, 63 N. C. 27; Boerum *v.* Schenck, 41 N. Y. 182; Coffee *v.* Ruffin, 4 Cold. (Tenn.) 487; Carter *v.* Thompson, 41 Ala. 375; Buell *v.* Buckingham, 16 Iowa 284. It has been held, however, that a court of equity will never aid a

even to remuneration for his services, and prevents him
from receiving anything beyond reimbursement of his
expenses, unless there be an express contrary stipulation.[1] So far as .such reimbursement extends, he is
entitled to claim it in the fullest extent. All payments
made and liabilities incurred by him, and all his reasonable costs, as between solicitor and client, of any suit
relating to the trust, are to be paid out of the estate, or
if that should prove deficient, by the *cestui que trust*
personally.[2] But if the trustee is himself a solicitor, he

---

trustee, under any circumstances, to enforce such a purchase, though it
might refuse to annul it: Monro *v.* Allaire, 2 Caines' Cas. 183. This
distinction is unquestionably a valid one in general; yet it may be
doubted of the modern authorities. See Hill on Trustees, 4th Am. ed. 249,
837; Salmon *v.* Cutts, 4 De G. & S. 131.

See, as to the power of a trustee to purchase the trust fund, if the beneficiary agree to the purchase: Field *v.* Arrowsmith, 3 Humph. (Tenn.)
442; and also, Coles *v.* Trecothick, 9 Ves. 244; Lacy, Ex parte, 6 Id. 626;
Henricks *v.* Robinson, 2 John. Ch. 311. A sale by a trustee to his *cestui
que trust*, stands on the same footing as a purchase by a trustee for his
cestui que trust, and is void, especially if the trustee has taken any advantage of the *cestui que trust*: McCants *v.* Bee, 1 McCord Ch. 383.

[1] The rule under consideration applies only to transactions *inter vivos*, for
gifts by will always implies bounty, and a trustee may receive a benefit
under the will of his *cestui que trust*: Hindson *v.* Weatherill, 5 De G., M.
& G. 361; Stump *v.* Gaby, 2 Id. 623; though see Waters *v.* Thorn, 22 Beav.
547.

[2] Expenses incurred unnecessarily and against the remonstrance of the
cestui que trust will not be allowed: Berryhill's Appeal, 35 Penn. St. 245.
Trustees are entitled to expense incurred in taking the opinion of counsel
as to the trust estate: Fearns *v.* Young, 10 Vesey 184; McElhenny's Appeal, 46 Penn. St. 347. A trustee is liable for the fraud of his solicitor,
although he may have used ordinary discretion in employing him: Bostock *v.* Floyer, L. R. 1 Eq. 26; Sutton *v.* Wilder, L. R. 12 Eq. 373; and
also for his negligence: Hopgood *v.* Parkin, L. R. 11 Eq. 74.

Whether the trustee, however, can claim compensation or not, he is entitled to be fully reimbursed for all expenses incurred and responsibilities
assumed in the management of the trust: Towle *v.* Mack, 2 Verm. 19;
Green *v.* Winter, 1 John. Ch. 27; Burr *v.* McEwen, 1 Bald. 154; Pennell's

cannot of course charge the trust for his own profes-
sioual services, so as to derive in that form a personal
benefit. $(x)^1$

If a trustee fail in performance of his trusts, whether
by exceeding or falling short of its proper limits, the
cestui que trust is entitled to a remedy in equity.

We have already seen that, if there be no trustee, or if
the trustee is desirous to be discharged from his trust, the
Court of Chancery will undertake the office.   If there be
an existing and acting trustee, who either refuses to perform a particular duty, or threatens to do an unauthorized

(x) Moore v. Frowd, 3 M. & C. 45; Bainbridge v. Blair, 8 Bea. 588.
Though see Cradock v. Piper, 1 Macn. & Gord. 668. [Cradock v. Piper,
was disapproved in Broughton v. Broughton, 5 De G., M. & G. 160. See
also, Lyon v. Baker, 5 De G. & Sm. 622; Mayer v. Gulluchat, 6 Rich. Eq.
1; Clack v. Carlon, 7 Jur. N. S. 441 and Id. part 2, p. 211].

App., 2 Penn. St. 216; Morton v. Adams, 1 Strobh. Eq. 76; Hatton v.
Weems, 12 G. & John. 83; Morton v. Barrett, 22 Maine 257. And this is
the case, even though the trust may have been afterwards declared void,
provided he acted in good faith: Hawley v. James, 16 Wend. 61; Stewart
v. McMinn, 5 W. & S. 100.

¹ The rule stated in the text was adopted in some of the earlier cases in
this country: see Green v. Winter, 1 John. Ch. 37, 38; Manning v. Manning, Id. 532; Mumford v. Murray, 6 Id. 17; State Bank v. Marsh, Saxton 288; Egbert v. Brooks, 3 Harring. 110; Miles v. Bacon, 4 J. J. Marsh.
457; Kendall v. The New Eng. Carpet Co., 13 Conn. 384; though commissions might be agreed upon at the creation of the trust: Boyd v. Hawkins, 2 Dev. Ch. 212.

But now, however, in most of the United States, trustees are allowed
compensation, either by express statutes or by analogy to compensation
allowed to executors.   Upon the subject of compensation to trustees, see
Meacham v. Sternes, 9 Paige Ch. 398; Ringgold v. Ringgold, 1 Har. &
Gill. 11; Boyd v. Hawkins, 2 Dev. Ch. 329; Miller v. Beverleys, 4 Hen. &
M. 415; Jenkins v. Eldredge, 3 Story 325; Matter of De Peyster, 4 Sandf.
Ch. 511; Burr v. McEwen, 1 Bald. 163; Nathans v. Morris, 4 Wh. 389;
Stehman's Appeal, 5 Penn. St. 413. The cases and statutes on this subject,
will be found fully collected in the American note to Robinson v. Pett, 2
Lead. Cas. Eq. 200.

act, he may be compelled to act in the one case, or restrained in the other; (*y*) or, if necessary, he may be removed altogether from the trust, and another appointed in his room.(*z*)[1]

If a breach of trust has been committed. the trustee [*62] *will be liable to make good any consequent loss, whether immediately resulting from it, or traceable as its effect. And if several trustees have concurred in its commission, each of them will, in favor of the *cestui que trust*, be severally liable for the whole loss. But if no actual fraud has been committed, a contribution may be enforced as between themselves. And if any third party has knowingly reaped the benefit of the breach of trust, the loss may be eventually cast on him.[2] If the *cestuis que trustent* themselves, being *sui juris*, have consented to the act, they cannot afterwards be heard to complain of it;[3] and if some only out of several have so consented, the trustees and the other *cestuis que trustent* must be indemnified out of their interest; nor can the trustee waive the right to such indemnity, because it is a security, not to himself alone, but to the other *cestuis que trustent*, also to be worked out through him.(*a*) If, after the commission of a breach of trust, the trustee has given full and complete information to the *cestuis que trustent*, and they have acquiesced in the existing state of things,

(*y*) Kirby *v*. Marsh, 3 Y. & C. 295 ; Att.-Gen. *v*. Mayor of Liverpool, 1 M. & C. 171, 210.

(*z*) Att.-Gen. *v*. Shore, 9 Cl. & F. 355 ; Att.-Gen. *v*. Caius College, 2 Keen 150.

(*a*) Walker *v*. Symonds, 3 Sw. 1, 75; Wilson *v*. Moore, 1 M. & K. 127; Greenwood *v*. Wakeford, 1 Bea. 576; Fyler *v*. Fyler, 3 Id. 550; Woodyatt *v*. Gresley, 8 Sim. 180; Fuller *v*. Knight, 6 Bea. 205.

---

[1] See note to page 38, ante.

[2] Trull *v*. Trull, 13 Allen (Mass.) 407.

[3] Campbell *v*. Miller, 38 Geo. 304.

and have dealt with the trustee on the footing of that acquiescence, the breach of trust will be considered as waived.(b) But unless there be acquiescence in the *cestuis que trustent*, the mere lapse of time will not bar the liability of an express trustee; for his possession is according to his title.[1] It is otherwise with regard to persons who, not being themselves express trustees, have acquired property with notice of a trust, or have otherwise become trustees by construction of equity; for such persons, though bound in equity to perform the trust, are not in strictness existing trustees, but are to be constituted trustees by a decree. Their possession, therefore, in the meantime is *adverse to the *cestui que trust*, and if left undisturbed, will ultimately exclude him.(c) [*63]

The extent of the remedy which equity affords, depends on the character of the wrong done. There does not appear to be any case where the Court has awarded damages for mere injury to the estate; but the trustee must account for what he has or ought to have received, with interest at four per cent. on moneys improperly retained.(d)[2]

(b) Brice v. Stokes, 11 Ves. 319; Walker v. Symonds, 3 Sw. 1, 64, 67; Roberts v. Tunstall, 4 Hare 257. [See Hill on Trustees, 4th Am. ed. pp. 267 and 460, et seq., where the American cases are collected.]

(c) Beckford v. Wade, 17 Ves. 99; Hovenden v. Annesley, 2 Sch. & L. 633; Wedderburn v. Wedderburn, 2 K. 722; s. c. 4 M. & C. 41; 3 & 4 Wm. 4, c. 27, s. 25.

(d) Ludlow v. Greenhouse, 1 Bligh, N. S. 17, 57; Rocke v. Hart, 11 Ves. 58: Tebbs v. Carpenter, 1 Madd. 290.

---

[1] If, however, there is negligence on the part of the *cestui que trust* in asserting his rights, a court of equity will not, after a long lapse of time, render the trustee liable: Bright v. Legerton, 2 De G., F. & J. 606. But the breach of trust must be distinctly brought to the notice of the *cestui que trust;* it is only from the time of such notice that the satutte begins to run in favor of the trustee: Hunter v. Hubbard, 26 Texas 537; see also, New Market v. Smart, 45 N. H. 87.

[2] See notes to pages 56, 57, ante.

The giving of interest, however, is merely an imperfect
method of estimating the indemnity which the *cestui que
trust* may claim, and does not preclude the adoption of a
more accurate rule. If, therefore, the property is at the
time of the trustee's misapplication actually invested in
stock, and is improperly sold out by him, or if the trust
deed contains a direction so to invest it, the amount of
such stock will be the measure of the indemnity; and the
trustee may, at the option of the *cestui que trust*, be compelled either to repay the money with interest, or to make
good the amount of stock which has been improperly sold,
or which a timely investment would have produced. The
effect in this respect of an option given by the instrument
of trust to invest either in stock or real security, but not
exercised by the trustee, appears to be doubtful.(e)[1] If
there is also an express direction to accumulate, the replacement may be extended to the amount of accumulation which would have been produced by a proper investment of the dividends.(f) If an improper investment
has been made, it is considered, as against the trustee
himself, equivalent to no investment. But in favor of
[*64]   the *cestui que trust* it gives an option to claim
either the investment made, or the replacement of
the original fund with interest, according as the one or
the other may be most for his benefit.(g)

If there be circumstances of actual malfeasance, as, for

' (e) Byrchall *v.* Bradford, 6 Madd. 235; Watts *v.* Girdlestone, 6 Bea.
188 ; Ames *v.* Parkinson, 7 Id. 379; Shepherd *v.* Mouls, 4 Hare 500.

(f) Pride *v.* Fooks, 2 Bea. 430.

(g) Lane *v.* Dighton, Amb. 409; Infra, Conversion.

---

[1] It is now held that the trustee is liable in such case only for principal
and interest, and not for the value of the stock. See Hill on Trustees, 4th
Am. ed. 567, in note.

instance, if the trustee has not only neglected to invest the fund but has applied it to his own purposes, as by using it in his trade, he may be charged with interest at five per cent., instead of four. And the same may be done where his misconduct has been very gross, as where an executor, being directed to lay out property in the funds, had unnecessarily sold out stock, kept large balances in his hands, and resisted payment of debts by a false pretence of outstanding demands. Where the improper application has produced an ascertainable profit, as, for example, where the trust money has been applied either solely or as mixed up with other property belonging to the trustee, in carrying on a trade or other speculation, the *cestui que trust* is entitled to claim the profits. And with this view he may insist on an account of the profits made, so that after they have been ascertained, he may have an option to accept either the amount realized, or interest at five per cent.(*h*)[1]

In some cases, where there has been an express direction to accumulate, accompanied by special circumstances of malfeasance, the account has been directed in such a form as to charge the trustee with compound interest.(*i*)

The cost of a suit for rectifying a breach of trust are to some extent dependent on the degree of misconduct.

(*h*) Tebbs *v.* Carpenter, 1 Mad. 290; Crackelt *v.* Bethune, 1 J. & W. 586 ; Docker *v.* Somes, 2 M. & K. 655.

(*i*) Raphael *v.* Boehm, 11 Ves. 92; 13 Ves. 407, 590 ; Walker *v.* Woodward, 1 Russ. 107 ; Tebbs *v.* Carpenter, 1 Mad. 290; Heighington *v.* Grant, 5 M. & C. 258.

[1] On the subject of the liability of a trustee to interest, the cases will be found collected in Hill on Trustees, 4th Am. ed. 568, in note. See supra note to page 56.

The general rule seems to be, that if the suit has been actually occasioned by the breach of trust, the trustee must pay the costs.   If a suit were necessary for other [*65] purposes, *as for administering the estate or construing the trusts, he may have his general costs, as between solicitor and client, notwithstanding that it includes a prayer for remedying the effect of his misconduct.   But he may, at the same time, be compelled to pay any additional costs, which that misconduct occasions.[1]

The jurisdiction for compelling admittance to copyholds seems analogous to that for compelling performance of a trust.   For the copyholder has the beneficial interest in the land, and the lord is bound to perfect his title by admittance, and to place the evidence of it on the manor rolls.   But the lord cannot *e converso* bring his bill against the copyholder, to compel him to come in and be admitted tenant; for he has his remedy by seizing the land after proclamation made.   It is said, too, that if there be error in any adversary proceeding in the lord's Court, the Court of Chancery will order the lord to examine it; and that if judgment be given in the lord's Court on a copyholder's petition, though no appeal or writ of error will lie, yet the Court of Chancery will correct the proceedings, if anything be done against conscience.(k)

Besides the ordinary trusts which we have just considered, there is another class of trusts, those for charitable and public purposes, where the legal ownership is

(k) Christian v. Corren, 1 P. Wms. 329 ; Clayton v. Cookes, 2 Atk. 449 ; Ash v. Rogle, 1 Vern. 367 ; Williams v. Lord Lonsdale, 3 Ves. 752 ; Widdowson v. Lord Harrington, 1 J. & W. 532.

---

[1] See Hill on Trustees, p. 856, *et seq.*, 4th Am. ed.

conferred on a fiduciary holder, but the trust is declared for general objects, and not for the benefit of a specific owner.[1]

---

[1] Upon the subject of charitable trusts, bequests for pious and charitable uses, and also the doctrine of *cy pres*, see the following authorities : Baptist Association *v.* Hart's Executors, 4 Wheaton 1 ; Inglis *v.* The Trustees of the Sailor's Snug Harbor, 3 Peters 99 ; Trustees of the Baptist Association *v.* Smith, 3 Peters' Appendix 481 ; Executors of Burr *v.* Smith et al., 7 Verm. 241 ; Gallego's Executors *v.* Attorney-General, and Id. *v.* Lambert and wife, 3 Leigh 450 ; Shotwell's Executor *v.* Mott et al., 2 Sandf. Ch. 46 ; Vidal et al. *v.* Girard Executors, 2 How. U. S. 127 ; City of Philadelphia *v.* Girard's Heirs, 45 Penn. St. 9 ; Miller *v.* Porter, 53 Penn. St. 292. Mr. Justice Baldwin, in the celebrated case of Magill *v.* Brown, which involved the construction of the will of Sarah Zane (reported in Brightly's (Pa.) Nisi Prius Reports, p. 347, &c.) gave to the subject of bequests for pious and charitable uses, a most profound investigation, and condensed in the elaborate and learned opinion, which he delivered in that cause, all the English and American learning upon this most interesting branch of equity jurisprudence. In some of the United States, where the Statute of 43 Elizabeth is not in force, it has been held that the same liberal principles as to charitable trusts, were applied in the Court of Chancery at common law, independently of that statute ; and that charities within its definition or analogies would be enforced, though the beneficiaries are too vaguely designated, to claim for themselves that assistance. All that is necessary is that a discretion in the application of the funds shall have been vested somewhere, by the donor : Vidal *v.* Girard, 2 How. S. C. 127 ; Brown *v.* Kelsey, 2 Cush. 243 ; Burr *v.* Smith, 7 Verm. 241 ; King *v.* Woodhull, 3 Edw. Ch. 79 ; Banks *v.* Phelan, 4 Barb. S. C. 80 ; Shotwell *v.* Mott, 2 Sandf. Ch. 46 ; Newcomb *v.* St. Peter's Church, Id. 636 ; Williams *v.* Williams, 4 Selden 525 ; McCaughal *v.* Ryan, 27 Barb. 376 ; Bascomb *v.* Albertson, 34 N. Y. 584 ; Whitman *v.* Lex, 17 S. & R. 88 ; Zane's Will, Brightly 350 ; McCord *v.* Ochiltree, 8 Blackf. 15 ; State *v.* McGowen, 2 Ired. Ch. 9 ; Griffin *v.* Graham, 1 Hawks 96 ; Att.-Gen. *v.* Jolly, 1 Rich. Eq. 99 ; Beall *v.* Fox, 4 Geo. 404 ; Wade *v.* American Col. Soc., 7 S. & M. 663 ; Dickson *v.* Montgomery, 1 Swan (Tenn.) 348 ; Carter *v.* Balfour, 19 Ala. 814 ; Urmey's Executors *v.* Woodon, 1 Ohio St. N. S. 160 ; White *v.* Fisk, 22 Conn. 31 ; Levy *v.* Levy, 33 N. Y. 97. In other states, the statute has been declared to be still in force : Griffin *v.* Graham, 1 Hawks. 96 ; Gass *v.* Wilhite, 2 Dana 170 ; Att.-Gen. *v.* Wallace, 7 B. Monr. 611 ; Tainter *v.* Clark, 5 Allen 66 ; Perin *v.* Carey, 24 Howard 465 ; Hill on Trustees 200, 201, 701.

In Virginia and Maryland, however, it has been decided that neither the

The meaning of the word charity, as applied to a trust, is different from any signification which it ordinarily bears.

The word in its widest sense denotes all the good affections which men ought to bear towards each other; in its most restricted and most usual sense, relief of the poor.

In neither of these senses is it employed by the Court of Chancery, but a signification has been affixed to it, de- [*66] rived *for the most part from the enumeration given in the Statute of Charitable Uses.(*l*)   And the purposes enumerated in that act, together with others analogous to them, are accordingly considered as the only charities which the Court will recognise.

The purposes enumerated in the statute as charitable are "the relief of aged, impotent, and poor people; the maintenance of maimed and sick soldiers and mariners; the support of schools of learning, free schools, and scholars of universities; repairs of bridges, &c.; education and preferment of orphans; the relief and maintenance of houses of correction; marriages of poor maids; help of young tradesmen, handicraftsmen, and persons decayed; redemption or relief of prisoners or captives; and the aid of poor inhabitants concerning payment of fifteenths, setting out of soldiers, and other taxes." These are the only uses which the statute in term reaches, but

---

(*l*) 43 Eliz. c. 4.

statute nor the principles which it embodies, are in force : Baptist Association *v.* Hart, 4 Wheat. 1 ; Wheeler *v.* Smith, 9 How. U. S. 58 ; Gallego *v.* Att.-Gen., 3 Leigh 451 ; Carter *v.* Wolfe, 13 Grat. 301 ; Dashiell *v.* Att.-Gen., 5 Harr. & J. 392 ; 6 Id. 1 ; Wilderman *v.* Baltimore, 8 Md. 551.

In the recent case of Fontain *v.* Ravenal, 17 How. U. S. 369, it was held by a majority of the court, that the courts of the United States had no independent power to administer the law of charitable uses, whether under the Statute of Elizabeth, or otherwise, except so far as it had been adopted into the *lex rei sitæ.*

it is not necessarily confined to them; and gifts, not within its letter, have been deemed charitable within its equity. Such, for instance, are gifts for religious or educational purposes; for the erection of a hospital or a sessions house; or for any other beneficial or useful public purpose, not contrary to the policy of the law. But a gift merely for useful or benevolent purposes, without specifying what the purposes are, does not constitute a gift to charity; because there may be many useful or benevolent purposes, which the Court cannot construe to be charitable; a gift also to mere private charity is not within the analogy of the statute; and although there are cases where the Court has apparently interfered in favor of private charity, yet such cases have in fact been those not of gifts to charitable purposes, but of gifts to individuals with a benevolent purpose. Such, for example, would be a gift to " poor relations." That is not a charity in the legal sense of the term, but a trust to give to poor relations; and the only question under such a trust is, whether the objects are sufficiently specified to enable *the Court to execute it, or whether the gift is void on the ground of uncertainty.(*m*)[1]   [*67]

(*m*) Morice *v.* Bishop of Durham, 9 Ves. 399, 405; 10 Id. 522, 541; Mitford *v.* Reynolds, 1 Ph. 185; Nash *v.* Morley, 5 Bea. 177; Kendall *v.* Granger, 5 Id. 300; Townsend *v.* Carus, 3 Hare 257; Nightingale *v.* Goulburn, 5 Hare 484; 1 Jarm. on Wills 192.

---

[1] See Saltonstall *v.* Sanders, 11 Allen 446. A charity is a gift to be applied consistently with existing laws, for the benefit of an indefinite number of persons, either by bringing their minds or hearts under the influence of education or religion, by relieving their bodies from disease, suffering or constraint; by assisting them to establish themselves in life, or by erecting or maintaining public works, or otherwise lessening the burdens of government: [Per Gray, J.,] Jackson *v.* Phillips, 14 Allen (Mass.) 539. A gift designed to promote the public good, by the encouragement of learning, science and the useful arts, without any particular reference to

In order to create a public or charitable trust, it is not necessary that the property on which the trust attaches should be derived from private bounty. The principle is equally applicable to a fund levied by authority of Parliament, and placed in the hands of public officers, in order to its application for public purposes. And in accordance with this view, it has been determined that since the passing of the Municipal Corporation Act,(n) directing the corporation property to be applied, first, for certain specified purposes, and afterwards, for other general purposes for the benefit of the town, a trust has attached on the property, giving jurisdiction in equity to control any improper dealing by the corporation.(o)

It should be observed, that trusts for charitable purposes, equally with those for individual benefit, must be of a character not prohibited by the policy of the law. A trust therefore to promote religion must not be directed to what the law calls a superstitious use; as, for example, the maintenance of a priest to pray for the soul of the donor.[1] If such a trust be created in terms which show that the illegal object alone was contemplated, e. g., that the only object was to obtain for the donor the benefit of the prayers, the gift will be simply void. If it appears that charity was the object contemplated, e. g., that it was

(n) 5 & 6 Wm. 4, c. 76, s. 92.

(o) Att.-Gen. v. Mayor of Dublin, 1 Bligh. N. S. 312; Att.-Gen. v. Compton, 1 N. C. C. 417; Att.-Gen. v. Aspinwall, 2 M. & C. 613; Att.-Gen. v. Corporation of Poole, 2 K. 190; 4 M. & C. 17; 8 Cl. & F. 409; Att.-Gen. v. Shrewsbury, 6 Bea. 220.

the poor, is a charity: American Academy v. Harvard College, 12 Gray (Mass.) 582.

[1] It has been held that there are no uses which can be denominated superstitious in the United States: Methodist Church v. Remington, 1 Watts 218; Gass v. Wilhite, 2 Dana 170.

intended to benefit the priest or to support his chapel, the illegality of the particular method will not exclude some other application, but the fund will be at the disposal of the Crown, to be applied *under the sign manual for some lawful object. (*p*) In respect also to gifts [*68] for any charitable purpose, whether religious or not, there is an express restriction by statute, invalidating all gifts of or charges on real estate, or on estate savoring of the realty, for charitable uses, unless made by indenture, twelve months previously to the donor's decease. By the operation of this act, if the trust is entirely for charity the gift is invalid at law; if the gift at law is good, yet the trust is invalid, and the estate must be reconveyed. (*q*)[1]

The incidents of a trust for charitable purposes are for the most part the same with those of an ordinary trust. The principal points of distinction are, first, that a charitable trust is not affected by lapse of time in the same manner as a trust for private persons ;[2] and secondly, that where an apparent charitable intention has failed, whether

(*p*) West *v.* Shuttleworth, 2 M. & K. 684; Infra, *cy pres*, Application.
(*q*) 6 Geo. 3, c. 136 ; Jarm. on Wills 198.

---

[1] See Philpott *v.* St. George's Hospital, 6 H. L. Cas. 338 : Hall *v.* Warren, 9 H. L. Cas. 420. The Statutes of Mortmain are not generally in force in the United States : 2 Kent's Com. 282; Vidal *v.* Girard, 2 How. U. S. 187 ; Hill on Trustees 76, 710, 4th Am. ed. There are, however, legislative provisions regulating charitable gifts in certain particulars.

[2] No neglect or perversion of the funds of a charity, by the trustees, will be permitted to affect it: Hadley *v.* Hopkins Acad., 14 Pick. 240 : Griffitts *v.* Cope, 17 Penn. St. 96 ; Wright *v.* Linn, 9 Id. 433 ; Att.-Gen. *v.* Wallace, 7 B. Monr. 611 ; Price *v.* Methodist Church, 4 Hamm. 542. Nor will the *cestui que trust* be affected by the declarations of the trustees : McKissick *v.* Pickle, 16 Penn. St. 148. But a general limitation over from one charity to another, contingent on the neglect of the trustees of the former, at any time, for a fixed period, to carry on the charity properly, is valid, and does not create a perpetuity: Christ's Hospital *v.* Grainger, 7 Macn. & Gord. 460.

by an incomplete disposition at the outset, or by subsequent inadequacy of the original object, effect may be given to it by a *cy pres* or approximate application, to the exclusion of a resulting trust for the donor.

The first of these peculiarities exists in reference to the rule which has been already stated, that, as between the *cestui que trust* and an express trustee, no length of time is a bar to the right; and that, on the other hand, with respect to constructive trustees, or parties who have acquired an estate with notice of a trust, the same principle does not apply. In case of charities, both branches of this rule are subject to modification. With respect to the first branch, it has been determined, that if the trustees of a charity have *bonâ fide* mistaken the right mode of application, and have actually disbursed the funds in accordance with that mistake, and without notice of the objection, the disbursements shall not be disallowed ; (r) and further, that although the mere length of an errone- [*69] ous usage *cannot alter the original trust, yet where trusts have been imposed on colleges or other existing corporations, who are under no obligation to accept them, traditional usage may be allowed an effect which in ordinary cases it might not possess. And it has been accordingly held that, if there are questions on the original instrument of foundation, and an arrangement be fairly made at the time of acceptance, and evidenced by cotemporaneous instruments or by constant subsequent usage; the Court will not disturb it, although in its own view of the original instrument, such arrangement was in effect a modification of that which might now be considered the best construction. (s)

(r) Att.-Gen. v. Pretyman, 4 Bea. 462; Att.-Gen. v. Draper's Company, 6 Id. 382; Att.-Gen. v. Mayor of Exeter, Jac. 443; 2 Russ. 362.

(s) Attorney-General v. Caius College, 2 K. 150; Attorney-General v. Draper's Company, 6 Bea. 382.

In these instances the lapse of time is allowed to operate against a charity to a greater extent than against an individual. But on the other hand, its operation under the second branch of the rule as a bar to claims against a constructive trustee, was not, until the late statute of 3 & 4 Wm. 4, c. 27, available to protect a purchaser with notice of a charitable trust, either by analogy to the Statute of Limitations, or as a presumptive bar by acquiescence. The precise effect of the statute does not appear to have been determined. Its enactments are in terms imperative, and it contains no exception in favor of charity. But it seems to have been doubted by Sir Edward Sugden whether charity is not a *casus omissus*, and whether the former rule does not continue.(*t*) [1]

The second and most singular peculiarity is, that where an apparent charitable intention has failed, whether by an incomplete disposition at the outset, or by subsequent inadequacy of the original object, effect will be given it by a *cy pres* or approximate application, notwithstanding that in ordinary cases the trust would be void for uncertainty, or would result to the donor or his representative.[2]

(*t*) 3 & 4 Wm. 4, c. 27, ss. 24, 25; Incorporated Society *v.* Richards, 1 Conn. & L. 68; Att.-Gen. *v.* Flint, 4 Hare 147; Commissioners of Donations *v.* Wybrants, 2 Jones and Latouche 182.

---

[1] Att.-Gen. *v.* Wilkins, 17 Bea. 285; but *contra* in the House of Lords, Magdalen College *v.* Att.-Gen., 6 H. L. Cas. 189; Att.-Gen. *v.* Davey, 4 De G. & J. 136. See Att.-Gen. *v.* The Federal Street Meeting House, 3 Gray 1.

[2] The *cy pres* doctrines of the English Chancery have not been generally adopted in the United States, in their application to charitable trusts: Carter *v.* Balfour, 18 Ala. 814; White *v.* Fisk, 22 Conn. 31; McAuley *v.* Wilson, 1 Dev. Eq. 276; Beekman *v.* The People, 23 N. Y. 298; Witman *v.* Lex, 17 S. & R. 88; see Brendle *v.* The German Reformed Congregation, 33 Penn. St. 418; Att.-Gen. *v.* Jolly, 2 Stroh. Eq. 379; Dickson *v.* Montgomery, 1 Swan 348; Venable *v.* Coffman, 2 W. Va. 310.

12

[*70]   *The soundness of the distinction thus drawn is
perhaps open to doubt; but its existence is established by many precedents; and it appears to rest, partly
on the favor due to charity, and partly on the hypothesis
that the details of a charitable gift are not, like those of a
gift to individuals, the primary object of the donor, but
that the true intention is, first to effectuate a charity, and
secondly, to do so in the particular way which the trust
denotes. Of course this doctrine, whether well or ill
founded, cannot apply to an ordinary trust: for there the
donor's object is to benefit the persons specified; and if
that benefit is not available, there is no ulterior intention
to which effect can be given.

In accordance with this principle two doctrines appear
to be established, viz.: 1. If in a gift to charity an intention be manifested of appropriating the entire fund, it
will be effectuated, to the exclusion of a resulting trust,
notwithstanding that the gift actually made is of a portion
only. And such intention may be evidenced, either by
words declaring an intention to give the whole; or by a
gift of specified sums out of the income, if it appear that
at the time of gift such specified sums exhausted the
whole available income. For such exhausting gift is considered equivalent to a gift of the whole, and will carry
any subsequent increase. If it appears from the instrument of gift that the specified payments were meant as
fixed charges, and not by way of illustration only, and

It was, however, recognised in Baker v. Smith, 13 Metcalf 41; Burr's
Exrs. v. Smith, 7 Verm. 287 (semble); Urmey's Exr. v. Wooden, 1 Ohio
N. S. 160. See Att.-Gen. v. Wallace, 7 B. Monr. 611; Brown v. Concord,
33 N. H. 285; Gilman v. Hamilton, 16 Illinois 225. By a recent Act of
Assembly in Pennsylvania, the *cy pres* doctrine has been introduced into
the law of that state to a certain extent: Brightly's Purd. 145; Zeisweiss
v. James, 63 Penn. St. 465.

that the *corpus* was meant for the benefit of the immediate donees, they will of course be entitled in exclusion of the charity, to any subsequent increase. The result of the decisions in this respect is, that an intention in favor of the donee will be presumed, first, if the gift be made to him subject to certain specified payments; secondly, if it be made on condition of making certain payments, and subject to forfeiture on non-performance; or thirdly, if the donor would be liable to make good the payments, notwithstanding a subsequent *deficiency of the fund. [*71] In like manner, if it is apparent that the charity was to have only a limited interest, but that the immediate donee was to have no benefit, the surplus or the subsequent increase will revert to the donor or his heir. (*u*)[1]

2. If in a gift to charity the intended object be not specified at all, or not with sufficient certainty; or if it cease to exist, or to afford the means of applying the entire fund, the presumed general object will be effectuated by an application *cy pres;* i.e., an application to some other purpose, having regard as nearly as possible to the original plan.

The assumption on which this doctrine is based, viz., that the general idea of charity was uppermost with the donor, and that the particular charity specified was merely illustrative, is one of a very doubtful character. Lord Eldon repeatedly expressed his disapprobation of it, but

(*u*) Thetford School Case, 8 Rep. 130; Att.-Gen. *v.* Arnold, Show. P. C. 22; Att.-Gen. *v.* Mayor of Bristol, 2 J. & W. 294; Att.-Gen. *v.* Skinners' Company, 2 Russ. 407; Att.-Gen. *v.* Smythies, 2 R. & M. 717; Att.-Gen. *v.* Wilson, 3 M. & K. 362; Att.-Gen. *v.* Drapers' Company, 2 Bea. 508; Att.-Gen. *v.* Coopers' Company, 3 Id. 29; Att.-Gen. *v.* Grocers' Company, 6 Id. 526; Jack *v.* Burnett, 12 Cl. & F. 812.

---

[1] See the Mayor of Beverly *v.* The Att.-Gen., 6 H. L. Cas. 310; Att.-Gen. *v.* Dean of Winsor, 8 H. L. Cas. 369.

considered it firmly established by precedent, and for that reason refused to overthrow it. (v)   It is, however, a mere presumption of law; and, therefore, if it appears from the wording of the instrument that the individual charity was the only one in the donor's mind, and that, if that should fail, he intended the property to revert to himself, there is no equity to alter his disposition. (w)

The manner in which the *cy pres* application is effected, is by referring it to the Master to settle a scheme, having a regard to the instrument of gift.   In ordinary cases this is not difficult; as, for example, in one instance, where a legacy was given to University College to purchase advowsons, and it was found that they already held as many advowsons *as the law would permit; [*72] and in another, where a devise was made to Trinity Hall, Cambridge, for the purpose of founding fellowships for the scholars of a particular school, and the college alleged that fellowships of this class were contrary to their statutes.   In both these cases the real intention of the doner was sufficiently obvious.   There could be no doubt in the one that he meant to increase the advowsons of the college, or in the other that he meant to provide endowments for the school; and accordingly the fund was applied in the former case for increasing the value of the existing advowsons, and in the latter it was suggested by Lord Thurlow that it would be near the purpose, if the college would admit the scholars as exhibitioners; or if any other college would receive them as fellows. (x)

(v) Moggridge v. Thackwell, 7 Ves. 36 ; Mills v. Farmer, 19 Id. 483.

(w) Corbyn v. French, 4 Ves. 418 ; De Themmines v. De Boneval, 5 Russ. 288 ; Att.-Gen. v. Whitchurch, 3 Ves. 141 ; Cherry v. Mott, 1 M. & C. 123.

(x) Att.-Gen. v. Green, 2 B. C. C. 492 ; Att.-Gen. v. Andrews, 3 Ves. 633.

In cases where the charity is of a compound character, it is sometimes difficult to determine in what part of the description its essence resides. A doubt of this kind arose in a case where a gift had been made for apprenticing the sons of poor Presbyterians, resident in the testator's parish; a surplus arose, to be applied *cy pres;* and it was contended on one side, that the proper objects would be poor Presbyterians resident out of the parish; on the other, that they would be poor persons in the parish, not being Presbyterians. The Court, on looking at all the circumstances came to the conclusion, that the profession of Presbyterianism, and not the residence in the parish was in the particular instance the primary object, and decreed in favor of the first scheme.(*y*)

In some instances the object specified is so peculiar that it is difficult to find anything substantially analogous. In this case, if other charities are mentioned in the will, they may afford a clue for the guidance of the Court. The application, however, must be a *cy pres* one to the object which has failed, and not a mere transfer to the other charities. The *principle on which such [*73] charities can be available as a guide, appears to be that of ascertaining how much of the original object it is possible to adopt, and then filling up the deficiencies from the other objects. An instance of this kind occurred under a bequest of property on three trusts; viz., as to one-half for the redemption of British slaves in Algiers; as to a quarter for Church of England schools in London; and as to the remaining quarter for poor freemen of the Ironmonger's Company. The first trust failed for want of objects. It was held, that so much of the first trust as conferred a benefit on all British subjects might still

(*y*) Att.-Gen. *v.* Wansay, 15 Ves. 231.

be effectuated, and that the mode of effectuating it might be borrowed from the second trusts; and the fund was accordingly applied for the maintenance of Church of England schools throughout England.(z) The difficulties. however, which may occur in discovering an analogy, will not obviate the necessity of doing it. If the fund is clearly dedicated to charity, the Court of Chancery must so apply it. And similarities of character, however remote, may properly warrant a proposed application, if no other plan of nearer affinity can be found.

The jurisdiction in equity for a *cy pres* application appears to exist in all cases where the original gift creates a trust for distribution in charity, although the trust as designated fails of effect. But if there be a general indefinite gift to charity or the poor, or a gift to a charity of a superstitious character, which is considered in law as equivalent to an indefinite gift, it seems that the disposition is in the Crown by sign manual.(a)[1]

The jurisdiction to superintend a charitable trust is set in motion by the information of the Attorney-General [*74] *suing on behalf of the Crown, or, if the nature of the trust is such that its non-performance has inflicted personal injury on an individual, then by a compound form of suit, uniting both the public and the private wrong, and called an information and bill. So far as its exercise is required for controlling the management of the property, it extends to all charities, whether corpo-

(z) Att.-Gen. v. Ironmongers' Company, 2 M. & K. 576; 2 Beav. 313 · Cr. & P. 208; 10 Cl. & F. 908.

(a) Moggridge v. Thackwell, 7 Ves. 36; Hayter v. Trego, 5 Russ. 113; De Themmines v. De Bonneval, 5 Russ. 292; Att.-Gen. v. Todd, 1 K. 803; Reeve v. Att.-Gen., 3 Hare 191.

---

[1] See article in the American Law Register, vol. 1, N. S. pp. 385–400.

rate or not, and is regulated by the same principles as in
the case of ordinary trusts. The trustee having the legal
dominion, may exercise that dominion for effectuating the
objects of his trust, but he cannot do so for any other
object; he may manage the property in a husbandlike
way, but he cannot waste or alienate it.(b)

So far as the jurisdiction is sought to be exercised for
directing the internal administration of the charity, and
determining the manner in which the funds shall be
applied, it is confined to charities at large, i. e., such charities as have no charter of incorporation, but are under
the management of private persons, or of some independent corporation, in whom, as trustees, their property is
vested.

In the case of eleemosynary corporations, i. e., corporations established by charter for the purposes of the
charity, and having endowments for that purpose, the
jurisdiction of equity is confined to the management of
the estate, and does not extend to the election or amotion
of corporators, or to the internal administration of the
charity. The proper jurisdiction for these purposes is
that of the visitor, which is incidental to all eleemosynary corporations, and, if not expressly or impliedly conferred by the charter itself, will arise of common right to
the founder and his heirs. If the King be founder, or
if the heir of the founder be unknown or a lunatic, the
jurisdiction will be in the Crown, to be exercised through
the Lord Chancellor on petition to him. If the visitor
refuses to hear and decide a dispute, he may be compelled
to do so by *mandamus; but his decision cannot [*75]
be controlled. If, however, the visitors are also

(b) Att.-Gen. v. Pargeter, 6 Bea. 150; Att.-Gen. v. Foord, 6 Id. 289;
Att.-Gen. v. Corporation of Newark, 1 Hare 395.

in receipt of the revenue, so that they are in fact trustees, subject to no independent control, the jurisdiction of equity will attach; and the same result will follow when the object sought is beyond the visitor's functions, such, for instance, as a new apportionment of the charity revenues. (c)

In addition to the jurisdiction of equity in matters of charity, a special jurisdiction was created by the statute 43 Eliz. c. 4, called the Statute of Charitable Uses, for remedying abuses of charitable gifts. And it is thereby enacted that commissioners may be appointed by the Crown for the regulation of charities, whose decision shall be subject to review by the Lord Chancellor, with a further appeal to the House of Lords. The statute, however, does not exclude the right to proceed in Chancery; and the proceeding under it has fallen into disuse. (d)[1]

There is also a statutory jurisdiction in the Court of Chancery itself for remedying abuses by a summary process, instead of the more regular course by information and bill. This jurisdiction is created by 52 Geo. 3, c. 101, commonly known as Sir Samuel Romilly's Act, which directs that, where a breach of trust has been committed by the trustees of a charity, or where the direction of a Court of equity is deemed necessary for its administration, the parties seeking relief may proceed summarily

, (c) Ex parte Wrangham, 2 Ves. Jun. 609; Re Queen's Coll. Jac. 1; 3 Steph. Bl. 183; Ex parte Inge, 2 R. & M. 591; Rex v. Archbishop of Canterbury, 15 East 117; Att.-Gen. v. Foundling Hospital, 2 Ves. Jun. 42; Att.-Gen. v. Dixie, 13 Ves. 519; Ex parte Kirby Ravensworth Hospital, 15 Ves. 305; Att.-Gen. v. Earl of Clarendon, 17 Ves. 491; Ex parte Berkhamstead Free School, 2 Ves. & B. 134; Att.-Gen. v. Lubbock, 1 Coop. Ch. Ca. 15; Att.-Gen. v. Smythies, 2 R. & M. 717, 737; 2 M. & C. 135.

(d) Att.-Gen. v. Mayor of Dublin, 1 Bl. N. S. 312, 347; Incorporated Society v. Richards, 1 Conn. & L. 58.

---

[1] See ante, note to page 65.

by a petition to be sanctioned by the fiat of the Attorney-General.   The summary jurisdiction thus conferred, if the statute had been construed in its widest acceptation, would have been one of a very *extensive character, but [*76] it is confined by the decisions to plain breaches of trust, or to cases where no contention exists, and where the trustees are merely asking the direction of the Court. If any question is involved as to who are to be intrusted with the estate, or who are to be entitled to the benefit of it, or if the interest of any stranger may be affected, or if a new application of the fund is sought, the proper course is by an information. (e)

In the particular case of Grammar Schools, an additional jurisdiction has been conferred on the Court by 3 & 4 Vict. c. 77.   And authority is given to make decrees and orders, either in the progress of an ordinary suit, or on petition under Sir Samuel Romilly's Act, for extending the system of education to other branches of learning besides Greek and Latin; for extending or restricting the right of admission; and for establishing schemes for the application of the revenue, having due regard to the intentions of the founder.   By the same act authority is given to the Court to enlarge and confer powers for regulating the discipline of such schools, and to appoint the mode of removing masters.

A summary jurisdiction is also conferred by statute for superintending and controlling the officers of Friendly Societies; (f) for apportioning charitable bequests between new parishes and districts formed under the Church

(e) 52 Geo. 3, c. 101; Corporation of Ludlow v. Greenhouse, 1 Bl. N. S. 17; Re Clark's Charity, 8 Sim. 34; Re Phillipott's Charity, Id. 381; Re West Retford, 10 Id. 101; Re Parke's Charity, 12 Id. 329.

(f) 10 Geo. 4, c. 56, ss. 14, 15, 16.

Building Acts and the remaining parts of the ol
and making a like apportionment of debts or ch
tracted or charged on the credit of church rate
for administering property which was formerly
the municipal corporations on charitable trusts.

(*g*) 8 & 9 Vict. c. 70, s. 22.
(*h*) 5 & 6 Wm. 4, c. 76, s. 71.

*CHAPTER II. [*77]

OF SPECIFIC PERFORMANCE——ELECTION——MERITORIOUS OR IM-
PERFECT CONSIDERATION——DISCHARGE BY MATTER IN PAIS OF
CONTRACTS UNDER SEAL——RELIEF AGAINST PENALTIES.

THE jurisdiction for compelling performance of a contract involves the consideration not merely of what is
technically termed specific performance, but also of the
doctrines of election, of meritorious or imperfect consideration, of the discharge by matter *in pais* of contracts
under seal, and of relief against penalties and forfeited
mortgages. The equities, therefore, which exist under
those heads, except those relating to forfeited mortgages,
will form the subject of the present chapter. The jurisdiction of equity over mortgages will be afterwards separately considered.

The equity to compel SPECIFIC PERFORMANCE of a contract
arises where a contract, binding at law, has been infringed,
and the remedy at law by damages is inadequate.[1] And

---

[1] The character of the relief which equity affords in decreeing the
specific performance of a contract does not differ in kind from that which
is administered by the same system of jurisprudence in other cases, for
the relief given in equity is always *specific*. See Introduction, page xxxv.,
ante. In cases of contracts the jurisdiction of equity arises in some instances from the inability to estimate damages for the breach; and, in
others, from the inadequacy of the compensation which damages afford;
and the jurisdiction having once attached, the Court goes on to apply its
usual remedy, viz., specific relief, or causing that to be actually done which

in order to originate this equity, it is essential that the contract shall have been made for valuable consideration, and that its enforcement in *specie* be practicable and necessary.[1] The validity of the contract at law is not

---

in good conscience ought to be done. Equity acts "specifically" in the enforcement of a trust, the reformation of a written instrument, and other instances, no less than in decreeing the performance of a contract; and the only reason why the term "specific" seems to have been more frequently applied to the last case, than to the others, is, perhaps, because in the performance of contracts the relief in equity is more striking, and more in contrast with the common law remedies, than in other instances.

The Act of 21 & 22 Vict. c. 27, commonly known as Sir Hugh Cairns's Act, provides that the Court may either in addition to or in substitution for the relief which is prayed, grant that relief which would otherwise be proper to be granted by another Court—that is to say, award damages. On the construction of this act see Ferguson v. Wilson, L. R. 2 Eq. 77; Soames v. Edge, Johns. 649; Norris v. Jackson, 1 Johns. & H. 319; Howe v. Hunt, 31 Beav. 420. In Indiana (by statute) specific performance is enforced through the common law medium of a trial by jury; and in Pennsylvania a similar result is attained as respects land by the action of ejectment. So too in California: Weber v. Marshall, 19 Cal. 447; and Wisconsin: Fisher v. Moolick, 13 Wis. 321.

[1] The requisites for the specific performance of contracts in equity are five: *First*, the performance in specie must be *necessary; Second*, it must be *practicable; Third*, there must be a *valuable consideration; Fourth*, the terms of the contract must be *certain;* and *Fifth*, it must be *reciprocal.* To these rules it may be added, generally, that the allowance of this relief is a matter of judicial discretion.

First. The relief must be necessary, and this necessity may result either from the inadequacy of the damages afforded at common law, or from the impossibility of ascertaining those damages. Of the former, instances will be found in Lloyd v. Loaring, 6 Vesey, Jr. 773; Nutbrown v. Thornton, 10 Id. 159; Earl of Macclesfield v. Davis, 3 Vesey & B. 16; Lowther v. Lowther, 13 Vesey 95; Fells v. Read, 3 Id. 71; Pusey v. Pusey, 1 Vern. 273; Duke of Somerset v. Cookson, 3 P. Wms. 389; Brown v. Gilliland, 3 Dessaus. 541; Phyfe v. Wardell, 2 Ed. Ch. 51; Bowman v. Irons, 2 Bibb 78; Faleke v. Gray, 5 Jur. N. S. 645; 4 Drew 651; Hill v. Rockingham Bank, 44 N. Hamp. 567. Of the latter, the following cases will furnish examples: Sullivan v. Tuck, 1 Md. Ch. 59; Waters v. Howard, Id. 112; Finley v. Aiken, 1 Grant Cas. 83. When some of the articles are capable of compensation in damages, and some are not, equity will

material to be here considered. And our attention will therefore be directed to those requisites alone which, as-

enforce performance as to the whole: McGowin v. Remington, 12 Penn. St. 56. As a general rule, specific performance of contracts relating to personal property will not be enforced: Cowles v. Whitman, 10 Conn. 121; Hoy v. Hansborough, 1 Free. Ch. 533; Cuddie v. Rutter, 1 Lead. Cas. Eq. 640. Though the rule is otherwise when the chattel has not merely a market value, but also a *pretium affectionis:* Pusey v. Pusey, 1 Lead. Cas. Eq. 654; Duke of Somerset v. Cookson, Id. 655. The fact that in an agreement to convey land, a penalty for non-compliance with the contract has been inserted expressly as " liquidated damages," does not deprive the party injured of his right to a specific performance: Hull v. Sturdivant, 46 Maine 34; Hooker v. Pynchon, 8 Gray 550; Moorer v. Kopmann, 11 Rich. Eq. 225; Daily v. Litchfield, 10 Mich. 38. See Dowling v. Betjemann, 2 Johns. & H. 544; Gillis v. Hall, 2 Brewster (Pa.) 342.

Second. The specific enforcement of the contract must be practicable: Tobey v. The County of Bristol, 3 Story 800; Blackett v. Bates. 12 Jur. N. S. 151; also Phillips v. Stauch, 20 Mich. 369; Burke v. Seeley, 46 Mo. 334. For instance, a contract to convey land will not be specifically enforced against a vendor who has no title: Fitzpatrick v. Featherstone, 3 Ala. 40. Mere pecuniary inability, however, is no defence: Hopper v. Hopper, 1 Green (N. J.) 147; see also Love v. Cobb, 63 N. C. 324. And an agreement to *devise* lands will not be specifically enforced: Stafford v. Bartholomew, 2 Carter 153; though see Maddox v. Rowe, 23 Geo. 431; Mundorf v. Kilbourne, 4 Md. 463; Whitridge v. Parkhurst, 20 Id. 62; Johnson v. Habbell, 2 Stockton, 332; Logan v. McGinnis, 12 Penn. St. 27. A specific performance by husband and wife of a contract for the sale of the wife's land will not be decreed on a bill filed by the vendee; Clarke v. Reins, 12 Gratt. 98; though in Massachusetts a wife may, by statute, make a binding contract for the sale of her lands; Baker v. Hathaway, 5 Allen 103. Under this head, too, fall the instances mentioned infra, p. 81, where the specific performance of a contract will not be decreed when the property affected by it has become vested, by descent or devise, in infants and persons from other reasons incapable of executing a conveyance. In most of the United States, however, there are statutes providing for the execution of decedents' contracts.

Third. The agreement must be supported by a valuable consideration. See infra, p. 78 note.

Fourth. The terms of the contract must be explicit and certain: Dodd v. Seymour, 2 Conn. 473; Rockwell v. Lawrence, 2 Halstead Ch. 190; McKibbin v. Brown, 1 McCart. 13; Aday v. Echols, 18 Ala. 353; Soles v. Hickman, 20 Penn. St. 180; Allen v. Burke, 2 Md. Ch. 534; Canton

suming the fact of its legal validity, are essential to the
equity for specific enforcement.

Co. v. The Railroad Co., 21 Md. 395; Maderia v. Hopkins, 12 B. Monr.
595; Parrish v. Koons, 1 Pars. Eq. 97; Robinson v. Ketlletas, 4 Edw. Ch.
67; Price v. Griffith, 1 De G., M. & G. 80; Hammer v. McEldowney, 46
Penn. St. 334; Taylor v. Portington, 7 De G., M. & G. 328; Parker v.
Taswell, 2 De G. & J. 571; Buckmaster v. Thompson, 36 N. Y. 558;
Waring v. Ayres, 40 Id. 357; Jordan v. Deaton, 23 Ark. 704; Potts v.
Whitehead, 20 N. J. Eq. 55; Lobdell v. Lobdell, 36 N. Y. 327; Brewer v.
Wilson, 2 Green (N. J.) 180; Mehl v. Von Derwulbeke, 2 Lans. (N. Y.)
267; Foot v. Webb, 59 Barb. (N. Y.) 38; Munsell v. Loree, 21 Mich. 491.
When the price to be paid was to be fixed by two persons, and a third
(their nominee), and they could not agree, the court refused specific per-
formance: Milnes v. Gery, 14 Vesey 400–407; Darbey v. Whitaker, 4
Drew. 134; Dike v. Greene, 4 R. I. 285. And the same rule applies to
other stipulations, besides those in regard to the price: Tillett v. The
Charing Cross Bridge Co., 26 Beav. 419. Though see Gregory v. Mighell,
18 Vesey 328. An agreement to sell at a *fair valuation* may be enforced:
Milnes v. Gery, supra; Van Doren v. Robinson, 1 Green (N. J.) 256.
Though an agreement is uncertain when first entered into, its terms may
be settled by user: Laird v. The Birkenhead Railway Co., John. 501;
Powell v. Thomas, 6 Hare 300. See, in this connection, Price v. Salusbury,
32 Beav. 446.

Fifth. The agreement must be mutual. See post 82, note 1. It may
be added, lastly, that the specific performance of a contract is a kind of
relief which rests in *judicial discretion*, that is a discretion not vacillating
or arbitrary, but one which is governed by sound and fixed rules, and
which is only exercised within certain defined limits. It is a discretion
which is to a considerable extent controlled by the circumstances of the
individual case: Rogers v. Saunders, 16 Maine 92; Griffith v. Frederick
County Bank, 6 Gill. & J. 424; Pigg v. Corder, 12 Leigh 69, 76; Meeker
v. Meeker, 16 Conn. 403; Seymour v. Delancy, 3 Cow. 445; 6 John. Ch.
222; King v. Morford, Saxton 274; Anthony v. Leftwich, 3 Rand. 238;
Prater v. Miller, 3 Hawks. 629; Turner v. Clay, 3 Bibb 52; Frisby v. Ballance, 4 Scam. 287; McMurtrie v. Bennette, Harring. Ch. 124; Dougherty
v. Humston, 2 Blackf. 273; St. John v. Benedict, 6 John. Ch. 111; Henderson v. Hays, 2 Watts 148; Perkins v. Wright, 3 Har. & McHen. 324;
Leigh v. Crump, 1 Ired. Ch. 299; Gould v. Womack, 2 Ala. 83; Tobey v.
The County of Bristol, 3 Story 800; Dalzell v. Crawford, 1 Parsons 45;
Waters v. Howard, 8 Gill 262; Tyson v. Watts, 1 Md. Ch. 13; Bennett
v. Smith, 16 Jurist 421; 10 Eng. L. & Eq. 272; Fish v. Lightner, 44 Mo.
268; but a discretion, nevertheless, which conforms itself to general rules

*The first requisite is that there be a valuable
consideration, either in the way of benefit be- [*78]
stowed, or of disadvantage sustained, by the party in
whose favor a contract is to be enforced.(a)¹ The neces-

(a) 2 Steph. Bl. 113.

---

and settled principles: Ash v. Daggy, 6 Ind. 259 ; Powell v. Central Plank
Co., 24 Ala. 441 ; Stoutenburgh v. Tompkins, 1 Stockt. 332; Chubb v.
Peckham, 2 Beas. 207 ; Haywood v. Cope, 25 Beav. 140. In the exercise
of this discretion, if the complainant has been guilty of laches : Parrish v.
Koons, 1 Pars. Eq. 97 ; Ins. Co. v. Union Canal Co. Bright. N. P. 48 ;
Miller v. Henlan, 51 Penn. St. 265 ; or has failed to perform his own part
of the contract: Roy v. Willink, 4 Sand. Ch. 525 ; Slaughter v. Harris, 1
Carter 238 ; Eastman v. Plumer, 46 N. H. 464 ; specific performance will·
be refused.

¹ To entitle a party in Chancery to the aid of the court in obtaining a
specific performance, the instrument must be supported by a valuable consideration, or at least by what a Court of equity considers a meritorious
consideration, as payment of debts, or making provision for a wife and
child: Minturn v. Seymour, 4 John. Ch. 500; Woodcock v. Bennett, 1
Cowen 733 ; Cabeen v. Gordon, 1 Hill Ch. 51 ; Shepherd v. Shepherd, 2
Md. Ch. 144 ; Vasser v. Vasser, 23 Miss. 378 ; Crompton v. Vasser, 19 Ala.
259 ; Clarke v. Lott, 11 Ill. 105 ; Banks v. May, 3 A. K. Marsh. 436 ; Butman v.
Porter, 100 Mass. 337 ; Tarbell v. Tarbell, 10 Allen 278 ; Walrond v. Walrond, Johns. 18 ; Allen v. Davison, 16 Ind. 416 ! Short v. Price, 17 Tex.
397–403 ; Lear v. Chouteau, 23 Ill. 39 ; Harkness v. Remington, 7 R. I.
134. Where the holder of shares of railway stock upon which no deposit
or other sums have been paid, agrees to transfer them to another who
agrees to receive them, and to do all acts necessary to relieve the former
from liability in respect to them, the agreement is not void for want of
consideration or mutuality, but a bill may be sustained against the latter
to compel him to take the stock: Cheale v. Kenward, 3 De G. & J. 27. A
contract to borrow a sum of money will not be specifically enforced :
Rogers v. Challis, 27 Beav. 175 ; nor a contract to lend: Sichel v. Mosen-
thal, 30 Beav. 371–377. Natural love and affection has been held to be a
good consideration in equity, in Taylor v. James, 4 Dessaus. 5 ; McIntire
v. Hughes, 4 Bibb 186 ; Caldwell v. Williams, 1 Bailey Eq. 175 ; and see
Hayes v. Kershow, 1 Sandf. Ch. 261. But in Pennsylvania, the opposite
doctrine has been held: Kennedy v. Ware, 1 Penn. St. 445 ; Campbell's
Est., 7 Id. 100 , and see Morris v. Lewis, 33 Ala. 353 ; and this is nuques-
tionably the result of the English cases. As to assignments for the benefit
of creditors, see ante 31, and note ; Hill on Trustees, 4th Am. ed. 507 in
note ; Burrill on Assignments 280, 306 ; notes to Thomas v. Jenks, 1 Am.
Lead. Cas. 80 ; and see Hickman v. Grimes, 1 A. K. Marsh. 87.

sity for such consideration exists at law, where the agreement is by simple contract only; but if it be an agreement under seal, technically called a contract by specialty, the solemnity of a deed is held at law to imply a consideration. In equity, however, where a special remedy is sought in addition to the ordinary one of pecuniary recompense, a valuable consideration is always requisite, and no additional force is given to the agreement, because it is evidenced by an instrument under seal. If there be no consideration, or if the only consideration be a moral duty or natural affection, which are termed good, but not valuable considerations, the Court of Chancery will not interfere; e. g., if a man contract after marriage, in consideration of duty or affection towards his wife and children.(b) If, on the other hand, the contract be made before marriage, it will be supported, in consideration of the subsequent marriage, and may be enforced on the application of any person claiming within that consideration.[1] It will not, however, be enforced on the application of a party not within the consideration, to whom a collateral interest has been voluntarily given,—although, if enforced at all, it will be enforced throughout.(c) The peculiar doctrine of equity with respect to meritorious or imperfect considerations, which are distinguished from valuable considerations on the one hand, and from an absolute want of consideration on the other, will be presently considered. It is sufficient here to remark, that where a decree for specific performance is asked,

(b) Jefferys v. Jefferys, Cr. & P. 141; [Moore v. Crofton, 3 Jones & Lat. 442.]

(c) 3 Sug. V. & P. 289; Davenport v. Bishopp, 2 N. C. C. 451; 1 Ph. 698.

---

[1] Neale v. Neales, 9 Wall. 1.

there must be a valuable consideration to support the equity. A distinction, however, must be noted between value and adequacy. It is essential that the consideration be valuable, but it is not essential *that it be also adequate. The parties themselves are the best [*79] judges of that; and therefore mere inadequacy, if not so gross as to prove fraud or imposition, will not warrant the refusal of relief.$(d)^1$

By parity of reasoning, if a benefit has been conferred as the consideration for any act, a party who knowingly accepts that benefit, though he may not be bound by an actual contract, or by a condition of performance annexed to the gift, is compellable in equity to do the act.(e) And in like manner it is a principle of the common law, that

(d) 1 Sug. V. & P. 440; Borell v. Dann, 2 Hare 440, 450; Bower v. Cooper, Id. 408.

(e) Edwards v. Grand Junction Railway, 1 M. & C. 650; Green v. Green, 19 Ves. 665; 2 Merv. 86; Gretton v. Haward, 1 Sw. 409, 427.

---

[1] Mere inadequacy of price is not *per se* sufficient to set aside a transaction: Park v. Johnson, 4 Allen 259; yet where it is so great as to give to the contract the character of unreasonableness and hardship, the Court may be induced to stay the exercise of its discretionary power, in enforcing the specific performance of a contract for the sale of land, and leave the party to seek his compensation in damages at law: Osgood et al. v. Franklin et al., 2 John. Ch. 23, s. c. on appeal, 14 John. 527; Howard v. Edgell, 17 Verm. 9; Shepherd v. Bevin, 9 Gill 32; Erwin v. Parham, 12 How. U. S. 197; Harrison v. Town, 17 Mo. 237; Powers v. Hale, 5 Foster 145; and so as to personalty: Falcke v. Gray, 4 Drew. 651. See also Seymour v. Delancy, 3 Cowen 445; 6 John. Ch. 222; Garnett v. Macon, 2 Brock. 185; Rodman v. Zilley, Saxton 320; White v. Thompson, 1 Dev. & Bat. Ch. 493; Fripp v. Fripp, Rice Ch. 84; Bean v. Valle, 2 Mo. 126; Davidson v. Little, 22 Penn. St. 245; Vick v. Troy & Boston R. R. 21 Barb. 381. If the inadequacy be very gross and manifest, so as has been said to "shock the conscience," the court will infer fraud or imposition, and, it seems, give active relief: Butler v. Haskell, 4 Dessaus. 687; Wright v. Wilson, 2 Yerg. 294; Barnett v. Spratt, 4 Ired. Eq. 171; Deaderick v. Watkins, 8 Humph. 520: see, however, Erwin v. Parham, 12 How. U. S. 197.

13

if a service has been rendered and accepted by any person, it will be implied, in the absence of a specific contract, that he shall pay as much as it is reasonably worth.(f)

The necessity for valuable consideration is confined in equity, as well as at law, to promises which rest *in fieri*.[1] If the promise has been already executed, whether at law by transfer of a legal ownership, or in equity by the creation of a final trust, the consideration on which it was made is immaterial. And it is therefore frequently contended, that effect should be given to a voluntary promise, on the ground that the party making it, though he has not absolutely perfected his gift, has gone sufficiently far to constitute himself a trustee for the claimant. The exact line of demarcation, where the contract ceases to be an executory agreement, and becomes a perfected trust in equity, is often difficult to distinguish; but the principle itself is sufficiently clear. If the donor has perfected his gift in the way which he intended, so that there is nothing left for him to do, and nothing which he has authority to countermand, the donee's right is enforceable as a trust, and the consideration is immaterial. Such, for instance, is the case where an instrument of gift has been fully [*80] executed, *although retained in the donor's possession;(g)[1] where the legal ownership of a right en-

(f) 2 Steph. Bl. 186.

(g) Coningham v. Plunkett, 2 N. C. C. 245; Hughes v. Stubbs, 1 Hare 476; Exton v. Scott, 6 Sim. 31; Fletcher v. Fletcher, 4 Hare 67.

---

[1] Equity will aid in enforcing an agreement executed, though voluntary, *aliter* if it be executory: Read v. Long, 4 Yerg. 68; Wyche v. Green, 16 Geo. 49; Morris v. Lewis, 33 Ala. 53. But, in Boze v. Davis, 14 Texas 331, it was held that equity will not enforce a voluntary agreement to convey land, although the grantee was put in possession and made improvements; but, if the bill is properly drawn, he may obtain compensation for the labor he expended and the improvements he made: Pinckard v. Pinckard, 23 Ala. 649, acc.

[2] Way's Settlement, 10 Jur. N. S. 1166.

forceable at law has been completely vested in a trustee for the claimant;(*h*) where the legal estate is already in a trustee, and the equitable ownership, retaining the old trustee, has been completely assigned to the claimant, or a trustee for him;(*i*) where a chose in action which is transferable in equity alone, has been transferred by a complete equitable assignment;(*k*) or where, by a formal declaration of trust, which purports to be and is a complete transaction, the donor has assumed the character of a trustee.(*l*) If, on the contrary, the transaction is incomplete, and its final completion is asked in equity, the Court will not interpose to perfect the author's liablity, without first inquiring into the origin of the claim, and the nature of the consideration given.(*m*)[1]

(*h*) Fletcher *v.* Fletcher, 4 Hare 67.

(*i*) Collinson *v.* Pattrick, 2 K. 123 ; Sloan *v.* Codogan, 3 Sug. V. & P. App. 66 ; Beatson *v.* Beatson, 12 Sim. 281.

(*k*) Ex parte Pye & Dubois, 18 Ves. 140 ; McFadden *v.* Jenkyns, 1 Hare 458 ; 1 Ph. 153 ; Fortescue *v.* Barnett, 3 M. & K. 36 ; Edwards *v.* Jones, 1 M. & C. 226.

(*l*) Meek *v.* Kettlewell, 1 Hare 464 ; 1 Ph. 342.

(*m*) Edwards *v.* Jones, 1 M. & C. 226 ; Dillon *v.* Coppin, 4 Id. 647 ; Meek *v.* Kettlewell, 1 Hare 464 ; 1 Ph. 342 ; Fletcher *v.* Fletcher, 4 Hare 67 ; Ward *v.* Audland, 8 Bea. 201.

---

[1] By the recent case of Kekewich *v.* Manning, 1 De G., M. & Gord. 176, it is now established in England, contrary to several previous decisions, that a voluntary assignment of an equitable or reversionary interest, or of a chose in action, will be enforced in equity, where the assignor has done all in his power to make the transaction complete. The fact that the legal title cannot pass in such case, is held to be immaterial : s. P. Voyle *v.* Hughes, 18 Jur. 341 ; 2 Sm. & Giffard 18. But the rule still remains the same where the assignor has not done all in his power, and which the nature of the property is capable of, as a transfer of stock, where it is assigned : Beech *v.* Keep, 18 Bea. 285 ; Bridge *v.* Bridge, 16 Id. 315 ; Hill *v.* The Rockingham Bank, 44 N. H. 567 ; see Milroy *v.* Lord, 8 Jur. N. S. 806 ; and the classification of the cases on this subject in Hill on Trustees 139, 142, notes, 4th Am. ed.

The second requisite is, that the mutual enforcement of the contract in *specie* be practicable, *i. e.*, that the contract be one which the defendant can fulfil; and the fulfilment of which on his part, and also on the part of the plaintiff, can be judicially secured.

If the defendant cannot fulfil the contract which he has made, it may be a ground for exempting the plaintiff from costs on the dismissal of his bill, but it cannot authorize the Court to decree an impossibility. Such, for example, is the case, where the vendor of property has no estate, or only a limited estate therein; (*n*) where he holds [*81] it as a *trustee without authority to sell; (*o*) or where, being the absolute owner at the time of his contract, he subsequently conveys to a stranger who is ignorant of the prior sale, and is therefore bound by no equity to give it effect. In this last case, the vendor's misconduct may be a ground for charging him with costs, but a decree for performance of the contract is obviously impossible, and there is no jurisdiction in equity to give damages for the breach. (*p*)

A similar obstacle is sometimes occasioned, where, after a contract has been made, the property which it affects descends or is devised to persons, who by reason of infancy or of the limited nature of their estate, are unable to make the requisite conveyance.[1] The effect of an incapacity of

(*n*) Malden *v.* Fyson, 9 Bea. 347.

(*o*) Mortlock *v.* Buller, 10 Ves. 292.

(*p*) Todd *v.* Gee, 17 Ves. 273 ; Jenkins *v.* Parkinson, 2 M. & K. 5 ; Sainsbury *v.* Jones, 2 Bea. 462 ; Nelson *v.* Bridges, Id. 239.

---

[1] The contract of the ancestor was decreed to be performed by the infant heir-at-law, who was allowed six months after coming of age to show cause: Glaze *v.* Drayton, 1 Dessaus. 109 ; Wilkinson *v.* Wilkinson, a minor, 1 Id. 201. The subject-matter must, however, have been fixed : Ferris *v.* Irving, 28 Cal. 645. Where specific performance of a contract would be

this kind is not to oust the jurisdiction of equity, but to delay its exercise until the requisite capacity is attained. The inconvenience, however, has been remedied by a recent statute, and it is enacted that in such cases, after a decree has been made for specific performance, the Court may direct a conveyance in the same manner as in the case of an incapacitated trustee.(q)⎯ A corresponding authority is given by another statute, where a contracting party becomes lunatic after a contract has been made.(r)

If the defendant, though able to fulfil his contract, cannot be judicially compelled to do so, the jurisdiction of equity is equally at an end. Such, for example, is the case where a tradesman has contracted to sell the goodwill of a business, unconnected with any specific property, or where an actor has engaged to perform at a particular theatre;[1] for the Court is incompetent to tell the

(q) 1 Wm. 4, c. 60, ss. 16 & 17.   (r) 1 Wm. 4, c. 65, s. 27.

decreed between the original parties to a contract, it will be decreed between all claiming under them, if there are no intervening equities controlling the case: Hays v. Hall, 4 Porter 374 ; McMorris v. Crawford, 15 Ala. 271 ; Brewer v. Brewer, 19 Id. 481 ; Nesbit v. Moore, 9 B. Monr. 508 ; Tiernan v. Roland, 15 Penn. St. 429 ; Guard v. Bradley, 7 Ind. 600 ; Hill v. Ressegieu, 17 Barb. (N. Y.) 162 ; Moore v. Burrows, 34 Id. 173 ; Hunter v. Bales, 24 Ind. 299 ; Laverty v. Moore, 33 N. Y. 658 ; see Van Doren v. Robinson, 1 Green (N. J.) 256.

[1] Hamblin v. Dinneford, 2 Edw. Ch. 529. A court will sometimes restrain the infringement of negative covenants though it cannot specifically enforce the whole contract: see Lumley v. Wagner, 1 De G., M. & G. 604 ; De Mattos v. Gibson, 4 De G. & J. 276 ; also Peto v. The Railroad Co., 1 Hem. & M. 468 ; post 207 note. A contract for personal services of an uncertain duration will not be enforced: Firth v. Ridley, 33 Bea. 516, approved by the Lord Justices June 30, 1864 ; or a contract for the performance of a continuous series of duties, the non-performance of which can only be punished by repeated attachments: Blackett v. Bates, L. R. 1 Ch. App. 117 ; though see Furman v. Clark, 3 Stockt. 306. The court will not

actor what parts he shall perform, or how he shall perform
them; or to tell the tradesman how he shall induce his
[*82] customers to employ his *asignees. (s)   Such again
is a contract for entering into a partnership, where
no term is fixed for its duration, and where the decree
might therefore be nullified by an immediate dissolution;
or for granting a lease, where the term contracted for
has expired before the hearing of the cause.   It seems,
however, that if special cause be shown, the Court may
insist on such a lease being executed; and dated as of
the time when it ought to have been made, and may compel the lessor to admit such date as the true one in any
proceeding at law. (t)

If, when the cause comes on for hearing, the plaintiff's
part of the agreement has not been performed, and its
fulfilment by him cannot be secured, there is a want of
mutuality between the parties.[1]   And such want of mu-

(s) Coslake v. Till, 1 Russ. 376; Kemble v. Kean, 6 Sim. 333; Dietrichsen v. Cabburn, 2 Ph. 52; [Fitzpatrick v. Nowlan, 1 Irish L. & Eq. N.
S. 671.]

(t) Hercy v. Birch, 9 Ves. 357; Nesbitt v. Meyer, 1 Sw. 223.

---

specifically enforce a contract to run a railroad: Port Clinton R. R. Co. v.
The Cleveland & Toledo R. R. Co., 13 Ohio N. S. 544. Specific performance
of a contract to build a railroad will not be decreed. Such a work requires
too long a time for its performance to be conducted under orders and decrees of chancery: Ross v. Union Pacific R. R., 1 Woolw. 26; Fallon v. R.
R. Co., 1 Dill. 121.

[1] The contract or agreement sought to be enforced, must be mutual, and
the tie reciprocal, or a Court of Equity will not enforce a performance:
McMurtrie v. Bennett, Harring. Ch. 124; Hawley v. Sheldon, Id. 420;
Hutcheson v. McNutt, 1 Ham. 14; Cabeen v. Gordon, 1 Hill Ch. 51;
Benedict v. Lynch, 1 John. Ch. 370; Ohio v. Baum, 6 Ham 383; Tyson
v. Watts, 1 Md. Ch. 13; Bronson v. Cahill, 4 McLean 19; Southern Life
Ins. Co. v. Cole, 4 Florida 359; Duvall v. Myers, 2 Md. Ch. 401; Stout-
enbergh v. Tompkins, 1 Stock. 332; Hoen v. Simmons, 1 Cal. 119; Cor-
son v. Mulvany, 49 Penn. St. 88; Hawralty v. Warren, 3 Green (N. J.)

tuality, though it may not in all cases absolutely exclude the jurisdiction, is a material ingredient in restraining its exercise. For example, where an agreement had been made between the plaintiff and the defendant, that the plaintiff should supply certain acids for the defendant, and that the defendant should purchase them from the plaintiff alone, the Court refused to restrain the defendant from purchasing elsewhere, because it could not compel the plaintiff to furnish all the acids which might be required. And it has been held on the same principle, that an infant cannot sustain a suit for specific performance of a contract made by him, for, if a decree were made in his favor, it would be impossible to compel him to execute that decree.(u)

The third requisite is, that an enforcement in *specie* be necessary, *i. e.*, it must be really important to the plaintiff, and not oppressive on the defendant.

*It must be really important to the plaintiff; for the equitable remedy is not concurrent with the legal one, but supplemental to it, and will not there- [*83]

(u) Hill v. Crolls, 2 Ph. 60; Fight v. Bolland, 4 Russ. 298; Bozon v. Farlow, 1 Meriv. 469; Pickering v. Bishop of Ely, 2 N. C. C. 249; Salisbury v. Hatcher, 2 N. C. C. 54; Dietrichsen v. Cabburn, 2 Ph. 52; Rolfe v. Rolfe, 15 Sim. 88; [Hargrave v. Hargrave, 12 Beav. 408.]

Eq. 124; Jones v. Noble, 3 Bush (Ky.) 694; Marble Co. v. Ripley, 10 Wall. 339. Thus, where by the terms of sale, title is to be absolute, and purchase-money to be paid within a certain period, or a re-sale, it seems specific performance will not be decreed in favor of the vendor, on a bill filed after the expiration of that period: Bodine v. Glading, 21 Penn. St. 54; see, however, Roberts v. Donny, 3 De G., M. & G. 284. As to the necessity of performance and diligence on the part of the complainant: see Thorp v. Pettit, 1 Gr. (N. J.) 448; Ely v. McKay, 12 Allen (Mass.) 323; Gentry v. Rogers, 40 Ala. 442; Gale v. Archer, 42 Barb. (N. Y.) 320. A tender of performance need not be made when it would be wholly nugatory: Kerr v. Purdy, 50 Barb. (N. Y.) 24.

fore be substituted for such legal remedy, unless a particular necessity be shown.[1] In accordance with this
principle, specific performance may be enforced of contracts for the sale of land, of shares in a public company, (v) or of a life annuity; (w) for refraining from specific
injurious acts, and generally for any purpose, where the
specific thing or act contracted for, and not mere pecuniary compensation, is the redress practically required. (x)[2]
On the other hand, it will not ordinarily be decreed on a
contract for the sale of stock or goods; because with a
sum equal to the market price, the plaintiff may buy
other stock or goods of the same description. (y)[3]   On the
same principle, a covenant to repair a house, or to put
lands into a particular state of cultivation, will not be enforced in equity; for the matter really in controversy is
nothing more than the cost of employing some other per-

(v) Duncuft v. Albrecht, 12 Sim. 189; Colombine v. Chichester, 2 Ph.
27.

(w) Withy v. Cottle, 1 S. & S. 174; Clifford v. Turrell, 1 N. C. C. 138.

(x) Adderley v. Dixon, 1 S. & S. 610.

(y) Cud v. Rutter, 1 P. W. 570; Doloret v. Rothschild, 1 S. & S. 590;
Adderley v. Dixon, 1 S. & S. 610.

---

[1] Mead v. Camfield, 3 Stockt. 38.

[2] An agreement between a creditor and a third person, founded on a
valuable consideration, to compromise the claim of the former against his
debtor, will be specifically enforced by a Court of equity : Phillips v. Berger, 8 Barb. S. C. 527.

Specific performance of an agreement for insurance may be decreed even
after a loss: Tayloe v. Merchants' Fire Ins. Co., 9 How. U. S. 390; Carpenter v. Mutual Safety Ins. Co., 4 Sandf. Ch. 408 ; see Neville v. Merchants' Ins. Co., 19 Ohio 452; and the Court, having obtained jurisdiction,
may then go on and give the suitable relief: Tayloe v. Ins. Co., ut sup.

[3] Maulden v. Armistead, 18 Ala. 500 ; and see ante, p. 77, note. It is
not by itself a sufficient ground of demurrer, that a bill seeks specific performance of a contract with regard to personal property: Carpenter v.
Mutual Safety Ins. Co., 4 Sandf. Ch. 408.   See Cheales v. Kenward, 3 De
G. & J. 27 ; stated ante, note to p. 80.

son to do the work. In the case of a contract for building a house, and not for repairing only, the application of the principle is doubtful; but if the building be one which the defendant only can erect, and the non-erection of which cannot be compensated by money, the jurisdiction is clear, and the Court will see that the work is properly done.(z)[1]

It must not be oppressive on the defendant. If its importance to the plaintiff be shown, a material step is gained towards obtaining a decree. But the establishment of this fact is not conclusive; for however important specific performance may be to the plaintiff, yet he has at all events another remedy by damages at law; and it is therefore open to the defendant to contend that a wrong *would be inflicted on him by going beyond the ordinary remedy, greater than would be inflicted [*84] on the plaintiff by refusing to interpose.(a)[2] Specific performance will accordingly be refused, if there has been misrepresentation by the plaintiff on a material point, although it may not be sufficient to invalidate the con-

(z) Errington v. Aynesly, 2 B. C. C. 342; Flint v. Brandon, 8 Ves. 164; Storer v. Great Western Railway, 2 N. C. C. 48. [See Birchett v. Bolling, 5 Munf. 442.]

(a) Wedgwood v. Adams, 6 Bea. 600.

---

[1] But an agreement to build a house of a given value, and according to a plan to be agreed upon, cannot be specifically enforced, when neither plan nor specifications have been under the consideration of the parties: Brace v. Wehnert, 27 L. J. Ch. 572; 4 Jur. N. S. 549. Specific performance will be decreed of land, though it appear that it is valuable only on account of the timber upon it; equity acting in such case merely on the ground of the subject being land: Kitchen v. Herring, 7 Ired. Eq. 190. In the recent case of Clayton v. Illingsworth, 10 Hare 451, however, specific performance of an agreement for a mere tenancy from year to year, was refused, because the breach was susceptible of compensation by damages.

[2] Webb v. Direc. London & Portsmouth R. R. Co., 1 De G., M. & Gord. 52; Bowles v. Woodson, 6 Gratt. (Va.) 78.

tract ; (b) if he has induced the defendant to execute a written agreement, on the faith of his verbal promise that it shall be subsequently altered; (c) or if after making a contract in writing, he has put an end to it by parol waiver,[1] although it is doubtful whether such a waiver would be good at law in respect of a contract affected by the Statute of Frauds.(d)[2]

(b) Cadman v. Horner, 18 Ves. 10 ; Clermont v. Tasburgh, 1 J. & W. 112 ; Brealey v. Collins, You. 317 ; 1 Sug. V. & P. 338 ; Nelthorpe v. Holgate, 1 Coll. 203.

(c) Clarke v. Grant, 14 Ves. 519 ; Omerod v. Hardman, 5 Id. 722 ; Att.-Gen. v. Jackson, 5 Hare 366.

(d) Goss v. Lord Nugent, 5 B. & Ad. 58 ; Robinson v. Page, 3 Russ. 114, 119 ; 1 Sug. V. & P. ciii, s. 9.

---

[1] Huffman v. Hummer, 3 Green (N. J.) 83 ; Ryno v. Darby, 20 N. J. Eq. 231.

[2] Where a contract is hard, and destitute of all equity, the court will leave the parties to their remedy at law ; and if such remedy has been lost by negligence, they must abide the consequences : King v. Hamilton, 4 Pet. 311 ; Western Railroad Corporation v. Babcock, 6 Met. 346 ; Perkins v. Wright, 3 Har. & McHen. 324 ; Leigh v. Crump, 1 Ired. Ch. 299 ; Hall v. Ross, 3 Heyw. 200 ; Rice v. Rawlings, Meigs 496 ; Eastland v. Vanarsdel, 3 Bibb 274 ; Wingart v. Fry, Wright 105 ; Edwards v. Handley, Hardin 602 ; Cannaday v. Shepard, 2 Jones Eq. 224 ; Bowen v. Waters, 2 Paine C. C. 1. And when one of the parties to a contract has been guilty of unfair conduct, in relation to the contract of which he seeks the specific performance, his bill will be dismissed, and he will be left to his legal remedy : Thompson v. Tod, Pet. C. C. 380 ; Frisby v. Ballance, 4 Scam. 287 ; Berry v. Cox, 8 Gill 466. So where the contract is unreasonable : McWhorter v. McMahan, 1 Clarke 400. And where it is entered into for the purpose of defrauding a creditor : St. John v. Benedict, 6 John. Ch. 111. Or was not originally honest and fair : Carberry v. Tennehill, 1 Har. & J. 224 ; Harris v. Smith, 2 Cold. (Tenn.) 306 ; Cuff v. Dorland, 55 Barb. (N. Y.) 481 ; McClellan v. Darrah, 50 Ill. 249 ; Wells v. Millett, 23 Wis. 64. But a mere increase of the value of the land subsequent to the contract, will not be a ground for refusing specific performance : Young v. Wright, 4 Wis. 144. The intoxication of a purchaser at the time of sale, will not be ground for refusing to enforce specific performance of the contract against him, unless it appear that his intoxication was produced or procured by the vendor, or that undue advantage was taken of it : Maxwell

In accordance with the same principle, it is held that where specific performance is asked of a contract for the purchase of real estate, the défendant may have the title examined by a master;[1] so that its validity may be sifted in a way which would not be possible on a mere abstract, authenticated as the vendor thinks proper, and that, in consideration of the relief sought beyond the law, he may have an assurance about the nature of his title, such as he cannot have elsewhere.(e)   If the investigation shows a reasonably clear and marketable title, specific performance will be compelled.   But if there be a rational doubt on its validity, the Court, though it may be of opinion that the title is good, will not compel the purchaser's acceptance, but will leave the parties to law.(f)[2]

(e) Jenkins v. Hiles, 6 Ves. 646, 653.

(f) Stapylton v. Scott, 16 Ves. 272; Jervoise v. Duke of Northumberland, 1 J. & W. 539, 549.

---

v. Pittenger, 2 Green Ch. 156; Rodman v. Zilley, Saxton 320; Whitesides v. Greenlee, 2 Dev. Ch. 152; Shaw v. Thackray, 17 Jur. 1045; 1 Sm. & Giff. 537; Morrison v. McLeod, 2 Dev. & Batt. Eq. 221; Harbison v. Lemon, 3 Blackf. 51; Belcher v. Belcher, 10 Yerg. 121; Crane v. Conklin, Saxt. Ch. 346; Calloway v. Witherspoon, 5 Ired. Eq. 128; contra, Prentice v. Achorn, 2 Paige 30.

[1] Where the court is satisfied on the hearing that there can be no fuller investigation of the title, and that all the facts are before the court, and is satisfied that objections exist to the title, which from their nature cannot be removed, it will not direct a reference to a master: Dominick v. Michael, 4 Sandf. S. C. 374.

[2] Butler c. O'Hear, 1 Dessaus. 382; Longworth v. Taylor, 1 McLean 395; Watts v. Waddle, 6 Pet. 389; Bates v. Delavan, 5 Paige Ch. 299; Winne v. Reynolds, 6 Id. 407; Dutch Church v. Mott, 7 Id. 77; Gans v. Renshaw, 2 Barr 34; Fitzpatrick v. Featherstone, 3 Ala. 40; Beckwith v. Kouns, 6 B. Monr. 222; Hepburn v. Auld, 5 Cranch 262, 275; Owings v. Baldwin, 8 Gill 337; Thompson v. Dulles, 5 Rich. Eq. 370; St. Mary's Church v. Stockton, 4 Halst. Ch. (N. J.) 520; Laurens v. Lucas, 6 Rich. Eq. 217; Lowry v. Muldrow, 8 Id. 241; Chambers v. Tulane, 1 Stockt. (N. J.) 146; Freetly v. Barnhart, 51 Penn. St. 279; Speakman v. Forepaugh, 44 Id. 363; Doebler's Appeal, 64 Id. 9; Littlefield v. Tinsley, 26

Specific performance may be refused where the defendant has by mistake, not originating in mere carelessness,

---

Tex. 353 ; Griffin *v.* Cunningham, 19 Gratt. (Va.) 571 ; Swain *v.* Fidelity
Ins. Co., 54 Penn. St. 455 ; Linkhouse *v.* Cooper, 2 W. Va. 67. For a discussion of doubtful title, see Mullings *v.* Trinder, 10 Eq. Cas. L. R. 449.
The cases in which courts of equity have refused their aid to the vendor,
where they have considered his title good, though disputable, are cases of
real and serious difficulty. Omissions in the judicial process through which
the title passed, which omissions could be supplied by amendment, by the
court in which the proceedings were had, will not be considered as sufficient: Dalzell *v.* Crawford, 1 Pars. Eq. 57. A purchaser will not be
compelled to accept a title depending upon an illegal sale, while it remains
open to revision at the discretion of a court of law : Young *v.* Rathbone, 1
Green (N. J.) 224.

If in the progress of a suit for specific performance of a real contract,
objections to a title are discovered, never made during the negotiations, the
defendant cannot insist on such objections as excusing him from performance, if the plaintiff is able and willing to remove them when first pointed
out: Dalzell *v.* Crawford, ut sup. In the same case it was laid down as
the doctrine of the court, that adverse opinions of conveyancers and counsel alone, are not sufficient ground to refuse a decree for specific performance of a contract for the purchase of land : Id. 37.

Perhaps the law was stated in Dalzell *v.* Crawford, rather more broadly
than in some other cases, and than was necessary for a decision on the
facts. It is certainly clear that a purchaser ought not to be forced into a
possible litigation, merely because the opinion of the court, which binds no
one but himself, happens to be in favor of the title. In a recent case in
England (Pyrke *v.* Waddingham, 10 Hare 1), a stricter rule was acted on.
The following propositions were deduced from a careful examination of
the authorities: A doubtful title, which a purchaser will not be compelled
to accept. is not only a title upon which the court entertains doubt, but includes also a title which, although the court has a favorable opinion of it,
yet may reasonably and fairly be questioned, in the opinion of other competent persons ; for the court has no means of binding the question as
against adverse claimants, or of indemnifying the purchaser, if its own
opinion in favor of the title should turn out not to be well founded. If
the doubts, as to a title, arise upon a question connected with the general
law, the court is to judge whether the general law on the point is or is not
settled ; and if it be not, or if the doubts as to the title may be affected by
extrinsic circumstances, which neither the purchaser nor the court can
satisfactorily investigate, specific performance will be refused.

The rules thus stated rest upon the fundamental principle, that every

*entered into a contract framed differently from his [*85] own intention; notwithstanding that there is no

---

purchaser is entitled to require a marketable title, and it is only an indubitable title that is a marketable one: Swayne *v.* Lyon, 67 Penn. St. 436. It is further the duty of the court on questions of title depending on the possibility of future rights arising, to consider the course which should be taken if the rights had actually arisen and were in course of litigation: Pyrke *v.* Waddingham, 10 Hare 1. See Sohier *v.* Williams, 1 Curtis C. C. 479. "To force a title on a purchaser," said the Vice-Chancellor in Rogers *v.* Waterhouse, 4 Drew. 329, "the opinion of the Court in favor thereof must be so clear that it cannot apprehend that another judge may form a different opinion." See also Pegler *v.* White, 33 Beav. 403; Howe *v.* Hunt, 31 Id. 420. A vendor may make an agreement for the sale of his title, such as it is, and this agreement will be specifically enforced: Hume *v.* Pocock, L. R. 1 Eq. 423–662; L. R. 1 Ch. App. 679.

Though equity will not compel a vendee to take a bad title, yet a pecuniary charge against a good title presents no objection, provided the purchaser can be protected against it: Tiernan *v.* Roland, 15 Penn. St. 441. See Cox *v.* Coventon, 31 Beav. 378; Wood *v.* Majoribanks, 3 De G. & J. 329; 7 H. L. Cas. 806. And the pendency of a suit for the land, which is found on investigation to be groundless, is no reason for refusing specific performance: Owings *v.* Baldwin, 8 Gill 337. When a proposed vendee buys in the reversion, and then refuses to complete the contract, he may be compelled to do so, with an allowance for what he has paid: Murrell *v.* Goodyear, 1 De G., F. & J. 432.

A court of equity will decree a specific performance of a contract for the sale of lands, if the vendor is able to make a good title at any time before the decree is pronounced: Hepburn *v.* Dunlop, 1 Wheat. 179; Baldwin *v.* Salter, 8 Paige 473; Hepburn *v.* Auld, ubi supra; Graham *v.* Hackwith, 1 Marsh. 423; Tyree *v.* Williams, 3 Bibb 366; Seymour *v.* Delancy, 3 Cowen 445; Moss *v.* Hanson, 17 Penn. St. 379; Tiernan *v.* Roland, 15 Id. 429; Richmond *v.* Gray, 3 Allen 25; Luckett *v.* Williamson, 37 Mo. 388. And where a vendor of land cannot make a valid title to the whole land sold, the vendee may insist upon the specific performance by the vendor, so far as such vendor can execute it: Jacobs *v.* Locke, 2 Ired. Ch. 286; Henry *v.* Liles, Id. 407; Ketchum *v.* Stout, 20 Ohio 453; Collins *v.* Smith, 1 Head 251. The court will order a return of the deposit money with interest, where the vendor cannot show a good title, and will give the vendee a lien on the estate for the same and for costs: Turner *v.* Marriott, 3 Eq. L. R. 744.

When the performance of a contract of purchase is resisted upon grounds wholly independent of the validity of the title, and the objections of the

unfairness on the plaintiff's part, and no defect or doubt
in his title;(*g*) and even the mere fact that the contract
is a hard one, and would press heavily on the defendant,
has in some cases been considered a ground for refusing
to interfere.(*h*)[1]

(*g*) Clowes *v.* Higginson, 1 Ves. & B. 524; commented on in 1 Sug. V.
& P. 228; Townsend *v.* Stangroom, 6 Ves. 328; Mallins *v.* Freeman, 2 K.
25; Kennedy *v.* Lee, 3 Meriv. 441.

(*k*) Wedgwood *v.* Adams, 6 Bea. 600; Talbot *v.* Ford, 13 Sim. 173;
Pickering *v.* Ely, 2 N. C. C. 249, 266.

---

purchasers are overruled; or when the purchaser, although doubtful of the
title, consents by his answer to accept it when in the judgment of the court it
can be rendered valid, it is sufficient to warrant a decree for a specific performance that a good title can be made within a reasonable time, before
the final decree. But when it appears that the purchaser rejected the
title offered, as insufficient, and upon that ground refused and still refuses
to complete the contract, the entire controversy turns upon the validity of
the objections, and if they are sufficient, the court will not decree a specific
performance: Dominick *v.* Michael. 4 Sandf. (S. C.) 374. When objections to the title must be taken, see Lyle *v.* Yarborough, John. 70.

[1] James *v.* State Bank, 17 Alab. 69; King *v.* Hamilton, 4 Peters 311;
Bradbury *v.* White, 4 Greenl. 391; Yancy *v.* Green, 6 Dana 444; Orear *v.*
Tanner, 1 Bibb 237; Frisby *v.* Ballance, 4 Scam. 287; Western Railroad
Company *v.* Babcock, 6 Met. 346; Morss *v.* Elmendorf, 11 Paige 277;
Coles et. al., Ex'rs., *v.* Bowne, 10 Id. 526; Schmidt *v.* Livingston, 3 Edw.
Ch. 213; Helling *v.* Lumley, 5 Jur. N. S. 301; where the defendant
was compelled to perform his contract, although the performance might
occasion a forfeiture of this lease.

But where a mistake is a matter deemed perfectly immaterial by both
parties at the time of the contract, which would not have varied it if it had
been known, and of which both parties were equally ignorant, and where
the contract is an advantageous one to the purchaser, *quære*, whether a
Court of equity should interfere: McFerran *v.* Taylor, 3 Cranch 270. And
a Court of equity will carry into effect the original intention of the parties
when defectively expressed in an instrument through fraud or mistake:
Hunt *v.* Freeman, 1 Ham. 490. For the principle in which the court proceeds in cases of mistake, see Swaisland *v.* Dearsley, 29 Beav. 430. It has
been held in several cases in the United States, that a bill will lie to correct an agreement as to lands, for mistake, upon parol evidence, and for

In applying the equity of specific performance to real estate, there are some modifications of legal rules, which at first sight appear inconsistent with them, and repugnant to the maxim, that "equity follows the law." The modifications here referred to are those of enforcing parol contracts relating to land, on the ground that they have been already performed in part; of allowing time to make out a title beyond the day which the contract specifies; and of allowing a conveyance with compensation for defects. The wisdom of permitting any deviation is a subject admitting of much doubt. But the particular doctrines now in question are firmly established by the course of

---

specific performance of the agreement as corrected; or, on the other hand, that the defendant in a bill for specific performance, may by his answer set up mistake, and entitle himself to specific performance of the reformed agreement, against the claim of the complainant to have his bill dismissed notwithstanding the Statute of Frauds: Wall v. Arrington, 13 Geo. 88 · Mosby v. Wall, 1 Cushm. (Miss.) 81: Philpott v. Elliott, 4 Md. Ch. 273; Moale v. Buchanan, 11 Gill & John. 325; Tilton v. Tilton, 9 N. H. 385; Bellows v. Stone, 14 Id. 175; Bradford v. Union Bank, 13 How. U. S. 57; Gillespie v. Moon, 2 John. Ch. 585; Keisselbrock v. Livingstone, 4 John. Ch. 144. And this doctrine is strongly approved by Judge Story, Eq. Jur. §§ 160, 161, &c. But in other American cases, as Elder v. Elder, 10 Maine 80; Osborn v. Phelps, 19 Conn. 63; Westbrook v. Habeson, 2 McCord Ch. 112; Brooks v. Wheelock, 11 Pick. 439; Miller v. Chetwood, 1 Green. Ch. 199; Dennis v. Dennis, 4 Rich. Eq. 307; Best v. Stow. 2 Sandf. Ch. 298; Climer v. Hovey, 15 Mich. 18; and in England, Woollam v. Hearn, 7 Ves. Jr. 211; Nurse v. Lord Seymour, 13 Beav. 254, it is held that though in such cases mistake is good ground for refusing specific performance, that being within the discretion of a chancellor, it cannot furnish a reason for active relief by the execution of the agreement, in the face of the Statute of Frauds. For, it is obvious that if any part of the agreement remain in parol, the whole must be so, to all intents and purposes. This view is supported also by Judge Hare, in the able note to Woollam v. Hearn, 2 Lead. Cases Eq., part i., 404. Where, however, the agreement is executed by part performance, it is agreed on all hands, that in this, as in other cases, the question is no longer governed by the statute: Ibid. See, Gilroy v. Alis, 22 Iowa 174.

precedent, and may perhaps be considered, not so much deviations from the rule of law, as subordinate equities, or developements from the original doctrine, that specific performance of a contract, and not pecuniary compensation for its breach, is the equitable measure of redress.

The first of these subordinate equities is that of enforcing parol contracts relating to land, on the ground that they have been already performed in part. It is enacted by the Statute of Frauds, that no action shall be brought on any contract for sale of lands, tenements, or hereditaments; or any interest in or concerning them, unless the agreement or some memorandum or note thereof shall be in writing and signed by the party to be charged therewith, or some other person thereunto by him lawfully [*86] *authorized.(*i*)[1] If the requirements of this statute are not complied with, a contract falling within its scope, so long as it remains *in fieri* cannot be enforced either at law or in equity. It sometimes, however, happens that a contract which is still *in fieri*, at law, has been already performed by construction of equity; for if it is one of which specific performance would be decreed, it is itself in some sort an equitable title; and if the parties have clothed that title with possession, or have otherwise acted on it as an existing ownership, they are held to have perfected their agreement in equity; and if the terms of their parol contract can be proved, may be decreed to perfect it by a conveyance at law.[2]

(*i*) 29 Car. 2, c. 3, s. 4.

---

[1] It is not necessary that the party seeking specific performance should have signed the agreement: Old Colony R. R. *v.* Evans, 6 Gray 25.

[2] In nearly every state in the Union, the rule is settled, that part performance takes a parol agreement out of the Statute of Frauds. Newton *v.*

The doctrine on this point is called the doctrine of part performance, and its principle appears to be that, if one of

---

Swazey, 8 N. H. 9; Downey v. Hotchkiss, 2 Day 225; Annan v. Merritt, 13 Conn. 478; Pugh v. Good, 3 W. & S. 56; Harris v. Knickerbacker, 5 Wend. 638; Parkhurst v. Van Cortland, 14 Johns. 15; Hall & Wife v. Hall et al., 1 Gill 383; Tilton v. Tilton, 9 N. II. 386; Wilde v. Fox, 1 Rand. 165; Gough v. Crane, 3 Md. Ch. 119; Johnson v. McGruder, 15 Miss. 365; Stoddart v. Tuck, 5 Md. 18; Dougan v. Blocher, 24 Penn. St. 28; McCue v. Johnston, 25 Penn. St. 306; Printup v. Mitchell, 17 Geo. 558; Offenhouse v. Burleson, 11 Texas 87; Parke v. Seewright, 20 Miss. 85; Despain v. Carter. 21 Id. 331; Arguello v. Edinger, 10 Cal. 150; and see the rules upon this subject stated in Purcell v. Miner, 4 Wall. S. C. 513; Chastain v. Smith, 30 Geo. 96. Though the agreement must be clearly and unequivocally proved: Charnley v. Hansbury, 13 Penn. St. 16; Owings v. Baldwin, 8 Gill. 337; Bracken v. Hambrick, 25 Texas 408; Broughton v. Coffer, 18 Gratt. (Va.) 184; Knoll v. Harvey, 19 Wis. 99; and must be shown distinctly to be referable exclusively to the contract set up in the bill: Duvall v. Myers, 2 Md. Ch. 401; Eyre v. Eyre, 4 Green (N. J.) 102; Patrick v. Horton, 3 W. Va. 23; and the remedy must be mutual: Smith v. McVeigh, 3 Stockt. 239; Meason v. Kaine, 63 Penn. St. 335; see also Van Doren v. Robinson, 1 Green (N. J.) 256.

But in some of the states, as in Tennessee, North Carolina, Massachusetts and Maine, the general rule is different. See Patton v. McClure, 1 Mart. & Yerg. 333; Ridley v. McNairy et al., 2 Humph. 174; Stearns v. Hubbard, 8 Greenl. 320; Parker v. Parker, 1 Gray 409; Wilton v. Harwood, 23 Maine 131; Patterson v. Yeaton, 47 Maine 308; Robeson v. Hornbaker, 2 Green. Ch. 60; Brooks v. Wheelock, 11 Pick. 439; Wingate v. Dail, 2 Har. & J. 76; Ellis v. Ellis, 1 Dev. Eq. 341; Albea v. Griffin, 2 Dev. & Bat. Eq. 9; Dunn v. Moore, 3 Ired. Eq. 364; Allen v. Chambers, 4 Id. 125. If, however, the statute is set up, the money will be decreed to be refunded with interest, and as against the vendors, it will be decreed a lien on the land agreed to be conveyed: Hilton v. Duncan, 1 Cold. (Tenn.) 313.

Payment or part payment of the purchase-money, is not such a part performance of a parol contract, as will take the case out of the Statute of Frauds: Parker v. Wills, 6 Wharton 153; Jackson v. Cutright, 5 Munf. 308; Haight v. Child, 34 Barb. 186; Hatcher v. Hatcher, 1 McMullan's Ch. 311; Smith v. Smith, 1 Rich. Ch. 130; Anderson v. Chick, 1 Bailey Ch. 118; Hood v. Bowman, 1 Freem. Ch. 290; Bean v. Valle, 2 Miss. 126; Johnston v. Glancy, 4 Blackf. 94; Sites v. Keller, 6 Ham. 483; contra, Townsend v. Houston, 1 Harring. 532; McMurtrie v. Bennett, Harring. Ch. 124. But where a party who has paid the purchase-money upon a

the contracting parties induce the other so to act, that, if
the contract be abandoned, he cannot be restored to his

---

parol contract, cannot be replaced in the same position by a recovery of
the money paid, he will be entitled to specific performance: Malins v.
Brown, 4 Comst. 403. See Nunn v. Fabian, L. R. 1 Ch. Ap. 35.

When a parol contract is entered into in consideration of marriage, the
solemnization of the marriage is not such a part performance as will take
the case out of the Statute: Caton v. Caton, L. R. 1 Ch. Ap. 137. Part
performance by the party sought to be charged does not take the case out
of the statute: Id.

The part performance of a parol agreement to devise lands will take the
case out of the statute: Davison v. Davison, 2 Beas. 246; Johnson v. Hubbell, 2 Stockt. 332; Watson v. Mahan, 20 Ind. 223.

. And where the purchaser has taken possession, paid the purchase-money,
and made improvements thereon, equity will enforce a specific performance: Casler v. Thompson, 3 Green Ch. 59; Wetmore v. White, 2 Cal. Ca.
87; Ellis v. Ellis, 1 Dev. Ch. 180 (contra, s. v. 341); Smith v. Smith, 1
Rich. Ch. 130; Massey v. McIlwain, 2 Hill Ch. 421; Cox v. Cox, Peck 443;
see also Johnston v. Glancy, 4 Blackf. 94; Tibbs v. Barker, 1 Blackf. 58;
Moreland v. Lemasters, 4 Id. 383; Brewer v. Brewer, 19 Ala. 481;
School Dist. No. 3 v. MacLoon, 4 Wis. 79; Ramsey v. Liston, 25 Ill. 114;
Stevens v. Wheeler, Id. 300; Neatherly v. Ripley, 21 Tex. 434; Mims v.
Lockett, 33 Ga. 9; Perkins v. Hadsell, 50 Ill. 216; Howe v. Rogers, 32
Tex. 218; Freeman v. Freeman, 43 N. Y. 34. Such improvements must be
of a permanent, nature, or of great value: Peckham v. Barker, 8 R. I. 17.

So it is a sufficient part performance to take the case out of the Statute
of Frauds for the purchaser to take possession of the lands sold by virtue
of the agreement, where the assent of the vendor is shown, or is inferable:
Smith v. Underdunk, 1 Sandf. Ch. 579; Pugh v. Good, 3 W. & S. 56;
Moale v. Buchanan, 11 Gill & J. 314; Hart v. Hart, 3 Dessaus. 592; Anderson v. Chick, 1 Bailey Ch. 118; Brock v. Cook, 3 Porter 464; Wagoner
v. Speck, 3 Ham. 292; Palmer v. Richardson, 3 Strobh. Eq. 16.

But it has been held that delivery of possession of a part of the land is
not sufficient: Allen's Est., 1 W. & S. 383; or where the party going into
possession made temporary improvements much less in value than the
rent of the premises: Wack v. Sorber, 2 Wharton 387; see also Mims v.
Lockett, 33 Ga. 9; neither is the remaining in possession of the purchaser,
if he was in possession at the time of the purchase: Hatcher v. Hatcher,
1 McMullan Ch. 311; Johnston v. Glancy, 4 Blackf. 94; Christy v. Barnhart, 14 Penn. St. 260; Mahana v. Blunt, 20 Iowa 142. The part performance must be such as would make the party asking the specific relief
a wrongdoer in case the specific performance were not decreed. And de-

former position, the contract must be considered as perfected in equity, and a refusal to complete it at law is in
the nature of a fraud.[1] Such, for instance, is the case,
where upon a parol agreement for the purchase of an
estate, a party, not otherwise entitled to the possession,
is admitted thereto; for if the agreement be invalid, he
is made a trespasser, and is liable to answer as a trespasser at law. The equity is still stronger if, after being
let into possession, he has been allowed to build and otherwise to expend money on the estate. If the possession
may be referred to an independent title, e. g., where it is
held under a previously existing tenancy, the same principle does not apply, unless the parties so conduct them-

---

livery of possession must have been in pursuance and part execution of
the agreement charged in the bill: Ham v. Goodrich, 33 N. H. 32.

Continuance of a previous possession may be a part performance: Blanchard v. McDougal, 6 Wis. 167; Spalding v. Conzelman, 30 Missouri 177.
See however Mahance v. Blunt, *supra*. Where a *vendor* files a bill for
specific performance, part performance by the *vendee* cannot be used to
take the case out of the statute: Luckett v. Williamson, 37 Mo. 388.

For other general instances of part performance, see Phillips v. Edwards,
33 Beav. 440; Pain v. Coombs, 1 De G. & J. 34; Rankin v. Lay, 2 De G.
F. &. J. 72; Daniels v. Lewis, 16 Wis. 140; Peckham v. Barker, 8 R. I.
17; Welsh v. Bayard, 21 N. J. Eq. 186; Richmond v. Foote, 3 Lans. (N. Y.)
244; Mason v. Blair, 33 Ill. 194; Hedrick v. Hern, 4 W. Va. 620.

The rule has recently been stated to be in Pennsylvania, that every parol
contract is within the Statute of Frauds, except where there has been such
performance *as cannot be compensated in damages.* "Without possession
taken and maintained under the contract, there can be no pretence of part
performance; but generally," say the Court, "that is an act which admits
of compensation, and therefore too much is made of it when it is treated
as sufficient ground for decreeing specific performance:" Moore v. Small,
19 Penn. St. 461. Proof of a parol contract for the sale of lands, delivery
of possession pursuant thereto, part payment of the purchase-money and
valuable improvements, are the full measure of what is required to take a
case out of the statute: Milliken v. Dravo, 67 Penn. St. 230.

[1] Gilbert v. The Trustees of the East Newark Co., 1 Beas. 180; Arguello
v. Edinger, 10 Cal. 150; Paine v. Wilcox, 16 Wis. 202.

selves, as to show that they are acting under the contract, nor does it apply to any acts which do not alter the position of the parties. Such, for instance, are the taking of surveys, the preparation of conveyances, the payment of earnest, and even the payment of purchase-money itself; for, although all these acts are in some sense a perform ance of the contract, yet their consequences may be set [*87] right by *damages at law, and they do not place the parties in a position from which they can only be extricated by its completion.$(k)^1$

The same principle which establishes a parol contract where the title under it is sustained by part performance, is also applicable where the purchaser of real estate has waived by his conduct any objection of title.[2] The general rule is, that a contract for the purchase of realty implies as one of its terms that a title shall be shown. And if

---

(k) Mitf. 266; 1 Sug. V. & P. c. iii, s. 7; Wills v. Stradling, 3 Ves. 378; Cooth v. Jackson, 6 Id. 12; Clinan v. Cooke, 1 Sch. & L. 22, 41; Sutherland v. Briggs, 1 Hare 26; Dale v. Hamilton, 5 Id. 369, 381; Mundy v. Joliffe, 5 M. & C. 167.

---

[1] A written agreement will be specifically enforced in equity, according to its terms, although verbally another provision had been agreed to at the same time, though not inserted in the agreement, if the person who is to perform the omitted term consents to its performance: Martin v. Pycroft, 2 De G., M. & G. 785.

[2] And there is a settled distinction between the case of a vendor, coming into a Court of equity to compel a vendee to performance, and of a vendee resorting to equity to compel a vendor to perform. In the first case, if the vendor cannot make out a title as to part of subject-matter of the contract, equity will not compel the vendee to perform the contract *pro tanto*. But where a vendee seeks a specific execution of an agreement, there is much greater reason for affording him the aid of the court, where he is desirous of taking the part to which a title can be made: Waters v. Travis, on appeal, 9 Johns. 450. See S. E. Railway v. Knoll, 10 Hare 122; Hopper v. Hopper, 1 Green (N. J.) 147.

there be no waiver of this right in the contract, it cannot be afterwards waived at law by parol, for such waiver would in effect create a new contract to be proved partly by the written agreement and partly by the subsequent parol waiver.(l) In equity, however, the purchaser may accept the defective title, and by treating the contract as already performed, may preclude himself from insisting on any further title. He may, for instance, thus bind himself by taking possession and doing acts of ownership after he is aware that objections exist, where such possession and acts of ownership are not authorized by his contract; or he may do so by simple acquiescence.[1] The waiver, however, must be intentional; and his conduct is merely evidence from which the intention may be presumed. If, therefore, there be a subsequent treaty respecting objections, the presumption of waiver is at an end.(m) And even if he has waived his right to call for a title, yet if the title be proved bad, he is not compelled to accept it, unless he has expressly contracted to take such title as the vendor has.(n)

The second equity is that of allowing time to make out *a title beyond the day which the contract speci- [*88] fies. It is an obvious principle, both of law and of equity, that no one can have a contract enforced in his

(l) Goss v. Lord Nugent, 5 B. & Ad. 58.

(m) Knatchbull v. Grueber, 1 Mad. 153, 170; Burroughs v. Oakley, 3 Sw. 159; Calcraft v. Roebuck, 1 Ves. J. 221; Osborne v. Harvey, 1 N. C. C. 116; 2 Sug. V. & P. c. viii, s. 1.

(n) Warren v. Richardson, You. 1; Blachford v. Kirkpatrick, 6 Bea. 232; Duke v. Barnett, 2 Coll. 337.

---

[1] Palmer v. Richardson, 3 Strob. Eq. 16. If the vendee wishes to rescind the contract, he must give up possession, or do some other act indicating his intention: Thompkins v. Hyatt, 28 N. Y. 347; Mullin v. Bloomer, 11 Iowa 360.

favor, unless he has performed, or is ready to perform, his own part. And it would apparently follow from this principle that, if the seller of an estate has contracted to show a title by a specified day, and has failed to do so, he cannot afterwards enforce his contract. This conclusion is accurate with respect to proceedings at law, but is modified in equity by the doctrine already noticed, that the·contract itself is in the nature of a title. And it is accordingly held that if a substantial ownership exists, though the title be not fully cleared on the appointed day, specific performance may be decreed; and the Court may rectify the incidental delay by giving the intermediate rents to the purchaser, and interest on the purchase-money to the vendor.

The doctrine on this point is expressed by the maxim that "time is not of the essence of a contract in equity."[1]

It is not, however, to be understood from this maxim that time cannot be made of the essence of the contract. The mere fact that a day has been specified for completion, will not *per se* render it essential. But the parties may contract on what terms they will, and may declare, if they think fit, that it shall be so considered. The same conclusion may be drawn by implication from the nature of the property to which the contract refers; as, for instance, if it be property in reversion, or if it be required for the purposes of a trade or manufactory, or be of a fluctuating value. If time is not originally declared essential, it cannot be made so by either party alone. But if delay takes place, the aggrieved party may give

---

[1] Remington *v.* Irwin, 14 Penn. St. 143; Bryson *v.* Peak, 8 Ired. Eq. 310; Glover *v.* Fisher, 11 Ill. 666; Tiernan *v.* Roland, 15 Penn. St. 429; Parkin *v.* Thorold, 16 Jur. 959; Pegg *v.* Wisden, 16 Beav. 246; Roberts *v.* Denny, 3 De G., M. & G. 284; Emmons *v.* Kiger, 23 Ind. 483.

notice that he abandons the contract, and if the other
makes no prompt assertion of his right, he will be cousidered as acquiescing in such notice, and as abandoning
his equity for specific performance.(*o.*)[1]

(*o*) Walker *v.* Jeffreys, 1 Hare 341, 348 ; King *v.* Wilson, 6 Bea. 124 ;
'1 Sug. V. & P. c. v.

---

[1] Time is not generally of the essence of the contract, but where it ap-
pears that time is really material to the parties, the right to a specific performance may depend on it: Garnett *v.* Macon, 2 Brock. 185 ; s. c. 6 Call.
308 ; Garretson *v.* Vanloon, 2 Iowa 128 ; Armstrong *v.* Pierson, 5 Clarke
(Ia.) 317 ; Scarlett *v.* Hunter, 3 Jon. Eq. 84 ; Morris *v.* Hoyt, 11 Mich. 9 ;
Du Bois *v.* Baum, 46 Penn. St. 537 ; Edwards *v.* Atkinson, 14 Texas 373 ;
Keller *v.* Fisher, 7 Ind. 718 ; Potter *v.* Tuttle, 22 Conn. 513 ; Wells *v.*
Maxwell, 32 Beav. 408 ; Morgan *v.* Scott, 26 Penn. St. 55 ; Hanna *v.* Rate-
kin, 43 Ill. 462 ; Andrews *v.* Bell, 56 Penn. St. 343 ; Miller *v.* Henlan, 51
Id. 265 ; Spaulding *v.* Alexander, 6 Bush (Ky.) 160. And where by lapse
of time the value of the property is greatly diminished, performance will
not be compelled : McKay *v.* Carrington, 1 McLean 50. So where the
vendee has purchased to sell, time is of the essence of the contract: Id.
See also, Benedict *v.* Lynch, 1 John. Ch. 370 ; Jackson *v.* Ligon, 3 Leigh
161. But see Brashier *v.* Gratz, 6 Wheaton 528 ; Bank of Columbia *v.*
Hagner, 1 Pet. 465 ; Hepburn *v.* Auld, 5 Cranch 262 ; where in the Supreme
Court of the United States, it was held, that time is not of the essence of
a contract of sale ; and a failure on the part of vendor or purchaser on a
stipulated day, does not of itself deprive him of the right to a specific
performance when he is able to comply with his part of the agreement.
Though in Goldsmith *v.* Guild, 10 Allen 239, the Court seemed to think
that in this country time should be made the essence of the contract. See
also, Macbryde *v.* Weekes, 22 Beav. 533. Mistake may sometimes prevent
time from becoming of the essence when it otherwise would : Todd *v.* Taft,
7· Allen 371. Very great delay, *e. g.*, twenty one years, will not be excused :
Green *v.* Covilland, 10 Cal. 317. See also, Francis *v.* Love,3 Jon. Eq.
321 ; Stretch *v.* Schenck, 23 Ind. 77. Time may be always made material
by either party if he choose. Either may demand performance on the
stipulated day, and if the other do not then comply, may elect to rescind,
which rescission will free him from the obligations of the contract in
law and equity: Dominick *v.* Michael, 4 Sandf. S. C. 374; Patchin *r.*
Lamborn, 31 Penn. St. 314; Ives *v.* Armstrong, 5 R. I. 567; Stow *r.*
Russell, 36 Ill. 18; Heckard *v.* Sayre, 34 Id. 142; King *v.* Ruckman,
20 N. J. Eq. 316. A reasonable time must, however, be given on a
demand for performance: Parkin *v.* Thorold, 16 Jurist 959. Time also

[*89]   *In the absence of any special matter, a wide liberty as to time is given to the vendor. He is permitted to make out his title after the commencement of a suit, or at any time before the making of a final decree, subject, however, to a liability for costs, where the title has not been shown before litigation began.(p) And in some cases where a person, being owner of a portion only of the estate, or having but a limited interest therein, has *bonâ fide* contracted for a sale of the whole, he has been allowed time to obtain a title to the rest, or to extend his interest into a fee.(q)

It has been sometimes attempted to extend the maxim, that "time is not of the essence of a contract," to cases where covenants have been contained in a lease that the lessor will renew, on request, within a specified time, and the lessee has failed in making the request. In cases of this kind, if the delay has been occasioned by unavoidable accident or misfortune, which has disabled the lessee from applying at the stated time, it seems that he may have relief in equity. But unless there be some special

(p) Townsend *v.* Champernowne, 3 Y. & C. 505; Scoones *v.* Morrell, 1 Bea. 251.

(q) Esdaile *v.* Stephenson, 2 Sug. V. & P. 30; Chamberlain *v.* Lee, 10 Sim. 444; Salisbury *v.* Hatcher, 2 N. C. C. 54.

---

becomes material, in connection with an important change in value, or circumstances: Southern Life Ins , &c., Co. *v.* Cole, 4 Florida 359. Or where there are not mutual remedies: Westerman *v.* Means, 12 Penn. St. 97. So, an alteration in the situation of the parties will be taken into consideration: Waters *v.* Howard, 8 Gill 262. So, time is material on an agreement for the leasing of a house, or surety for the rent being procured before a day fixed: Mitchell *v.* Wilson, 4 Edw. Ch. 697. So also, where by the original agreement a re-sale may be made if the vendor does not comply within a fixed period: Bodine *v.* Glading, 21 Penn. St. 50; Magoffin *v.* Holt, 1 Duvall (Ky.) 95. But if time is to be considered of the essence of a contract, the point must be made promptly: Monro *v.* Taylor, 8 Hare 62; Price *v.* Griffith, 1 De G., M. & G. 80.

circumstances of excuse, a specific performance will not be decreed; for the contract is, that the question of renewal or non-renewal shall be determined at the time appointed, and if the lessee were relievable, notwithstanding the delay, the effect would be to bind the lessor, and to leave himself unbound.(r)

The third equity is that of allowing a conveyance with compensation for defects where a contract has been made for sale of an estate, which cannot be literally performed *in toto*, whether by reason of an unexpected failure in the title to part, of inaccuracy in the terms of description or of diminution in value by liability to a charge. It is not unusual to provide against these contingencies by a *condition that misdescriptions and errors shall [*90] not vitiate the sale, but that a compensation shall be given for the difference in value. But, unless there be such a condition, the contract cannot be partially enforced at law; for a Court of law has no adequate machinery by which it may investigate the several points of variance, and determine how far they affect the essence of the contract, and how far they may be remedied by compensation. The vendor, therefore, cannot at law recover part of the purchase-money, if unable to convey the entire property, nor can the purchaser insist on paying a part only in respect of a partial failure in the sale.(s) In equity, on the other hand, there is no difficulty in making the requisite investigation; and therefore, on a bill for specific performance, inquiry will be made whether the property can be either literally or substantially transferred. If a substantial transfer can be made, it has been considered

(r) Bayley v. Corporation of Leominster, 3 B. C. C. 529; City of London v. Mitford, 14 Ves. 41; Harries v. Bryant, 4 Russ. 89.
(s) Johnson v. Johnson, 3 B. & P. 162.

against conscience to take advantage of small circumstances of variation.[1]

In such a case, therefore, where the mistake made has
been *bonâ fide*, and not material to the purchaser's enjoyment, the vendor may insist on performance with compensation.[2] But it must be clear that the defect is not
substantial, for a purchaser cannot be required against his
will to pay for anything but what he has bought. He is
not, for example, compellable to accept a lease instead of

---

[1] But where there is a great deficiency in the quantity of land the Court
will not, in the absence of fraud, compel the vendor to complete the sale,
making a deduction in the price for the deficiency: Rugge v. Ellis, 1 Dessaus.
160. A deficiency of 171 acres out of 662 is not such a deterioration as
will entitle the purchaser to have a contract rescinded, notice being given
at the sale that a claim existed, and that if it succeeded a proportional deduction would be made: Wainwright v. Read, 1 Dessaus. 573. See also
Cordingley v. Cheesebrough, 3 Giff. 496.

[2] Hepburn v. Auld, 5 Cranch 262; Evans v. Kingsberry, 2 Rand. 120;
Rankin v. Maxwell, 2 A. K. Marsh. 488; King v. Bardeau, 6 John. Ch.
38; Wiswall v. McGowan, 1 Hoff. Ch. 125; Harbers v. Gadsden, 6 Rich.
Eq. 284. Damages may in some cases also be decreed: Wiswall v. Mc-
Gowan, ubi supra; Slaughter v. Tindle, 1 Lit. 358; Fisher v. Kay, 2 Bibb
434; Wright v. Young, 6 Wis. 127. And the rule of compensation on a
bill for a specific performance, where a conveyance cannot be enforced, is
the value of the land at the time the contract should have been performed:
Dustin v. Newcome, 8 Ham. 49. See, on this subject, note to Seton v.
Slade, 2 Lead. Cas. Eq., p. ii. 33. Compensation in money, however, is not
always proper; thus, on a bill for specific performance of an agreement for
a partition of coal mines owned in common by complainant and defendant,
and for an account of coal already taken out, it was held that the most
equitable mode of partition was, that coal should be assigned to the complainant, in order to make up his full share, regard being had to quantity
and quality, and to accessability and convenience in mining, with reference
to all the parties interested, instead of decreeing the value in money of the
coal taken out and sold: Young v. Frost, 1 Md. 377; King v. Ruckman,
20 N. J. Eq. 316. See also Coleman's Appeal, 62 Penn. St. 252.

In Pennsylvania it is competent for a jury, on principles of equity, to
find conditional damages, to be released on specific performance of a contract: Decamp v. Feay, 5 S. & R. 322; Hauberger v. Root, 5 Penn. St. 112.

an underlease; a copyhold instead of a freehold; a life estate instead of a fee; an estate of reversion instead of one in possession; nor to take a part only of the estate contracted for, whether the other part is a large portion of the entire subject-matter, or is in its nature material to the enjoyment of the rest. (t)

In favor of the purchaser the equity is of wider application, and the rule is that, although he cannot have a partial interest forced upon him, yet if he entered into the contract *in ignorance of the vendor's inca- [*91] pacity to give him the whole and chooses afterwards to take as much as he can get, he has generally, though not universally, a right to insist on that, with compensation for the defect. (u)[1]

In both cases alike, whether the claim be made by the vendor or the purchaser, the defect must be one admitting

(t) Stewart v. Alliston, 1 Meriv. 26; Knatchbull v. Grueber, 1 Mad. 153; 1 Sug. V. & P. c. vii; [Tiernan v. Roland, 15 Penn. St. 429.]

(u) Thomas v. Dering, 1 K. 729; Wheatley v. Slade. 4 Sim. 126; Graham v. Oliver, 3 Bea. 124; Nelthorpe v. Holgate, 1 Coll. 103.

---

[1] Waters v. Travis, 9 Johns. 464; Erwin v. Myers, 46 Penn. St. 96–107; Collins v. Smith, 1 Head 251. Where a purchaser of land, who, on faith of a parol contract, has entered into possession and has made valuable improvements, but, on bill filed, fails to make out such a case as would entitle him to relief, the bill may be retained for the purpose of allowing him compensation, if he have not a full and adequate remedy at law: Aday v. Echols, 18 Ala. 353; Rockwell v. Lawrence, 2 Halst. Ch. 190. In such case the land should be charged as against the vendor and his representatives for the amount of compensation found to be due, unless there be some circumstances which would make this improper. The insolvency of the vendor's estate, he being dead, is not a sufficient reason for refusing so to charge it: Aday v. Echols, ut supra. On the death of a vendor, and bill for specific performance by vendee, the dower right of the widow is to be compensated for, not by the deduction of a gross sum on its estimated value, but one-third of the purchase-money is to be retained till the death of the dowress, without interest, secured by a lien on the land: Springle v. Shields, 17 Ala. 295.

of compensation, and not a mere matter of arbitrary
damages.(*v*)   And the compensation given must be really
compensation for a present loss, and not indemnity against
a future risk.   For the offer to give such indemnity is in
truth merely an offer of a defective title, with pecuniary
compensation in the event of its failure.   In some cases
where an estate has been liable to a contingent charge, a
purchaser has been compelled to accept the title with a
security protecting him against the charge.[1]   But it has
been doubted whether the doctrine of these cases is sound,
and whether in the absence of an express contract, the
Court ought to compel either a vendor to give or a purchaser to accept an indemnity.(*w*)[2]

A corresponding relief to that by specific performance
is given, even in the absence of a contract, in the case of
title deeds or specific chattels of peculiar value detained
from the legitimate owner, by directing them to be delivered up or secured.[3]

The remedies at law for such unlawful detainer are by

(*v*) White *v.* Cuddon, 8 Cl. & F. 766, 792 ; Lord Brooke *v.* Rounthwaite,
5 Hare 298.

(*w*) Fildes *v.* Hooker, 3 Mad. 193 ; Aylett *v.* Ashton, 1 M. & C. 105, 114
2 Surg. V. & P. c. x, s. 2.

---

[1] See Tiernan *v.* Roland, 15 Penn. St. 441.

[2] A Court of Chancery will not decree compensation as a distinct head
of equitable relief ; but when the jurisdiction of the Court has once
attached by reason of mistake, part-performance, or other equitable ground
of relief, and the vendor has rendered specific performance impossible,
compensation will be decreed. See Denton *v.* Stewart, 1 Cox Ch. 258 ;
Andrews *v.* Brown, 3 Cush. 134 ; Harrison *v.* Deramus, 33 Ala. 463 ; Bell
v. Thompson, 34 Id. 633 ; Lee *v.* Howe, 27 Missouri 521 ; Smith *v.* Fly, 24
Tex. 345 ; Phillips *v.* Thompson, 1 John. Ch. 149 ; Parkhurst *v.* Van Cortland, Id. 273 ; Scott *v.* Bilgerry, 40 Miss 119. See, however, Sainsbury *v.*
Jones, 5 Myl. & Cr. 1 ; Todd *v.* Gee, 17 Ves. 278·

See McGowin *v.* Remington, 12 Penn. St. 56 ; Pooley *v.* Budd, 14
Beav. 34.

an action of trespass for the unlawful taking, by trover for the unlawful conversion to the defendant's use, or by detinue for the actual detainer. In the two former actions, the judgment at law is for damages only; in the third the judgment is for restoration of the deed or chattel, if it can be found, or for the value, if it has been destroyed or eloigned. The remedy, however, though in terms specific, *is inferior to that by suit in equity; for there is [*92] no power to prevent destruction or defacement whilst the suit is pending. The defects thus existing in the remedy at law originate a jurisdiction in the Court of Chancery, and suits have accordingly been entertained for recovery of an ancient silver altar, claimed by the plaintiff as treasure-trove; for a cabinet of family jewels; for a picture or statue by a particular artist; and for other objects of a like kind. (x)

The two next subjects which fall under our notice are those of ELECTION and of MERITORIOUS OR IMPERFECT CON-SIDERATION; and both these subjects are closely connected with the principle of enforcing those contracts, and those only, which are based on valuable consideration.

We will first consider the equity of election.[1] It has

(x) Mitf. 117; Duke of Somerset v. Cookson, 3 P. W. 389; Earl of Macclesfield v. Davis, 3 Ves. & B. 16; Wood v. Rowcliffe, 3 Hare 304.

---

[1] See an elaborate discussion of the Doctrine of Election in Spence on the Equitable Jurisdiction of the Court of Chancery, Vol. II, page 585, et seq Story's Equity Jurisprudence, § 1076, et seq.; Gretton v. Haward, 1 Swanst., cited post, and in the notes to Streatfield v. Streatfield, 1 Lead. Cas. Eq. 273. See. also, Hall v. Hall, 1 Bland 130, 134; McGinnis et al. v. McGinnis, 1 Kelly 496; Clay and Craig v. Hart, 7 Dana 1; Field v. Eaton, 1 Dev. Ex. 283, 286; Brown v. Ricketts, 3 John. Ch. 553; Allen v. Getz, 2 Penna. R. 311; Marriott v. Sam Badger, 5 Md. 306; McElfresh v. Schley, 2 Gill 182; Cauffman v. Cauffman, 17 S. & R. 16; Upshaw v. Upshaw and Others, 2 Hen. & Munf. 381; Pemberton v. Pemberton, 29 Mo. 408; Van Duyne v. Van Duyne, 1 McCart. 49; Lewis v. Lewis, 33 Penn.

been stated as a general principle that the equity to enforce contracts made for value, is extended by parity of
reasoning to cases where a benefit has been conferred as
the consideration for an act, and knowingly accepted,
although the party so accepting it may not be bound by
an actual contract, or by a condition of performance annexed to the gift.(y)   The equity of election is analogous to this.   It applies not to cases of contract or of
conditional gifts, but to those on which the donor of an
interest by will has tacitly annexed a disposition to his
bounty, which can only be effected by the donee's assent,
e. g., where a testator leaves a portion of his property to
A., and by the same will disposes of property belonging
to A.   In this case there is no contract by A. to relinquish his own property; nor is there any condition annexed to the testator's gift, as a term of its acceptance,
which requires him to do so.   But the double disposition
made by the testator implies that he did not intend that
A. should have both the interests ; and he must therefore
[*93]   elect between the two, *and either relinquish his
own property or compensate the disappointed
donee out of the property bequeathed.

From the definition given of this equity, it is obvious
that two things are essential to originate it, viz., 1. That
the testator shall give property of his own; and 2. That
he shall profess to give also the property of his donee.

1. The testator must give property of his own; for
otherwise, if the recipient refuse to give effect to the will,
there is nothing on which the right to compensation can

(y) Edwards v. Grand Junction Railway, 1 M. & C. 650 ; Green v. Green,
19 Ves. 665 ; 2 Meriv. 86 ; Gretton v. Haward, 1 Swanst. 409, 427.

St. 66 ; Gable v. Daub, 40 Id. 217 ; Reaves v. Garrett, 34 Ala. 558 ; Brown
v. Brown, L. R. 2 Eq. 481 ; Brown v. Pitney, 39 Ill. 468.

attach. In the case, therefore, of an appointment under a power which is void as to some appointees, but good as to the rest, the doctrine does not apply; but the legitimate appointees may claim their appointed shares without giving effect to the invalid appointment. If, on the other hand, they have independent legacies out of the testator's property, they must elect between those legacies and their claim to the fund of which the appointment fails.(z)[1]

2. The testator must profess to dispose of property belonging to his donee.[2] There will therefore be no equity for election, if the gift of such property be not judicially cognisable; as, for example, where, previously to the late Wills Act, a will was made by an infant, or without proper attestation, professing to devise real estate, the heir-at-law might take a personal legacy under such will, and yet dispute the validity of the devise; for such a will was judicially read, as if the devise were blotted out, and an intention to give the realty did not appear.(a)[3] So again,

(z) Bristowe v. Warde, 2 Ves. Jr. 336; Kater v. Roget, 4 Y. & C. 18.
(a) Brodie v. Barry, 2 V. & B. 127; Sheddon v. Goodrich, 8 Ves. 481.

---

[1] Fowler's Trusts, 27 Beav. 362.

[2] Melick v. Darling, 11 Ohio 351. It is not material, however, whether the testator knew that the property he has attempted to dispose of belonged to another, or whether he mistakingly supposed it to be his own: Stump v. Findlay, 2 Rawle 168.

[3] Snelgrove v. Snelgrove, 4 Dessaus. 274; Melchor v. Burger, 1 Dev. & Bat. Eq. 634. So where a will is made in one state, professing to pass both real and personal estate, but is not executed so as to pass real estate in another state, the heir is not put to an election in the latter: Maxwell v. Maxwell, 2 De G., M. & G. 705; Jones v. Jones, 8 Gill 197. See also Kearney v. Macomb, 1 Green (N. J.) 189. In Maxwell v. Maxwell, ut supra., the principle was stated by L. J. Knight Bruce, to be "that the generality merely, or the universality merely, of the gift of the property, is not sufficient to demonstrate or create a ground of inference that the giver meant it to extend to property incapable, though his own, of passing by the particular act."

But a case for election may arise, even where a will is incapable of

where a *feme coverte* has made a will in exercise of a testator's power of appointment, and assumed to dispose of other property also, the gift of such other property is judicially non-existent; and her husband may take a benefit under the appointment, without relinquishing his marital right.(*b*) The same principle applies where a testator, having a limited power of appointment, exer-[*94] cises it in favor of the *legal object, and then attempts to cut down the gift in violation of the power. In this case, the original legal disposition is not affected by the subsequent illegal one; but the will is read as if it stopped at the original gift. A claimant, therefore, under it, though in one sense claiming against the illegal gift, is in law claiming in conformity with the will, and need not elect in respect of other interests which he may take under it.(*c*)[1]

If, on the other hand, the devise is in itself a valid devise, but is ineffectual to pass the particular property, the doctrine of election is not excluded. Such, for example, was the case where a will of earlier date than 1 Vict. c. 26, professed to extend to after-acquired lands. The lands did not pass by the will; but if the heir claimed an interest under it, he was put to his election.(*d*)[2]

(*b*) Rich *v.* Cockell, 9 Ves. 369.

(*c*) Carver *v.* Bowles, 2 R. & M. 301; Kater *v.* Roget, 4 You. & Col. 18; [Blacket *v.* Lamb, 14 Beav. 482.]

(*d*) Churchman *v.* Ireland, 4 Sim. 520; 1 Russ. & My. 250; Thelluson *v.* Woodward, 13 Ves. 209.

passing realty, as where the legacy and devise cannot be separated. Thus where, in such case, the real estate is devised away, but charged with a legacy for the heir-at-law, the latter must elect: Nutt *v.* Nutt, 1 Freem. Ch. 128.

[1] So where there is a recital of an intention, under a belief on the part of the testator that is erroneous, there is not a case of election: Box *v.* Barrett, L. R. 3 Eq. 244.

[2] s. p. McElfresh *v.* Schley, 2 Gill 182; *contra* City of Philadelphia *v.*

In accordance with the same principle, there is no equity for election, if the testator has himself a partial interest, which might satisfy the terms of his gift ;[1] *e. g.*, where a testator gives a legacy to his widow entitled to dower, and devises his real estate to another person, under circumstances to which the Dower Act does not apply. If such devise be expressly made free of dower, or if its natŭre be inconsistent with the contrary hypothesis, the widow is bound to elect. But it is otherwise, if the devise be in general terms. For it may be intended as a gift of what was strictly his own, viz., the estate subject to dower; and it will not be needlessly presumed that he intended to dispose of another's property.(e)[2] For the

(e) Birmingham *v.* Kirwan, 2 Sch. & Lef. 444; Holdich *v.* Holdich, 2 N. C. C. 18; Ellis *v.* Lewis, 3 Hare 310; 1 Jarm. on Dev. 366, 408; Lowes *v.* Lowes, 5 Hare 501.

Davis, 1 Whart. 490, though the point was not directly decided. Where, however, it is not clear on the face of the will that the testator intended to refer to after-acquired lands, it is not a case for election. See 1 Lead. Cas. Eq. 407, American note; Hall *v.* Hall, 2 McCord Ch. 269; City of Philadelphia *v.* Davis, ut sup. See Schroder *v.* Schroder, 18 Jur. 987.

[1] It must be clear, beyond reasonable doubt, that the testator designedly assumed to dispose of the property of the beneficiary, and did not intend to dispose of any expectant or other interest of his own in the property: Havens *v.* Sackett, 15 N. Y. 365; Miller *v.* Thurgood, 33 Beav. 499. A devise of an estate does not impart a devise free of encumbrances, so as to put the encumbrancers to their election: Stephens *v.* Stephens, 3 Drew. 697; 1 De G. & J. 62. The rule as to election is applicable only as between a gift under a will and a claim *dehors* the will and adverse to it, and not as between one clause in a will and another clause in the same will: Wollaston *v.* King, L. R. 8 Eq. 165.

[2] See, as to the application of the doctrine of election to the case of a devise or bequest made to the widow of a testator, when the estate of which she is dowable, is disposed to others: Adsit *v.* Adsit, 2 Johns. Ch. 448, and Gordon, Adm'r., *v.* Stevens, 2 Hill Ch. 46; Brown *v.* Caldwell, 1 Speer's Eq. 322; Whilden *v.* Whilden, Riley's Ch. 205; Timberlake *v.* Parrish's Ex'r., 5 Dana 345; Kinsey *v.* Woodward, 3 Harring. 459; Smith *v.* Kniskern, 4 John. Ch. 9; Wood *v.* Wood, 5 Paige 597; Havens *v.* Havens et al., 1

15

same reason, it has been decided, that the doctrine of election does not apply to creditors, but that they may take the benefit of devise of lands for payment of debts, and at the same time enforce their legal claims against [*95] personal estate, to the exclusion of *specific legatees. For it will be presumed that the testator bequeathed no more than what really belonged to him, and that the legatees were to take the personal estate subject to its ordinary liabilities.$(f)^1$

In like manner, no case of election will arise, if the testator shows by the terms of his gift, that he is doubtful whether the property in fact belongs to him, and that he only intends to dispose of it, if it is his own; e. g., if he directs a different disposition, in the event of its proving that he has no power to give, or if he expressly makes the deposition, in case he has power, or so far as he lawfully can or may.(g)

(f) Kidney v. Coussmaker, 12 Ves. 136.
(g) Bor. v. Bor., 3 B. P. C. by Toml. 167; Church v. Kemble, 5 Sim. 525.

Sandf. Ch. 325; Fuller v. Yates, 8 Paige 325; Sandford v. Jackson, 10 Id. 266; Webb v. Evans, 1 Binney 565: Kennedy v. Nedrow, 1 Dal. 415; Snelgrove v. Snelgrove, 4 Dessaus. 274; Ambler v. Norton, 4 H. & M. 23; Tobias v. Ketchum, 36 Barb. 304; Bending v. Bending, 3 K. & J. 257; Bradford v. Kents, 43 Penn. St. 474; Pollard v. Pollard, 1 Allen 490; Dodge v. Dodge, 31 Barb. 413; Pemberton v. Pemberton, 29 Missouri 408 · Sandoe's Appeal, 65 Penn. St. 314; Carder v. Commissioners of Fayette Co., 16 Ohio 353. This subject has been very fully and ably discussed in the notes to Streatfield v. Streatfield, 1 Lead. Cas. Eq. 225.

[1] That the doctrine of election does not apply to creditors, has been denied as a general rule in Pennsylvania: Irwin v. Tabb, 17 S. & R. 419; Adlum v. Yard, 1 Rawle 163; and it has been frequently held there that creditors taking a benefit under an assignment, fraudulent in law, elect not to disaffirm it. See Lanahan v. Latrobe, 7 Md. 268. It is otherwise, however, as to assignments fraudulent in fact: Hays v. Heidelberg, 9 Penn. St. 207; and an inclination was there manifested not to carry the doctrine of Adlum v Yard any further. The actual point decided in Kidney v. Coussmaker, as stated in the text, however, was never questioned in any of the cases. See also Waters v. Howard, 1 Md. Ch. 112.

It was at one period doubted whether evidence *dehors* the will itself was not admissible in cases of election in contravention of the ordinary rule of law, for the purpose of showing that a testator in making a bequest of his estate, intended to include property which was not strictly his own, although in some sense subject to his dominion; *e. g.*, lands of which he was tenant in tail, or leaseholds and mortgages belonging to his wife. The weight of authority, however, seems to be against its admissibility, and in favor of abiding by the ordinary rule.(*h*)[1]

If both the requisites concur, which have been here explained; if the testator has conferred a benefit out of his own property, and has professed to dispose of the property of the donee, the equity of election arises, and the donee must choose between the conflicting interests.

The election may be either express or implied: and if not made voluntarily, may be compelled by decree. But the electing party is entitled to know the value of both interests; and the mere fact that the benefit has been conferred, or even that it has been accepted in ignorance of the *conveyance, does not bind his right.[2] If, therefore, a bill be filed against him, he may insist [*96]

(*h*) Druce *v.* Dennison, 6 Ves. 385; Dummer *v.* Pitcher, 2 M. & K. 262; Clementson *v.* Gandy, 1 K. 309; 1 Jarm. on Wills 391; Wigram on Wills 39.

---

[1] The intention to raise an election must clearly appear on the face of the will: Jones *v.* Jones, 8 Gill 197; McElfresh *v.* Schley, 2 Id. 182; Waters *v.* Howard, 1 Md. Ch. 112; Wilson *v.* Arny, 1 Dev. & Batt. Eq. 376. It cannot be raised by evidence *dehors*: City of Phila. *v.* Davis, 1 Whart. 490; Timberlake *v.* Parish, 5 Dana 345; Waters *v.* Howard, 1 Md. Ch. 112. Though there will be no objection to such evidence so far as it goes only to show the state and circumstances of the property: Waters *v.* Howard, ut sup.

[2] Snelgrove *v.* Snelgrove, 4 Dessaus. 274; Adsit *v.* Adsit, 2 John. Ch. 448; Pinckney *v.* Pinckney, 2 Rich. Eq. 219; Upshaw *v.* Upshaw, 2 Hen. & Munf. 381; Duncan *v.* Duncan, 2 Yeates 302; Sopwith *v.* Maughan, 30

on the values being ascertained before a decree to elect is
made; or he may himself as plaintiff sustain a bill to
have the accounts taken and the property ascertained.(*i*)
If he be incompetent to make his election, as in the case
of infancy or coverture, the Court will do so in his stead,
and will refer it to the Master to inquire what election
should be made.(*k*)[1]

The principle which gives the right of choice to the
donee necessarily leads to the result that his election, when
made, binds himself alone, and does not affect the interests of donees in remainder. A contrary election by
them may possibly create some inconvenience; but this

(*i*) Pusey *v.* Desbouvre, 3 P. W. 315; Dillon *v.* Parker, 1 Swans. 359,
381.

(*k*) Gretton *v.* Haward, 1 Swanst. 413, n.

Beav. 235; Dewar *v.* Maitland, L. R. 2 Eq. 834; Douglas *v.* Webster, 12
Ib. 617. An election, however, made in ignorance of the law, but with
full knowledge of all material facts, as in the case of a widow taking
under her husband's will to the exclusion of dower, is binding, unless there
were fraud or imposition: Light *v.* Light, 21 Penn. St. 407; Bradfords *v.*
Kents, 43 Id. 475. An election once made, though by matter *in pais*, is
binding: Upshaw *v.* Upshaw, 2 Hen. & Munf. 381; Caston *v.* Caston, 2
Rich. Eq. 1; Buist *v.* Dawes, 3 Id. 281. As to what circumstances will
amount to proof of such election where the party to elect has remained in
possession of both estate: see Padbury *v.* Clark, 2 M. & G. 298; 2 H.
& Twells 341, s. *v.* See the result of the authorities in this point stated
by the Master of the Rolls in Miller *v.* Thurgood, 33 Beav. 496; also
Fitzsimons *v.* Fitzsimons, 28 Id. 417; Honywood *v.* Forster, 30 Id. 14;
Howells *v.* Jenkins, 2 John. & H. 706; 1 De G., J. & Sm. 617; Marriott *v.*
Sam Badger, 5 Md. 306; Spread *v.* Morgan, 11 H. L. Cas. 588; Whitridge *v.* Parkhurst, 20 Md. 85. Where both rights are legal, an election
operates as an estoppel at law: Buist *v.* Dawes, 3 Rich. Eq. 281. When
a married woman can elect: see Barrow *v.* Barrow, 4 K. & J. 409.

[1] See Robertson *v.* Stevens, 1 Ired. Eq. 247; Sledds *v.* Carey, 11 B.
Monr. 181; Addison *v.* Bowie, 2 Bland 606; Kavanaugh *v.* Thompson, 16
Ala. 817; McQueen *v.* McQueen, 2 Jones Eq. 16. An election by a *feme
covert* may be presumed after a great lapse of time: Tiernan *v.* Roland,
15 Penn. St. 429.

is no ground for allowing a preceding taker to bind their rights, or for depriving them of an independent election as their respective interests accrue. Nor will such donees be affected in their choice by acquiring derivative interests under the first elector; for such derivative interests are incidental to his estate, and not to their own. If, for instance, a married woman elect to take an estate of inheritance against a will, her husband may have his curtesy of that estate, and nevertheless claim a legacy under the will.(*l*)

The effect of election is not to divest the property out of the donee, but to bind him to deal with it as the Court shall direct.

If he elects to relinquish his own property, conforming throughout to the testator's disposition, he is said to take under the will, and must convey accordingly. If he elects to retain it, he is said to take against the will and must convey the estate devised to him to the disappointed donee, or must compensate him thereout for his disappointment. With respect, however, to this last point, some doubt exists. And it appears to be uncertain whether the consequence of an election to take against the will is confined to a liability *to compensate, [*97] or is a forfeiture of the property devised.[1] In the

(*l*) Cavan *v*. Pulteney, 2 Ves. Jr. 544; Ward *v*. Baugh, 4 Ves. 623.

---

[1] This doubt seems now to be settled in England in favor of compensation, and against a forfeiture : Spread *v*. Morgan, 11 H. L. Cas. 588. In this country, it has frequently been held, that it is compensation and not forfeiture, upon which equity proceeds in cases of this kind : Cauffman *v*. Cauffman, 17 S. & R. 16 ; City of Philadelphia *v*. Davis, 1 Whart. 490 ; Stump *v*. Findlay, 2 Rawle 168; Key *v*. Griffin, 1 Rich. Eq. 67 ; Marriott *v*. Sam Badger, 5 Md. 306 ; and the general rule was admitted so to be, in Lewis *v*. Lewis, 13 Penn. St. 82. But in this last case, it was held, that where the estate retained, is greater in value than that devised, compen-

case of a contract for valuable consideration, the result would be clearly forfeiture; for if the party claiming will not give the price, he must relinquish the benefit for which it was to be paid. But in the case of election it seems to be otherwise. For the equity does not originate in a gift on consideration, but in the intention presumable from the double gift, that the disappointed donee shall have some benefit. This intention is at once effected if compensation be the result; but will be manifestly defeated by forfeiture, unless the Court can imply a gift to the disappointed donee, for which the testator has given no authority, or can decree the heir taking as on an intestacy, to be a constructive trustee for him. It seems, however, difficult to conceive how the heir can be thus affected with a trust on the election of a devisee, which would not have attached if there had been an express condition of forfeiture in the will, or if the devisee instead of electing had disclaimed the interest devised.(m)

The next equity which requires notice is that of meritorious, or imperfect consideration.

The doctrine of meritorious consideration originates in the distinction between the three classes of consideration on which promises may be based; viz., valuable consider-

(m) 2 Sug. on Powers 145; 1 Roper, Hus. & Wife, by Jacob, 156 n.; Gretton v. Haward, 1 Sw. 433 n.; 2 Roper on Legacies 571-8; Ker v. Wauchope, 1 Bligh 1.

sation would be useless, and therefore a decree should be made in favor of the disappointed devisee directly, on the ground of forfeiture; and that, as a consequence, under the peculiar system of Pennsylvania, he could recover in ejectment. In Marriott v. Sam Badger, 5 Md. 306, where a slave belonging to a legatee was emancipated by will, it was held that no case of election arose, because, the principle being compensation, if the slave received the legacy as compensation, his master would be immediately entitled to it again, *jure domini.*

ation, the performance of a moral duty, and mere voluntary bounty. The first of these classes alone entitles the promisee to enforce his claim against an unwilling promisor; the third is for all legal purposes a mere nullity until actual performance of the promise.

The second, or intermediate class, is termed meritorious, and is confined to the three duties of charity,[1] of payment of creditors, and of maintaining a wife and children; and under this last head are included provisions made for persons, not being children of the party promising, but in *relation to whom he has manifested an intention [*98] to stand *in loco parentis,* in reference to the parental duty of making provision for a child.(n)

Considerations of this imperfect class are not distinguished at law from mere voluntary bounty, but are to a modified extent recognised in equity. And the doctrine with respect to them is, that although a promise made without a valuable consideration cannot be enforced against the promisor, or against any one in whose favor he has altered his intention, yet if an intended gift on meritorious consideration be imperfectly executed, and if the intention remains unaltered at the death of the donor, there is an equity to enforce it in favor of his intention, against persons claiming by operation of law without an equally meritorious claim.

The principal applications of this equity are in supplying surrenders of copyholds against the heir, and in supporting defective executions of powers, when the defect is formal, against the remaindermen.

(n) Perry v. Whitehead, 6 Ves. 544; Ex parte Pye, 18 Id. 140; Powys v. Mansfield, 3 M. & C. 359; Pym v. Lockyer, 5 Id. 29.

---

[1] Equity will relieve against the defective execution of a power in favor of a charity: Innes v. Sayer, 3 Macn. & Gord. 606; affirming s. v. 7 Hare 377.

The equity for supplying surrenders of copyholds originates in the doctrine, that a copyhold does not pass by
grant or devise, but by a surrender into the hands of the
lord to the use of the grantee, or of the will.   In the one
case, the grantee is entitled to immediate admission ; in
the other, the person designated in the will is entitled to
admission on the testator's death.   If a grant or devise
were made without a previous surrender, it was formerly
inoperative at law ; but if it were made for meritorious
consideration, the surrender might be supplied in equity.
The jurisdiction thus to supply a surrender existed whether
the gift were by deed or will,(o) but it was ordinarily
called into exercise in the case of wills ; and it is now
rendered of little practical importance by the enactment
that all real estate may be devised by will, and that copy-
[*99]   holds *shall be included under that description,
notwithstanding that the testator may not have
surrendered them to the use of his will, nor have even
been himself admitted to them.(p)

The exercise, therefore, of the equity in question is now
principally confined to defective executions of powers.[1]

(o) Rodgers v. Marshall, 17 Ves. 294.   (p) 1 Vict. c. 26, s. 3.

---

[1] Equity relieves against the defective execution of a power, in favor of
purchasers, creditors, children, or a wife: Schenck v. Ellingwood, 3 Edw.
Ch. 175 ; Porter v. Turner, 3 S. & R. 108 ; Dennison v. Goehring, 7 Penn.
St. 175 ; Bradish v. Gibbs, 3 John. Ch. 523.   Upon a somewhat analogous
principle, it is held, that where a person has a general power of appointment over property, which he actually exercises, either by deed or will,
he thereby subjects the property to the claims of his creditors in preference to the claims of his appointee.   But a Court of equity will not interfere, unless the party upon whom the power has been conferred, or to
whom it is tendered, has done some act indicating an intention to execute
it ; and the power of appointment must be a general power.   A power of
appointment is general, or not, within the meaning of the rule, according
to the person or uses to which the property may be appointed under it,

And the powers to which it applies are those which have been created by way of use, as distinct from bare authorities conferred by law.   Acts done under authorities of this latter kind, as, for example, leases or conveyances by a tenant in tail, are only binding when regular and complete. The principle of the distinction appears to be that powers limited by use · are mere reservations out of the original ownership, constituting the donee a *quasi* owner, and the remainderman a *quasi* heir; and consequently that, in conformity with this hypothesis, the donee's contracts for value ought to bind the remainderman, and his meritorious intention, if unaltered, ought to have the same effect.   The soundness of this equity has been questioned by Sir William Grant, and its principle seems difficult to sustain.   For the power given, though doubtless in some sense a modified ownership, does not confer an absolute right to dispose of the property, but a right to do so in a specific way.   And the chance that the power may never be executed, or that it may not be executed in the man-

and not according to the time when its exercise takes effect in possession, or the instrument by which its exercise is to be manifested. If a party may by will or deed dispose of property, to whom, and for such uses as he pleases, to take effect at his death, and may thus apply it to the payment of his debts, or direct any other disposition to be made of it, he has as great a power of disposal as he has of his own estate to take effect at the same time, and having undertaken to exercise the authority, it may be treated as a part of his estate upon his decease, so far as to require that that he should first provide for his debts out of it ; and if he fails so to do, equity may apply it as a part of his estate, so far as it is necessary for that purpose : Johnson *v.* Cushing, 15 N. H. 298 ; Fleming *v.* Buchanan, 3 De G., M. & G. 976 ; see 2 Sug. on Powers, 7th ed. 27.   But it would appear in England to be the opinion that equity will not aid a *defective* execution in favor of a stranger, for the benefit of the creditors of the appointor : 2 Sug. 102. This doctrine of treating a fund appointed to a volunteer, as assets for creditors, was strongly disapproved by Gibson, C. J., in Comm. *v.* Duffield, 12 Penn. St. 277.

ner prescribed, is an advantage given to the remainderman.
If, therefore, his interest is to be regarded, it is difficult to
see why he should be bound by any other than the prescribed act; for he is a stranger to any equity or consideration. If, on the other hand, his interest is subordinate to
the donee of the power, the intention of such donee ought
to be sustained, whatever be the consideration on which
it rests. The objection, however, which is noticed in these
remarks, appears not to be peculiar to the execution of
powers, but to apply generally to the equity of meritorious
[*100] consideration, and to the principle of enforcing *a
gift on the ground of intention alone, as distinct
from any binding contract, and yet inquiring into the consideration on which that intention was based. (q)

Whatever opinion may be entertained as to the original
soundness of the equity, there is no question that it is established by precedent; but it is confined to cases of
execution formally defective, or of contract amounting to
such defective execution. If there be no such execution
or contract the Court cannot interpose; [1] for, unless when
the power is in the nature of a trust, the donee has his
choice whether to execute it or not; and if he does not
execute or attempt to execute, there is no equity to execute for him. If the defect be not formal, but in the
substance of the power, the execution cannot be aided
in equity; for such aid would defeat the intention of the
donor. A power, for example, which is given to be executed by deed, may be effectuated where the execution

(q) Holmes v. Goghill, 7 Ves. 499; 12 Id. 206; 2 Sug. on Powers, c. 10.

[1] Lippincott v. Stokes, 2 Hals. Ch. 122. If the court is left in doubt
whether an execution was at all intended, it will not interfere; such an
intention must clearly appear: Id. See, also, Drusadow v. Wilde, 63
Penn. St. 170; Bingham's Appeal, 64 Id. 345.

has been by will; for the mode of execution is immaterial. But if given to be executed by will, its execution by deed is altogether invalid; for it was meant to have continuance until the death of the donee, and the deed, if it avail at all, must avail to its destruction.(r)

The rule that the intention must remain unaltered does not require any special notice. It might perhaps have been originally contended, that the very fact of the appointment being left imperfect was evidence that the intention had not continued. The doctrine, however, is clearly otherwise; but if there be any subsequent act of the donor showing that his original intention is recalled, the equity is at an end; for it is not one to enforce a contract against him, but to effectuate his intention in his own favor.(s)

The only remaining requisite is, that the party against whom relief is asked must not have an equally meritorions claim. If, therefore, the heir-at-law or remainderman be a *child unprovided for, it seems the better opinion that the equity will not be enforced; [*101] and the same rule prevails where relief is sought against a grandchild, although a defective execution cannot be supplied in his favor.[1] It is not, however, sufficient that the heir is disinherited; for if he is provided for, it is immaterial from whom the provision moved.[2] Nor will the Court inquire into the relative amount of the provisions made; for on that point the parent is the best judge.(t)

(r) Tollett $v.$ Tollett, 2 P. W. 489; Reid $v.$ Shergold, 10 Ves. 370.

(s) Finch $v.$ Finch, 15 Ves. 51; Antrobus $v.$ Smith, 12 Id. 39.

(t) Rodgers $v.$ Marshall, 17 Ves. 294; Hills $v.$ Downton, 5 Id. 557; 2 Sug. on Powers, c. 10, and App. 24.

---

[1] See Porter $v.$ Turner, 3 S. & R. 108.

[2] See Morse $v.$ Martin, 34 Beav. 500.

Another class of cases, to which the doctrine of meritorious consideration applies, are those where a man, subject to a moral duty, does an act which may reasonably have been meant in satisfaction of that duty; and is therefore presumed to have so intended it.

In accordance with this principle acts, which as between strangers would bear one construction, may be construed differently where meritorious consideration exists; *e. g.*, a purchase made by one person in the name of another, may be construed an advancement in favor of a child, instead of a resulting trust for the purchaser; a legacy may be construed a provision, instead of mere bounty, and may on that ground bear interest from the testator's death. And in like manner, if there be a prior legacy bequeathed or promise made to a child, a subsequent gift or legacy may be construed as a substituted portion, instead of being a cumulative benefit.

With respect to purchases by one person in the name of another, it has been already stated to be a presumption of law that the purchase is intended for the benefit of the purchaser, and that the conveyance is taken on trust for him. If, however, the conveyance is taken in the name of a child, or of one towards whom the purchaser stands *in loco parentis,* a counter presumption arises. And the *primâ facie* probability is, that the purchase was meant as a provision or advancement for the child.[1] In either

---

[1] The general rule of equity is, that if a father makes a purchase in the name of the son, even though illegitimate, it will not be deemed a resulting trust, but an advancement: Page *v.* Page, 8 N. H. 187. See, however, Tucker *v.* Burrow, 2 Hem. & M. 515; and see, also, Williams *v.* Mears, 2 Disney (Ohio) 604. And a purchase in the name of a wife or child will be considered an advancement until the contrary is proved, and no trust will result to the husband or father. It seems to be doubtful whether the doctrine under consideration applies to purchases made by a

case the *doctrine is one of presumption, not of the
construction of the conveyance itself.   There is] [*102]
therefore no rule of law which prohibits the use of parol
evidence, either to counteract or to support the presumption.[1] But the only difference is that, in the case of a
stranger, the onus lies on those who allege that he was
intended to take beneficially; in the case of a child, it lies
on those who allege that he was to take as a trustee.(u)
It may, for instance, be shown that the child was already
fully provided for, which affords a presumption that no
further advancement was intended.   It may be shown

(u) Hall v. Hill, 1 Conn. & L. 120.

---

mother. It was held not to apply in Re De Visme, 2 De G., J. & Sm. 17;
but Murphy v. Nathans, 46 Penn. St. 508, is the other way. See also
Garrett v. Wilkinson, 2 De G. & Sm. 244; Loyd v. Read, 1 P. Wms. 607;
Hill on Trustees 160, 4th Am. ed. ; Astreen v. Flanagan, 3 Edw. Ch. 279;
Livingston v. Livingston, 2 John. Ch. 537 ; Sampson v. Sampson, 4 S. & R.
329 ; Taylor v. James, 4 Dessaus. 1; Partridge v. Havens, 10 Paige 618 ;
Knouff v. Thompson, 16 Penn St. 357 ; Dennison v. Goehring, 7 Id. 182
n.; Dudley v. Bosworth, 10 Humph. 12; Tremper v. Barton, 18 Ohio 418 ;
Taylor v. Taylor, 4 Gilm. 303 ; Jackson v. Matsdorff, 11 John. 91 ; Creed
v. Lancaster Bank, 1 Ohio St. 1; Smith v. Smith, 21 Ala. 76. Advancement is always a question of intention: Weaver's Appeal, 63 Penn. St.
309; Dillman v. Cox, 23 Ind. 440.   In Sterry v. Arden, 1 John. Ch. 261,
a voluntary advancement to a child was decided to be void against a purchaser, for valuable consideration, with only constructive notice ; and also
where the notice is direct, the rule seems to be the same.   In equity
the estate will be subjected to the claims of the parent's creditors : Guthrie v. Gardner, 19 Wend. 414; Croft v. Arthur, 3 Dessaus. 223 ; Jencks v.
Alexander, 11 Paige 619; Abney v. Kingsland, 10 Ala. 355; Doyle v.
Sleeper, 1 Dana 531 ; Rucker v. Abell, 8 B. Monr. 566 ; and in Pennsylvania, the land may be levied upon directly : Kimmel v. McRight, 2 Penn.
St. 38. See, also, ante, p. 34, in note.

[1] This presumption of advancement may be rebutted by parol evidence :
Dudley v. Bosworth, 10 Humph. 12; Jackson v. Matsdorff, 11 John. 91 ;
Taylor v. Taylor, 4 Gilm. 303 ; Tremper v. Burton, 18 Ohio 418. The
clearest evidence of a present gift, accompanied by exclusive possession
and valuable improvements, are necessary to establish a valid parol gift
between father and son : Miller v. Hartle, 53 Penn. St. 108.

that at the time of the purchase, or in immediate connection therewith, the father dealt with the property as his own; but the mere receipt of rent, which may possibly be by the child's permission, will not alter the presumption; or again, it may be shown that at the time of making the purchase, the father declared his intention either against, or in favor of the presumed advancement.[1] It must be observed, however, that the only question to which the evidence can apply is, what the father intended at the time of the purchase, and not whether his intention has been afterwards changed. And for this reason his subsequent acts and declarations cannot be admitted as evidence in his favor, although those of the child might be so used.(v)

With respect to legacies, the distinction between legacies to strangers and those to children is that, in the case of a stranger, the legacy is considered mere bounty, and is dealt with by the ordinary rules of law; in the case of a child, it is presumed to be meant as a provision for him, and the ordinary rules are modified by that presumption.

One instance in which ˙this distinction occurs, regards the period from which interest is given. The ordinary rule is that, if the testator has not expressed a different [*103] *intention, a legacy shall bear interest from the time fixed for payment of the principal, or if no time be fixed, then from the end of a twelvemonth after the testator's death. But if it be given by a parent, or

(v) Murless v. Franklin, 1 Sw. 13; Grey v. Grey, 2 Id. 594; Sidmouth v. Sidmouth, 2 Bea. 447; Scawin v. Scawin, 1 N. C. C. 65; Skeats v. Skeats, 2 Id. 9.

---

[1] Subsequent declarations of the father, however, are incompetent: Tremper v. Barton, 18 Ohio 418. They were admitted, however, in Speer v. Speer, 1 McCart. 240.

by one who stands *in loco parentis*, it is treated as a gift by way of provision; and the legatee, if he be not adult, and there be no other provision for his maintenance, will be allowed interest by way of maintenance from the time of the death.(*w*)[1] Another instance of the same distinction occurs in the case of successive legacies or gifts, viz., where a legacy has been bequeathed or a promise made, which has been followed by a gift *inter vivos*, or by a a legacy of later date.

(*w*) Raven *v.* Waite, 1 Sw. 553; Donovan *v.* Needham, 9 Bea. 164.

---

[1] Generally, when no time is fixed by a will, a pecuniary legacy is payable in a year after the testator's death, and not before, and interest is not payable until the end of the year, or the expiration of the period fixed by the will: Sullivan *v.* Winthrop, 1 Sumner 1; Eyre *v.* Golding, 5 Binn. 475; Bitzer *v.* Hahn, 14 S. & R. 238. So in Virginia and New York: Shobe *v.* Carr, 3 Munf. 10; Williamson *v.* Williamson, 6 Paige Ch. 298; Marsh Hague, 1 Edw. Ch. 174. See Hammond *v.* Hammond, 2 Bland 306. But where a legacy is given to an infant child who is otherwise unprovided for, interest will be allowed from the testator's death, whether a time is fixed for the payment of interest or not, and this doctrine applies to testators placing themselves *in loco parentis*: Sullivan *v.* Winthrop, ubi supra; Hite *v.* Hite, 2 Rand 409; Miles *v.* Wister, 5 Binn. 479; Bitzer *v.* Hahn, 14 S. & R. 232. So, though the legacy is payable at twenty-one, and without mention of interest, Ibid.; or is given for life, for separate use: Bird's Est., 2 Pars. Eq. 168; Bowman's Appeal, 34 Penn. St. 19. This exception does not extend to the case of a grandchild: Lupton *v.* Lupton, 2 John. Ch. 614. See Smith *v.* Moore, 25 Verm. 127; Walker *v.* Walker, 27 Ala. 396; but see Bitzer *v.* Hahn, 14 S. & R. 232, *semb. contr.*, also Bowman's Appeal, 34 Penn. St. 19; nor to grand-nephews: Miles *v.* Wister, 5 Binn. 479; nor to the widow: Martin *v.* Martin, 6 Watts 67; Gill's Appeal, 2 Penn. St. 231.

As a legacy to a child carries interest, in the accepted cases, on the ground of the duty of maintenance, where the parent has fulfilled that duty by providing maintenance out of another fund, the legacy does not necessarily carry interest: Rouse's Est., 9 Hare 649. When it is apparent that a legacy is intended for the immediate support of the legatee, it will bear interest from the death of the testator. If, however, it is charged on the *income* of the estate, it cannot be considered due till one year has elapsed: Morgan *v.* Pope, 7 Cold. (Tenn.) 541.

It will be convenient to consider each case separately, taking first that of a prior legacy, and afterwards that of a prior promise.

In the case of a prior legacy, followed by a gift or legacy of later date, the question which arises is, whether the later gift or legacy, was intended to be identical with the first, so as to operate either by way of anticipated payment or as a reiteration of the original gift. If it was so intended, and the intention is proved by admissible evidence, the first legacy is a obviously at an end, as if a man were to bequeath a particular horse, and were afterwards to give the horse in his lifetime, or again bequeath it to the same person. The construction put by law on the later gift or legacy is *primâ facie* against its being meant as identical, and in favor of its being held an independent benefit. And if it be conferred by a written instrument, extrinsic evidence of the intention is not admissible.(x) The construction, however, may be altered by a presumption of law, to be raised by a comparison of the two gifts, and of the motives respectively assigned for each, or by the relative position in which the parties [*104] stand. The first *ground of presumption, arising from the similarity of the gifts and motives, is not material to our present purpose. It is sufficient to observe, that mere equality of amount is not such an identification of the gifts as will prevent their cumulative effect. But if, in addition to this, the same motive is expressed for both, the double coincidence gives rise to a presump-

(x) Ex parte Dubost, 18 Ves. 140; Kirk v. Eddowes, 3 Hare 509; 2 Will. on Exors., 2d ed. 924; Hurst v. Beach, 5 Madd. 351; Suisse v. Lord Lowther, 2 Hare 424; Lee v. Paine, 4 Id. 201; Hall v. Hill, 1 Conn. & L. 120.

tion that repetition was intended, and not accumulation. (y) [1] The second ground of presumption arises out of the relative position of the parties, and is that with which we are now more immediately concerned. If the donor be a parent, or *in loco parentis*, the presumption is that the first legacy was intended as a provision, proportioned to the then existing claims of the legatee, and that the later gift or legacy had the same object, and was intended as an immediate payment or a modified repetition, either in full or *pro tanto*, by reason of altered circumstances, of the first. And the circumstance, that the second benefit differs in amount or disposition from the first, is not inconsistent with such presumption. The doctrine on this point is expressed by the maxim, that "the presumption is against a double portion." (z) [2] The presumption thus

---

(y) Hurst *v.* Beach, 5 Madd. 351 ; Suisse *v.* Lord Lowther, 2 Hare 424.

(z) Wharton *v.* Earl of Durham, 3 M. & K. 472 ; 3 Cl. & F. 146 ; Pym *v.* Lockyer, 5 M. & C. 29 ; Suisse *v.* Lord Lowther, 2 Hare 424 ; Lady Thynne *v.* Earl Glengall, 2 House Lds. Cas. 153. In Scotland the law is otherwise : Campbell *v.* Campbell, L. R. 1 Eq. 383.

---

[1] See the cases of Dewitt *v.* Yates, 10 Johns. 156 ; Jones *v.* Creveling's Ex'rs., 4 Harrison 127 ; Id., 1 Zabriskie 573.

The rule, as established by these cases, is, that where the two bequests occur in the same instrument, the presumption is most strongly in favor of repetition ; but if in different instruments, then the presumption is, in general, in favor of cumulation. See also, Wilson *v.* O'Leary, L. R. 12 Eq. 525. In the former case, the fact that the second legacy is charged upon land, will not rebut the presumption of repetition : Dewitt *v.* Yates, ut sup. ; Hooley *v.* Hatton, 1 Lead. Cas. Eq. 285.

[2] Ademption only takes place where a parent bequeaths a legacy to a child, and afterwards gives a portion to the same child, which is *ejusdem generis*. A house and lot is not *ejusdem generis* with a pecuniary legacy, and cannot adeem it : Swoope's Appeal, 27 Penn. St. 58. See also, Rogers *v.* French, 19 Geo. 316.

In New York, it has been held that the intention of a testator that a subsequent gift or advancement shall operate as a satisfaction of a legacy cannot be presumed, for in such a case, there is an implied revocation of

16

raised, whether it be based on a comparison of the two gifts, or on the relative position of the two parties, is against the *primâ facie* construction of the second gift. And therefore it may be rebutted by extrinsic evidence of intention, and sustained by counter evidence of the same kind, notwithstanding that the gift is by a written instrument. (*a*)

The second case is that of a promise *inter vivos*, followed by a gift or legacy of later date.[1]

If the benefit promised and the benefit conferred are precisely identical, no question arises; for the promisor has done that which he undertook to do; and his promise [*105] is in *fact performed. (*b*) But if they are not precisely identical, then a question arises whether the gift or legacy was meant in satisfaction, either wholly or in part, of the original promise. If an intention to that effect be shown, the promisee must elect between the two benefits. The principle of decision in this case is the same as in that of double legacies. The *primâ facie* construction of the second gift is in favor of its being considered independent of the first. And that construction may be rebutted, either by a comparison of the promise and the gift, and of the motives for which they are respectively expressed to be made; or by the presumption that both are by way of portion, and consequently that

. (*a*) Hurst *v.* Beach, 5 Madd. 351; Hall *v.* Hill, 1 Conn. & L. 120; Kirk *v.* Eddowes, 3 Hare 509.

(*b*) Blandy *v.* Widmore, 1 P. W. 324; Goldsmid *v.* Goldsmid, 1 Sw. 211.

the will, which is forbidden by the Rev. Sts.: Langdon *v.* Astor's Executors, 3 Duer 477.

[1] The subject of the satisfaction of debts, portions, and legacies, is very fully discussed in the notes to Ex Parte Pye, 2 Lead. Cas. Eq. 303, where all the American cases are cited and commented upon. The rules on the subject are in general the same in this country as in England.

the second is in lieu of the first.(c)[1] The effect, however, of differences between the promise and the benefit, is much greater than in the case of successive legacies; for the donor must know that he cannot alter his promise, and therefore any variation from its terms tends to the conclusion that it was not in his mind.(d)

The presumption which arises from the relationship of parent and child, exists also in a less degree with respect to creditors, whether mere strangers or children, to whom, by transactions independent of the relationship, the parent has become indebted. In such cases, the presumption is, that a payment by the debtor, equal to or exceeding the debt, is meant in discharge, and the same doctrine applies to a legacy, provided it be substantially equivalent to payment.(e)[2] But the presumption is much weaker than with respect to portions, and may be excluded by a less degree of difference; as, for example, if the legacy be

(c) Ansley v. Bainbridge, 1 R. & M. 657; Jones v. Morgan, 2 Y. & C. 403; Weall v. Rice, 2 R. & M. 251; Plunkett v. Lewis, 3 Hare 316; Hall v. Hill, 1 Conn. & L. 120.

(d) Wharton v. Earl of Durham, 3 M. & K. 472; 3 Cl. & F. 146, 155; [Lady Thynne v. Earl of Glengall, 2 H. Lds. Cas. 153.]

(e) Plunkett v. Lewis, 3 Hare 316; Jeffs v. Wood, 2 P. W. 129; Chancey's Case, 1 P. W. 408; Wallace v. Pomfret, 11 Ves. 542.

---

[1] Hopwood v. Hopwood, 7 H. L. Cas. 728. A residuary legacy may be adeemed, and the ademption need not be entire, but may be *pro tanto:* Montefiore v. Guedalla, 1 De G., F. & J. 93; Coventry v. Chichester, 2 Hem. & M. 149. See further, on this subject, McClure v. Evans, 29 Bea. 422; Ravenscroft v. Jones, 32 Id. 669; Hine v. Hine, 39 Barb. 507; Miner v. Atherton's Executor, 35 Penn. St. 528. Substituted and added legacies are to be raised out of the same fund and are subject to the same conditions: Leacroft v. Maynard, 1 Ves. Jr. 279; Crowder v. Clowes, 2 Id. 449; Johnstone v. The Earl of Harrowby, 1 De G., F. & J. 183; Note to Hooley v. Hatton, 1 Lead. Cas. Eq. 301.

[2] This was termed a "false principle" by the Vice-Chancellor of England in Hassell v. Hawkins, 4 Drew. 468.

less than the debt, or if it be payable at a different time.(ƒ)

Whenever the presumption arises, it may, as we have

[*106] seen, *be rebutted or confirmed by evidence, notwithstanding that the gift is by a written instrument.[1] But it must be evidence in rebuttal or confirmation of the presumption, and not evidence to construe the instrument itself.[2] The presumption, therefore, must first arise, and if the instrument is so worded that its *primâ facie* construction is not altered by the relationship alone, extrinsic evidence of intention is not admissible.(g)

The last equity which will be considered in the present chapter, is the converse to that of specific performance, and consists in giving effect to discharges by matter *in pais* of contracts under seal, and in confining the claim on a contract with a penalty to the specific performance of its terms.

We will first consider the doctrine as to DISCHARGES BY MATTER IN PAIS OF CONTRACTS UNDER SEAL.[3]

It is a rule of law, that an agreement under seal, technically termed an agreement by specialty, can only be avoided by a like specialty; and it is therefore unaffected

(ƒ) 2 Will. on Executors 929 ; 2 Story on Equity, s. 1122.

(g) Wallace v. Pomfret, 11 Ves. 542; Hall v. Hill, 1 Conn. & L. 120.

---

[1] Miner v. Atherton's Executor, 35 Penn. St. 528.

[2] Eaton v. Benton, 2 Hill 576 ; Jones v. Mason, 5 Rand. 577 ; Brady v. Cabitt, 1 Dougl. 30 ; Zeigler v. Eckert, 6 Penn. St. 13 ; Zeiter v. Zeiter, 4 Watts 212.

[3] See post, notes to pp. 111, 112.

It is settled, in Pennsylvania, that verbal stipulations by one party, on the faith of which a written agreement is executed by the other, will control the writing, even in the absence of evidence of a fraudulent design : Hultz v. Wright, 16 S. & R. 345; Christ v. Diffenbach, 1 Id. 464; Miller v. Henderson, 10 Id. 292; Clark v. Partridge, 2 Penn. St. 13 ; 4 Id. 166. See Keisselbrack v. Livingston, 4 John. Ch. 114.

by an accord by parol, or other matter *in pais*, which would operate as a discharge of a simple contract.(*h*) In equity, however, the rule is otherwise. For the form of agreement is immaterial; and if the act done is in substance a discharge, it will warrant a decree for the execution of a release, or for delivery up and cancellation of the specialty.[1]

The most ordinary application of this equity is in favor of sureties, where a guarantee has been given under seal, and the creditor, without the surety's consent, has discharged or modified the principal's liability. In this case the doctrine of the law is, that by such discharge or modification of the principal's liability, the surety is absolutely discharged; for he has contracted to guarantee a specific agreement; and if a new agreement be substituted without his assent, his contract is at an end.(*i*)[2]

*The same effect is produced if the creditor enters into a binding contract to give time for payment to the principal. For it would be a fraud on the contract, if he were afterwards to receive his debt from [*107]

(*h*) 1 Selw. N. P. 518, 549.

(*i*) Samnell *v.* Howarth, 3 Meriv. 272; Mayhew *v.* Crickett, 2 Sw. 186; Smith's Merc. Law 423; 3 Jarman's Bythewood, 3d ed., p. 298–305.

---

[1] Hurlbut *v.* Phelps, 30 Conn. 42. In general, however, the court will not decree that to be a release in equity which is not so at law, unless there be a valuable consideration : Cross *v.* Sprigg, 6 Hare 552; Tufnell *v.* Constable, 8 Sim. 69; Peace *v.* Hains, 17 Jurist 1091; 11 Hare 151; Campbell's Estate, 7 Penn. St. 100; Kidder *v.* Kidder, 33 Id. 268. See, also, Yeomans *v.* Williams, L. R. 1 Eq. 184; Taylor *v.* Manners, L. R. 1 Ch. Ap. 48; and the party claiming the benefit of this equitable doctrine, must, as in all other instances, do equity : Headley *v.* Goundry, 41 Barb. 279.

[2] On the subject of the discharge of a surety by the conduct of the creditor, see post, 268, note; also, Pledge *v.* Buss, Johns. 663; Brubaker *v.* Okeson, 36 Penn. St. 519; Henderson *v.* Ardery, Id. 449; and the notes to Rees *v.* Berrington, 2 Lead. Cas. Eq. 814, where the American cases are cited.

the surety, and thus confer on him an immediate right of action against the principal. The position of the surety is therefore varied, and he is in consequence discharged altogether from his guarantee. If, however, the creditor, in agreeing to give time, expressly reserve his remedies against the surety, there is no discharge; for although he undertakes not to sue the principal directly, he does not preclude himself from enabling the surety to do so. Nor will the surety be discharged by mere forbearance to sue, unless there be a stipulation in the guarantee, binding the party guarantied to use due diligence against the principal.(k)

The doctrine which has just been laid down is not peculiar to the Court of Chancery; but its operation at law is confined to guarantees by simple contract. If the guarantee be by specialty, the rule that its discharge must be by a like specialty, prevents the creditor's conduct being pleaded at law. And a consequent equity arises to restrain him from suing at law, and to compel him, if requisite, to give up or cancel the guarantee.(l)

The equity for relief against enforcement of PENALTIES, originates in the rule which formerly prevailed at law, that on breach of a contract secured by penalty, the full penalty might be enforced without regard to the damage sustained.[1]

(k) Ex parte Glendinning, Buck 517; Boultbee v. Stubbs, 18 Ves. 20; Eyre v. Everett, 2 Russ. 381.

(l) Archer v. Hale, 1 Moore & P. 285; Aldridge v. Harper, 3 Moore & Sc. 518; Blake v. White, 1 Y. & C. 420; Brooks v. Stuart, 1 Bea. 512.

---

[1] A Court of equity will always relieve against a penalty, where compensation can be made: Hackett v. Alcock, 1 Call. 533; Mayo v. Judah, 5 Munf. 495; and also against back interest, secured by way of penalty: Mosby v. Taylor, Gilm. 172; and will not aid the recovery of a penalty of forfeiture, or anything in the nature of one: Livingston v. Tompkins, 4 John. Ch. 431; McKim v. White Hall Co., 2 Md. Ch. 510; Shoup v. Cook,

The Court of Chancery, in treating contracts as matters for specific performance, was naturally led to the conclusion that the annexation of a penalty did not alter their character; and in accordance with this view, would not on the one hand permit the contracting party to evade performance by paying the penalty; and on the other hand, would restrain *proceedings to enforce the penalty [*108] on a subsequent performance of the contract itself; viz., in the case of a debt, on payment of the principal, interest, and costs; or in that of any other contract, on reimbursement of the actual damage sustained.

An authority of a similar kind has been now conferred on, courts of law by two statutes, the first of which applies to penalties for non-performance of covenants, and the second to those of non-payment of money.$(m)^1$ The effect of these statutes has been to diminish the frequency

(m) 8 & 9 Wm. 3, c. 11, s. 8; 4 & 5 Ann. c. 16, ss. 12, 13; 1 Selw. N. P. 542, 569, 588.

---

1 Carter 135. But where the sums covenanted to be paid are in the nature of stipulated damages, a Court of Chancery will not relieve: Skinner v. Dayton, 2 John. Ch. 526; s. c. Skinner v. White, 17 John. 357. See also, White v. Dingley, 4 Mass. 433; Pierce v. Fuller, 8 Id. 223; Tingley v. Cutler, 7 Conn. 291; Slosson v. Beadle, 7 Johns. 72; Myers v. Hay, 3 Missouri 98; Gammon v. Howe, 14 Maine 250. Where a stipulation is designated in the contract as a penalty, how far a Court will consider a sum stipulated as liquidated damages, see Taylor v. Sandiford, 7 Wheat. 19; Curry v. Larer, 7 Penn. St. 470; Streeper v. Williams, 48 Id. 450; Shreve v. Brereton, 51 Id. 175. See on this subject the notes to Peachy v. Somerset, 2 Lead. Cas. Eq. 895; where the American and English cases are collected and very fully considered.

A proviso in a mortgage, that the whole sum shall become due upon the failure to pay any one of the instalments on the day, is in the nature of a penalty, against which equity will relieve upon adequate compensation, viz., payment of instalment due, interest and costs: Tiernan v. Hinman, 16 Ill. 400; Martin v. Melville, 3 Stockt. 222; Thompson v. Hudson, L. R. 2 Eq. 612. See, however, Sterne v. Beck, 1 De G., J. & Sm. 598.

1 These or similar statues are in force generally in the United States.

of equitable interference.   But they do not affect the authority to interfere.   The jurisdiction is not limited to the
case of bonds or of instruments which in terms impose a
penalty ; but extends to all agreements where a stipulation is made in the event of non-performance, which on
the whole matter appears intended as such.   If it be not
in truth meant as a penalty, but be merely an agreement
between the parties that a fixed sum shall be paid, as
ascertained or liquidated damages, for doing or omitting
a particular act, there is no equity to substitute a new
agreement.   The mere use, however, of the words " liquidated damages," will not of itself decide the question ;
but it depends on the substantial meaning of the contract.[1]
If, for example, the payment of a smaller sum is secured
by a larger, or if there be a series of covenants of varying
importance, and the same specific sum is made payable in

---

[1] It is stated by Judge Hare, in his lucid and able notes to Peachy v.
Somerset, 2 Lead. Cas. Eq., Pt. ii., 472, upon a full examination of the cases,
that the result " seems to be, that equity will not permit a recovery for
the breach of a contract, to an extent manifestly greater than the injury
suffered, but that the parties may fix upon that amount of compensation,
which does not come in conflict with this limitation.   Hence, when the injury is susceptible of definite admeasurement, as in all cases where the
breach consists in the non-payment of money, the parties will not be
allowed to make a stipulation for a greater amount, whether in the form
of a penalty or of liquidated damages.   But when, on the other hand, the
injury in question is uncertain in itself, and insusceptible of being reduced
to certainty by a legal computation, it may be settled beforehand, by special
agreement. . . . . But even when the subject-matter is one which
admits of compensation fixed by agreement, and not by the law, still it
must be a question, whether the parties have so meant to fix it, and
whether a stipulation for the payment of a sum certain, in case of default,
is intended as a penalty, or as a liquidation of the damages.   This is obviously a question of intention, determinable, in the first place, by what
appears on the face of the contract itself; and next, by a resort to extrinsic circumstances."   See also a full discussion of the law on this subject
in Cotheal v. Talmage, 5 Selden 551.

respect of each, the stipulated payment will be held a penal one, notwithstanding that it may be otherwise named in the contract.(n) The distinction thus drawn between a penalty for securing the performance of the contract, and a stipulation which makes part of the contract itself, may be illustrated by the rule, that if a certain rate of interest be reserved on a mortgage, with an agreement that if it be not paid punctually, the rate shall be increased, the larger *interest is in the nature of a penalty, and [*109] may be relieved against in equity. But on the other hand, if the larger rate be originally reserved, with an agreement for reduction on punctual payment, the condition for such punctual payment is part of the contract, and relief cannot be given if it is not fulfilled.(o)[1]

The same relief which is granted in the case of penalties has also been extended to clauses of re-entry for non-performance of the covenants in a lease.[2] In respect to covenants for payment of rent, the jurisdiction for this purpose has been long established on the principle that payment of the rent with interest is a complete compensation for the damage sustained. Its soundness, even in this case, has been questioned by Lord Eldon, for it is by no means true that subsequent interest is an equivalent for punctuality; but its exercise is established by pre-

(n) Rolfe v. Peterson, 2 B. P. C. by Toml. 436; Kemble v. Farren, 6 Bing. 141; Boys v. Ancell, 5 Bing. N. C. 390; 3 Jarm. Byth. 325–336.

(o) Nicholls v. Maynard, 3 Atk. 519.

---

[1] A stipulation in a mortgage, that if it becomes necessary to forclose, a reasonable amount shall be added as attorney's fees, is not in the nature of a penalty and is valid: Nelson v. Everett, 29 Iowa 184; Williams v. Meeker, Id. 292.

[2] Or breach of conditions subsequent: Smith v. Jewett, 40 N. H. 530. See, also, Warner v. Bennett, 31 Conn. 468; Robinson v. Loomis, 51 Penn. St. 78; Mahoning Co. Bank, 32 Id. 158.

cedent, and has been for the last century recognised by
an express statute, defining the circumstances to which
it shall apply, and conferring a similar jurisdiction on
Courts of law.(p)   To this extent therefore the jurisdiction is settled; but it is not carried beyond this limit.
Relief will be granted where a forfeiture is incurred by
non-payment of money, and perhaps in other cases also,
if a special equity be raised on the ground of unavoidable
ignorance or accident; but it will not be granted without
such special equity, in respect of covenants for repairing,
insuring, or doing any specific act, where the compensation must be estimated in damages.(q)

(p) 4 Geo. 2, c. 28; Adams on Ejectment 122.

(q) Hill v. Barclay, 18 Ves. 56; Reynolds v. Pitt, 19 Id. 134; Ex parte
Vaughan, T. & R. 434; Green v. Bridges, 4 Sim. 96; White v. Warner, 2
Meriv. 459; Elliott v. Turner, 13 Sim. 477.

*CHAPTER III.   [*110]

OF MORTGAGES, BOTH PERFECT AND IMPERFECT.

THE equity for relief against penalties applies most extensively to the case of FORFEITED MORTGAGES, where a loan has been secured by the transfer of property, with a condition to redeem on a specified day, and the right of redemption has been forfeited at law by non-payment at the appointed time.   There are other methods of charging loans on property, which will be presently noticed as imperfect mortgages.   But a regular mortgage is in the form which has been just mentioned, and may be defined as a "security for a debt, created by conveyance of the legal ownership in property, either to the entire extent of the mortgagor's estate, or for a partial estate carved out of it, with a proviso that, on payment at a specified time the conveyance shall be void or the mortgagee shall reconvey."[1]

---

[1] It is perfectly well settled that a mortgage is a mere security for a debt: Wilson v. Troup, 2 Cow. 195; Simpson v. Ammons, 1 Binney 177; Ragland v. Justices, 10 Geo. 65; 4 Kent's Com. 160; Williams on Real Prop. 391; note to Thornborough v. Baker, 2 Lead. Cas. Eq. 857. And from this doctrine several consequences arise.

First. The interest of the mortgagee in fee, or for a smaller estate, is personalty, and his executor, and not the heir, is entitled to the money secured by the mortgage: Thornborough v. Baker, *supra.*

Second. It is not necessary that there should be any independent evidence of the debt, or any personal or collateral security for the same. The mortgage alone is sufficient: Mitchell v. Burnham, 44 Maine 299. See also Chappell v. Allen, 38 Mo. 213; Bank v. Anderson, 14 Iowa 544.

Third. The payment or discharge of the mortgage debt revests the estate

Until the day of redemption is passed, the debtor is
not invested with any special equity.(a)   He may pay

(a) Brown v. Cole, 14 Sim. 427.

at law in the mortgagor without the necessity of a reconveyance: 4 Kent's
Com. 194, and notes; Williams on Real Prop. 391; McNair v. Picotte, 33
Mo. 57; Large v. Van Doren, 1 McCart. 211; Gray v. Jenks, 3 Mason
526; Martin v. Mowlin, 2 Burrow 978. Though see Cross v. Robinson, 21
Conn. 379. It must be done before condition broken: Stewart v. Crosby,
50 Maine 130; Grover v. Flye, 5 Allen 543.

Fourth. The transfer or extinguishment of the debt will operate as a
transfer or extinguishment of the mortgage: Hawkins v. King, 2 A. K.
Marsh. 109; Barnes v. Lee, 1 Bibb 526; Ackla v. Ackla, 6 Penn. St. 228;
Wallis v. Long, 16 Ala. 738; Smith v. Smith, 15 N. H. 55; Moore v. Bea-
som, 44 Id. 215; Armitage v. Wickliffe, 12 B. Mon. 488; Marriott v.
Handy, 8 Gill 31; Hadlock v. Bulfinch, 31 Maine 246, 308; Wilson v.
Drumrite, 21 Mo. 325; Blodgett v. Wadhams, Hill & Denio 65; Ledyard
v. Chapin, 6 Ind. 320; Keyes v. Wood, 21 Vt.˙332; Mapps v. Sharpe, 32
Id. 13; Dearborn v. Taylor, 18 N. H. 153; Potter v. Stevens, 40 Mo. 229;
Moore v. Cornell, 68 Penn. St. 320; Hyman v. Devereux, 63 N. C. 624;
though see Dwinel v. Perley, 32 Maine 197; Chappell v. Allen, 38 Mo.
213; Bank v. Anderson, 14 Iowa 544; Olds v. Cummings, 31 Ill. 188. An
assignment of the mortgage without the debt is a nullity: Polhemus v.
Trainer, 30 Cal. 685; Merritt v. Bartholick, 36 N. Y. 44.

Fifth. But the fact that a simple contract debt is barred by the Statute
of Limitations, will not prevent recovery upon a mortgage given to secure
it: Elkins v. Edwards, 8 Geo. 326; Thayer v. Mann, 19 Pick. 535; Bush v.
Cooper, 26 Miss. 599; Whipple v. Barnes, 21 Wis. 327. Though in California, under the statute in that state, the rule is otherwise: Lord v. Morris, 18 Cal. 482.

Sixth. It has been held that a tender of the debt on or after the day upon
which it falls due, discharges the lien of the mortgage: Kortright v. Cady,
21 N. Y. 343; Caruthers v. Humphreys, 12 Mich. 270; Van Husen v.
Kanouse, 13 Mich. 303. But it may well be doubted whether these decisions
are not opposed to the policy of the recording acts, and whether the courts
in other states will not hold a different doctrine.

Seventh. A mortgage being a mere security for a debt, it may be given
to secure future advances, as well as an existing indebtedness: Shirras v.
Craig, 7 Cranch 34; Johnson v. Richardson, 38 N. H. 353; Seymour v.
Darrow, 31 Vt. 122. And see, moreover, Rowan v. Sharpe's Rifle Co., 29
Conn. 282; Thomas v. Kelsey, 30 Barb. 268; Bell v. Fleming, 1 Beasley
13-490; Robinson v. Williams, 22 N. Y. 380; Ladue v. The Railroad Co.,
13 Mich. 380; Joslyn v. Wyman, 5 Allen 62; 4 Kent's Com. 175; Ward

his money according to the proviso, and may thus avoid
the conveyance at law; or if the proviso is not for an

---

v. Cooke, 2 Green (N. J.) 93; Tully *v.* Harloe, 35 Cal. 302; Goddard *v.*
Lawyer, 9 Allen 78 ; Collins *v.* His Creditors, 18 La. Ann. 235; Foster *v.*
Reynolds, 38 Mo. 553 ; Philadelphia, Wilmington & Baltimore R. R. *v.*
Woelpper, 64 Penn. St. 366. And the general rule appears to be that such
advances, if made in pursuance of the original agreement, will be protected against intervening encumbrancers and purchasers with notice
of the agreement, otherwise not: see Farnum *v.* Bennett, 21 N. J. 87 ;
see also, Summers *v.* Roos, 42 Miss. 749 ; D'Meza *v.* Generis, 22 La. Ann.
285. In Hopkinson *v.* Rolt, 9 House Lds. Cas. 514, however, it was held
that where there is a first mortgage to secure future advances, and a second
mortgage is afterwards given of which the first mortgagee has notice, all
advances made after such notice will be postponed to the second mortgage ;
and see The Bank of Montgomery County's Appeal, 36 Penn. St. 170.
This decision overruled the early case of Gordon *v.* Graham, 2 Eq. Cas.
Abr. 598, which was, however, erroneously reported, the decision being in
fact the other way. But the doctrine in Gordon *v.* Graham, *as reported*,
was followed in Wilson *v.* Russell, 13 Md. 495. How far it is essential
that the terms of the agreement for future advances should appear on the
face of the mortgage is not quite clear: 4 Kent 175. If the advances do
not exceed the nominal amount of the lien when recorded, it is decided
that it is not necessary that they should so appear, or that the creditor
should have notice: Craig *v.* Tappin, 2 Sandf. Ch. 78 ; Cadwalader *v.* Montgomery, 3 Am. Law Reg. 169; s. c. Moroney's Appeal, 12 Har. 372; Miller *v.* Lockwood, 32 N. Y. 293. In some of the states, bond debts may be
tacked to a mortgage as against heirs and devisees, but not as against encumbrancers. See note to Marsh *v.* Lee, 1 Lead. Cas. Eq. 494; Trescott
v. King, 2 Selden 147. A mortgage of personal property given to secure
future advances, as well as an existing debt. is valid for the sum due at
the time the mortgagees assert their title: Fairbanks *v.* Bloomfield, 5 Duer
434. See also, Chapin *v.* Cram, 40 Maine 561 ; Hamilton *v.* Rogers, 8 Md.
301. In the former case a mortgage of stock provided that all additions
subsequently made, should be held in the same manner as the goods then
in store. It was held that this clause could have no effect to vest such additions in the mortgagee, without some further act by the mortgagor. See,
in this connection, Carpenter *v.* Simmons, 1 Rob. (N. Y.) 360; Barnard *v.*
Moore, 8 Allen (Mass.) 273 ; Speer *v.* Skinner, 35 Ill. 282. In regard to
mortgages of personal property to be acquired in future, a very clear statement of the law upon the subject will be found in the opinion of the chancellor, in Holroyd *v.* Marshall, 9 Jur. N. S. 213; 10 H. L. Cas. 191. See
also, Smithurst *v.* Edmunds, 1 McCart. 413. As to mortgages by railroads

avoidance of the estate, but for a reconveyance to be made by the mortgagee, he may call on the mortgagee to reconvey accordingly, and on his refusal may file a bill for specific performance. After the day of redemption is passed, a special equity arises for redemption. The express remedy under the proviso is gone; the mortgagee's estate is absolute at law; and the mortgagor's right, to the extent to which it was originally transferred to the mort-[*111] gagee, is *at law finally extinguished. If he has mortgaged his entire estate, *e. g.*, if he has mortgaged land in fee simple, he has no interest remaining; if he has mortgaged a partial estate carved out of his own, *e. g.*, if, being tenant in fee, he has mortgaged for a term, he has only the reversion expectant thereon.[1]

The equity is, that the real transaction was a loan on security, and the forfeiture by non-payment a mere penalty, which may be relieved against on a subsequent satisfaction of the debt. And in accordance with this equity the mortgagor may file a bill, notwithstanding forfeiture, praying for an account and redemption of the estate, and insisting on a reconveyance by the mortgagee on repayment of the principal and interest due, together with all costs in equity or at law properly incurred by the mortgagee in protecting his right.(*b*) Under this head are included costs fairly incurred in defending the title to the estate, in keeping the property in necessary repair, in procuring a renewal of leasehold interests, and so forth ; but not the costs of mere improvements, unless

(*b*) Dryden *v.* Frost, 3 M. & C. 670 ; Morley *v.* Bridges, 2 Coll. 621.

---

of subsequently acquired property, see Morrill *v.* Noyes, 56 Maine 458 ; Pierce *v.* Milwaukee R. R. Co., 24 Wis. 551 ; Philadelphia, Wilmington & Baltimore Railroad Co. *v.* Woelpper, 64 Penn. St. 366.

[1] Alden *v.* Garver, 32 Ill. 32.

they were made by the mortgagor's consent, or acquiesced in by him after notice.(*c*)[1]

If the transaction be not in fact a loan, but a *bonâ fide* sale, with power to repurchase, there is no equity to interfere.(*d*) A clause of redemption, however, is *primâ facie* evidence of a loan. And even if on the face of the conveyance the transaction is termed a purchase, yet its true character may be proved by parol evidence, or by the subsequent conduct of the parties themselves, *e. g.*, if the alleged vendee, instead of entering into receipt of the rents, demands and receives interest for his purchase-money.(*e*)[2]

(*c*) Sandon *v.* Hooper, 6 Bea. 246 ; 14 L. J. 120.

(*d*) Davis *v.* Thomas, 1 R. & M. 506 ; Williams *v.* Owen, 10 Sim. 386 ; Reversed, 12 L. J. 207 ; Bulwer *v.* Astley, 1 Ph. 422 ; Belcher *v.* Varden, 2 Coll. 162 ; [Ford *v.* Irwin, 18 Cal. 117.]

(*e*) Maxwell *v.* Mountacute, Prec. Chanc. 526.

---

[1] See post, note to page 118.

[2] A deed absolute on its face may be shown to be a mortgage by parol evidence, and when it appears that a deed was intended as security for a debt, the debt being paid, the debtor will be entitled to a reconveyance of the estate : Kenton *v.* Vandergrift, 42 Penn. St. 339 ; Taylor *v.* Luther, 2 Sum. 228 ; Morris *v.* Nixon, 1 How. U. S. 118 ; Slee *v.* The Manhattan Company, 1 Paige 48 ; Whittick *v.* Kane, 1 Id. 202 ; Van Buren *v.* Olmstead, 5 Id. 1 ; Strong *v.* Stewart, 4 John. Ch. 167 ; Ross *v.* Norvell, 1 Wash. (Va.) 14 ; Kunkle *v.* Wolfersberger, 6 Watts 126 ; Reitenbaugh *v.* Ludwick, 31 Penn. St. 131 ; Wilson *v.* Shoenberger, Id. 295 ; (though see Alderson *v.* White, 2 De G. & J. 97) ; Todd *v.* Campbell, 32 Penn. St. 250 ; Kellum *v.* Smith, 33 Id. 158 ; Wing *v.* Cooper, 37 Vermont 169 ; Clark *v.* Conceit, 3 Green (N. J.) 358 ; McNeill *v.* Narsworthy, 39 Ala. 156 ; Gay *v.* Hamilton, 33 Cal. 686 ; Shays *v.* Norton, 48 Ill. 100 ; Turner *v.* Kerr, 44 Mo. 429 ; Phillips *v.* Hulsizer, 20 N. J. Eq. 308 ; Whiting *v.* Eichelberger, 16 Iowa 422 ; Halo *v.* Shiek, 57 Penn. St. 320 ; Parmalee *v.* Lawrence, 44 Ill. 405 ; Odenbaugh *v.* Bradford, 67 Penn. St. 96 ; Sweet *v.* Parker, 22 N. J. Eq. 453 ; Horn *v.* Keteltas, 46 N. Y. 605 ; Harper's Appeal, 64 Penn. St. 315 ; Keinck *v.* Price, 4 W. Va. 4 ; Crane *v.* De Camp, 21 N. J. Eq. 414. A court of law will not treat an absolute deed as a mortgage : Farley *v.* Goocher, 11 Iowa 570 ; Johnson's Ex'rs. *v.* Clark, 5

If the character of a security is once impressed on the
[*112] *conveyance, it is a rule never departed from,
that no contemporaneous stipulation can clog the

Ark. 321 ; McDonald v. McLeod, 1 Ired. Eq. 221 ; Randall v. Phillips, 3
Mason 378 ; McLaurin v. Wright, 2 Ired. Ch. 94; Hudson v. Isbell, 5 Stew.
& Port. 67 ; Murphy v. Trigg, 1 Monr. 72 ; Lewis v. Robards, 3 Id. 406 ;
Blair v. Bass, 4 Blackf. 539 ; Delahay v. McConnel, 4 Scam. 156 ; Sellers
v. Stalcup, 7 Ired. Eq. 13 ; Hinson v. Partee, 11 Humph. 387 ; Bank of
Westminster v. Whyte, 1 Md. Ch. 536 ; Conner v. Banks, 18 Ala. 42 ;
Crews v. Threadgill, 35 Id. 334 ; Murphy v. Calley, 1 Allen 107 ; Steel v.
Steel, 4 Id. 417 ; Vanderhaize v. Hughes, 2 Beas. 244 ; Lockerson v. Still-
well, Id. 357 ; Artz v. Grove, 21 Md. 456 ; Rowan v. The Sharpe Rifle
Co., 31 Conn. 1 ; Lee v. Evans, 8 Cal. 424 ; Hovey v. Holcomb, 11
Ill. 660 ; Carter v. Carter, 5 Texas 93 ; Russell's Appeal, 15 Penn. St.
322 ; Bragg v. Massie's Ex'rs., 38 Ala. 89. But see Thomas v. McCormack, 9 Dana 108 ; Streator v. Jones, 1 Mur. 449 ; Thompson v. Patton,
5 Litt. 74 ; Bryant v. Crosby, 36 Maine 562 ; Brown v. Carson, 1 Busbee
Eq. 283 ; Mann's Ex'rs. v. Falcon, 25 Texas 271 ; Cunningham v. Hawkins,
27 Cal. 603. But the proof in such case must be clear, strong, and satisfactory, especially against an answer denying the facts : English v. Lane,
1 Porter 328 ; Conwell v. Evill, 4 Blackf. 67 ; Scott v. Britton, 2 Yerg. 215 ·
Fay v. Eastin, 2 Porter 414 ; Lane v. Dickerson, 10 Yerg. 373 ; Elliott v.
Maxwell, 7 Ired. Eq. 246 ; Chapman v. Hughes, 14 Ala. 218 ; Arnold v.
Mattison, 3 Rich. Eq. 153 ; Sweet v. Mitchell, 15 Wis. 641 ; Tillson v.
Moulton, 23 Ill. 648 ; Kent v. Lasley, 24 Wis. 654 ; McGinity v. McGinity,
63 Penn. St. 38. See the American note to Thornbrough v. Baker, 2
Lead. Cas. Eq., p. 857, 3d Am. ed. ; and to Woollam v. Hearn, Id., page
404, where the question of the admissibility of parol evidence, in such
case, is discussed at large, and placed upon its true ground, the establishment of an equity of redemption in the grantor, and not the creation of a
parol defeasance.

On the same principle, equity leans towards considering an absolute
deed, with an agreement for reconveyance on certain conditions, as a
mortgage, and not a conditional sale : Pearson v. Seary, 35 Ala. 612 ; Pen-
soneau v. Pulliam, 47 Ill. 58 ; Sharkey v. Sharkey, 47 Mo. 543 ; Robinson
v. Willoughby, 65 N. C. 520. See also Holton v. Meighen, 15 Minn. 69 ;
Fiedler v. Darrin, 59 Barb. (N. Y.) 651. Parol evidence of all the material
facts will be admitted, and, if it appear to have been really intended as a
security for money, it will be decreed a mortgage. Great inadequacy of
consideration tends strongly to establish such a conclusion, and the fact
that the agreement for reconveyance contains no promise by the mortgagee
to repay the money, and that no personal security is taken, will not dis-

right of redemption, or entitle the creditor to more than repayment of his principal, interest, and costs. This rule is expressed by the maxim that " Once a mortgage always a mortgage :" and stipulations repugnant to this maxim have been frequently set aside.[1] Such, for ex-

prove it: Russell v. Southard, 12 How. U. S. 139; McLaughlin v. Shepherd, 32 Maine 143; Turnipseed v. Cunningham, 16 Ala. 501; Poindexter v. McCannon, 1 Dev. Eq. 377; Whitney v. French, 25 Verm. 663.; Cross v. Hepner, 7 Ind. 359; Kerr v. Gilmore, 6 Watts 405; Brown v. Nickle, 6 Barr 390; Pearson v. Seay, 38 Ala. 643; Anthony v. Anthony, 23 Ark. 479; Stephenson v. Haines, 16 Ohio St. 478; Snyder v. Griswold, 37 Ill. 216; Tibbs v. Morris, 44 Barb. (N. Y.) 138; Trucks v. Lindsey, 18 Iowa 504; Sears v. Dixon, 33 Cal. 326; Carpenter v. Snelling, 97 Mass. 452; Tabor v. Hamlin, Id. 489. But a conditional sale will unquestionably be supported where the intention of the parties is clear: Conway v. Alexander, 7 Cranch 218; cases cited, note to Thornbrough v. Baker, ut supr., p. 634; Forkner v. Stuart, 6 Gratt. 197; Vasser v. Vasser, 23 Miss. (Cushm.) 378; Galt v. Jackson, 9 Geo. 151; 4 Kent 144; Pitts v. Cable, 44 Ill. 103. A deed conveying land in lieu of a debt cannot be construed a mortgage : Kearney v. Macomb, 1 Green (N. J.) 189. No instrument can be construed a mortgage, in which there does not exist both the right to foreclose and the right to redeem : Chaires v. Brady, 10 Florida 133. The test of the distinction is said to be whether the relation of debtor and creditor in fact subsisted between the parties: see Kent 143, note. Or, to borrow the distinction laid down in Marvin v. Titsworth, 10 Wis. 320, if there is a conveyance directly to the creditor, and the trust is to be executed by him, it is a mortgage; if to a third party, who acts as the agent of both the debtor and the creditor, it is not a mortgage, but a trust. As to which, see infra, 126; see also Slowey v. McMurray, 27 Missouri 119; Hickox v. Lowe. 10 Cal. 197.

[1] This is the universal rule in equity, and no agreement in a mortgage to change it into an absolute conveyance, upon any condition or event whatever, will be allowed to prevail: Clark v. Henry, 2 Cow. 324; Wheeland v. Swartz, 1 Yeates 579; Johnston v. Gray, 16 S. & R. 361; Bloodgood v. Zeily, 2 Cai. Ca. 124; Stoever v. Stoever, 9 S. & R. 434; Wharf v. Howell, 5 Binn. 499; Cooper v. Whitney, 3 Hill 95; Palmer v. Guernsey, 7 Wend. 248; Nugent v. Riley, 1 Metc. 117; Dey v. Dunham, 2 John. Ch. 182; 15 John. 555; Hiester v. Madeira, 3 W. & S. 384. See also Rogan v. Walker, 1 Wis. 527; Knowlton v. Walker, 13 Id. 264; Woods v. Wallace, 22 Penn. St. 171; Locke v. Palmer, 26 Ala. 312. Although in the writing creating an equitable mortgage the time of redemp-

ample, are agreements for restricting the right of redemption to a limited time, (f) for restricting it to a particular line of heirs, (g)[1] for entitling the mortgagee after default to purchase at a specific sum,(h) for converting arrears of interest into principal, so as in effect to give compound interest,(i) for allowing the mortgagee a percentage as receiver, beyond interest on the money advanced,(k) or for allowing him, when in possession under a West Indian mortgage, a like percentage as consignee of the produce. There is a different, and apparently exceptional, rule in favor of a West Indian mortgage out of possession.

(f) Newcomb v. Bonham, 1 Vern. 7.
(g) Howard v. Harris, 2 Ch. Ca. 147.
(h) Willett v. Winnell, 1 Vern. 488.
(i) Blackburn v. Warwick, 2 Y. & C. 92.
(k) Davis v. Dendy, 3 Madd. 170; Langstaffe v. Fenwick, 10 Ves. 405.

---

tion is limited, yet such limitation has no effect on the right to redeem. Once a mortgage always a mortgage: Stover v. Bounds, 1 Ohio St. 107. See also note to Thornbrough v. Baker, 2 Lead. Cas. Eq. 857; Clark v. Condit, 3 Green (N. J.) 358. The purchase of the equity of redemption by a mortgagee is viewed with great disfavor in equity, and will be avoided, for constructive fraud or unconscientious advantage: Russell v. Southard, 12 How. U. S. 139; Platt v. McClure, 3 Wood. & M. 151; note to Thornbrough v. Baker, ut sup. But if perfectly fair it will be sustained: Sheckell v. Hopkins, 2 Md. Ch. 89; McKinstry v. Conly, 12 Ala. 678; Torill v. Skinner, 1 Pick. 213; Green v. Butler, 26 Cal. 595; Decker v. Hall, 1 Edm. (N. Y.) Sel. Cas. 279. Such a purchase will generally create a merger of the mortgage: Jenning's Lessee v. Wood, 20 Ohio 261; Bailey v. Richardson, 9 Hare 734; though not necessarily: Polk v. Reynolds, 31 Md. 106. But this may be prevented by taking the conveyance of the equity of redemption in the name of a trustee, with a declaration of the intention to that effect: Bailey v. Richardson, 9 Hare 734. And equity will in general relieve against such merger, if necessary: Slocum v. Catlin, 22 Verm. 137. A decree of foreclosure does not merge the lien of the mortgagee; that continues until the debt is paid or discharged: Hendershott v. Ping, 24 Iowa 134.

[1] See Johnston v. Gray, 16 S. & R. 361; Slowey v. McMurray, 27 Miss. 113.

And he is allowed to insist on being consignee of the produce, with the usual percentage on the consignments made.(*l*)

The relief thus given on a forfeited mortgage was at first confined to Courts of equity, and the forfeiture at law continued absolute. A partial jurisdiction has been now created at law, but it is confined to cases of the simplest kind, and does not apply even to them if any suit of foreclosure or redemption has been commenced.

The enactment on this subject is, that where an action is brought by a mortgagee, either for payment of the money or for possession of the estate, and no suit of foreclosure or of redemption is pending, if the mortgagor shall appear and become defendant in the action, and shall *pay to the mortgagee, or on his refusal, [*113] shall bring into Court the principal, interest, and costs, the Court of law may discharge him from the mortgage, and may compel the mortgagee to reconvey. By the same statute it is enacted, that where a bill of foreclosure is filed, the Court of equity may, on the defendant's application, and on his admitting the plaintiff's title, make such order or decree before the hearing as it might have made if the suit had been brought to a hearing. But the act does not apply to cases where the right of redemption or the sums chargeable are in controversy.(*m*)

The mortgagor's right to redeem is technically called his " Equity of Redemption," and is treated as a continu-

(*l*) Bunbury *v.* Winter, 1 Jac. & W. 255; Leith *v.* Irvine, 1 M. & K. 277; Falkner *v.* Daniel, 3 Hare 218.

(*m*) 7 Geo. 2, c. 20; Bastard *v.* Clarke, 7 Ves. 489; Praed *v.* Hull, 1 S. & S. 331; Piggin *v.* Cheatham, 2 Hare 80; Reeves *v.* Glastonbury Canal Company, 14 Sim. 351.

ance of his old estate, subject to the mortgagee's pledge
for repayment.[1]

It therefore remains subject to the ordinary incidents of

---

[1] Contracts made with the mortgagor to lessen or embarrass the right of
redemption, are regarded with jealousy: Holridge v. Gillespie, 2 John. Ch.
34. And a mortgagee before foreclosure can do no act to bind the mortgagor when he offers to redeem: Wilson v. Troup, 7 Johns. Ch. 25. But
a contract not to prefer a bill to redeem within a limited time is good.
Such a contract, however, with a further stipulation that at the expiration
of the time stipulated, there should be a foreclosure, unless the debts were
paid, is void, or at least voidable: Daniels v. Mowry, 1 R. I. 151. See,
however, Stover v. Bounds, 1 Ohio St. 197. A Court of equity will restrain a mortgagee from proceeding at law to sell the equity of redemption,
or put him to his election either to proceed directly on his mortgage or to
seek other property (where the rights of creditors do not interfere), or the
person of the debtor for the satisfaction of the debt: Tice v. Annin, 2
John. Ch. 125. As a general rule, no person can come into a Court of
equity for a redemption, unless he is entitled to the estate of the mortgagor, or claims a subsisting interest under it: Grant v. Duane, 9 John.
591; Welch v. Beers, 8 Allen (Mass.) 151; Gage v. Brewster, 31 N. Y.
218.

As to the right of redemption by the mortgagor, his executors, administrators, heirs and assigns, see Smith v. Manning's Ex'rs., 9 Mass. 422;
Wilkins v. Sears, 4 Monr. 347; Douglas v. Sherman, 2 Paige 358; Skinner
v. Miller, 5 Litt. 85; Bell v. Mayor of New York, 10 Paige 49; Beach v.
Cooke, 28 N. Y. 508; Merriam v. Barton, 14 Verm. 501; Sheldon v.
Bird, 2 Root 509; Craik v. Clark, 2 Hay. 22; Farrell v. Parlier, 50 Ill.
274. By judgment creditors, see Hitt v. Holliday, 2 Litt. 332; Dabney v.
Green, 4 Hen. & Munf. 101; Bigelow v. Willson, 1 Pickering 485; and by
subsequent encumbrancers, see Burnet v. Denniston, 5 John. Ch. 35;
Cooper v. Martin, 1 Dana 25; Brown v. Worcester Bank, 8 Metc. 47; Watt
v. Watt, 2 Barb. Ch. 371; McHenry v. Cooper, 27 Iowa 137; Johnson v.
Harmon, 19 Id. 56. See also, Pearce v. Morris, L. R. 8 Eq. 217; and
the right of a subsequent mortgagee to pay off a debt secured by a prior
mortgage, is not affected by an agreement by the parties to such mortgage
for a higher rate of interest than that specified in the mortgage: Gardner
v. Emerson, 40 Ill. 296.

He who redeems must pay the whole debt: Adams v. Brown, 7 Cush.
220; Knowles v. Rablin, 20 Iowa 101; though the debt secured, or part
of it, has become separated from the mortgage by becoming the property
of a different person: Johnson v. Candage, 31 Maine 28; or has become
barred by the statute: Balch v. Onion, 4 Cush. 559.

the estate; it passes in the same course of devolution; it may be devised, settled, or conveyed in the same way; or may be transferred to a new claimant by mere length of enjoyment.(n) And the parties making title by these or any other means to the mortgagor's estate, have the same right with himself to sue for redemption. If there be several persons all claiming under the mortgagor, they will be entitled to redeem successively according to their priorities. Where the mortgagor's estate has altogether determined, and the only claim is in the lord by escheat, a different question arises; for escheat is a mere incident of the law of tenure, and that law, as we have already seen, does not apply to equitable estates.(o) In accordance with this principle, the rule appears to be, that if the mortgage be in fee, so that the whole estate is transferred to the mortgagee, and nothing remains in the mortgagor *which can escheat at law, the lord is not entitled; [*114] but if the mortgage be for a term only, so that a reversion is left which may escheat at law, the incidental equity will pass with it.(oo)

Another result of the principle which treats the equity of redemption as a continuance of the old estate, is that so long as the mortgagor is left in possession, he is considered to hold in respect of his ownership.[1] The ordi-

(n) Cholmondely v. Clinton, 4 Bligh, O. S. 1; 3 & 4 Wm. 4, c 27, s. 24.
(o) Supra.
(oo) Burgess v. Wheate, 1 Eden 177; Downe v. Morris, 3 Hare 394.

---

[1] As between the mortgagor and third persons, the mortgagor is to be considered as possessed of the freehold : Wilkins v. French, 20 Maine 111; Ellison v. Daniels, 11 N. H. 274; Wellington v. Gale, 7 Pick. 159; Groton v. Roxborough, 6 Mass. 50; Hitchcock v. Harrington, 6 John. 295; White v. Whitney, 3 Met. 81; Norwich v. Hubbard, 22 Conn. 587; Whitney v. French, 25 Verm. 663; Johnson v. Brown, 11 Foster 405; Carpenter v. Bowen, 42 Miss. 28; Woods v. Hilderbrand, 46 Mo. 284. A conveyance

nary practice now is, that he should be so left in possession, and that the mortgagee should receive regular payments

---

of the land by the mortgagee, before entry, without a transfer of the debt, passes no interest or title in the land: Smith v. Smith, 15 N. H. 55. A parol assignment of a mortgage, though endorsed on the mortgage deed, and delivered and recorded with it, will not support a writ of entry by the assignee to foreclose the mortgage : Adams v. Parker, 12 Gray (Mass.) 53. And in Pennsylvania, it has never been understood that such privity exists as that the mortgagee can compel the tenant of the mortgagor to pay him the rent whether the lease was executed before or after the mortgage: Myers v. White, 1 Rawle 355. In New York, it has been held that the mortgagee has no right to the freehold, or to anything more than a bare possession, even as between himself and the mortgagor: Runyan v. Mersereau, 11 John. 534; Astor v. Miller, 2 Paige 68. See Hughes v. Edwards, 9 Wheat. 499; Tucker v. Keeler, 4 Verm. 161; Northampton Paper Mills v. Ames, 8 Metcalf 1; Smith v. Moore, 11 N. H. 55; Frothingham v. McKusick, 24 Maine 403; Covell v. Dolloff, 31 Id. 104; Henshaw v. Wells, 9 Humph. 568; 4 Kent Com. 160. A mortgagee has no title, only a lien: Jackson v. Lodge, 36 Cal. 28. Fletcher v. Holmes, 32 Ind. 497; Williams v. Beard, 1 S. C. 309; compare Mack v. Wetzlar, 39 Cal. 247. The contrary doctrine is held in Tennessee: Carter v. Taylor, 3 Head 30. In most of the United States, an equity of redemption is subject to dower, and liable to sale on execution. See 4 Kent Com. 161; though see Otley v. Haviland, 36 Miss. 19; Decker v. Hall, 1 Edm. (N. Y.) Sel. Cas. 279. See also, Hitchcock v. Merrick, 18 Wis. 357; Williams v. Townshend, 31 N. Y. 411.

Though a mortgagor in possession is thus treated in most respects as owner, yet he may be restrained by injunction from such acts of waste as will impair the value of the security: Cooper v. Davis, 15 Conn. 556; Brady v. Waldron, 2 John. Ch. 148. Or an action will lie: Van Pelt v. McGraw, 4 Comst. 110. See Langdon v. Paul, 22 Verm. 205; though see 4 Kent Com. 161.

The owner of the equity of redemption is liable for the taxes, before possession by the mortgagee. Hence, if he buys at a sale of the land for taxes, it will be considered merely a form of payment, and he will acquire no greater title than he had before: Frye v. Bank of Illinois, 11 Ill. 367; Ralston v. Hughes, 13 Id. 469. The payment of taxes by the mortgagor is to be credited in satisfaction of interest and not of principal: Cook v. Smith, 1 Vroom (N. J.) 387.

In Maine, where mortgaged lands are taxed in the name of the mortgagee, no title passes on a sale therefor: Coombs v. Warren, 34 Maine 89.

A mortgagee not having been in possession recovering in ejectment against an occupant, cannot recover for mesne profits prior to his entry

of interest, and should be entitled to call for his principal at six months' notice. If there be an express agreement that the mortgagor shall have possession for a specified period, he is a termor for that period at law; if there be no express agreement, or if he continue to hold after determination of the specified period, he is at law merely an occupant by permission, and may be ejected at any moment by the mortgagee. So long, however, as the mortgagee does not exert his power, the mortgagor is considered in equity to hold as owner, and is entitled to the rents in that character. He cannot, therefore, be made accountable for bygone rents.(p)[1] But if the security be insufficient he may be restrained, at the instance of the mortgagee, from cutting timber on the mortgaged premises.(q) If the possession of the mortgagor continue for twenty years, the mortgagee may under the circumstances be altogether barred of his right. The effect of such possession, under the old law, without demand of possession by the mortgagee, or receipt or demand of principal or interest, was to raise a presumption that the debt was satisfied. And by the present law it is expressly declared, that a mortgagee out of possession shall not proceed, either at law or in equity, to recover the land, except within twenty years after he last had posses-

(p) Ex parte Wilson, 2 Ves. & B. 252.
(q) King v. Smith, 2 Hare 239.

---

under the judgment in ejectment: Litchfield v. Ready, 5 Exch. 939. Nor, prior to a judgment in ejectment, or entry, can he maintain trespass: Turner v. Cameron's, &c., Co. 5 Exch. 932. See Northampton Paper Mills v. Ames, 8 Met. 1.

[1] The mortgagor may authorize a second mortgagee to collect the rents, and apply them as payments on his mortgage, and the court will not restrain him, on application of the first mortgagee, even after the filing of a bill for foreclosure: Best v. Schermier, 2 Halst. Ch. 154.

[*115] sion, *or after the last payment of any principal or interest. (r)[1]   The same principle which treats the mortgagor's equity as the actual ownership, necessarily involves the conclusion, that the mortgagee's legal estate is *e converso* a mere pledge for repayment.

In some sense, therefore, the mortgagee is treated as a trustee for the mortgagor, or rather he is liable to be

(r) Christophers v. Sparke, 2 J. & W. 223 ; 3 & 4 Wm. 4, c. 27, ss. 2, 3 ; 7 Wm. 4 & 1 Vict. c. 28 ; 3 & 4 Wm. 4, c. 42, s. 3.

---

[1] The general rule is, that there may be redemption within twenty years ; but upon equitable circumstances it may be allowed after a much longer time : Ross v. Norwell, 1 Wash. (Va.) 19. The possession to bar the equity of redemption must be actual, quiet and uninterrupted possession for twenty years, or a period of time sufficient to toll the right of entry at law : Moore v. Cable, 1 Johns. Ch. 385 ; Demarest v. Wynkoop, 3 Id. 129 ; Slee v. Manhattan Co., 1 Paige 48 ; Fenwick v. Macey, 1 Dana 279 ; Morgan v. Morgan, 10 Geo. 297 ; Cromwell v. Bank of Pittsburgh, 2 Wallace, Jr. 569 ; Blithe v. Dwinal, 35 Maine 556. But so long as the mortgagee recognises the mortgage in any way, the presumption will not begin to run : Morgan v. Morgan, ut supr. It is not so much the possession, as the nature of the possession, which operates in equity as a bar to redemption. Time does not begin to run against the right to redeem so long as the mortgagee continues to hold as such : Richmond v. Aiken, 25 Verm. 324. In a suit by the mortgagor to redeem, the Statute of Limitations will not avail the mortgagee, unless he has been in actual possession of the land. In Missouri, payment of taxes on wild land is not equivalent to possession : Bollinger v. Chouteau, 20 Mo. 89. So where a mortgage was given on wild land, of which neither party was in possession, there being evidence that the debts were unpaid, the lapse of thirty years was held no bar to a foreclosure : Chouteau v. Burlando, 20 Mo. 482.

In some of the states, fifteen years' possession, where no statute disabilities or special circumstances equivalent thereto exist, will bar an equity of redemption : Skinner v. Smith, 1 Day 124 ; Crittenden v. Brainard, 2 Root, 485 ; Richmond v. Aiken, 25 Verm. 324 ; see Robinson v. Fife, 3 Ohio N. S. 551.

On the other hand, after the lapse of twenty years, the mortgagor being in possession and no interest paid, there is a presumption of satisfaction of the mortgage debt : Boyd v. Harris, 2 Md. Ch. 210 ; Roberts v. Welch, 8 Ired. Eq. 287 ; Ayres v. Waite, 10 Cush. 72 ; Cheever v. Perley, 11 Allen 584. Otherwise where the possession has been in the mortgagee : Crooker a. Jewell, 31 Maine 306. See Martin v. Jackson, 27 Penn. St. 504.

made a trustee by payment of his claim. But nothing
short of payment can affect his right. He is not bound
to reconvey on a deposit of the money in Court, however
inconvenient his refusal may prove; nor is he even bound
to allow an inspection of the title deeds until the money
is actually in his hands.(s)[1] And so long as the mortgage
remains undischarged, he is entitled to settle and deal
with it as his own, and if his so doing renders the redemption more expensive, the mortgagor must nevertheless defray the expense.(t)

The parties to whom the mortgagee may transfer his
interest, or who may otherwise make title to his estate,
are of course bound by the same equity as himself; but
if his estate has escheated, and redemption is asked
against the lord, there appears to be some question
whether the equity is binding. It has been contended
that there is a difference in this respect between a trust
and an equity of redemption, and that although the lord
is not bound by a trust, unless he is party or privy to it,
yet that he shall be bound by an equity of redemption,
whether he were privy or not.(u)[2] The distinction, however, it would probably be difficult to sustain.

(s) Brown v. Lockhart, 10 Sim. 421; Richards v. Platel, Cr. & P. 79;
Postlethwaite v. Blythe, 2 Sw. 256.

(t) Wetherell v. Collins, 3 Madd. 255; Bartle v. Wilkins, 8 Sim. 238;
Barry v. Wrey, 3 Russ. 465; Re Marrow, Cr. & P. 142; Re Townsend, 2
Ph. 348.

(u) Burgess v. Wheate, 1 Eden 177; Attorney-General v. Duke of Leeds,
2 M. & K. 343.

---

[1] The renewal of a note secured by mortgage, is not such a payment as
will discharge the mortgage unless so intended: Parkhurst v. Cummings,
56 Me. 135; nor is it defeated or impaired by partial payments; the mortgage lien remains so long as the debt is unpaid: Chase v. Abbott, 20 Iowa
154. Though see Smith v. Smith, 32 Ill. 198. Money paid to the mortgagee
designed at the time to be applied as payment, will operate to extinguish
the mortgage to that amount: Champney v. Coope, 32 N. Y. 543.

[2] In most of the United States it is provided by statute that on the

[*116]   *The statutory remedy against escheat in the case of a trustee, has already been considered, under the subject of trusts. And we had, at the same time, occasion to notice the analogous remedies provided by another statute, in the event of lunacy or infancy of a trustee, and in the event of a trustee being out of the jurisdiction, of doubts as to survivorship or heirship, and of a refusal to convey when properly required.(v) The provisions with respect to lunacy and infancy, are expressly made applicable to mortgages also. The applicability of the other provisions has been a subject of some discussion. But the doubts are now cleared up by a later statute, which after reciting the two former acts, provides for the case of a mortgagee who has died without having been in possession and to whose executor or administrator the mortgage-money has been paid, and expressly confines the operation of the former acts to that particular case.(w) The enactments of the statute referred to are that, "where any person seised of land by way of mortgage, shall have departed this life without having been in possession of such land, or in the receipt of the rents and profits thereof, and the money due in respect of such mortgage shall have been or shall be paid to his executor or administrator, and the devisee or heir or other real representative, or any of the devisees or heirs, or real representatives, of such mortgagee shall be out of the jurisdiction, or not amenable to the process of the Court of Chancery, or it shall be uncertain, where

(v) 3 & 4 Wm. 4, c. 23 ; 11 Geo. 4 & 1 Wm. 4, c. 60, supra.
(w) 1 & 2 Vict. c. 69.

escheat of land it shall be held upon the same trusts and under the same encumbrances as before: 4 Kent's Com. 425 ; 1 Greenleaf's Cruise 417 ; note to Hill on Trustees, 4th Am. ed. 78.

there are several devisees or representatives who were
joint tenants, which of them was the survivor, or it shall
be uncertain whether any such devisee or heir or representative be living or dead, or if known to be dead, it
shall not be known who was his heir, or where such
mortgagee or any such devisee or heir, or representative
shall have died without an heir, or if any such devisee or
heir or representative shall neglect or refuse to convey
such land for the space of twenty-eight *days next [*117]
after a proper deed for making such conveyance
shall have been tendered for his execution by, or by an
agent duly authorized by, any person entitled to require
the same, then and in every such case it shall be lawful
for the Court of Chancery to direct any person whom such
Court may think proper to appoint for that purpose, in
the place of the devisee, heir, or representative (whether
such devisee, heir, or representative shall or shall not
have a beneficial interest in the money paid to the executor or administrator as aforesaid), to convey such land in
like manner as by the said first recited act, the said
Court is empowered to appoint a person to convey in the
cases therein mentioned in the place of a trustee or the
heir of a trustee, and every such conveyance shall be as
effectual as if such devisee or heir or representative had
executed the same." And it is further enacted, that the
provisions of this act shall embrace the same objects as
they would have done if they had formed part of the
said recited acts, and should not extend to the case
of any person dying seised of any land by way of mortgage other than such as are in such act expressly provided for.(x)

(x) Re Goddard, 1 M. & K. 25; Prendergast v. Eyre, Ll. & G. 181; Ex
parte Whitton, 1 K. 279; Green v. Holden, 1 Bea. 207.

If the mortgagee is dissatisfied with the security for his debt, he may enforce payment by an action at law, or may take possession of the mortgaged estate ; or he may, if he choose, pursue both these remedies at the same time, and any other which his contract confers. For the right to do so is part of his security, and if the mortgagor is inconvenienced by its exercise, his proper remedy is payment of the debt.$(y)^1$

If the mortgagee takes possession of the estate, he is treated in equity as holding in respect of his security, and must deal with the estate in conformity with that character. He is bound therefore to keep the premises [*118] in necessary *repair, but is not bound to spend more than is strictly necessary. He must account for all the moneys which he in fact has received, or which without wilful default he might have received, but is not bound to take the trouble of making the most of the property. He is entitled to receive any incidental benefit, provided it be of a pecuniary kind, and therefore applicable in liquidation of his debt; but if it be not of that character, as, for example, if it be the presentation to a

---

(y) Schoole v. Sall, 1 Sch. & L. 176; Drummond v. Pigou, 2 M. & K. 168; Lockhart v. Hardy, 9 Bea. 349.

---

[1] The mortgagee may enter or maintain ejectment: Hughes v. Edwards, 9 Wheaton 489; Dunkley v. Van Buren, 3 John. Ch. 330; Callum v. Emanuel, 1 Ala. 22. See also Fluck v. Replogle, 13 Penn. St. 406; Smith v. Schuler, 12 S. & R. 240; Martin v. Jackson, 27 Penn. St. 504; Clay v. Wren, 34 Maine 187; Wilhelm v. Lee, 2 Md. Ch. 322; Brown v. Stewart, 1 Id. 87; Wheeler v. Bates, 1 Foster (N. H.) 460; Youngman v. Elmira R. R., 65 Penn. St. 278; Allen v. Ranson, 44 Mo. 263. See, in Vermont, under the statute of that state, Pierce v. Brown, 24 Verm. 165. The mortgagee is entitled to pursue all his remedies at once: Brown v. Stewart, ut sup. A mere entry for a particular purpose will not, however, be deemed to be a taking possession: Great Falls Co. v. Worster, 15 N. H. 412.

vacant living, the mortgagor must have it as the real owner.(z)[1]

(z) Mackensie v. Robinson, 3 Atk. 559.

---

[1] A mortgagee in possession is accountable for the profits really made, and no further, except in case of gross negligence: Bainbridge v. Owen, 2 J. J. Marsh 465; Van Buren v. Olmstead, 5 Paige 9; Bell v. The Mayor, &c., of New York, 10 Paige 49; Strong v. Blanchard, 4 Allen 538; Anthony v. Rogers, 20 Mo. 281; and is not, in general, chargeable with interest on rents: Breckenridge v. Brooks, 2 A. K. Marsh. 339. But see Shaeffer v. Chambers, 2 Halst. Ch. 548; Boston Iron Co. v. King, 2 Cush. 400; as to where rests will be allowed. See also Smith v. Pilkington, 1 De G., F. & J. 120. Rents received by a mortgagee should be applied to keep down the interest: Saunders v. Frost, 5 Pickering 260; McConnel v. Holobush, 11 Ill. 61; Moore v. Cable, 1 John. Ch. 385; Bell v. New York, 10 Paige 49; Rawling v. Stewart, 1 Bland 22. Then to the payment of the principal: Mahone v. Williams, 39 Ala. 202. But a mortgagee is not entitled to compensation for his trouble in managing the estate, whether the parties have agreed to make such allowance or not: Breckenridge v. Brooks, 2 A. K. Marsh. 339. The only repairs made by the mortgagee, without the mortgagor's consent, which will be allowed to the mortgagor, are strictly necessary repairs. Beneficial expenditures, if unnecessary, will not be allowed: Quinn v. Brittain, 1 Hoff. Ch. 353; Hagthorp v. Hook, 1 Gill & J. 270; Lowndes v. Chisolm, 2 McCord Ch. 455; McConnel v. Holobush, 11 Ill. 61; Boston Iron Co. v. King, 2 Cush. 400; Hidden v. Jordan, 32 Cal. 397. Taxes will be allowed: Goodrich v. Friedersdorff, 27 Ind. 308. With few exceptions, it is a general rule in Chancery that a mortgagee in possession is not entitled to any allowance for new improvements erected on the premises: Dougherty v. McColgan, 6 Gill & J. 275. See Boston Iron Co. v. King, ut sup.; Harper's Appeal, 64 Penn. St. 315. Where a mortgagee insures, without contract, and the loss is paid him, it is not to be deducted from his charges for repairs: White v. Brown, 2 Cush. 412; Garden v. Ingram, 23 L. J. Ch. 478. On the other hand, as the mortgagor is not bound to insure, the mortgagee cannot charge him with premiums: Dobson v. Land, 8 Hare 216.

A mortgagee by taking possession, assumes the duty of treating the property as a provident owner would treat it: Shaeffer v. Chambers, 2 Halst. Ch. 548. If it be a farm, for instance, he is not at liberty to let it lie untilled, because the house on it, or the house and farm together, were not rented, but must keep it in good ordinary repair, and is bound to good ordinary husbandry: Shaeffer v. Chambers, ut sup. And he will be charged with the rent he might have obtained for it, although by cultivating it

In taking the account of a mortgagee in possession,
where the rents h́ave exceeded the interest on his mortgage, a question occurs, whether he shall be charged with
interest on the surplus rents.   If he is not to be charged
with such interest, the account is taken by ascertaining
on the one hand the aggregate amount of principal and
interest down to the period of redemption, and on the
other hand the aggregate amount of rent, down to the
same period, and striking a balance of the two accounts.
If he is to be charged with interest, the account is taken
by making rests from time to time, and striking a balance
at each rest, so as to apply the surplus rents in gradual
reduction of the principal debt, and in consequent diminution of the subsequent interest.   The effect of this
course is equivalent to allowing interest throughout on
the entire principal, and charging interest on the surplus
rents.

In order to authorize the rests, an express direction of

---

himself he has actually sustained a loss : Sanders v. Wilson, 34 Verm. 321 ;
and see Miller v. Lincoln, 6 Gray 556.

So a mortgagee in possession of slaves is bound to exercise reasonable
diligence in keeping them engaged in useful employments, so as not only
to pay their expenses, but also to obtain a reasonable compensation for
their labor : Bennett v. Butterworth, 12 How. U. S. 367.

So, in general, a mortgagee of personalty in possession, after condition
broken, is responsible for ordinary diligence, and liable for ordinary ne-
gleet.

If the property is destroyed without fault of his, he cannot be held to
account for it ; but he is accountable for the net profits before its destruction : Covell v. Dolloff, 31 Maine 104.

How the account of the rents and profits is to be taken, see Powell v.
Williams, 14 Ala. 476 ; Shaeffer v. Chambers, 2 Halst. Ch. 548.

A mortgagee in possession is liable to an action for waste : Givens v. Mc-
Calmont, 4 Watts 460.   He cannot be dispossessed by the holder of the
legal title.   Being in possession he is entitled to retain it until his mortgage is satisfied : Sahler v. Signer, 44 Barb. (N. Y.) 606.

the Court is necessary,(a) and the *primâ facie* presumption is against allowing them. For the mortgagee is not bound to take payments by instalments, and his possession is in consequence of the mortgagor's default. If, however, he take possession when no interest is in arrears, he is not compelled to do so by the mortgagor's default, and rests will be decreed against him. It is otherwise if interest is in *arrear at the time; and he will not in that [*119] case become liable to account with rests until both principal and interest have been discharged. If he continue in possession after that time, annual rests will be decreed for the subsequent period.(b)

The liability of a mortgagee in possession to account is confined to a period of twenty years, unless continued by his own acknowledgment. The rule formerly was, that if a mortgagee were in possession for twenty years, without keeping accounts or otherwise dealing with the property as mortgagee, a presumption arose that the equity was released. And by the present law it is expressly declared that the mortgagor out of possession shall not be entitled to redeem, except within twenty years after the mortgagee took possession, or after a written acknowledgment of his right, signed by the mortgagee, has been given to him or his agent.(c)

The remedy of the mortgagee by taking possession is practically very inconvenient. Yet if the forfeiture by non-payment had been taken away, and not replaced by any substitute, it would have been the only one attainable under his security. In order to remedy this objection,

(a) Webber v. Hunt, 1 Mad. 13.

(b) Quarrell v. Beckford, 1 Mad. 269; Wilson v. Metcalf, 1 Rus. 530· Wilson v. Cluer, 3 Bea. 136; Horlock v. Smith, 1 Coll. 287.

(c) Hodle v. Healey, 6 Mad. 181; Cholmondeley v. Clinton, 4 Bl. O. S. 1; 3 & 4 Wm. 4, c. 27, s. 28, supra.

the mortgagee is allowed after forfeiture to file a bill praying foreclosure of the equity to redeem. A new day for payment is then fixed by decree, and if default be made, the mortgagor's right is destroyed. The foreclosure, however, may be opened and the right of redemption revived, if the decree appear to have been unfairly obtained, or if the mortgagee treat the loan as still continuing; as, for example, if he proceed against the mortgagor on bond or other collateral security. If he sell the estate, and thus render it impossible to reopen the foreclosure, he will be restrained from suing on the [*120] collateral securities, although the sale *may have been *bonâ fide* made for less than the amount due.(d)

The effect of foreclosure is also produced by the dismissal of a redemption bill on default in payment, for the Court will not again interfere, but will leave the parties to their rights at law.

It must be observed, that the right of the mortgagee on such a bill is a right merely to foreclose the equity, and does not extend to warrant a sale. For although a sale would be often more convenient than a foreclosure, yet it is not stipulated for by the contract, and the Court has no more authority to sell the mortgaged estate for payment of the debt, than to sell the mortgagor's other estates for the same purpose. If; however, the property mortgaged be a right of presentation to a church,(e) or a dry reversion, incapable of producing present profit,(f) the mortgagee in entitled to a sale, is respect of the special

(d) Tooke v. Hartley, 2 B. C. C. 125; Perry v. Barker, 8 Ves. 527; 13 Ves. 198; Lockhart v. Hardy, 9 Bea. 349.

(e) Mackensic v. Robinson, 3 Atk. 559.

(f) How v. Vigues, 15 Viner's Abr. 475.

character of the mortgaged property, and its incapacity of constituting, except by a sale, a practical security for the debt. And in cases where stock has been transferred by way of mortgage, the mortgagee is entitled by the custom of business to sell immediately on default, without the necessity of obtaining a decree.(*g*) In those cases also where there is a special supervening jurisdiction, and where the Court does not act in respect of the mortgage alone, a decree for sale may be obtained. If, for example, the mortgagor be dead, there is an independent jurisdiction to administer his assets, and therefore if the personalty be insufficient, the mortgaged estate may be sold by consent of the mortgagee, and the produce applied, first in discharge of the mortgage, and then in payment of the other debts,(*h*) or if the estate has *been vested in an infant, a sale may be directed as indispensable for [*121] his benefit, lest the estate should be foreclosed and lost.(*i*) In Ireland, and some of the American courts, a different rule prevails, and the mortgagee may in all cases require a sale.(*k*)[1] If an express power of sale is given by the

(*g*) Tucker *v.* Wilson, 1 P. W. 261.

(*h*) Daniel *v.* Skipwith, 2 B. C. C. 155.

(*i*) Mondey *v.* Mondey, 1 Ves. & B. 223; Brookfield *v.* Bradley, Jac. 634; Davis *v.* Dowding, 2 K. 245.

(*k*) 2 Story on Eq. Jur. s. 1025; [Brinkerhoff *v.* Thallhimer, 2 John. Ch. 486; Mills *v.* Dennis, 3 Id. 369.]

---

[1] In England, by Stat. 15 & 16 Vict. c. 86, s. 48, the Court of Chancery is now empowered in a foreclosure suit, to direct a sale of the property at the request of either party; and recent statutes have regulated the mortgagee's remedy by powers of sale. See Williams on Real Property 396. In some of the United States the remedy in equity obtains: 4 Kent's Com. 181; in others the proceedings are regulated by statute: Williams on Real Property 395, note.

In many of the states the ancient practice of procuring a strict foreclosure is not adopted: Nelson *v.* Carrington, 4 Munf. 332; Rodgers *v* Jones, 1 McCord's Ch. 221; Downing *v.* Palmateer, 1 Monr. 66; Pannell

18

mortgage, such a power forms an additional remedy for the
mortgagee, and does not interfere with his right to foreclose.[1]

If the mortgagor become bankrupt, the position of the
mortgagee as to foreclosure is changed. He loses the
right, which he previously had, of enforcing payment as
a general creditor, and retaining in the meantime his
power to foreclose. For the principle of the Bankrupt
Law, which aims at distributing a debtor's property among

---

v. Farmers' Bank, 7 Har. & J. 202; Humes *v.* Shelly, 1 Tenn. 79; Hord *v.*
James, Id. 201; David *v.* Grahame, 2 Har. & G. 94. See Henderson *v.*
Lowry, 5 Yerg. 240; Smith *v.* Bailey, 1 Shaw (Verm.) 163; Lockwood
v. Lockwood, 1 Day 295; Baylies *v.* Bussey, 5 Greenleaf 153; Gilman
v. Hidden, 5 N. H. 31; Erskine *v.* Townsend, 2 Mass. 493; 5 Ham.
554.

The practice in the New England states seems to be similar to that of
the English Courts: Mix *v.* Hotchkiss, 14 Conn. 32; but see Gibson *v.* Bailey,
9 N. H. 168; and, in North Carolina, see Spiller *v.* Spiller, 1 Hayw. 482;
see, in Maine, Chamberlain *v.* Gardner, 38 Maine 548. In Pennsylvania
a mortgage may be foreclosed by *scire facias;* so in Illinois and in Missouri by petition and summons. It was held in Riley *v.* McCord, 24
Missouri 265, that a mortgagee had still a right to come into equity, notwithstanding the remedy provided by statute; and see Hall *v.* Hall, 46
N. H. 240; McCumber *v.* Gilman, 13 Ill. 542. In Pennsylvania, however,
the Courts have no equitable jurisdiction to compel the sale of the mortgaged premises at the suit of the mortgagee; the remedy is by *scire facias*
under the statute: Ashhurst *v.* The Montour Iron Co., 35 Penn. St. 30;
Bradley *v.* The Chester Valley R. R. Co., 36 Id. 141.

[1] Carradine *v.* O'Connor, 21 Ala. 573; Walton *v.* Cody, 1 Wis. 420. A
power to mortgage includes a power to execute a mortgage containing a
power to the mortgagee to sell the premises in default of payment, it being
one of the usual and lawful remedies given to a mortgagee, known to the
law and·regulated by statute: Wilson *v.* Troup, 7 John. Ch. 25; 2 Cowen
195, s. *v.* See Russell *v.* Plaice, 18 Bea. 21. And a power to sell in a
mortgage deed, on default of payment, is a power coupled with an interest,
and does not die with the mortgagor: Bergen *v.* Bennett, 1 Caines Cas.
in Eq. 1; Varnum *v.* Meserve, 8 Allen (Mass.) 158. A sale under a power in
a mortgage must pursue strictly, as to time and place, the stipulation in the
mortgage: Hall *v.* Towne, 45 Ill. 493.·

all his creditors, will not permit a creditor to keep back part of that property, and at the same time to share in the distribution of the rest. The mortgagee therefore must elect between two courses. He must either relinquish his security and prove for the whole debt; or he must realize his security, and afterwards prove for so much of the debt as the produce is insufficient to discharge. And in order to effectuate this latter course, it is directed that the commissioner acting under the fiat, on being satisfied of the creditor's title as mortgagee, shall take an account of the moneys due; shall cause the mortgaged premises to be sold, and the produce to be applied, first in payment of the expenses, and then in satisfaction of the claim; and if the moneys produced shall be insufficient to satisfy it, shall admit the mortgagee as a creditor for the deficiency, and to receive dividends thereon.(*l*)[1]

In addition to regular or perfect mortgages, which *convey the legal estate to the mortgagee, and specify a day of forfeiture at law, there are other [*122] securities of an analogous character, but defective in one or both of these respects.

These imperfect securities are seven in number: viz., 1. Mortgages of a trust or equity of redemption, and

---

(*l*) General Order in Bankruptcy of 8th March, 1794; 1 Mont. & Ayrton's Bankruptcy 243; Greenwood *v.* Taylor, 1 R. & M. 185; Mason *v.* Bogg, 2 M. & C. 443; Davis *v.* Dowding, 2 K. 245.

---

[1] Where a mortgagor becomes bankrupt, and a deficiency of his property is apprehended, and a prior mortgagee obtains the appointment of a receiver to collect the rents, such mortgagee acquires a lien upon the rents, and, upon motion, they may be applied to the mortgage debt: Post *v.* Dorr, 4 Edw. Ch. 412. See, as to the appointment of a receiver, Cortleyeu *v.* Hathaway, 3 Stockt. 39; Finch *v.* Houghton, 19 Wis. 149; Hyman *v.* Kelly, 1 Nev. 179. A receiver cannot be appointed at the commencement of the foreclosure suit: Ibid.

equitable mortgages by imperfect conveyance, or by contract to convey; 2. Equitable mortgages by deposit of title deeds unaccompanied by a written contract; 3. Welsh mortgages; 4. Trust deeds in the nature of mortgage; 5. The equitable lien of a vendor or purchaser of real estate; 6. Equitable *fi. fa.* and *elegit ;* and 7. Judgment charges under 1 and 2 Vict. c. 110, s. 13 and 14.

The first class of imperfect mortgages are, mortgages of a trust or equity of redemption. In a mortgage of this kind the legal estate is *ex concessis* outstanding in the trustee or prior encumbrancer, and cannot be transferred to the mortgagee. He is therefore disabled from obtaining possession at law, and is entitled in consequence of that disability, to have a receiver appointed in equity, by whom the rents of the estate may be received, and applied in satisfaction of his mortgage. A receiver, however, will not be appointed, if a prior legal encumbrancer is in possession, unless the applicant will pay off his demand. If the prior encumbrancer be not in possession, the appointment may be made, without prejudice to his right of applying for the possession. A legal mortgagee cannot have a receiver, but must take possession under his legal title. (*m*)

It should be observed that where an equity of redemption is the subject of mortgage, the mortgagor is bound to disclose the prior mortgage; and that if he conceals it and represents the land as unencumbered, he is liable by statute to forfeit his equity, and to be *ipso facto* foreclosed in favor of the second mortgagee. (*n*) By the same act it is [*123] *enacted that if a person bound by judgment, statute or recognisance, borrow money on mort-

(*m*) Berney *v.* Sewell, 1 Jac. & W. 627; Brookes *v.* Greathed, Id. 176.
(*n*) 4 & 5 Wm. 3, c. 16; Stafford *v.* Selby, 2 Vern. 589.

gage, without giving notice thereof in writing, he must discharge the judgment, statute, or recognisance, within six months after requisition by the mortgagee, and that in default in so doing, he shall be *ipso facto* foreclosed.

Mortgages of the kind just considered may be properly called "mortgages of an equity;" there are also other imperfect mortgages, which may be termed "equitable mortgages," consisting of mortgages by imperfect conveyances, or by an uncompleted contract to convey. Mortgages of this latter class entitle the mortgagee to claim specific performance and the execution of a legal mortgage. In the meantime, they stand on the same footing as mortgages of an equity, and entitle the mortgagee to a receiver of the rents.[1]

The second class of imperfect mortgages are equitable mortgages by deposit of title deeds, unaccompanied by a written contract.[2]

---

[1] A Court of equity will often pronounce that to be an equitable mortgage, which at law would be considered a conditional sale, and if a conveyance resolves itself into a security for the performance or non-performance of any act, it is a mortgage, whatever be its form: Flagg v. Mann, 2 Sum. 486. It has been held in several of the United States, that any agreement *in writing* to give a mortgage, or imperfect attempt to create a mortgage, or to appropriate specific property in discharge of a particular debt, will be treated in equity as a mortgage, or a specific lien, which will have precedence of subsequent judgment creditors: Read v. Simons, 2 Dessaus. 552; Welsh v. Usher, 2 Hill Eq. 167; Dow v. Ker, 1 Spear Eq. 414; In the matter of Howe, 1 Paige 125; Bank of Muskingum v. Carpenter, 7 Ohio 21; Lake v. Doud, 10 Ohio 415. See Brown v. Nickle, 6 Penn. St. 390; Locke v. Palmer, 26 Ala. 312; note to Russel v. Russel, 1 Lead. Cas. Eq. 541; Racouillat v. Sansevain, 32 Cal. 376. This is a question, however, which depends to some extent upon the policy of the recording acts.

There can be no mortgage of property not yet in existence, at law, and in equity an instrument of such a character will be regarded as a mere contract, giving no right over the property when it is acquired, and so far as it entitles the mortgagee to specific performance, is subordinate to intervening liens: Otis v. Sill, 8 Barb. S. C. 102.

[2] Equitable mortgages by deposit have been sustained in Rockwell v.

The *primâ facie* effect of such deposit is, that, until payment, the debtor cannot get back his title deeds, and therefore cannot conveniently deal with the estate; and if the right conferred on the creditor had stopped here, it would not have been in the nature of a mortgage at all, but would have been very similar to a solicitor's lien, viz., a right to hold the deeds so as to enforce payment by embarrassing the debtor, but unaccompanied by any charge on the estate.   The attempt to carry the security beyond this limit, and to make such deposits a charge on the estate was seriously impeded by the enactment of the Statute of Frauds, that no interest in land shall be created otherwise than by writing; but it has been held that the fact of the deeds being delivered to the creditor, raises an implication of law, not only that they were to operate as a security for the debt, but that such security was to be [*124]   effectuated by a mortgage.(*o*)   *The conclusion, however, on this latter point seems unsatisfactory; for although there may be a sufficient ground to presume that a security was meant, yet the deposit might effectuate that object by embarrassing the debtor without necessarily charging the land.   The doctrine was several times commented on by Lord Eldon, who admitted that

(*o*) Russel *v.* Russel, 1 B. C. C. 269 ; Ex parte Whitbread, 19 Ves. 209 ; Ex parte Hooper, 1 Meriv. 7 ; Parker *v.* Housefield, 2 M. & K. 419.

Hobby, 2 Sandf. Ch. 9 ; Williams *v.* Stratton, 10 Smed. & M. 418 ; and see Welsh *v.* Usher, 2 Hill Eq. 170 ; Jarvis *v.* Dutcher, 16 Wis. 307. In Pennsylvania, it has been decided that an equitable mortgage by delivery of title deeds, or otherwise by *parol*, is not valid : Shitz *v.* Dieffenbach, 3 Penn. St. 233 ; Bowers *v.* Oyster, 3 Penna. R. 240 ; Thomas's Appeal, 30 Penn. St. 378 ; see also as to Kentucky : Vanmeter *v.* McFaddin, B. Monr. 435. See Edwards Ex'rs. *v.* Trumbull, 50 Penn. St. 509. So also, in Ohio : Probasco *v.* Johnson, 2 Disney 96.

It seems such a mortgage would not be valid in Vermont, though the point was not decided : Bicknell *v.* Bicknell, 31 Verm. 498.

it was established by precedent, but said that it ought never to have been so established.

In conformity with this doctrine a mere delivery of deeds, by way of security, unaccompanied by any written contract, will constitute in equity a charge on the land. And by parity of reasoning, the security may be extended to future advances, if they are made under a parol agreement to that effect, although in the case of an ordinary mortgage, or of a contract for conveyance as distinct from deposit, a writing would be necessary under the Statute of Frauds.(p)

Mortgages of this kind are not unusual, especially in the case of persons in trade where loans are required for a short period, and the parties are desirous of saving time and expense.

Their essentials are, as we have already seen, that the deeds be delivered to the creditor, and that the delivery be by way of pledge, and not *diverso intuitu*.[1] A delivery to a third person on behalf of the creditor would probably be sufficient if the intention were proved. But if the deeds are retained by the mortgagor a parol agreement to deposit them is ineffectual.(q) If a portion only of the deeds be delivered, it appears to be sufficient, provided the delivery be with the intention to create a security.

But if part be delivered to one creditor. and part to another, there may be much difficulty in considering either of them as an equitable mortgagee, or as entitled

(p) Ex parte Whitbread, 19 Ves. 209 ; Ex parte Hooper, 1 Meriv. 7.

(q) Ex parte Coming, 9 Ves. 115; Ex parte Whitbread, 19 Ves. 209 ; Ex parte Coombe, 4 Madd. 249.

---

[1] The mere fact that the title deeds are in a bond-creditor's possession, is not sufficient evidence by itself of an equitable mortgage in his favor : Chapman *v.* Chapman. 13 Beav. 308.

to more than his right of detainer.(r)[1] If the delivery [*125] is not strictly by way of *pledge, but in order to the preparation of a regular mortgage, there seems to be additional difficulty in sustaining it as an equitable mortgage. For the implication arising out of the mere deposit, that such deposit itself was meant as a charge, is expressly negatived by the proved intent. And if that intent is specifically enforced by directing a mortgage to be made, the direction will be based, not on an implication of law, but on express parol evidence, admitted in contravention of the Statute of Frauds. The authorities, however, are in favor of the mortgagee's claim.(s)

The effect of a mortgage by deposit is that the mortgagee has an equitable charge on the land. He is not invested with the legal ownership; and for this reason he is entitled, like the mortgagee of an equity, to have a receiver appointed of the rents. His mortgage specifies no day of payment, and a doubt therefore has existed whether his proper remedy is by foreclosure or by a decree for sale. The decisions on this point are not uniform,

(r) Ex parte Wetherell, 11 Ves. 401; Ex parte Pearse, Buck 525; Ex parte Chippendale, 2 M. & A. 299.

(s) Norris v. Wilkinson, 12 Ves. 192; Ex parte Bruce, 1 Rose 374; Hockley v. Bantock, 1 Russ. 141; Keys v. Williams, 3 Y. & C. 55.

---

[1] In Roberts v. Croft, 24 Beav. 223, the equitable mortgagor deposited with one creditor all the deeds except the last conveyance to himself, and this he subsequently placed with another person. It was held that the first creditor was entitled to priority, on the ground that title papers deposited by way of mortgage need not necessarily show the mortgagor's title. In Daw v. Terrell, 33 Beav. 218, the deposit of deeds of two lots, and an order on the mortgagor's bankers for the deeds of a third, were held to constitute a good equitable mortgage as to the whole. The deeds of the third property had been deposited with the bankers by way of mortgage, and, on payment, had been returned to the mortgagor.

but their result appears to be that the implied contract is one for a legal mortgage, and therefore carries with it all the rights which a legal mortgage would confer, including the right of foreclosure. Whether he is bound to abide by that right, or may claim in the alternative a sale of the estate, seems to be still in doubt.(t)[1]

The third and fourth classes of imperfect mortgages are Welsh mortgages, and trusts deeds in the nature of mortgages.

A Welsh mortgage is a conveyance of an estate redeemable at any time on payment of principal and interest, and its chief imperfection is the want of a specified day of forfeiture. The consequence of this want is that the mortgagee's remedy is confined to perception of the rents, and *that he is not entitled to foreclosure [*126] or sale, nor will his liability to account be determined by the lapse of time, unless he has continued in possession for twenty years after the debt was fully paid and satisfied.(u)[2]

Trust deeds in the nature of mortgage are mere conveyances to the creditor, on trust for the debtor until default; and after default, on trust to sell and to retain the

(t) Pain v. Smith, 2 M. & K. 417; Parker v. Housefield, 2 M. & K. 419; Brocklehurst v. Jessop, 7 Sim. 438; Moores v. Choat, 8 Sim. 508, 515, 523; Price v. Carver, 3 M. & C. 157, 161; Lister v. Turner, 5 Hare 281.

(u) Yates v. Hambley, 2 Atk. 360; Fenwick v. Reed, 1 Meriv. 114; Teulon v. Curtis, Younge 610; Balfe v. Lord, 1 Conn. & L. 519.

---

[1] Sale and not foreclosure was held to be the remedy in Tuckley v. Thompson, 1 Johns. & H. 126; but Redmayne v. Forster, L. R. 2 Eq. 467, is the other way.

[2] In Louisiana, the *antichresis*, which resembles the Welsh mortgage, in that the creditor is entitled to take the rents and profits in discharge of his debt, but differs, in his being entitled to a decree of sale, is the form of pledge of real estate authorized by the Civil Code. See Livingston v. Story, 11 Peters S. C. 351.

debt out of the proceeds. The imperfection of these
securities, like that of Welsh mortgages, consists in the
want of any day of forfeiture, and in the consequent
absence of a right to foreclosure. The estate never
vests absolutely in the creditor, and he is placed rather
in the position of a trustee, though to some extent for
his own benefit, than in that of an independent mortgagee. (v)

The inconvenience resulting from the want of ability
to foreclose, both in the case of Welsh mortgages, and
in that of trust deeds, is very great; and such securities
are of comparatively unfrequent occurrence.

The fifth class of imperfect mortgages is the equitable
lien of a vendor or purchaser of real estate [1]

The term lien, when accurately used, signifies a right
to retain a personal chattel, until a debt due the person
retaining is satisfied; and it exists at common law independently of liens by agreement or usage, in three
cases, viz., 1. Where the person claiming the lien has,
by his labor or expense, improved or altered the chattel;
2. Where he is bound by law to receive the chattel or to
perform the service in respect of which the lien is claimed;
and 3. Where his claim is for salvage, as on a rescue of
goods from perils of the sea, or from capture by an
enemy.

The foundation of this right is the actual possession,
and therefore, if the possession be abandoned, the lien
is gone; and if there be any agreement to postpone the
[*127] time of payment, *the same effect follows; for it
cannot be supposed that the creditor was intend-

(v) Ex parte Pettit, 2 Gl. & J. 47 ; Sampson v. Pattison, 1 Hare 533.

---

[1] This equitable lien gives the vendor, at least at law, no right to detain
the title deeds : Goode v. Burton, 1 Exch. 189.

ed to detain the chattel during the whole period of post-ponement.(w) There is also a right at law in the nature of lien, entitling the vendor of a chattel who has not sold on credit, and has not actually or constructively delivered it to a purchaser, to retain it in his possession until the whole price is paid,[1] notwithstanding that by payment of a portion, the right of property may have passed to the purchaser. The right, however, seems to be merely a right of detention, and not a right to rescind the contract, or to make up the deficiency by a resale; and when the chattel has been delivered, the right is at an end.(x)

The equitable lien on a sale of realty is very different from a lien at law; for it operates after the possession has been changed, and is available by way of charge, instead of detainer.

The distinction may, perhaps, be traced to the same principle which prevails in regard to specific performance; viz., that where the possession of a chattel has been parted with, the Courts of common law cannot compel its restoration, but can only give damages for its deten-tion, which could be equally well obtained in an action for its price. A right of lien, therefore, when the posses-sion has been parted with, would be a nullity at law; and as damages are a sufficient remedy for detention of chattels, there is no ground for equitable interference. But, on the other hand, where real estate is concerned, a specific decree is required, and will be made.

(w) Smith's Merc. Law. 510, 518; Jarm. Byth. 3–13.
(x) Ibid, 436–9, 457–63, 500–9.

---

[1] Or, if the sale is on credit, to exercise the well known right of *stoppage in transitu.* And the vendor may come into a Court of Equity, and ob-tain its aid to enforce this lien by an injunction: Schotsmans *v.* The Lan-cashire and Yorkshire R. R. Co., L. R. 2 Chan. Ap. 332.

Whatever be the origin of the distinction, its existence
is clear.   And it is an established principle of equity,
that where a conveyance is made prematurely before payment of the price, the money is a charge on the estate in
the hands of the vendee; and where the money is paid
[*128] prematurely *before conveyance, it is, in like
manner, a charge on the estate in the hands of
the vendor. $(y)^1$

(y) Mackreth v. Symmons, 15 Ves. 329.   [See Rose v. Watson, 10 House
of Lords Cas. 672.]

---

[1] The subject of the equitable lien of the vendor for unpaid purchase-
money will be found discussed in the notes to Mackreath v. Symmons, 1
Lead. Cas. Eq. 235.   "The true nature of this claim appears to be this:
It had its origin in a country where lands were not liable, both during
and after the life of the debtor for all personal obligations, indiscriminately, including debts by simple contract; and it seems to be an original
and natural equity, that the creditor whose debt was the consideration of
the land, should by virtue of that consideration be allowed to charge the
land upon failure of personal assets.   It is not a lien until a bill has been
filed to assert it; before that is done it is a mere equity or capacity to acquire a lien, and to have satisfaction of it.   When a bill is filed it becomes
a specific lien:" 1 Lead. Cas. Eq. 373.   The states in the Union may, as
to this subject, be divided into five classes :
First, those in which the lien is recognised by judicial decision: such
are New York—Stafford v. Van Rensselaer, 9 Cowen 316; Warren v. Fenn,
28 Barb. 335 ; New Jersey—Vandoren v. Todd, 2 Green Ch. 397; Herbert
v. Scofield, 1 Stockt. 492; Dudley v. Matlack, 1 McCart. 252; Indiana—
Deibler v. Barwick, 4 Blackf. 339; McCarty v. Pruet, 4 Ind. 226; Cox v.
Wood, 20 Id. 54; Ohio—Williams v. Roberts, 5 Ohio 35; Mississippi—
Stewart et al. v. Ives et al., 1 Sm. & M. 197; Trotter v. Irwin, 27 Miss.
772; Littlejohn v. Gordon, 32 Id. 235; Missouri—Marsh v. Turner, 4 Mo.
253; Bledsoe v. Games, 30 Id. 448; Illinois—Dyer v. Martin, 4 Scam. 148;
Trustees v. Wright, 11 Ill. 603; Maryland—Moreton v. Harrison, 1 Bland.
491; Carr v. Hobbs, 11 Md. 285; Bratt v. Bratt, 21 Id. 578; Minnesota—
Selby v. Stanley, 4 Minn. 65; Tennessee—Eskridge v. McClure, 2 Yerg.
84; Brown v. Vanlier, 7 Humph. 239; Alabama—Hall's Ex'rs. v. Click, 5
Ala. 363; Burns v. Taylor, 23 Id. 255; California—Truebody v. Jacobson,
2 Cal. 269; Williams v. Young, 17 Id. 403; Burt v. Wilson, 28 Id. 632;
Arkansas—English v. Russell, Hemp. 35; Georgia—Mounce v. Byars, 16
Georgia 469; Chance v. McWhorter, 26 Id. 315; Florida—Woods v. Bailey,

The lien thus attaching on the estate is obviously useless by way of detainer, and can only be available by way

---

3 Flor. 41; *Iowa*—Pierson v. David, 1 Iowa 23; *Michigan*—Sears v. Smith,
2 Mich. 243; Converse v. Blumrich, 14 Id. 124; *Texas*—Pinchain v. Collard, 13 Texas 333; Glasscock v. Glasscock, 17 Id. 480.

Second. Those states in which the lien is expressly recognised and maintained by statute: *Maryland*—General Laws, Art. 16, ? 130; *Iowa*—Revised Laws of 1860, page 653.

Third. Those in which the lien is abolished or confined within narrow
limits by statute: *Virginia*—where the vendor's lien is abolished unless
expressly reserved in the conveyance: 2 Mat. Dig. 397; Yancey v. Mauck,
15 Gratt. 300; though it formerly existed: Tompkins v. Mitchell, 2 Rand.
428; Kyles v. Tait, 6 Gratt. 44; *Kentucky*—where there is a statute to the
same effect: Digest, vol. ii, 230; Gritton v. McDonald, 3 Metc. 252; *Vermont*—where the Statute of 1851 abolishes the lien entirely.

Fourth. Those states in which the lien has never been recognised by
the courts: *Pennsylvania*—Kauffelt v. Bower, 7 S. & R. 64; Hepburn v.
Snyder, 3 Penn. St. 72; Zentmyer v. Mittower, 5 Id. 403; Hiester v.
Green, 48 Id. 96; though a lien may be created by express charge in the
conveyance: Heist v. Baker, 49 Penn. St. 9; *North Carolina*—Womble v.
Battle, 3 Ired. Eq. 182; Henderson v. Burton, 3 Id. 259; Cameron v.
Mason, 7 Id. 180; *South Carolina*—Wragg's Rep. v. Comp. Gen., 2
Dessaus. 509; *Maine*—Phillbrook v. Delano, 29 Maine 410; *Massachusetts*
—Gilman v. Brown, 1 Mason 191; though see Wright v. Dame, 5 Metc. 503.

Fifth. Those states in which the question seems yet to be undecided:
New Hampshire—Arlin v. Brown, 44 N. H. 102; *Connecticut*—Watson v.
Well, 5 Conn. 468; Dean v. Dean 6 Id. 285; Atwood v. Vincent, 17 Id.
575; *Delaware*—Budd v. Busti, 1 Harrington 69. No vendor's lien exists
in *Kansas* when a deed absolute on its face is given: Simpson v. Mun-
dee, 3 Kansas 172; Brown v. Simpson, 4 Id. 76.

In the United States Courts this lien is recognised: Bayley v. Greenleaf, 7 Wheat. 46; Chilton v. Braiden's Adm'x., 2 Black 458.

As against creditors or purchasers, the existence of this lien is a point
upon which the decisions are contradictory and conflicting. See Bayley
v. Greenleaf, 7 Wheat. 46; Moore v. Holcombe, 3 Leigh 597; Harper v.
Williams, 1 Dev. & Bat. Eq. 379; Roberts v. Rose et al., 2 Humph. 145;
Brown v. Vanlier et al., 7 Humph. 239; Repp et al. v. Repp, 12 Gill & J.
341; Duval v. Bibb, 4 Hen. & M. 113; Clark v. Hunt, 3 J. J. Marsh. 533;
Eubank v. Poston, 5 Monr. 285; Kyles v. Tait, 6 Gratt. 44; Kilpatrick v.
Kilpatrick, 23 Miss. (Cushm.) 124; Green v. Demos, 10 Humph. 371;
Webb v. Robinson, 14 Geo. 216; MacAlpine v. Burnett, 23 Texas 649;
Chance v. McWhorter, 26 Geo. 315; Selby v. Stanley, 4 Minn. 65. See
note to Mackreth v. Symmons, supra.

of charge. It is treated, therefore, as a security in the
nature of mortgage;[1] and the remedy under it is by suing
in equity to have the estate resold, and the deficiency, if
any, made good by the defendant; or else to have the
contract rescinded, retaining the deposit as forfeited,
which is practically equivalent to a foreclosure of the
charge.(z)

The character of this lien as an enforceable charge, pro-

(z) 1 Sug. V. & P. 427.

The lien arises on the conveyance of an equitable, as well as a legal
estate : Warren v. Fenn, 28 Barb. 335; Bledsoe v. Games, 30 Missouri
448; 1 Lead. Cas. Eq. 363; Hill v. Grigsby, 32 Cal. 55. And on the sale
of a term of years: Bratt v. Bratt, 21 Md. 578. In Burns v. Taylor, 23
Ala. 255, it was said to apply to an exchange with the same force as to a
sale for money ; and see Wickman v. Robinson, 14 Wis. 493. See also,
Child v. Burton, 6 Bush 617 ; where a lien was held to have attached on
other land exchanged by the vendee for the land sold.

The *lien* of a vendor *after conveyance* is to be distinguished from the
interest of the vendor under articles before conveyance. The former is a
mere *charge;* the latter is an *estate.* See, however, Hall v. Jones, 21 Md.
439; and Haughwout v. Murphy, 7 C. E. Green 531. After conveyance
the whole estate both legal and equitable passes to the vendee, and the
vendor has a mere naked right to the purchase-money enforceable against
the land. Before conveyance, however, and while there is a contract of
sale only, the vendor has the legal *estate* in the land, and the vendee has
the equitable interest, the former being a trustee of the beneficial interest
in the land for the latter ; the latter being a trustee of the purchase-money
for the former. See Chapter on Conversion, post. This distinction has
in many cases in this country been disregarded, and the interest of a vendor
under articles or a title-bond treated as if it were the same as the equitable lien for purchase-money after a conveyance has been executed. Such,
however, is by no means the case, and the distinction above stated should
always be kept in view.

The lien of the vendee who has prematurely paid his purchase-money
has been recognised in this country : Wickman v. Robinson, 14 Wis. 493.
And as to this lien, see Rose v. Watson, 10 House of Lords Cas. 672.

[1] It is contended by the author of the American note to Mackreth v.
Symmons (supra), that this lien does not partake of the nature of a mort-
gage : 1 Lead. Cas. Eq. 373 ; and ees Shoffner v. Fogleman, 1 Wins. (N. C.)
No. 2 (Eq.) 12.

ects it from being lost by postponing the day of payment.[1] For such postponement, though inconsistent with a
right of detainer, is not inconsistent with a right of charge.
Nor will it be lost by taking a bill, note, or bond, as
a security for the consideration, although such security
be payable at a future day.(a)[2] It is different if the

(a) Winter v. Anson, 3 Russ. 488.

---

[1] Whether the lien is barred when the debt is barred by the Statute of
Limitations seems not be settled. See 1 Lead. Cas. Eq. 370; also Littlejohn v. Gordon, 32 Miss. 235.

[2] It is incumbent upon the party contesting the vendor's lien to show
that it has been relinquished; and the acceptance of personal security, is
no evidence of such relinquishment: Garson v. Green, 1 John. Ch. 308;
Tompkins v. Mitchell, 2 Rand. 428; Campbell v. Baldwin, 2 Humph. 248;
Gilman v. Brown, 1 Mason 192; Tiernan v. Beam. 2 Ham. 383. See also,
Evans v. Goodlet, 1 Blackf. 246; Cox v. Fenwick, 3 Bibb 183; White v.
Williams, 1 Paige 502; Thornton v. Knox's Ex'rs., 6 B. Monr. 74; Ross
v. Whitson, 6 Yerg. 59; Mims v. Macon, 3 Kelly 333. See note to Mackreth v. Symmons, ut sup., where it is stated to be the result of the American authorities, "that the implied lien will be sustained wherever the
vendor has taken the personal security of the vendee only, by whatever
kind of instrument it be manifested, and therefore that any note, bond, or
covenant, given by the vendee alone, will be considered as intended only
to countervail the receipt for the purchase-money contained in the deed, or
to show the time and manner in which the payment is to be made, unless
there is an express agreement between the parties to waive the equitable
lien; and on the other hand, that the lien will be considered as waived
whenever any distinct and independent security is taken, whether by
mortgage of other land, or pledge of goods, or personal responsibility of
a third person (as the endorsement of the vendee's note), and also when
the security is taken upon the land, either for the whole or a part of the
unpaid purchase-money, unless there is an express agreement that the
implied lien shall be retained." See also, Truebody v. Jacobson, 2 Cal.
269; Griffin v. Blanchar, 17 Id. 70; Delassas v. Posten, 19 Miss. 425;
Tiernan v. Thurman, 14 B. Monr. 277; Hare v. Deusen, 32 Barb. 92;
Parker County v. Sewell, 24 Tex. 238; Harris v. Harlan, 14 Ind. 439;
Selby v. Stanley, 4 Minn. 65; Daughaday v. Paine, 6 Id. 443; Hummer v.
Schott, 21 Md. 307; Fogg v. Rogers, 2 Cold. (Tenn.) 290; Schwartz v.
Stein, 29 Md. 112; Hadley v. Pickett, 25 Ind. 450; Porter v. Dubuque, 20
Iowa 440; McGonigal v. Plummer, 30 Md. 422; Sullivan v. Ferguson, 40

security be itself the consideration, as, for example, if the conveyance profess to be in consideration of a covenant to pay, and not in consideration of actual payment.(b) If, however, the security is inconsistent with a continuance of the charge, the lien is at an end; as, for example, if a mortgage be made on the same estate for part of the price, or on part of the estate for the whole price; for either of these securities contradicts the notion that the whole price is to be a charge on the whole estate.(c) The question whether in each particular case the lien is relinquished, can only be determined by the special circumstances. If the nature of the thing bought, and of the consideration for it, exclude the supposition that the lien was relied on, that circumstance will have weight in the decision; or if a security be taken of *a character and value which show that credit was exclusively given to that security, that fact also will have its weight. But the question is always one of intention, to be collected from circumstances which have taken place.(d)[1]

[*129]

(b) Clarke v. Royle, 3 Sim. 499; Parròtt v. Sweetland, 3 M. & K. 655; Bucknell v. Pocknell, 13 Sim. 406.

(c) Capper v. Spottiswoode, Taml. 21; Bond v. Kent, 2 Vern. 281.

(d) Nairn v. Prowse, 6 Ves. 752; Mackreth v. Symmons, 15 Id. 329; Winter v. Anson, 3 Russ. 488; 3 Sug. V. & P. c. xviii.

Mo. 79; Yaryan v. Shriner, 26 Ind. 364; Armstrong v. Ross, 20 N. J. Eq. 109. See, however, Burrus v. Roulhac, 2 Bush (Ky.) 39; where it was held that the acceptance of a guaranteed note did not waive the lien; and see also, Anketel v. Converse, 17 Ohio 11; where a purchase-money mortgage was held not to extinguish the lien. Also Dodge v. Evans, 43 Miss. 570; Fonda v. Jones, 42 Miss. 792; Sanders v. McAfee, 41 Ga. 684; Durette v. Briggs, 47 Mo. 356; Carrico v. Farmers' Bank, 33 Md. 235.

[1] The lien may be waived by conduct showing that intention: see Clark v. Hunt, 3 J. J. Marsh. 553. In some of the states the lien may be enforced without a judgment: High and Wife v. Batte, 10 Yerg. 186; Gal-

· The sixth and seventh classes of imperfect mortgages, are those of equitable *fieri facias* and *elegit*, and judgment charges under 1 & 2 Vict. c. 110, ss. 13, 14.

The writs of *fieri facias* and *elegit* are writs of execution after judgment, respectively requiring the sheriff to levy the debt out of the debtor's personal or real estate. And being writs issued out of the common law Courts, they are confined in their operation to legal interests. If the debtor be entitled to a trust or equity of redemption, his interest is exempt from execution at law, and must be attached, if at all, by suit in equity. A partial exception to this rule was introduced by the Statute of Frauds, giving legal execution against the real estate of which any person was seised in trust for the debtor at the time of execution sued out. But the enactment did not extend to chattels real, to trusts under which the debtor has not the whole interest, to equities of redemption, or to any equitable interest which had been parted with before execution sued out.(*e*)

The remedy afforded to the creditor in equity, when either of these writs has been issued, is termed an equitable *fieri facias*, or *elegit*, according as it is sought against personal or real estate.

(*e*) 29 Car. 2, c. 2, s. 10; Forth *v.* Duke of Norfolk, 4 Mad. 503.

---

loway *v.* Hamilton's Heirs, 1 Dana 576 ; Richardson *v.* Baker, 5 J. J. Marsh. 323.

As to whether this lien passes, on the assignment of the debt for the unpaid purchase-money, to the assignee, the authorities are in conflict in the different states : see the note to Mackreth *v.* Symmons, ut supr., where the matter is fully discussed. And see Fisher *v.* Johnson, 5 Indiana 492 ; Kern *v.* Hazlerigg, 11 Id. 443 ; Keith *v.* Horner, 32 Ill. 524 ; Simpson *v.* Montgomery, 25 Ark. 365 ; Wells *v.* Morrow, 38 Ala. 125 ; Lindsey *v.* Bates, 42 Miss. 397 ; Carter *v.* Sims, 2 Heisk. (Tenn.) 166.

Its *modus operandi* is of a threefold character, first by injunction against setting up an outstanding estate in bar of execution at law; secondly, by appointment of a receiver; and, thirdly, in the case of an equity of redemption, by permitting the judgment creditor to redeem. But it is strictly confined to its legitimate object, viz., the imposing *on the equitable interest the liability [*130] which would attach at law on a corresponding legal interest. In accordance with this principle, no relief can be obtained in equity until the title is perfected at law by suing out the writ; but it is not necessary that the writ should be returned. There is an apparent exception to this rule where the judgment creditor is seeking to redeem a mortgage, or where the debtor is dead, and administration of his assets is wanted. In the former case, the Court, finding the creditor in a condition to acquire a power over the estate by suing out the writ, acts, as it does in all similar causes, and enables him to redeem other encumbrances; in the latter, if under any circumstances the estate is to be sold, it pays off the judgment, because it will not sell subject to the debt, and it cannot otherwise make a title to the estate. In accordance with the same principle, a sale will not be decreed on an equitable *elegit,* unless a special jurisdiction supervenes, *e. g.,* in a suit to administer the debtor's assets; but the relief is confined to perception of rents. Nor will a decree be made for charging property by way of equitable *fieri facias* or *elegit,* if the property be of a kind exempt from execution at law, *e. g.,* stock or shares; nor for charging (independently of the late statute) more than the moiety of a trust in land; but it is otherwise with respect to an equity of redemption, for the judgment creditor is obliged to redeem the entirety, and cannot be afterwards deprived of it without payment of his demand. (f)

The rights of a judgment creditor, except as against purchasers and mortgagees without notice, are much increased by a late statute. The operation of the *fieri facias* and *elegit* at law is extended, and a new right is introduced by way of equitable charge, enforceable in like manner with a charge by contract. It is enacted by the same statute, that decrees and orders of Courts of equity, and all rules *of Courts of law and orders in bankruptcy and lunacy for payment of money, [*131] shall have the effect of judgments. And that judgments, rules, and orders of certain inferior Courts, may be removed into a superior Court, and acted on as a judgment thereof; but not so as to operate against purchasers or creditors until delivery of the writ. (g)

The operation of the *elegit* at law is extended, so as to bind the entirety, instead of a moiety of the debtor's land, to include lands of copyhold and customary tenure, lands over which the debtor has a sole disposing power exer‑ cisable for his own benefit, and lands of which the debtor, or any person in trust for him, is seised or possessed at the time of entering the judgment. It appears, therefore, to include leaseholds and trust estates, belonging to the debtor at the date of the judgment, and to render his alienation of the one before the delivery of the writ, or of the other before execution is sued out, no longer material. (h)

(f) Mitf. 126; Neate *v.* Duke of Marlborough, 3 M. & C. 407; Stileman *v.* Ashdown, 2 Atk. 608; Rider *v.* Kidder, 10 Ves. 360, 368; Skeeles *v.* Shearley, 3 M. & C. 112.

(g) 1 & 2 Vict. c. 110, s. 9–22; 2 Vict. c. 11, s. 5.

(h) 1 & 2 Vict. c. 110, s. 11; 2 Sug. V. & P. 401; 5 Jarm. Byth. 48; 1 Id. 107; Prideaux on Judgments 58.

The operation of the *fieri facias* at law is extended by authorizing the sheriff to seize money, bank notes, bills of exchange, and other securities, to pay the money or notes to the creditor, and to sue on the bills or securities in his own name, paying over the money to be recovered to the creditor.(*i*)

The remedies by equitable *fieri facias* and *elegit* will of course be extended in a corresponding degree; but they are still far from satisfactory remedies. The *elegit* is imperfect, because it can only operate by perception of profits, and does not authorize acceleration of payment by a sale; the *fi. fa.* is imperfect because it cannot operate on stock or shares.

In order to obviate these difficulties the judgment charge has been introduced.

[*132]   *The right to an *elegit* or *fieri facias*, whether legal or equitable, is left untouched, and in the case of personal estate, other than stock or shares, no alteration has been made. But with respect to real estate, whether legal or equitable, and whether liable to execution or not, and with respect to interest in stock or shares, whether legal or equitable, the operation of the judgment is still further extended, and it is constituted, under certain restrictions, an actual charge in equity; but the operation of such charge, as well as the extended execution under the preceding clauses, is declared of no effect as against purchasers or mortgagees without notice.(*k*)

The judgment charge on real estate is created by an enactment, that a judgment properly registered shall operate as a charge in equity on all lands and hereditaments, including copyholds and customary holds, to which the debtor may, at or after the time of entering

(*i*) 1 & 2 Vict. c. 110, s. 12.   (*k*) 2 & 3 Vict. c. 11, s. 5.

the judgment, be entitled, for any estate or interest at law or in equity, whether in possession, reversion, or remainder, or expectancy, or over which he may at either of such times have a sole disposing power exercisable for his own benefit, and shall be binding against himself and all persons claiming under him, and also against his issue and persons whom, without assent of any other person, he might bar, with the like remedies in equity for its enforcement, as if he had by writing under his hand agreed to charge them with the debt and interest.   But it is enacted, that no judgment creditor shall be entitled to proceed in equity to obtain the benefit of such charge, until after the expiration of one year from the time of entering up the judgment; and that no such charge shall operate to give any preference in bankruptcy, unless such judgment shall have been entered up one year at least before the bankruptcy.(*l*)

*The judgment charge on stocks and shares is created by enactments, that if a judgment debtor [*133] have an estate or interest in stock or shares, or in the dividends or interest of stock or shares standing in his name in his own right, or in the name of any other person in trust for him, or in the name of the Accountant-General, a judge's order may be obtained, to be made in the first instance *ex parte,* and afterwards made absolute on notice, charging such stock or shares, or any part thereof, or the dividends or interest thereon, with payment of the judgment debt and interest; and that such order shall entitle the judgment creditor to the same remedies as if the charge had been made by the debtor himself; provided that no proceedings shall be taken to have the benefit of

(*l*) 1 & 2 Vict. c. 110, s. 13 ; Smith *v.* Hurst, 1 Coll. 705 ; Clare *v.* Wood, 4 Hare 81 ; Harris *v.* Davison, 15 Sim. 128.

such charge until after the expiration of six calendar months from the date of the order.(m)

Under these clauses the right of the judgment creditor is no longer restricted to property which is capable of seizure, nor to the inconvenient remedy by perception of profits; but is extended to all property, both legal and equitable, and may be made available by sale.

A clause is contained in the act for the purpose of precluding a creditor from enforcing his remedies under it against the debtor's property, and at the same time taking the debtor's person in execution.   The common law rule on this subject is, that if part only of the debt be levied on a *fi. fa.*, or on execution had of goods under an *elegit*, the plaintiff may have a *capias ad satisfaciendum* for the residue; but that if lands be seized under an *elegit*, the execution is of so high a nature that after it the body of the defendant cannot be taken.(n)   The statutory enactment is that, if a judgment creditor who under the powers of the act shall have obtained a charge, or be entitled to [*134] the benefit *of a security, shall afterwards and before the property so charged or secured shall have been realized, and the produce applied towards payment of the debt, cause the person of the debtor to be taken in execution, he shall be deemed to have relinquished such charge or security.(o)

(m) 1 & 2 Vict. c. 110, ss. 14 & 15; 3 & 4 Vict. c. 82, s. 1 ; Bristed v. Wilkins, 3 Hare 235.

(n) 3 Steph. Bl. 650, 652.

(o) 1 & 2 Vict. c. 110, s. 16 ; Houlditch v. Collins, 5 Bea. 497.

*CHAPTER IV. [*135]

OF CONVERSION—PRIORITIES—NOTICE—TACKING.

IN immediate connection with the subjects just considered, of trusts, contract, and mortgage, we have to consider the doctrines of equitable conversion, and of priority among conflicting equities; doctrines which, though applicable to all subjects of equitable jurisdiction, are more especially important in regard to these

The doctrine of EQUITABLE CONVERSION is embodied in the maxim that "What ought to be done, is considered in equity as done;" and its meaning is, that whenever the holder of property is subject to an equity in respect of it, the Court will, as between the parties to the equity, treat the subject-matter as if the equity had been worked out, and as impressed with the character which it would then have borne.

The simplest operation of this maxim is found in the rule already noticed, that trusts and equities of redemption are treated as estates; but its effect is most obvious in the constructive change of property from real to personal estate, and *vice versa*, so as to introduce new laws of devolution and transfer.

Let us first consider the doctrine in its operation under a trust.

The rule in respect to trusts is, that if an imperative trust is created either for employing money in the pur-

chase of land, or for selling land and turning it into
[*136] *money, the money or land, of which a conversion is directed, will be dealt with in equity during the continuance of the trust, and for objects within
the scope of the trust, as if the purchase or sale had been
actually made. (a)[1]

(a) Fletcher v. Ashburner, 1 B. C. C. 497.

---

[1] The rule is well settled that where there is an absolute and imperative
direction that land shall be sold and turned into money, or money be employed in the purchase of land, the money is considered in equity in all
respects as converted into land, or the land into money, as the case may
be: Craig v. Leslie, 3 Wheat. 564; Peter v. Beverly, 10 Peters 532; Tay-
lor v. Benham, 5 How. 233; Hawley v. James, 5 Paige 320; Smith v.
McCrary, 3 Ired. Eq. 204; Gott v. Cook, 7 Paige 534; Commonwealth v.
Martin's Ex'rs., 5 Munf. 117; Kane v. Gott, 24 Wend. 660; Johnson v.
Bennett, 39 Barb. 251; Pratt v. Taliaferro, 3 Leigh 419; Rutherford v.
Green, 2 Ired. Eq. 122; Siter v. McClanachan, 2 Gratt. 280; Harcum v.
Hadnall, 14 Id. 369; Wilkins v. Taylor, 8 Rich. Eq. 294; Reading v.
Blackwell, 1 Bald. 166; Hurtt v. Fisher, 1 Har. & G. 88; Leadenham v.
Nicholson, Id. 267; Morrow v. Brenizer, 2 Rawle 185; Burr v. Sim. 1
Whart. 265; Smith v. Starr, 3 Id. 65; Rice v. Bixler, 1 W. & S. 445; Wil-
ling v. Peters, 7 Penn. St. 287; Parkinson's Appeal, 32 Id. 455; Brolasky
v. Gally's Ex'rs., 51 Id. 509; Scudder v. Vanarsdale, 2 Beas. 109; Lorillard v. Coster, 5 Paige 172; Drake v. Pell, 3 Edw. Ch. 251; Thomas v.
Wood, 1 Md. Ch. 296; Collins v. Champ's Heirs, 15 B. Monr. 118. A collection of the English authorities on this subject will be found in Fon-
blanque's Eq., Vol. I., Book 1, Ch. 6, Sec. ix., notes s and t. See the notes
to Fletcher v. Asburner, 1 Lead. Cas. in Eq. 659. Where one by will
directed real estate to be sold, and the proceeds divided among residuary
legatees, and one of them, a feme coverte, died before the time of payment,
it was held that the land must be considered as money; and there being
no election by the feme coverte to take the legacy as land, the devise passed
to the husband and his representatives as personalty: Rinehart v. Harrison,
Baldw. 177. And where a will directs executors to sell the real estate, and
distribute the proceeds in a manner specified, the land will be treated as
personal property, and upon the death of one of the distributees before
the time appointed for the sale, his share will descend as personal estate:
Marsh v. Wheeler, 2 Edw. Ch. 156; Pratt v. Taliaferro, 3 Leigh 419;
Reading v. Blackwell, Baldw. 166; Smith v. McCrary, 3 Ired. Eq. 204;
Hurtt v. Fisher, 1 Har. & G. 88; Morrow v. Brenizer, 2 Rawle 185.

Where the sale is made by the act of the law, as under proceeding for

The points which require notice under this rule are the requirement that the converting trust shall be imperative, and the limitation of the continuance and purposes of the conversion so as to coincide with the continuance and purposes of the trust.

First, the conversion must be directed by an imperative trust; for if the trustees are entitled to exercise a discretion, there is no duty imposed on them to make the change and no reason to deal with the property as if they had done so.[1] If, for example; the trustee is authorized to "sell or not sell," as he may think best, or if he is directed to purchase "freeholds or leaseholds," or to invest "on

---

payment of debts or to make partition, there is no conversion until all the conditions of sale are complied with, at least so far as to entitle the purchaser to a deed: Biggert's Est., 20 Penn. St. 17; and see Betts *v.* Wirt, 3 Md. Ch. 113; Jones *v.* Plummer, 20 Id. 416.

Where land is not converted out and out, and at all events into personal property, but on the contrary its conversion depends upon a condition, it will not be considered in equity as personal estate: Evans *v.* Kingsberry, 2 Rand. 120. So if it depend upon a contingency: Naglee *v.* Ingersoll, 7 Penn. St. 197.

[1] If there is an absolute direction to sell it is not material that the time of sale, if fixed, is postponed: Reading *v.* Blackwell, Baldw. C. C. 166; Rinehart *v.* Harrison, Id. 177; Hocker *v.* Gentry; 3 Metc. 473; see, also, Barnett *v.* Barnett's Adm'r., 1 Id. 258. Where the power of sale, however, is discretionary, there is no conversion till it is actually exercised: Dominick *v.* Michael, 4 Sandf. S. C. 374; Bleight *v.* Bank, 10 Penn. St. 132; Pratt *v.* Taliaferro, 3 Leigh 419; Montgomery *v.* Milliken, 1 Sm. & M. Ch. 495; Greenway *v.* Greenway, 2 De G., F. & J. 128. So where the power is to be exercised with the consent of the parties interested: Nagle's Appeal, 13 Penn. St. 262; Stoner *v.* Zimmerman, 21 Id. 394; Ross *v.* Drake, 37 Id. 373; Anewalt's Appeal, 42 Id. 414. But a mere discretion given as to the *time* when the power is to be exercised, will not prevent a conversion where the direction to sell is absolute: Stagg *v.* Jackson, 1 Comstock 206; Tazewell *v.* Smith, 1 Rand. 313; though see *contra*, Christler's Ex'rs. *v.* Meddis, 6 B. Monr. 35. A *mere* power to sell will not work a conversion: Phelps *v.* Pond, 23 N. Y. 69; Chew *v.* Nicklin, 45 Penn. St. 84.

land or good security," there is no positive expression of intention to convert, and the Court *in dubio* will not interfere ; but the use of such expressions, or of others which in terms imply an option, will not deprive the trust of an imperative character, if other portions of the instrument show a contrary intent.   A mere declaration that the property shall be considered as converted is immaterial ; for it is not the declaration, but the duty to convert, which creates the equitable change.(*b*)[1]

Secondly, the duration of the converted character is coincident with that of the trust.   For the conversion originates in the duty of the trustee; and if the trust be countermanded either by the exercise of a revoking power in the donor, or by the act of those in whom the absolute dominion has vested, the duty is at an end; and the constructive conversion is determined with it.

Where the trust is countermanded by the subsequent [*137] *owners, their act is denominated a reconversion.[2] And such act must be equally unequivocal with

(*b*) Thornton *v.* Hawley, 10 Ves. 129 ; Polley *v.* Seymour, 2 Y. & C. 708 ; Cookson *v.* Cookson, 12 Cl. & F. 121 ; Attorney-General *v.* Mangles, 5 Mee. & W. 128.

---

[1] Taylor *v.* Taylor, 3 De G., M. & G. 190 ; Robinson *v.* The Governors, &c., 10 Hare 29.

[2] Though land directed to be sold is considered as money, yet an election may be made by those having a right to elect to take it as land : Tazewell *v.* Smith, 1 Rand. 313 ; Craig *v.* Leslie, 3 Wheat. 578 ; Burr *v.* Sim, 1 Whart. 252 ; Broome *v.* Curry, 19 Ala. 805.   But this election must be by some unequivocal act, and all the parties interested must join : Willing *v.* Peters, 7 Penn. St. 290 ; Pratt *v.* Taliaferro, 3 Leigh 428 ; Harcum *v.* Hudnall, 14 Gratt. 369 ; High *v.* Worley, 33 Ala. 196 ; Beatty *v.* Byers, 18 Penn. St. 105 ; Dixon *v.* Gayfere, 1 De G. & J. 655.   Mere lapse of time, however great, is not sufficient: Beatty *v.* Byers.   Nor the mere entering into and taking possession of the estate: Dixon *v.* Gayfere.   As to the power of an infant to make an election, see Burr *v.* Sim ; Pratt *v.* Taliaferro ; Fletcher *v.* Ashburner (supra).

the original trust. It need not, however, be evidenced by an express declaration of change. It is sufficient if the conduct of the parties distinctly shows an intention to deal with the property in its original, instead of its converted charàcter ; as, for example, by entering on and demising land which is directed to be sold,(c) or by receiving or reinvesting money which is directed to be laid out in land.(d) But if an estate is directed to be sold, and the proceeds to be divided among several persons, a reconversion cannot be effected until all are competent and willing to join ; for the duty imposed on the trustee, is to convert the entire estate for the benefit of all, and that duty continues until countermanded by all.(e)

The receipt by the *cestui que trust* of money convertible into land operates, as we have seen, as a reconversion. And the same result follows where a covenant has been entered into for purchasing land on trust, and the covenantee has become the only *cestui que trust*. In this case the money is said to be " at home " in his hands ; and the union of the double character in himself operates as a constructive receipt, and determines the trust.(f) .

It has been contended that the right to countermand the converting trust renders a gift of the proceeds of conversion equivalent to a gift of the unconverted property ; and, consequently, that a gift of land to a trustee, on trust to sell and pay the proceeds to an alien, is invalid as against the policy of law. But it is decided otherwise ; for the trust is in truth a compliance with the law by direct-

(c) Crabtree v. Bramble, 3 Atk. 680.

(d) Lingen v. Sowray, 1 P. W. 172; Cookson v. Cookson, 12 Cl. & F. 121.

(e) Fletcher v. Ashburner, 1 B. C. C. 497, 500; Deeth v. Hale, 2 Moll. 317 ; Seeley v. Jago, 1 P. W. 389.

(f) Pulteney v. Darlington, 1 B. C. C. 223, 238 ; 7 B. P. C. by Toml. 530 ; Wheldale v. Partridge, 8 Ves. 227, 235.

ing that the land shall be sold to persons who may [*138] *legally hold it, in order to raise the money which the alien may legally hold. And, although the alien would be entitled to elect against the conversion, there is no reason to force that election on him, or to inflict a forfeiture of money, which he can enjoy, because he might have elected to take land, which he cannot.(g)[1]

Thirdly, the conversion will operate for those purposes only which fall within the scope of the trust.

The principal doubts on this point have arisen in regard to resulting trusts; viz., where conversion is directed for a particular purpose, which fails to exhaust the entire interest. The question then arises, whether the owner under the resulting trust shall be determined according to the original, or according to the converted, nature of the property.

The law on this subject has been, to some extent, stated under the head of Resulting Trust; but it will be convenient to restate it here.

The general principle is, that the conversion is limited to the purpose of the donor, and that, therefore, in the event of failure, the property will devolve according to its original character.[2] If, for example, land be devised for sale with a direction to apply the produce for purposes altogether illegal, or which altogether fail, the heir-at-law is entitled. If the purposes are partially illegal, or par-

(g) Fourdrin v. Gowdey, 3 M. & K. 383; Du Hourmelin v. Sheldon, I Bea. 79.; 4 M. & C. 525.

---

[1] Craig v. Leslie, 3 Wheat. 564; Commonwealth v. Martin, 5 Munf. 117; Taylor v. Benham, 5 How. U. S. 269; Anstice v. Brown, 6 Paige 448.

[2] The student will find a clear statement of the rule upon this subject in Bective v. Hodgson, 10 House of Lords Cas. 656. See also, Hill on Trustees 127–128, and notes.

tially fail, or if they require the application of a part only of the land devised, he is entitled to so much of the land or of its produce as was destined for the ineffective purpose, or so much as is not required for the purpose of the will. And *e converso*, if a purchase of land be directed for purposes which are altogether or partially illegal, or which altogether or partially fail, the next of kin are entitled to the money, or to so much of it, as cannot or need not be applied to the purposes of the will.(*h*)[1]

(*h*) Cogan *v.* Stephens; Lewin on Trustees, App. vii.; Hereford *v.* Ravenhill, 1 Bea. 481; Eyre *v.* Marsden, 2 K. 564, 574; Ackroyd *v.* Smithson, 1 B. C. C. 503.

---

[1] The result of the authorities on this subject is, that where land is devised to be sold for purposes which are illegal, or fail, in whole or part, or do not exhaust the whole interest, the heir takes the disappointed interest, to the exclusion of the next of kin. Where there is only a partial failure or lapse, so that a sale is still necessary, or as to any undisposed of surplus, the heir takes the money as land: Craig *v.* Leslie, 3 Wheat. 564; Burr *v.* Sim, 1 Whart. 252; Morrow *v.* Brenizer, 2 Rawle 185; Pratt *v.* Taliaferro, 3 Leigh 419; Owens *v.* Cowan, 7 B. Monr. 152; Lindsay *v.* Pleasants, 4 Ired. Eq. 320; Slocum *v.* Slocum, 4 Edw. Ch. 613; Bogert *v.* Hertell, 4 Hill (N. Y.) 493. The converse of this rule applies as to money to be laid out on land: Hawley *v.* James, 5 Paige 323; except that where the money is disposed of only for a limited interest, it, or the land when purchased, beyond that interest, goes to the heir: 2 Jarm. Pow. on Dev. 74; Thorn *v.* Coles, 3 Edw. Ch. 330. In De Beauvoir *v.* De Beauvoir, 3 House Lords Cas. 524, where there was a power to lay out money on land, and a blended disposition of the realty and personalty, so as to produce a conversion of the latter, and to show an intention to impress it with the character of real estate, and the whole was devised to designated persons in tail male, with a limitation over to the testator's right heirs, it was therefore held that the intention did not cease with the failure of issue male under the limitations, so as to make the real estate go one way and the uninvested personalty another.

The rights of the heir are not affected, in these respects, by the fact that the produce of the real estate is blended with the personalty as a joint fund: Lindsay *v.* Pleasants, 4 Ired. Eq. 321; Wood *v.* Cone, 7 Paige 476. In some of the American cases, however, it has been held that where it appears to have been the testator's intention that the land shall change its character

[*139] In like manner, a conveyance of *real estate in the owner's lifetime, on trust to convert it into money and to pay the proceeds to him or to his executors, will not, if the estate is unsold at his death, work an equitable conversion in favor of the crown, so as to subject it to probate duty. (i)[1]

To this extent the general rule is clear. But where real estate is devised for sale, and its produce, either alone, or in union with the personal estate, is constituted a fund

(i) Matson v. Swift, 8 Bea. 368; Taylor v. Haygarth, 14 Sim. 8. [See Cradock v. Owen, 2 Sm. & Giffard 241.]

for all purposes, and be considered as personalty, the next of kin will be entitled in the failure of any particular purpose: Craig v. Leslie, 3 Wheat. 383; Burr v. Sim, 1 Whart. 263; Morrow v. Brenizer, 2 Rawle 185. But in England the rule is now that not the most express directions in the will, as that the proceeds of real estate shall constitute a fund of personalty, or the like, will exclude the right of the heir, unless, perhaps, there is a distinct bequest to the next of kin on the occurrence of such failure: Taylor v. Taylor, 3 De G., M. & G. 190; Robinson v. The Governors, 10 Hare 29; Fitch v. Weber, 6 Id. 145; Gordon v. Atkinson, 1 De G. & Sm. 478; Sammons v. Rose, 25 L. J. Ch. 615; 20 Jurist 73.

Though the undisposed of interest in land devised to be sold for particular purposes is treated as land, so as to descend to those who would have been entitled had it remained unconverted, yet after actual conversion the surplus descends as money: Pennell's App., 20 Penn. St. 515; Whitebread v. Bennet, 18 Jurist 140.

[1] Where a settlor conveys real estate upon trusts for sale, and directs the proceeds to be applied to certain purposes, some of which fail, whether the sale is directed in the lifetime of the settlor or after his decease, the property will, to the extent to which the purposes fail, result to the settlor as personal estate. *Secus*, if there is a failure of the whole purposes for which the sale is directed: Clarke v. Franklin, 27 L. J. Ch. 567; 4 Kay & Johns. 257. In Wilson v. Coles, 28 Bea. 215, there was a direction to sell real estate, to invest the proceeds, to pay the income thereof to the testator's wife for life, and after her death to pay the principal to a charity. The gift to the charity failed; but it was held that there had been a conversion out and out, that the testator's heir took the residue, which remained undisposed by reason of the failure of the gift to the charity, as personalty, and that as such it passed to his personal representatives, and not to his heir-at-law.

for particular payments, a contention sometimes arises as to the purpose really in view; viz., whether it was confined to those particular payments, or extended to a total change of character, so that the surplus may be liable as personal assets to creditors, may pass to a legatee of the personal residue, and may have the benefit of augmentation by lapse, independently of the enactment of 1 Vict. c. 26. The *primâ facie* construction is in favor of the more limited view; but if the will shows an intention to convert *quoad* the ulterior object, there is no reason to confine its effect. The question, however, is one of construction only, and it is sufficient here to notice that it exists. (*k*)[1]

The circumstance that the conversion has been *de facto* made, is immaterial in determining who is entitled to the surplus. But the necessity of such conversion for the other purposes of the gift, may be material in determining in what character the party takes. The former question

---

(*k*) 1 Jarm. on Wills, c. xix, ss. 4 & 5; Amphlett *v.* Parke, 1 Sim. 275; 4 Russ. 75; 2 R. & M. 221.

---

[1] The heir-at-law has a resulting trust in land directed to be sold, after debts and legacies are paid, and may come into equity and restrain the trustee from selling more than is necessary to pay the debts and legacies, or may offer to pay them himself, and pray to have a conveyance of a part of the land not sold in the first case, and the whole in the latter, which property will in either case be land and not money; but, if the intent of the testator appears to be to stamp upon the proceeds of lands the quality of personalty, not only for the particular purposes of the will, but to all intents, the claim of the heir-at-law to a resulting trust is defeated, and the estate is considered to be personal: Craig *v.* Leslie, 3 Wheat. 582, 583. See also Burr *v.* Sim, 1 Whart. 252; Pratt *v.* Taliaferro, 3 Leigh 419; Wright *v.* Trustees of Methodist Episcopal Church, 1 Hoff. Ch 205; Morrow *v.* Brenizer, 2 Rawle 185; but see note to previous page.

Equity will extend the same privilege to the residuary legatees which is allowed to the heir, viz., to pay debts and legacies, and call for a conveyance of the real estate, or to restrain the trustee from selling more than is necessary to pay debts and legacies: Craig *v.* Leslie, ubi supra.

depends on the original character of the property; the latter on the character which at the time of his taking it has been impressed on it by the creator of the trust. The test, therefore, by which the question should be tried, is the inquiry whether the effective trusts do or do not require the conversion to be made. If they do require it, the undisposed-of interest will be held by him in its converted character; if they do not, in its original one. Let us, for [*140] example, assume that land is devised on trust *to sell, and to divide the proceeds between A. and B. A dies in the testator's lifetime; B. survives him. In this case, there is a resulting trust of A.'s moiety for the heir; but a sale for convenience of division is just as necessary between B. and the heir, as it was between A. and B. The execution of the trust therefore requires a sale, although its purposes do not exhaust the proceeds; and, accordingly, the heir will take his share as money; and if he die without altering its destination, it will go to his executor and not to his heir. If, on the contrary, both A. and B. die in the testator's lifetime, there is a resulting trust of the entirety for the heir. A sale, therefore, is no longer wanted; the heir will take the estate as land; and on his death it will devolve on his heir. (l)

We will next consider the doctrine of conversion in its operation under contracts.[1]

(l) Smith v. Claxton, 4 Madd. 484; Jessopp v. Watson, 1 M. & K. 665; Hereford v. Ravenhill, 5 Bea. 51.

---

[1] The rules as to conversion apply to agreements between parties to a sale for the purposes of division : Hardy v. Hawkshaw, 12 Bea. 552; Naglee v. Ingersoll, 7 Penn. St. 197. Or to a conveyance for the benefit of creditors on trusts for sale : Griffiths v. Ricketts, 7 Hare 299. An infant's share in the proceeds of realty sold under proceedings in partition, will be treated as real estate until he comes of age : Bateman v. Latham, 3 Jones Eq. 35.

The rule in respect to contracts is, that if a binding contract be made for the sale of land, enforceable in equity, such contract, though in fact unexecuted, is considered as performed; so that the land becomes in equity the property of the vendee, and the purchase-money that of the vendor. The vendee, therefore, is entitled to the rents from the day named for completion, or, if a good title be not then shown, from the day when such title was first shown; and he must bear any loss, and will be entitled to any benefit occurring between the contract and the conveyance. And, *vice versâ,* the vendor is entitled to interest from the same time, if the purchase-money be not paid unless such non-payment originate in his own fault.(*m*) On the same principle, if either party die before completion, the equitable right to the land or purchase-money will devolve as real or personal estate. On the death of the vendee it will pass to the devisee or heir; who will be entitled to have the price paid out of the personalty, or, if the contract be rescinded after the death, [*141] *will be entitled to the purchase-money instead.(*n*) On the death of the vendor it will pass to his executor, for whom the devisee or heir will be a trustee.(*o*)

In the case of contracts, as in that of trusts, it is essential that the contract be a binding one, and that the object of the conversion be within its scope.[1]

(*m*) 1 Sug. V. & P. c. iv., s. 1; c. vi., s. 2; 3 Sug. V. & P. c. xvi., s. 1.
(*n*) Broome *v.* Monck, 10 Ves. 597.
(o) Knollys *v.* Shepherd, cited 1 J. & W. 499; 1 Jarm. on Wills 147; 1 Sug. V. & P. 291; Lumsden *v.* Frazer, 12 Sim. 263.

---

[1] See ante, note p. 136, upon the subject of equitable conversion generally, and also Story's Eq. Jurisprudence, ss. 790–793, and ss. 1212–1214; Henson *v.* Ott, 7 Ind. 512. An equitable conversion occurs though the election to purchase rests entirely with the vendee: Collingwood *v.* Row, 26 L. J. Ch. 649; Kerr *v.* Day, 14 Penn. St. 112. If there be a rescission

The first essential is that the contract be binding, and such as the Court will specifically execute.

If, therefore, the vendee die before completion of the contract, and the contract be one which, either from defect in the title or for any other reason, was not obligatory on him at his decease, the heir or general devisee of realty cannot require that the executor shall complete the purchase. If, however, it were binding on the deceased contractor it is immaterial that it was optional with the other party. When there is an option, if it be declared against the contract, the property will go according to its original character, and so long as the option is undeclared, the intermediate interest will follow the same course; but when the option is made in favor of enforcing the contract, the conversion will take effect from the date of its being declared.(*p*)

The second essential is that the object for which conversion is assumed be within the scope of the contract.

There is no equity for assuming a conversion in favor of or against any person who is not a party to the contract.[1]

(*p*) Broome *v.* Monck, 10 Ves. 595; Rose *v.* Cunynghame, 11 Id. 550; Townley *v.* Bedwell, 14 Id. 591; 1 Jarm. on Wills 49.

---

after the death of the vendor it amounts to a reconversion into land, and his distributees, who would be entitled to the money, will take the land instead: Leiper's Ex'rs. *v.* Irvine, 26 Penn. St. 54. An interest in a contract for the purchase of land descends on the heirs of the purchaser; his administrator must account to them for the rents; or for moneys derived from sales: Griffith *v.* Beecher, 10 Barb. S. C. 432. So, on the other hand, the interest of the vendor is held by the heir in trust for the next of kin, and if the land is recovered back in ejectment, it is still held as personalty: Rose *v.* Jessup, 19 Penn. St. 280.

A devise of lands is revoked by an agreement to sell in the devisor's life, and the purchase-money passes not to the devisee, but the residuary legatee: Donohoo *v.* Lea, 1 Swan (Tenn.) 119.

[1] Equitable conversion by a contract of sale, does not affect the rights of

It was at one time supposed that when an equitable
interest had been acquired in leasehold property by a
deposit of the lease for securing a debt, or by any other
contract in the nature of an assignment, the contract was
not only binding as between the intermediate parties, but
that the landlord had a right to treat it as executed, and
to proceed in equity against the assignee. A case might
certainly *occur in which the person having the [*142]
equitable right might so conduct himself as to
raise an equity in favor of the landlord, but it is decided
that the mere existence of the contract cannot confer on
the landlord any equity to interfere.(q) It has also been
contended that a husband's assignment of his wife's choses
in action should exclude the wife's right by survivorship,
on the ground that such an assignment implies a contract
to reduce the chose into possession, and is equivalent in
equity to such reduction. This proposition was first overruled in respect to bankruptcy, and it was decided that
whatever might be the rights of purchasers for value, the
assignees in bankruptcy were entitled to no such equity.
It was next overruled with respect to all assignments,
although for valuable consideration, if the chose were reversionary, and therefore incapable of present possession;
leaving the question still open, whether, if it were capable
of immediate possession or become so during the coverture, the wife should be excluded. The principle is now
extended to all cases; and it is held that, although the
husband's contract for value may, as between himself and

(q) Moores v. Choat, 8 Sim. 508; Close v. Wilberforce, 1 Bea. 112;
Robinson v. Rosher, 1 You. & Coll. N. C. C. 7.

the creditors of the vendor: Leiper's Ex. v. Irvine, 26 Penn. St. 54. The
rights of the widow and distributees in the fund are not changed by the
reconversion: Leiper's Appeal, 35 Penn. St. 420.

the assignee, be equivalent to a reduction into possession,
yet as against the wife, who is no party to the contract,
it cannot have that effect.(r)[1]

On an analogous principle to that of conversion, it is
held that where property subject to a trust has been unduly changed, the substituted property is bound by the
incidents of that which it represents.[2] If, therefore, the
guardian or trustee of an infant invest his personal estate
in land without authority for so doing, the land will be
affected in equity as personal estate, and will pass to the
administrator on the infant's death.[3] Or again, if timber
be cut by a guardian or trustee on the estate of an infant
tenant in fee, the proceeds will be realty, and will go to
[*143] the *heir; it is otherwise if the infant be tenant
in tail, for the conversion into personalty is then
palpably for his benefit, and the act ceases to be a breach
of trust. If the timber is blown down by accident, or is
cut down by a stranger tortiously, or if the act of the
guardian or trustee is authorized by the Court, there is
no breach of trust, and therefore no equity.(s)

In like manner, if an estate or fund has been changed
by breach of trust, the *cestui que trust* may, at his option,
waive its restoration, and may attach and follow it in its
altered form, *e. g.*, if a trustee or executor purchase an
estate with his trust-money or assets, and the fact of his

(r) Ashby v. Ashby, 1 Coll. 553; Rees v. Keith, 11 Sim. 388; Ellison v.
Elwin, 13 Sim. 309; Burnham v. Bennett, 2 Coll. 254.

(s) Tullit v. Tullit, Amb. 370; Witter v. Witter, 3 P. W. 99; Pierson v.
Shore, 1 Atk. 480; Ex parte Bromfield, 1 Ves. J. 453; 3 B. C. C. 510;
Oxenden v. Lord Compton, 2 Ves. J. 69.

---

[1] See, however, in the United States, note to Hill on Trustees, p. 642,
4th Am. ed.

[2] See Philips v. Crammond, 2 W. C. C. R. 441; and note, ante, page 33.

[3] Collins v. Champ's Heirs, 15 B. Monr. 118.

having done so be admitted or distinctly proved, the parties interested in the money may claim the estate, or if the purchase be made, partly out of the trust fund and partly out of the trustee's own property, they may claim a lien for the amount misapplied. It is essential, however, that the one property shall have been produced by the other; and therefore the doctrine will not apply if the estate be purchased with borrowed money, and a trust fund misapplied in payment of the debt. The principle of this doctrine is identical with that which originates a resulting trust, that when one man pays for an estate and has it conveyed to another, the grantee, who has the legal estate, is a trustee by operation of law for the purchaser. If a trust fund be applied in paying for the estate, and the *cestui que trust* affirms the purchase, it becomes a purchase with his money, and entitles him to the estate. It is therefore unnecessary that the trust should be evidenced in writing, notwithstanding that the claim may be for real estate. But the application of the trust fund must be admitted by the answer or proved by convincing evidence. And unless there be corroborating circumstances, such as a written account by the trustee showing how the *money was used, or a clear [*144] inability in him to make the purchase with other funds, mere parol evidence of declarations supposed to be made by him will be received with great caution.(*t*)[1]

(*t*) Lane *v.* Dighton, Amb. 409; Lewis *v.* Maddocks, 8 Ves. 150; 17 Id. 48; Denton *v.* Davis, 18 Id. 499; Taylor *v.* Plumer, 3 M. & S. 575; Lench *v.* Lench, 10 Ves. 511; Wilkins *v.* Stevens, 1 You. & Coll. V.-C. C. 431; 3 Sug. V. & P. c. xx., s. 3 and 4.

---

[1] See Murray *v.* Lylburn, 2 John. Ch. 442; and note, page 33: Olds *v.* Cummings, 31 Ill. 188; Pryor *v.* Wood, 31 Penn. St. 142. See also, May *v.* Le Claire, 11 Wall. (U. S.) 217.

The same rule has been applied where a contract had been rescinded upon the ground of fraud, and the purchase-money had been traced to a subsequent investment. It was held that where a contract is avoided on the ground of fraud, no property delivered under it passes from the owner; that the money, therefore, which had been paid still belonged to the vendee, who had paid it; and that inasmuch as the money thus obtained by fraud, had been laid out in the purchase of stock which was traced and identified, the person on whom the fraud has been practised was entitled to an injunction against its sale or assignment. It does not appear to have been contended, that this principle could be resisted in the case of a mere naked fraud, which vitiates a contract both at law and in equity. But it was argued by Sir Edward Sugden, on behalf of the defendant, that its application was not justified where the contract was rescinded on the ground of what may be called fraud in equity, rather than for absolute legal nullity. The distinction did not prevail with the Court; but it is still considered by Sir Edward Sugden that, in the event of an appeal, the decree could hardly have been maintained.(*u*)[1]

(*u*) Small *v.* Attwood, Younge 507 ; 1 Sug. V. & P. 400.

---

[1] The doctrine of conversion applies to a legislative direction for a sale : Snowhill *v.* Snowhill, 2 Green Ch. 20 ; see In re Arnold, 32 Beav. 591 ; Dixie *v.* Wright, Id. 662. The same principle has been applied in the working of the Act of Parliament for the emancipation of negroes in the West Indies, there treated as realty, giving compensation to the owners thereof: Richards *v.* Att.-Gen. of Jamaica, 6 Moore Priv. Coun. Cas. 381. But in England it has been held that money paid into court for land taken under the compulsory powers of an Act of Parliament, was to be treated as realty : Re Horner's Est., 5 De G. & Sm. 483 ; Re Steward's Est., 1 Drew. 636 ; Re Stewart, 1 Sm. & Giff. 39 ; Taylor's Settlement, 9 Hare 596 ; but see Ex parte Hawkins, 13 Sim. 569 ; Ex parte Flamank, 1 Sim. N. S. 260. See also, Bank of Auburn *v.* Roberts, 45 Barb. 419.

The doctrine of conversion, by changing the character of trusts and contracts, and altering them from mere rights of action into actual though imperfect titles in equity, gives rise to questions between them and the legal title, and also to questions between conflicting equities, where several have been created in reference to the same [*145] *thing. It therefore becomes necessary to consider the principle which determines the PRIORITY between such conflicting claims.

The rule of priority in regard to transfers and charges of the legal estate, whether made spontaneously by a conveyance, or compulsorily by a judgment at law, is that the order of date prevails. Conveyances take place from the date of the conveyance; judgments against realty from the date of the judgment; and judgments against personalty from the delivery of the writ; nor does the mere absence of valuable consideration affect the priority, except where it is provided otherwise by statute. There are, however, several statutes which have this effect, viz., the statute of 27 Eliz. c. 4, by which certain grants of real estate are avoided as against subsequent purchasers; that of Eliz. c. 5, by which certain grants either of real or personal estate are avoided against creditors; and the Statutes of Bankruptcy and Insolvency, by which certain grants made by a bankrupt or insolvent are avoided as against his assignees.[1]

---

[1] The subject of conveyances of land and chattels in fraud of purchasers or creditors, upon which there is a very considerable diversity of decision and legislation in the different states, will be found discussed very fully, and with remarkable ability, in the notes to Sexton v. Wheaton, 1 Am. Lead. Cas. 17; and to Twyne's Case, 1 Smith Lead. Cas. 33, 6th Am. ed., by the late Mr. Wallace. By Act of Congress of March 2d, 1867, to "Establish a uniform system of Bankruptcy throughout the United States," certain conveyances by persons in contemplation of bankruptcy and with an intention to defeat the operation of that act, are declared void. The

By the statute of 27 Eliz. c. 4, it is enacted, that conveyances, grants, &c., of or out of any lands or hereditaments had or made of purpose to defraud and deceive
such persons as shall purchase the same lands or hereditaments, or any rent, profit, or commodity out of the same,
shall be deemed and taken, only as against such persons
and their representatives as shall so purchase the same
for money or other good consideration, to be utterly void.
And further, that if any person shall make a conveyance
of lands or hereditaments, with a clause of revocation at
his pleasure, and shall afterwards sell the same lands or
hereditaments for money or other good consideration,
without first revoking the prior conveyance, then the
prior conveyance shall be void as against the vendee.

A conveyance may be rendered voidable under this
act in three ways: viz., First, if it be designedly fraudulent; and in this case it may be avoided by a subsequent
[*146] conveyance *from the heir of the grantor,[1] as
well as by one from the grantor himself.(v) Secondly, if it contain a power of revocation.(w) And
thirdly, if it be made without valuable consideration, and
followed by a conveyance or contract for value by the
grantor. For it has been held that a voluntary grant,

(v) Burrel's Case, 6 Rep 72; 3 Sug. V. & P. 282.
(w) 3 Sug. V. & P. 307.

---

assignee in bankruptcy is entitled to recover the property thus improperly
disposed of from the person to whom it has been transferred; and in certain cases, as where there has been collusion between the bankrupt and
the transferree, the latter, if a creditor, loses his right to prove his debt
against the estate.

[1] This has been overruled in England by the recent case of Doe d. Newman v. Rusham, 17 Q. B. (79 E. C. L. R.) 723; and Burrel's Case shown
not to support the proposition for which it is usually cited. See also, Doe
v. Lewis, 11 C. B. (73 E. C. L. R.) 1035.

coupled with such subsequent conveyance or contract, is sufficient to establish fraud as a conclusion of law.(*x*) But the grant may cease to be voluntary by matter *ex post facto*, and be thus made good against a subsequent purchaser, *e. g.*, if there be a subsequent conveyance from the volunteer to a purchaser for value.(*y*) If the grant be voluntary in part, it will be voidable to that extent, *e· g.*, if it be made in consideration of marriage, and there be an ultimate remainder to the brothers of the settlor, the marriage will not *per se* support that remainder, and it may be set aside by the purchaser.(*z*) The grant when made cannot be recalled by the grantor, but he will not be restrained from defeating it by a sale.(*a*) When a *bonâ fide* sale for value has been made, the purchaser may set aside the prior grant, and his *bona fides* will not be affected by notice of it.(*b*)[1] If he claims under an executed conveyance, the prior grant will be invalid at law; if under an executory contract, he may insist on a specific performance in equity; but it cannot be enforced against him at the suit of the vendor.(*c*)

(*x*) Doe *v.* Manning, 9 East 59; Pulvertoft *v.* Pulvertoft, 18 Ves. 84; 3 Sug. V. & P. 286, et seq.

(*y*) Prodgers *v.* Langham, 1 Sid. 133; George *v.* Milbanke, 9 Ves. 190; Brown *v.* Carter, 5 Ves. 862; 3 Sug. V. & P. 297.

(*z*) Johnson *v.* Legard, 6 M. & S. 60; T. & R. 281; Doe *v.* Rolfe, 8 A. & E. 650 (35 E. C. L. R.); Davenport *v.* Bishopp, 2 N. C. C. 451.

(*a*) Petre *v.* Espinasse, 2 M. & K. 496; Pulvertoft *v.* Pulvertoft, 18 Ves. 84.

(*b*) Gooch's Case, 5 Rep. 60 a.; Pulvertoft *v.* Pulvertoft, 18 Ves. 84; Buckle *v.* Mitchell, 18 Id. 100.

(*c*) Buckle *v.* Mitchell, 18 Ves. 100; Metcalfe *v.* Pulvertoft, 1 Ves. & B. 180; Smith *v.* Garland, 2 Meriv. 123; Johnson *v.* Legard, T. & R. 281; 3 Sug. V. & P. 305; Willats *v.* Busby, 12 Law Jur. N. S. 105; 3 Sug. V. & P. 300, et seq.

---

[1] A different rule obtains in many of the United States: Note to Sexton *v.* Wheaton, 1 Am. Lead. Cas. 36, 4th Am. ed.

[*147] *By the statute of 13 Eliz. c. 5, it is enacted, that all conveyances, grants, &c., of any lands hereditaments, goods, or chattels, had or made of purpose to delay or defraud creditors and others of their actions or debts, shall be taken, only as against such persons and their representatives as shall or might be so delayed or defrauded, to be utterly void; provided that the act shall not extend to any conveyance or assurance made on good consideration and *bonâ fide* to a person not having notice of such fraud.

The provisions of this statute, like those of the statute in favor of purchasers,[1] invalidate all conveyances and assignments made with a fraudulent design;(d) but they do not affect mere voluntary gifts, although the donor may afterwards become indebted; for he may fairly intend to give away his property; and if he were never allowed to do so effectively, it would produce mischiefs equally great with those which the act was intended to prevent. If, however, the party making a voluntary gift is deeply indebted at the time, it affords presumptive evidence that it was meant to defeat his creditors.[2]   If the amount given constitutes a large proportion of his estate, it increases the probability of such intent; and if he is in a state of actual insolvency, it appears to be conclusive evidence of fraud. The presumption, however, does not arise except in favor of persons who were creditors when the gift was made.[3]

(d) Twyne's Case, 3 Rep. 80.

[1] See Danbury v. Robinson, 1 McCart. 213.

[2] As to the extent of indebtedness which will render a voluntary conveyance fraudulent as to creditors, the decisions in the United States are not uniform.   See note to Sexton v. Wheaton, ut supr.

[3] See McLane v. Johnson, 43 Verm. 48.

But if the gift is set aside by them, the subsequent creditors will be let in to partake of the fund.(e)

In order to invalidate a gift under this statute, the property must be of a kind to which the creditors can resort for payment; for otherwise they are not prejudiced by the *gift. For this reason, if relief be asked in [*148] the lifetime of the debtor, the creditor must obtain judgment for his debt, and the property must be such as can be taken in execution. It was, therefore, formerly held, that during the debtor's lifetime, and so long as he was not bankrupt or insolvent, an assignment of a chose in action could not be set aside; but that it was otherwise on his bankruptcy, insolvency, or death, because the creditors might then reach all his personal property. It may be presumed that the same result will follow from the provisions of 1 & 2 Vict. c. 110.(f)

The effect of bankruptcy, or of a discharge under the insolvent acts, in avoiding prior conveyances by the bankrupt or insolvent, is dependent on peculiar principles and enactments, and is foreign to our present subject.

The rule of priority which governs transfers and charges of a legal estate, governs also, in the absence of a special equity, transfers and charges of an equitable interest.[1] But if legal and equitable titles conflict, or if, in the absence of a legal title, there is a perfect equitable title by conveyance on the one hand, and an imperfect one by

---

(e) Cadogan v. Kennett, Cowp. 432; Kidney v. Coussmaker, 12 Ves. 136. Richardson v. Smallwood, Jac. 552; Holloway v. Millard, 1 Mad. 414; Townsend v. Westacott, 2 Bea. 340; Ede v. Knowles, 2 N. C. C. 172, 178; Norcutt v. Dodd, Cr. & P. 100; 1 Story on Eq. Jur. s. 355, et seq.

(f) Colmun v. Croker, 1 Ves. Jr. 160; Dundas v. Dutens, Id. 196; Norcutt v. Dodd, 1 Cr. & P. 100; Story on Eq. s. 366, et seq.

---

[1] See Cory v. Eyre, 1 De G., J. & Sm. 167.

contract on the other, a new principle is introduced, and priority is given to the legal title, or, if there is no legal title, to the perfect equitable one. This doctrine is embodied in the maxim, that "between equal equities the law will prevail."

In order, however, that this maxim may operate, it is essential that the equities be equal. If they are unequal, the superior equity will prevail; and such superiority may be acquired under any of the three following rules:

1. The equity under a trust or a contract *in rem*, is superior to that under a voluntary gift, or under a lien by judgment.

2. The equity of a party who has been misled, is superior to his who has wilfully misled him.

3. A party taking with notice of an equity, takes subject to that equity.

[*149]   *The first of these rules is, that the equity under a trust or a contract *in rem*, is superior to that under a voluntary gift, or under a lien by judgment.

The principle on which this doctrine rests is, that the claimant under a trust or contract *in rem*, has acquired an equity to the specific thing which binds the conscience of the original holder, whilst the voluntary donee has no right of his own, but is entitled only to that which his donor could honestly give;[1] and even the judgment creditor, though he has in some sense given a consideration, has not advanced his money on the specific security, and is entitled to his debtor's real interest alone, viz., his interest, subject to his equities as they existed at the date of the judgment.[2] In accordance with this

---

[1] See Green *v.* Givan, 33 N. Y. 343.

[2] The rule is the same in the United States generally, in the absence of statutory regulation : Note to Basset *v.* Nosworthy, 2 Lead. Cas. Eq. 1.

principle, it has been decided that the rights of a *cestui que trust*, of a purchaser for value by imperfect conveyance or executory contract, and of a mortgagee by deposit of deeds, have priority over a judgment of a later date, against the trustee, vendor, or mortgagor, notwithstanding that by means of an *elegit*, the judgment may have been clothed with the legal estate.(*g*) Nor is this doctrine affected by the late statute, transforming a judgment into a charge by contract. For the statute treats the legal estate as separate from the equitable interest, and makes each of them subject to the judgments against their respective owners. When, therefore, it is enacted that the judgment shall operate as a charge on the estate, it means a charge on the beneficial estate of the debtor. If he has a legal estate, subject to an equity, it will be a charge on the estate subject to the same equity. If he has an equitable interest, it will be a charge on that interest.(*h*)

The second rule of superior equity is, that "the equity *of a party who has been misled, is superior to his who has wilfully misled him."   [*150]

This rule is, in fact, merely a specific application of the general doctrine of law with respect to fraud, where the fraud complained of is a representation, express or implied, false within the knowledge of the party making it.(*i*) Its effect, however, on the priority of conflicting equities, renders it proper to be noticed here.

(*g*) Newlands *v.* Paynter, 4 M. & C. 408 ; Lodge *v.* Lyseley, 4 Sim. 70 ; Langton *v.* Horton, 1 Hare 549, 560 ; Whitworth *v.* Gaugain, 3 Id. 416 ; 1 Ph. 728.

(*h*) 1 & 2 Vict. c. 110 ; Whitworth *v.* Gaugain, 3 Hare 416 ; 1 Ph. 728.

(*i*) Infra, Rescission of transactions on the ground of fraud.

In Cadbury *v.* Duval, 1 Am. Law Reg. 105 (affirmed on appeal), the doctrine was applied to a creditor by judgment for contemporaneous advances.

The meaning of the rule is, that if a person interested in an estate knowingly misleads another into dealing with the estate as if he were not interested, he will be postponed to the party misled, and compelled to make his representation specifically good. If, therefore, a person, intending to buy an estate or to advance money on it, inquires of another whether he has any encumbrance or claim thereon, stating at the same time his intention to make the purchase or advance, and the person of whom the inquiry is made untruly deny the fact, equity will relieve against him; and if he has acquired the legal ownership, will decree him a trustee for the puisne claimant.[1] And even though he do not expressly deny his own title, yet if he knowingly suffers another to deal with the property as his own, he will not be permitted to assert it against a title created by such other person.(k)[2] The same principle will apply if he lie by and allow another to expend money in improvements, without giving notice of his own claim. But the fact of improvements having been made in error, where such error was not abetted by himself creates no equity for reimbursement of their expense.(l)

(k) 3 Sug. V. & P. 429 ; Nicholson v. Hooper, 4 M. & C. 179.

(l) Pilling v. Armitage, 12 Ves. 78, 84; Cawdor v. Lewis, 1 Y. & C. 427 ; E. I. Company v. Vincent, 2 Atk. 83 ; Williams v. Earl of Jersey, Cr. & P. 91 ; 3 Sug. V. & P. 437.

---

[1] Otis v. Sill, 8 Barb. S. C. 102; Lesley v. Johnson, 41 Barb. 359; Lee v. Kirkpatrick, 1 McCart. 264 ; Crocker v. Crocker, 31 N. Y. 507 ; Chapman v. Hamilton, 19 Ala. 121 ; Folk v. Beidelham, 6 Watts 339 ; McKelvey v. Truby, 4 W. & S. 323. It has been held, however, that a party will not be postponed on the ground of silence alone, where his title is upon record : Goundie v. Northampton Co., 7 Penn. St. 239 ; Knouff v. Thompson, 16 Id. 361 ; Hill v. Epley, 31 Id. 331 ; Clabaugh v. Byerly, 7 Gill 354. Neither infancy nor coverture will excuse parties guilty of fraudulent concealment: Schmithermen v. Eisernan, 7 Bush (Ky.) 298.

[2] Carr v. Wallace, 7 Watts 400.

In order to the introduction of this equity, it is essential that there be intentional deceit in the defendant, or at all *events, that degree of gross negligence [*151] which amounts to evidence of an intent to deceive. If, therefore, the party standing by be ignorant of his right, or if he has been merely careless or negligent; *e. g.*, where a mortgagee or trustee, by not taking the title deeds, or by subsequently parting with them, has enabled the mortgagor or *cestui que trust* to commit a fraud, the mere circumstance of his having done so will not warrant relief against him.[1] It may, however, exclude him from equitable aid as against a subsequent purchaser or mortgagee.(*m*)

Cases of concealed or undisclosed interest, whether the non-disclosure be fraudulent or accidental, are obviously distinct from those where the interest was in its creation fraudulent and void, and where therefore its non-disclosure is not treated as a substantial equity, but as mere evidence of a pre-existent fraud. In respect to lands, such non-disclosure is not *primâ facie* evidence of fraud; for the possession of land does not ordinarily follow the permanent ownership, but may belong to a mere tenant at will. In respect to personalty it is otherwise, for the ordinary proof of ownership is possession of the pro-

(*m*) Evans *v.* Bicknell, 6 Ves. 174 ; Martinez *v.* Cooper, 2 Russ. 198.

---

[1] A legal mortgagee will be postponed on account of not retaining the title deeds; when he displays fraud, or gross or wilful negligence, or when he gives up the deeds to the mortgagor for the express purpose of raising a sum of money, and thus puts it in the power of the latter to raise a larger sum : Perry Herrick *v.* Attwood, 2 De G. & J. 21 (see Lloyd *v.* Attwood, 3 De G. & J. 614) ; Waldron *v.* Sloper, 1 Drewry 193. But where there is no such negligent and deliberate action on the part of the mortgagee, he will not be postponed : Hewitt *v.* Loosemore, 9 Hare 449 ; Colyer *v.* Finch, 5 House Lds. Cas. 905. See also, Dowle *v.* Saunders, 2 Hem. & M. 242.

perty; and therefore, if such possession be left in an assignor, it, is *primâ facie* a badge of fraud in the assign-·ment, though subject to be rebutted by counter proof. (*n*)[1]

The third, and. most important rule of equity is, that " a party taking with notice of an equity takes subject to that equity."[2]

(*n*) Twyne's Case, 3 Rep. 80; Manton *v.* Moore, 7 T. R. 67; Leonard *v.* Baker, 1 M. & S. 251; Arundell *v.* Phipps, 10 Ves. 139, 145; Martindale *v.* Booth, 3 B. & Ad. 498.

---

[1] Twyne's Case, 1 Sm. Lead. Cas. 33, 6th Am. ed.

[2] The subject of notice will be found discussed in the notes to Le Neve *v.* Le Neve, 2 Lead. Cas. Eq. 23. Notice may be either actual or construct-ive. Actual notice arises from distinct knowledge or means of knowledge; constructive notice springs from a presumption of law which fastens know-ledge upon a person conclusively supposed to be affected by the notice. Instances of the former are not needed; of the latter, the notice afforded by the recording acts is an illustration. Notice must be certain, and not vague: Massie *v.* Greenhow, 2 P. & H. 255; Williamson *v.* Brown, 15 N. Y. 354–364. It must be clear enough to put a party on inquiry, and enable him to prose-cute that inquiry to a successful termination: Kerns *v.* Swope, 2 Watts 78. If this is done, it will be sufficient: Hawley *v.* Cramer, 4 Cow. 717; Pearson *v.* Daniel, 2 Dev. & Bat. Ch. 360; Sigourney *v.* Munn, 7 Conn. 324; Booth *v.* Barnum, 9 Id. 286; Peters *v.* Goodrich, 3 Id. 146; Lasselle *v.* Barnett, 1 Blackf. 150; Cotton *v.* Hart, 1 A. K. Marsh. 56; Pitney *v.* Leonard, 1 Paige 461; Woodfolk *v.* Blount, 3 Hey 147; Harris *v.* Carter, 3 Stew. 233; Benzein *v.* Lenoir, 1 Dev. Ch. 225. And the notice need not be distinct and formal, for if a purchaser has the means of knowledge he cannot wilfully neglect them, but will be affected with notice: Graff *v.* Castleman, 5 Randolph 195; Pendleton *v.* Fay, 2 Paige 202; Doyle *v.* Teas, 4 Scam. 202; Cook *v.* Gaiza, 14 Tex. 201; Wilson *v.* Miller, 16 Iowa 111; Tilling-hast *v.* Champlin, 4 R. Island 173, 215; Price *v.* McDonald, 1 Md. 403; Hoxie *v.* Carr, 1 Summer 193; Harper *v.* Reno, 1 Freem. Ch. 323; Green *v.* Slayter, 4 J. C. R. 47; Kerns *v.* Swope, 2 Watts 78; Churcher *v.* Guern-sey, 39 Penn. St. 84; Flagg *v.* Mann, 2 Sum. 486; Hackwith *v.* Damron, 1 Mon. 327; Miller *v.* Shackleford, 2 Dana 264; Billington's Lessee *v.* Welsh, 5 Binn. 132; 2 Lead. Cas. Eq. 154; Allen *v.* McCalla, 25 Iowa 464; Bell *v.* Twilight, 18 N. H. 159; Parker *v.* Foy, 43 Miss. 260. The notice should come from parties interested, and vague representations by strangers will have no effect: Butler *v.* Stevens, 26 Maine 484; The City Council *v.* Page, 1 Spear's. Eq. 159; Barnhart *v.* Greenshields, 28 Eng. L. & Eq. 77. But full and direct information, even from a stranger, cannot be disre-

The meaning of this doctrine is, that if a person acquiring property has, at the time of acquisition,[1] notice of a

garded: Ripple v. Ripple, 1 Rawle 386. Notice to an agent is of course
notice to the principal, but it must as a general rule be in the course of
the same transaction. See Hill on Trustees 165, and notes; post 157, note.
And notice to one of several trustees is notice to all: see Willes v. Greenhill, 29 Beav. 376; also Brazelton v. Brazelton, 16 Iowa 417. A purchaser
who is bound to take notice of a deed will be affected with notice of everything that appears upon its face: note to Le Neve v. Le Neve, 2 Lead.
Cas. Eq. 169, and cases cited; George v. Kent, 7 Allen 16; Montefiore v.
Browne, 7 House of Lords Cas. 241. See Hetherington v. Clark, 30 Penn.
St. 393. And where it is the duty of a person to demand the production
of title-deeds, he will be held to have notice of all the facts of which the
production would have informed him: Peto v. Hammond, 30 Beav. 509;
Kellogg v. Smith, 26 N. Y. 18. Possession is notice, because it ought to
put parties upon inquiry: Krider v. Lafferty, 1 Whart. 303; see Patton v.
The Borough, 40 Penn. St. 206; Hughes v. United States, 4 Wall. S. C. 232;
Morrison v. March, 4 Minn. 422; Bank of Newbury v. Eastman, 44 N. H.
431; Warren v. Richmond, 53 Ill. 52; Perkins v. Swank, 43 Miss. 349;
and even when the possession is not exclusive: Boggs v. Anderson, 50
Maine 161; Hill on Trustees 798, note (4th Am. ed.). A bonâ fide purchaser will not be affected by the notice of his vendor: Demarest v. Wynkoop, 3 John. Ch. 147; and on the other hand a purchaser who has notice
will, as a general rule, be protected by the want of notice on the part of
his vendor: Curtis v. Lunn, 6 Munf. 42; Lindsey v. Rankin, 4 Bibb 482;
Bumpus v. Platner, 1 John. Ch. 213; McNitt v. Logan, Litt. Sel. Cas. 69;
Wood v. Chapin, 13 N. Y. 509; Webster v. Van Steenbergh, 46 Barb. 211;
Hagthorp v. Hook's Adm'r., 1 G. & J. 273. And the same rule applies to
cases of constructive notice under the recording acts: American note to
Le Neve v. Le Neve, 2 Lead. Cas. Eq. 184.

[1] In England and some of the United States, the rule is that notice before the execution of the conveyance, though after payment of the purchase-
money, is sufficient. But in others, as Pennsylvania, Virginia and Iowa,
the notice must be before payment of the purchase-money: Hill on Trustees (4th Am. ed.) 259; notes to Basset v. Nosworthy, 2 Lead. Cas. 1;
Barney v. McCarty, 15 Iowa 514. In some of the states also, contrary to
the English rule, and that prevailing in other states, payment of part of
the purchase-money will be a protection pro tanto: Juvenal v. Jackson,
14 Penn. St. 519; Frost v. Beekman, 1 John. Ch. 288; Flagg v. Mann, 2
Sumn. 486; Paul v. Fulton, 25 Missouri 156; but compare Fraim v.
Frederick, 32 Texas 294. See note to Basset v. Nosworthy, ut sup. To
entitle a party to the status of a bonâ fide purchaser, without notice, there

prior equity binding the owner in respect of that property, he shall be assumed to have contracted for that only which the owner could honestly transfer, viz., his interest, subject to the equity as it existed at the date of the notice.

[*152]   *In accordance with this principle, the purchaser of property from a trustee with notice of the trust, is himself a trustee for the same purposes; the purchaser of property which the vendor has already contracted to sell, with notice of such prior contract, is bound to convey to the claimant under it; and the purchaser of land which the vendor has covenanted to use in a specified manner, having notice of that covenant, is bound by its terms. The exact extent to which this doctrine will be carried, where a covenant has been made by the owner of land, the burden of which does not at law run with the land, does not appear to be positively settled. If, however, the covenant be one respecting the land, and not purely collateral, there appears to be no reason why the doctrine of notice should not apply, or why the assignee of the land, knowing that the covenant has modified his assignor's ownership, should not be presumed to have contracted for it, subject to that modification.(o)[1]

It will be observed, that the notice required by this doctrine is a notice of an equity, which if clothed with

(o) Whatman v. Gibson, 9 Sim. 196; Schreiber v. Creed, 10 Sim. 9; Keppell v. Bailey, 2 M. & K. 517; 2 Sug. V. & P. 500.

must be a want of notice both at the time of the purchase and at the time of payment: Blanchard v. Tyler, 12 Mich. 339

[1] It was accordingly so decided in Tulk v. Moxhay, 2 Phill. 774, in which an assignee of land with notice of a covenant not to build, was restrained, without any regard to the technical rules in Spencer's Case; and the case has been followed frequently since. See Coles v. Sims. 5 De G., M. & G. 1; Wilson v. Hart, L. R. 1 Ch. Ap. 463; Western v. MacDermott, L. R. 2 Ch. Ap. 72.

legal completeness would be indefeasible, and not merely notice of a defeasible legal interest, or of an interest, which, if legal, would be defeasible. For the principle is that an interest, which if legal, would be indefeasible, shall not be defeated by reason of its equitable character, by a party who has notice of it. If, being legal, it may be defeated at law, there is no equity to preserve it.

Instances of the first class will be found in trusts and contracts, including the lien of a vendor of real estate; and in judgments against the owners of an equitable interest; for if the trust or contract were perfected by conveyance, or the legal ownership were vested in the judgment debtor, the right of the *cestui que trust* or vendee in the one case, or of the judgment creditor in the other, could not be subsequently defeated. The case of dower was until *recently an exception to this rule. We [*153] have already seen that by an anomalous distinction in the law of trusts, the widow was excluded from dower in a trust estate, although she would have been entitled to it in a legal one of the same character. The same distinction was continued in respect to notice; and it was held, that although the mere existence of an outstanding term would not exclude the widow in favor of the husband's heir, yet it would exclude her in favor of her vendee, notwithstanding that the purchase was made with notice of her right. This anomaly, as well as that of her exclusion from a trust estate, has been abolished by the recent act.

Instances of the second class will be found in judgments defeated under the old law by a power of appointment in legal titles destroyed by fine;(p) in contracts

(p) Langley v. Fisher, 9 Bea. 90; Story v. Windsor, 2 Atk. 630.

which the purchaser had *ab initio* a right to nullify;(*q*) and in voluntary conveyances avoided by subsequent alienation for value;(*r*) for in all these cases the legal right of the claimant is legally defeasible, and he has no independent equity to sustain it.

There is an apparent exception to this rule in regard to unregistered conveyances and undocketed judgments, which, although mere legal titles, and invalid at law, have been enforced as equities on the ground of notice.

By several acts of Parliament,[1] all deeds and wills concerning estates within the North,(*s*) East,(*t*) or West(*u*) Ridings of the county of York, or within the town and county of Kingston-upon-Hull,(*v*) or within the county of Middlesex, are directed to be registered.(*w*)[2]   And it is

(*q*) Lufkin *v.* Nunn, 11 Ves. 170; 3 Sug. V. & P. 441.
(*r*) Pulvertoft *v.* Pulvertoft, 18 Ves. 84; Buckle *v.* Mitchell, Id. 100.
(*s*) 8 Geo. 2, c. 6.   (*t*) 6 Ann. c. 35.
(*u*) 2 & 3 Ann. c. 4; 5 Ann. c. 18.   (*v*) 6 Ann. c. 35.
(*w*) 7 Ann. c. 120.

---

[1] Two acts have been recently passed in England in regard to real estate, which ought to be noticed here. The Stat. 25 & 26 Vict. c. 67 provides for an examination of title by the Court of Chancery, and a declaration thereupon; and Ch. 53 of the same statute furnishes a system of registration for such titles as, after official investigation, appear good and marketable.

[2] The rule under the recording acts, in force generally in the United States, is different from that under the registry acts in England, and it is held that the registry of a deed or mortgage, is notice of its contents, and of equities created thereby, or arising therefrom, to all persons claiming under the grantor, any title held by him at the time of conveyance: 4 Kent's Com. 174; American notes to Le Neve *v.* Le Neve, 2 Lead. Cas. Eq., p. i., 178, and cases cited, among which are Cushing *v.* Ayer, 25 Maine 383; McMechan *v.* Griffing, 3 Pick. 149; Peters *v.* Goodrick, 3 Conn. 146; Parkist *v.* Alexander, 1 J. C. 394; Wendell *v.* Wadsworth, 20 John. 663; Plume *v.* Bone, 1 Green 63; Evans *v.* Jones, 1 Yeates 174; Irvin *v.* Smith, 17 Ohio 226; Martin *v.* Sale, Bail. Eq. 1; Shults *v.* Moore, 1 McLean 520; Hughes *v.* Edwards, 9 Wheat. 489; Hickman *v.* Perrin, 6 Cold. (Tenn.) 135; Digman *v.* McCollum, 47 Mo. 372. This does not apply, however,

enacted, that all such deeds shall be adjudged fraudulent
and void against any subsequent purchaser or mortgagee

---

where the recording of an instrument is not legally requisite, or it is defectively executed or acknowledged : cases in notes to Le Neve *v.* Le Neve,
ut supra ; Moore *v.* Auditor, 3 Hen. & Munf. 232 ; Sumner *v.* Rhodes, 14
Conn. 135 ; Walker *v.* Gilbert, 1 Freem. Ch. 85 ; Harper *v.* Reno, Id. 323 ;
Isham *v.* Bennington Iron Co., 19 Verm. 230 ; Graham *v.* Samuel, 1 Dana
166 ; Pitcher *v.* Barrows, 17 Pick. 361 ; Thomas *v.* Grand Gulf Bank,
9 Sm. & M. 201 ; Green *v.* Drinker, 7 W. & S. 440 ; Shults *v.* Moore, 1
McLean 520 ; Brown *v.* Budd, 2 Carter (Ind.) 442 ; Choteau *v.* Jones, 11
Illinois 300 ; Work *v.* Harper, 24 Miss. 517 ; Pope *v.* Henry, 24 Verm.
560 ; Lally *v.* Holland, 1 Swan 396 ; Parret *v.* Shaubhut, 5 Minn. 323 ;
Racouillat *v.* Rene, 32 Cal. 450 ; nor where it is recorded in a different
county from that in which the lands lie : Aster *v.* Wells, 4 Wheat. 466 ;
Kerns *v.* Swope, 2 Watts 75 ; or, *à fortiori*, in another state : Hundley *v.*
Mount, 8 S. & M. 387 ; Lewis *v.* Baird, 3 McLean 56 ; Crosby *v.* Huston,
1 Texas 203. But in De Lane *v.* Moore, 14 How. U. S. 253 ; U. S. Bank
v. Lee, 13 Peters 107 ; Crenshaw *v.* Anthony, M. & Y. 110 ; Bruce *v.*
Smith, 3 H. & J. 449 ; Crosby *v.* Huston, 1 Texas 203, it was held that
the registration of a settlement of personal property in the state where
the parties reside at the time, and the property then was, is valid as
against creditors and purchasers in another state, into which the property
is afterwards removed : though see Hundley *v.* Mount, 8 Sm. & M. 387.
The record also is not notice to those not claiming title under the
same grantor : Stuyvesant *v.* Hall, 2 Barb. Ch. 151 ; Lightner *v.* Mooney,
10 Watts 412 ; Woods *v.* Farmere, 7 Id. 282 ; Bates *v.* Norcross, 14 Pick.
224 ; Crockett *v.* Maguire, 10 Mo. 34 ; Tilton *v.* Hunter, 24 Maine 29 ;
Leiby *v.* Wolfe, 10 Ohio 80 ; Hoy *v.* Bramhall, 4 Green (N. J.) 563 ; Iglehart *v.* Crane, 42 Ill. 261 ; Calder *v.* Chapman, 52 Penn. St. 359. An unrecorded deed, is in general, good between the parties : 4 Kent 456, cases
cited. And where a subsequent purchaser has knowledge of the existence of such a deed, it is equivalent, as to him, to registry, and is treated
as such, both at law and in equity : Jackson *v.* Leek, 19 Wend. 339 ;
Jackson *v.* Sharp, 9 John. 163 ; Porter *v.* Cole, 4 Maine 20 ; Farnsworth
v. Childs, 4 Mass. 637 ; Martin *v.* Sale, Bail. Eq. 1 ; Corry *v.* Caxton, 4
Binn. 140 ; Speer *v.* Evans, 47 Penn. St. 141 ; Pike *v.* Armstead, 1 Dev.
Eq. 110 ; Vanmeter *v.* McFaddin, 8 B. Monr. 442 ; Ohio Ins. Co. *v.* Ledyard, 8 Ala. 866 ; McRaven *v.* Maguire, 9 Sm. & M. 34 ; McConnell *v.* Read,
4 Scam. 117 ; Dearing *v.* Lightfoot, 19 Ala. 28 ; McCullough *v.* Wilson, 21
Penn. St. 436 ; Center *v.* P. & M. Bank, 22 Ala. 743 ; Gibbes *v.* Cobb, 7
Rich. Eq. 54 ; notes to Le Neve *v.* Le Neve, ut supra ; Conover *v.* Von Ma-
ter, 3 Green, (N. J.) 481 ; Nice's Appeal, 54 Penn. St. 200. Though a

[*154] for valuable *consideration, unless a memorial thereof be registered, in the manner thereby pre-

mortgage is falsely recited in the records, it is notice of the actual mortgage: Smallwood v. Lewin, 2 McCarter (N. J.) 60. Recital of one unregistered in a registered one is sufficient notice: Hamilton v. Nutt, 34 Conn. 501. But see in Ohio as to mortgages, Mayham v. Coombs, 14 Ohio 428. In regard to judgment creditors, and purchasers at sales under judgments, actual notice is, without doubt, too late after judgment obtained, and, it would seem, after the *status* of creditor has been acquired: Davidson v. Cowen, 1 Eq. 470; Uhler v. Hutchinson, 23 Penn. St. 110, overruling Solms v. McColloch, 5 Id. 473; American note to Bassett v. Nosworthy, 2 Lead. Cas. in Eq. 111. See, also, Benham v. Keane, 1 Johns. & H. 685; Barker v. Bell, 37 Ala. 354. Under the statute in Iowa, however, the rule is different; see Seevers v. Delashmutt, 11 Iowa 174; Parker v. Pierce, 16 Id. 227; Hays v. Thode, 18 Iowa 51. But the authorities are at variance with regard to the character of the notice which will postpone a recorded to a prior unrecorded deed. The cases in England, since Hine v. Dodd, 2 Atkyns 275, place the relief given against the subsequent purchaser, which is there only in equity, on the ground of fraud (see Le Neve v. Le Meve, ut supra; Fleming v. Burgin, 2 Ired. Eq. 584; Ohio Ins. Co. v. Ross, 2 Md. Ch. Dec. 35); on which alone, it is supposed, the Act of Parliament could be broken in upon; and therefore, require clear proof of actual notice, which is considered equivalent to fraud: Chadwick v. Turner, L. R. 1 Ch. 310. In some of the states this doctrine has been adopted, and constructive notice is held to be insufficient: Norcross v. Widgery, 2 Mass. 509; Bush v. Golden, 17 Conn. 594; Harris v. Arnold, 1 Rhode Island 125; Frothingham v. Stacker, 11 Mo. 77; Martin v. Sale, Bail. Eq. 1; Fleming v. Burgin, 2 Ired. Eq. 584; Ingram v. Phillips, 5 Strobh. 200; see Burt v. Cassedy, 12 Ala. 734; McCaskle v. Amarine, 12 Id. 17; Hopping v. Burnham, 2 Green (Iowa) 39. Thus, possession of the prior grantee, except, perhaps, where distinctly brought home to the knowledge of the purchasers, is held to be insufficient: Harris v. Arnold; Frothingham v. Stacker. In other states, there are statutory provisions to the same effect: Spofford v. Weston, 29 Maine 140; Butler v. Stevens, 26 Id. 489; Curtis v. Mund, 3 Metc. 405; Hennessey v. Andrews, 6 Cush. 170. In Pennsylvania and New York, the decisions are not consistent. In Scott v. Gallager, 14 S. & R. 333, and Boggs v. Varner, 6 W. & S. 469, the language of the court is in accordance with the doctrine just stated. But there is no doubt that in the former state, open and notorious possession is sufficient notice of an unrecorded deed: Krider v. Lafferty, 1 Whart. 303; Randall v. Silverthorn, 4 Penn. St. 173; Patton v. The Borough, 40 Id. 206. So in New York,

scribed, before the registering of the memorial of the deed under which such subsequent purchaser or mortgagee shall claim. And that all devises by will shall be adjudged fraudulent and void against subsequent purchasers or mortgagees, unless a memorial of such will be registered within the space of six months after the death of the testator, dying within Great Britain; or within the space of three years after his death, dying upon the sea or in parts beyond the seas. And it is by the same acts further provided, that no statute, judgment, or recognisance (other than such as shall be entered into the name and upon the proper account of the King, his heirs, and successors), shall bind any such estates as aforesaid, but only from the time that a memorial thereof shall be duly entered.(x)

The question which has arisen under these acts is,

(x) 3 Sug. V. & P. c. xxi., s. 5.

Tuttle v. Jackson, 6 Wend. 213, has established, contrary to Dey v. Bunham, 2 J. C. 182, and other cases, that constructive notice is enough to postpone a subsequent purchaser. See Troup v. Hurlbut, 10 Barb. S. C. 354. And in Grimstone v. Carter, 3 Paige 421, it was held in general, that equities and agreements to convey, were not within the recording acts. In Maryland, in the case of Price v. McDonald, 1 Md. 414, a similar doctrine was held by the Court of Appeals; though in Ohio Ins. Co. v. Ross, 2 Md. Ch. Dec. 35, and Gill v. McAttee, Id. 268, the English rule was supported and followed by Chancellor Johnson. That possession is notice, has been also held in Webster v. Maddox, 6 Maine 256; Kent v. Plummer, 7 Id. 464 (before the statute referred to above); Boggs v. Anderson, 50 Id. 161; Buck v. Halloway, 2 J. J. Marsh. 163; Hopkins v. Garrard, 7 B. Monr. 312; Colby v. Kenniston, 4 N. H. 262; Williams v. Brown, 14 Ill. 200; Morrison v. Kelly, 22 Id. 610; Wyatt v. Elam, 19 Geo. 335; Vaughan v. Tracy, 22 Mo. 4; see, also, Bell v. Twilight, 2 Foster (N. H.) 500; Griswold v. Smith, 10 Verm. 452; and in Landes v. Brant, 10 How. U. S. 348; where, indeed, the point was considered to be unquestioned. This, however, is a mistake. This subject is treated of with great ability and acuteness in notes to Le Neve v. Le Neve, ut supra, where the cases will be found collected. See, also, Hart v. The Farmers' Bank, 33 Verm. 252.

whether a person buying an estate with notice of a prior encumbrance, not registered, shall be bound in equity by such encumbrance, although he has obtained a priority at law by registration of his deed.[1] And it has been held that he shall; but that the notice must be clear and undoubted, amounting in effect to evidence, that knowing the situation of the prior encumbrances, he registered in order to defraud them. A mere *lis pendens* is not such notice.

The doctrine as to notice of unregistered deeds has been a subject of regret, as breaking down the operation of the acts; and it is perhaps difficult to reconcile it altogether to principle. For if it be assumed that the unregistered conveyance evidences a mere legal title, invalidated by a mere legal flaw, it is difficult to see how an equity can arise, because an act of Parliament has made it invalid; if it evidences an equitable title by contract, which the want of registration has deprived of legal completeness, it is difficult to see why the same degree of [*155] *notice, which would bind in other cases, should not bind in this.(*y*)

The question with respect to undocketed judgments has arisen as follows: It was directed by the old law, that a particular of all judgments entered in the Courts should be made and put in an alphabetical docket, and that no undocketed judgment should affect any lands or tenements as against purchasers or mortgagees.(*z*) The first decision in favor of the undocketed judgments was, that if the purchaser had notice of it, and did not pay

(*y*) Jolland *v.* Stainbridge, 3 Ves. 478; Wyatt *v.* Barwell, 19 Id. 435; 3 Sug. V. & P. 372–3; Tyrrell's Suggestions 230.

(*z*) 4 & 5 Wm. & Mary, c. 20; 7 & 8 Wm. 3, c. 36.

---

[1] Butler *v.* Viele, 44 Barb. (N. Y.) 166.

the value of the estate, it should be presumed that he agreed to pay it off, and he should be compelled in equity to do so. The question afterwards came before Lord Eldon, on a bill for specific performance, where the purchaser had notice of undocketed judgments. Lord Eldon refused to force the title on him, stating at the same time an opinion, grounded on the decisions under the Registry Acts, that he would be bound by notice. He expressed, however, some doubt whether the doctrine could be perfectly reconciled to principle; and it is perhaps attended with the more difficulty, because the undocketed judgment is only an invalid title by an act of law, and is not, like an unregistered conveyance, evidence of a title by contract in equity.(a) The doctrine itself, however, is now at an end. The system of dockets has been abolished, a new method of registration substituted;(b) and it is declared that notice shall be immaterial.(c)

A remarkable illustration of the doctrines of notice is presented by the rule which requires the purchaser under a trust for sale, to see to the application of his purchase-money.[1] This rule assumes that the trustee is expressly or impliedly authorized to sell, and that he does not, so far as *the purchaser is aware, intend to misapply [*156] the price. For if either of these ingredients be wanting, the purchaser, having notice of a breach of trust committed or intended, would be obviously responsible

(a) Davis v. Strathmore, 16 Ves. 419; 2 Sug. V. & P. 394.
(b) 1 & 2 Vict. c. 110.   (c) 3 & 4 Vict. c. 82.

---

[1] By statute 23 & 24 Vict. (1860) c. 145, § 29, it is provided that the receipts in writing of any trustee for any money payable to him in the exercise of his trust shall be a sufficient discharge, and shall exonerate the purchaser from seeing to the application of the purchase-money.

for aiding it.(d)   The rule, however, goes beyond this,
and requires the purchaser to ascertain that his purchase-
money is in fact rightly applied.[1]   If the trust be to pay
it over to other persons, he must see that such payments
are made; if it be to invest the amount in the names of
the trustees, he must see that the investment is duly
made, though he need not interfere with its subsequent
application.(e)   In order to obviate this inconvenience, it
is usual to declare by an express clause, that the trustee's
receipt shall be a discharge; and a corresponding autho-

(d) Watkins v. Cheek, 2 S. & S. 199; Eland v. Eland, 4 M. & C. 420, 427.
(e) 3 Sug. V. & P. 158.

---

[1] Where there is a general charge or power to sell for debts, or for debts
and legacies, the purchaser is not bound to look to the application of the
purchase-money: Williams v. Otey, 8 Humph. 568; Garnett v. Macon, 6
Call 308; Bruch v. Lantz, 2 Rawle 392; Cadbury v. Duval, 10 Penn. St.
267; Dalzell v. Crawford, 1 Pars. Eq. 57; Hauser v. Shore, 5 Ired. Eq.
357; Gardner v. Gardner, 3 Mason 178; Andrews v. Sparhawk, 13 Pick.
393; Nicholls v. Peak, 1 Beas. 69. So, as to legacies, where there is a
trust for reinvestment, or the application cannot be made immediately:
Wormley v. Wormley, 8 Wheat. 421; Coonrod v. Coonrod, 6 Hamm. 114;
Hauser v. Shore, 5 Ired. Eq. 357. But where the trust is for the payment
of scheduled or specified debts, the cases generally hold that the purchaser
is bound to see to the application of the purchase-money: Gardner v. Gardner, 3 Mason 178;' Cadbury v. Duval, 10 Penn. St. 267; Dalzell v. Crawford, 1 Pars. Eq. 57; Wormley v. Wormley, 8 Wheat. 422; Duffy v. Calvert,
6 Gill 487; though see the remarks of Mr. Wallace's note to Elliott v. Mer-
ryman, 1 Lead. Cas. Eq. 45, as to devises for payment of debts. It has also
been doubted by Mr. Wallace, ut sup., whether, under a devise for the payment of legacies simply, the rule would be applied in this country, inasmuch as the debts of a decedent are always an implied charge on land here,
and therefore it is supposed such a charge would be equivalent to a devise
for the payment of both debts and legacies. But the analogy between the
two cases can only hold, if, on a sale for the payment of legacies alone,
the lien of debts would be discharged, which is by no means clear. In
Duffy v. Calvert, 6 Gill 487, and Downman v. Rust, 6 Rand. 587, accordingly, a purchaser was held bound to see to the application of the purchase-
money under such circumstances. See on this subject Hill on Trustees,
pp. 342–363.

rity will arise by implication, if the nature of the trust be inconsistent with the contrary view. If, for instance, the sale be directed at a time when the distribution could not possibly be made, it will be assumed that the trustees were meant to give a discharge, for the money cannot be paid to any other person.(f_1) The same assumption is made on a trust for general payment of debts, or for payment of debts and legacies; for it is impossible that the purchaser should ascertain the creditors; and if he were held liable to see the legacies paid, he would be necessarily involved in the account of debts. If the original trust be for payment of debts and legacies, the power to give a discharge is not affected, although the purchaser may know that the debts have been paid, and that the legacies alone remain as a charge.(g) Where leasehold estates are purchased from an executor, their price is necessarily applicable in a course of administration, which is tantamount to a trust for general payment of debts. And it is, therefore, settled that such a purchaser is not bound to see to the application of the purchase-money, when he *purchases *bonâ fide*, and without notice that there are no debts.(h)[1] [*157]

(*f*) Balfour *v.* Welland, 16 Ves. 151; Sowarsby *v.* Lacy, 4 Mad. 142.
(*g*) Forbes *v.* Peacock, 1 Ph. 717; Sug. V. & P. c. xvii., s. 1.
(*h*) 2 Sug. V. & P. c. xvii., s. 2.

[1] It has been recently held, however, that it is immaterial on a trust for sale for the payment of debts and legacies, that the purchaser has notice there are no debts, or even that there were none at the testator's death. The principle in such cases was said by the Lord Chancellor to be, that the testator in creating such a trust is to be supposed to have intended to give his trustees full power of receiving and applying the money; and not to rest upon the ground of the difficulty a purchaser would have in determining whether there were any debts or not: Stroughill *v.* Anstey, 1 De G., M. & Gord. 635. See article in 17 Jurist, part ii., 251; Hill on Trustees 553, note, 4th Am. ed.

The only remaining question as to notice is what degree of information will amount to notice.[1] It is not essential that the notice be given to the party himself; but notice to his counsel, solicitor, or agent, is sufficient, whether given in the same or in another transaction, provided there be adequate reason to conclude that the facts continued in remembrance.(i) Where, however, a solicitor had obtained for himself an estate from a client, by fraud, and afterwards on his selling it acted as the purchaser's solicitor, it was considered by Lord Brougham, in opposition to Sir John Leach, that as the solicitor had in fact defrauded both parties, the purchaser could not, from the mere circumstance of his having employed the same soliciter, be held to have notice of the fraud, any more than the party on whom it was first committed.(k)[2]

The ordinary instances of notice by actual information do not require any special remark. But it should be observed, that under this head is included notice by *lis pendens* or an interlocutory decree.[3] For it is presumed

(i) Fuller v. Bennett, 2 Hare 394.
(k) Kennedy v. Green, 3 M. & K. 699.

---

[1] See on the subject of notice, notes to Le Neve v. Le Neve, 2 Lead. Cas. Eq. 23.

[2] Knowledge acquired by an agent, in the course of his agency, is notice to the principal: Hough v. Richardson, 3 Story 660; Bowman v. Wathen, 1 How. 195; Astor v. Wells, 4 Wheat. 466; Westervelt v. Haff, 2 Sandf. Ch. 98; Watson v. Wells, 5 Conn. 468; Bracken v. Miller, 4 W. & S. 108. See Hood v. Fahnestock, 8 Watts 489. But it must generally be acquired in the same transaction: Bracken v. Millar, 4 W. & S. 111; Henry v. Morgan, 2 Binn. 497; Martin v. Jackson, 27 Penn. St. 404. See Smith's Appeal, 47 Penn. St. 128; Espin v. Pemberton, 3 De G. & J. 547. Where the agent acts for both parties, it is notice to the purchaser: Sergeant v. Ingersoll, 15 Penn. St 343; 7 Id. 340.

[3] Murray v. Ballou, 1 John. Ch. 566; Murray v. Lylburn, 2 Id. 441; Zeiter v. Bowman, 6 Barb. S. C. 133; Owongs v. Myers, 3 Bibb 279; Bolling v. Carter, 9 Ala. 921; Green v. White, 7 Blackf. 242; Tongue v.

that legal proceedings during their continuance, are pub-
lically known throughout the realm.` But no *lis pendens,*

Morton, 6 Harr & John. 21 Walker *v.* Butz, 1 Yeates 574; Diamond *v.*
Lawrence Co., 37 Penn. St. 353. It has been held, however, in one or two
cases, that the doctrine of *lis pendens* was inconsistent with the policy of
the recording or registration acts in this country: Newman *v.* Chapman,
2 Rand. 93; City Council *v.* Page, Spear's Eq. 159. In King *v.* Bill, 28
Conn. 593, it was doubted whether the doctrine of notice by *lis pendens.*
obtains in Connecticut. The principle of *lis pendens* is, that the specific
property must be so pointed out by the proceedings as to warn the whole
world that they meddle with it at their peril: Lewis *v.* Mew, 1 Strobhart's
Eq. 180. See Green *v.* Slayter. 4 John. Ch. 38; but the doctrine does not
apply in a case where the Court has no jurisdiction of the thing in controversy: Carrington *v.* Brents, 1 McLean 167; and it applies only to rights
or interests acquired from a party after the institution of a suit, and not to
the case of a right previously contingent or conditional becoming perfect:
Hopkins *v.* McLaren, 4 Cow. 667; Clarkson *v.* Morgan, 6 B. Monr. 441.
Lis pendens is notice only in relation to the property which is the immediate subject of the suit: Edmonds *v.* Crenshaw, 1 McC. Ch. 252; and the
property affected must be definitely described: Miller *v.* Sherry, 2 Wallace
S. C. 250; and can only affect a purchaser from the party to the suit of
the subject of controversy: French *v.* The Loyal Company, 5 Leigh 627.
Notice to a purchaser, arising from a bill filed, is notice of what the bill
contains, and nothing more: Griffith *v.* Griffith, 1 Hoff. Ch. 153; and a suit
not prosecuted to decree or judgment, is not constructive notice to a person
who is not a *pendente lite* purchaser: Alexander *v.* Pendleton, 8 Cranch
462; but the pendency of a suit duly prosecuted, is notice to a purchaser
of the subject of a suit, so as to bind his interest; and a pendency of a
suit commenced from the service of the subpœna, after the bill is filed:
Murray *v.* Ballou, 1 John. Ch. 566; Goodwin *v.* McGehee, 15 Ala. 232;
Lytle *v.* Pope, 11 B. Monr. 318. Publication as to a non-resident defendant
is equivalent to service of subpœna: Chaudron *v.* Magee, 8 Ala. 570.
Notice, however, by *lis pendens,* cannot continue after a final decree or
judgment: Blake *v.* Heyward, 1 Bailey's Eq. 208; Turner *v.* Crebill, 1
Ohio 372; Winborn *v.* Gorrell, 3 Ired. Eq. 117. See on this subject Hill
on Trustees, 4th Am. ed., 794; notes to Le Neve *v.* Le Neve, 2 Lead. Cas.
Eq. 23. The doctrine of *lis pendens* has been recently considered in the
Court of Appeal in England, and finally decided not to stand on the ground
of notice express or implied, but to follow from the general rule that pending litigation, neither party can be permitted to alienate the contested
property, so as to affect the rights of the other. The doctrine in question
was therefore held, not to apply as between co-defendants: Bellamy *v.*
Sabine, 3 Jur. N. S. 943.

of which a purchaser has not express notice, w
bind him, unless it be duly registered.(*l*)   On th
hand, a final decree or judgment is not notice;(*m*
fiat in bankruptcy;(*n*) nor the Court Rolls of a ma
nor the registration of a deed; nor the docketing
registration of a judgment.   But if it appear that
was actually made, it will be presumed that th
was found, and the purchaser will be affected wit
[*158] of its contents   *In the absence of an
information of the equity, the party may
affected with notice by information of any fact or
ment relating to the subject-matter of his contract
if properly inquired into would have led to its as
ment.[1]   If, for instance, he purchases land wb
knows to be in the occupation of another th
vendor, he is bound by all the equities of the ʃ
occupation.

If he knows that the title deeds are in anothe
possession, he may be held to have notice of th
sessor's claim on the estate.   If he knows of any
ment, forming directly or presumptively a link in t
he will be presumed to have examined it, and ther
have notice of all other instruments or facts to w
examination of the first could have led him.   But
not be presumed to have examined instruments wl
not directly or presumptively connected with th
merely because he knows that they exist, and th

(*l*) 3 Sug. V. & P. 458 ; Shallcross *v.* Dixon, 5 Jarm. on Con\
493 ; 2 Vict. c. 11, s. 7.

(*m*) 2 Sug. V. & P. 461.

(*n*) Hithcox *v.* Sedgwick, 3 V. & P. 467.

(*o*) 3 V. & P. 478.

---

[1] See notes to Le Neve, 2 Lead. Cas. Eq. ut sup.

may by possibility affect it, for that may be predicated of almost any instrument; *e. g.*, if he be informed that the vendor made a settlement on his marriage, but is informed at the same time that it does not relate to the property, he is not bound by notice of its contents. The mere want of caution is not notice. If indeed there be a wilful abstinence from inquiry, or any other act of gross negligence, it may be treated by the Court as evidence of fraud; but, though evidence of fraud, it is not the same thing as fraud. The party may have acted *bonâ fide*, and if he has done so there is no equity against him. The neglect, therefore, of a purchaser to inquire for the title deeds is not equivalent to notice that they are deposited with the mortgagee. For though he may have acted incautiously in taking a coveyance without them, yet the other party has been equally imprudent in taking the deeds without a conveyance, and each, in the absence of fraud, is at liberty to make the best use he can of his imperfect title. In conformity with the same principle, it seems that the mere notice of a fact, which may or may not, according to circumstances, be held *in a [*159] Court of equity to amount to fraud, will not affect a purchaser for value denying actual notice of the fraud. But where a lease was granted to a trustee and agent at a rent palpably below the value, it was held that the fact of its being granted at such undervalue, coupled with a recital that it was for faithful services, was a sufficient notice to the purchaser of such lease to put him on his guard.(*p*)

We have now considered the three rules of superior

(*p*) Jones *v.* Smith, 1 Hare 43; 1 Ph. 244; West *v.* Reid, Id. 249; Borell *v.* Dann, Id. 440; Kerr *v.* Lord Dungannon, 1 Conn. & L. 335; 3 Sug. V. & P. 468–480.

equity originating in contracts *in rem*, wilful misrepre-scutation, and purchasers without notice. If no superior equity exists, the common course of law is not interfered with. The equities are equal, and the law, or the analogy of law, will prevail.

If there be a legal right in either party, the Court of Chancery remains neutral; as, for example, if the purchaser of property without notice of a prior equity has procured a conveyance of the legal estate, either to himself or to an express trustee for him, this legal estate will secure him at law, and his priority therefore will be absolute over all claimants.[1] A similar result will follow if he can procure the assignment of an outstanding term, or of an estate by *elegit*. In the one case he has priority during the continuance of the term; in the other until the *elegit* is determined at law, *i. e.*, until the judgment has been satisfied at the extended value, which is always much below the real. It has been enacted by the late statute that the duration of an *elegit* shall in future be ascertained at law by a computation at the real, and not at the extended value; but this enactment, as well as the other statutory changes in respect to judgment, is subject to an exception in favor of purchasers without notice.(q)

The recent enactment as to the cesser of outstanding terms, when they become attendant on the inheritance,

(q) 1 & 2 Vict. c. 110; 2 & 3 Vict. 11, s. 5.

---

[1] See Story, J., in Flagg v. Mann, 2 Sumn. 557; Gibler v. Trimble, 14 Ohio 323. In Sergeant v. Ingersoll, 7 Penn. St. 340; 15 Id. 343; however, where the purchaser of an equitable title got the legal title from the trustee at the same time, he was held, nevertheless, bound by a covenant of the *cestui que trust*, of which he had no notice, the Court being of opinion under the circumstances that the separation of the legal and equitable titles was so suspicious a circumstance that it ought to have put him on inquiry.

has *been already explained.(r)   If a purchaser **[*160]** without notice of a prior equity, fails in obtaining the legal estate, he may still protect himself to some extent by getting possession of the title deeds, whether of the fee or of an outstanding term; for the possession of the deeds, though not equivalent to ownership, is so far available at law, that if he can otherwise get possession of the estate, it may serve him as a shield to protect his holding, or, at all events, may so far inconvenience his opponent as to compel the satisfaction of his claim.(s) If he cannot obtain either a conveyance or the deeds, he may take his chance of defects in his opponent's evidence, and will not be compelled to answer a bill of discovery.(t)

If there be no legal right in either party, the Court of Chancery cannot be neutral; for it is the only tribunal competent to take cognisance of the dispute. In this case, therefore, it acts on the analogy of law, and gives priority to that title which most nearly approximates to a legal one; viz., to an executed and perfect title in equity, rather than to one which is executory and imperfect.[1]

The methods by which a title may be perfected in equity differ according to the subject-matter of conveyance. Where an equity of redemption, whether in real or personal estate, is the subject, the conveyance will be perfected by the joinder of the mortgagee, and by his

(r) 8 & 9 Vict. c. 112, supra, Attendant Terms.

(s) Head v. Egerton, 3 P. Wms. 280, cited 2 Ves. & B. 83 ; Wallwyn v. Lee, 9 Ves. 24; Bernard v. Drought, 1 Moll. 38.

(t) 3 Sug. V. & P. c. xxiv.

---

[1] See Bellas v. McCarty, 10 Watts 13. Where a purchaser, the day after the completion of his purchase, deposited the title deeds by way of equitable mortgage, the mortgagee was held to have a better equity than the vendor as to his lien for unpaid purchase-money : Rice v. Rice, 23 L. J. Ch. 289 ; 2 Drew. 77.

22

declaration that the purchaser shall be entitled to redeem.(u). Where a trust estate in realty is the subject, the conveyance will be perfected if the trustee acknowledge a trust for the purchaser, either by executing a declaration to that effect, or by joining in the conveyance of his *cestui que trust*, though without purporting to pass [*161] his own estate.(v)   Where a trust *estate in personalty or a *chose in action* is the subject, the assignment is perfected by notice to the trustee or debtor, which operates as a constructive transfer of possession.(w)[1] If, in any of these cases, the party acquiring an equitable interest neglects to perfect it in the manner pointed out, he incurs the risk of some subsequent purchaser without notice being more diligent, and thus acquiring a priority over him.

It has been contended, that on the conveyance of a trust estate in realty, notice of such conveyance may be given to the trustee, and that the title will be thereby perfected, so as to exclude a subsequent purchaser from obtaining priority. The probability is, that a notice so given would practically prevent a priority being gained, because few persons would purchase without inquiring of the trustee, and few trustees would convey the legal estate after such a notice had come to their hands. But

(u) 3 Sug. V. & P. 422.

(v) Maundrell v. Maundrell, 10 Ves. 246, 270 ; Wilmot v. Pike, 5 Hare 14, 22

(w) Dearle c. Hall, 3 Russ. 1 ; Foster v. Cockerell, 3 Cl. & F. 456 ; Timson v. Ramsbottom, 2 K. 35 ; Meux c. Bell, 1 Hare 73 ; Etty v. Bridges, 2 N. C. C. 486 ; Holt v. Dewell, 4 Hare 446 ; Gardner v. Lachlan, 4 M. & C. 129 ; Ex parte Arkwright, 3 M., D. & D. 129, 141 ; [Consolidated Co. v Riley, 1 Giff. 371 ; Barr's Trusts, 4 K. & J. 219 ; Scott v. Hastings, Id. 633.]

[1] Notice to the debtor is not generally considered necessary in the United States to perfect the assignment of a chose in action. See ante, 53, note·

assuming that the purchase were made without inquiry, and that the trustees were afterwards induced to convey the estate, the notice seems immaterial; for it is merely a constructive taking possession of the estate, and therefore can have no greater effect in equity than possession without conveyance would have had at law.(x)

It has been already stated, that in order to avoid the postponement of the latter equity, freedom from notice is indispensable. The notice, however, here referred to, is a notice existing at the acquirement of the equity, not a notice at the completion of the right. The latter purchaser or encumbrancer, on payment of his money, becomes an honest claimant in equity, and is entitled, if he can, to protect his claim. But he is not bound to look for protection *until he has ascertained that danger [*162] exists; and his right to obtain it will continue, notwithstanding the institution of a suit to settle the priorities of the conflicting claimants. A decree, however, to settle priorities, is a bar to any protection being afterwards gained; for it is in effect a judgment for all the claimants, according to the order in which they then stand.(y)

If there be no legal right, or, in respect of equitable subject-matter, no perfect equitable right in any of the claimants, as, for example, if the estate be still outstanding in the original owner, or in some third person not constituted a trustee for any claimant individually, the claims will be satisfied in order of date.(z)

(x) Peacock v. Burt, Coote on Mortgages, Appendix; Jones v. Jones, 8 Sim. 633; Wilmot v. Pike, 5 Hare 14; Wiltshire v. Rabbits, 14 Sim. 76; Ex parte Knott, 11 Ves. 609, 612; 2 Sug. V. & P. 83.

(y) Brace v. Duchess of Marlborough, 2 P. Wms. 491; Wortley v. Birkhead, 2 Ves. 571; Belchier v. Butler, 1 Eden 523; Ex parte Knott, 11 Ves. 609, 619.

(z) Brace v. Duchess of Marlborough, 2 P. Wms. 491; Frere v. Moore,

The same rule seems applicable to cases where, in respect of legal subject-matter, both the titles are legal, and the jurisdiction of Chancery is not to enforce an equity, but to give the same relief as at law by more convenient means. On this principle, a plea of purchase without notice has been held inapplicable to a bill for assignment of dower, or for an account of tithes, although the soundness of the decision has been questioned.(a) And it would seem also that a bill to perpetuate testimony may be sustained, notwithstanding that the defendant is a purchaser without notice; for such a bill asks no relief or discovery from the defendant, but merely prays to secure the testimony, which might be had at the time if the circumstances called for it.(b)[1]

8 Price 475; commented on, 3 Sug. V. & P. 81, 422; Jones v. Jones, 8 Sim. 633.

(a) Collins v. Archer, 1 R. & M. 284; 3 Sug. V. & P. 495; Hare on Discovery 98.

(b) Seaborne v. Clifton, cited 6 Ves. 263; 3 Sug. V. & P. 438

---

[1] The prevailing doctrine in the United States is, that the purchaser of an equitable title takes it subject to all prior equities: Snelgrove v. Snelgrove, 4 Dessaus. 274; Winborn v. Gorrell, 3 Ired. Eq. 117; Shirras v. Craig, 7 Cranch 48; Vattier v. Hinde, 7 Peters 252; Boone v. Chiles, 10 Id. 177; Hallett v. Collins, 10 How. U. S. 185; Chew v. Barnet, 11 S. & R. 389; Kramer v. Arthurs, 7 Penn. St. 165; Sergeant v. Ingersoll, Id. 347; s. c. 15 Penn. St. 343. And the plea of purchase without notice, would not, therefore, be sufficient in such case. But the principle just before stated in the text (p. 160), that "if there be no legal right in either party," the court "acts on the analogy of law, and gives priority to that title which most nearly approximates to a legal one," was substantially followed in Bellas v. McCarty, 10 Watts 13, where a purchaser of the equitable estate in land under articles of agreement, who had recorded his deed (such an interest being within the recording acts of Pennsylvania), was preferred to a prior sheriff's vendee of the same interest, who had neglected to have his deed registered. And this was approved in Rhines v. Baird, 41 Penn. St. 265, where the doctrine in Chew v. Barnet, supra, was said to be contrary to the policy of the recording acts. So in Flagg v. Mann, 2 Sumn. 486, it was the opinion of Story, J., though the point

The maxim of non-interference between equal equities is the foundation of the doctrine of Tacking in Equity.[1]

---

was not directly decided, that a purchaser of an equity who subsequently obtains a conveyance from the trustee, is protected against any antecedent secret trust of which he has no notice. See also, the note to Bassett v. Nosworthy, 2 Lead. Cas. Eq., part i., 97, where this subject is discussed; though, notwithstanding some doubts suggested by the learned American editor of the work above cited, it appears to be clear upon the authorities both in this country and in England, that, except in the cases just put, among equal equities, the prior in time, whether it be original or intermediate, is the prior in right.

It has been held in some cases in the United States, following certain of the English decisions, such as Williams v. Lambe, 3 Bro. C. C. 264, and Collins v. Archer, 1 Russ. & Mylne 284, that a plea of a purchase for a valuable consideration is no defence in equity to a claim under a legal title: Snelgrove v. Snelgrove, 4 Dessaus. 274; Blake v. Heyward, 1 Bail. Eq. 208; Larrowe v. Beam, 10 Ohio 498; Jenkins v. Bodley, 1 Sm. & M. Ch. 338; Wailes v. Cooper, 24 Miss. 208; Brown v. Wood, 6 Rich. Eq. 155. But an opposite doctrine has been held in a number of cases, and principally in Wallwyn v. Lee, 9 Ves. 24; Joyce c. De Moleyns, 2 Jones & Lat. 374: Stackhouse v. The Countess of Jersey, 1 John. & H. 721; Att.-Gen. v. Wilkins, 17 Beav. 285; see also, Flagg v. Mann, ut supr. In the very recent case of Finch v. Shaw, 18 Jur. 935, 19 Beav. 500, an attempt was made to reconcile the conflicting authorities on this question. " The true distinction," said the Master of the Rolls, " appears to be this: where the suit is for the enforcement of a legal claim, and the establishment of a legal claim, there, although the court may have jurisdiction in the matter, it will leave the parties to their remedies at law; but where the legal title is perfectly clear and distinct, and attached to that legal title is an equitable remedy, or an equitable right, which can only be enforced in this court, I am not aware of any case in which the legal title being clearly established, this court refuses to enforce the equitable remedy which attaches to it." It was accordingly decided that the plea of purchase for a valuable consideration was no answer to a bill by a legal mortgagee for foreclosure. This case was affirmed in the House of Lords, under the name of Colyer v. Finch, 5 H. L. Cas. 905. See also, Carter v. Carter, 3 K. & J. 917, where the authorities are reviewed.

[1] See Lloyd v. Attwood, 3 De G. & J. 614. The English doctrine of tacking mortgages does not generally apply in the United States: Bridgen v. Carhartt, Hopkins 234; Grant v. U. S. Bank, 1 Cai. Ca. E. 112; Siter & Co. v. McClanachan, 2 Grat. (Va.) 280; Brazee and Others v. Lancaster Bank, 14 Ohio 318; Osborn v. Carr, 12 Conn. 196; Chandler v. Dyer, 37

[*163] The *cases to which this doctrine applies are those where several encumbrances have been created on an estate, and two or more of them, not immediately successive to each other, have become vested in a single claimant.

Under these circumstances the question arises, whether an intermediate claimant may redeem one of such eucumbrances, and postpone the other to his own charge, or whether the party holding the two may tack or consolidate them, so that the earlier in date cannot be separately redeemed. The doctrine on this subject is, that if the double encumbrancer is clothed with a legal or superior equitable right, he may, as against the mesne claimants tack to his original claim a claim for any further amount due to him in the same character, which was advanced expressly or presumptively on credit of the estate without notice of the mesne equity. If, for example, a third mortgagee, having advanced his money without notice of a second mortgage, should afterwards get a conveyance of the legal estate from the first mortgagee, the second mortgagee would not be permitted to redeem the first mortgage, after forfeiture at law, without redeeming the third also.

It is essential to the existence of this equity that there shall be a legal right in the party claiming to tack, or such a superior equitable right as gives him a preferable claim

---

Verm. 345; Anderson v. Neff, 11 S. & R. 223; it being inequitable and unjust in itself, and the system of registration being adopted throughout the Union; though the point seems doubtful in Kentucky: Nelson v. Boyce, 7 J. J. Marsh. 401; Averill v. Guthrie, 8 Dana 82. In some of the states, further advances to the mortgagee, for which a bond binding the heirs has been given, may be tacked to the mortgage as against an heir or devisee, though not as against intervening encumbrancers. See note to Marsh v. Lee, 1 Lead. Cas. Eq. 494, where the cases are collected.

to the legal estate; (c) that both the claims shall be vested in him in the same character, and not the one in his own right, and the other as executor or trustee; (d) and that the advance, in respect of which the equity is claimed, shall have been made expressly or presumptively on the credit of the estate without notice of the mesne equity. It seems doubtful what would be the effect of such notice, where a mortgage has been made for a specific sum, with a clause extending the security to future advances, and such future advances had been made after notice of an intermediate *charge. (e) It may, however, be observed, that in such a case the priority of the [*164] future advances, if sustained, would not be based on the equity of tacking, but on the construction of the security itself, as incorporating such advances with the original loan.[1]

The requirement that the moneys shall have been advanced on the credit of the estate, is obviously complied with in the instance already given, where the second advance is made on mortgage. But it is not confined to mortgages: it extends also to advances on judgment or statute, where the creditor was previously a mortgagee; for it is presumed in such a case that the prospect of tacking was in his contemplation at the time. It does not, on the other hand, include advances on judgment or statute, where the creditor was not previously a mortgagee, unless the judgment has been matured under the statute into a charge by contract, for a creditor by judgment or statute

(c) Willoughby v. Willoughby, 1 Term 763; 3 Sug. V. & P. 83.

(d) Barnett v. Weston, 12 Ves. 130; Morret v. Paske, 2 Atk. 52. [See Tassell v. Smith, 2 De G. & J. 713.]

(e) Gordon v. Graham, 7 Vin. Abr. 52, E. pl. 3; Blunden v. Desart, 2 Conn. & L. 111, 131.

---

[1] As to the incorporation of future advances in a mortgage security, see ante, note to p. 110.

does not lend his money on contemplation of the land; and cannot, therefore, by getting in a prior mortgage, convert a personal loan into a real encumbrance.(*f*) It is otherwise if redemption is asked by the debtor himself; for then the equity of tacking is in the nature of an equitable *elegit*, and is the proper method of enforcing the creditor's claim.(*g*) For the same reason a bond-debt may be tacked as against the heir or devisee, unless other creditors would be thereby prejudiced; for the equity of redemption is assets in his hands. And if a chattel real be mortgaged, a simple contract debt may be tacked as against the personal representative. The same right would, perhaps, be now allowed under 3 & 4 Wm. 4, c. 104, as against the heir or devisee, when there is not a devise for payment of debts. *If the heir or [*165] devisee has aliened the equity of redemption, it is not assets in the hands of the alienee, and the mortgage may be redeemed alone.(*h*)

It is also held, that an equity in the nature of tacking accrues where two mortgages of different estates are made to one person, or being originally made to two become vested in one, whilst the equities of redemption remain united in a single hand. In such a case, neither the mortgagor, nor any person making title under him, can after forfeiture redeem one without redeeming both.(*i*)[1]

(*f*) Brace *v.* Duchess of Marlborough, 2 P. Wms. 491; Baker *v.* Harris, 16 Ves. 397 ; Ex parte Knot, 11 Id. 609, 617.

(*g*) Supra. Equitable fieri facias and elegit.

(*h*) Coleman *v.* Winch, 1 P. Wms. 775 ; Morret *v.* Paske, 2 Atk. 52 ; Adams *v.* Claxton, 6 Ves. 226 ; Coote on Mortgages, 402.

(*i*) Margrave *v.* Le Hooke, 2 Vern. 207; Pope *v.* Onslow, 2 Id. 286; Jones *v.* Smith, 2 Ves. Jr. 372, 376 ; Ireson *v.* Denn, 2 Cox 425 ; White *v.* Hilacre, 3 Y. & C. 597 ; Grugeon *v.* Gerrard, 4 Id. 119; Coote on Mortgages 483–491.

---

[1] See, on the subject of Tacking: Neve *v.* Pennell, 2 Hem. & M. 170 ; Lloyd *v.* Attwood, 3 De G. & J. 614 ; Bates *v.* Johnson, Johnson 304.

*CHAPTER V. [*166]

OF RE-EXECUTION, CORRECTION, RESCISSION, AND
CANCELLATION.

THE subjects hitherto considered in the present Book
are the equities of trust, contract, and mortgage, and the
incidental doctrines of conversion and priority. In considering these subjects we have assumed, that the original
transaction and its evidence are unimpeached and clear,
and that the relief asked is merely the enforcement of a
consequent equity. If the instrument evidencing a transaction is destroyed or lost, if through mistake or accident
it has been incorrectly framed, or if the transaction is
vitiated by illegality or fraud, or as having been carried
on in ignorance or mistake of facts material to its operation, a new equity arises to have the instrument re-
executed, the error corrected, or the vicious transaction
rescinded and set aside. The equities for such re-execution, correction, and rescission, like the equity for per
formance in specie, are incapable of enforcement at
common law, and fall, therefore, within the province of
the Court of Chancery.

The jurisdiction for re-execution and other similar relief
arises, not only on a destruction or concealment by the
defendant, but also on an accidental destruction or loss,
where the missing instrument is such, that its non-
production would perpetuate a defect of title, or would

preclude the plaintiff from recovering at law.[1] If, for
instance, a conveyance to a purchaser has been acciden-
[*167]   tally burned, so *that the purchaser is unable to
show a title to the estate, the vendor may be
compelled to reconvey.(a)[2]

The most ordinary instances in which this jurisdiction
is exercised, are those of lost bonds and negotiable securities, the non-production of which would defeat an action.
And in these cases the decree is not confined to re-
execution, but, to avoid circuity of action, extends to
payment. In order, however, that the jurisdiction may
attach, it is essential that an affidavit be annexed to the
bill, averring that the instrument is destroyed or lost, or
that it is not in the plaintiff's custody or power, and that
he knows not where it is, unless it is in the hands of the
defendant.[3] The same facts must be also admitted or
proved at the hearing; for the instrument, if in existence,
would be cognisable at law, and the alleged loss or destruction is the only ground for shifting the jurisdiction

(a) Bennett v. Ingoldsby, Finch 262; 2 Sug. V. & P. 98.

---

[1] And the loss of an article of agreement containing mutual covenants is
sufficient to confer jurisdiction on a Court of Chancery in favor of the injured party: Bolware v. Bolware, 1 Litt. 124; see Owen v. Paul, 16 Ala. 130.

[2] But a bill for the re-execution of a deed of land, lost or destroyed while
in the possession of the grantee, cannot be sustained unless there be some
additional grounds for relief: Hoddy v. Hoard, 2 Carter (Ind.) 474.

[3] In a suit in Chancery praying relief for a lost writing, though strictly
the party should make affidavit of loss: Chewing v. Singleton, 2 Hill Eq.
371; Hill v. Lackey, 9 Dana 81; Owen v. Paul, 16 Ala. 130; Pennington
v. The Governor, 1 Blackf. 78; yet, if the proof of the loss is clear, the
affidavit may be dispensed with: Graham v. Hackwith, 1 A. K. Marsh.
424; Parsons' Admr. v. Wilson, 2 Tenn. 260; Webb v. Bowman's Ex'rs.,
3 J. J. Marsh. 73. In Lawrence v. Lawrence, 42 N. H. 109, where there
was a decree for the re-execution of a lost mortgage, the defendant was
ordered to pay the costs, because he had improperly denied the existence
of the mortgage.

into Chancery. If the relief sought extends merely to the delivery of the instrument, or is otherwise such as can only be given in a Court of equity, the affidavit is not required.(b) We have already seen, that a similar affidavit is requisite where a bill is filed for an examination *de bene esse,* as auxiliary to an action at law.(c)

The jurisdiction in the case of lost bonds originates in the doctrine of profert at law. It was anciently a rule of pleading in the common law Courts, that they could give no remedy for a debt secured by bond, unless the creditor offered to produce his bond in Court. This was called making profert of the bond. If the bond were lost, profert was impossible; and the remedy at law was gone. But the Court of Chancery, on proof that the bond was really lost, entertained jurisdiction to compel its re-execution and payment of the money secured. The rule requiring profert is now dispensed with at law in the event of loss; but the *change of practice at common law does not annul the jurisdiction in equity.(d)[1] [*168]

The jurisdiction in the case of negotiable securities originates in a different way. These securities not being under seal, are so far different from a bond, that in an action brought on them at common law, it has never been requisite to make profert. An action may be commenced on a bill or note, a plea called for, and the cause brought on for trial, without production being offered or made. And therefore, up to this point, there is no ground for

(b) Mitf. 124.　　　　　(c) Supra, Examination *de bene esse.*
(d) Ex parte Greenway, 6 Ves. 812; East India Company v. Bodham, 9 Id. 464.

---

[1] See Shields v. Commonwealth, 4 Rand. 541. And the finding of the lost bond or note after a suit in Chancery is instituted does not oust the chancellor of his jurisdiction: Crawford v. Summers, 3 J. J. Marsh. 300; Miller v. Wells, 5 Missouri 6; Hamlin v. Hamlin, 3 Jones' Eq. 191.

equitable interference. If, however, the bill or note be negotiable, it follows, that a plaintiff alleging it to have been lost, may, in fact, have assigned it to a third party, against whose claim the Court of law cannot indemnify the debtor. For this reason it is held at law, that a plaintiff suing on a negotiable instrument shall not recover the amount, unless he delivers up the security. And therefore a Court of equity, which can enforce a proper indemnity from the plaintiff, will entertain jurisdiction to compel payment on such indemnity being given. If the security be not negotiable, its loss will not prevent the creditor from recovering at law, and will not therefore create a jurisdiction in equity. (e)[1]

The jurisdiction to correct written instruments which have been erroneously framed is obviously appropriate to equity alone. A Court of law may construe and enforce the instrument as it stands, or may set it aside altogether if there be adequate cause. But it cannot compel any alteration to be made; and avoidance of the entire instrument would, in the case which we are now considering, be a nullification, and not an affirmance, of what was really meant.[2]

(e) Hansard v. Robinson, 7 B. & C. 90 (14 E. C. L. R.); Macartney v. Graham, 2 Sim. 285; Walmsley v. Child, 1 Ves. 341; Glynn v. Bank of England, 2 Id. 38; Mossop v. Eadon, 16 Id. 430.

---

[1] The loss of a negotiable note is a ground for equitable relief: Irwin v. The Planter's Bank, 1 Humph. 145; Tindall v. Childress, 2 St. & Porter 250; Smith v. Walker, 1 Sm. & Marsh. Ch. 432; Chewning v. Singleton, 2 Hill Eq. 371; Savannah Nat. Bank v. Haskins, 101 Mass. 370. But if the note has not been negotiated at bank, the bill must contain an allegation of all the facts necessary to be shown to manifest due diligence in attempting to obtain the money from the assignor: West v. Patton, Litt. Sel. Cas. 405. The general rule is the same as to bonds: Kerney v. Kerney, 6 Leigh 478; Harrison v. Turbeville, 2 Humph. 242; Rich v. Catterson, 2 J. J. Marsh. 135. See, as to statutory bonds: Webb v. Bowman, 3 J. J. Marsh. 70.

[2] The present English rule in regard to the reformation of instruments

*The most obvious and easy exercise of this [*169]
jurisdiction is where an instrument has been exe-

---

is well stated by the Chancellor in Fowler v. Fowler, 4 De G. & J. 265:
"It is clear," he says, " that a person who seeks to rectify a deed on the
ground of mistake must be required to establish in the clearest and most
satisfactory manner that the alleged intention to-which he desires it to be
made conformable continued concurrently in the minds of all parties
down to the time of its execution, and also must be able.to show exactly
and precisely the form to which the deed ought to be brought." See
also Malmesbury v. Malmesbury, 31 Beav. 417; Clark v. Malpas, 31 L. J.
Ch. (N. S.) 696; Garrard v. Frankel, 30 Beav. 459; Bradford v. Romney,
Id. 431.

In the United States there is no question as to the jurisdiction of a Court
of equity to reform a written instrument, on the ground of mistake, upon
parol evidence, where no statutory provision intervenes: Gillespie v. Moon,
2 John. Ch. 585; Newsom v. Bufferlow, 1 Dev. Eq. 379; Shipp v. Swann,
2 Bibb 82; Bellows v. Stone, 14 N. H. 175; and cases collected in note to
Woollam v. Hearn, 2 Lead. Cas. Eq. (3d Am. ed.) 684; Bradford v. Union
Bank of Tennessee, 13 How. U. S. 57; Runnell v. Read, 21 Conn. 586;
Stedwell v. Anderson, 21 Id. 139; Craig v. Kittredge, 3 Foster 231;
Lavender v. Lee, 14 Ala. 688; Wall v. Arrington, 13 Geo. 88; see Miller
v. Fichthorn, 31 Penn. St. 252; Wesley v. Thomas, 6 Har. & J. 23; see
Tilton v. Tilton, 9 N. H. 385; Durant v. Bacot, 2 Beas. 201; Hook v. Craighead, 32 Missouri 405; Gump's Appeal, 65 Penn. St. 476; Firmstone v.
DeCamp, 2 Green (N. J.) 317. Though the evidence must be very strong,
clear and precise, especially where it is against the answer: Reese v.
Wyman, 9 Geo. 430; Mosby v. Wall, 23 Miss. 81; Ligon's Admr. v. Rogers,
12 Geo. 281; Galdsborough v. Ringgold, 1 Md. Ch. 239; Beard v. Hubble,
9 Gill 420; Lea's Ex'rs. v. Eidson, 9 Gratt. 277; U. S. v. Monroe, 5 Mason
572; Lyman v. Ins. Co., 17 John. 373; Preston v. Whitcomb, 17 Verm.
183; Greer v. Caldwell, 14 Geo. 207; Leikensdorfer v. Delphy, 15 Mo. 160;
Carnall v. Wilson, 14 Ark. 482; Coffing v. Taylor, 16 Ill. 457; Wright v.
Delafield, 23 Barb. (N. Y.) 498; Wemple v. Stewart, 23 Id. 498; Farley
v. Bryant, 32 Maine 474; Tucker v. Madden, 44 Id. 206; Adams v. Robertson 37 Ill., 45; Clearly v. Babcock, 41 Ill. 271; Goltra v. Sanasack, 35
Id. 456; Shively v. Welch, 2 Oregon 288; Edmonds' Appeal, 59 Penn. St.
220. A Court of equity relieves more readily against a mistake in the
execution of a power than in a contract: Oliver v. Mutual Comm. Marine
Ins. Co., 2 Curtis C. C. 277. A misunderstanding of the facts is not
sufficient ground for asking a reformation of a contract; fraud or mistake
is indispensable: Story v. Conger, 36 N. Y. 673.

As to the parties *against whom* equity will afford this relief, they con-

cuted in order to the performance of a pre-existing trust, or where it purports to have been executed in pursuance of an agreement which it recites.

---

sist not only of the original parties, but also of all those claiming under them in privity, as heirs, legatees, devisees, assignees, voluntary grantees, judgment creditors, and purchasers with notice of the facts: Simmons v. North, 3 S. & M. 67; Whitehead v. Brown, 18 Ala. 682; Stone v. Hale, 17 Id. 557; Davis v. Rogers, 33 Maine 222; Wall v. Arrington, 13 Geo. 88; Godwin v. Yonge, 22 Ala. 553; Adams v. Stevens, 49 Maine 365; Cady v. Potter, 55 Barb. (N. Y.) 463; though see Dennis v. Dennis, 4 Rich. Eq. 307; see Quirk v. Thomas, 6 Mich. 76. But between creditors who have equal equities, there can be no relief for a mistake: Knight v. Bunn, 7 Ired. Eq. 77; Smith v. Turrentine, 2 Jones Eq. 253. Equity will correct as against sureties as well as others: Butler v. Durham, 3 Ired. Ch. 589.

As to cases within the Statute of Frauds, however, the authorities in the United States are somewhat conflicting where such parol evidence is resorted to, not for the purpose of rescinding or resisting execution of a contract, but in order to compel a specific performance with a variation, though the prevailing opinion appears to be that it is admissible. See ante, note to page 85, and the American note to Wollam v. Hearn, ut sup.; also Thompsonville v. Osgood, 26 Conn. 16; Ring v. Ashworth, 3 Clarke (Ia.) 458; White v. Port Huron, &c., R. R. Co., 13 Mich. 356; Glass v. Hulbert, 102 Mass. 24. In the absence of mistake or fraud, a provision or stipulation omitted from a contract by the express agreement of the parties, cannot be made, in general, the ground of a reformation upon parol evidence. See cases cited in American note to Woollam v. Hearn, ut sup.; Ligon's Admr. v. Rogers, 12 Geo. 281; Chamness v. Crutchfield, 2 Ired. Eq. 148; Whitehead v. Brown, 18 Ala. 682; Dwight v. Pomeroy, 17 Mass. 303; Andrew v. Spurr, 8 Allen 417; Betts v. Gunn, 31 Ala. 219. But in Pennsylvania, it has been constantly held, that contemporaneous verbal stipulations or provisions, on the faith of which a contract has been entered into, will control its operation: Christ v. Diffenbach, 1 S. & R. 464; Rearich v. Swinehart, 11 Penn. St. 238; Chalfant v. Williams, 35 Id. 212.

In general, a Court of equity will not relieve for ignorance or mistake of law: Hunt v. Rousmaniere, 1 Pet. S. C. 1; Shotwell v. Murray, 1 John. Ch. 512; Lyon v. Richmond, 2 Id. 60; Brown v. Armistead, 6 Rand. 594; Farley v. Bryant, 32 Maine 474; Freeman v. Curtis, 51 Id. 140; Peters v. Florence, 38 Penn. St. 194; Wintermute v. Snyder, 2 Green Ch. 498; Hall v. Reed, 2 Barb. Ch. 503; Lyon v. Sanders, 23 Miss. 533; Shafer v. Davis, 13 Ill. 395; Mellish v. Robertson, 25 Verm. 603; Smith v. McDougal, 2 Cal. 586; Bently v. Whittemore, 3 Green (N. J.) 366. It has been said,

In the former case the parties bound by the trust have no authority to vary it, or to execute any instrument inconsistent with its terms ; and if they do so, whether intentionally or not, there is a manifest equity to correct their error. For example, if a conveyance is improperly made in supposed pursuance of an executory trust by following its precise language, instead of working out by a set of formal limitations what it was intended to effect, the error will be rectified by decree.$(f)^1$

(f) Supra, Executory Trusts.

that whatever exceptions there may be to this rule, they will be found to be few in number, and to have something peculiar in their character, and to involve other elements of decision : Hunt v. Rousmaniere, ut sup. ; Bank U. S. v. Daniel, 12 Pet. 32. See Moreland v. Atchison, 19 Tex. 303. A distinction has sometimes been drawn between ignorance and mistake of law, and the latter, when distinctly proved, has been held ground for interference : Hopkins v. Mazyek, 1 Hill Eq. 242 ; State v. Paup, 8 Eng. (Ark.) 135 ; Lawrence v. Beaubin, 2 Bailey 623 ; but see Champlin v. Laytin, 18 Wend. 407 ; Jacobs v. Morange, 47 N. Y. 57. Mistake as to the legal effect of a conveyance, will not be relieved against, where the conveyance is such as the parties intended at the time : Hunt v. Rousmaniere, ut sup. ; Gilbert v. Gilbert, 9 Barb. S. C. 532 ; Arthur v. Arthur, 10 Id. 9 ; Mellish v. Robertson, 25 Verm. 608 ; Farley v. Bryant, 32 Maine 474 ; Larkins v. Biddle, 21 Ala. 252 ; Hawralty v. Warren, 3 Green (N. J.) 124 ; Burt v. Wilson, 28 Cal. 632 ; Hoover v. Reilly, 2 Abb. U. S. 471. Though see Clayton v. Freet, 10 Ohio (N. S.) 544 ; Kennard v. George, 44 N. H. 440 ; also Green v. The Morris and Essex R. R. Co., 1 Beas. 165 ; Canedy v. Marcy, 13 Gray 373 ; King v. Doolittle, 1 Head 77 ; Gross v. Leber, 47 Penn. St. 520 ; Clayton v. Bussey, 30 Ga. 946 ; Lister v. Hodgson, L. R. 4 Eq. 30. Where, however, one of the parties to a contract knows that the other is ignorant of some matter of law involved in it, and takes advantage of that ignorance, relief will be granted on the ground of fraud : Cooke v. Nathan, 16 Barb. 342 ; Dill v. Shahan, 25 Ala. 694. This subject has been much discussed in the United States, and there is no little diversity of opinion upon it. See Story on Equity, § 136, &c., where it is treated of at large.

See upon this subject generally the note to Wollam v. Hearne, 2 Lead. Cas. Eq. supra.

^{1} Equity will not reform a voluntary deed as against the grantor : Broun

In the second case where the instrument purports to
carry into execution an agreement which it recites, and
exceeds or falls short of that agreement, there is no difficulty in rectifying the mistake ; for then there is clear
evidence in the instrument itself that it operates beyond
its real intent.[1] If, however, there is no recital of any
agreement, but a mistake is alleged, and extrinsic evidence tendered in proof that it was made, the limits of
the equity for correction are more difficult to define.
The *primâ facie* presumption of law is, that the written
contract shows the ultimate intention, and that all previous proposals and arrangements, so far as they may be
consistent with that contract. have been deliberately
abandoned.   It seems, however, that the instrument may
be corrected, if it is admitted or proved to have been
made in pursuance of a prior agreement, by the terms of
which both parties meant to abide, but with which it is in
fact inconsistent; or if it is admitted or proved that an
instrument intended by both parties to be prepared in one
form, has, by reason of some undersigned insertion or
omission, been prepared and executed in another.   If, for
[*170] instance, a contract were made *for the purchase
of certain hereditaments, and the conveyance were
to omit a portion, or were to pass more than was intended,
there would be an equity to correct the deficiency or excess.   So again, where a solicitor, being instructed to
prepare a settlement of a particular sum, inserted by mistake double the amount, and the settlement was executed

---

v. Kennedy, 33 Beavan 147 ; Phillipson *v.* Kerry, 32 Id. 637 ; Henderson
v. Dickey, 35 Mo. 126.   But see Thompson *v.* Whitmore, 1 Johns. & H.
268 ; Mitchell *v.* Mitchell, 40 Ga. 11.

[1] Where there is an express ageeement for a policy of insurance in a
particular form, and the policy is drawn in a different form by the insurer,
equity will reform, on the face of the instruments: Collett *v.* Morrison, 9
Hare 162 ; Powell *v.* Fireman's Ins. Co., 13 B Monr. 311.

without discovery of the mistake, a bill was sustained to rectify it; and the same course was pursued where the solicitor, being directed to strike out a particular clause, had by mistake extended his erasure to the one which followed it.(*g*) But it is not sufficient that there is a mistake as to the legal consequences of the instrument; for to admit correction on this ground would be indirectly to construe by extrinsic evidence, and the proper question is not what the document was intended to mean, of how it was intended to operate, but what it was intended to be.[1] For example, where an annuity had been sold by the plaintiff, and was intended to be redeemable, but it was agreed that a clause of redemption should not be inserted in the grant, because both parties erroneously supposed that its insertion would make the transaction usurious, it was held that the omission could not be supplied in equity; for the Court was not asked to make the deed what the parties intended, but to make it that which they did not intend, but which they would have intended if they had been better informed. So also it has been decided, that where a party making a voluntary deed supposes that he will have a power of subsequent revocation though no such power is reserved, the deed cannot afterwards be altered to give him the power, for the evidence is not that its insertion was prevented by mistake, but that it was never intended to be made.(*h*)[2]

(*g*) Beaumont *v.* Bramley, T. & R. 41 ; Breadalbane *v.* Chandos, 2 M. & C. 711 ; Young *v.* Young, 1 Dick. 295 ; Rogers *v.* Earl, Id. 294 ; Wilson *v.* Wilson, 14 Sim. 405 ; 1 Sug. V. & P. c. iii., s. 11 ; Okill *v.* Whittaker, 2 Ph. 338.

(*h*) Irnham *v.* Child, 1 B. C. C. 92; Townshend *v.* Stangroom, 6 Ves. 328, 332 ; Worall *v.* Jacob, 3 Meriv. 267, 271.

---

[1] See note, ante, 168.

[2] See as to rectification of a settlement where the solicitor preparing has exceeded his instructions : Walker *v.* Armstrong, 25 L. J. Ch. 638.

23

[*171]   *In order to sustain a bill for relief under this equity, it is essential that the error be on both sides, and that it be admitted by the defendant or distinctly proved.[1] It must be a mistake on both sides, for if it be by one party only, the altered instrument is still not the real agreement of both.[2] A mistake on one side may be a ground for rescinding a contract, or for refusing to enforce its specific performance ; but it cannot be a ground for altering its terms. And the mistake must be admitted or distinctly proved. In determining whether such proof has been given, great weight will be allowed to what is reasonably and properly sworn by the defendant; but his oath is not conclusive, and may be counterbalanced by evidence. It has been suggested that in all cases where the Court has reformed a settlement, there has been something beyond mere parol evidence ; such, for instance, as the instructions for preparing the conveyance, or a note by the attorney, and the mistake properly accounted for. But it does not seem that evidence would be absolutely inadmissible even though there were nothing in writing to which it might attach. It would, however, be difficult to support the allegation of mistake, if the defendant positively denied it, and there were nothing to depend on but the recollection of witnesses.(i)

(i) Townshend v. Stangroom, 6 Ves. 328 ; Beaumont v. Bramley, T. & R. 41 ; Alexander v. Crosbie, L. & G. 145; Mortimer v. Shortall, 1 Conn. & L. 417.

---

[1] Lanier v. Wyman, 5 Rob. (N. Y.) 147; Mills v. Lewis, 55 Barb. (N. Y.) 179; Nevius v. Dunlap, 33 N. Y. 676.

[2] Thus a policy of insurance will not be reformed in consequence of a mistake of the assured alone : Cooper v. The Farmers' Ins. Co., 50 Penn. St. 299. And see Bentley v. Mackay, 31 Beav. 151 ; Sawyer v. Hovey, 3 Allen 331 ; Woodbury Savings Bank v. Insurance Company, 31 Conn. 517 ; Diman v. Providence R. R. Co., 5 Rhode Island 130. But mistake on the one side and fraud on the other will authorize a reformation : Wells v. Yates, 44 N. Y. 525.

Where land is the subject of the erroneous instrument, the reformation of an executed conveyance on parol evidence is not precluded by the Statute of Frauds, for otherwise it would be impossible to give relief. And where a mistake in an executory agreement relating to land is alleged, parol evidence may be admitted in oppositiou to the equity for specific performance. But it does not appear, that where the defendant has insisted on the benefit of the statute, the Court has ever reformed such an executory agreement on parol evidence, and specifically enforced *it with the variation.(*k*)[1] [*172] A will cannot be corrected by evidence of mistake, so as to supply a clause or word inadvertently omitted by the drawer or copier; for there can be no will without the statutory forms, and the disappointed intention has not those forms.[2] But it seems that if a clause be inadvertently introduced, there may be an issue to try whether it is part of the testator's will.(*l*)

In addition to the cases of correction on direct evidence of mistake, there are others where it has been decreed on a presumption of equity; as, for example, where bonds given for payment of a joint and several debt, but drawn up as merely joint, have been reformed in equity and made joint and several, so as to charge the estate of a deceased obligor.[3] The principle on which this presumption

(*k*) Attorney-General *v.* Sitwell, 1 Y. & C. 559; Townshend *v.* Stangroom, 6 Ves. 328; Higginson *v.* Clowes, 15 Ves. 516; 1 V. & B. 524; Okill *v.* Whittaker, 2 Ph. 338.

(*l*) 8 Vin. Abr. 188, G. a, pl. 1; Newburgh *v.* Newburgh, 5 Madd. 364; 1 Jarm. on Wills 353; Wigram on Wills s. 121.

---

[1] See Osborn *v.* Phelps, 19 Conn. 63; but see note, ante, p. 85 and 168; notes to Woollam *v.* Hearne, 2 Lead. Cas. Eq. 670.

[2] See Jackson *v.* Payne, 2 Metcalfe (Ky.) 567; Hunt *v.* White, 24 Texas 643.

[3] Story's Eq. s. 162; Weaver *v.* Shryock, 6 S. & R. 262; Stiles *v.* Brock, 1 Penn. St. 215.

depends is, that if the debt itself were joint and several, and a bond were given to secure that debt, it must be supposed that the liability on the bond was to be coextensive with the liability for the debt. On the same principle it is held that where a loan has been made to several persons jointly, it must be presumed that every debtor was to be permanently liable, until the money should be paid; and that therefore a debt so arising, though at law it is the joint debt of all the co-debtors, shall be treated in equity as the several debt of each.(m)[1] If, however, there be no independent liability, as for example, if the bond be of indemnity or of suretyship, there is no presumption that the instrument is erroneous, and no jurisdiction to vary its effect. If therefore, it be a joint obligation in form, it can have only the effect of a joint obligation. For its construction is the same in equity and at law; and unless there be evidence, direct or [*173] *presumptive, that its form is contrary to what was meant, it cannot be altered on mere conjecture.(n)[2]

An important instance of the equity in respect to co-

(m) Simpson v. Vaughn, 2 Atk. 31; Bishop v. Church, 2 Ves. 100; Thorpe v. Jackson, 2 Y. & C. 553; Clarke v. Bickers, 14 Sim. 639.

(n) Sumner v. Powell, 2 Meriv. 30; Underhill v. Horwood, 10 Ves. 209, 227; Rawstone v. Parr, 3 Russ. 539.

---

[1] This proposition, that a joint loan creates a joint and several debt in equity, for which Thorpe v. Jackson, is cited, was doubted in Jones v. Beach, 2 De G., M. & G. 886, by L. J. Knight Bruce.

[2] Jones v. Beach, 2 De G., M. & G. 886; U. S. v. Price, 9 How. U. S. 83; Moser v. Libenguth, 2 Rawle 428. Such evidence must be of mistake of fact, as by the draftsman of his instructions, but not of law, as of the legal effect of the words used: Moser v. Libenguth, ut sup. The rule has been also applied to the case of a joint judgment, entered on a joint and several bond, and the estate of the surety held discharged by his death after the rendering of the judgment: U. S. v. Price, ut supr.

debtors occurs in the case of debts owing by a partnership. On the death of a partner, the liability survives at law, and the debt is chargeable on the surviving partners alone. But the deceased partner's assets remain liable in equity; and the liabilities may be enforced either by the creditor or by the surviving partners. The duration of the liability is sometimes doubtful; and so also is the duration of a partner's liability who has retired from the firm, and is afterwards sued by an anterior creditor. The doubt, however, is not of law, but of fact. The principle of decision is clear; viz., that the deceased or retiring partner's estate must remain liable until the debts which affected him are discharged. But the discharge may take place in various ways; e. g., by actual payment on account of such debts; by the regular application of unapropriated payments to their reduction, as the earliest items on the account; by the express or implied agreement of the creditor to substitute the continuing partners as his debtors; or by the effect of the Statute of Limitations in barring the claim; and the question in each case is, whether, as against the particular partner, the debt has been in fact discharged.(o)

The equity for correction on presumptive evidence is applied also to mortgages by husband and wife, of the wife's estate, which have limited the equity of redemption to the husband. If the instrument does not recite an intention[1] to do more than make a mortgage, the presump-

(o) Wilkinson v. Henderson, 1 M. & K. 582; Winter v. Innes, 4 M. & C. 101 ; Brown v. Weatherby, 12 Sim. 6 ; Tatam v. Williams, 3 Hare 347 ; Way v. Bassett, 5 Id. 55; Thompson v. Percival, 5 B. & Ad. 925 ; Hart v. Alexander, 2 M. & W. 484; Blair v. Bromley, 5 Hare 542, 555 ; Smith's Merc. Law 55.

[1] It is not necessary, however, as was decided in Innes v. Jackson, cited below, that such intention should appear in the recitals in the deed, it is

tion is that nothing more was intended; and the instru-
[*174] ment will be *reformed by restoring the equity
of redemption to the wife.[1] And in like manner
it is held, that if a lease be made by tenant for life, under
a power created by a settlement, and a rent reserved to
the lessor and his heirs, these words shall be interpreted
by the prior title, and applied to the remainderman under
the settlement, and not to the heir of the lessor.(z)

The jurisdiction for Rescission and Cancellation arises
where a transaction is vitiated by illegality or fraud, or
by reason of its having been carried on in ignorance, or
mistake of facts material to its operation.[2]   And it is

(z) Innes v. Jackson, 1 Bl. O. S. 104, 114; Clark v. Burgh, 2 Coll. 221;
[see also, Plowden v. Hyde, 2 De G., M. & G. 684.]

---

sufficient if it appear from the whole transaction; and see Demarest v.
Wynkoop, 3 John. Ch. 129   In the recent case of Whitbread v. Smith, 3
De G., M. & G. 737, it was held that the Court would not on slight expressions in the proviso for redemption, infer an intention to exclude the
wife. Where there has been a different construction, it was said, there
were special circumstances independently of the limitations of the equity
of redemption. See also, Plowden v. Hyde, 2 De G., M. & G. 684.
Where a wife mortgages her property for a husband's debt, she stands in
the position of surety, and is entitled to exoneration out of his estate:
Sheidle v. Weishlee, 16 Penn. St. 134; Neimcewicz v. Gahn, 3 Paige 614;
and if her estate is joined with her husband's in one mortgage under such
circumstances, the latter must be first sold: Loomer v. Wheelwright, 3
Sandf. Ch. 135; Johns v. Reardon, 11 Md. 465; or if her estate has been
sold, she is entitled to subrogation to the mortgage, as against her husband: Sheidle v. Weishlee. On the other hand, where the mortgage by
the husband and wife is of the wife's separate estate, parol evidence is admissible to show that the money was really advanced to the wife, and the
husband the surety: Gray v. Downman, 27 L. J. Ch. 702.

[1] On the other hand, equity will not relieve against a deed of a married
woman which is defective through non-compliance with statutory regulations: Dickinson v. Glenney, 27 Conn. 104.

[2] To justify the rescission of an executed contract, there must be some
objection affecting the substance of the contract; and a contract can never

exercised for a double purpose; first, for cancelling executory contracts, where such contracts are invalid, but

---

be rescinded, except in case of fraud or palpable mistake: Thompson v.
Jackson, 3 Rand. 504.

Inadequacy of price by itself is no ground of rescission, as has been
held in a great number of cases: Osgood v. Franklin, 2 Johns. Ch. 1; Hill
on Trustees 236, 237 (4th Am. ed.), and cases cited: Potter v. Everett, 7
Ired. Eq. 152; Robinson v. Robinson, 4 Md. Ch. 183; Judge v. Wilkins,
19 Ala. 765; Erwin v. Parham, 12 How. U. S. 197; Harrison v. Guest, 8
H. L. Cas. 481. Yet it may, in connection with suspicious circumstances,
be evidence of fraud: Wormack v. Rogers, 9 Geo. 60; McArtee v. Engart,
13 Ill. 242; Coffee v. Ruffin, 4 Cold. (Tenn.) 487; particularly in view of
the mental capacity of the seller, or the relations of the parties; see post
182 and notes. And it has been often said, though not often acted on,
that where the inadequacy is very gross indeed, so as to shock the conscience and understanding of any man, the Court from that alone would
infer fraud or imposture: Wright v. Wilson, 2 Yerg. 294; Butler v. Haskell, 4 Dessaus. 652; Gist v. Frazier, 2 Litt. 118; Barnett v. Spratt, 4 Ired.
Eq. 171; Deaderrick v. Watkins, 8 Humph. 520; Juzan v. Toulmin, 9 Ala.
662; Eye v. Potter, 15 How. U. S. 60; Gifford v. Thorn, 1 Stockt. 702;
Surget v. Byers, 1 Hempst. C. C. 715; Marlatt v. Warwick, 3 Green (N.
J.) 108; but see Erwin v. Parham, 12 How. 197

On the other hand, a purchase of land at an exorbitant price, made on
condition of a loan of money, by a party whose necessities compel him to
borrow, will be set aside: Cockell v. Taylor, 15 Beav. 147.

The cancellation of an instrument may be decreed, though it has become
a nullity, on the ground of its creating a cloud in the title, or because it
may subject the party to litigation when the facts are forgotten: Cook v.
Cole, 2 Halst. Ch. 522, 627; but see, De Hoghton v. Money, L. R. 1 Eq.
154, where it was held that a purchaser for value could not require a
voluntary agreement affecting the land to be delivered up.

A Court of Chancery may refuse to rescind a contract, where it would
refuse to enforce a specific performance of it, at the suit of the other party:
Beck v. Simmons, 7 Ala. 71; Watkins v. Collins, 11 Ohio 31; Kirby v.
Harrison, 2 Ohio N. S. 326.

Application for a rescission must usually be made as soon as the cause
for rescission is discovered: Ayres v. Mitchell, 3 S. & M. 683; and the
Court will not rescind a contract, unless it can put the parties in *statu quo.*
Pintard v. Martin, 1 S. & M. Ch. 126; Garland v. Bowling, 1 Hemp. C. C.
170; Coppedge v. Threadgill, 3 Sneed 377. See also, Skinner v. White,
17 John. 357; Clay v. Turner, 3 Bibb 52; Lane v. Latimer, 41 Ga. 171.
The court will refuse to rescind where the plaintiff has acted in a manner

their invalidity is not apparent on the instrument itself, so that the defence may be nullified by delaying to sue until the evidence is lost;(a) and secondly, for setting aside executed conveyances or other impeachable trans- actions, where it is necessary to replace the parties in *statu quo.* And in such cases, though pecuniary damages might be in some sense a remedy, yet, if fraud be com- plained of, there is jurisdiction in the Court of Chan- cery.(b) The mode of relief under this equity, may be by cancellation of the instrument, or reconveyance of the property which has been unduly obtained, or by an injunc- tion against suing at law on a vitiated contract, or against taking other steps to complete an incipient wrong.(c)

We will first consider the case of Rescission and Can- cellation for illegality.

It is a maxim of law, that "*ex turpi causâ non oritur actio;*" and, therefore, if a contract of such a character be made, its invalidity will be a defence at law whilst it [*175] *remains unexecuted; and *pari ratione*, if its illegal character be not apparent on the face of it, will be a ground for cancellation in equity.[1] Such, for instance, are contracts entered into for the purposes of gaming[2] or smuggling, for inducing or aiding prostitution,[3]

(a) Peake v. Highfield, 1 Russ. 559; Jones v. Lane, 3 Y. & C. 281, 294; Simpson v. Lord Howden, 3 M. & C. 97.

(b) Evans v. Bicknell, 6 Ves. 174; Blair v. Bromley, 2 Ph. 354.

(c) Infra, Injunction.

---

inconsistent with the repudiation of the contract: Ex parte Briggs, L. R. 1 Eq. 483. Equity will also, upon a proper case being made, rescind con- tracts in relation to *personal* as well as real estate: Bradberry v. Keas, 5 J. J. Marsh. 446.

[1] W—— v. B——, 32 Beav. 574.

[2] Rucker v. Wynne, 2 Head 617.

[3] Walker v. Gregory, 36 Ala. 180.

for compromising a criminal prosecution, for giving usurious interest on a loan; or even for purposes which, though not strictly illegal, are against the policy of the law,[1] *e. g.*, for an unreasonable restraint of trade.

If the contract be already executed, it cannot be set aside as illegal or immoral; for it is a maxim that " *in pari delicto melior est conditio defendentis.*"[2] But it is otherwise where a law is made to prevent oppression, and the oppressed party is asking relief, *e. g.*, on a breach of the statutes against usury; for in such a case, although the complainant has joined in violating the law, he is not considered *in pari delicto*, but may defeat the contract after completion.[3]

So long as the contract continues executory, the maxim of " *in pari delicto*" does not apply; for the nature of the

---

[1] See Brown *v.* Speyers, 20 Gratt. 296.

[2] See Blystone *v.* Blystone, 51 Penn. St. 373.

[3] Courts of equity will not set aside an executed conveyance to compound a felony: Swartzer *v.* Gillett, 1 Chand. (Wis.) 207; nor a conveyance of a slave, upon a secret trust for his emancipation, when it is against law: Grimes *v.* Hoyt, 2 Jones Eq. 271.

A debtor, however, may always obtain relief in equity against a usurious contract; but he is obliged to tender by his bill the principal of the debt and legal interest, except in New York, where this is dispensed with by statute: Story Eq., § 301; see Vilas *v.* Jones, 1 Comst. 274; Rexford *v.* Widger, 2 Id. 131; West *v.* Beanes, 3 Harr. & John. 568; Anon., 2 Dessaus. 333.

So, where the parties to a contract contrary to public policy, or illegal, are not *in pari delicto*, and where public policy is considered as advanced in allowing either, or at least the more excusable of the two, to sue for relief, as in the case of bargains "savoring of champerty," equity will relieve, though against an executed conveyance: Reynell *v.* Sprye, 1 De G., M. & G. 660; 21 L. J. Ch. 633; affirming s. c. Hare 222. Where a party is injured by an act which is a felony at common law, or by statute, there is no remedy at law or in equity till after a conviction or acquittal on the criminal charge; but this does not apply where the injury is not discovered till after the criminal's death: Wickham *v.* Gattrell, 18 Jur. 768.

contract would be a defence at law, and the decree of cancellation is only an equitable mode of rendering that defence effectual. The prayer, however, must be confined to cancellation of the contract, and must not couple relief in affirmance of it, such as specific performance or reformation of error.(d)

Next, of Rescission and Cancellation by reason of fraud.[1]

The avoidance of transactions on the ground of fraud is a copious source of jurisdiction in equity. With respect to fraud used in obtaining a will, this jurisdiction does not exist. If the will be of real estate, it is exclusively cognisable at law; if of personal estate, in the Ecclesiastical Court.(e) In other cases of fraud, the Court of Chancery has concurrent jurisdiction with the [*176] Courts of law;[2] and *this jurisdiction will be exercised against any one who has abetted or profited by the fraud, and after any length of time. The infancy of the defrauding party will not exonerate him, for though the law protects him from binding himself by contract, it gives him no authority to cheat others.(f)[3]

(d) Batty v. Chester, 5 Beav. 103.

(e) Infra 248, Establishment of Wills. [But see note, Ibid.]

(f) Overton v. Banister, 3 Hare 503; Stikeman v. Dawson, 1 De G. & Sm. 90; [Wright v. Snowe, 2 Id. 321; Stoolfoos v. Jenkins, 12 S. & R. 399.]

---

[1] In equity nothing can be called fraud, or treated as fraud, except an act which involves grave moral guilt: Smallcomb's Case, L. R. 3 Eq. 769.

[2] See Relf v. Eberly, 23 Iowa 467; McHenry v. Hazard, 45 N. Y. 580.

[3] So of a feme coverte: Jones v. Kearney, 1 Dr. & Warr. 134; see Davis v. Tingle, 8 B Monr. 539; Hobday v. Peters, 28 Beav. 603. In the recent case of Vaughan v. Vanderstegan, 2 Drewry 363, it was held that a married woman, fraudulently representing herself as sole, made her separate estate liable for debts so contracted, and that where she had a general power of appointment and exercised it, equity would treat the property as assets on her death. See Hobday v. Peters, 28 Beav. 603; Hill on Trustees 663, 4th Am. ed.

The absence of personal benefit is no excuse; for if a man has aided or abetted a fraud he may be justly made responsible for its result, and even if no other relief be asked against him, may be compelled to pay the costs of suit.(*g*) The lapse of time is no bar to relief, for so long as the fraud remains unknown, it is a daily aggravation of the original wrong;(*h*) and even the innocence of a party who has profited by the fraud, will not entitle him to retain the fruit of another man's misconduct, or exempt him from the duty of restitution.(*i*) On the other hand, all unfounded allegations of fraud are discouraged by the Court; and if such allegations are made, and not established, the plaintiff will not in general be allowed to resort to any secondary ground of relief.(*k*)[1]

With respect to what will constitute fraud, it is impossible to lay down a specific rule; but the most ordinary instances of its occurrence, and those to which our attention will be now directed, are the procuring contracts to

(*g*) Supra, Priority of Equity on the ground of Fraud. Beadles *v.* Burch, 10 Sim. 332; Attwood *v.* Small, 6 C. & F. 232.

(*h*) Alden *v.* Gregory, 2 Eden 280; South Sea Company *v.* Wymondsell, 3 P. Wms. 143; Hovenden *v.* Lord Annesley 2 Sch. & L. 607, 639.

(*i*) Huguenin *v.* Baseley, 14 Ves. 273, 289.

(*k*) Glascott *v.* Lang, 2 Ph. 310.

---

[1] Price *v.* Berrington, 3 Macn. & G. 486; Eyre *v.* Potter, 15 How. U. S. 56; Fisher *v.* Boody, 1 Curtis 211; see Waters *v.* Mynn, 14 Jur. 341. It is not sufficient to allege fraud, in order to the rescission of a transaction, it must also be made to appear that the complainant has suffered some injury thereby: Cunningham *v.* Ashley, 7 Eng. (Ark.) 296; Cook *v.* Cook, Id. 381; Jewett *v.* Davis, 10 Allen (Mass.) 68. In general, an allegation of fraud is necessary: Gouveneur *v.* Elmendorff, 5 Johns. Ch. 79; Thompson *v.* Jackson, 3 Rand. 504; Booth *v.* Booth, 3 Lit. 57; Miller *v.* Cotten, 5 Ga. 346; Conway *v.* Ellison, 14 Ark. 360; McLane *v.* Manning, 1 Wins. (N. C.) No. 2, (Eq.) 60; though, where the facts are stated with distinctness and precision, an allegation of fraud *totidem verbis* is not required: McCalmont *v.* Rankin, 8 Hare 1; Skrine *v.* Simmons, 11 Ga. 401; Kennedy *v.* Kennedy, 2 Ala. 571.

be made or acts to be done by means of wilful misrepresentation, either express or implied, and the procuring them to be made or done by persons under duress or incapacity.[1]

In order to constitute a fraud of the first class, there must be a representation, express or implied, false within the knowledge of the party making it, reasonably relied [*177] on by the other party, and constituting a material inducement *to his contract or act.[2] If the

---

[1] In Chesterfield v. Janssen, 2 Ves. 125, Lord Hardwicke made the celebrated division of fraud, since so often recognised, into four classes, viz.: 1st. Fraud arising from facts and circumstances of imposition; 2d. Fraud arising from the intrinsic value and subject-matter of the bargain itself; 3d. Fraud presumed from the circumstances and condition of the parties contracting; 4th. Fraud affecting third persons not parties to the agreement. See the notes to this case in 1 Lead. Cas. Eq. 428.

[2] A false and fraudulent representation of a material fact, constituting an inducement to the contract, and on which the vendee relied, and had a right to rely, is a ground for rescission; and it appears to be generally held in the United States, that the principle equally applies, where the party making the representation was ignorant whether it were true or false: Hough v. Richardson, 3 Story 659; Harding v. Randall, 15 Maine 332; Pratt v. Phillbrook, 33 Id. 17; Lewis v. McLemore, 10 Yerg. 206; Turnbull v. Gadsden, 2 Strob. Eq. 14; Rosevelt v. Fulton, 2 Cowen 129; Smith v. Babcock, 2 Wood. & M. 246; Hunt v. Moore, 2 Penn. St. 105; Smith v. Richards, 13 Peters 26; Joice v. Taylor, 6 Gill & John. 54; Taylor v. Black, 13 How. U. S. 230; Reese v. Wyman, 9 Ga. 439; Taymon v. Mitchell, 1 Md. Ch. 496; Smith v. Robertson, 23 Ala. 312; Belknay v. Sealey, 2 Duer (N. Y.) 570; Lanier v. Hill, 25 Ala. 554; York v. Gregg, 9 Texas 85; Oswald v. McGehee, 28 Miss. 340; see Pulsford v. Richards, 17 Jurist 865; 17 Beav. 87; Reynell v. Sprye, 8 Hare 222; 1 De G., M. & G. 660. The tendency both in England and in this country, seems to be to make a party liable for representations *not known by him to be true*, as well as for those which he actually knows to be false: Hill on Trustees 146; Sharp v. Mayor, 40 Barb. 256; Thompson v. Lee, 31 Ala. 292: Wheelden v. Lowell, 50 Maine 499. It is not material that the misrepresentation was merely by an agent: Fitzsimmons v. Goslin, 21 Verm. 129; Brooke v. Berry, 2 Gill 83; or by partner: Blair v. Bromley, 2 Phillips 425; Beebe v. Young, 14 Mich. 136; May v. Snyder, 22 Iowa 525; Phillips v. Hollister, 2 Cold. 269. But if the agreement be fair between the parties, it is not invalid because

fact concerning which the representation is made is not a
material inducement to the contract or act, there is no
reason why a misstatement of it should vitiate what has

---

brought about by a third person to benefit himself: Bellamy *v.* Sabine, 2
Phillips 425; Blackie *v.* Clarke, 22 L. J. Ch. 377. Or even though brought
about by fraudulent misrepresentations on the part of such third person :
Fisher *v.* Boody, 1 Curtis 206.

In Turner *v.* Navigation Co., 2 Dev. Eq. 236, however, it was held that
in the case of a written ·contract, representations made *bonâ fide*, must
have been inserted in the contract to be relieved against; and this, though
the language of some of the cases seems to go much further, is on principle
the true doctrine. See Attwood *v.* Small, 6 Cl. & Finn. 232. Where both
parties have equal means of information, so that by the exercise of ordinary prudence and diligence, either may rely upon his own judgment,
misrepresentations, though false, will not be considered fraudulent : Hobbs
v. Parker, 31 Maine 143; Yeates *v.* Pryer, 6 Eng. (Ark.) 68; Hall *v.* Thomson, 1 Sm. & Marsh. 443; Tindall *v.* Harkinson, 19 Ga. 448; Rockafellow
v. Baker, 41 Penn. St. 319. And so if a vendee becomes acquainted with
the fraud before completing his bargain, and chooses to go on, a court of
equity will not help him : Pratt *v.* Philbrook, 33 Maine 17; Knuckolls *v.*
Lea, 10 Humph. 577; see Yeates *v.* Pryor, 6 Eng. (Ark.) 68; Scott *v.* Gamble, 1 Stockt. 218. But a contract may be set aside for fraudulent misrepresentations, though the means of obtaining information were fully open
to the party deceived, where, from the circumstances, he was induced to
rely upon the other party's information : Reynell *v.* Sprye, 8 Hare 222; 1
De G., M. & G. 660. Misrepresentations of value, or of other matters
which are only of opinion, also will not be relieved against : Warner *v.*
Daniels, 1 Wood. & Min. 90; Hough *v.* Richardson, 3 Story 659; Speigle-
myer *v.* Crawford, 6 Paige Ch. 254; Juzan *v.* Toulmin, 9 Ala. 662; Smith
v. Richards, 13 Pet. 26 ; Glasscock *v.* Minor, 11 Mo. 655; Hutchinson *v.*
Browne, 1 Clark Ch. 408 ; Coil *v.* Pittsburgh College, 40 Penn. St. 445. See
also, Wambaugh *v.* Bimer, 25 Md. 368. If, however, there is some fiduciary
relationship between the parties : Spence *v.* Whittaker, 3 Porter 297 ; or
in resisting specific performance, misrepresentations of value may become
important. Misrepresentations must be made in respect to matters of fact
and not of law : People *v.* San Francisco, 27 Cal. 655; and see also,
Jordan *v.* Stevens, 51 Maine 78.

As to false representations and concealment in a prospectus or advertisement of a projected railway or similar company, by which parties are induced to become shareholders, see Jennings *v.* Broughton, 17 Jur. 905; 17
Bea. 234 ; Pulsford *v.* Richards, 17 Jur. 865; 17 Bea. 87; Denton *v.* Mac-
Neil, L. R. 2 Eq. 352.

been done; (*l*) and if the misstatement has not been relied on, or not reasonably relied on, by the complaining party, the same reasoning will apply. Such, for example, will be the case, if the party to whom the representation is made resorts to the proper means of verification, so as to show that he in fact relied on his own inquiries; or if the means of investigation and verification are at hand, and his attention is drawn to them; or if the representation regards a mere matter of opinion or inference, with respect to which both parties have equal means of forming a judgment.[1] But it would be different if he were prevented by any artifice of the other party from making such full inquiry as he would otherwise have made. (*m*)   For this reason a contract is not vitiated by a mere false assertion of value on the part of the seller; nor by vague and indefinite terms of commendation; (*n*) nor by a mere misstatement by the buyer of his motive in purchasing or in limiting the amount of his offer; for these are not representations on which a man can reasonably rely. (*o*)   Nor will the mere employment of one person to bid at an auction on the owner's behalf, though not notified, be a fraud in equity, provided he be *bonâ fide* employed to prevent a

(*l*) Attwood *v.* Small, 6 Cl. & F. 232, 502; Phillips *v.* Duke of Buckingham, 1 Vern. 227; Fellowes *v.* Lord Gwydyr, 1 R. & M. 83; Crosbie *v.* Tooke, 1 M. & K. 431; Nelthorpe *v.* Holgate, 1 Coll. 203; 1 Sug. V. & P. 348–351.

(*m*) Clapham *v.* Shillito, 7 Bea. 146; Attwood *v.* Small, 6 Cl. & F. 232, 503. .

(*n*) 1 Sug. V. & P. 3, 4; White *v.* Cuddon, 8 Cl. & F. 766.

(*o*) Vernon *v.* Keys, 12 East 632.

---

[1] False reasoning upon facts truly stated is no ground for relief in equity: Bowman *v.* Bates, 2 Bibb 47.   So, also, if a vendor falsely assert that he paid a much greater price than he actually paid for the land: Best *v.* Blackburns, 6 Litt. 51; Nicol's Case, 3 De G. & J. 437.

sale at an under value.[1] But it is otherwise if the intention is to take advantage of the eagerness of bidders in screwing up the price, or if there is an announcement that the sale is without reserve, which implies that such a course will not be takeu.(*p*)

*The requirement that the representation shall [*178] be not only false, but false within the knowledge of the party making it, distinguishes a fraudulent representation inducing to a contract from an erroneous affirmation embodied in it by way of warranty or covenant.[2] Affirmations of this latter kind bind the party making them, although he were himself honestly mistaken, because he has explicity agreed that they shall do so; but if a warranty or covenant is not given, a mere representation honestly made, and believed at the time to be true by the party making it, though not true in fact, does not amount to fraud.(*q*)

Where no statement has been expressly made a misrepresentation may nevertheless be implied from conduct. But mere nondisclosure is generally not equivalent to fraud. The ordinary maxim of law is "*caveat emptor;*" and this maxim authorizes a contracting party to remain silent, and to avail himself so far as he can of his superior knowledge. If, for example, I treat for the purchase of an estate, knowing that there is a mine under it, and the

(*p*) Smith *v.* Clarke, 12 Ves. 477; Woodward *v.* Miller, 2 Coll. 279; Thornett *v.* Haines, 15 Mee. & W. 367; 15 Law. J. Exch. 230; 1 Sug. V. & P. c. i., s. 2.

(*q*) Pasley *v.* Freeman, 3 T. R. 51; Freeman *v.* Baker, 5 B. & Ad. 797; Ormrod *v.* Huth, 14 Mee. & W. 651; 14 Law J. Exch. 366.

[1] Though see Pennock's App., 14 Penn. St. 446; Staines *v.* Shore, 16 Id. 200, *contra*.

[2] See Spence *v.* Duren, 3 Ala. 251.

other party makes no inquiry, I am not bound by law to
inform him of the mine.(*r*)[1]

There are, however, cases of a different character,
where the contract is necessarily based on the assumption
of a full disclosure, and where for that reason, any degree
of reticence on a material point is fraud. Such, for instance, is the case where the seller of real estate, knowing a fact material to the validity of his title, delivers an
abstract which does not disclose it; for the knowledge of
his title is confined to himself; and the purchaser contracts on the assumption that the real title will be shown.(*s*)
It has been further decided at law that, even though an
[*179] article be sold *with all the faults, so as expressly
to free the seller from responsibility, yet if he
falsely represent that a particular defect does not exist,
or if he use any artifice to disguise a defect or to prevent
its discovery, the contract may be set aside.(*t*)[2]

(*r*) Turner *v.* Harvey, Jac. 169, 178; Dykes *v.* Blake, 4 B. N. C. 463;
Gibson *v.* D'Este, 2 N. C. C. 542; [*aliter*, if there were artifices used to
conceal the fact: Bowman *v.* Bates, 2 Bibb 47.]

(*s*) Edwards *v.* McLeay, Coop. 308; 2 Swanst. 287.

(*t*) Baglehole *v.* Walters, 3 Camp. 154; Schneider *v.* Heath, Id. 506;
1 Sug. V. & P. 545–552.

---

[1] In a recent case in Pennsylvania it was held, following the dictum of
Lord Thurlow, cited above, that a sale of land could not be rescinded on
the ground that the purchaser had not disclosed the existence of a valuable
mine on the property, which he had discovered, there being otherwise no
fraud in the transaction: Harris *v.* Tyson, 24 Penn. St. 369.

[2] Where concealment amounts to a wilful suppression by one party, for
his own benefit and to the injury of the other, of material facts which the
former was bound not merely morally but legally to communicate, it will
amount to a case of fraud against which equity will relieve. See Wall *v.*
Thompson, 1 Sm. & M. 443; Young *v.* Bampass, 1 Freeman Ch. 241; Armstead *v.* Hundley, 7 Gratt. 52; Torrey *v.* Buck, 1 Green Ch. 366; White *v.*
Cox, 3 Heyw. 79; Jopling *v.* Dooley, 1 Yerg. 290; Napier *v.* Elam, 6 Id.
108; Snelson *v.* Franklin, 6 Munf. 210; Bryant's Ex'rs. *v.* Boothe, 30 Ala.
311; Story's Eq., §207; Laidlaw *v.* Organ, 2 Wheat. 178; Lancaster Co.

The principle which treats nondisclosure as equivalent to fraud, when the circumstances impose a duty that the disclosure should be made, is especially material in respect to contracts of insurance and suretyship. For the risk which the insurer undertakes and the contract which the surety guarantees, can only be learned from the representation of the party insured or guarantied. If, therefore the insured does not state to the insurer truly and fully all the facts within his private knowledge, which would vary materially the object of the policy and change the risk understood to be run, the policy is void. Nor is it an excuse that the concealment was attributable to the

---

Bank v. Albright, 21 Penn. St. 223. The limits beyond which concealment becomes fraudulent are very difficult to determine. Chancellor Kent at one time advanced the doctrine that "each party is bound to communicate to the other his knowledge of material facts, provided he knows him to be ignorant of them, and they be not open or naked:" 2 Kent Comm. 482. But this, in later editions of his Commentaries, he considerably modified. It would seem, indeed, that in ordinary circumstances the concealment must have something active in its character to amount to fraud. Where, however, the parties stand towards each other in any relation of a fiduciary or quasi-fiduciary character, as in the case of solicitor and client: Higgins v. Joyce, 2 Jones & Lat. 282; or of co-partners: Ogden v. Astor, 4 Sandf. S. C. 312; Farnam v. Brooks, 9 Pick. 234; or of members of the same family dealing in that character as to their rights: Gordon v. Gordon, 3 Swans. 400; the obligation to disclosure becomes imperative. See Story Eq., § 217-18. See, however, Crane v. Hewitt, 2 Halst. Ch. 631; but qu. as to that case.

Where it does not appear that a party knew a fact alleged to have been concealed, or had had better opportunity to know it than the other, equity will not interfere: Perkins v. McGavock, Cooke 415.

Where an encumbrance is concealed by the vendor from the vendee, but is removed by the vendor before decree in a bill for rescission filed by the vendee, the Court refused to rescind the contract: Davidson v. Moss, 5 How. (Miss.) 673. But when an encumbrance is not removed, although it be recorded at the time the contract was entered into, equity will rescind the contract: Campbell v. Whittingham, 5 J. J. Marsh. 96; Napier v. Elam, 6 Yerg. 108.

24

fraud or neglect of an agent, or that the account concealed was false, or in no way referred to the subsequent cause of loss, or was not believed by the insurer to be material or was not concealed with a fraudulent design.(*u*) And in like manner if a contract is guarantied by a surety, and a fact materially affecting the nature of that contract is misrepresented to him or concealed from him, with the knowledge or consent of the party accepting the guarantee, the surety ceases to be liable.(*v*)[1]

Another case of the same character occurs in compositions by a debtor with his creditor, where a secret bargain has been made with particular creditors.   The very circumstances that some creditors have already executed, [*180] is an inducement *to the rest to follow their example.   The reason why they have so executed can only be known by the other creditors from the representation of the debtor; and if the real reason is the result of any secret arrangement, the influence of their example is a fraud on the rest.   All such secret arrangements, therefore, are utterly void; they cannot be enforced even against the debtor himself, and money paid under them may be recovered back, as having been obtained against the clear principles of public policy.(*w*)

In like manner a secret agreement on marriage, in

(*u*) Carter *v.* Boehm, 3 Burr. 1906 ; Smith Merc. Law, 358–363, 374 ; De Costa *v.* Scandret, 2 P. Wms. 170 ; Whittingham *v.* Thornburg, 2 Vern. 206 ; Fenn *v.* Craig, 3 Y. & C. 216 ; Kemp *v.* Pryor, 7 Ves. 237, 249 ; Jervis *v.* White, Id. 413.

(*v*) Pidcock *v.* Bishop, 3 B. & C. 605 ; Stone *v.* Compton, 5 B. N. C. 142 ; Hamilton *v.* Watson, 12 Cl. & F. 109.

(*w*) Jackman *v.* Mitchell, 13 Ves. 581 ; Ex parte Sadler and Jackson, 15 Id. 52 ; Smith Merc. Law 702.

[1] But not if misrepresentation was of the law : Reed *v.* Sidener, 32 Ind. 373.

fraud of the relations or friends of one of the parties, will be relieved against in equity; *e. g.*, an agreement under which a fortune paid is in part privately received back, or a bond of indemnity given for the amount; for it is a deception practised on the other parties to induce a larger settlement than they would otherwise have made.(*x*) And a bond given for assisting a clandestine marriage has been set aside, though given voluntarily after the marriage, and without any previous arrangement.(*y*)

Another class of transactions which have been held void, as amounting to a fraud on the marriage contract, are conveyances by an unmarried woman of her property, pending a treaty of marriage, without the knowledge of her intended husband.[1]

If a woman entitled to property enters into a treaty for marriage, and during the treaty represents to her intended husband that she is so entitled, that upon the marriage he will become entitled *jure mariti;* and if, during the same treaty, she clandestinely conveys away the property, either for the benefit of a third person, or

(*x*) Palmer *v.* Neave, 11 Ves. 165; Turton *v.* Benson, 1 P. Wms. 496; Thompson *v.* Harrison, 1 Cox 344.

(*y*) Williamson *v.* Gihon, 2 Sch. & L. 357.

---

[1] See Linker *v.* Smith, 4 Wash. C. C. 224; Logan *v.* Simmons, 3 Ired. Eq. 487; Tucker *v.* Andrews, 13 Maine 124; Waller *v.* Armistead, 2 Leigh 11; Manes *v.* Durant, 2 Rich. Eq. 404; Wrigley *v.* Swainson, 3 De G. & Sm. 458; Freeman *v.* Hartman, 45 Ill. 57; Chambers *v.* Crabbe, 34 Bea. 457; see notes to Countess of Strathmore *v.* Bowes, 1 Lead. Cas. Eq. 325, 3d Am. ed. In Petty *v.* Petty, 4 B. Monr. 215, the same rule was applied to the case of a husband who conveyed his property in fraud of the rights of his second wife. See Lewellen *v.* Cobbold, 1 Sm. & Giff. 376. So, on the other hand, a conveyance by a husband, pending proceedings for a divorce on the part of a wife, in order to avoid the effects of a decree for alimony, will be set aside: Blenkinsopp *v.* Blenkinsopp, 1 De G., M. &. G. 495. See Krupp *v.* Scholl, 10 Penn. St. 193; see also Kline's Estate, 64 Id. 122.

to secure to himself the separate use of it, and the concealment continues till the marriage takes place, there
can be no doubt that a fraud is practised on the husband.
If both the property and the mode of its conveyance,
[*181] pending the marriage *treaty, were concealed
from the intended husband, there still is, or may
be, a fraud practised on him.   It is true that the non-
acquisition of the property is no disappointment, but still
his legal right is defeated; and the conveying of the property for the benefit of a third person, or the vesting and
continuance of separate property in his wife, is a surprise
upon him, and might if previously known, have induced
him to abstain from the marriage.   The mere fact, however, of concealment from the husband, or rather the
non-existence of communication to him, is not necessarily
and under all circumstances equivalent to fraud.   In the
absence of any representation as to specific property,
there is no implied contract on the part of the lady that
her property shall not be in any way diminished before
the marriage; but it is for the Court to determine in each
case whether, having regard to the condition of the parties,
and the other attendant circumstances, a transaction complained of by the husband should be treated as fraudulent.[1]
Several circumstances appear to have been thought material as negativing the imputed fraud; such, for instance,
as the poverty of the husband—the fact that he has made
no settlement upon the wife—the fulfilment of a moral
or legal obligation, as in the case of a settlement upon the
children of a former marriage,[2] or of a bond given to secure
a debt contracted for a valuable consideration,—and the
ignorance of the husband that his wife possessed the pro-

---

[1] See Wrigley v. Swainson, 3 De G. & Sm. 458.
[2] Green v. Goodall, 1 Cold. (Tenn.) 404.

perty. There can be no doubt that any of these facts would be a good ground for insisting that the husband should make a settlement, and for determining the marriage contract if he should refuse to do so; but it is not so easy to understand why they should constitute reasons for practising concealment on him, or for treating such concealment as immaterial. Where, however, in addition to these circumstances, there was this further fact in extenuation of the concealment, that the husband had brought the intended wife to his house, and had induced her to cohabit with him before the marriage, it was held conclusive against relief. For, it was said by the Court, *that by the husband's conduct towards her, retirement from the marriage on her part [*182] was made impossible. She must have submitted to a marriage with her seducer, even though he should have insisted on receiving and spending the whole of her fortune; and the only method of protection left her was to make a settlement without his knowledge.(z)

Besides that kind of fraud, which consists in misrepresentation, express or implied, there is another, not less odious, which vitiates contracts made by persons, who, at the time of making such nominal contracts, are under duress or incapacity.

If an act be done under actual duress, it may be afterwards avoided even at law; e. g., if a man is induced to execute a deed through fear of death or mayhem, or by an illegal restraint of his liberty. And in such case, though its execution be accompanied by all requisite solemnities, yet he may allege the duress and avoid the extorted deed. But if a man be lawfully imprisoned,

(z) Goddard v. Snow, 1 Russ. 485; England v. Downs, 2 Beav. 522; Taylor v. Pugh, 1 Hare 608.

and either to procure his discharge, or on any other fair
account, seals a deed, this is not by duress of imprisonment, and he is not at liberty to avoid it. (a)[1]

The conveyances and contracts of idiots and lunatics
(except during a lucid interval) are also, generally speaking, void at law. But the feoffment of an insane person
is held not to be absolutely void, but voidable only, owing
to the solemnity of livery with which it is accompanied;
and for this reason it is held that he cannot himself set it
aside at law after his recovery; although it may be avoided by the committee, during his lunacy, or by the heir
after his death. (b)[2]

The principle on which a deed is held fraudulent, on
the ground of lunacy, is that it has been obtained from
[*183]   *a person who at the time of execution was not
capable of apprehending its effect, but the mere
fact that the party was in a state of lunacy, or even that
he was under confinement, will not *per se* induce the Court
to interfere, if it be distinctly shown that the act was

(a) 2 Steph. Bl. 131, 137.
(b) 1 Steph. Bl. 440; 2 Sug. on Pow. 179; 1 Story on Eq. s. 223–229.

---

[1] McDaniel v. Moorman, 1 Harp. Ch. 108; Underwood v. Brockman, 4
Dana 319; Brown v. Peck, 2 Wisc. 261; Thurman v. Burt, 53 Ill. 129;
Jones v. Bridge, 2 Sweeny (N. Y.) 431.

[2] A present interest passes by the deed of a lunatic, which is not void,
but voidable: Breckenridge v. Ormsby, 1 J. J. Marsh. 245; Allis v. Bil-
lings, 6 Metc. 415; Price v. Berrington, 3 Macn. & G. 486; Ballard v.
McKenna, 4 Rich. Eq. 358; Ingraham v. Baldwin, 5 Selden 45; see Mol-
ton v. Camroux, 2 Exch. 487; 4 Id. 17; Beals v. See, 10 Penn. St. 60;
though see Desilver's Est., 5 Rawle 111.

As to the parties who may avoid the deed of a lunatic, see Breckenridge v. Ormsby, 1 J. J. Marsh. 248–250, 254; Cates v. Woodson, 2 Dana
454; Ingraham v. Baldwin, 5 Selden 45.

A deed made by the grantor, while a lunatic, would require a re-execution when he was of sound mind, to give it validity: Jones et al. v. Evans,
7 Dana 96.

beneficial to him, that no coercion or imposition was used, and that he knew clearly what he was doing. (c)[1]

It has been held also that, independently of that utter imbecility which will render a man legally *non compos*, a conveyance may be impeached for mere weakness of intellect, provided it be coupled with ōther circumstances to show that the weakness, such as it was, has been taken advantage of by the other party. But the mere fact that a person is of weak understanding, if there be no fraud or surprise, is not an adequate cause for relief. (d)[2]

(c) Selby v. Jackson, 6 Beav. 192; 13 L. J. 249.

(d) Blachford v. Christian, 1 Knapp 73; Ball v. Mannin, 3 Bligh. N. S. 1; 1 Story on Eq. s. 234–237.

---

[1] There is a distinction between cases of rescission and a defence in equity to the enforcement of an incidental equitable remedy on a deed *primâ facie* good, upon similar grounds. Thus, though insanity would be a sufficient ground for the rescission of a mortgage, yet on a bill for forclosure, such a defence cannot be set up, where the deed has been duly proved, but the mortgagor or his representatives must establish the invalidity of the security at law, or by an issue: Jacobs v. Richards, 5 De G., M. & G. 55.

[2] Whipple v. McClure, 2 Root 216; Whitehorn v. Hines, 1 Munf. 557; Buffalow v. Buffalow, 2 Dev. & Bat. Ch. 241; Rutherford v. Ruff, 4 Dessaus. 350; Deatley v. Murphy, 3 A. K. Marsh. 472; McCormick v. Malin, 5 Blackf. 509; Hunt v. Moore, 2 Penn. St. 105; Ex parte Allen, 15 Mass. 58; Rippy v. Gant, 4 Ired. Eq. 447; Mann v. Betterly, 21 Verm. 326; Mason v. Williams, 3 Munf. 126; Harding v. Handy, 11 Wheat. 103; Brogden v. Walker, 2 Har. & Johns. 285; Whelan v. Whelan, 3 Cowen 537; Rumph v. Abercrombe, 12 Ala. 64; Gratz v. Cohen, 11 How. U. S. 1; Brice v. Brice, 5 Barb. S. C. 533; Brooke v. Berry, 2 Gill 83; Craddock v. Cabiness, 1 Swan. (Tenn.) 474; Lansing v. Russell, 13 Barb. S. C. 511; Long v. Long, 9 Md. 348; Cain v. Warford, 33 Id. 23; Hill v. McLaurin, 28 Miss. 288; Marshall v. Billingsly, 7 Ind. 250; Smith v. Elliott, 1 Patt. & Heath 307; Graham v. Pancoast, 30 Penn. St. 89; Nace v. Boyer, Id. 99; Aiman v. Stout, 42 Id. 114; see further on this subject, Prideaux v. Lonsdale, 1 De G., J. & Sm. 443; Clarke v. Malpus, 31 Beav. 80; Prewett v. Coopwood, 30 Miss. 369; Gass v. Mason, 4 Sneed 497; Graham v. Little, 3 Jones Eq. 152; Oldham v. Oldham, 5 Id. 89; Futrill v. Futrill, Id. 62; Hunt v. Hunt, 2 Beas. 161; Maddox v. Simmons, 31

A person drunk to the extent of complete intoxication, so as to be no longer under the guidance of reason, appears to be absolutely incapable of making a contract, so that his deed is void at law.   If the degree of intoxication fall short of this, a Court of equity will generally not assist the other party in enforcing his claim.   But it seems that it will confine itself to standing neuter, and will not relieve against the instrument, unless the contracting party was drawn in to drink by the contrivance of the other.(e)[1]

The same principle which vitiates a contract with an incapacitated person is extended in equity to avoid benefits

(e) 2 Sug. on Pow. 178; Cooke v. Clayworth, 18 Ves. 12; Lightfoot v. Heron, 3 Y. & C. 586; 1 Story on Eq. s. 230–233.

Ga. 512; Tally's Ex'rs v. Smith, 1 Cold. (Tenn.) 291; Beller v. Jones, 22 Ark. 92; though not from loss of memory: Thompson v. Gossitt, 23 Ark. 175.   As to contracts by illiterate persons, see Price v. Price, 1 De G., M. & G. 308 ; Wilkinson v. Fawkes, 9 Hare 592.

Monomania, not connected with the subject of the contract, has been held not to be a cause of invalidity: Boyce v. Smith, 9 Gratt. 704.   A contract will not be set aside on the ground of greater superiority of intellect in one of the parties, if the other party was of legal capacity to contract: Thomas v. Sheppard, 2 McC. Ch. 36.   And the mere fact that an agreement is improvident, is no ground for setting it aside: Green v. Thompson, 2 Ired. Ch. 365.

[1] And see to the same effect Morrison v. McLeod, 2 Dev. & Bat. Eq. 221; Hotchkiss v. Fortson, 7 Yerg. 67; Hutchinson v. Brown, 1 Clarke Ch. 408; Harbison v. Lemon, 3 Blackf. 51; Maxwell v. Pittenger, 2 Green Ch. 156; Whitesides v. Greenlee, 2 Dev. Eq. 152; Crane v. Conklin, Saxt. 346; Calloway v. Witherspoon, 5 Ired. Eq. 128; Phillips v. Moore, 11 Mo. 600; Marshall v. Billingsly, 7 Ind. 250.   As to specific performance, however, see ante, 84, note.   But when from continued habits of intoxication, or from excessive drunkenness at the time, the party is deprived of the use of reason and understanding, this is sufficient, by itself, to invalidate a contract: Gore v. Gibson, 13 Mees. & Welsby 626; Clifton v. Davis, 1 Pars. Eq. 31; French v. French, 8 Hamm. (Ohio) 214; Harbison v. Lemon, 3 Black. 57.   And see further on this subject, Lavette v. Sage, 29 Conn. 577; Futrill v. Futrill, 5 Jones Eq. 61; Dunn v. Amos, 14 Wis. 106.

obtained by trustees from their *cestuis que trustent*, or by other persons sustaining a fiduciary character from those in regard to whom that character exists.[1]

The most obvious instance of this doctrine is in the case of actual trustees. If a trustee be appointed for the sale or purchase of property, he cannot sell to or purchase from *himself, however honest, in the particular [*184] case, the transaction may be. For if he were permitted to buy or sell in an honest case, he might do so in one having that appearance, but which, from the infirmity of human testimony, might be grossly otherwise. It is not, therefore, necessary to show that an improper advantage has been made; but the *cestui que trust*, if he has not confirmed the transaction with full knowledge of the facts, may, at his option, set it aside. The rule, however, which imposes this absolute incapacity, applies to those cases only where a trustee attempts to purchase from or sell to himself. There is no positive rule that he cannot deal with his *cestui que trust;* but in order to do

---

[1] This rule is very constantly acted upon in the United States. It is applied to trustees, guardians, executors and administrators, agents, assignees in bankruptcy, or attorneys; and in general to all persons standing in any fiduciary position. See the American cases collected, Hill on Trustees, 4th Am. ed. 243–256; and see ante, note, p. 61. In Smith *v.* Kay, 7 H. L. Cas. 750, it was said by Lord Cranworth that the cases of parent and child, guardian and ward, &c., are but instances of the application of a general principle; while Lord Kingsdown remarked that the rule applied to every case "where influence is acquired and abused—where confidence is reposed and betrayed." See also the remarks of Turner, L. J., in Rhodes *v.* Bate, L. R. 1 Ch. Ap. 257.

The director of a railway company is a trustee, and, as such, is precluded from dealing, on behalf of the company, with himself, or with a firm of which he is a partner: Aberdeen Ry. Co. *v.* Blaikie Brothers, 1 Macq. Scott. App. Cas. 461; 23 L. T. 315 (H. of L.). It was there held, indeed, that the rule was applicable to all contracts, indifferently, whether as to real estate, or personalty, or mercantile transactions.

so, he must fully divest himself of all advantage which
his character as trustee might confer, and must prove, if
the transaction be afterwards impugned, that it was in all
respects fair and honest.(ƒ) In like manner an agent,
who is employed to sell, cannot himself become secretly
the purchaser; nor can an agent, who is employed to buy,
buy from himself or from his own trustee, or for his own
benefit.(g) And where even any person stands in a relation of special confidence towards another, so as to acquire an habitual influence over him, he cannot accept
from him a personal benefit without exposing himself to
the risk, in a degree proportioned to the nature of their
connection, of having it set aside as unduly obtained.[1]

(ƒ) Supra, Prohibition of personal benefit to a trustee.

(g) Gillett v. Peppercorne, 3 Beav. 78 ; Taylor v. Salmon, 4 Myl. & Cr.
134.

---

[1] See notes to pages 57 and 61, ante.

A court of equity looks with extreme jealousy on transactions between
parties who stand in any fiduciary relations, or relations of a similar character, by which an undue influence may be obtained by one over the other,
and unless he who receives the benefit can show that it was conferred un-
derstandingly, and with full knowledge of the circumstances, and apart
from the bias of that connection, will set them aside. This rule applies to
attorney and client: Greenfield's Est., 14 Penn. St. 504; Leisenring v.
Black, 5 Watts 303; Hockenbury v. Carlisle, 5 W. & S. 350; Stockton v.
Ford, 11 How. U. S. 232; Poillon v. Martin, 1 Sandf. Ch. 569; Salmon v.
Cutts, 4 De G. & Sm. 131; Robinson v. Briggs, 1 Sm. & G. 184; Merritt v.
Lambert, 10 Paige 357; 2 Denio 607; Howell v. Ransom, 11 Paige 538;
Mott v. Harrington, 12 Verm. 199; Brock v. Barnes, 40 Barb. 521; Tyrrell v. The Bank, 10 H. Lds. Cas. 26; Spring v. Pride, 10 Jur. N. S. 646;
Wall v. Cockerell, 10 H. Lds. Cas. 229; Gresley v. Mousley, 4 De G. & J.
78; and where a client, indebted to a solicitor, made an absolute conveyance, it has been held to stand as a mortgage merely: Pearson v. Benson,
28 Beav. 598; Morgan v. Higgins, 5 Jur. N. S. 236. But the rule is different when the solicitor has assumed the hostile attitude of a pressing
creditor: Johnson v. Fesemeyer, 3 De G. & J. 13. And agreements between attorney and client were, under the circumstances, upheld in Moss
v. Bainbrigge, 6 De G., M. & G. 292; Blagrave v. Routh, 2 K. & J. 509;
Clanricarde v. Henning, 30 Beav. 175; and a gift was held valid in Nesbit

An attorney, therefore, purchasing or taking a benefit from his client, whilst the relationship of attorney and client exists, and in respect of that matter wherein it exists, must show that he took no advantage of his influence or knowledge, but gave his client all that reasonable advice against himself which it was his duty to have given him against a third person.(h) A guardian, taking from his ward, is bound by the same rule ; a minister of religion, *taking from those under his spiritual charge, may be bound by it with even greater [*185] stringency.(i)¹ The same general principle applies to all

(h) Edwards v. Meyrick, 2 Hare 60.

(i) Huguenin v. Basely, 14 Ves. 273 ; Thompson v. Heffernan, 4 Dru. & W. 285.

v. Lockman, 34 N. Y. 167. The rule applies also to parent and child: Slocum v. Marshall, 2 Wash. C. C. 397; Taylor v. Taylor, 8 How. U. S. 183; Jenkins v. Pye, 12 Peters 249; Houghton v. Houghton, 15 Beav. 278; Baker v. Bradley, 7 De G., M. & G. 597; King v. Savery, 1 Sm. & G. 271; 5 H. L. Cas. 627; though the transaction may be validated by lapse of time: Wright v. Vanderplank, 2 K. & J. 1; 8 De G., M. & G. 133; guardian and ward: Johnson v. Johnson, 5 Ala. 90; Caplinger v. Stokes, Meigs 175 ; Bostwick v. Atkins, 3 Const. 53; Williams v. Powell, 1 Ired. Eq. 460; Scott v. Freeland, 7 Sm. & M. 410; Sullivan v. Blackwell, 28 Miss. 737; Wright v. Arnold, 14 B. Monr. 638 ; Witman's Appeal, 28 Penn. St. 378; Hawkins's Appeal, 32 Id. 263 ; physician and patient: Billage v. Southee, 9 Hare 534; Aherne v. Hogan, 1 Drury 310; Whitehorn v. Hines, 1 Munf. 559; see, however, Daggett v. Lane, 12 Mo. 215; clergymen: Greenfield's Estate, 24 Penn. St. 232; Nachtrieb v. The Harmony Settlement, 3 Wallace, Jr. 66; or other relation, connection, or position in which an undue advantage, influence, or control may be obtained or exercised over the judgment of another. See Cooke v. Lamotte, 15 Beav. 234; Ahearne v. Hogan, 1 Drury 310; Espey v. Lake, 16 Jur. 1106; 10 Hare 260; James v. Holmes, 8 Jur. N. S. 553, 732; Sears v. Shafers, 2 Seld. 268; Harkness v. Fraser, 12 Fla. 336. It has been recently held, however, that a provision in a will, in favor of the solicitor by whom the will be drawn, will not be held void in equity, unless where it would be so held at law, or in the ecclesiastical courts: Hindson v. Wetherell, 5 De G., M. & G. 301.

As to contracts by trustees, agents, &c., see ante, 61, note.

¹ Greenfield's Estate, 24 Penn. St. 232.

the variety of relations in which dominion may be exercised by one person over another; but in proportion as the relationship is less known and definite, the presumption of fraud is less strong. Where the known and definite relationship exists of trustees and *cestui que trust*, attorney and client, or guardian and ward, the conduct of the party benefited must be such as to sever the connection, and to place him in the same circumstances in which a mere stranger would have stood, giving him no advantage beyond the kindly feeling which the connection may have caused. Where the only relation is that of friendly habits and habitual reliance on advice and assistance, accompanied by partial employment in business, care must be taken that no undue advantage shall be made.[1] But no rigorous definition can be laid down, so as to distinguish precisely between the effects of natural and often unavoidable kindness, and those of undue influence or undue advantage.(k)

Another instance of fraud where there is a fiduciary relation is when a person having a power of appointment for the benefit of others, uses it by contrivance for his own benefit. Thus, if a parent has a power to appoint to such of his children as he may choose, he cannot appoint it to one of the children upon a bargain beforehand for his own benefit.(l)[2] It was also formerly held, that illusory

(k) Hunter v. Atkins, 3 M. & K. 113; Dent v. Bennett, 4 M. & C. 269.

(l) Daubeny v. Cockburn, 1 Meriv. 626; 2 Sug on Powers, c. xi., s. 2; [or for the benefit of a husband: 19 Jur. 50.]

---

[1] See Miller v. Welles, 23 Conn. 21.

[2] The fraudulent exercise of a power upon a corrupt bargain as to one portion, may be sustained as to a distinct part uninfluenced by such bargain, though both by the same deed: Rowley v. Rowley, 18 Jur. 306; 1 Kay 242; 23 L. J. Ch. 275. A benefit to the appointer, is a corrupt motive, though such benefit does not come out of the fund appointed, *semble*: Rowley v. Rowley, ut supra. See, also, on this subject, Aga v. Squire, 19 Jur. (1 Id. N. S.) 50.

appointments under a power were void in equity; *i. e.*, appointments of a nominal, instead of a substantial share to one of the members of a class, where power was given to appoint amongst them all. An appointment of this kind was clearly valid at law; and it would perhaps be difficult *to reconcile with principle its avoidance in equity. The doctrine is now abolished by statute.(*m*)[1] [*186]

On the same principle it is held, that where a marriage is required to be by consent of trustees, and the trustees withhold consent from a corrupt motive, the Court of Chancery may interfere. And it has been contended, that if the person whose consent is required is interested in refusing it, he must show a reason for his dissent. If, however, the creator of a trust chooses to require the consent of a person, whom he knows at the time to have an interest in refusing it, it is difficult to conceive an equity for interfering with his choice. And at all events no equity will arise if the trustee has meant to act honestly, though his decision may not be the same at which the Court would have arrived.(*n*)

The acts which have been hitherto the subject of inquiry are either directly fraudulent at law, or are held fraudulent in equity by analogy to law. There is another class of equitable fraud in which the legal analogy is less perceptible. The fraudulent transactions here

(*m*) Butcher *v.* Butcher, 9 Ves. 382; 1 Sug. on Powers, c. vii., s. 6; 11 Geo. 4 & 1 Wm. 4, c. 46.

(*n*) Clarke *v.* Parker, 19 Ves. 1.

---

[1] Stolworthy *v.* Sancroft, 10 Jur. N. S. 762; Ward *v.* Tyrrell, 25 Beav. 563. This doctrine has been disapproved of in the United States: see Fronty *v.* Fronty, 1 Bail. Eq. 529; Cowles *v.* Brown, 4 Call 477; Graeff *v.* De Turk, 44 Penn. St. 527; note to Aleyn *v.* Belchier, 1 Lead. Cas. Eq. 304, 3d Am. ed.

referred to are bargains made with expectant heirs or remaindermen, during the lifetime and without the knowledge of the parent or other ancestor.[1] Bargains of this kind are not necessarily and absolutely void. They may be sustained *ab initio*, if they are proved free of unfairness or inadequacy; or they may be made good afterwards by the bargainer, either by express confirmation or by continued acquiescence, after the original pressure of his necessities has ceased. (o) But, unless they can be sustained on one of these grounds, they may be set aside at the suit of the bargainer, partly as having been made under the pressure of necessity, but principally as being a fraud on [*187] the parent or ancestor, who is misled into leaving his *estate not to his heir or family, but to a set of artful persons, who have divided the spoil beforehand. The decree in such a case will be that the conveyance shall be set aside as an absolute sale, but shall stand as a security for the principal and interest of the money ad-

(o) King v. Hamlet, 2 M. & K. 456; 3 Cl. & Fin. 218; Roberts v. Tunstall, 4 Hare 257.

---

[1] See Jenkins et al. v. Pye et al., 12 Peters 241; and also Varick v. Edwards, 1 Hoff. Ch. 383, where it was held that the sale of the expectation of an heir of an inheritance, in real as well as in personal estate, will be supported, if made *bonâ fide* and for a valuable consideration. And see Larrabee v. Larrabee, 34 Maine 477; Powers' Appeal, 63 Penn. St. 443; Mastin v. Marlow, 65 N. C. 695; Lowry v. Spear, 7 Bush (Ky.) 451. The purchaser of a reversionary interest, at least from an expectant heir, is bound, if the transaction be impeached within a reasonable time, to satisfy the court that he gave the market value: Lord Aldborough v. Trye, 7 Cl. & Fin. 436; Edwards v. Burt, 2 De G., M. & G. 55. The mere reference to an actuary, to determine such value, without regard to local circumstances or the like, is not enough: Edwards v. Burt, ut sup. An heir in tail, who is entitled to an immediate possession of one-half the land, and to the other half on the death of a tenant by the curtesy, is not, it would seem, an heir expectant, within the rule: Davidson v. Little, 22 Penn. St. 252. On the subjcet of sales by reversioners and expectant heirs, see Hill on Trustees, 4th Am. ed. 238, note.

vanced, and generally, though not necessarily, for the costs of suit as on a common decree to redeem.(p) The soundness of this equity, when applied to reversioners, even assuming it to be well founded with regard to expectant heirs, seems open to much doubt. For a reversioner deals with property which is already his own, although its enjoyment is postponed. There is, therefore, no fraud on any third party; and an equity to set aside a sale, in the absence of fraud or trust as between the immediate parties, can rest on little more than mere improvidence in the bargain.(q) It may be doubted too, whether the rule has been productive of much good, even to the parties whom it was meant to protect, and whether it has not prevented them from selling their interest at the fair value, and compelled them to accept less favorable terms on account of the attendant risk.

On the same principle a bond by a young woman, secretly given to a man, conditioned to pay him a sum of money if she did not marry him on her father's death, he giving a bond to the same effect, has been set aside; and chiefly on the ground that it was a fraud on the parent, who disapproved of the marriage, and who would be misled into making a provision for his daughter, which, had he known of the bond, he might not have done, or might have done in such a manner as would have prevented the marriage.(r)

*The third ground on which a transaction may be rescinded, though not vitiated by illegality or [*188]

(p) Earl of Chesterfield v. Janssen, 1 Atk. 301; 2 Ves. 125; Peacock v. Evans, 16 Id. 512; King v. Hamlet, 2 M. & K. 456; 3 Cl. & Fin. 218; Newton v. Hunt, 5 Sim. 511; Edwards v. Browne, 2 Coll. 100; 1 Sug. V. & P. 444–464; 1 Story on Equity, s. 334–348.

(q) Wood v. Abrey, 3 Mad. 417; Davis v. Duke of Marlborough, 2 Sw. 140, note.

(r) Woodhouse v. Shepley, 2 Atk. 535; Cock v. Richards, 10 Ves. 429.

fraud is that it has been carried on in ignorance[1] or mistake of facts material to its operation.

The most direct illustration of this principle occurs in the doctrine of the common law, the money paid voluntarily under a mistake of fact may be recovered back as money had and received.[2] On the same principle, acts which have been done voluntarily under a like mistake may be recalled or annulled by a suit in equity; as, for example, where a deed of covenant, stipulating that any moneys which might be received by the defendant under certain circumstances should be held for the use of the plaintiffs, had been delivered up under a mistaken belief that no such moneys had been received.(s)   In accordance with the same doctrine a contract may be set aside if made for a consideration which is really non-existent, but which both parties mistakenly suppose to exist.   Such, for example, would be the case where the subject of sale is a remainder after an estate tail; and the estate tail, without

(s) East India Company v. Donald, 9 Ves. 275.

---

[1] A party relying on ignorance must show that he could not have obtained the necessary information with due diligence : Wason v. Wareing, 15 Bea. 151.

[2] The court will open settlements made by mistake, although receipts in full have passed : McCrae v. Hollis, 4 Dessaus. 122; Russell v. Church, 65 Penn. St. 9; and money paid by mistake, and on a usurious agreement above the legal interest, was recovered back by English bill: Ashbrook v. Watkins, 3 Monr. 82.   Where there is error in a settlement, and notes are given in consequence of such error or mistake, equity will relieve : Barnett v. Barnett, 6 J. J. Marsh. 499.   But see Clarke v. Dutcher, 9 Cow. 674 ; Bispham v. Price, 15 How. U. S. 162.   On the subject generally, see notes to Stapilton v. Stapilton, 2 Lead. Cas. Eq. 684, 3d Am. ed.; Larrabee v. Larrabee, 34 Maine 477 ; Hoge v. Hoge, 1 Watts 216 ; Steele v. White, 2 Paige 478; Currie v. Steele, 2 Sandf. S. C. 542; Bradley v. Chase, 22 Maine 524.   Equity has jurisdiction to cancel a patent for land granted by the United States under mistake or ignorance : United States v. Stone, 2 Wall. S. C. 525 ; Hughes v. United States, 4 Id. 232.

the knowledge of either party, has been previously barred.$(t)^1$

The most ordinary applications for this class of relief occur where releases or compromises have been made affecting rights, of which the existence was unknown or the character mistaken by the party executing the release or compromise; and there are three forms in which such ignorance or mistake may exist, viz. : 1. Where the release or compromise refers to other matters, and the facts originating the particular right are unknown to the parties, or are mistaken by them; 2. Where the uncertainty either of the facts or of the law is present to the parties' minds, and they intend to compromise their rights; and 3. Where the facts are known, but the law is mistaken.

In the first class of cases, where the instrument is executed, not by the way of releasing or compromising a *particular right, but in ignorance or mistake as to the facts which originate that right, such in- [*189] strument would be set aside in equity.$(u)^2$ There appears, however, to be an exception in the case of family arrangements, which are governed by a special equity of their own, and may be enforced, if honestly made, although they have not been meant as a compromise of doubts, but have proceeded on an error of all parties.

(t) Hitchcock v. Giddings, 4 Price 135; 1 V. & P. 389; Colyer v. Clay, 7 Bea. 188.

(u) Farewell v. Coker, cited 2 Meriv. 353; Naylor v. Winch, 1 S. & S. 555, 562; Pritt v. Clay, 6 Beav. 503.

---

[1] In Cochrane v. Willis, 34 Beav. 359, the court relieved against a sale of timber to a remainderman which had been made under the mistaken impression, common to both parties, that a tenant for life was alive, when, in fact he was dead, and the remainderman was therefore entitled to the timber.

[2] See note to pp. 168, 169 ; Broughton v. Hutt, 3 De G. & J. 501.

25

originating in mistake or ignorance of facts as to what their rights actually are. (v)

In the second class of cases, where the uncertainty either of the facts or of the law is present to the parties' minds and they intend to compromise their rights, whatever they may be, i. e., knowing the facts, to compromise the law, or being doubtful of the facts, to compromise both fact and law, there is no reason to set aside the transaction; for it is based on the existence of a doubt; there is no mistake in what is done, and the mere fact that one of the parties was in error as to the amount of benefit which he relinquished, cannot create an equity. (w)[1]

The third class of cases, where the facts are known but the law is mistaken, have been to some extent the subject of conflicting authorities. The rule at law is clear, that "money paid by a man with full knowledge of all the circumstances, or with the means of such knowledge in his hands, cannot be recovered back again on account of such payment having been made in ignorance of the law." (x)[2] The principle ought to be the same in equity.

(v) Stockley v. Stockley, 1 Ves. & B. 23, 30; Dunnage v. White, 1 Swanst. 137; Neale v. Neale, 1 K. 672; Westby v. Westby, 1 Conn. & L. 537; Gordon v. Gordon, 3 Swanst. 400.

(w) Attwood v. ——, 1 Russ. 353; 5 Id. 149; Leonard v. Leonard, 2 Ball. & B. 171; Stewart v. Stewart, 6 Cl. & F. 911.

(x) Bilbie v. Lumley, 2 East 469.

---

[1] See Ray and Thornton v. Bank of Kentucky, 3 B. Monr. 510.

[2] See note to p. 170. See, also, the case of Underwood v. Brockman, 4 Dana 309; and vol. 23 of the American Jurist, pp. 143–371, where the authorities are collected and compared upon this point. Where there is a mistake all round as to the legal effect of a marriage settlement, and a family arrangement is effected, not as to the right thus mistaken, but as to a collateral matter arising therefrom, such arrangement will be set aside: Lawton v. Campion, 18 Jurist 818; 23 L. J. Ch. 505; 18 Beav. 87.

So if a party, in ignorance of a plain and settled principle of law, is induced to give up his property, that ignorance is a ground for equitable

The authorities which appear most opposed to it are those of Bingham *v.* Bingham, (*y*) and Lansdown *v.* Lansdown. (*z*) In the *first case the defendant had sold to the plaintiff an estate, which in fact belonged to him [*190] already, but which both parties believed, under a mistake of law, to belong to the defendant. The Master of the Rolls decreed repayment of the purchase-money, saying there was a plain mistake. It has been said by Lord Cottenham, that if it were necessary to consider the principle of that decree it might not be easy to distinguish the case from any other purchase in which the vendor turns out to have no title. In both there is a mistake, and the effect in both is that the vendor receives, and the purchaser pays money without the intended equivalent. (*a*) In the second case one of four brothers died. his next brother and the son of his elder brother had a controversy which was heir, and were advised by the village schoolmaster that the former had the right because lands could not ascend. He recommended, them, however, to take further advice, but the nephew afterwards told him that he would agree to share the land with his uncle, let it be whose right it would, and thereby prevent all disputes and lawsuits. The land was accordingly divided and a conveyance made.

(*y*) 1 Ves. Sr. 126.　　　　　(*z*) Mosley 364; 2 Jac. & W. 205.
(*a*) 6 Cl. & F. 968.

---

relief. But if the question be one which is in any way doubtful, and the doubtfulness of that question is made the basis of any arrangement or agreement, especially a family one, the court will give no relief: Stone *v.* Godfrey, 18 Jur. 165, affirmed Id. 524; 5 De G., M. & G. 76.

A compromise effected in a suit, where the complainant untruly alleged himself tenant in tail, but set forth documents which showed him only tenant for life, will not be set aside on the ground of mistake arising from such erroneous allegation: Richardson *v.* Eyton, 2 De G., M. & G. 79. See also, as to setting aside family arrangements on mistake of law, Ashhurst *v.* Mill, 7 Hare 502, affirmed 12 Jur. 1035.

But the arrangement was afterwards set aside at the nephew's suit, the Court saying that the maxim *"ignorantia juris neminem excusat,"* meant only that ignorance cannot be pleaded in excuse of crimes, and did not hold in civil cases. Lord Cottenham has observed of this case that it was a very strong one of setting aside a compromise, but that it is impossible to ascertain the real facts, and that the restriction of the maxim to criminal cases is not recognised by modern decisions.(*b*)   It is said, too, that if a party acting in ignorance of a plain and settled principle of law is induced to give up a portion of his undisputable property to another, under the name of a compromise, he shall be relieved from the effect of his mistake.(*c*)[1]   Subject, however, to any exception which may exist on this ground, it seems now to be clearly [*191] established that in *equity as well as at law, a mere mistake of law, where there is no fraud or trust, and no mistake of fact, is immaterial.(*d*)

The remedy which the Court affords on a void transaction is the replacement of the parties in *statu quo*.[2] If,

(*b*) Stewart *v.* Stewart, 6 Cl. & Fin. 968.

(*e*) Naylor *v.* Winch, 1 S. & S. 555, 564; see also Stockley *v.* Stockley, 1 Ves. & B. 31 ; Saunders *v.* Lord Annesley, 2 Sch. & L. 73, 101.

(*d*) Cholmondeley *v.* Clinton, 2 Meriv. 171, 233, 328 ; Stewart *v.* Stewart, 6 Cl. &. F. 911 ; Denys *v.* Shuckburgh, 4 Y. & C. 42 ; 1 Story on Equity, s. 116–132.

---

[1] Equity will relieve against a mistake of law acted upon and brought about by undue influence: Jordan *v.* Stevens, 51 Maine 78 ; Freeman *v.* Curtis, Id. 140.

[2] Brown *v.* Lamphear, 35 Verm. 252, is a good illustration of the relief afforded. In that case the complainant had conveyed a lot to the defendant, intending to reserve the use of a spring therein situated by which other property of the complainant was supplied with water ; but, owing to a mistake of the scrivener, the reservation was not made. The purchaser was, at the time of the conveyance, ignorant of the existence of the spring, but subsequently discovered it, and attempted to stop the vendor's use thereof. Upon a bill filed by the vendor, it was held that the mistake was

for example, a bill be filed by the obligor of a usurious bond to be relieved against it, the Court, in a proper case will cancel the bond, but only on his refunding the money advanced. The equity is to have the entire transaction rescinded, and if the obligor will have equity, he must also do equity.[1] The Court will remit both parties to their original positions, and will not relieve the obligor from his liability, leaving him the fruits of the transaction of which he complains. (e)[2] If, again, a decree be asked for the cancellation of an invalid annuity deed, it must be on the terms of having an account taken of all receipts and payments on either side, and payment made of the balance. (f) It has been already stated, in accordance with the same principle, that a purchase from an expectant heir or reversioner will not be set aside absolutely, but will be ordered to stand as a security for the amount paid. And therefore, if the party complaining has done any act, when relieved from his necessities, by which the rights of the other are affected, so that he cannot be replaced in *statu quo*, he cannot afterwards repudiate the contract. (g)

(e) Hanson v. Keating, 4 Hare 1-6.
(f) Byne v. Vivian, 5 Ves. 604.
(g) King v. Hamlet, 2 M. & K. 456 ; 3 Cl. & Fin. 218.

one against which equity would relieve, and that the defendant must either execute a conveyance of the right to the spring, or reconvey the lot upon repayment of his purchase-money.

[1] Daniell v. Mitchell, 1 Story 173 ; Harding v. Handy, 11 Wheat. 103 ; Dower v. Fortner, 5 Port. 9 ; Brogden v. Walker, 2 Har. & Johns. 285 · Waters v. Lemon, 4 Hamm. 229 ; Lowry v. Cox, 2 Dana 469 ; White v. Trotter, 14 Sm. & Marsh. 30 ; Bruen v. Hone, 2 Barb. S. C. 586 ; Doggett v. Emerson, 1 Wood. & M. 195 ; Shaeffer v. Slade, 7 Blackf. 128 ; Mill v. Hill, 3 H. Lds. Cas. 828 ; Johnson v. Walker, 25 Ark. 196. This obligation of "doing equity" in such cases, does not extend to transactions unconnected with the one in suit: Wilkinson v. Fowkes, 9 Hare 592.

[2] See Skilbeck v. Hilton, L. R. 2 Eq. 587 ; Stewart v. Ludwick, 29 Ind. 230.

In addition to the jurisdiction for setting aside contracts on the ground of a mistake by the parties, there is
a jurisdiction to set aside awards on the ground of miscarriage in the arbitrators, where the fact of such miscarriage does not appear on the award, and cannot, therefore,
be made a ground for impeaching it at law

A dispute may be referred to arbitration in three ways.[1]
1. The reference may be by mere agreement of the par-
[*192]   ties, unaided by the direction *of any Court; 2.
It may be by a rule of Court, made by consent
in an action actually depending; and 3. It may be by
agreement to refer existing disputes, which might be the
subject of a personal action or suit in equity, but with respect to which no proceedings are actually depending.
In those cases where the submission is by mere agreement, it is revocable by either party until the award is
made at the peril of an action for breach of contract; but
where the agreement has been made a rule of Court,.
under the provisions of 9 and 10 Wm. 3, c. 15, it is now
by statute declared irrevocable, unless by leave of the
Court or one of its judges.(h)

After the award has been made, the power of revocation is at an end;[2] and the award may be enforced by
either party, either by action on the award or on the contract to refer,(i) or in a proper case by suit in equity for
specific performance,(k)[3] or, if it has been made a rule of
Court, by an attachment for contempt.

(h) 3 & 4 Wm. 4, c. 42, s. 39.
(i) Warburton v. Storr, 4 B. & C. 103 (10 E. C. L. R.)
(k) Hall v. Hardy, 3 P. Wms. 187; Wood v. Griffith, 1 Sw. 43–54.

---

[1] The subject of arbitration is regulated in most of the states, as in
Pennsylvania, by special statute.

[2] See Tobey v. County of Bristol, 3 Story 800.

[3] Smith v. Smith, 4 Rand. 95; McNear v. Bailey, 18 Maine 251; Paw-
ling v. Jackman, 6 Litt. 1; McNeil v. Magee, 5 Mason 244; Jones v. Bos-

In order to resist the enforcement of the award, it is necessary that its-validity be impeached. It is not sufficient for this purpose to contend, or even to prove, that it is unreasonable or unjust; for the reason and justice of the case are the very points referred to the arbitrators, and on which their decision must be conclusive. But if any fraud or partiality be shown, it will palpably vitiate the award.[1] And even in the absence of actual misconduct, the same result may follow, if the arbitrators have failed in performance of their duty; e. g., if they have not declared their decision with certainty; if their award be not final on all points referred; if it exceed the authority given; if they have acted on a mistake of law, when the law itself is not referred, but the reference was to decide on facts according to law :(l)[2] or if they have acted

(l) Young v. Walter, 9 Ves. 364; Steff v. Andrews, 2 Mad. 6.

---

ton Mill Corp., 4 Pick. 507; Cook v. Vick, 2 How. (Miss.) 882; Kirksey v. Fike, 27 Ala. 383; Wood v. Shepherd, 2 Patt. & H. 452; Story v. Norwich & Worcester, 24 Conn. 94. An agreement to refer will not, however, be specifically enforced: Conner v. Drake, 1 Ohio N. S. 166.

[1] See Schenck's Admr. v. Cuttrell, 1 Green Ch. 297; Herrick v. Blair, 1 John. Ch. 101; Shermer v. Beale, 1 Wash. 11; Pleasants et al. v. Ross, 1 Wash. 156; Van Cortlandt v. Underhill, 17 John. 405; Head v. Muir, 3 Rand. 122; Hardeman v. Burge, 10 Yerg. 202; Bispham v. Price, 15 How. U. S. 162; Tracy v. Herrick, 3 Foster 381.

[2] A mistake in law must be a plain one, and upon a material point affecting the case: Schenck's Admr. v. Cuttrell, ubi supra. So an award will be set aside, when it is not final and is indefinite: Hattier v. Etinaud, 2 Dessaus. 570; and also where it exceeds the submission, the excess will either be set aside, or the award in toto: Taylor's Admr. v. Nicolson, 1 Hen. & Munf. 66; McDaniell v. Bell, 3 Heywood 264; Gibson et al. v. Broadfoot, 3 Dessaus. 11. As to where the decision is given intentionally against the law, see West Jersey R. R. v. Thomas, 21 N. J. Eq. 205.

A mere mistake of judgment in arbitrators, is not sufficient evidence of improper conduct on their part, to justify the setting aside of their award in a Court of Chancery: Campbell v. Western, 3 Paige Ch. 124; Roloson v. Carson, 8 Md. 208; Bridgman v. Bridgman, 23 Mo. 272. When, how-

on a mistake as to a material fact, admitted by themselves
to have been made and to have influenced their judgment.[1]

---

ever, the arbitrators heard evidence, without giving the opposite party an
opportunity to cross-examine or of being heard, the award was set aside:
Shinnie v. Coil, 1 McC. Ch. 478. So, also, when they refused to hear evidence pertinent and material to the controversy: Van Cortlandt v. Underhill, 17 John. 405; see Severance v. Hilton, 32 N. H. 289; McGuire v.
O'Halloran, Hill & Denio 85.

[1] And where the award does not carry out the intention of the arbitrators, chancery will rectify it: Williams v. Warren, 21 Ill. 541. The more
recent authorities in England, have thrown very considerable doubt upon
the question of the admissibility of evidence of arbitrators, to show that
they made their award under a mistake as to some material fact. In the
case of Hall and Hinds, 2 M. & G. 847, evidence of this nature was admitted; but this decision was severely criticised in Phillips v. Evans, 12
M. & W. 309, and though not overruled directly, yet it was considered as
hardly to be supported. So in Re Stroud, 8 C. B. 501, the question was
considered very doubtful. In Hutchinson v. Shepperton, 13 Q. B. 955,
however, the admission of the evidence was held to be a matter of discretion, rarely to be exercised, but not to be refused in a case of gross injustice, as in that, which was one of account, where the parties agreed
upon the amount due, on a particular claim, but the arbitrator misunderstanding them, and supposing that it was no longer a matter of difference,
omitted it from his award. It seems, however, clear on the English authorities that no mistake upon the evidence itself, however gross, will be ground
for relief. In the United States, there has been a number of decisions on
the subject, from which no certain rule can be drawn, except that such
evidence would not be received except in peculiar cases. Thus in Boston
Water Power Co. v. Gray, 6 Metcalf 169, it was held that mistake as to
conclusion of fact, or of scientific principles applied in an award, could
not be cured by the after admission of the arbitrators, but it was said that
it was different where the mistake was in some preliminary fact, inadvertently assumed and believed, as in the use of false measures or weights;
see Roloson v. Carson, 8 Md. 208. And in Eaton v. Eaton, 8 Ired. Eq. 102,
the rule of the inadmissibility of such evidence, was stated, on the authority
of Phillips v. Evans, to be without exception. Ruffin, C. J., dissented,
however, in a forcible opinion; and certainly it is not difficult to imagine
cases in which such an extreme doctrine would be productive of most absurd injustice. See further, Bell v. Price, 2 Zabriskie 591; Bigelow v.
Maynard, 4 Cush. 316; Hartshorne v. Cuttrell, 1 Green. Ch. 297; Bumpass
v. Webb, 4 Port. (Ala.) 71. The rules on this subject are the same in equity
as law. See Russell on Arbitrators 301, &c.; Eaton v. Eaton, ut supr.

But unless *they voluntarily make the admission, [*193]
they cannot be compelled to disclose the grounds
of their judgment.(m)

If any of these objections appear on the face of the
award, they invalidate it, and preclude its enforcement
at law; and if there be actual fraud, it may be pleaded
in avoidance at law. If there be mere miscarriage, not
apparent on the face of the award, it cannot be pleaded
in avoidance at law, but must be made available by an
independent application to set aside the award.(n) And
where the submission rests on mere agreement, and is
not a rule of any Court, the jurisdiction for this purpose
is exclusive in equity.(o) If the submission is by rule at
nisi prius, the jurisdiction is concurrent in law and equity
For the Court of law which directed the reference retains
a superintending power, and the Court of Chancery has
its ancient jurisdiction over the parties to the action, of
which the reference is merely a modified continuance.(p)
In the third class, where a submission by agreement, not
made in any cause, has been made a rule[1] of Court under
the statute, the jurisdiction is exclusive in the Court of
which the submission has been made a rule. For it is
expressly enacted, that the Court of which it is made a
rule may set aside the award, if procured by corruption
or any undue means (which has been held to include mistake), if complaint be made before the last day of the
next term after its publication, that no other Court, either
of law or of equity, shall interfere.

(m) Knox v. Simmons, 1 Ves. J. 369; Anon., 3 Atk. 644.
(n) Braddick v. Thompson, 8 East 344; Pedley v. Goddard, 7 T. R. 73.
(o) Goodman v. Sayers, 2 J. & W. 249.
(p) Nichols v. Chalie, 14 Ves. 265; [Elliott v. Adams, 8 Black. 103;
but see Waples v. Waples, 1 Harring. 392.]

---

[1] Or has been agreed to be made such: Heming v. Swinnerton, 1 Coop.
C. C. 386; Nichols v. Roe, 3 M. & K. 431.

OF INJUNCTION AGAINST PROCEEDINGS AT LAW——BILLS OF
PEACE——INTERPLEADER——INJUNCTION AGAINST TORT.

It has been already observed, in treating of the equity
for rescission, that it is effectuated, not only by cancellation of an instrument or by reconveyance of property, but
by injunction against suing at law on a vitiated contract,
or against taking other steps to complete an incipient
wrong. The right to injunctive relief is not confined to
the equity for rescission, but extends to all cases where
civil proceedings have been commenced before the ordinary tribunals in respect of a dispute which involves an
equitable element, or where an act is. commenced or
threatened, by which an equity would be infringed.[1] The
restraint may be imposed either by a final decree, forbidding the act *in perpetuum* on establishment of the adverse
right, or by interlocutory writ, forbidding it *pro tempore*
whilst the right is in litigation.

The injunction against proceedings in another Court is
an auxiliary decree or writ, made or issued to restrain
parties from litigation before the ordinary tribunals where

---

[1] The common injunction no longer exists in New. York, the Courts of
that state being competent to administer relief on equitable as well as
legal grounds: Grant *v.* Quick, 5 Sand. S. C. 612. In Wisconsin injunctions have been abolished, and relief is afforded under express statutory
provisions: Trustees *v.* Hoessli, 13 Wis. 348.

equitable elements are involved in the dispute; as, for example, to restrain an ejectment by a trustee against his *cestui que trust*, or by a vendor, bound to specific performance, against the purchaser.[1] The ground for imposing

---

[1] The subject of the power of courts of equity to enjoin proceedings at law will be found discussed in the notes to the Earl of Oxford's Case, 2 Lead Cas. Eq. 504. As a general rule, whenever, through fraud, mistake, accident, or want of discovery, one of the parties in a suit at law obtains, or is likely to obtain, an unfair advantage over the other, so as to make the legal proceedings an instrument of injustice, a court of equity will interfere by injunction: Story's Equity, § 885; Daniel's Chan. Prac. 1725; and see How v. Mortell, 28 Ill. 478; Pierson v. Ryerson, 1 McCart. 181; Ferguson v. Fisk, 28 Conn. 511; Weed v. Grant, 30 Id. 74; Dehon v. Foster, 4 Allen 545; Davis v. Hoopes, 33 Miss. 173; Hine v. Handy, 1 Johns. Ch. 6; Atlantic DeLaine Co. v. Tredick, 5 R. I. 171; Dale v. Roosevelt, 5 Johns. Ch. 174; Matter of Merritt, 5 Paige 125; Miller v. McCan, 7 Paige 457; Dealafield v. State of Illinois, 26 Wend. 192; Beaty v. Beaty, 2 Johns. Ch. 430; Denton v. Graves, Hopkins 306; Bulows v. Committee of O'Neall, 4 Dessaus. 394; Vennum v. Davis, 35 Ill. 568.

But equity will not interfere to restrain criminal proceedings: Holderstaffe v. Saunders, 6 Mod. 16; The Mayor, &c., of York v. Pilkington, 2 Atk. 302; Montague v. Dudman, 2 Vesey 396; see Turner v. Turner, 15 Jur. 218. Nor where the ground for relief is equally available at law: Harrison v. Nettleship, 2 Myl. & K. 423; Philhower v. Todd, 3 Stockton 54. In England equitable pleas and replications may be made use of at law under the Procedure Act of 1854; but as this statute has been narrowly construed, a party has still, in many instances, to come into Chancery for relief: see Gompertz v. Pooley, 4 Drew. 448; Waterlow v. Bacon, L. R. 2 Eq. 514. A court of equity will not interfere to prevent a party from applying to Parliament for relief by special statute: Heathcote v. The North Staffordshire R. R. Co., 2 Macn. & G. 100; or to the legislature of a foreign country: Bill v. The Sierra Nevada Co., 1 De G., F. & J. 177. For further instances of the Court's refusal, on the other hand, to grant an injunction to restrain proceedings before judgment, see Peck v. Woodbridge, 3 Day 508; Mitchell v. Oakley, 7 Paige 68; Perrine v. Striker, Id. 598; Tone v. Brace, 8 Id. 597; Glenn v. Fowler, 8 Gill & J. 340; Caldwell v. Williams, 1 Bailey's Ch. 175; Mactier v. Lawrence, 7 Johns. Ch. 206; Chadoin v. Magee, 20 Texas 476. Equity will sometimes leave the parties to their mere legal rights: Bankhart v. Houghton, 27 Beav. 425.

No injunction to stay proceedings at law can be had against the United

this restraint is, that the ordinary tribunals cannot adjudicate on an equity ; and they would decide, therefore, on a part only, and not on the whole of the dispute. The [*195] *existence, however, of such an equitable element, or the pendency of a suit respecting it, is not recognised by those tribunals as a bar to their own procedure; but the bar must be made effectual by an injunction out of Chancery, which does not operate as a prohibition to the ordinary Court, but restrains the plaintiff personally from further steps.(a)

The proceedings to which this injunction most commonly applies are those before the common law. Courts. The interlocutory writ is attainable as of course within a very limited period after the commencement of a suit, so as to restrain proceedings at law, until the defendant in equity has answered the bill, and has thus enabled the Court to judge of their propriety. In order to prevent its issue, he must appear within four days after the *subpœna* has been served, and answer within eight days after his appearance. This writ is termed the common injunction.[1]

(a) Sheffield v. Duchess of Buckinghamshire, 1 Atk. 624 ; Lord Portarlington v. Soulby, 3 Myl. & K. 104, 107.

States: Hill v. The United States, 9 How. 386. In the well-known and important case of The State of Mississippi v. Johnson, President, 4 Wallace S. C. 475, the Court refused to allow a bill to be filed, the object of which was to enjoin the President of the United States from carrying out the provisions of the Acts of Congress of March 2d and 23d, 1867, commonly known as the Reconstruction Acts. This decision was made upon the ground that a court of equity had no right to interfere with the exercise of executive discretion

[1] The distinction between common and special injunctions has been abolished in England by statute 15 & 16 Vict. c. 85. In the United States, as a general rule, the common injunction does not exist, but all injunctions are granted on the merits. See Buckley v. Corse, Saxton 504 ; Hoffman's Ch. Prac. 78 ; Perry v. Parker, 1 Wood. & M. 280; Daniel's Ch. Prac. 1716. In Pennsylvania, injunctions may be obtained at once, on

The extent of its operation depends on the stage which the proceedings at law have reached. If it be obtained before a declaration is delivered, it stays all the proceedings at law. If afterwards, it only restrains execution, and leaves the plaintiff at liberty to proceed to judgment. But if the plaintiff in equity make affidavit that he believes the answer will afford discovery material to his defence at law, he may obtain by another motion an order extending it to stay trial. If the defendant, is diligent enough to prevent the common injunction from issuing, by filing a sufficient answer within the time allowed, the only way to obtain the injunction is by moving specially on the admissions in the answer. If the proceedings at law have been commenced under such circumstances that the plaintiff in equity has no opportunity of obtaining the common injunction, a special injunction may sometimes be obtained on affidavit under very special circumstances before answer.(b)

*As soon as the defendant has put in a full answer, he may move to dissolve the injunction.[1]   [*196]

(b) Drummond v. Pigou, 2 M. & K. 168; Bailey v. Weston, 7 Sim. 666.

security being given, without notice to the opposite party; but whenever so granted, it shall be taken to be dissolved, if the motion be not argued within five days after the notice is given, unless otherwise specially ordered. See the 75th of the Rules of Equity Practice of that state.

[1] The defendant may move to dissolve an injunction for want of equity appearing on the face of the bill; and such a motion is like a demurrer: Titus v. Mabee, 25 Ill. 259. It is an almost universal practice to dissolve the injunction, where the answer fully denies all the circumstances upon which the equity of the bill is founded; and likewise to refuse the writ, if application is made after the coming in of such answer: Hoffman v. Livingstone, 1 Johns. Ch. 211; McFarland v. McDowell, 1 Car. Law Rcp. 110; Cowles v. Carter, 4 Ired. Eq. 105; Livingston v. Livingston, 4 Paige Ch. 111; Gibson v. Tilton, 1 Bland. Ch. 355; Perkins v. Hallowell, 5 Ired. Eq. 24; Williams v. Berry, 3 Stew. & Port. 284; Green v. Phillips, 6 Ired. Eq. 223; Wakeman v. Gillespy, 5 Paige 112; Stoutenburgh v. Peck, 3

And it is then a question for the discretion of the Court, whether on the facts disclosed by the answer, or as it is

---

Green Ch. 446; Leigh v. Clark, 3 Stockt. 113; Hollister v. Barkley, 9 N. H. 230; Eldred v. Camp, Harring Ch. 163; Freeman v. Elmendorf, 3 Halst. Ch. 655; Adams v. Whiteford, 9 Gill 501; Dorsey v. The Hagerstown Bank, 17 Md. 408; West v. Rouse, 14 Ga. 715; Mahone v. Central Bank, 17 Id. 111; Greenin v. Hoey, 1 Stockt. (N. J.) 137; Kohler v. Los Angeles, 39 Cal. 510; Van Houten v. First Ref. Dutch Church, 2 Green (N. J.) 126; Manhattan Gas Co. v. Barker, 7 Rob. (N. Y.) 523. For the practice in New York, see Brewster v. Hodges, 1 Duer 609; Loomis v. Brown, 16 Barb. 325. But there is no inflexible rule to this effect; the granting and continuing an injunction must always rest in the sound discretion of the court, to be governed by the nature of the case: Roberts v. Anderson, 2 Johns. Ch. 204; Poor v. Carlton, 3 Sumn. 70; Bank of Monroe v. Schermerhorn, 1 Clark 303; Canton Co. v. Northern, &c., R. R., 21 Md. 383; Hine v. Stephens, 33 Conn. 497. The injunction will not be dissolved when the answers of the parties most interested admit the allegations in the bill; although the party restrained denies them: Zabriskie v. Vreeland, 1 Beas. 179. The answer of a corporation must be verified by the oath of some one of its officers: Bouldin v. The Mayor of Baltimore, 15 Md. 21.

Where the defendant in his answer admit, or does not deny the equity of the bill, but sets up new matter of defence, on which he relies, the injunction will be continued to the hearing: Minturn v. Seymour, 4 Johns. Ch. 497; Lindsay v. Etheridge, 1 Dev. & Bat. Eq. 38; Hutchins v. Hope, 12 Gill & J. 244; Lyrely v. Wheeler, 3 Ired. Eq. 170; Nelson v. Owen, Id. 175; Drury v. Roberts, 2 Md. Ch. 157; Rembert v. Brown, 17 Ala. 667; Wilson v. Mace, 2 Jones' Eq. 5; State v. Northern Central Railway Co., 18 Md. 193; West Jersey R. R. v. Thomas, 21 N. J. Eq. 205.

It is a general rule, that an injunction will not be dissolved, on answer, until the answers of all the defendants are put in. See Mooney v. Jordan, 13 Beav. 229; Balt. & Ohio R. R. v. Wheeling, 13 Gratt. 40; School Commissioners v. Putnam, 44 Ala. 506; Garrett v. Lynch, Id. 683. But there are many exceptions: e. g., it will be considered unnecessary, if those who have not answered are merely formal parties: Higgins v. Woodward, Hopkins' Ch. 342. So may it be dissolved upon the answer of one or more defendants within whose knowledge the facts charged especially or exclusively lie, although other defendants have not answered: Dunlap v. Clements, 7 Ala. 539; Coleman v. Gage, 1 Clarke 295; Ashe v. Hale, 5 Ired. Eq. 55. So also where that defendant against whom the gravamen of the charge rests, has fully answered; Depeyster v. Graves, 2 Johns. Ch. 148; Noble v. Wilson, 1 Paige 164; Stoutenburgh v. Peck, 3 Green Ch.

technically termed, on the equity confessed, the injunction shall be at once dissolved, or whether it shall be continued to the hearing. The general principle of decision
is, that if the answer shows the existence of an equitable
question, such question shall be preserved intact until the
hearing. But the particular mode of doing this is matter
of discretion.

If the plaintiff is willing to admit the demand at law,
and to give judgment in the action, but is unwilling to pay
money to the defendant, which, if once paid, it might be

446; Vliet v. Lowmason, 1 Id. 404; Price v. Clevenger, 2 Id. 207. See
also Goodwin v. State Bank, 4 Dessaus. 389. And this, too, where all the
defendants are implicated in the same charge, and the answer of all can
and ought to come in, but the plaintiff has not taken the requisite steps,
with reasonable diligence, to expedite his cause: Depeyster v. Graves, ubi
supra. See also Bond v. Hendricks, 1 A. K. Marsh. 594. The injunction cannot be dissolved, if the answer be evasive and apparently deficient
in frankness, candor, or precision: Little v. Marsh, 2 Ired. Eq. 18; Williams v. Hall, 1 Bland Ch. 193; Thomas v. Hall, 24 Ga. 481. Nor if it be
contradictory: Tong v. Oliver, Id. 199. Nor if there be extreme improbability in its allegations: Moore v. Hylton, 1 Dev. Eq. 429. Nor if it be
merely upon information and belief: Ward v. Van Bokkelen 1 Paige 100;
Apthorpe v. Comstock, Hopkins 143; Poor v. Carleton, 3 Sumn. 70;
Holmes v. Georgia, 24 Ga. 636; Pidgeon v. Oatman, 3 Rob. (N. Y.) 206.
And, moreover, where the equity of an injunction is not charged to be in
the knowledge of the defendant, and the defendant merely denies all
knowledge and belief of the facts alleged therein, the injunction will not
be dissolved, on the bill and answer alone: Rodgers v. Rodgers, 1 Paige
426; Quackenbush v. Van Riper, Saxton 476; Everly v. Rice, 3 Green
Ch. 553.

Upon an application to dissolve an injunction on bill and answer, the
defendant's answer is entitled to the same credit as the complainant's bill.
It, therefore, makes no difference on such an application that the bill is
supported by the oaths of several complainants: Manchester v. Dey, 6
Paige 295.

An injunction cannot be obtained on an amended bill having been dissolved on the original bill, for default, before appearance: Zulueta v. Vincent, 14 Beav. 209; contra, Eyton v. Mostyn, 3 De G. & Sm. 518. See
further, post, note to p. 356.

difficult to recover, he may have the injunction continued on payment of the money into Court.[1] If he is desirous to try his liability at law, the injunction will be dissolved with liberty to apply again after a verdict; but unless the defendant's right at law be admitted, he will not be restrained from trying it, except where it is obvious from his own answer that the relief sought must ultimately be decreed. Where the question has been already tried at law, and judgment obtained by the plaintiff there, he will be restrained from issuing execution, if it appear that there is an equitable question(c) to be decided before the matter can be safely disposed of. If at the hearing the decision is with the plaintiff in equity, the injunction is made perpetual.

The right to grant this injunction after judgment, was at one time the subject of a violent contest. It was alleged by the common law judges, that after judgment there was no power in Chancery to enjoin against execution.[1] And it was said, that if after judgment, the Chancellor grant an injunction and commit the plaintiff at law to the Fleet, the Court of King's Bench will discharge him by *habeas corpus*. In the reign of Henry 8, the assertion

---

(c) Playfair v. Thames Junction Railway Company, 9 L. J. N. S. 253; 1 Railway Cases 640; Barnard v. Wallis, Cr. & P. 85; Bentinck v. Willink, 2 Hare 1.

---

[1] See Anderson v. Noble, 1 Drewry 143. A debtor who seeks an injunction against a void judgment is not obliged to bring money into court before he can claim its interposition: Edrington v. Allsbrooks, 21 Texas 186.

[2] In Macon, &c., R. R. Co. v. Parker, 9 Ga. 394, an injunction was granted to restrain the sale under several *fi. fa.'s* of a railroad of a hundred miles long, and running through six counties, on the ground of irreparable injury, and the court proceeded, instead, to decree a sale of the whole at one time.

of this jurisdiction *was one of the articles of im-　[*197]
peachment against Cardinal Woolsey.　The same
opposition was continued against Woolsey's successor, Sir
Thomas More.　And in the reign of James I., under the
Chancellorship of Lord Ellesmere, a vehement discussion
took place on the subject, in which Lord Coke came forward as the chief opponent of the jurisdiction.　The question at last was brought before the King, and was decided
by him in favor of the jurisdiction.(d)　The exercise of
the jurisdiction is not frequent, for it is seldom that a
plaintiff in equity delays his application until judgment
has been obtained at law; and where such delay takes
place, it is itself a ground for refusing aid, unless the reasons for requiring it were not, and could not by reasonable diligence have been discovered before the trial.　The
rule on this subject appears to be as follows : First : that
if, after judgment, additional circumstances are discovered
not cognisable at law, but converting the controversy into
matter of equitable jurisdiction, the Court of Chancery
will interpose.　Secondly : that even though the circumstances so discovered would have been cognisable at law,
if known in time, yet if their non-discovery has been
caused by fraudulent concealment, the fraud will warrant
an injunction.　But, thirdly, that if the newly-discovered
facts would have been cognisable at law, and there has
been no fraudulent concealment, the mere fact of their
late discovery will not of itself create an equity; although
if a bill of discovery has been filed in due time, the proceedings at law might have been stayed until the discovery was obtained.　And still less can any equity arise,
if the facts were known at the time of the trial, and the
grievance complained of has been caused either by a mis-

(d) Note on Crowley's Case, 2 Sw. 22, n.

26

take in pleading, or other mismanagement, or by a supposed error in the judgment of the Court.$(e)^1$

(e) Bateman v. Willoe, 1 Sch. & L. 201; Harrison v. Nettleship, 2 M. &
K. 428; Taylor v. Sheppard, 1 Y. & C. 271.

---

[1] Any fact which clearly proves it to be against conscience to execute a
judgment at law, and of which the injured party could not have availed
himself in a Court of law, or of which he might have availed himself, but
was prevented by fraud or accident, unmixed with any fault or negligence
in himself or his agents, will authorize a Court of equity to interfere by
injunction: Marine Ins. Co. v. Hodgson, 7 Cranch 332. Especially in case
of fraud: Lee v. Baird, 4 Hen. & Munf. 453; Wierich v. De Zoya, 2 Gilman
385; Powers v. Butler, 3 Green Ch. 465; Wingate v. Haywood, 40 N. H.
437; Emerson v. Udoll, 13 Verm. 477; Rust v. Ware, 6 Gratt. 50; Humphreys v. Leggett, 9 How. U. S. 297; Hahn v. Hart, 12 B. Monr. 426;
Deaver v. Erwin, 7 Ired. Eq. 250; Nelson v. Rockwell, 14 Illinois 375;
Burton v. Wiley, 26 Verm. 430; Conway v. Ellison, 14 Ark. 360; Trevor
v. McKay, 15 Ga. 550; Moore v. Gamble, 1 Stockton 246; Clifton v. Livor,
24 Georgia 91; Clute v. Potter, 37 Barb. 201; Blakesley v. Johnson, 13
Wis. 530; Day v. Welles, 31 Conn. 344; Hendrickson v. Hinckley, 17 How.
U. S. 443; Givens v. Campbell, 20 Iowa 79; Roebuck v. Harkins, 38 Ga.
174. An injunction may be granted against a judgment on the ground of
a subsequent release, though both a motion to set aside and for an *audita
querela* have been made and refused in the Court in which the judgment
was obtained: Williams v. Roberts, 8 Hare 315. As to injunction against
a decree in equity on the ground of after discovered evidence, see Bayse
v. Beard, 12 B. Monr. 581. An injunction was refused in Forsythe v.
McCreight, 10 Rich. Eq. 308. In Ridgway v. Bank of Tennessee, 11 Humph.
523, it was held that a judgment on which the sheriff, by collusion, had
falsely returned a service on the defendant, could be enjoined: followed
in Bell v. Williams, 1 Head 229; see also Owens v. Ranstead, 22 Ill. 167;
but *contra*, Walker v. Robbins, 14 How. U. S. 584. In general, however,
a Court of equity will not enjoin on the ground of the irregularity of a
judgment: Suydam v. Beals, 4 McLean 12; Methodist Church v. Mayor,
&c., of Baltimore, 6 Gill 391; Boyd v. The Chesapeake Co., 17 Md. 195;
Saunders v. Albritton, 37 Ala. 716. Nor for a defect of jurisdiction merely:
Stokes v. Knarr, 11 Wis. 391; Sanches v. Carriaga, 31 Cal. 170; see also
Crandall v. Bacon, 20 Wis. 639; nor for errors of law in a Court of competent jurisdiction: Reeves v. Cooper, 1 Beas. 223. And no injunction
will be granted against a judgment where there has been negligence on
the part of the complainant in availing himself of a defence at law, or
other neglect. See Truly v. Wanser, 5 How. U. S. 141; Essex v. Berry, 2

The jurisdiction to enjoin against proceedings in other Courts is not limited *to proceedings in the Courts of law, although it is more usually exerted with reference to them. But it is equally applicable to proceedings in the Ecclesiastical and Admiralty Courts, in the Colonial Court, and even in the Courts of foreign and independent countries, where the parties are personally within the jurisdiction, and are attempting to proceed elsewhere in respect of part of a transaction, the whole of which can be investigated by the Court of Chancery alone. (f_t)[1] The injunction, however, in these cases, is not

[*198]

(*f*) Duncan *v.* McCalmont, 3 Beav. 409; Glascott *v.* Lang, 3 M. & C.

Verm. 161; Williams *v.* Lockwood, 1 Clarke 172; Southgate *v.* Montgomery, 1 Paige Ch. 41; Stanard *v.* Rogers, 4 Hen. & Munf. 438; Farmers' Bank *v.* Vanmeter, 4 Rand. 553; Brickell *v.* Jones, 2 Hay. 357; Fentris *v.* Robins, N. C. Term 177; Cullum *v.* Casey, 1 Ala. N. S. 351; Haughy *v.* Strang, 2 Port. 177; Mock *v.* Cundiff, 6 Id. 24; Lucas *v.* Bank of Darien, 2 Stew. 280; Thomas *v.* Phillips, 4 S. & M. 358; Little *v.* Price, 1 Md. Ch. 182; Lyday *v.* Douple, 17 Md. 188; Sample *v.* Barnes, 14 How. U. S. 70; Warner *v.* Conant, 24 Verm. 351; Lockard *v.* Lockard, 16 Ala. 423; Foster State Bank, 17 Id. 672; Skinner *v.* Deming, 2 Cart. (Ind.) 558; Prewitt *v.* Perry, 6 Texas 260; Briesch *v.* McCauley, 7 Gill 189; Hood *v.* N. Y. & N. H. Railroad Co., 23 Conn. 609; Wynn *v.* Wilson, 1 Hempst. C. C. 698; Harnsberger *v.* Kinney, 13 Gratt. 511; Conway *v.* Ellison, 14 Ark. 360; Dickerson *v.* Comm'rs., 6 Ind. 128; Vaughn *v.* Johnson, 1 Stockt. 173; George *v.* Strange, 10 Gratt. 499; Schricker *v.* Field, 9 Iowa 372; McCollum *v.* Prewitt, 37 Ala. 573; Franklin Mill Co. *v.* Schmidt, 50 Ill. 208; Bryan *v.* Hickson, 40 Ga. 465. Nor where the only ground is discovery, which might have been sought and obtained before the judgment: Lansing *v.* Eddy, 1 John. Ch. 49; Brown *v.* Swann, 10 Pet. 497; Thompson *v.* Berry, 3 John. Ch. 395; Bartholomew *v.* Yaw, 9 Paige 165; McGrew *v.* Tombeckee Bank, 5 Porter 547. An administrator, however, who must derive his information chiefly from others, is not bound by the strict rules on this subject, and may obtain an injunction for a pretermitted defence, after permitting a judgment in ignorance thereof: Hewlett *v.* Hewlett, 4 Edw. Ch. 9.

In Gough *v.* Pratt, 9 Md. 526, it was held, that even after judgment at law upon a security given for a gaming debt, the defendant may have relief in equity, although he did not resist the suit at law on that ground.

[1] A Court of Chancery will not, by injunction, restrain a suit or pro-

obtained as of course on the defendant's default, but must
be the subject of a special application to the Court.(*g*)

451; Bunbury *v.* Bunbury, 1 Bea. 318. [See Hope *v.* Carnegie, L. R. 1
Ch. Ap. 320.]

(*g*) Anon., 1 P. Wms. 301; Macnamara *v.* Macquire, 1 Dick. 223.

---

ceeding previously commenced in a Court of a sister state, or in any of
the federal Courts: Mead *v.* Merritt, 2 Paige 402; Burgess *v.* Smith, 2
Barb. Ch. 276; Williams *v.* Ayrault, 31 Barb. 366; Coster *v.* Griswold, 4
Edw. Ch. 364. The United States Courts, in general, are prohibited by
statute (1793) from granting injunctions against proceedings in state
courts. See Rogers *v.* Cincinnati, 5 McLean 337; Orton *v.* Smith, 18 How.
263; Kittredge *v.* Emerson, 15 N. H. 227. An injunction issued by a state
court is inoperative in any manner to affect proceedings in the federal
Courts: U. S. *v.* Keokuk, 6 Wall. (U. S.) 514. By the 2d section of the
United States Bankrupt Act of March 2, 1867, general jurisdiction under
the Act is conferred upon the Circuit Courts, with authority on application
in proper form of any party aggrieved, to hear and determine the case in
a court of equity; and by the 40th section of the same Act, the District
Courts, during the pendency of the rule to show cause why the defendant
should not be adjudged a bankrupt on a creditor's petition, may by injunction restrain the debtor and any other person " from making any transfer
or disposition of any part of the debtor's property not excepted by this
Act from the operation thereof, and from any interference therewith."
Under the first of these sections the Circuit Court, sitting in equity, has
jurisdiction in cases of involuntary bankruptcy, to restrain by injunction
a plaintiff in an execution in a state Court, from proceeding to the collection of a judgment, when the same was confessed, or the levy thereunder
procured to be made, with the knowledge on the part of the plaintiff, that
the defendant was insolvent or contemplated insolvency, and with an intent
to give a preference, or to defeat or delay the operation of the bankrupt
law. And in case of voluntary bankruptcy, the District Court will restrain
proceedings in state courts under state insolvent laws. But the United
States courts will not interfere in cases of voluntary bankruptcy involving
questions which a state court is fully competent to decide; nor to disturb
a lien properly acquired: Irving *v.* Hughes, 7 Am. Law Reg. N. S. 209
(U. S. Circuit Court, E. Dist. of Penna.). One Circuit Court cannot control or restrain proceedings in another: Roshell *v.* Maxwell, 1 Hemp. 25.
The execution of a judgment can be enjoined by no other court than that
from which the writ issued: Dufossat *v.* Berens, 18 La. Ann. 339.

In an action on the judgment of another state, proceedings may be
stayed by injunction, where such judgment was fraudulently obtained, or
has been since reversed: Sumner *v.* Marcy, 3 Wood. & Min. 105; McJilton

Injunctions have also been granted on special equities, to restrain parties from filing affdavits of debt, with the intent of issuing a fraudulent fiat of bankruptcy.(*h*) And it has been argued, that there is an equity to restrain assignees from making a dividend, during the pendency of a suit for an equitable claim. But it is decided that no such equity exists, and that the administration of a bankrupt's property, when once it is determined what the property is, falls wholly within the province of the Court of Bankruptcy.(*i*)

If the Court in which the proceedings complained of have been taken, is itself a Court of equitable jurisdiction, and competent to adjudicate on the whole matter, an injunction cannot be obtained, unless the suitor against whom it is asked, has been previously bound by a decree of the Court of Chancery, or has voluntarily submitted to the jurisdiction of that Court.(*k*)

In addition to the injunctive jurisdiction in regular suits, there is a similar authority exercised in a summary

(*h*) Attwood *v.* Banks, 2 Bea. 192; Perry *v.* Walker, 1 N. C. C. 672.

(*i*) Halford *v.* Gillow, 13 Sim. 44; Thompson *v.* Derham, 1 Hare 358.

(*k*) Jackson *v.* Leaf, 1 J. & W. 229; Harrison *v.* Gurney, 2 Id. 563; Boulter *v.* Boulter, 2 Bea. 196, n.; Infra, Administration.

v. Love, 13 Ill. 486; Pearce *v.* Olney, 20 Conn. 544; which last case was affirmed in Dobson *v.* Pearce, 1 Duer 143; affirmed on appeal, see 3 Am. Law Reg. 206; which was the original suit. See also, Engel *v.* Schewerman, 40 Ga. 206.

Where an administration suit was pending in England, a Scotch corporation was restrained from proceeding against the intestate's estates in Scotland, the service of the subpœna being at an office of the corporation in London: McLaren *v.* Stainton, 22 L. J. Ch. 274. In Pennell *v.* Roy, 17 Jur. 247, 3 De G., Macn. & G. 126, however, it was held that the English assignees of a bankrupt owning real estate in Scotland, could not maintain a bill for an injunction against an alleged creditor not proving under the commission, who had attached the rents of the real estate by suit in Scotland, though it appeared that the suit was entirely frivolous.

way, where proceedings have been taken in another Court,
[*199] against or by officers of the Court of *Chancery
in respect of claims arising out of their official
acts. In this as well as the former cases, the principle
on which the Court proceeds is that of giving efficacy to
its own authority by rejecting foreign interference. If its
processes are improperly or irregularly issued, that is a
matter to be dealt with by itself alone ; and if redress be
sought elsewhere an injunction will lie. If in acting under
a regular authority, its officers misconduct themselves,
that is a matter which may, at the discretion of the Court,
be either left to the ordinary tribunals, or examined by
itself. But the latter course is generally adopted, and
the parties are enjoined from having recourse to law.(*l*)
The officers of the Court may, *e converso*, be restrained at
law in respect of claims arising to them in their official
capacity.(*m*)

The relief by injunction against proceeding at law is
also applied under a distinct equity on bills of peace and
bills of interpleader.

A bill of peace is a bill filed for securing an established
legal title against the vexatious recurrence of litigation,
whether by a numerous class insisting on the same right,
or by an individual reiterating an unsuccessful claim.
The equity is, that if the right be established at law, it
is entitled to adequate protection.[1]

(*l*) Frowd *v.* Lawrence, 1 J. & W. 635; Phillips *v.* Worth, 2 R. & M.
638; Astou *v.* Heron, 2 M. & K. 390; Chalie *v.* Pickering, 1 K. 749;
Empringham *v.* Short, 3 Hare 461 ; Evelyn *v.* Lewis, 3 Id. 472; Darley
v. Nicholson, 1 Conn. & L. 207 ; [Peck *v.* Crane, 25 Verm. 146.]

(*m*) Re Weaver, 2 M. & C. 441 ; Blundell *v.* Gladstone, 9 Sim. 455 ; Ambrose *v.* Dunmow Union, 8 Bea. 43.

---

[1] Sheffield Water Works *v.* Yeomans. L. R. 2 Ch. Ap. 8. See Black *v.*

Bills of peace of the first class are those where the same right is claimed by or against a numerous body; as, for example, where a parson claims tithes against his parishioners, or the parishioners allege a *modus* against the parson; where the lord of a manor claims a right against the tenants, or the tenants claim a common right against the lord;[1] or where the owner of an ancient mill claims service to his mill from all the tenants of a *particular district. In all these cases, the only form of procedure at common law would be that [*200] of a separate action by or against each parishioner or tenant, which would only be binding as between the

---

Shreve, 3 Halst. Ch. 440; Bond v. Little, 10 Ga. 395. In order to the maintenance of a bill of peace, the complainant must have first established his title at law: Eldridge v. Hill, 2 Johns. Ch. 281; Bond v. Little, 10 Ga. 395; Morgan v. Smith, 11 Ill. 194; Gunn v. Harrison, 7 Ala. 585; Lowe v. Lowry, 4 Hammond 78; Harmer v. Gwynne, 5 McLean 313; Paterson & Hudson River R. R. Co. v. Jersey City, 1 Stockt. (N. J.) 434; Smith v. McConnell, 17 Ill. 135; unless where the parties to the controversy are so numerous that a suit in equity is indispensable to comprehend them all, and to prevent a multiplicity of suits: Eldridge v. Hill, ut supra; Nicholl v. Trustees, &c., 1 Johns. Ch. 166; Lupeer Co. v. Hart, Harring. Ch. 157; Nevitt v. Gillespie, 1 How. (Miss.) 108.

Where a bill is filed for the purpose of preventing a multiplicity of suits at law, and to have the title to land finally settled in one suit, under the direction of the chancellor, it seems that the bill will be sustained, though there has been but one trial at law: Trustees of Huntington v. Nicoll, 3 John. 566. Bills to enjoin the defendant from repeated acts of trespass resemble bills of peace: Livingston v. Livingston, 6 Johns. Ch. 497. Such are bills to restrain the interference with or obstruction of a watercourse: Corning v. The Troy Iron Factory, 39 Barb. 327; Holsman v. The Boiling Spring Co., 1 McCart. 335; Lyon v. McLaughlin, 32 Verm. 423; Angell on Watercourses, § 444; Scheetz's Appeal, 35 Penn. St. 88. Courts of equity will also interfere by injunction to restrain the back flowage of water: Sheldon v. Rockwell, 9 Wis. 166. See post 211, Nuisance.

[1] A bill of peace will not lie to establish the rights of one commoner alone; it must be filed for himself and others: Phillips v. Hudson, L. R. 2 Ch. Ap. 242.

immediate parties, and would leave the general right still open to litigation.   In order to remedy this evil, a suit may be sustained in the Court of Chancery, in which all parties may be joined, either individually or as represented by an adequate number.   If any question of right be really in dispute it will be referred to the decision of a Court of law; and when the general right has been fairly ascertained, an injunction will be granted against further litigation.(*n*)   If particular individuals have special grounds of claim, those claims will be left untouched.

In order to originate this jurisdiction, it is essential that there be a single claim of right in all arising out of some privity or relationship with the plaintiff.

A bill of peace, therefore, will not lie against independent trespassers, having no common claim and no appearance of a common claim to distinguish them from the rest of the community ; as, for example, against several booksellers who have infringed a copyright, or against several persons who, at different times, have obstructed a ferry. For if a bill of peace could be sustained in such a case, the injunction would be against all the people of the kingdom.(*o*)[1]

There are two cases which constitute apparent exceptions to this rule, which are known respectively

(*n*) Mitf. 145, 146; How *v.* Bromsgrove, 1 Vern. 22; Tenham *v.* Herbert, 2 Atk. 483.

(*o*) Mitf. 147, 148; Dilly *v.* Doig. 2 Ves. J. 486.

---

[1] No bill of peace will lie where the rights and responsibilities of the defendants neither arise from, nor depend upon, nor are in any way connected with each other: Randolph *v.* Kinney, 3 Rand. 394. See Miller *v.* Grandy, 13 Mich. 540. An allegation that the defendants have fraudulently confederated to harass the plaintiff with suits will not uphold an injunction when the defendants claim adversely to each other: McHenry *v.* Hazard, 45 Barb. (N. Y.) 657.

as the "Case of the Duties," and the "Case of the Fisheries."(*p*)

In the first of these cases, the claim was for a duty on all imported cheese. And the case has been sometimes treated as if the City of London had filed a bill, in the nature of a bill of peace, against several importers, claiming to have the *duties permanently established. [*201] From the report, however, that does not appear to have been the case. It appears that the corporation filed distinct bills against several importers; first against A., then against B., and then the bill in question against C. Decrees being obtained against A. and B., they claimed a right, not to enforce those decrees against C., but to give in evidence the depositions on which they had been founded; alleging, however, at the same time, that, even without those depositions, they had, in the suit against C. himself, given other proof sufficient to establish their right. The decree decides, that the right was established against C.; but the reasons for the decision are not reported; and it does not appear whether any weight was in fact given to the previous suits. The case, therefore, appears to be no authority for the doctrine, that a number of defendants, who were severally liable to the duties, might have been united in a bill of peace.

In the second case, the plaintiff claimed a fishery in the river Ouse; and filed a bill of peace against several trespassers. Lord Hardwicke's first impression was against the bill; but he ultimately allowed it, partly on the authority of the City of London *v.* Perkins, and partly because the defendants were in fact distinguished from the community at large, as being owners of adjacent grounds, and as claiming fisheries in that character. The

(*p*) City of London *v.* Perkins, 3 B. P. C. by Toml. 602; Mayor of York *v.* Pilkington, 1 Atk. 282; Story on Pleading, s. 124, 125.

first of these grounds, as I have already suggested, is hardly warranted by the report of that case. The second ground appears to be that on which Lord Hardwicke mainly relied, and is consistent with the terms in which the case was spoken of by Lord Eldon. (*q*)

Bills of peace of the second class are those where a right, claimed by an individual, is indefinitely litigated by him without success. The necessity for bills of this [*202] class originates *in the nature of the action of ejectment, which is based on a fictitious dispute between fictitious parties, so that the rights of the real litigants are only indirectly tried. The consequence of this is, that the result of the action is not conclusive, but that fresh actions may be repeatedly brought, and the successful party harassed by indefinite litigation. In order to remedy this oppression, a jurisdiction has been assumed by the Court of Chancery; and a bill will lie, after repeated trials at law and satisfactory verdicts, to have an injunction against further litigation.[1] The right to this jurisdiction was formerly much questioned. Lord Cowper, in a celebrated case, where the title to land had been five times tried in ejectment, and five uniform verdicts given, refused to exercise it; but his decision was overruled by the House of Lords. (*r*)[2]

(*q*) City of London *v.* Perkins, 3 B. P. C. 602 ; Mayor of York *v.* Pilkington, 1 Atk. 282 ; Weale *v.* West Middlesex Waterworks, 1 J. & W. 356, 369.

(*r*) Earl of Bath *v.* Sherwin, Prec. Ch. 261 ; s. *v.* 4 B. P. C. by Toml. 373 ; Mitf. 143, 144.

[1] See Marsh *v.* Reed, 10 Ohio 347. By statutory provisions in Pennsylvania, and perhaps in other states, two verdicts in ejectment, for either party, are an absolute bar to any future suit. Such provision will not interfere with the right of a court of the United States, to entertain a bill of peace, as to ejectment, in its own jurisdiction, and the bill may be maintained in a proper case, though the technical bar of the statute does not apply : Craft *v.* Lathrop, 2 Wall. Jr. 103.

[2] On a principle similar to that which governs bills of peace of the

A bill of interpleader is a bill filed for the protection of a person, from whom several persons claim legally or equitably the same thing, debt, or duty; but who has incurred no independent liability to any of them, and does not himself claim an interest in the matter. The equity is that the conflicting claimants should litigate the matter amongst themselves, without involving the stakeholder in their dispute.[1]

The principle on which the jurisdiction is based, that of protecting a mere stakeholder between conflicting claimants, was always recognised at common law, and was applied where a chattel had come to a man's possession by accident, or by bailment from both claimants jointly, or from those under whom both made title.

The technical forms of pleading at law excluded the

---

second class, Courts of Equity will interfere to quiet the enjoyment of a right, or to establish it by a decree, or to remove a cloud from a title. See Crews v. Burcham, 1 Black 352; Cross v. De Valle, 1 Wall. S. C. 1; Kennedy v. Kennedy, 43 Penn. St. 417; Bean v. Coleman, 44 N. H. 539. As to bills to remove a cloud from a title, see Doe v. Doe, 37 N. H. 268; Kimberly v. Fox, 27 Conn. 307; Munson v. Munson, 28 Id. 582; Eldridge v. Smith, 34 Verm. 484; Story's Eq. § 700; Chapter on Rescission and Cancellation, ante.

[1] Strange v. Bell, 11 Ga. 103; Farley v. Blood, 10 Foster (N. H.) 354. A bill of interpleader, strictly so called, is where the complainant claims no relief against either of the defendants, but only asks for leave to pay the money, or deliver the property, to the one to whom it of right belongs, and that he may thereafter be protected from the claims of both: Bedell v. Hoffman, 2 Paige Ch. 199; Lincoln v. Rutland, &c., R. R. Co., 24 Verm. 639; Mount Holly Turnpike Co. v. Ferree, 2 Green (N. J.) 117; Burton v. Black, 32 Ga. 53; Hathaway v. Foy, 40 Mo. 540; Cady v. Potter, 55 Barb. (N. Y.) 463. The right of interpleader is given now by statute, in England and many of the United States, to defendants at law in most cases. In Missouri such a bill may be maintained against non-residents in certain cases: Freeland v. Wilson, 18 Mo. (3 Bennett) 380. The defendants to a bill of interpleader may compromise the dispute; and the complainant has no right to prevent this: Horton v. The Church, 34 Verm. 309.

application of this principle, except where the possession had arisen from bailment or accident; but the principle itself was acknowledged; and in equity, where those forms did not exist, its operation was extended to all cases [*203] where *the same thing, debt, or duty was the subject of both claims.(s)   The equity originates in the double claim made on the complainant and the inadequate protection afforded him at law,   The fact, therefore, that both the claims are legal, does not preclude the party sued from resorting to equity; as, for example, when the assignees of a bankrupt and the bankrupt himself, being unable to agree on the validity of the *fiat*, threaten separate actions against a debtor.(t)   The necessity, however, for bills of interpleader, where both the claims are legal, is much diminished, although the jurisdiction is unaffected, by a late statute, enacting that on the application of the defendant in any action of assumpsit, debt, detinue, or trover, showing that he claims no interest and that the right is claimed by, or supposed to belong to, some third party, who has sued or is expected to sue, and that the defendant does not collude with such third party, but is ready to bring into Court or otherwise dispose of the subject-matter as the Court shall direct, such third party may be ruled to appear, the proceedings in the action may be stayed, and directions may be given for trying the right between the real claimants.(u)

If one of the claims be equitable, the statute does not apply, and the jurisdiction is in equity alone.(v)[1]

(s) Mitf. 141; Crawshay v. Thornton, 2 M. & C. 1, 21.

(t) Lowndes v. Cornford, 18 Ves. 299.

(u) 1 & 2 Wm. 4, c. 58.

(v) Langton v. Horton, 3 Bea. 464.

[1] A bill of interpleader may be filed, although the claim of one of the claimants is actionable at law, and that of the other in equity: Lozier's

It is apparent from the definition already given that, in order to originate the equity of interpleader, three things are essential; viz., 1. That the same thing, debt, or duty be claimed by both the parties against whom relief is asked; 2. That the party seeking relief have incurred no independent liability to either claimant; and 3. That he claim no interest in the matter.

1. The same thing, debt, or duty, must be claimed by both.[1]

*If the subject in dispute has a bodily exist- [*204] tence, as in the original cases of interpleader at law, no difficulty can arise on the ground of identity; but where it is a *chose in action,* it becomes necessary to determine what constitutes identity. And this is a question attended occasionally with much difficulty, and which, in each case, must be determined by the original nature and constitution of the debt. Where, for example, an auctioneer, by direction of the owner, had sold to two persons successively, and had received a deposit from each, it was held that the auctioneer could not support a bill of interpleader against the owner and the two purchasers; because, although there was one question in

---

Ex'rs. *v.* Van Saun's Adm'rs., 2 Green's. Ch. 325 ; Yates *v.* Tisdale, 3 Edw. Ch. 71 ; Hamilton *v.* Marks, 3 De G. & Sm. 638. But see Hurst *v.* Sheldon, 13 C. B. N. S. 750.

And where a person is in danger of being doubly vexed by adverse claimants, whether by suit commenced or only threatened, he may file a bill of interpleader: Gibson *v.* Goldthwaite, 7 Ala. 281 ; Yates *v.* Tisdale, supra ; Richards *v.* Salter, 6 Johns. Ch. 445. But it seems that where the double claim has been occasioned by the act of the stakeholder, he has no right to file a bill of interpleader: Desborough *v.* Harris, 4 De G., M. & G. 439.

[1] See City Bank *v.* Bangs, 2 Paige Ch. 570; Hayes *v.* Johnson, 4 Ala. 267 ; Briant *v.* Reed, 1 McCart. 271. If the bill shows affirmatively that neither of the defendants has a right to the fund it will be dismissed on demurrer: Barker *v.* Swain, 4 Jon. Eq. 220.

common between the purchasers, viz., which was to be
the purchaser of the estate, their claims as against the
auctioneer were for two different things, viz., by each for
his own deposit. The bill, therefore, was dismissed as
against a second purchaser with costs, and it was decreed
that the seller and the first purchaser should interplead
as to the first deposit. And again at law, where a purchaser of tea was sued by the seller for the price, and was
also sued in trover by a person who alleged himself to be
the real owner, it was held not to be a case of interpleader;
for the parties were not seeking the same thing. The one
was endeavoring to obtain the price of the goods, the
other damages for their conversion.(*w*)

2. The party seeking relief must have incurred no independent liability to either claimant.

In the case, therefore, of a tenant sued by his landlord,
or an agent by his principal, a claim adverse to the landlord or principal will not warrant a bill of interpleader,
unless it originate in his own act, done after the commencement of the tenancy or agency, and creating a
doubt who is the true landlord or principal, to whom the
tenancy or agency refers.[1]   In like manner a bill of inter-

---

(*w*) Glyn *v.* Duesbury, 11 Sim. 139 ; Hoggart *v.* Cutts, Cr. & P. 197 ;
Slaney *v.* Sidney, 14 Mee. & W. 800 ; 15 Law J. Exch. 72.

---

[1] Whitewater, &c., Co. *v.* Comegys, 2 Cart. (Ind.) 469 ; Crane *v.* Burn-
trager, 1 Cart. 165 ; Cook *v.* Rosslyn, 1 Giff. 167. A strict bill of interpleader cannot be maintained by a bailee or agent, to settle the conflicting
claims of bailor or principal, and a stranger who claims the property by a
distinct and independent title. Neither can an attorney maintain such a
bill to settle the claim for money which he has collected for his client :
Marvin *v.* Elwood, 11 Paige Ch. 365. But, it seems, a bill of interpleader,
as between principal and agent, is admissible, where the claim is under a
derivative and not under an adverse title. And hence, an attorney who
has collected money, may file a bill of interpleader in respect of the same,
against defendants who set up a derivative claim from the person for whom

pleader will not lie, if the party seeking relief has acknowledge a title *in one of the claimants, and [*205]
has thus incurred an independent liability to him.
If misrepresentation was used to obtain that acknowledgment, it may create an equity to be released from the
liability ; but the right of the party deceived to insist on
such release is not matter of interpleader between the
real ánd apparent owners.(x)

3. He must claim no interest.[1]

It has been held, therefore, that if a deposit is made by
a purchaser at an auction, and the auctioneer is afterwards
sued for the deposit by the purchaser and vendor, he cannot sustain a bill of interpleader against them, if he
claims to deduct from his deposit his commission and the
duty.(y)[2]

(x) Crawshay v. Thornton, 2 M. & C. 1; Stuart v. Welch, 4 Id.
305 ; Jew v. Wood, Cr. & P. 185.

(y) Mitchell v. Hayne, 2 S. & S. 63; Moore v. Usher, 7 Sim. 384; Bignold v. Audland, 11 Sim. 24.

---

the attorney undertook the collection ; and this, although he may be entitled to retain a part of it to compensate his services : Gibson v. Goldthwaite, 7 Ala. 281. So, an executor, standing between two claimants, one
of whom claims by title paramount to the testator's, and the other as a
legatee under the will, is not entitled to an interpleader; his duty being
clearly to protect the legatees : Adams v. Dixon, 19 Ga. 513. He may,
however, file a bill in the nature of an interpleader to determine whether,
under a proper construction of a will, slaves in his possession are entitled
to their freedom, making the legatees and next of kin of the testator
parties : Osborne v. Taylor, 12 Gratt. (Va.) 17. See Crosby v. Mason, 32
Conn. 482.

[1] Anderson v. Wilkinson, 10 Sm. & M. 601. Yet it is no objection to a
bill of interpleader, that the complainant has an interest in respect of other
property not in the suit, but which might be litigated, that one party,
rather than the other, should succeed in the interpleader, so as to increase
his own chance of success, in respect of such other property. This is only
an interest in the question, not in the particular suit : Oppenheim v. Leo
Wolf, 3 Sandf. Ch. 571 ; see also, Gibson v. Goldthwaite, 7 Ala. 281 ; Mc-
Henry v. Hazard, 45 Barb. (N. Y.) 657.

[2] But, although he claims a lien he may subsequently withdraw his

If the circumstances be such as to sustain the jurisdiction, the party against whom the double claim is made. may, for his own protection, file a bill praying that the claimants may interplead together, and that he may be indemnified ;[1] and on payment into Court of the amount due may obtain an injunction against any proceeding commenced or threatened at law or in equity. The injunction may be obtained *ex parte* immediately on the bill being filed, and stays proceedings both at law and in equity, but it stays them until further order only, and not, like the common injunction, till answer and further order.(*z*)[2] It is granted only on the terms of payment into Court, in order that it may not be abused to delay payment of a debt under a pretence of doubting to whom it is due. And the order must be so drawn as to make the payment a condition precedent   But the mere absence of an offer to that effect in the bill is not a ground of demurrer.(*a*)[3]
When an answer has been put in by the enjoined defend-
[*206]   ant, he may move to dissolve *the injunction, on
notice to the plaintiff and his co-defendant ; and

(*z*) Crawford *v.* Fisher, 10 Sim. 479 ; Moore *v.* Usher, 7 Id. 383.
(*a*) Sieveking *v.* Behrens, 2 M. & C. 581 ; Pauli *v.* Von Melle, 8 Sim. 327 ; Meux *v.* Bell, 6 Id. 175.

---

claim and file a bill of interpleader: Jacobson *v.* Blackhurst, 2 John. & H. 486.
[1] The bill must in general be filed before or immediately after the commencement of the action, and not delayed till after verdict or judgment : Union Bank *v.* Kerr, 2 Md. Ch. 460. But where the suit is allowed to go to verdict for the purpose of ascertaining the amount, it is no objection : Hamilton *v.* Marks, 5 De G. & Sm. 638.
[2] See Nelson *v.* Barter, 2 Hem. & M. 334.
[3] Nash *v.* Smith, 6 Conn. 421. And yet the plaintiff ought to offer to bring the money into court ; and an injunction will be allowed only upon compliance with such offer : Shaw *v.* Chester, 2 Edw. Ch. 405 ;* see, also, Biggs *v.* Kouns, 7 Dana 411.

if such co-defendant has also answered, an order may -be made for inquiry as to the respective titles. But such inquiry cannot be directed whilst either answer is outstanding, because the Court cannot know what claim such answer will make.(b) If the cause is carried to a hearing, a like inquiry or an action will -be directed by the decree; but the more usual practice is to obtain the direction at an earlier stage.(c) The decree, when made, may terminate the suit as to the plaintiff, though the litigation may continue between the co-defendants; and in that case it may proceed without reviver, notwithstanding the plaintiff's death.(d)

The only equity on which the jurisdiction of interpleader rests, is the danger of injury to the plaintiff from the doubtful titles of the defendants. He is required, therefore, to satisfy the Court that this equity exists by annexing to his bill an affidavit that he does not collude with either claimant; and the want of that affidavit is a ground of demurrer.(e)[1] For the same reason he should so conduct his proceedings as not to cause hardship and expense to the litigant parties, beyond what his own protection may require.(f) But he will be entitled to have his costs properly incurred out of the fund in dispute, and

(b) Masterman v. Lewin, 2 Ph. 182.

(c) Townley v. Deare, 3 Beav. 213, 216; Crawford v. Fisher, 1 Hare 436, 441.

(d) Mitf. 60. [See Lyne v. Pennell, 1 Sim. N. S. 113.]

(e) Mitf. 49, 143; Bignold v. Audland, 11 Sim. 23.

(f) Sieveking v. Behrens, 2 M. & C. 581; Crawford v. Fisher, 1 Hare 436.

[1] Gibson v. Goldthwaite, 7 Ala. 281; Atkinson v. Manks, 1 Cowen 691; Shaw v. Coster, 8 Paige Ch. 339. See also, Marvin v. Elwood, 11 Paige Ch. 365. An objection to the form of the affidavit should not be made at the time of the motion, but on demurrer: Hamilton v. Marks, 5 De G. & Sm. 638.

27

the Court will adjudicate on their ultimate paym
between the co-defendants.$(g)^1$

There is also another class of cases, somewhat ε
to those of interpleader, originating in the provisi
53 Geo. 3, c. 169, by which the responsibility o
owners for any damage done without their fault
other vessel or her cargo, is limited to the value o
[*207]   *ship, and the freight she is earning at th
of the accident.   By the provisions of thε
if several persons suffer such damage, and the value
ship and freight is not sufficient to pay them all, ε
the owners may file a bill in equity against the clai
to ascertain such value, and to obtain a rateable diε
tion thereof, annexing to the bill an affidavit that t]
no collusion, that all claimants are made parties, th
value does not exceed an amount specified in the affi
and that the claims exceed such value.   And on su
and affidavit being filed, and payment made into Co
the specified amount, he may obtain an injunction a
proceedings at law.(h)

The injunction against an act commenced or threa
by which an equity would be infringed, like that a
suing in the Courts of law, is often used as an au$\mathfrak{x}$
process in respect of ordinary equities; $e. g.$, where a t
is enjoined from committing a breach of trust, a cove$\mathfrak{l}$

(g) Cowtan $v.$ Williams, 9 Ves. 107; Campbell $v.$ Solomans, 1
462; Jones $v.$ Gilham, Coop. 49; Fenn $v.$ Edmonds, 5 Hare 514.

(h) 53 Geo. 3, c. 159; Walker $v.$ Fletcher, 12 Sim. 420; 1 Ph. 1]
Act Cong. 1851, Ch. xliii., § 4; 9 Stat. at L. 635.]

---

¹ The stakeholder is entitled to costs out of the fund : Canfield
gan, 1 Hopkins 224; Aymer $v.$ Gault, 2 Paige Ch. 284.   The c
to be paid, in the first instance, out of the fund, but eventually
losing party: Thomson $v.$ Ebbets, 1 Hopkins 272; Farley $v.$ Bl
Foster 354.

from infringing his covenant,[1] or a fraudulent holder of a
negotiable security from indorsing it to a stranger.   But
there is one class of cases in which the necessity for in-

---

[1] With regard to injunctions to restrain a breach of covenant, it may not
be out of place to state, that the rule frequently referred to, based upon
Kemble v. Kean, 6 Sim. 333, and Kimberly v. Jennings, Id. 340, that
equity will not restrain by injunction in cases of contract, where it cannot
enforce specific performance, has been modified to a very considerable
degree in England, by the recent case of Lumley v. Wagner, 1 De G.,
M. & G. 604 ; affirming s. c. 5 De G. & Sm. 485.   See also, Great Northern
R. R. Co. v. Manchester R. R. Co., 5 De G. & Sm. 138 ; Gelston v. Sigmund,
27 Md. 334.   In the former case it was laid down, that where a contract
contains covenants to do certain acts, and also to abstain from doing certain
acts, the Court has jurisdiction to restrain the breach of the negative covenants, though it has no power to compel specific performance of the affirmative covenants ; as in the case of an agreement by a musician to sing
at a particular theatre, and not to sing at any other, in which case an
injunction may be granted against the breach of the latter portion of the
agreement.   (Kemble v. Kean, overruled.)   But in such cases the Court
will decline to interfere when its jurisdiction cannot be beneficially exercised, or where its exercise would work injustice, as where the consideration for the negative covenant of the one party, is the affirmative covenant
of the other, which latter the Court cannot specifically enforce : Lumley v.
Wagner, supra ; Stocker v. Wedderburne, 26 L. J. Ch. 703. See also, De Mattos
v. Gibson, 4 De G. & J. 276 ; Peto v. R. R. Co., 1 Hem. & M. 468, ante 81.

In Hamblin v. Dinneford, 2 Edw. Ch. 529, however, the case of Kemble
v. Kean was followed, and the Court refused to enjoin an actor, who had
contracted to perform at the complainant's theatre and no other, from performing at another theatre in violation of his agreement.   Equity will not
indirectly by injunction compel the specific performance of a contract for
personal services : De Poe v. Sohlke, 7 Rob. (N. Y.) 280.

An injunction may be granted against a distinct breach of covenant,
though no damage be shown, or even, indeed, if such be shown to be positively harmless, or perhaps beneficial : Steward v. Winters, 4 Sandf. Ch.
587 ; Dickenson v. Grand Junction Canal Co., 15 Beav. 260.   A Court has
jurisdiction to restrain by injunction acts which the defendant is bound
by duty or contract to abstain from : Dietrichsen v. Cabburn, 2 Phillips
52 ; Beckwith v. Howard, 6 R. I. 1.   But not where there is a complete
remedy at law : Pusey v. Wright, 31 Penn. St. 387 ; Gallagher v. Fayette
Co. R. R., 38 Id. 102.   Covenants not to do a particular act can be enforced
by injunction, although accompanied by a clause providing for stipulated
damages : Gillis v. Hall, 2 Brewst. (Pa.) 342.

junctive relief constitutes *per se* an independent equity; viz., that of torts as a class of civil wrongs distinct from cases of trust, of contract, and of fraud.

The principle of injunctive relief against a tort is, that whenever damage is caused or threatened to property, admitted or legally adjudged to be the plaintiff's, by an act of the defendant, admitted or legally adjudged to be a civil wrong, and such damage is not adequately remediable at law, the inadequacy of the remedy at law is a sufficient equity, and will warrant an injunction against the commission or continuance of the wrong.[1] And though damages cannot be given in equity for the plaintiff's loss, yet if the defendant has made a profit, he will be decreed to account.[2]

The equity is not confined in principle to any particular acts, but those in respect of which it is most commonly *enforced, are five in number; viz., waste, [*208] destructive trespass, nuisance, infringement of patent right, and infringement of copyright. And, therefore, the first point which requires notice is the nature of these wrongs, and the remedy given at law to the party injured.

Waste is substantial damage to the reversion, done by one having an estate of freehold or 'for years, during the continuance of the estate. The principal acts of waste are cutting timber, opening new mines, converting arable land into pasture, or pasture into arable, and removing articles affixed to the freehold.[3] With

---

[1] See, in Pennsylvania, Denny *v.* Branson, 29 Penn. St. 382.

[2] See Duvall *v.* Waters, 1 Bland 576.

[3] Everything is waste which occasions a permanent injury to the inheritance, but the situation of this country requires an application of the rule different from that which might be proper in England: Williams on Real

respect, however, to waste of this latter kind, there is a special exception, in favor of a tenant who has put up

Prop. 23, note; Hill on Trustees 590, 4th Am. ed.; Drown v. Smith, 52 Maine 143; Keeler v. Eastman, 11 Verm. 293. Where a tenant for life cuts down more timber than is necessary for the enjoyment of his estate, and has injured the remainder, he is guilty of waste, and will be restrained from a continuance. See Johnson v. Johnson, 2 Hill Ch. 277; Livingston v. Reynolds, 26 Wend. 115; Smith v. Poyas, 2 Dessaus. 65. Not so, if it does not produce a lasting injury to the inheritance: Shine v. Wilcox, 1 Dev. & Batt. Eq. 631. Or if the clearing is not unreasonable, according to the usage of the country: Crawley v. Timberlake, 2 Ired. Eq. 460. And, although it amounts to a considerable change of woodland into arable: Alexander v. Fisher, 7 Ala. 514. Firewood for the houses of the tenant and servants may be taken: Gardiner v. Dering, 1 Paige 573; and see McCullough v. Irvine, 13 Penn. St. 438; Morehouse v. Cotheal, 2 Zabriskie 521.

Where a farm is occupied and used for mining purposes, any proper use of it in mining operations is not waste: Capner v. Flemington Mining Co., 2 Green Ch. 467; Findlay v. Smith, 6 Munf. 134; Crouch v. Puryear, 1 Rand. 258. Working a gold mine so as to produce irreparable damage may be restrained: McBrayer v. Hardin, 7 Ired. Eq. 1; and so of opening a new mine of any kind: Owings v. Emery, 1 Gill 260. A tenant for life has no right to take clay or wood from the premises for the manufacture of bricks, and such acts are waste: Livingston v. Reynolds, 2 Hill 157. An injunction will issue to prevent the commission of waste by one who has but a limited interest in or possession of the property, when the acts about to be done will work a lasting injury to the inheritance: Jones v. Whitehead, 1 Parsons's Sel. Eq. Cas. 304. See Denny v. Branson, 29 Penn. St. 382.

An injunction will be granted to prevent the lessee from making material alterations in a dwelling-house, by changing it into a warehouse or store, which would produce permanent injury to the building: Douglass v. Wiggins, 1 Johns. Ch. 435; or which he is bound not to make by covenant running with the premises, or by agreement of which he has notice: Parker v. Nightingale, 6 Allen 344; Piggott v. Stratton, 1 De G., F. & J. 33. See McCullough v. Irvine, 13 Penn. St. 438. But it is not waste by the tenant to make erections upon the demised premises, which may be removed, leaving the property in the state in which it was at the commencement of the tenancy, and the materials of which, if left on the premises, would more than compensate the lessor for the expense of their removal: Winship v. Pitts, 3 Paige Ch. 259.

An injunction may be granted, not only against a tenant who commits

ornamental fixtures, or erections for the purposes of his
trade. (*i*)¹

The essential character of waste is, that the party committing it is in rightful possession. And, therefore, the
remedy at law is by trespass on the case for the injury
done to the reversion. Under the old law, the place
wasted might also have been recovered in the now abolished action of waste. There are, however, no means at
law of stopping the waste itself whilst the tenancy continues; and for that purpose, if the reversioner's title be
admitted or proved at law, the prohibitive jurisdiction of
equity has been always exercised.²

(*i*) 2 Steph. Bl. 261; 3 Id. 593 ; 1 Cruise, tit. iii., c. 2.

---

waste, but also against one who colludes with him : Rodgers *v.* Rodgers,
11 Barb. S. C. 595; see Earl Talbot *v.* Scott, 27 L. J. Ch. 273 ; 4 K. & J.
96. A Court of equity, however, has no means of interfering in the case
of permissive waste by a tenant for life : Powys *v.* Blagrave, 1 Kay 495.

¹ In a case of equitable waste, the court may, in addition to injunction,
direct an account, and satisfaction : Rodgers *v.* Rodgers, 11 Barb. S. C.
395.

² In order to the injunction, there must be no dispute as to the title.
See Zinc Co. *v.* Franklenite Co., 2 Beas. 350; Bogey *v.* Shute, 4 Jones Eq.
174. In Nevitt *v.* Gillespie, 1 How. (Miss.) 108, it was held that an injunction should never be granted to stay waste, where it appears that the
defendant to the bill is in possession, claiming and holding adversely.
See also Storm *v.* Mann, 4 Johns. Ch. 21; and Davenport *v.* Davenport, 7
Hare 217; United States *v.* Parrott, 1 McAll. Ch. 271. But pending an
action to try the title to land, an injunction will sometimes be granted to
restrain the defendant from waste, especially where it appears that he will
not be able to respond in damages, in case of a recovery by the plaintiff :
Kinsler *v.* Clarke, 2 Hill Ch. 617 ; Shubrick *v.* Guerard, 2 Dessaus. 616 ;
Duvall *v.* Waters, 1 Bland. 569. For other instances of the granting of
the writ pending a suit at law, see Hawley *v.* Clowes, 2 Johns. Ch. 122 ;
Camp *v.* Bates, 11 Conn. 51. In Earl Talbot *v.* Hope Scott, 4 K. & J. 96,
there will be found a full discussion of the English cases on this subject.
The court will not appoint a receiver of the rents, when a plaintiff claims
only on *a legal title which is denied by a defendant in possession ;* nor, as
a general rule will waste, under such circumstances, be restrained, unless

In addition to waste, strictly so called, and cognisable as such in the Courts of law, there is also a kind of waste cognisable in equity alone, and called equitable waste, where the owner of a particular estate, made unimpeachable of waste at law, is committing waste *mala fide*, or in a manner not contemplated by the donor.

Where an estate for life is comprised among the limitations of a settlement it is not unusual to make it " unimpeachable of waste," and the object of this is that the owner may be enabled to cut timber, open mines, and avail himself of other modes of profit which are derived out *of the *corpus* of the estate, and not from the annual produce, and are therefore, in law, con- [*209]

---

it is of a very malicious and destructive character. See the notes to Garth *v.* Cotton, 1 Lead. Cas. Eq. 567.

The injunction will not be granted, where there is an adequate remedy at law: Cutting *v.* Carter, 4 Hen. & Munf. 424; Poindexter *v.* Henderson, Walker 176. Yet in some cases it may be granted, notwithstanding a statute giving a remedy at law: Harris *v.* Thomas, 1 Hen. & Munf. 18. See, however, Brown's Appeal, 66 Penn. St. 155.

The writ will not be granted, unless the injury will probably be irreparable, or not capable of compensation by damages in a suit at law: Atkins *v.* Chilson, 7 Metc. 398 ; Poindexter *v.* Henderson, supra ; Spooner *v.* McConnell, 1 McLean 338 ; Works *v.* Junet. R. R., 5 Id. 425 ; Clark's Appeal, 62 Penn. St. 447.

The court will not, unless under very special circumstances, grant an injunction to prevent the removal of timber already cut, but only to prevent *future* waste: Watson *v.* Hunter, 5 Johns. Ch. 169. Yet a threat to commit waste is sufficient: Loudon *v.* Warfield, 5 J. J. Marsh. 196 ; Livingston *v.* Reynolds, 26 Wend. 115, 123.

The appropriate remedy for a mortgagee against a mortgagor in possession, who is impairing the security by committing waste, is by bill in Chancery for an injunction: Cooper *v.* Davis, 15 Conn. 556 ; Brady *v.* Waldron, 2 Johns. Ch. 148 ; Salmon *v.* Clagett, 3 Bland 125 ; Capner *v.* Flemington Mining Co., 2 Green Ch. 467. See on the general subject, Sarles *v.* Sarles, 3 Sandf. Ch. 601: Brashear *v.* Macey, 3 J. J. Marsh. 93 ; Herr *v.* Bierbower, 3 Md. Ch. 456 ; Carlisle *v.* Stephenson, Id. 499; Burden *v.* Stein, 27 Ala. 104 ; Bunker *v.* Locke, 15 Wis. 635 ; Nelson *v.* Pinegar, 30 Ill. 481.

sidered waste. So long as he is *bonâ fide* acting on this authority, and endeavoring to make a profit by its exercise, the Court of Chancery cannot interfere with his discretion. If, however, he is not acting *bonâ fide*, but is maliciously attempting to destroy the property, his conduct is a fraud on the power, and will be restrained by injunction.(*k*) The same restriction will be imposed if he is attempting to cut down timber which was planted for ornament, or which is evidently unfit to be cut, and which was, therefore, not meant to be included in his authority.(*l*)

Destructive trespass is damage, amounting to the destruction of the estate, done by a stranger, whose possession or entry is unlawful. In this case the remedy at law, if the trespass amount to an actual ouster, is by ejectment to recover the land; or if it fall short of ouster, by trespass *quare clausum fregit*, to recover satisfaction in damages for the wrong.

The equitable jurisdiction over this class of injuries, where the damage is by a mere wrongdoer without color of right, and not by a person having a limited interest, was at first doubtful. The point arose in a case before Lord Thurlow, where a man having a parcel of land on lease began to get coal there, and then proceeded to get more coal out of the adjoining parcel, which belonged to a different person. It was held that the former act, being waste, would be restrained; but that the latter, being a bare trespass, could not be interfered with by the Court of Chancery. It was said, however, by Lord Eldon, that

(*k*) Vane *v.* Barnard, 2 Vern. 738.

(*l*) Marquis of Downshire *v.* Sandys, 6 Ves. 107; Day *v.* Merry 16 Id. 375; Wellesley *v.* Wellesley, 6 Sim. 497; Brydges *v.* Stephens, 6 Mad. 279; Leeds *v.* Amherst, 2 Ph. 117; [Clement *v.* Wheeler, 5 Foster 361.]

· Lord Thurlow had afterwards changed his mind; and it is now settled that an injunction will lie for protection of a title, admitted or proved at law, whenever the act complained of is not a mere ouster or temporary trespass, but is attended *with permanent results, destroy- [*210] ing or materially altering the estate; as, for example, if a man be pulling down his neighbor's house, felling his timber, working his quarries, or the like.[1] If it

---

[1] See Davis v. Reed, 14 Md. 152; Merced Mining Co. v. Fremont, 7 Cal. 321. There must be something particular in the case, so as to bring the injunction under the head of quieting possession, or preventing irreparable injury : Livingston v. Livingston, 6 Johns. Ch. 497. The injury threatened or begun must not be susceptible of compensation in damages at law : Smith v. Pettingill, 15 Verm. 82; Stevens v. Beekman, 1 Johns. Ch. 318; Hart v. The Mayor of Albany, 9 Wend. 571; Jerome v. Ross, 7 Johns. Ch. 315; Scudder v. The Trenton Delaware Falls Co., Saxton 694; Bethune v. Wilkins, 8 Ga. 118; George's Creek Coal Co. v. Detmold, 1 Md. Ch. 371; Catching v. Terrell, 10 Ga. 576; Justices of Pike Co. v. Griffin & West Point Plank Road Co., 11 Id. 246; Shipley v. Ritter, 7 Md. 408; Mulvaney v. Kennedy, 2³ Penn. St. 44; Cherry v. Stem, 11 Md. 1; Earl Talbot v. Scott, 4 K. & J. 96; De Veney v. Gallagher, 20 N. J. Eq. 33. That the trespasser is insolvent is not by itself sufficient: Turnpike, &c., v. Burnet, 2 Carter 536. See, however, Hawley v. Clowes, 2 Johns. Ch. 122; Hart v. Mayor of Albany, 3 Paige 214; Winnipiseogee Lake Co. v. Worster, 9 Foster 449; James v. Dixon, 20 Mo. 79. The facts which show the irreparable nature of the injury must be set out in the bill, a mere general averment is not enough: Chesapeake & Ohio Co. v. Young, 3 Md. 480. Where the alleged trespass was committed more than a year before the application for an injunction, and there was no allegation of a threatened renewal of the trespass, held, the injunction could not be granted: Southard v. Morris Canal, Saxton 518. See also, Duval v. Waters, 1 Bland 569; Amelung v. Seekamp, 9 Gill & J. 468.

Equity will not restrain, by injunction, the working of a mine, or other trespass, until the title, if disputed, has been settled at law, except in extreme cases : Irvin v. Davidson, 3 Ired. Eq. 311; Lining v. Geddes, 1 McCord Ch. 304; Powers v. Heery, Charl. R. M. 523; West v. Walker, 2 Green Ch. 279. See Elliott v. North Eastern R. R. Co., 10 H. L. Cas. 333.

So on a question between two bodies, each claiming to be the trustees of a religious society, and a refusal by one to permit the other to use the bury-

be a mere ouster or temporary trespass, the recovery of
the land by an action of ejectment, or of pecuniary damages by an action of trespass, are sufficient remedies, and
an injunction will not lie.(m)[1]

Nuisances are of two kinds; Public and Private. A
public nuisance consists in the doing anything to the an-
noyance of all the King's subjects, e. g., the obstructing a
highway or public river, or the carrying on of offensive or.
dangerous trades, or the neglecting to do anything which
the common good requires, e. g., the omission to repair a
highway or public bridge. A private nuisance is an act
done unaccompanied by an act of trespass, which causes
a substantial prejudice of the hereditaments, corporeal or
incorporeal, of another; e. g., diverting a watercourse, so
as to interrupt the right of another person, that it should
run undisturbed to his meadow or mill; obstructing ancient windows, so that the owner cannot enjoy the light
so freely as before ; or disturbing a franchise, by setting
up, without license from the Crown, a fair, market,
or ferry, so near to a more ancient one, as to diminish
its custom. And a public nuisance may also be a private
one, if there be special damage to an individual; as
where, by reason of an obstruction to the highway, he
meets with an accident, or is compelled to travel by a

(m) Thomas v. Oakley, 18 Ves. 184; Goulson v. White, 3 Atk. 21 ; Ridgway v. Roberts, 4 Hare 106, 116.

ing ground, a forcible entry by the latter for that purpose on several occasions, was held not to be ground for injunction : Miller v. English, 2 Halst.
Ch. 304.

[1] See a full discussion of this subject in Earl Talbot v. Scott, 27 L. J.
Ch. 273 ; 4 K. & J. 96.

An injunction may be granted in favor of a married woman to restrain
a party from cutting down trees under an authority from her husband as
trustee of her separate estate: Thomas v. James, 32 Ala. 726; and see
Smith v. The Bank, 4 Jon. Eq. 303.

longer or more difficult way; or where an offensive or dangerous trade is carried on or so near his premises as to do them special prejudice.(n)[1]

The remedy at law for nuisance is by indictment in respect of public nuisances, and by action in respect of private nuisances or of the private injuries resulting from public ones. And the party aggrieved may also abate or remove the nuisance by his own act, so as he commit no riot in doing it, nor occasion, in the case of *a private nuisance, any unnecessary damage.(o) [*211]

The remedies, however, at law can at the utmost only abate or afford compensation for, an existing nuisance, but are ineffectual to restrain or prevent such as are threatened or in progress; and for this reason there is a jurisdiction in equity to enjoin, if the fact of nuisance be admitted or established at law, whenever the nature of the injury is such that it cannot be adequately compensated by damages, or will occasion a constantly recurring grievance.(p)[2]

(n) 2 Steph. Bl. 10–16; 3 Id. 499–502; 4 Id. 295. [See Hepburn v. Lordan, 2 Hem. & M. 345.]

ˈ (o) 3 Steph. Bl. 361, 503.

(p) Mitf. 144; Attorney-General v. Nichol, 16 Ves. 338; Attorney-General v. Cleaver, 18 Id. 211; Attorney-General v. Forbes, 2 M. & C. 123; Crowder v. Tinkler, 19 Ves. 617; Earl of Ripon v. Hobart, 3 M. & K. 169; Hudson v. Maddison, 12 Sim. 416; Blakemore v. Glamorgan Canal, 1 M. & K. 154, 181.

---

[1] The student will find an excellent summary of the rules regulating the relief afforded by equity in cases of private nuisances, in the opinion of Mr. Justice Swayne in Parker v. Winnipiseogee Lake Cotton & Woollen Co., 2 Black 545. The term "public nuisance" applies only to something occasioned by acts done in violation of law: Hinchman v. Patterson, &c., R. R., 2 Green (N. J.) 75. A work which is authorized by law cannot be a nuisance: Ibid.

[2] In England by stat. 21 & 22 Vict. c. 27, damages may be assessed in cases of nuisance in such manner as the court may think proper. The

Injunctions for the restraint of trespass and nuisance'
are often issued against railway companies, and other

---

right of the complainant ought generally to be admitted or established at
law, before the granting of an injunction: White v. Booth, 7 Verm. 131;
Shields v. Arndt, 3 Green Ch. 234; Caldwell v. Knott, 10 Yerg. 209; Hart
v. Mayor of Albany, 3 Paige 213; Reid v. Gifford, 6 Johns. Ch. 19; Biddle v. Ash, 2 Ashmead 211; Porter v. Witham, 17 Maine 292; Arnold v.
Klepper, 24 Mo. 273; Coe v. The Winnipiseogee Manuf. Co., 37 N. H.
254; Rhea v. Forsyth, 37 Penn. St. 507; Frizzle v. Patrick, 6 Jones' Eq.
(N. C.) 354; Eastman v. Amoskeag Co., 47 N. H. 71. But when the right
has once been established, an alteration in the nuisance complained of
will not render a fresh action necessary. Chancery can judge whether
the nuisance has been increased or diminished: Gas Company v. Broadbent, 7 H. L. Cas. 600. And in Holsman v. Boiling Spring Co., 1 McCart.
335, a perpetual injunction was granted without any trial at law. Yet he
will not be first required to establish his right at law, unless it is doubtful
and in dispute: White v. Forbes, Walk. Ch. 112; Duncan v. Hayes, 22 N. J.
Eq. 25. In the case of great injury to a prescriptive right, the injunction
may be granted without first sending the plaintiff to law to establish his
title: Gardner v. Newburgh, 2 Johns. Ch. 162; Robeson v. Pittenger, 1
Green Ch. 57. The fact that the complainant has not established his title
at law is no ground for *demurrer* to the bill: Soltau v. De Held, 2 Sim.
N. S. 133. It is sufficient if damages have been once recovered at law, no
matter how small an extent, if the legal title has been clearly established:
Rochdale Canal Co. v. King, 2 Sim. N. S. 78. The Court, however, is not
always bound by the mere fact that damages, even if substantial, have
been recovered, and the legal title is established. It will consider whether
the complainant be entitled to the equitable relief; and moreover will not
grant it where an injunction could not restore the party to his former
position. Thus an injunction will be refused against a manufacturer for
polluting the water of a stream by dye-stuffs, &c., in favor of another
manufacturer, when the real damage to the stream and to its use by the
latter, is produced by causes over which the Court has no control, as by
the growth of population on the banks of the stream, so that the granting
the injunction would not be of real benefit; though the complainant has
recovered damages at law: Wood v. Sutcliffe, 2 Sim. N. S. 163.

The fact of nuisance ought to be clear, for the Court will not interfere
by injunction to restrain an erection not in itself noxious, though it may,
according to circumstances, prove so, until a trial of the right at law;
except where an action could not be framed to meet the question, when
the Court may direct an issue. But if the injury apprehended is great,
and the danger imminent, an injunction will not be refused on the ground

bodies of a similar nature, where the act complained of is done in alleged pursuance of a Parliamentary power. In

---

that there is a possibility that the injury anticipated may not result from the erection complained of: Mohawk Bridge Co. *v.* Utica and Schenectady Railroad Co., 6 Paige Ch. 554. On the other hand, the mere *tendency* of an erection to produce the result complained of, has never been considered sufficient to warrant the restraining process of a Court of equity : Gwin *v.* Melmoth, 1 Freem. Ch. 505 ; Ellison *v.* The Commissioners, 5 Jones Eq. 57 ; Ross *v.* Butler, 4 Green (N. J.) 294.

To authorize the Court's interference by injunction, there should appear imminent danger of great and irreparable damage, and not of that for which an action at law would furnish full indemnity : Wingfield *v.* Crenshaw, 4 Hen. & Munf. 474; City of Rochester *v.* Curtiss, 1 Clarke 336 ; Bradsher *v.* Lea, 3 Ired. Eq. 301 ; Spooner *v.* McConnell, 1 McLean 337 ; Webb *v.* Portland Manuf. Co., 3 Sumner 189 ; Croton Turnpike *v.* Ryder, 1 Johns. Ch. 611 ; Wall *v.* Cloud, 3 Humph. 181 ; Vaughn *v.* Law, 1 Id. 123 ; Bemis *v.* Upham, 13 Pick. 169 ; Vanwinkle *v.* Curtis, 2 Green Ch. 422 ; Smith *v.* Cummings, 2 Pars. Eq. 92 ; Wallace *v.* McVey, 6 Ind. 540 ; Clark *v.* White, 2 Swan 540 ; Webber *v.* Gage, 39 N. H. 186 ; Thebaut *v.* Canova, 11 Florida 143 ; Richards's App., 57 Penn. St. 105.

An injunction may be granted to restrain a public nuisance at the suit of a private person, who suffers a special injury thereby : Corning *v.* Lowerre, 6 Johns. Ch. 439 ; Milhau *v.* Sharp, 27 N. Y. 611. See as to this point, Rosser *v.* Randolph, 7 Porter 238 ; Mayor of Georgetown *v.* Alexandria Canal Co., 12 Peters 91 ; Bigelow *v.* Hartford Bridge Co., 14 Conn. 565 ; Attorney-General *v.* Utica Ins. Co., 2 Johns. Ch. 379, 380 ; Delaware and Maryland R. R. Co. *v.* Stump, 8 Gill & J. 479 ; Biddle *v.* Ash, 2 Ashmead 211 ; Rowe *v.* Granite Bridge Co., 21 Pick. 344 ; Soltau *v.* De Held, 2 Sim. N. S. 133 ; Smith *v.* Lockwood, 13 Barb. S. C. 209 ; Peck *v.* Elder, 3 Sandf. S. C. 126 ; Frink *v.* Lawrence, 20 Conn. 117 ; Hartshorn *v.* South Reading, 3 Allen 501; Allen *v.* The Board of Freeholders, 2 Beas. 74 ; Zabriskie *v.* The Jersey City R. R. Co., 2 Id. 314; Att.-Gen. *v.* Sheffield Gas Consumers Co., 3 De G., M. & G. 304; Smith *v.* Bangs, 15 Ill. 399 ; Hamilton *v.* Whetridge, 11 Md. 128 ; Mississippi & Missouri R. R. Co. *v.* Ward, 2 Black 485. See Roosevelt *v.* Draper, 23 N. Y. 323 ; Buck Mt. Co. *v.* Lehigh Co., 50 Penn. St. 99 ; People *v.* Third Avenue R. R. Co., 45 Barb. (N. Y.) 63 ; Columbus *v.* Jaques, 30 Ga. 506 ; City of Phila. *v.* Collins, 68 Penn. St. 106.

In Catlin *v.* Valentine, 9 Paige 575, and Brady *v.* Weeks, 3 Barb. S. C. 157, it was held that to constitute a nuisance, it is not necessary that a trade or business complained of, should endanger the health of the neighborhood. It is sufficient if it produces that which is offensive to the senses,

these cases, if the company are acting *bonâ fide* w
their authority, there is no equity to interfere, alth
the Court may think that the power was unadvisedly
ferred, or that the company are not exercising a
discretion. If, however, their conduct is not *bonâ*
there is jurisdiction to enjoin ; as, for example, if ha
authority to take land for a particular purpose, they
tend to take it for that purpose, but want it for
other.(*q*) And if they are acting beyond their autho
there is the same jurisdiction as in ordinary cases
for example, if having authority to do a certain tl
upon certain terms, and in a certain manner, they ar
tempting to do some other thing, or to do it on some c

(*q*) Webb *v.* Manchester & Leeds Railway, 4 M. & C. 116 ; [see C
v. Pittsburgh & Conn. R. R., 24 Penn. St. 139.]

---

and which renders the enjoyment of life and property uncomfo1
See also, Peck *v.* Elder, 3 Sandf. S. C. 126 ; Howard *v.* Lee, Id. 181 ;
v. Cummings, 2 Pars. Eq. 92 ; Cleveland *v.* Citizens' Gas Light Co.,
J. Eq. 201. The rule on this subject was laid down with great cle
in Walker *v.* Selfe, 4 De G. & Sm. 315 ; and see Wolcott *v.* Melick, 3
204 ; Crump *v.* Lambert, L. R. 3 Eq. 409.

See also generally as to injunction to restrain nuisance, Soltau
Held, 2 Sim. N. S. 133 ; Bostock *v.* North Stafford R. R. Co., 5 De G.
584 ; Auburn Co. *v.* Douglass, 12 Barb. 553 ; Harrell *v.* Ellsworth, 1
576 ; Gilbert *v.* Mickle, 4 Sandf. Ch. 357 ; Cunningham *v.* The Ro
R. Co., 27 Ga. 499 ; Wood *v.* Sutcliffe, 2 Sim. (N. S.) 163 ; Hole *v.* B
4 C. B. N. S. (93 E. C. L. R.) 334 ; St. Helen's Smelting Co. *v.* Ti
11 H. L. Cas. 642 ; Crossley *v.* Lightowler, L. R. 2 Ch. Ap. 478 ; Att.
v. Bradford Canal, L. R. 2 Eq. 71 ; Robson *v.* Whittingham, L. R.
Ap. 442.

A state may obtain an injunction in the Supreme Court of the
States to restrain a company incorporated by another state from bri
a navigable river, within the limits of the latter state, which runs th
the former, so as to obstruct the navigation : Pennsylvania *v.* Wh
Bridge Co., 13 How. U. S. 518 ; see Mississippi & Missouri R. R.
Ward, 2 Black 485.

A corporation owning a toll bridge may maintain a bill in equity
a nuisance, to restrain a city from unlawfully laying it out as a high
Central Bridge *v.* Lowell, 4 Gray (Mass.) 474. See also Green *v.* O
17 Ill. 249 ; Walker *v.* Shepardson, 2 Wis. 384.

terms, or in some other manner. Such, for instance, would be the case, if their authority were to cross a man's land coming to it in a particular direction, and they claimed to alter the direction, and, nevertheless to take the land. And perhaps the same result would follow, if they were to make an important alteration in the *termini* of their line, or if the sum which *they had power to raise were palpably insufficient to complete their works; for, in both these cases, they would not be using their powers for the purpose for which they were conferred.(*r*) [*212]

The same principles are equally applicable to all other persons who have been authorized by the Legislature to do specified acts, which without such authority they would be incompetent to do. So long as they are acting within their prescribed limits, the Court of Chancery has no control; but if they exceed those limits, if they are assuming to do that which the Legislature has not said they may do, then, in so far as the excess is concerned, they have no authority; and, if their acts be of a nature to warrant an injunction, it will be granted against them.(*s*)

Patent right is the exclusive liberty conferred by letters-patent from the Crown on an inventor, or his alienee, of making articles according to his invention.(*t*)[1]

(*r*) Agar *v.* Regent's Canal Company, Coop. 77; Salmon *v.* Randall, 3 M. & C. 439; Blakemore *v.* Glamorgan Canal, 1 M. & K. 154; Lee *v.* Milner, 2 Y. & C. 611.

(*s*) Attorney-General *v.* Forkes, 2 M. & C. 123; Frevin *v.* Lewis, 4 M. & C. 249; Birley *v.* Chorlton, 3 Beav. 499; Dawson *v.* Paver, 5 Hare 415; [Winch *v.* Birkenhead, &c., R. R. Co., 16 Jur. 1035; Beman *v.* Rufford, 1 Sim. N. S. 550.]

(*t*) 2 Steph. Bl. 86: 5 Jarm. Byth., tit. Patent; Godson on Patent and Copyright, bk. ii.

---

[1] The American cases and statutes on this subject will be found collected in Curtis on Patents.

The patent, of itself, and in the absence of treaty stipulation, creates no

The powers of the Crown to grant such letters-patent, both as regards the parties to whom they may be granted, and the periods to which they must be limited, are regulated by statute;(u) and the qualities essential to sustain a patent are foreign to this Treatise. But the patent right of an inventor is personal property, and assignable by writing under hand and seal; and if it be infringed, the inventor or his alienee has a remedy at law by an action for damages. And in consideration of the inefficiency of that remedy, he may also, if the validity of his patent and the fact of infringement are admitted or established at law, have a remedy in equity by injunction and account. The right originates in the character of the patent as private *property, and not in the mere exclusive privilege. And therefore, a patent to keep a theatre, which is a mere privilege granted to the party, will give no right to enjoin other parties, who are infringing the law by keeping theatres without license.(v)

[*213]

The validity of the patent itself, and the fact of infringement, are matters which, if doubtful, must be determined at law.

Copyright is the exclusive liberty conferred, either by common law or by statute, on an author or his

(u) 21 Ja. 1, c 3, s. 1; 5 & 6 Wm. 4, c. 83; 2 & 3 Vict. c. 67.
(v) Calcraft v. West, 2 Jones & Lat. 128.

---

exclusive right in a foreign country: yet it has been recently held that an English patent would be enforced by injunction against a foreigner bringing a patented article into England, to the same extent as against English subjects: Caldwell v. Van Vlissengen, 16 Jur. 115; 9 Hare 429. This was the case of a Dutch steam vessel, using an English patented screw propeller without license, coming into England. The same point arose in Brown v. Duchosne, 2 Curtis C. C. 371, affirmed 19 Howard 183, and received a contrary decision under the Patent Laws of the United States.

alienee, of printing or otherwise multiplying copies of his work(w)[1]

The property of an author in his work before publica tion is absolute and perpetual;(x)[2] nor is it lost by send- ing the manuscript as a letter to a correspondent;(y)[3] nor by reading it orally as a public lecture. But where the lecture has not been first committed to writing, it has been doubted whether there can be property in the senti- ments and language; although a pupil may be restrained, on the basis of an implied contract, from publishing it for profit.(z)

Lectures are now protected by 5 & 6 Wm. 4, c. 65, giving to the author and his alienee the sole right of first printing and publishing, and, after publication, the ordi nary term of copyright. But this statute gives no exclu- sive right of oral delivery; it requires that notice of the

---

(w) 2 Steph. Bl. 94; 5 Jarm. Byth., tit. Copyright; Godson on Patent and Copyright, bk. iii.

(x) Miller $v.$ Taylor, 4 Burr. 2303; Donaldson $v.$ Becket, 2 B. P. C. 129; Tonson $v.$ Walker, 3 Sw. 672, 680.

(y) Gee $v.$ Pritchard, 2 Sw. 402; Palin $v.$ Gathercole, 1 Coll. 565.

(z) Abernethy $v.$ Hutchinson, 3 Law J. O. S. Ch. 209; Miller $v.$ Tay- lor, 4 Burr. 2303; Donaldson $v.$ Beckett, 2 B. P. C. 129.

---

[1] See Curtis on Copyright.

The power given to Congress to pass copyright laws extends only to such as " promote the progress of science and useful arts:" Martinette $v.$ Ma- guire, 1 Abb. (U. S.) 356.

[2] This subject will be found very fully considered in the case of Prince Albert $v.$ Strange, 2 De G. & Sm. 652; aff'd 1 Macn. & G. 25. There a workman, who had been intrusted with some etchings on copper, for the purpose of working off the engravings, which were not intended for publi- cation, was restrained from publishing a descriptive catalogue of the etch- ings and compelled to destroy certain impressions which he had taken for himself.

[3] See Woolsey $v.$ Judd, 4 Duer 379; Wetmore $v.$ Scovill, 3 Edw. Ch 515; Hoyt $v.$ Mackenzie, 3 Barb. Ch. 320; Bartlett $v.$ Crittenden, 5 McLean 32.

28

intended lectures shall have been given to two justices
before delivery; it does not extend to lectures delivered
in a university, public school, or college, or under any
gift, endowment, or foundation; and it contains a saving
of the common law in respect to all lectures which it does
not include.

[*214]   *The property of an author in his work after
publication is also regulated by statute ;(a) and
of late years the rights of authors have been considerably
amended, improved, and extended.(b)   Protection is not
only afforded to printed books, but also to engravings,(c)
sculptures,(d) dramatic compositions,(e) and registered
designs,(f) and also under certain limitations, to works
published abroad.(g)

In addition to the copyright conferred by statute, there
is also a prerogative copyright in the Crown of printing
at the royal press all Acts of Parliament, Proclamations,
and Orders in Council, and Liturgies, and Service-books
of the Church, and the authorized translation of the Bible.
The same privileges extend to the grantees of the Crown,
viz., to the Queen's printer, and to the Universities of
Oxford and Cambridge.   A similar privilege of printing
almanacs was formerly claimed, but was adjudged to be
void.   The Universities of Oxford and Cambridge, and
the Colleges of Eton, Westminster, and Winchester also
enjoy, by Act of Parliament, a perpetual copyright in
all books given or bequeathed to them, so long as such

(a) 54 Ga. 3, c. 156.
(b) 5 & 6 Vict. c. 45.
(c) 8 Geo. 2, c. 13 ; 7 Geo. 3, c. 38, 57 ; 6 & 7 Wm. 4, c. 59.
(d) 38 Geo. 3, c. 71 ; 54 Geo. 3, c. 56.
(e) 3 & 4 Wm. 4, c. 15; 5 & 6 Vict. c. 45.
(f) 5 & 6 Vict. c. 100 ; 6 & 7 Vict. c. 65.
(g) 7 & 8 Vict. c. 12.

books shall be published at their own presses and for their own benefit.(*h*)

The question as to what will constitute an infringement of copyright is sometimes attended with considerable doubt. It is declared by the late statute that it is equally piracy, either to print the copyright work within the British dominions for sale or exportation, or to import for sale or hire copies so printed, or copies printed abroad. or to sell or publish, or expose or possess for sale or hire, copies known to have been so printed or imported, or to cause any such *printing, importation, sale, [*215] publication, or exposure for sale or hire.(*i*)[1] But in the case of partial imitation or copying, and of piracy from compilations of pre-existing matter, it is sometimes difficult to determine whether the latter work is, or is not, a copy of its predecessor. The doctrine on these points appears to be : 1. That in regard to original works, it is no piracy to extract passages for the purpose of *bonâ fide* criticism or quotation, or for that of combining them with new matter so as to constitute a new original work, or even to make a fair abridgment of the work himself. But it is otherwise if the criticism, &c., be merely colorable.(*k*) 2. That in regard to compilations of pre-existing matter, such as maps and road-books, the true subject of copyright is the selection and

(*h*) 2 Steph. Bl. p. 98.
(*i*) 5 & 6 Vict. c. 45, ss. 15 and 17.
(*k*) Campbell *v.* Scott, 11 Sim. 31 ; Bell *v.* Whitehead, 8 L. J. Ch. 141 ; Wilkins *v.* Aikin, 17 Ves. 427 ; Saunders *v.* Smith, 3 Myl. & Cr· 711 ; Bramwell *v.* Halcomb, Id. 737 ; D'Almaine *v.* Boosey, 1 Y. & C. 288.

[1] After much discussion in England, it has been recently held in the House of Lords, that a foreigner, not residing there, can have no copyright under the statutes, nor does his English assignee before publication stand in any better position : Jefferyes *v.* Purday, L. J. Exch. 350.

arrangement. The materials for the work are open to all; any man may avail himself of them, and may compile a work, which will probably be similar to the first, and may perhaps be identical with it. But he must create the work by his own labor and skill, and must not copy the result of his predecessor's. And if, on comparison of the two works, he appears to have done so, his own work will be declared a piracy.(*l*)[1]

The copyright of an author, like the patent right of an inventor, is personal property, and transferable by assignment.[2] Such assignment may be made, in cases falling within the Copyright Amendment Act, by entry in the registry at Stationers' Hall; but if not so made, it must be by an instrument in writing, though not necessarily under seal.(*m*)[3]

(*l*) Longman *v.* Winchester, 16 Ves. 269; Lewis *v.* Fullarton, 2 Beav. 6.
(*m*) Power *v.* Walker, 3 M. & S. 7; Rundell *v.* Murray, Jac. 311, 315; 5 & 6 Vict. c. 45, s. 13.

---

[1] A work in part a *bonâ fide* abridgment of another, and in part mere compilation without original labor, may be restrained as to the latter: Story's Ex'rs. *v.* Holcombe, 4 McLean 306. A translation is not a violation of a copyright: Stowe *v.* Thomas, 2 Am. Law Reg. 210; 2 Wall. Jr. 547. See Kelly *v.* Morris, L. R. 1 Eq. 697; Hotten *v.* Arthur, 1 Hem. & M. 603. It is no infringement of a copyright to represent a play dramatized from a novel written by another author, but it is an infringement to print and publish a play so constructed: Tinsley *v.* Lacy, 1 Hem. & M. 747. See also, Reade *v.* Lacy, 1 Johns. & Hem. 524.

[2] But property in a work, is distinct from property in the means of its reproduction. Thus a sale on execution of the engraved plate of a map does not pass the copyright in the map, and the purchaser may be restrained by injunction from the multiplication of copies thereof: Stephens *v.* Cady, 14 How. U. S. 528.

[3] Where an author is employed by the proprietor of a periodical, to write for it articles for a certain compensation, but without any mention of the copyright, it is to be inferred that the copyright was to belong to such proprietor: Sweet *v.* Benning, 16 Com. Bench 459.

So it was held to be piracy, for a proprietor of an analytical digest of

If the right be infringed, the remedy of the author or his alience at law is by an action of trespass on the case for damages ; and by an action of detinue or trover for the *pirated copies, or their value.(*n*) He may also sue in equity for an injunction and account [*216] if the right and infringement are admitted or established at law. It will be observed, that the jurisdiction to enjoin in equity is expressly for the protection of copyright as property, and not for the prevention of improper publications. There is, therefore, no jurisdiction to enjoin against a wicked or libellous work, merely on the ground of its mischievous character ; and, on the other hand, if a work alleged to be copyright be tainted by immorality, libel, or fraud, it is not acknowledged as property at law; and in that case, or even if it be of a doubtful tendency, the Court of Chancery will not interfere.(*o*)

The existence of the right itself, and the fact of the infringement, are matters which, if doubtful, must be determined at law.

The jurisdiction to restrain infringement of patent and copyright is based on the exclusive property which the complainant has. There is also a jurisdiction, of a not very dissimilar character, to enjoin against the use of a secret of trade which has been fraudulently obtained, and to enjoin against damaging the plaintiff's business by representing a spurious article to be his.

If a person, having made a discovery, does not choose

(*n*) 5 & 6 Vict. c. 45, s. 23.

(*o*) Gee *v.* Pritchard, 2 Sw. 402; Du Bost *v.* Beresford, 2 Camp. N. P. C. 511; Wright *v.* Tallis, 1 Man., Gr. & Sc. 893; 4 Law J. C. P. 283; Southey *v.* Sherwood, 2 Meriv. 438; Lawrence *v.* Smith, Jac. 471.

---

equity, common law, and other cases, to copy *verbatim* the head notes of cases from reports, the copyright of which was in the plaintiffs, without their consent: Id.

to protect it by a patent, and thus to limit his enjoyment
of it within the statutory period, he has no exclusive
right to the invention; and if another person can discover
the secret, there is no equity to restrain him from using
it. It must, however, be discovered by legitimate means;
and therefore if the party acquiring it has resorted to a
breach of trust or a fraud, he will be restrained from availing himself of what he has learnt.(*p*)

[*217]   *If, again, a person has adopted a particular
device, with a view to denoting a particular article or manufacture as his own, he does not necessarily
acquire a copyright in such device, and cannot restrain
on that ground, its user by another man. But he is
entitled, on the ordinary principles of law, to insist that
no other person shall injure his business by representing
a spurious article to be his, although the genuine article
may be one to which he has no exclusive right. And
therefore, if such a representation be made, either by
direct misstatement or by imitation of his device, he may
recover damages at law for the injury to his business, and
pari ratione may have an injunction in equity.(*q*)[1]

(*p*) Williams *v.* Williams, 3 Meriv. 157; Youatt *v.* Winyard, 1 J. & W.
394; [Morrison *v.* Moat, 9 Hare 266; affirmed 16 Jur. 321; 21 L. J. Ch.
248.]

(*q*) Sykes *v.* Sykes, 3 B. & C. 541; Bloefield *v.* Payne, 4 B. & Ad. 410;
Crutwell *v.* Lye, 17 Ves. 336; Motley *v.* Downman, 3 M. & C. 1; Millington *v.* Fox, 3 M. & C. 338; Perry *v.* Truefitt, 6 Beav. 66; Croft *v.* Day, 7
Id. 84; Spottiswoode *v.* Clark, 2 Ph. 154; Clark *v.* Freeman, 17 L. J. Ch.
142; 11 Beav. 112.

[1] On the subject of injunction to restrain the use of trade-marks, the following recent decisions may be referred to: Coffeen *v.* Brunton, 4 McLean
516; Rogers *v.* Nowill, 3 De G., M. & G. 614; 17 Jur. 109; Burgess *v.*
Burgess, 3 De G., M. & G. 896; 17 Jur. 292; Flavell *v.* Harrison, 10 Hare
467; 17 Jur. 368; Edleston *v.* Vick, 18 Id. 7; Holloway *v.* Holloway, 13
Beav. 209; Taylor *v.* Taylor, 2 Eq. 290; 23 L. J. Ch. 255; Woollam *v.*

Having now examined the chief objects of the injunctive equity, we must, in conclusion, notice the chief incidents of the equity itself. These incidents are three in number. The equity attaches only on an admitted or legally adjudged right in the plaintiff, admitted or legally adjudged to be infringed by the defendant; it prohibits continuance as well as commission of a wrong; and it extends to an account of the defendant's profit.

First, it attaches only on an admitted or legally adjudged right in the plaintiff, admitted or legally adjudged to be infringed by the defendant. The existence of the right, and the fact of its infringement, must be tried, if disputed, in a Court of law. And therefore, if the plaintiff resorts to equity in the first instance, he should forthwith move for an interlocutory injunction to protect his alleged right until decree, and thus give an opportunity of directing a trial at law, so that when the cause comes on

---

Ratcliffe, 1 Hem. & M. 259; Batty v. Hill, Id. 264; Braham v. Bustard, Id. 447; Farina v. Silverlock, 4 K. & J. 650; Welch v. Knott, Id. 747; Edelsten v. Edelsten, 1 De G., J. & Sm. 185; Leather Cloth Co. v. The American Leather Cloth Co., 11 H. L. Cas. 523; Boardman v. Meriden Brittania Co., 35 Conn. 402; McCartney v. Garnhart, 45 Mo. 593; Palmer v. Harris, 60 Penn. St. 156; Filley v. Fassett, 44 Mo. 168; Rowley v. Houghton, 2 Brewst. (Pa.) 303; Dixon Crucible Co. v. Guggenheim, Id. 321; Bradley v. Norton, 33 Conn. 157; Smith v. Woodruff, 48 Barb. (N. Y.) 438; Congress Spring Co. v. High Rock Spring Co., 45 N. Y. 291; Canal Co. v. Clark, 13 Wall. (U. S.) 311; Howard v. Henriques, 3 Sandf. S. C. 725, in which the name of a hotel was treated in the same light as a trade-mark. See also Coffeen v. Brunto, 5 McLean 256; Ames v. King, 2 Gray (Mass.) 379; Samuel v. Berger, 24 Barb. (N. Y.) 163. No property can be acquired in marks or devices which indicate merely the nature, kind or quality of articles, and not the goods or property, or particular place of business: Stokes v. Landgraff, 17 Barb. (N. Y.) 608; Sherwood v. Andrews, 5 Am. Law Reg. (N. S.) 588; Ferguson v. Davol Mills, 2 Brewst. (Pa.) 314.

In case of patent medicines, &c., see Heath v. Wright, 3 Wall. Jr. 141; but see Smith v. Woodruff, supra.

for hearing it may be ready for immediate adjudication. When the motion for an interlocutory injunction is made, the Court, having regard to the extent of *primâ facie* title [*218] shown, the probability *of mischief to the property, and the balance of inconvenience on either side, will either grant the injunction, accompanied by a provision for putting the legal right into an immediate course of trial; or will send the parties to law, directing the defendant to keep an account; or will merely retain the bill, with liberty for the plaintiff to proceed at law.(r)

Secondly, the equity extends to prohibit continuance, as well as commission. Where an interlocutory injunction is granted against the continuance of a nuisance, the abatement of which cannot be ordered on motion in direct terms, it becomes what is called a mandatory injunction, *i. e.*, an injunction so framed that it restrains the defendant from permitting his previous act to operate, and, therefore, virtually compels him to undo it. Injunctions of this class have been granted in various instances; *e. g.*, against continuing the removal of the stop-gate of a canal; against permitting stables to remain which had been improperly built in an ornamental garden; and against permitting a railway tunnel to continue, which had the effect of completely destroying the road.(s)[1]

(r) Hill v. Thompson, 3 Meriv. 622; Kay v. Marshall, 1 M. & C. 373; Ansdell v. Ansdell, 4 M. & C. 449; Bacon v. Jones, 1 Beav. 382; 4 M. & C. 433; Collard v. Allison, 4 M. & C. 487; Hilton v. Granville, Cr. & P. 283; Harman v. Jones, Id. 299; Stevens v. Keating, 2 Ph. 333.

(s) Robinson v. Byron, 1 B. C. C. 558; Lane v. Newdigate, 10 Ves. 194; Blakemore v. Glamorgan Canal, 1 M. & K. 154, 183; Rankin v. Huskisson, 4 Sim. 13; Spencer v. Birmingham Railway, 8 Id. 193, 198; 1 Railway Ca. 159; Attorney-General v. Manchester and Leeds Railway, Id. 436; Hooper v. Brodrick, 11 Sim. 48; Earl of Mexborough v. Bower, 7 Beav. 127, 133; Great North of England Junction Railway v. Clarence Railway, 1 Coll. 507.

---

[1] But such an injunction is not granted, except in rare and peculiar

Thirdly, the equity extends to an account of the defendant's profits. The grant of an injunction necessarily presupposes that the plaintiff has sustained a loss by the defendant's act, and that the defendant has probably derived a profit, which may or may not, according to circumstances, be coextensive with the plaintiff's loss. The strict right of the plaintiff, so far as the past wrong is concerned, is to *a recompense in damages for his own loss, irrespectively of the defendant's profit.

[*219]

A claim, however, for such damages would involve the necessity of proceeding in two Courts at once, in equity for an injunction, and at law for damages; and therefore the Court of Chancery, having jurisdiction for the purpose of the injunction, will prevent that circuity and expense; and although it cannot decree damages for the plaintiff's loss, will substitute an account of the defendant's profits.(*t*)   The equity for the account is strictly an incident to the injunction, and therefore, if an injunction is refused, an account cannot be given; but the plaintiff must resort to a Court of law.(*u*)

(*t*) Crossley *v.* Derby Gas Gompany, 3 Myl. & Cr. 428; Bacon *v.* Spottiswoode, 1 Beav. 382, 385; Colburn *v.* Simms, 2 Hare 543, 560.

(*u*) Baily *v.* Taylor, 1 R. & M. 73.

cases : Bradbury *v.* Manchester, &c., R. R. Co., 5 De G. & Sm. 624; Washington University *v.* Green, 1 Md. Ch. 97. On final hearing, however, the decree may, of course, require the abatement of a nuisance : Lamborn *v.* The Covington Co., 2 Md. Ch. 409. In Durell *v.* Pritchard, 13 W. R. 981, the Master of the Rolls, relying on Deere *v.* Guest, 1 Myl. & Cr. 516, laid down the rule that a mandatory injunction would not be granted where the act complained of was completed before the filing of the hill. But this ruling was reversed by the Court of Appeals : L. R. 1 Ch. Ap. 249.

*BOOK III.

OF THE JURISDICTION OF THE COURTS OF EQUITY IN C
IN WHICH THE COURTS OF ORDINARY JURISDICTION
NOT ADMINISTER A RIGHT.

CHAPTER I.

OF ACCOUNT.

THE equities under the second head of our divi
viz., where the Courts of ordinary jurisdiction ca
administer a right, are those for investigation of acco
for severance of co-tenancies, and other analogous r
for winding up partnerships and administering testa
tary assets, for adjusting liabilities under a common ch
and for protection of the persons and estates of in
and lunatics.[1]

---

[1] In matters of account, Courts of equity possess a concurrent ju
tion in most, if not in all cases, with courts of law: see Mitchell *v.*
facturing Co., 2 Story 648; Post *v.* Kimberly, 9 Johns. 470; Jo
Bullock, 2 Dev. Ch. 368; Nelson *v.* Harris, 1 Yerg. 360; Bruce *v.* B
1 J. J. Marsh. 80; Wilson *v.* Mallett, 4 Sandf. S. C. 112; Seym
Long Dock Co., 20 N. J. Eq. 396; in all cases in which an action
count would be a proper remedy at law: Fowle *v.* Lawrason, 5 Peter
and in some cases in which assumpsit, or other action at law, wou
Hickman *v.* Stout, 2 Leigh 6; Hay *v.* Marshall, 3 Humph. 623. E
ally where equity has acquired cognisance of a suit for the purpose

One important instance of the jurisdiction over accounts occurs in the case of trustee and *cestui que trust*, where the *cestui que trust* demands an account of moneys received under the trust. The equity of this particular case is included under the general equity for enforcement of trusts,(a) but a corresponding one exists as against an agent or steward, or a person employed in any similar character, who is bound by his office to render regular accounts. If this duty is performed, and the accounts are regularly rendered, his employer can recover the balance at law on the evidence of the accounts themselves, and a suit *in equity is not required. If it is neglected, he can recover damages at law for the neglect,(b) and will also have an equity, arising out [*221]

(a) Supra, Trusts. (b) Smith Merc. Law 96.

---

covery: Handley v. Fitzhugh, 1 A. K. Marshall 24; see, also, Pearl v. Nashville, 10 Yerg. 179. And a bill for discovery and account will sometimes lie upon a purely legal claim: see Pleasants v. Glasscock, 1 Sm. & Mar. Ch. 23. So, also, where a multiplicity of suits will be avoided, or the remedy at law is not full and adequate, or fraud, accident, or mistake is connected with the subject: McLaren v. Steapp, 1 Kelly 376; Cummins v. White, 4 Blackf. 356. And between partners and the assignees of their copartners: Pendleton v. Wambersie, 4 Cranch 73; Collins v. Dickinson, 1 Haywood 240. In Ludlow v. Simond, 2 C. C. E. 1, it was held that chancery has jurisdiction of all matters of account, though no discovery is required, and a bill for account against principal and surety may be sustained, although the account has been stated as to the principal; see, in addition, on this subject, Randolph v. Kinney, 3 Rand. 394; Ship v. Jameson, 6 Litt. 190; Sturtevant v. Goode, 5 Leigh 83; McKim v. Odom, 3 Fairfield 94; Reybold v. Dodd, 1 Harring. 402; Dunwidie v. Kerley, 6 J. J. Marsh. 501. It seems that mere delay of a defendant at law coming into equity in matters of account, forms no reason for refusing relief where the nature of the account in such that a court of law cannot deal with it: Southeast R. R. Co. v. Brogden, 3 Macn. & G. 8. See the remarks in this case as to the difference between the cases where equity assumes original jurisdiction in a matter of account, and those where it withdraws a matter of account from a court of law.

of the agent's failure in duty, to have the accounts ta
in the Court of Chancery, where the evidence may
supplied by discovery on oath.(c)   It will be obser
that this equity does not originate in the mere war
discovery, which will not, as we have already seen,
fer a jurisdiction for relief;(d) but in the additiona
gredient that such want has been caused by the def
ant's fault. It is otherwise in the case of a mere stran
He is compellable to answer on oath to the best of
information, but there is no original duty to posses
formation, and, therefore, no equity on the ground of
absence, to withdraw his rights from the Court of (
nary jurisdiction.

It obviously follows from this doctrine, that a bill
an account by an agent against his principal will
generally lie; for it is the agent's duty, and not the p
cipal's, to keep the account.[1] But this rule is subje
a special exception in favor of a steward, the natui
whose employment is such, that money is often pa
confidence without vouchers, embracing a variety o
counts with the tenants, so that it would be impossib
do him justice without an account in equity.(e)[2]

(c) Mackenzie v. Johnston, 4 Mad. 373 ; Massey v. Banner, 4 Id.
Anon. 2 Hare 289, n.; Bowles v. Orr, 1 Y. & C. 464.

(d) Supra, Discovery.

(e) Dinwiddie v. Bailey, 6 Ves. 136; Allison v. Herring, 9 Sim. 5£

[1] An account will lie on behalf of an agent against his principal
has received certain sums upon which the former was entitled to a
mission : Smith v. Leveaux, 1 Hem. & M. 123.

[2] An agent or factor may file a bill against his principal for an acc
Ludlow v. Simond, 2 C. C. E. 1, 39, 53 ; Kerr v. Steamboat Co., 1 C
2d part, 189. See Wilson v. Mallet, 4 Sandf. S. C. 112. But in ge
a bill will not lie by a factor against his principal, for discovery a
count, merely in aid of a suit at law ; nor will a bill for relief, wher

In taking the account against an agent, he will be charged with the moneys of his principal which he has actually received, and, if a special case of negligence be

---

bill is dependent on the right to discovery: Wilson v. Mallett, 4 Sandf. S. C. 112. See Dunning v. Stearns, 9 Barb. S. C. 903.

In the recent case of Pennell v. Deffell, 4 De G., M. & G. 372, the following rules were established as governing the practice of the Court of Chancery in the analogous case of trusts. Where a trustee pays trust money into a bank to his credit, the account being a simple account with himself, not marked or distinguished in any other manner, the debt thus constituted from the bank to him, belongs, so long as it remains due, specifically to the trust, as between the *cestui que trust* on the one side, and the trustee or his representatives on the other ; and this state of things is not varied by the circumstance of the bank holding also for the trustee, or owing to him money in every sense his own. And where the account consists of a series of items in respect of moneys paid in, and drawn out by general checks by the trustee, the mode of ascertaining what part of the balance is trust property, and what part of the trustee's own money is to hold (as in Clayton's Case, 1 Mer. 572), that each check drawn out by the trustee is to be applied in payment of the earlier items of the opposite side of the account, *i. e.*, in diminution of the trust fund *pro tanto*, if those items arise from trust moneys paid into the account, or of the customer's own moneys *pro tanto*, if they arise from moneys paid in on his own private personal account. See also, Frith v. Cartland, 34 L. J. Ch. 301.

Where an agent is intrusted with money to be disbursed, his principal may sustain a bill against him for an account of his agency, and in some instances although no discovery is sought. See Kerr v. Steamboat Co., ut supra ; Hale v. Hale, 4 Humph. 183 ; Halstead v. Rabb, 8 Porter 63 ; Mason v. Man, 3 Dessaus. 116. If an agent does not, within a reasonable time, apply money to the purposes for which it is sent to him, he will be chargeable with interest: Harrisson v. Long, 4 Dessaus. 110. See on the subject of interest, Hill on Trustees, 4th Am. ed. 568, and notes. But an agent having no authority to invest, is not liable for interest, until a demand made by his principal: Rowland v. Martindale, Bailey Eq. 226 ; Lever v. Lever, 2 Hill Ch. 158. So an agent will be charged with moneys which, but for his default, he might have received: Short v. Skipwith, 1 Brock. 103 ; see also, Prentice v. Buxton, 3 B. Monr. 35. If an agent mixes the property of his principal with his own, he will be obliged to show clearly which part of the property belongs to himself; and so far as he is unable to do this, it is treated as the property of his principal: Kelly v. Greenleaf, 3 Story 105, 106.

made out, with such moneys also as but for his wilful default he might have received. In the absence of a special case an inquiry as to wilful default will not be granted against a trustee or agent, although it is otherwise in the case of a mortgagee.(*f*) But if the agent neglect to account, he will be charged with interest on [*222] moneys improperly *retained; if he has unduly used his principal's moneys for the purpose of profit to himself, he will be charged with the profits which he has made; and if, by his neglect, his own property has become mixed up with that of his principal, so that they cannot readily be distinguished, the burden of separation will be thrown on him, and the whole will be treated as belonging to the principal, until the agent shows clearly what portion is his own.(*g*)

Another instance of the jurisdiction is in the case of mutual accounts, where items exist on both sides, not constituting mere matters of set off, but forming a connected transaction, and requiring an account to ascertain the balance, more complicated than can practically be taken at law.(*h*) The mere fact that such complicated mutual accounts exist is a sufficient equity to sustain a bill. But it is otherwise with respect to mere matters of set-off; for right of set-off can be effectually tried at law, and can only be transferred to Chancery by some special equity.[1]

(*f*) Pelham *v.* Hilder, 1 N. C. C. 3.

(*g*) Pearse *v.* Green, 1 J. & W. 135 ; Lupton *v.* White, 15 Ves. 432, 441.

(*h*) Kennington *v.* Houghton, 2 N. C. C. 620 ; Ranger *v.* Great Western Railway, 1 Railway Ca. 1 ; Taff Vale Company *v.* Nixon, 1 House of Lords Reports 111.

[1] In matters of account which are mutual and complicated, Courts of equity have complete jurisdiction : Hay *v.* Marshall, 3 Humph. 623 ; The Governor *v.* McEwen, 5 Id. 241 ; Power *v.* Reeder, 9 Dana 9 ; Hickman *v.*

The right of set-off is that right which exists between two persons, each of whom, under an independent contract, owes an ascertained amount to the other, to set-off their respective debts by way of mutual[1] deduction, so that in any action brought for the larger debt, the residue only after such deduction shall be recovered. At the common law there was no such right; but if the party

---

Stout, 2 Leigh 6; Long v. Majestre, 1 John. Ch. 305; Hunter's Ex'rs. v. Spotswood, 1 Wash. 146; Cummins v. White, 4 Blackf. 356; Dubourg de St. Colombe's Heirs v. The United States, 7 Peters 625; Kirkman v. Vanlier, 7 Ala. 217. So also in cases of insolvency: Blake v. Langdon, 19 Verm. 485; White v. Wiggins, 32 Ala. 424; though the rule on this subject is not, perhaps, satisfactorily settled: see American note to Rose v. Hart, 2 Smith's Lead. Cas. 374 (6th Am. ed.), where the cases are discussed. But to sustain a bill for an account, there must be *mutual* demands, not merely payments by way of set-off,—there must be a series of transactions on one side, and of payments on the other. See Bowen v. Johnson, 12 Ga. 9; Porter v. Spencer, 2 John. Ch. 169; Pearl v. Nashville, 10 Yerg. 179; McLin v. McNamara, 2 Dev. & Bat. Eq. 83; Wilson v. Mallett, 4 Sandf. Ch. 112; Pointup v. Mitchell, 17 Ga. 558; Phillips v Phillips, 9 Hare 471; Cullum v. Bloodgood, 15 Ala. 34; Padwick v. Hurst, 18 Jur. 763; 18 Beav. 575; see Burlingame v. Hobbs, 12 Gray (Mass.) 367, and Haywood v. Hutchins, 65 N. C. 574. Complication of accounts, where the receipts are all on one side, if it ever alone constitutes sufficient ground for intervention of a Court of equity, must show a very strong case of entanglement: Padwick v. Stanley, 9 Hare 627; see Taylor v. Tompkins, 2 Heisk. (Tenn.) 89.

Upon demurrer, a general allegation that accounts are of a complicated nature is not sufficient, unless supported by specific allegation of facts showing their complex character: Padwick v. Hurst, 18 Jur. 763; 18 Beav. 575. See Lesley v. Rosson, 39 Mississippi 368.

A bill will not lie, even against an agent, as to a single transaction not tainted by fraud, and where there is a legal remedy: Navulshaw v. Brownrigg, 1 Sim. N. S. 573; 2 De G., M. & G. 441; Barry v. Stevens, 31 Beav. 258.

[1] The consideration that the nominal parties to a contract are not strictly mutual is no objection to set-off, if the real parties on whom the burden is ultimately to fall are the same: Smith v. Wainwright, 24 Verm. 97. One demanding account must himself account: Fairchild v. Valentine, 7 Rob. (N. Y.) 564.

suing for a debt were himself indebted to the defendant, he would nevertheless recover in his action, and the defendant would be driven to a cross action for his own claim.   To obviate this inconvenience it was enacted " that where there are mutual debts between the plaintiff and defendant, or (if either party sue or be sued as executor or administrator), where, there are mutual debts between the testator or intestate and either party, one may be set against the other."(i)   And *in the event [*223] of bankruptcy a still wider remedy is given, and the right of set-off is extended to cases where mutual credit has been given by the bankrupt and any other person, although strictly speaking, there may not be actual debts on both sides.(k)   If the cross demands are of legal cognisance, the right of set-off is also legal ; and unless one of the demands involves an equitable element, their existence creates no equity for resorting to the Chancery.   If one or both be matter of equitable cognisance, as, for example, if there be a question of trust or fraud, the set-off may be enforced in the Court of Chancery.(l)[1] There are also some cases occasionally spoken of as depending on an equitable set-off, but which would be more correctly termed retainers in the nature of set-off.   As, for example, where a legatee is indebted to his testator's estate, and the executor, instead of paying the legacy, is entitled to balance it against the debt.   In such a case as

(i) 2 Geo. 2, c. 22 ; 8 Geo. 2, c. 24.

(k) 6 Geo. 4, c. 16, s. 50; Smith's Merc. Law 608; Gibson v. Bell, 1 B. N. C. 748.

(l) Vulliamy v. Noble, 3 Meriv. 593, 618 ; Rawson v. Samuel, Cr. & P. 161 ; Dodd v. Lydall, 1 Hare 333.

---

[1] The equitable right of set-off was said, in Freeman v. Lomas, 9 Hare 116, not to be derived from or dependent upon any statutory right, but founded on the Roman law.   See Meriwethen v. Bird, 9 Ga. 594.

this there are not, in strictness, any mutual demands to which the term set-off can be applied; and the right of the executor is rather a right to retain the debt out of the legacy as a fund in hand, than to set it off against the amount. (*m*)

The right of account is essentially different from this. It is not a right to amalgamate independent cross demands, for the purpose of enabling one action or suit to suffice; but it assumes that the several demands have no independent existence, but have been so connected by the original contract or course of dealing, that the only thing which either party can claim is the ultimate balance. The only right, therefore, is that of taking the account; and the forms of procedure, both at law and in equity, are framed for that purpose. An account of this kind is not confined to mere receipts and payments of money, although *it ordinarily occurs in that form. But it is applicable to any dealings which have been [*224] treated as equivalent to receipts and payments. An account, for instance, will lie in respect of reciprocal deliveries of goods, provided that in the course of dealing between the parties, such deliveries have been treated as items in an account, and not as creating mere cross demands ; or it will lie in respect of a claim for work done and partially paid for by advances from time to time, so that a balance only of the price is ultimately due. (*n*)[1]

(*m*) Cherry *v.* Boulbee, 4 M. & C. 442; Courtney *v.* Williams, 3 Hare 539 ; Jones *v.* Mossop, 8 Id. 568 ; McMahon *v.* Burchell, 2 Ph. 127 ; [see Keim *v.* Muhlenberg, 7 Watts 79.]

(*n*) Wellings *v.* Cooper, cited 6 Ves. 139, and 9 Id. 473 ; O'Conner *v.* Spaight, Sch. & L. 305 ; Cottam *v.* Partridge, 4 Man. & Gr. 271; Ranger *v.* Great Western Railway, 1 Railw. Ca. 1.

[1] Where a contractor to build a house has performed his part of the

29

The remedy at law on a mutual account is in ordinary cases by assumpsit for the balance, and, in the case of account between merchants, by the action of account.

The inefficiency of the common action of assumpsit is too evident to require explanation; for in such an action the jury must investigate the account, item by item, so as to return the verdict for the ultimate balance. And the practical impossibility of their so doing generally results in a reference to arbitration.

The action of account is less unsuitable than that of assumpsit, but it is far from meeting the exigencies of the case. In this action the investigation of items is not intrusted to a jury at nisi prius, but is referred, under a judgment "that the defendant do account," to auditors assigned by the Court. After the auditors have made their report, a final judgment is given that the "plaintiff do recover against the defendant" so much as the latter is found to be in arrear. The tribunal, however, to which the account is subjected, though superior to a jury, is attended with much delay and expense. The auditors have no power of deciding on controverted items, so as to carry on a continuous inquiry, but must from time to time, as any question occurs, interrupt their proceedings by referring it to the Court or to the jury, as a distinct [*225] issue of *law or fact, and must resume them again when a decision has been obtained. And even in respect to items not controverted they had not, until 3 & 4 Anne, c. 16, any general power to give effect to their inquiry by administering an oath, or by examining the

---

contract, on account of which partial payments have been made, that is *not* such matter of account as will sustain a bill to recover the balance: Smith *v.* Marks, 2 Rand. 449; City Council *v.* Page, Speer's Ch. 159; *sed vide* Sturtevant *v.* Goode, 5 Leigh 83.

parties. There is also an inconvenience in taking the account at law, by reason of the incapacity of the legal procedure to operate beyond the immediate plaintiff and defendant, or to include rights or claims which may be collaterally involved.(o)

In addition to these objections, the remedy itself is of very partial operation. It was originally applicable to one class of accounts only, those of bailiffs, receivers, and guardians in socage, in respect of the trust or privity of contract existing therein, and, by special extension of the benefit of trade, to accounts between merchants. And so strictly was this privity of contract construed, that the action did not lie by or against executors or administrators. The statute of 13 Edw. 1, st. 1, c. 23, gave it to the executors of a merchant; the statute of 25 Edw. 3, st. 5, c. 5, gave it to the executors of executors; and the statute of 31 Edw. 3, st. 1, c. 11, to administrators. But it was not until the statute of 3 & 4 Anne, c. 15, that it lay against executors and administrators of guardians, bailiffs, and receivers.

The difficulties thus existing at law are effectually obviated by the procedure in equity. A foundation is first laid for all necessary inquiries by the discovery elicited from the defendant's answer. The account is then referred to a Master, who is armed with power not only to examine witnesses, but also to examine the parties themselves, and to compel production of books and documents. It is not liable to interruption by controversies on particular items, but is carried on continuously to its close. The Master reports the final result to the Court. The report may be *excepted to on any points which [*226] are thought objectionable, and all such points

(o) 1 Selw. N. P. 1 ; 1 Story on Equity, s. 446–449.

are simultaneously re-examined by the Court, and either at once determined, or, if necessary referred back to him for view. As soon as the report is finally settled and confirmed, a decree is made for payment of the ultimate balance. If the interests of other persons are entangled in the account, the Court may require that they be made parties to the suit, or may direct, if necessary, the institution of cross suits; and thus having all their interests before it, may so modify a single decree, as effectually to embrace and arrange them all.

If the account is one which might be readily investigated by a jury, the necessity for equitable interference does not exist, and it seems that in that case no equity will arise. And if the facts stated in the bill show no practical difficulty in proceeding at law, a mere indefinite allegation that the accounts are intricate will not prevent a demurrer.(p)[1]

The same result will follow if the parties themselves have disposed of the matter and have struck a balance of their account, for there is then no difficulty in proceeding at law.

If, therefore, there has been an account stated between the parties, it may be pleaded as a bar to both discovery and relief, or may be set up by answer as a bar to relief. And in this latter case, if the allegation in the answer be not proved, it is usual on referring the account to the Master, to direct that, if he find any account stated, he

---

(p) Foley v. Hill, 1 Ph. 399; Darthez v. Clemens, 6 Beav. 165; [Padwick v. Hurst, 18 Jurist 763; 18 Beav. 575; see ante, note, p. 222.]

---

[1] Courts of equity will not entertain jurisdiction when there is no difficulty in the remedy at law: Monk v. Harper, 3 Ed. Ch. 109; Turnpike Co. v. Allen, 2 Dev. & Batt. Eq. 115; Butler v. Ardis, 2 McCord Ch. 60, 71; Gloninger v. Hazard, 42 Penn. St. 401.

shall not disturb it.(q)[1] The account, however, may be
opened on the ground of fraud, or if important errors are
specified and proved ; but a general allegation that it is
erroneous will not suffice.(r) In some cases where a
*stated account is impeached, the Court will re- [*227]
open the whole and direct it to be taken *de novo*.
In others, when it is faulty in a less degree, it will allow
it to stand, with liberty to surcharge and falsify. This
leaves it in full force as a stated account, except so far as
it can be impugned by the opposing party. If he shows
the omission of a credit, that is a surcharge ; if he shows
the insertion of an improper charge, that is a falsification.(s)
The question of what will constitute a stated account is
in some measure dependent on the circumstances of the
case. The mere delivery of an account, without evidence
of contemporaneous or subsequent conduct, will not prove
it to be a stated account ; but an acceptance, implied from
circumstances, will suffice. Between merchants at home
an account which has been presented, and which has not
been objected to after the lapse of several posts, is treated
under ordinary circumstances as a stated account. Between merchants in different countries a similar rule prevails; and if an account is transmitted from one to another,
showing a balance due to himself, and the other keeps it
two years without objection, the rule is to consider it as
allowed.(t)[2]

(q) Seton on Decrees 47 ; Connop v. Hayward, 1 N. C. C.-35.

(r) Taylor v. Haylin, 2 B. C. C. 310; Johnson v. Curtis, 3 B. C. C. 266 ;
Mr. Belt's notes ; [Coleman v. Mellersh, 2 Macn. & Gord. 309.]

(s) Pit v. Cholmondeley, 2 Ves. 565 ; Seton on Decrees, 48 ; Millar v.
Craig, 6 Beav. 433.

(t) Irvine v. Young, 1 S. & S. 333 ; Willis v. Jernegan, 2 Atk. 251 ;

----

[1] An account stated may be set up by way of plea, as a bar to all discovery and relief: Weed v. Smull, 7 Paige 573 ; Bullock v. Boyd, 2 Ed.
Ch. 293 ; Deil's Ex'rs. v. Rogers, 4 Dessaus. 175.

[2] The Court may direct a stated account to be opened and taken *de novo*

It is also material to the equity for an account that it
be claimed within the proper time. Where the account is

Sherman v. Sherman, 2 Vern. 276; Tickel v. Short, 2 Ves. 239; 1 Dan.
C. P. 632.

---

upon a bill brought for the purpose, or where a sufficient foundation has
been laid in the answer; but only for fraud or errors specified, and which
are palpable or clearly proved: Slee v. Bloom, 20 Johns. 669; s. c. 5
Johns. Ch. 366; Lee's Admr. v. Reed, 4 Dana 112; Botifeur v. Weyman
et al., 1 McCord's Ch. 156; Barrow v. Rhinelander, 1 Johns. Ch. 550;
Johnson's Ex'rs. v. Ketchum, 3 Green Ch. 364; Bloodgood v. Zeily, 2 C. C.
E. 124; Gray v. Washington, Cooke 321; Roberts v. Tottan, 13 Ark. 609;
Lockwood v. Thorne, 1 Kern. (N. Y.) 170. And although in England the
Court has gone the length of holding, that where an account has been sur-
charged or falsified in one or more items, the complainants may then have
liberty before a master to surcharge and falsify it at large; yet in this
country, the Court will not allow the inquiry to be opened beyond the special matter charged; the account can only be corrected in the items which
the bill points out as erroneous or alleges should be supplied: Consequa v.
Fanning, 3 Johns. Ch. 587; Troup v. Haight, Hopk. 239; Chappedelaine
v. Dechenaux, 4 Cranch 306; Redman v. Green, 3 Ired. Eq. 54; Bullock v.
Boyd, 1 Hoff. Ch. 294; Nourse v. Prime, 7 Johns. Ch. 69; Phillips v.
Belden, 2 Ed. Ch. 1; Grover v. Hall, 3 Har. & J. 43; Freeland v. Cocke,
3 Munf. 352; Compton v. Greer, 2 Dev. Ch. 93; Miller v. Womack's
Adm'rs., Freeman's Miss. Ch. 486. Lilly v. Kroesen, 3 Md. Ch. 83; Williams v. Savage Manufact. Co., 1 Id. 306. In cases of gross fraud the
Court will direct the whole account to be opened and taken de novo: Bankhead v. Alloway, 6 Cold. (Tenn.) 56. Where an account stated is opened
a long time, as sixteen years, after it has been rendered, it will not be
opened generally. It will be opened as to fraud or mistakes charged in
the bill, and so far proved that the court is satisfied that they ought to be
corrected; and when some such errors are proved, then as to other errors
charged, which the court is satisfied ought to be made the subjects of further
examination. In restating a stated account between partners, thus opened,
which has been made up of separate adventures and transactions, undertaken under an agreement for the mutual rendering of annual accounts
of the whole business, the decree directed the account to be restated in the
form of a general account of the whole business: Ogden v. Astor, 4 Sandf.
S. C. 311.
   A suit to impeach an account ought to be brought within a reasonable
time, or, at farthest, within the statutory period for commencing an action
at law upon matters of account: Lupton v. Janey, 13 Peters 381. And
where the bar of the statute is inapplicable, as e. g., where the demand is

sought under a legal title, or under an equitable title of like nature with a legal one, that limit of time will be adopted in equity which is prescribed by the Statute of Limitations at law. When the bar of the statute is inapplicable, there may nevertheless be a bar in equity, originating in long acquiescence by the party, and in the cousequent presumption that he has either been satisfied *his demand, or that he intended to relinquish [*228] it.(u) And in a case where the account was carried back into remote transactions, of which accounts had been regularly kept by a deceased party at the time, it was ordered that they should be received as *primâ facie* evidence, so as to throw on the other side the *onus* of impeaching them.(v)[1]

(u) Smith v. Clay, 3 B. C. C. 639, n.; Stackhouse v. Barnston, 10 Ves. 453, 466; Bond v. Hopkins, 1 Sch. & L. 413, 428; Hovenden v. Lord Annesley, 2 Id. 607, 629; 3 & 4 Wm. 4, c. 27, s. 24–27.

(v) Chalmer v. Bradley, 1 J. & W. 51–65.

purely equitable, the court is loath to interfere after a considerable lapse of time; particularly after the death of parties whose transactions are involved in the inquiry: Baker v. Biddle, Baldwin C. C. R. 418; Ellison v. Moffat, 1 Johns. Ch. 46; Ray v. Bogart, 2 Johns. Cas. 432; Rayner v. Pearsall, 3 Johns. Ch. 578, 586; Mooers v. White, 6 Id. 360, 370; Bolling v. Bolling, 5 Munf. 334; Randolph v. Randolph, 2 Call 537; Dexter v. Arnold, 2 Sumner 108; Wilde v. Jenkins, 4 Paige 481; Dakin v. Demming, 6 Paige 95; Bloodgood v. Zeily, 2 C. C. E. 124; Gregory's Ex'r. v. Forrester, 1 McCord Ch. 318, 332; Ex'rs of Radcliffe v. Weightman, Id. 408; Hutchins v. Hope, 7 Gill 119; Chesson v. Chesson, 8 Ired Eq. 141.

Where there has been fraud, however, the court will open and examine accounts after any length of time, even though the person who committed the fraud be dead: Botifeur v. Weyman, 1 McCord Ch. 156. But it must be shown that the fraud was not, and could not with reasonable diligence be discovered, until within six years before the commencement of suit: Ogden v. Astor, 4 Sandf. S. C. 311. And so of fraud apparent on the face of the account, or which would be discovered with slight examination: Ibid.

[1] As to when an account ought to be claimed, and what constitutes a stated account, see Langdon v. Roane's Adm'r., 6 Ala. 518; Murray v. Tol-

[*229]   *CHAPTER II.

OF PARTITION——OF ASSIGNMENT OF DOWER——SUBTRACTION
OF TITHES——ASCERTAINMENT OF BOUNDARY——PAYMENT OF
RENTS.

THE equity for the severance of co-tenancy and other
analogous relief originates in the fact, that the co-tenants

---

land, 3 Johns. Ch. 575; Burden v. McElmoyle, 1 Bailey Eq. 375; Sherwood v. Sutton, 5 Mason 143; Freeland v. Heron et al., 7 Cranch 147;
Philips v. Belden, 2 Ed. Ch. 1. It is generally held now that an account
rendered, not objected to in a reasonable time, becomes an account stated:
Thompson v. Fisher, 13 Penn. St. 313; Porter v. Patterson, 15 Id. 236;
Beers v. Reynolds, 12 Barb. 288; Dows v. Durfee, 10 Id. 213; Coopwood
v. Bolton, 26 Miss. 212; Brown v. Van Dyke, 4 Halst. Ch. 795. In Ogden v. Astor, 4 Sandf. S. C. 311, it was held that an account by a surviving
partner, rendered to the representatives of his deceased copartner, one of
whom was a female unacquainted with accounts, and the other a nephew
of the accountant, who had entire confidence in him, which account was
without vouchers, and showed the results merely, and not the details of
various transactions and adventures, would become a stated account after
long acquiescence without objection on these grounds, no fraud or collusion
being charged. But it is otherwise where the party receiving the account
is so deficient in mental capacity as to be unable to give it proper examination: Williams v. Savage Manufact. Co., 1 Md. Ch. 306. See Rembert
v. Brown, 17 Ala. 667.

Where, in restating an account after a great lapse of time, there is to
be a correction of errors, charged in respect of which the account would
not have been opened if they had stood alone, it will be ordered that the
books, papers and vouchers in possession of the accounting party shall be
taken as *primâ facie* correct and genuine, without further proof than his
oath, or that of his clerk or agent having their management and custody,
that they are the original entries, papers and vouchers: Ogden v. Astor,
4 Sandf. S. C. 311.

have a rightful unity of possession, and that its severance
cannot be adequately effected at law.(a)[1] It is most frequently applied in effecting partition between co-owners,
but its principle extends to suits for assignment of dower
and for relief against substraction or non-payment of tithes.

There is also an equity for ascertainment of boundary
between the estates of independent proprietors, where the
confusion has arisen from the defendant's act; and for
compelling payment of rents, where by confusion of
boundary, or other cause, the remedy by distress is gone
without the plaintiff's default.

The manner of enforcing a partition at law, until abolished by a late statute, was by a writ of partition, issued
to the sheriff, requiring him to make partition by the verdict of a jury, and to assign to each co-owner his part in
severalty. In the case of coparceners, who acquire their
united estate by act of law, this writ always lay as of
common right. It did not orginally lie in favor of a
joint tenant or tenant in common, whose united estate is
conferred by gift or contract, but it was afterwards extended to them by statute.(b) The partition of copyholds
*was effected by a plaint in the lord's Court in [*230]
the nature of a writ of partition. The writ and
the plaint are now abolished.(c)

(a) Pulteney v. Warren, 6 Ves. 73, 89.
(b) 31 Hen. 8, c. 1; 32 Id. c. 32.   (c) 3 & 4 Wm. 4, c. 27, s. 36.

---

[1] The partition of real property is regulated in nearly all of the United
States by special statutes, and the efficiency and adaptability of the common
law action greatly increased. These statutes will be found collected in a
note to Washburn on Real Property, vol. i., p. 433. The flexibility and
neatness of the equitable partition must nevertheless, in many instances,
render that method preferable to the more unyielding forms of the common
law action. Upon the subject of partition in equity, see the notes to Agar
v. Fairfax, 2 Lead. Cas. Eq. 374.

The inconvenience of the remedy by writ of partition originated a concurrent jurisdiction in equity, the exercise of which may be demanded as matter of right, notwithstanding the difficulties by which a division may be embarrassed, or the mischief which it may entail on the property.$(d)^1$ The jurisdiction was originally confined

(d) Agar v. Fairfax, 17 Ves. 533; Warner v. Baynes, Amb. 589; Turner v. Morgan, 8 Ves. 143.

---

[1] Partition between tenants in common of real property is a matter of right in equity where both the parties cannot, or either of them will not, consent to hold and use such property in common. See Wright v. Marsh, 2 Greene (Iowa) 94; Howey v. Goings, 13 Ill. 95; Donnell v. Mateer, 7 Ired. Eq. 94; Holmes v. Holmes, 2 Jones Eq. 334. In Georgia, it appears that a bill for equitable partition will only lie, where there is some difficulty or obstruction in the way, so that the remedy at law is inadequate and imperfect, as where a discovery and account of rents and profits is necessary: Boggs v. Chambers, 9 Ga. 1; Rutherford v. Jones, 14 Id. 521; Hall v. Piddock, 21 N. J. 311. But the title of the complainant must be undisputed, otherwise the bill will be dismissed, or else retained until the title has been settled at law: Castleman v. Veitch, 3 Rand. 598; Straughan v. Wright, 4 Id. 493; Smith v. Smith, 10 Paige 470; Steedman v. Weeks, 2 Stroh. Eq. 141; Albergottie v. Chaplin, 10 Rich. Eq. 428; Pell v. Ball, 1 Id. 361; Collins v. Dickinson, 1 Hay. 240; Davis v. Davis, 2 Ired. Ch. 607; Wilkin v. Wilkin, 1 Johns. Ch. 111; Manners v. Manners, 1 Green Ch. 384; Wisely v. Findley, 3 Rand. 361; Stuart v. Coalter, 4 Id. 74; Garrett v. White, 3 Ired. Ch. 131; Bruton v. Rutland, 3 Humph. 435; Hosford v. Merwin, 5 Barb. S. C. 51; Burhans v. Burhans, 2 Barb. Ch. 398; Trayner v. Brooks, 4 Hey. 295; Maxwell v. Maxwell, 8 Ired. Eq. 25 · Foust v. Moorman, 2 Carter 17; Boone v. Boone, 3 Md. Ch. 497; Whillock v. Hale, 10 Humph. 64; Corbett v. Corbett, 1 Jones Eq. 114; Walker v. Laflin, 26 Ill. 472; Williams v. Wiggand, 53 Ill. 233; Gourley v. Woodbury, 43·Verm. 89; Hassam v. Day, 39 Miss. 392; Dewitt v. Ackerman, 2 Green (N. J.) 215; but see, Cuyler v. Ferrill, 1 Abb. (U. S.) 169; Morenhaut v. Higuera, 32 Cal. 289; Bollo v. Navarro, 33 Id. 459. The bill must in general allege seisin in both complainant and respondent: Maxwell v. Maxwell, 8 Ired. Eq. 25; Adams v. Ames Iron Co., 24 Conn. 230; though see Howey v. Goings, 13 Ill. 95. But actual possession on the part of the complainant is not necessary; it is sufficient if there be not a legal disseisin: Foust v. Moorman, 2 Carter 17; Denton v. Woods, 19 La. Ann. 356; Florence v. Hopkins, 46 N. Y. 182. Though in general a partition will

to land of freehold tenure, but has been extended to copyholds by statute.(e)

(e) Horncastle v. Charlesworth, 11 Sim. 315; Jope v. Morshead, 6 Beav. 213; 4 & 5 Vict. c. 35, s. 85.

---

not be decreed where the title is disputed, this applies only to the legal title. In cases of equitable estates, or defences, chancery has of necessity jurisdiction over the whole matter: Donnell v. Mateer, 7 Ired. Eq. 94; Foust v. Moorman, 2 Carter 17; Carter v. Taylor, 3 Head. (Tenn.) 30; Leverton v. Waters, 7 Cold. (Tenn.) 20. Where the defendant, in an action of partition at law, has an equitable defence, he may go into equity and obtain an injunction to stay proceedings at law, till the matter is settled in equity, or if the suit be already in equity, the respondent must set up his defence by a cross bill; though his omission to do so, will not prevent his filing a separate bill for relief: Donnell v. Matee, ut supra. On this principle that equity does not determine upon conflicting legal titles in partition, a decree therein is not conclusive evidence in ejectment: Whillock v. Hale, 10 Humph. 64.

Partition can be had of a mere equitable estate: Hitchcock v. Skinner, 1 Hoff. Ch. 21; or of an incorporeal hereditament: Bailey v. Sisson, 1 R. I. 233.

If land sought to be parted is subject to a mortgage, the equity of redemption only can be divided: Wotton v. Copeland, 7 John. Ch. 140.

In a partition among heirs or devisees, notice must be given to all the parties interested, or they will not be bound by the acts of the court: Vick v. The Mayor of Vicksbug, 1 How. (Miss.) 379.

Parties to proceedings in partition, acquire no new title thereby; and where they are made such by publication, without actual notice are not estopped thereby from setting up their legal title: McBain v. McBain, 15 Ohio St. 337.

The wife of a tenant in common is not a necessary party to a suit for partition: Matthews v. Matthews, 1 Ed. Ch. 565. Yet see Graydon v. Graydon, 1 McMullan Eq. 63.

Judgment creditors and mortgagees of tenants in common, are not proper parties: Sebring v. Mersereau, 9 Cowen 344; Harwood v. Kirby, 1 Paige 469; Low v. Holmes, 2 Green (N. J.) 148; Speer v. Speer, 1 McCarter (N. J.) 240; Thruston v. Minke, 32 Md. 571. Though a mortgagee may be joined where his interests would otherwise be injured: Whitton v. Whitton, 38 N. Hamp. 135. Nor a widow entitled to her "living" upon a tract of land, the heirs of the fee seeking a partition: McClintic v. Manns, 4 Munf. 328. Nor a railroad corporation, which has laid out its road over lands held by tenants in common: Weston v. Foster, 7 Metc. 297. A decree of partition of the estate of an intestate conveys only a contingent in-

The principal inconveniences attending partition at law were, that the writ could only be issued by and against the tenants in possession, so that an estate in remainder or contingency could not be bound; that the judgment was for partition according to the title proved, so that the plaintiff must prove the defendant's title as well as his own; and that the partition being made, not by mutual conveyances, but by the sheriff's actual division and the subsequent judgment of the Court was often incapable of being conveniently modelled. In the Court of Chancery these difficulties do not exist. Parties having limited interests, as, for example, tenants for life or years, may, if they please, have a partition in equity as well as at law, in respect of their own interests only.(*f*) But if a complete partition be desired, all parties interested may be brought before the Court, and all estates, whether in possession or expectancy, including those of infants and of persons not *in esse,* may be bound by the decree.(*g*) The defendant's titles need not be proved by the plaintiff, but *may be ascertained by a reference to the Master;(*h*) and the partition itself, being effectuated by mutual conveyances, may be made in a

[*231]

(*f*) Baring *v.* Nash, 1 Ves. & B. 551.

(*g*) Brook *v.* Lord Hertford, 2 P. Wms. 518 ; Gaskell *v.* Gaskell, 6 Sim. 643 ; Wills *v.* Slade, 6 Ves. 498 ; Seton on Decrees 275.

(*h*) Jope *v.* Morshead, 6 Beav. 213 ; Agar *v.* Fairfax, 17 Ves. 533, 542.

terest, defeasible in behalf of the creditors of the intestate: Dresher *v.* Allentown, &c., Co., 52 Penn. St. 225. See as to dower, post, 233. In New York, a doweress cannot be sole plaintiff or defendant: Wood *v.* Clute, 1 Sandf. Ch. 199. In Maryland, by statute, a widow's dower must be set off to her in an action of partition. See Phelps *v.* Stewart, 17 Md. 240; Stallings *v.* Stallings, 22 Id. 41. A tenant by the curtesy initiate may be a party to a bill for partition: Riker *v.* Drake, 4 Edw. Ch. 668 ; as may tenants by curtesy consummate. See 1 Roper on Husband and Wife 36.

more convenient form. Its general principle is of course the same as that of a partition at law, viz., a division of the estate; but if the estate is not susceptible of an exact division, an allotment may be made in unequal shares, with compensation for the inequality by creation of a rent or charge. A partition, however, must be *bonâ fide* made, and the pecuniary charge confined to corrections of inequality. There cannot, under the name of such correction, be substituted a mere sale to one co-tenant; and therefore, if the estate consist of a single house, the entire house must be divided, however inconvenient such division may be.(*i*)[1]

(*i*) Clarrendon *v*. Hornby, 1 P. Wms. 446; Turner *v*. Morgan, 8 Ves. 143; Story *v*. Johnson, 2 Y. & C. 586, 611; Horncastle *v*. Charlesworth, 11 Sim. 315; Mole *v*. Mansfield, 15 Id. 41; Vin. Ab. Partition, Z., Pl. 2.

---

[1] In case the estate cannot be exactly divided, the court will decree a pecuniary compensation to one or more of the parties for owelty or equality of partition, or charge part of the land with a rent, servitude, or easement, for their benefit. See Smith *v*. Smith, 10 Paige 470; Graydon *v*. Graydon, 1 McMullan Eq. 63; Haywood *v*. Judson, 4 Barb. S. C. 228; Warfield *v*. Warfield, 5 Har. & J. 459; Wynne *v*. Tunstall, 1 Dev. Ch. 23; Cox *v*. McMullin, 14 Gratt. 82; Phelps *v*. Green, 3 Johns. Ch. 302; Larkin *v*. Mann, 2 Paige 27; Norwood *v*. Norwood, 4 Har. & J. 112.

One party may have given to him a right of way over another's share: Cheswell *v*. Chapman, 38 N. H. 17; see also, Hoffman *v*. Savage, 15 Mass. 130; Chandler *v*. Goodrich, 23 Maine 78.

In most of the states, chancery has power to order a sale of the premises in a suit for partition. See Pell *v*. Ball, 1 Rich. Ch. 361; Thompson *v*. Hardman, 6 John. Ch. 436; Steedman *v*. Weeks, 2 Strob. Eq. 145; Dunham *v*. Minard, 4 Paige 441; Reynolds *v*. Reynolds, 5 Id. 161; Calwell *v*. Boyer, 8 Gill & J. 136; Matter of Skinner, 2 Dev. & Batt. Eq. 63; Smith *v*. Brittain, 3 Ired. Ch. 347; Royston *v*. Royston, 13 Ga. 425. So in Pennsylvania: Acts of April 18, 1853, s. 2, and April 22, 1863, s. 1. But see, on the other hand, Deloney *v*. Walker, 9 Porter 497; Norment *v*. Wilson, 5 Humph. 310.

In case of a sale, the shares of infant defendants ought not to be paid to their guardians, *ad litem*, but should be brought into court, and invested for the benefit of such infants: Carpenter *v*. Schermerhorn, 2 Barb. Ch. 314. So, if such infant is a wife, her share should not be paid to the husband: Sears *v*. Hyer, 7 Paige 483.

The mode in which a partition is effected in equity is that after the interests of all parties have been ascertained, either by evidence in the cause, or by the Master's report, a commission is issued to persons nominated by the parties, or if necessary by the Court, directing them to enter on and survey the estate, to make a fair partition thereof, to allot their respective shares to the several parties, and to make a return of their having done so to the Court. The commissioners in making their division are guided by the principles already explained. After making it, they allot to the several parties their respective shares; and in doing this they ought to look to their respective circumstances, and to assign to each that part of the property which will best accommodate him.$(k)^1$

The return of the commissioners, when made, is confirmed by the Court.[2] The confirmation, however, does not, like the judgment on a writ of partition, operate on the actual ownership of the land, so as to divest the parties of their undivided shares, and reinvest them with [*232] corresponding *estates in their respective allotments, but it requires to be perfected by mutual conveyances; and the next step, therefore, after confirmation of the return, is a decree that the plaintiffs and de-

(k) Story v. Johnson, 1 Y. & C. 538 ; 2 Id. 586.

---

[1] A less expensive mode than the appointment of commissioners is for the court to make a declaration that the estate ought to be divided, with liberty to the parties interested therein to bring before the judge at chambers proposals for partition. See Clarke v. Clayton, 2 Giff. 333.

[2] The report of the commissioners is regarded in the same light as a verdict at law, and will only be set aside for such cause as would induce a Court to grant a new trial: Livingston v. Clarkson, 3 Edw. Ch. 596. See Wilhelm v. Wilhelm, 4 Md. Ch. 330. For the practice in New Jersey on the commissioners' report, see Bentley v. The Dock Co., 1 McCart. 480. Commissioners have no judicial powers to determine any question of the title: Allen v. Hall, 50 Maine 253.

fendants do respectively convey to each other their respective shares, and deliver up the deeds relating thereto, and that in the meantime the allotted portions shall respectively be held in severalty.[1] If any of the co-owners have settled or mortgaged their shares, directions will be given for framing the conveyance so that all parties shall have the same interests in the divided shares, which they before had in the undivided shares.(*l*) If the infancy of the parties or other circumstances prevent the immediate execution of conveyances, the decree can only extend to make partition, give possession, and order enjoyment accordingly until effectual conveyances can be made. If the defect arises from infancy, the infant must have a day after attaining twenty-one years to show cause against the decree.(*m*)[2]

(*l*) Horncastle *v.* Charlesworth, 11 Sim. 315, 317 ; Story *v.* Johnson, 2 Y. & C. 586.

(*m*) Brook *v.* Lord Hertford, 2 P. Wms. 518 ; Seton on Decrees 275.

---

[1] The effect of a decree of partition is no more than that of an ordinary conveyance at law, and does not create of itself an adverse possession : Anderson *v.* Hughes, 5 Strobh. Law 74.

In Maryland, the decree does not direct the execution of conveyances, but that the parties hold in severalty, which is of equivalent effect: Young *v.* Frost, 1 Md. 377. In Pennsylvania it is provided by the Act of 1857, that the decree of a Court of equity shall have the same effect in vesting the titles of the several purparts, as the judgment in the common law action that the partition remain firm and stable forever ; and it has been held that under this statute conveyances are unnecessary: Griffith *v.* Phillips, 3 Grant's Cas. 381. The right of property passes from the date of the commissioners' report: Dixon *v.* Warters, 8 Jones L. (N. C.) 449.

[2] Where some of the owners are infants, the return of the commissioners for a partition will not be confirmed until the infants have been brought before the Court by bill : House *v.* Falconer, 4 Dessaus. 86. Independently of statutes, the Court has power to decree a conveyance by an infant party in a suit for partition to be binding on him, unless he shows cause within six months after becoming of age: Jackson *v.* Edwards, 7 Paige 386, 405. See also, Latimer *v.* Rogers, 3 Head. (Tenn.) 692 ; Long *v.* Mulford, 17 Ohio St. 484.

But in New York, where all the parties are infants, proceedings in par-

In addition to the decree for a partition, the Court may also, if either of the co-owners has been in the exclusive reception of the rents, decree an account of his receipts.[1] But the mere fact of his having occupied the property will not of itself make him liable for an occupation rent; for the effect of such a rule would be that one tenant in common, by keeping out of the actual occupation of the premises, might convert the other into his bailiff, and prevent him from occupying them, except upon the terms of paying rent.(n)   The period over which the account will extend was originally unlimited in the case of joint tenants and coparceners, on the ground that a mutual trust existed between them.   In the case of tenants in common, it was confined to six years, by analogy to the statute which gave them *an account at law.   It is now confined in all cases to six years.(o)[2]

[*233]

(n) Lorimer v. Lorimer, 5 Mad. 363; McMahon v. Burchell, 2 Ph. 127; Henderson v. Eason, 2 Ph. 308.

(o) Prince v. Heylin, 1 Atk. 493; 4 Ann. c. 16, s. 27; 3 & 4 Wm. 4, c. 27.

---

tition are invalid: Gallatian v. Cunningham, 8 Cowen 361. Nor can an infant maintain a bill alone: Postley v. Kain, 4 Sandf. Ch. 508. See Johnson v. Noble, 24 Mo. 252.

[1] Rozier v. Griffith, 31 Mo. 171. See also, Leach v. Beattie, 33 Verm. 195; Early v. Friend, 16 Gratt. 21.

[2] A tenant in common in sole possession, is chargeable, upon partition, with an occupation rent: Hitchcock v. Skinner, 1 Hoff. Ch. 21; Backler v. Farrow, 2 Hill Ch. 111. And sometimes interest on the rents from the time of bill filed: Carter v. Carter, 5 Munf. 108. But he will be allowed for substantial improvements made by himself or his ancestors: Respass v. Breckenridge, 2 A. K. Marsh. 581; Louvalle v. Menard, 1 Gilman 39; Conklin v. Conklin, 3 Sandf. Ch. 64; Hitchcock v. Skinner, supra. Or, as is most usual, his share shall include the improvements: St. Felix v. Rankin, 3 Ed. Ch. 323; Brookfield v. Williams, 1 Green Ch. 341; Sneed v. Atherton, 6 Dana 276; Borah v. Archer, 7 Id. 176; Dean v. O'Meara, 47 Ill. 120.

When a ship is the subject of tenancy in common, it is obviously impossible to make partition, and a decree for sale is beyond the jurisdiction of the Court.[1] The co-ownership, therefore, is incapable of compulsory severance, and if it were governed during its continuance by the ordinary rule of law, exempting each of the co-owners from any control by the rest, would enable any one of them, by resisting the employment of the ship, to render it valueless to all. In order to obviate this inconvenience, there is a jurisdiction in the Court of Admiralty to entertain the application of a majority in value or interest, for liberty to employ the ship in a particular adventure, giving security to their co-owners, either to bring her back or to pay the value of their shares. When this is done the dissentient owners bear no portion of the expenses, and have no share in the profits. It is considered that the same right exists where the owners are equally divided, but its extension to a minority is more doubtful. (*p*)[2]

(*p*) Story on Partnership, ss. 427–439; Smith's Merc. Law 174; Davis *v.* Johnston, 4 Sim. 539

---

[1] See as to the jurisdiction of equity in case of part-owners: Crapster *v.* Griffith, 2 Bland 5; Milburn *v.* Guythur, 8 Gill 92; Brenan *v.* Preston, 2 De G., M. & G. 813; 10 Hare 331; Darby *v.* Baines, 9 Id. 369; Southworth *v.* Smith, 27 Conn. 335; Mustard *v.* Robinson, 52 Maine 54. Equity has undoubted jurisdiction to enforce agreements of part-owners, as in other cases: Darby *v.* Baines. It will also have jurisdiction to aid by injunction the process of a Court of Admiralty in a possessory suit. Thus part-owners, who had taken possession of the machinery of a steam vessel, so as to prevent her sailing under a charter-party, were restrained from continuing that possession; there appearing to be difficulty in the relief in Admiralty, either on account of the delay, or because the complainants were in possession of the vessel: Brenan *v.* Preston, 2 De G., M. & G. 813·

[2] In Davis & Brooks *v.* The Brig Seneca, 6 Penn. L. J. 213, it was held by the Circuit Court of the United States for the Eastern District of Pennsylvania, that a sale might be decreed in Admiralty, where part-owners are equally divided. See The Orleans *v.* Phœbus, 11 Peters 175.

30

The equity for assignment of dower originates, in like manner with that for partition, out of the unity of possession of the widow and heir.[1]

---

[1] See Phares v. Walters, 6 Clarke (Iowa) 106. Courts of Chancery have a concurrent jurisdiction with courts of law, in assigning dower: Herbert v. Wren, 7 Cranch 370. To entitle the wife to dower, the husband must have been seised of a present freehold, as well as of an estate of inheritance: Dunham v. Osborn, 1 Paige 634.

She is, in most of the states, endowable of an *equitable* interest held by her husband in land, provided he continues to hold it to the time of his death: Hawley v. James, 5 Paige 318; Lawson v. Morton, 6 Dana 471; Hamilton v. Hughes, 6 J. J. Marsh. 581; Gillespie v. Somerville, 3 Stew. & Port. 447; Winn v. Elliott, Hardin 482; Lewis v. Moorman, 7 Porter 522; Shoemaker v. Walker, 2 S. & R. 554; Stevens v. Smith, 4 J. J. Marsh. 64; Rowton v. Rowton, 1 Hen. & Munf. 92; Bailey v. Duncan's Rep., 4 Monr. 262; Fleeson v. Nicholson, Walker (Miss.) 247; Bowie v. Berry, 1 Md. Ch. 452; Thompson v. Thompson, 1 Jones (N. C.) 430; Stewart v. Heard, 4 Md. Ch. 319. See on the other hand, Kirby v. Dalton, 1 Dev. Ch. 195; Milledge v. Lamar, 4 Dessaus. 638; Nicoll v. Ogden, 29 Ill. 323, where the authorities are reviewed; also Gano v. Gilruth, 4 Greene (Iowa) 453.

She is endowable of an equity of redemption: Smith v. Jackson, 2 Ed. Ch. 28; Titus v. Neilson, 5 Johns. Ch. 452; Keith v. Trapier, 1 Bailey Ch. 63; Bell v. Mayor of N. Y., 10 Paige 49; Evertson v. Tappen, 5 Johns. Ch. 497; Russell v. Austin, 1 Paige 192; Reed v. Morrison, 12 S. & R. 18; Kittle v. Van Dyck, 1 Sandf. Ch. 76; Hartshorne v. Hartshorne, 1 Green Ch. 349; Criswell v. Morris, 1 McCart. 101; Eldridge v. Eldridge, Id. 195; Heth v. Cocke, 1 Rand. 344; Wheatley v. Calhoun, 12 Leigh 264; Manning v. Laboree, 33 Maine 343; Rossiter v. Cossit, 15 N. H. 38; Mantz v. Buchanan, 1 Md. Ch. 202; though she joined in the mortgage: Simonton v. Gray, 34 Maine 50. See ante, 193, note; Davis v. Wetherill, 13 Allen (Mass.) 60; but see Decker v. Hall, 1 Edm. (N. Y.) Sel. Cas. 279. Of a rent: Herbert v. Wren, 7 Cranch 370; Williams v. Cox, 3 Ed. Ch. 178. Her right is superior to the vendor's lien for purchase-money: Clements v. Bostwick, 38 Ga. 1; contra, Thorn v. Ingram, 25 Ark. 52; Walton v. Hargreaves, 42 Miss. 18; Cooke v. Bailey, Id. 81; see also, Wing v. Ayre, 53 Maine 138. Of land bought with partnership funds, if it is not properly the partnership property: Wheatley v. Calhoun, 12 Leigh 264. Of a fee simple, determinable by executory devise, on her husband dying without issue living at the time of his death: Evans v. Evans, 9 Penn. St. 190; Milledge v. Lamar, 4 Dessaus. 637. And even of railroad shares, although a part of the amount due on the stock has been paid since the death of the

By the old law the widow's right of dower was a right
to have assigned to her on the death of her husband, a

---

holder : Price *v.* Price, 6 Dana 107 ; Copeland *v.* Copeland, 7 Bush (Ky.)
349.

But where there is but a momentary seisin of the husband, dower doe
not attach : Mayburry *v.* Brien, 15 Peters 21 ; Bullard *v.* Bowers, 10 N.
H. 500 ; Gammon *v.* Freeman, 31 Maine 243 ; Foster *v.* Gordon. 49 Id.
54 ; Welsh *v.* Buckins, 9 Ohio (N. S.) 331 ; Eslava *v.* Lepetre, 21 Ala.
504 ; Edmonson *v.* Welsh, 27 Id. 578. The widow is not endowed of land
given, and of land received in exchange. See Stevens *v.* Smith, 4 J. J.
Marsh. 64. Nor of a reversion : Blow *v.* Maynard, 2 Leigh 30. Nor of a
vested remainder, where the husband dies or aliens during the continuance
of the particular estate : Dunham *v.* Osborn, 1 Paige 634 ; Cocke *v.*
Philips, 12 Leigh 248. Nor of an estate of which her husband was merely
trustee : Powell *v.* Manufacturing Co., 3 Mason 347 ; Robison *v.* Codman,
1 Sumner 121 ; Derush *v.* Brown, 8 Ham. 412 ; Bartlett *v.* Gouge, 5 B.
Monr. 152 ; Cowman *v.* Hall, 3 Gill & J. 398 ; Thompson *v.* Murray, 2 Hill
Ch. 204, 213 ; Dean *v.* Mitchell, 4 J. J. Marsh. 451 ; Lenox *v.* Notrebe, 1
Hempst. 251 ; White *v.* Drew, 42 Mo. 561 : Buffalo, &c., R. R. *v.* Lampson,
47 Barb. (N. Y.) 533. She is however entitled to dower until such trust
is established : Bailey *v.* West, 41 Ill. 290. Nor of partnership property
as against creditors of the firm : Greene *v.* Greene, 1 Ham. 535. See also
Sumner *v.* Hampston, 8 Ham. 338 ; Richardson *v.* Wyatt, 2 Dessaus. 471 ;
Pierce *v.* Trigg, 10 Leigh 406 ; Goodburn *v.* Stevens, 1 Md. Ch. 420 ; Gal-
braith *v.* Gedge, 16 B. Monr. 631 ; and post, 246, note ; *sed vide* Smith *v.*
Jackson, 2 Ed. Ch. 28, wherein the doctrine of Greene *v.* Greene, supra, is
questioned. Nor of the land of husband, found, before marriage, to be of
unsound mind, and who continued so until death : Jenkins *v.* Jenkins, 2
Dana 102. Nor of the estate of a joint tenant : Mayburry *v.* Brien, 15
Peters 21. Nor of a mere privilege : Kingman *v.* Sparrow, 12 Barb. 201.
Nor of a pre-emption right : Wells *v.* Moore, 16 Mo. 478. Nor of land of
which her husband was in possession under an executory contract, the
terms of which he had not complied with during his lifetime : Lobdell *v.*
Hayes, 4 Allen 187.

Nor shall the widow entitled to dower in land sold by her husband, take
any advantage from the improvements made by the purchaser. but may
from the increased value of the land : Thompson *v.* Morrow, 5 S. & R.
290 ; Braxton *v.* Coleman, 5 Call 433 ; Hazen *v.* Thurber et al., 4 Johns.
Ch. 604 ; Bowie *v.* Berry, 1 Md. Ch. 452 ; Dashiel *v.* Collier, 4 J. J. Marsh.
603 ; Beavers *v.* Smith, 11 Ala. 20 ; Mosher *v.* Mosher, 15 Maine 371 ;
Powell *v.* Manufacturing Co., 3 Mason 347 ; Dunseth *v.* Bank U. S., 6 Ohio
77 ; Manning *v.* Laboree, 33 Maine 343 ; Johnstown *v.* Van Dyke, 6

third part of the lands and tenements of which he was
seised during the marriage in fee simple or fee tail, and
which her issue (if any) might by possibility have inhe-
rited. If the thing of which she was endowed were divisible, her dower must have been set out by metes and
bounds : if it were indivisible, she must have been endowed specially, as of the third presentation to a church ;
the third toll dish of a mill ; the third part of the profits
[*234] of an office, and the like. Upon *the death of the
husband her right to dower became perfect, but
unless her precise portion of land has been already specified, she could not enter till dower was assigned. It was,
therefore, the duty of the heir, or his guardian, to assign
dower within forty days after the husband's death. If
he did not assign it, or assigned it unfairly, the widow
had her remedy at law by writ of dower, or of dower
unde nihil habet, and the sheriff was appointed to assign it.
The recent Statute of Limitations, which abolished other
real actions, has retained these writs.(*q*)

The inconveniences attending assignment at law,
coupled with the difficulties to which the dowress was
exposed, by reason of her evidence being in possession
of the heir, gave rise to a concurrent jurisdiction in equity
for issuing a commission to set out her dower, or making
a reference to the Master for the same purpose.(*r*)[1]

(*q*) 1 Steph. Bl. 249-254 ; 3 Steph. Bl. 657-661 ; 3 & 4 Wm. 4, c. 27, s.
36.

(*r*) Curtis *v*. Curtis, 2 B. C. C. 620 ; Mundy *v*. Mundy, 2 Ves. J. 122 ;
Pulteney *v*. Warren, 6 Id. 73, 89 ; Agar *v*. Fairfax, 17 Id. 533, 552 ; Seton
261.

McLean 422. See also Fritz *v*. Tudor, 1 Bush (Ky.) 28. Yet see, as to
her advantage from the land's rise in value, Tod *v*. Baylor, 4 Leigh 498 ;
Hale *v*. James, 6 Johns. Ch. 258 ; Humphrey *v*. Phinney, 2 Johns. 484.
A widow, who was not a citizen of the United States, at the time of her
husband's death, cannot be endowed : Alsberry *v*. Hawkins, 9 Dana 177.

[1] Courts of equity have concurrent jurisdiction with courts of law, in the

At the same time with the decree for assigning dower, an account might, before the late statute, 3 & 4 Wm. 4, c. 27, s. 40, have been directed of the rents and profits received since the husband's decease, and payment of one-third to the widow. At common law the demandant in a writ of dower, as in any other real action, was not entitled to damages in respect of bygone rents; but by the Statute of Merton a special relief was given, and it was enacted that "if a widow were deforced of her dower, and should subsequently recover the same by plea, she should recover damages to the amount of the value of the dower from the death of the husband to the day of her recovering seisin." In accordance with this rule of law, a dowress was entitled in equity to an account of rents and profits from the death of her husband; and although at law her right to damages would be lost by the death of the heir, yet such death, if occurring *pendente lite*, was not allowed in equity to *prejudice her claim.(s)   It [*235] is now enacted by 3 & 4 Wm. 4, c. 27, s. 40, that no arrears of dower, nor any damages on account of such arrears, shall be recovered by action or suit for a longer period than six years next before the commencement of such action or suit.[1]

(s) 20 Hen. 3, c. 1; Curtis *v.* Curtis, 2 B. C. C. 620; Oliver *v.* Richardson, 9 Ves. 222.

---

assignment of dower, yet they always treat it as a strictly legal right, and are governed by the same rules of right with Courts of law, and will not permit an equity to be interposed to defeat the dower: Blain *v.* Harrison, 11 Ill. 384; Potier *v.* Barclay, 15 Ala. 439; Kiddall *v.* Trimble, 1 Md. Ch. 143; Gano *v.* Gilruth, 4 Greene (Iowa) 453; Palmer *v.* Casperson, 2 Green (N. J.) 204; Brooks *v.* Woods, 40 Ala. 538. But, where the widow applies for equitable relief in relation to dower which a Court of law cannot grant, she cannot resist an equitable defence as against a purchaser, for a valuable consideration, who is ignorant of her claim of dower: Blain *v.* Harrison, ut sup.

[1] A widow is entitled in equity to an account of the rents and profits

The right of the widow under certain modifications. still exists; but by the recent Dower Act it has been reduced, as to all women married after 1st January, 1834, to a right of a very .precarious description, which the husband may defeat by conveyance or devise, or by a simple declaration that his estate shall be exempt.(*t*)

The equity for relief against subtraction or non-payment of tithes originates in the fact that the tithes, with the remaining produce, continue rightfully in possession of the tithe-payer, who is bound to set them apart and to account for them to the tithe-owner; and it is accordingly an equity against the tithe-payer alone, and not against any third person who may have received the tithes under an adverse claim. In this latter case an ejectment is the proper remedy.(*u*)

The right to tithe is a right capable of enforcement at the common law, and also to some extent in the Ecclesiastical Courts. The exact nature of the right, and of the remedies in the common law and Ecclesiastical Courts, are not material to be here considered. It is sufficient to observe that the tithe-owner, suing in those Courts, is in some cases enabled by statute to recover the treble value of the tithe, and that, inasmuch as the treble liability is

(*t*) 3 & 4 Wm. 4, c. 105.

(*u*) Pulteney *v.* Warren, 6 Ves. 73, 90; St. Asaph *v.* Williams, Jac. 349.

---

until her dower is assigned, independently of the Statute of Merton: Keith *v.* Trapier, 1 Bailey Eq. 63. In Sellman *v.* Bowen, 8 Gill & J. 50, and Steiger *v.* Hillen, 5 Id. 121, it was held that she was entitled to damages from her husband's alienee from the time of demand made by her. In Tod *v.* Baylor, 4 Leigh 498, it was held that she was entitled to an account of the profits only, from the date of the *subpœna.* And in Garton *v.* Bates, 4 B. Monr. 366; Golden *v.* Maupin, 2 J. J. Marsh. 240; and Kendall *v.* Honey, 5 Monroe 283, that she was not entitled to profits even from the commencement of the suit. The widow is entitled to an account of rents and profits, only from the time of assignment, where the husband does not die seised: Bolser *v.* Cushman, 34 Maine 348.

in the nature of a forfeiture, he is required to waive it if he sues in equity.(v)

The relief prayed by a bill for tithes may be resisted in two ways: the defendant may either deny the plaintiff's title *ab origine*, alleging an adverse right in some third *person, and establishing it by proof of an actual grant, or by presumption arising from long [*236] enjoyment;(w) or he may admit a primary title in the plaintiff, and insist on an absolute or partial discharge, either by a prescription *de non decimando*, which is when lands are absolutely discharged from tithe, on the ground that from time immemorial they have not been liable ; or by a prescription *de modo decimandi*, commonly called a *modus*, which is where by immemorial usage, a particular mode of tithing has been allowed, different from the payment of a tenth in kind; or by a composition real, which is an agreement made between the owner of lands and the parson or vicar, with the consent of the ordinary and patron that such lands shall be discharged from tithe by reason of land, or other real recompense, given to the person in their stead.(x) If the primary title is disputed, it must be established in a regular action at law, before the equity for an account can arise; but if that right is admitted, and met by a specific ground of exemption, *e. g.*, a *modus* or prescription *de non decimando*, the Court may either decide the question itself, or may refer it to a jury on a feigned issue.(y)

There is also a cross equity for establishing a *modus* against the tithe-owner, where the tithe-payer has been disturbed by proceedings, either in equity or elsewhere, to enforce payment in kind. But if the rector insists on

(v) 3 Steph. Bl. 123–125, 708.　　　　(w) Id. 125–127.

(x) 3 Steph. Bl. 127–133.

(y) Knight v. Waterford, 11 Cl. & F. 657 ; Raine v. Cairns, 4 Hare 327 333 ; 12 Cl. & F. 833.

trying the existence of the *modus* at law, he is entitled to demand an issue for that purpose.(*z*)

The equitable jurisdiction over tithes and moduses was originally vested in the Court of Exchequer. That of the Court of Chancery over the same subject is of much later origin, or at least was a matter of controversy to a much later period, and was not firmly established until after the [*237] *Restoration. Since that period the Court of Chancery has always been held to have a concurrent authority with the Exchequer; and when the equitable jurisdiction of that Court was abolished, it obtained the sole jurisdiction on the subject.

The jurisdiction was originally exercised without reference to the value of the tithe. But by a recent statute it is confined to cases where the yearly value is upwards of 10*l.*, or where the actual title to the tithe, composition, or *modus*, or the actual liability or exemption of the property sought to be charged, is *bonâ fide* in question.(*a*) And by the gradual operation of the Tithe Commutation Acts, for converting all tithes into fixed rent-charges, recoverable by distress and entry, it is becoming practically extinct.(*b*)

The equity for ascertainment of boundary arises when lands are held in severalty by independent proprietors, but the boundaries have been confused by the misconduct of the defendant, or of those under whom he claims.[1] The

(*z*) Gordon *v.* Simkinson, 11 Ves. 509 ; 2 Dan. C. P. 1056 ; 1 Madd. C. P. 334.

(*a*) 5 & 6 Wm. 4, c. 74 ; 4 & 5 Vict. c. 36 ; 3 Steph. Bl. 709.

(*b*) 6 & 7 Wm. 4, c. 71 ; 1 Vict. c. 69 ; 1 & 2 Vict. c. 64 ; 2 & 3 Vict. c. 62 ; 3 & 4 Vict. c. 15 ; 5 & 6 Vict. c. 54 ; 3 Steph. Bl. 133, 137.

[1] See Mayor, &c., of Basingstoke *v.* Lord Bolton, 1 Drew. 170 ; 17 Jur. 57.

A court of equity has no jurisdiction to fix boundaries of legal estates, unless some equity is superinduced by the act of the parties: Norris's Appeal, 64 Penn. St. 275 ; Tillmes *v.* Marsh, 67 Id. 507.

mere confusion of boundary will not create it, for the fact that a man cannot ascertain his property does not constitute an equity against another person. But it must be shown that the confusion has been caused by the defendant's misconduct, or by the misconduct of those under whom he claims. As, for example, where a tenant has confounded the boundaries to prevent a distress ; or a copyholder has confounded the copyholds with his own freehold. In this case the Court will issue a commission to ascertain the boundaries, or will set out an equivalent portion of the lands in the defendant's possession. It will, at the same time, if necessary, decree an account of rents and profits.(c)

The equity for payment of rent arises where, by confusion of boundaries, *by fraudulent removal of goods, or by the incorporeal nature of the hereditaments charged, the remedy at law by distress is gone, without default in the owner of the rent. A bill seeking this relief may be supported merely by proof of long-continned payment, and is then termed a bill founded on the *solet.* The same remedy has been given where the days on which the rent was payable were uncertain, and even where the nature of the rent (of which there are many kinds at law) was unknown.(d)[1]

[*238]

(c) Wake v. Conyers, 1 Eden 331 ; Speer v. Crawter, 2 Meriv. 410 ; Miller v. Warmington, 1 J. & W. 464.

(d) Duke of Bridgewater v. Edwards, 6 B. P. C. by Toml. 368 ; Holder v. Chambury, 3 P. Wms. 256 ; Benson v. Baldwyn, 1 Atk. 598 ; Bouverie v. Prentice, 1 B. C. C. 200 ; Duke of Leeds v. New Radnor, 2 Id. 338 ; Attorney-General v. Jackson, 11 Ves. 365 ; [Mayor, &c. of Basingstoke v. Lord Bolton, 17 Jur. 57 ; 1 Drew. 170.]

---

[1] Although a Court of chancery will not ordinarily take jurisdiction of a case of rent. yet when the time of payment, or the amount to be paid is uncertain, or when the distress is evaded or obstructed by fraud, the Court will take jurisdiction, and give relief: Dawson v. Williams, 1 Freem. Ch. 99. So where the lease has been lost: Lawrence v. Hammitt, 3 J. J. Marsh. 287.

[*239]   *CHAPTER III.

OF PARTNERSHIP.

THE equity for winding up the business of a partnership originates in the peculiar character of that relationship, as involving not merely a community of interest,
but the employment of a common stock, whether consisting of property or of mere labor and skill, in some
common undertaking, with a view to a common profit.$(a)^1$ In order that such common profit may be ob-

(a) 2 Steph. Bl. 150; Coope v. Eyre, 1 H. Blacks. 37.

---

[1] The law of partnership is a branch of the law of agency, each partner
holding towards the other the double relation of principal and agent. This
is expressed with great clearness in Cox v. Hickman, 8 H. Ld. Cas. 268.
In that case Lord Cranworth, after commenting upon the insufficiency of
the test usually applied, viz., that participation in profits is a criterion of
partnership, went on to observe: "It is not strictly correct to say that
a partner's right to share in the profits makes him liable to the debts of
the trade. The correct mode of stating the proposition is to say that the
same thing which entitles him to the one makes him liable to the other,
namely, the fact that the trade has been carried on in his behalf, *i. e.*, that
he stood in the relation of principal towards the persons acting ostensibly
as the traders, by whom the liabilities have been incurred, and under
whose management the profits had been made." A careful attention to
the rules as stated by Lords Cranworth and Wensleydale, in this case, will
help to solve the question of partnership or no partnership in very many
instances. See also, Bullen v. Sharp, L. R. 1 Com. Pleas 86, and the note
to Waugh v. Carver, 1 Smith's Lead. Cas. 1174 (6 Am. ed.). Practically,
the general rule is that participation in profits, *quâ profits*, will constitute
a person a partner as to third parties: Motley v. Jones, 3 Ind. Ch. 144;
Turner v. Bissell, 14 Pick. 194 ; Simpson v. Feltz, 1 McCord Ch. 218 ; Pur-

tained, it is essential that there be a capacity to contract partnership debts, and to acquire partnership assets, independent of the debts and assets of the individual part-

viance v. McClintee, 6 S. & R. 259; Dob v. Halsey, 16 Johns. 34; Brown v. Higginbotham, 5 Leigh 583; Bromley v. Elliott, 38 N. H. 301; Julio v. Ingalls, 1 Allen 41; Voorhees v. Jones, 5 Dutch. 270; Goldsmith v. Berthold, 24 How. 536; Manhattan Brass Co. v. Sears, 45 N. Y. 797. But a share in the profits, as a measure of compensation for services and labor, does not render the party receiving the compensation a partner. There must be an interest in the profits *as profits:* Waugh v. Carver (supra); Ogden v. Astor, 4 Sandf. S. C. 311; Reed v. Murphy, 2 Greene (Iowa) 574; Kerr v. Potter, 6 Gill 404; Potter v. Moses, 1 R. I. 430; Stocker v. Brockelbank, 3 M. & G. 250; Bull v. Schuberth, 2 Md. 38; Hodgman v. Smith, 13 Barb. 302; Pierson v. Steinmyer, 4 Rich. 389; Clarke v. Gilbert, 32 Barb. 576. And see Newmen v. Bean, 1 Foster 93; Dunham v. Rogers, 1 Penn. St. 255; Pattison v. Blanchard, 1 Selden 186; Merrick v. Gordon, 20 N. Y. 93; Radcliffe v. Rushworth, 33 Beav. 484; Parker v. Fergus, 43 Ill. 437; Merwin v. Playford, 3 Rob. (N. Y.) 702; Conklin v. Barton, 43 Barb. (N. Y.) 435; Lentner v. Milliken, 47 Ill. 178; Edwards v. Tracy, 62 Penna. St. 374; but see Morgan v. Stearns, 41 Verm. 398.

A joint stock company is a partnership, the capital of which is divided or agreed to be divided into shares, so as to be transferable without express consent of all the partners: Hedge & Horn's Appeal, 63 Penn. St. 273.

In England it is now provided by the Stat. 28 & 29 Vict. c. 86, that an advance of money, on a contract to receive a share of the profits, is not to constitute the lender a partner; and that the remuneration of agents, &c., by shares of profits, shall not render them partners.

An association of persons for a special purpose, distinct from making profits, is not a partnership: Caldecott v. Griffith, 8 Exch. 898; Bright v. Hutton, 3 H. L. Cas. 341; Flemyng v. Hector, 2 M. & W. 172; Irvine v. Forbes, 11 Barb. S. C. 587; Thomas v. Ellmaker, 1 Pars. Eq. 98. See also Pomeroy v. Sigerson, 22 Missouri 177; Wright v. Cumsty, 41 Penn. St. 102; Fay v. Noble, 7 Cushing 188; Parsons on Partnership 42, note (b).

There may be a partnership for dealing in real estate: Dalton City Co. v. Dalton Manuf. Co., 33 Ga. 243. Therefore, land bought with partnership money, for partnership purposes, and applied to those purposes, will in equity be treated as a partnership fund: Clegett v. Kilbourne, 1 Black (S. C.) 346; Wallis v. Freeman, 35 Verm. 44; Abbott's Appeal, 50 Penn. St. 234; 3 Kent's Com. 37; Parsons on Partnership 369; infra, page 246, note.

ners, the ultimate balance of which is the profit or loss of the firm. And, therefore, before the interest of an individual partner can be known, an account must be taken of the business, the assets, and the liabilities, so that the divisible surplus may be ascertained.

The common law Courts cannot take this account. The mere existence of a partnership does not necessarily exclude this jurisdiction; for it may happen that litigation exists between the partners, with which they are fully competent to deal. Such, for example, is the case where the transaction in respect of which relief is sought is wholly independent of the partnership; or is merely preliminary to it; or consists in the breach of a covenant or [*240] of an undertaking *to perform some specific act, so that the decision is unconnected with the partnership account;[1] or where a dissolution has already taken place, and the balance of account has been struck, so that further investigation is not requisite. But if it be necessary to investigate the account, it cannot be done at law, unless by the adoption of the action of account, the inconveniences of which have been already explained.(b)[2]

(b) 3 Steph. Bl. 532; Smith's Merc. Law 38 ; Foster v. Allanson, 2 T. R. 479; Jackson v. Stopherd, 4 Tyrw. 330; Elgie v. Webster, 5 M. & W. 518; Brown v. Tapscott, 6 Id. 119.

---

[1] Kinloch v. Hamlin, 2 Hill Ch. 19 ; Duncan v. Lyon, 3 Johns. Ch. 360; Hunt v. Gookin, 6 Verm. 462. See Cross v. Cheshire, 7 Exch. 43. In Addams v. Tutton, 39 Penn. St. 447, it was held that covenant would lie for a breach of partnership articles by a wrongful dissolution, and by wrongful acts tending to that dissolution.

[2] Where there is a distinct promise to pay an ascertained sum, as where a balance of accounts is struck, assumpsit will lie between partners : Hall v. Stewart, 12 Penn. St. 213; Hamilton v. Hamilton, 18 Id. 20; Halderman v. Halderman, 1 Hempstead 557 ; see Morrow v. Riley, 15 Ala. 710 ; Gridley v. Dole, 4 Comst. 486 ; Miller v. Andress, 13 Ga. 366 ; Knerr v. Hoffman, 65 Penn. St. 126 ; and where an account stated, resulting in

If a dissolution, as well as an account, be sought, the common law jurisdiction is altogether excluded.[1]

The incapacity thus existing in the Courts of law confers a jurisdiction on the Court of Chancery; and accordingly, if the partnership has been already dissolved, or if there be misconduct or incompetency in either partner sufficient to warrant its dissolution, a bill will lie to have the assets converted into money, the debts discharged out of their produce, and the surplus distributed among the partners, or the deficiency made good by contribution.(c)

There may of course be grounds for relief under general equities, at the suit of one partner against another, independently of this special equity for taking the account,[2]

(c) Ex parte Ruffin, 6 Ves. 119; Ex parte Williams, 11 Id. 3.

---

such balance, is retained by a partner without objection, a promise will be implied, as in other cases: Van Amringe v. Ellmaker, 4 Penn. St. 281.

[1] In matters of difficulty or controversy between partners it is now most usual to resort to a Court of equity for their final adjudication and settlement: Bracken v. Kennedy, 3 Scam. 558; Holyoke v. Mayo, 50 Maine 385; and see Raymond v. Crane, 45 N. H. 201. It will entertain jurisdiction, although account or other action would lie between the parties: Gillett v. Hall, 13 Conn. 426; Cunningham v. Littlefield, 1 Ed. Ch. 104. And although one partner cannot bind the firm by deed: Donaldson v. Kendall, 2 Ga. Decis. 227; Napier v. Catron, 2 Humph. 534; Dickinson v. Legare, 1 Dessaus. 537; Skinner v. Dayton, 19 Johns. 513; Fisher v. Tucker, 1 McCord's Ch. 170; Williams v. Hodgson, 2 Har. & Johns. 474; yet in some cases a Court of equity will regard a debt secured by the specialty of one partner as a simple contract debt, and hold all the partners bound for it. See Galt v. Calland, 7 Leigh 594: McNaughton v. Partridge, 11 Ohio 223; Christian v. Ellis, 1 Gratt. 396; Anderson v. Tompkins, 1 Brock. 456; Kyle v. Roberts, 6 Leigh 495; James v. Bostwick, Wright 142.

[2] A Court of equity may compel specific execution of a partnership contract, and may restrain one partner from persisting in a course jeopardizing the rights of another, or depriving him of his due share in the direc-

e. g., for performance of covenants in the partnership deed, for recovery of assets fraudulently withdrawn, for an injunction against threatened misapplication of assets, and the like; and if the misconduct of a partner has been knowingly abetted by a stranger, the abettor may be also sued in equity, for the injured partners cannot sue him at law, because the fraudulent co-partner must be joined as a plaintiff in the action.[1] The subject, however, of these general equities is not now under consideration. Our present subject is, the special equity for winding up a partnership on the ground that the account cannot be taken [*241] at law. And the essential characteristic of this *equity is that it contemplates the winding up of the partnership, and not its continuance. A bill will not lie for an account and distribution of the profits, which contemplates at the same time a continuance. of the business; for if a decree could be obtained for such an account, the result would fluctuate in each successive year, and would only be settled when the partnership was at an end.[2] The ordinary course is to pray that the part-

---

tion of the business: see Gillett *v.* Hall, 13 Conn. 426 ; Pirtle *v.* Penn, 3 Dana 248.

So where one of the parties to an agreement of partnership has been induced to enter into it upon fraudulent representations, equity will interfere and declare it void, except as against creditors: Hynes *v.* Stewart, 10 B. Monr. 429 ; Fog *v.* Johnstone, 27 Ala. 432.

[1] Where the same person is a member of two distinct firms, one of those firms cannot sue the other at law, even on an account stated, because one cannot sue himself; the remedy is in equity : Calvit *v.* Markham, 3 How. (Miss.) 343. In Pennsylvania, such suit lies at law by statute ; with this restriction, that no act or declaration of one party shall be given in evidence in his own favor to the prejudice of others: Purdon's Digest, tit. Partnership. See, also, for the construction of it, Hepburn *v.* Certs, 7 Watts 300; Pennock *v.* Swayne, 6 W. & S. 231; Tassey *v.* Church, Id. 465 ; Meconkey *v.* Rodgers, Bright. R. 450.

[2] It has often been held that there can be no division of partnership pro-

nership may be dissolved, and the surplus assets distributed; but this practice has been relaxed in favor of joint stock companies, and of other numerous partnerships, and bills have been sustained which asked more limited relief, viz., that the assets of an abandoned or insolvent partnership might be collected and applied in discharge of the debts, leaving questions of distribution and contribution as between the partners entirely open for future settlement.(d)

The first topic which occurs in examining this equity is, as to the circumstances which will cause or warrant a dissolution.

A dissolution may be caused in various ways: first, by mere effluxion of the time, or completion or extinction of the business for which the partnership was created; secondly, by mutual agreement of all the partners, or, if, no specific term of duration has been fixed, by the declaration of any one partner that the connection is

(d) Goodman v. Whitcomb, 1 J. & W. 572; Marshall v. Colman, 2 Id. 266; Glassington v. Thwaites, 1 S. & S. 124; Loscombe v. Russell, 4 Sim. 8; Wallworth v. Holt, 4 M. & C. 619; Richardson v. Hastings, 7 Bea. 301, 323; Apperly v. Page, 1 Ph. 779; Fairthorne v. Weston, 3 Hare 387; infra, Pleading, Parties.

perty until all the accounts of the partnership have been taken, and the clear interest of each partner ascertained; that the chancellor may, in a proper case, dissolve the partnership, but cannot aid in carrying it on· Baird v. Baird, 1 Dev. & Bat. 524; McRae v. McKenzie, 2 Id. 232; Camblatt v. Tupery, 2 La. Ann. 10; Kennedy v. Kennedy, 3 Dana 240. But in Pennsylvania. it has been decided that a Court of equity will entertain a bill for an account by one partner against the other, although the bill does not contemplate a dissolution of the partnership: Hudson v. Barret, 1 Parsons's Sel. Eq. Cas. 414. Equity will enjoin one partner from violating the rights of his copartner in partnership matters, although no dissolution of the partnership be contemplated: Marble Co. v. Ripley, 10 Wall. (U. S.) 339.

dissolved; $(e)^1$ and thirdly, by the death or bankruptcy of a partner, or by an execution against him, followed by seizure and sale of his share.[2]   And when a dissolution

(e) Peacock v. Peacock, 16 Ves. 49; Crawshay v. Maule, 1 Sw. 495, 508; Featherstonhaugh v. Fenwick, 17 Ves. 298.

---

[1] Even where a partnership is formed for a definite period, it is said, it may be dissolved at the pleasure of one of the partners: Skinner v. Dayton, 19 Johns. 538; Mason v. Connell, 1 Whart. 381; Slemmer's Ap., 58 Penn. St. 168; sed vide Bishop v. Breckles, 1 Hoff. Ch. 534. A dissolution of a partnership, by sealed articles, by agreement before the time limited, is good, though not under seal: Wood v. Gault, 2 Md. Ch. 433.

But a partnership is to be considered in existence till it is wound up, and the partner in possession of the place of business of the partnership, has no right, by giving notice of dissolution, to exclude immediately the other partner therefrom, or from the disposal of the effects: Roberts v. Edenhart, 1 Kay 148. And see Western Stage Co. v. Walker, 2 Clarke 504.

One partner may sell the whole of the partnership property, if the sale be free from fraud on the part of the purchaser, and such sale dissolves the partnership, although the term has not expired: Whitton v. Smith, 1 Freem. Ch. 231; Deckard v. Case, 5 Watts 22. The latter case differing as to the effect of such sale; sed vide Hewitt v. Sturdevant, 4 B. Monr. 453.

As to his power to make an assignment for the benefit of the firm creditors, see McCullough v. Somerville, 8 Leigh 415; Harrison v. Sterry, 5 Cranch 289; Egberts v. Wood, 3 Paige 517; Robinson v. Crowder, 4 McCord L. R. 519; Havens v. Hussey, 5 Paige 30; Hitchcock v. St. John, 1 Hoff. Ch. 511; Mills v. Argall, 6 Paige 577; Pearpoint v. Graham, 4 W. C. C. R. 232; Graser v. Stellwagen, 25 N. Y. 315; Sheldon v. Smith, 28 Barb. 599; Ormsbee v. Davis, 5 R. I. 442: Cullum v. Bloodgood, 15 Ala. 34; Clark v. Wilson, 19 Penn. St. 414. In Deming v. Colt, 3 Sandf. S. C. 284, it was decided, upon much deliberation, that an assignment by one partner, without the consent of the rest, where they are present, and actually engaged in the business of partnership, was invalid; and this is undoubtedly the better and sounder opinion: Hook v. Stone, 34 Mo. 329; Welles v. March, 30 N. Y. 344. In Forkner v. Stuart, 6 Gratt. 197, however, such an assignment, in the absence of one partner, was held good. See also, Kemp v. Carnley, 3 Duer 1; Norris v. Vernon, 8 Rich. 13; National Bank v. Sackett, 2 Daly (N. Y.) 395.

[2] By the general rule of law, every partnership is dissolved by the death of one of the partners, and the dissolution is so effectual, that want of

is thus effected, the executor or administrator of the partner, the assignee under his fiat, or the sheriff's vendee, becomes entitled to *his interest in the partner- [*242] ship assets, as it shall appear on adjustment of the partnership account.$(f_t)^1$

A partnership may also be in some sense dissolved by sale of a partner's share, if such sale be authorized by the deed of partnership.[2] The ordinary rule is that no

---

(*f*) Taylor *v.* Fields, 4 Ves. 396 ; Young *v.* Keighly, 15 Id. 557 ; Dutton *v.* Morrison, 17 Id. 193 ; Re Wait, 1 J. & W. 585 ; Habershon *v.* Blurton, 1 De G. & S. 121.

---

notice of it does not have the effect of making the estate of the deceased partner liable to debts contracted by the surviving partners, or for their misconduct: Caldwell *v.* Stileman, 1 Rawle 212, 216 ; Williamson *v.* Wilson, 1 Bland 418. But a partner may, by will, provide that the partnership shall continue after his death, and if it be assented to by the surviving partner, it becomes obligatory: Burwell *v.* Mandeville, 2 Howard U. S. 560. And see Laughlin *v.* Lorenz's Admr., 48 Penn. St. 275 ; Davis *v.* Christian, 15 Grattan 11. The surviving partner has a reasonable time to close up the affairs: Tillotson *v.* Tillotson, 34 Conn. 335 ; and he is not entitled to compensation for so doing: Ibid.

[1] As to dissolution by the seizure and sale of one partner's share, see Moody *v.* Payne, 2 Johns. Ch. 548 ; Place *v.* Sweetzer, 16 Ohio 142 ; Brewster *v.* Hammet, 4 Conn. 540 ; Sitler *v.* Walker, 1 Freem. Ch. 77 ; Doner *v.* Stauffer, 1 Penna. R. 198 ; Phillips *v.* Cook, 24 Wend. 389 ; Renton *v.* Chaplain, 1 Stockt. 62.

[2] A voluntary assignment, by one partner, of all his interest in the concern, dissolves the partnership, although the articles provide that the partnership is to continue until two of the contracting parties shall demand a dissolution: Marquand *v.* N. Y. Man. Co., 17 Johns. 525 ; Whitton *v.* Smith, 1 Freem. Ch. 231 ; see, also, Mason *v.* Connell, 1 Whart. 381 ; Conwell *v.* Sandidge, 5 Dana 213 ; Horton's App., 13 Penn. St. 67 ; Ormsbee *v.* Davis, 5 R. I. 422. See, also, Coope *v.* Bowles, 42 Barb. (N. Y.) 87 ; Eden *v.* Williams, 36 Ill. 252. A partner may, however, assign his interest to another, who, being substituted, may, after the expiration or dissolution of the partnership, maintain a bill for his share of the profits: Mathewson *v.* Clarke, 6 Howard U. S. 122. So a partnership may be dissolved by the act of God, by the act of the government, as, by a war between the countries of the partners, or by some of the members becoming a body politic: The Cape Sable Co's Case, 3 Bland 674.

31

partner can sell or dispose of his share without the concurrence of the rest. He may alien his interest in the
surplus to be ascertained by taking the partnership account, but he cannot substitute his alienee to the position
of a partner, nor give him any right to interfere in the
business. A right, however, to alien the share itself may
be, and in the case of very large partnerships often is
conferred. And the effect of such alienation, when
properly made, is to determine the relation of partnership as between the alienor and the other members of
the firm, and to substitute a similar relation with the
alienee.(*g*) This power of alienation is usually confined
to joint stock companies, and regulated by the provisions
of express statutes.(*h*)

A decree for dissolution will be warranted if it is impossible that the partnership should be beneficially continued, *e. g.*, if the principles on which the scheme is
based are found on examination to be erroneous and impracticable;(*i*) if one partner excludes, or claims to exclude the other from his proper share of control in the
business, or if, though not in terms excluding him, he is
so conducting himself as to render it impossible that the
[*243] business should be conducted *on the stipulated
terms;(*k*)[1] if he is dealing fraudulently with the

(*g*) Young *v.* Keighley, 15 Ves. 557 ; Duvergier *v.* Fellows, 5 Bing. 248 ;
Blundell *v.* Windsor, 8 Sim. 601 ; Harrison *v.* Heathorn, 6 Scott N. R. 735 ;
12 Law J. C. P. 282; Pinkett *v.* Wright, 2 Hare 120, 130.

(*h*) Joint Stock Companies' Acts, 7 Wm. 4 and 1 Vict. c. 73 ; 7 & 8 Vict.
c. 110 and 111 ; Companies' Clauses Consolidation Act, 8 & 9 Vict. c. 16 ;
3 Steph. Bl. 182; Joint Stock Banks' Acts, 7 Geo. 4, c. 46 ; and 1 and 2
Vict. c. 96 ; 5 & 6 Vict. c. 85 ; 7 & 8 Vict. c. 113 ; 3 Steph. Bl. 340.

(*i*) Beaumont *v.* Meredith, 3 Ves. & B. 180; Clough *v.* Radcliffe, 1 De
G. & S. 164.

(*k*) Goodman *v.* Whitcomb, 1 J. & W. 569 ; Hale *v.* Hale, 4 Beav. 369 ;
Smith *v.* Jeyes, Id. 503 ; Waters *v.* Taylor, 15 Ves. 10; 2 Ves. & B. 299, 304.

---

[1] Where a partnership is formed for a definite term, neither partner can,

business or assets of the partnership;(*l*) or if he is incapacitated by incurable lunacy from performing his own part in the partnership business. The lunacy of a partner does not *per se* amount to a dissolution; but if it be not a mere temporary malady, but a confirmed state of insanity, without a fair prospect of speedy recovery, it will warrant a decree for the purpose; and the partnership will be dissolved as from the date of the decree.(*m*)[1]

Assuming a dissolution to be proved or decreed, the next topic for consideration is the mode of winding up the concern.

The first step is, that the partnership debts should be ascertained, and the assets applied in their discharge.[2]

(*l*) Marshall *v.* Colman, 2 J. & W. 266.

(*m*) Waters *v.* Taylor, 2 Ves. & B. 299, 303; Jones *v.* Noy, 2 M. & K. 125; Besch *v.* Frolich, 1 Ph. 172.

during the term, file a bill for a dissolution merely on the ground that he is dissatisfied, or that the partners quarrel: Henn *v.* Walsh, 2 Ed. Ch. 129. But only little more is needed, and dissolution will be granted, where dissension prevents all hope of advantage: Bishop *v.* Breckles, 1 Hoff. Ch. 534; Watney *v.* Wells, 30 Beav. 56; Stevens *v.* Yeatman, 19 Md. 480; Seighortner *v.* Weissenborn, 20 N. J. Eq. 172; Meaher *v.* Cox, 37 Ala. 201. Especially where one partner assumes the exclusive control of the business, and is guilty of breaches of faith. See Kennedy *v.* Kennedy, 3 Dana 239; Howell *v.* Harvey, 5 Ark. 270; Gowan *v.* Jeffries, 2 Ashmead 296; Maude *v.* Rodes, 4 Dana 144; Story *v.* Moon, 8 Id. 226; s. c. 3 Id. 331; Garretson *v.* Weaver, 3 Ed. Ch. 385. Breaches of articles of partnership are not necessarily the foundation of a decree of dissolution: Anderson *v.* Anderson, 25 Beav. 190. But where they are of such a nature, as to show that a partnership cannot be carried on for the benefit of the parties according to the original intention, as apparent from the articles, the partner thus affected may be relieved from the partnership, although there is no express provision that the partnership should determine upon the breaches complained of, or any other: Hall *v.* Hall, 3 Macn. & G. 79. See as to what amounts to such breach: Smith *v.* Mules, 9 Hare 556.

[1] Leaf *v.* Coles, 1 De G., M. & G. 171. See s. c., Id. 417, as a proof of the caution necessary in such cases: Rowlands *v.* Evans, 30 Beav. 302.

[2] The rule, that co-partnership funds are to be applied in the first place

484 ADAMS'S DOCTRINE OF EQUITY.

If the parties cannot agree on the intermediate management, whilst the process of dissolution is going on, a re-

to payment of the debts of the firm, and the separate funds of the partners
to the payment of their individual debts, before paying joint debts out of
the same, is very generally administered in this country. See McCulloh v.
Dashiel, 1 Har. & Gill 96; Lucas v. Atwood, 2 Stewart 378; White v.
Dougherty, 1 Mart. & Yerg. 409; Hubble v. Perrin, 3 Ham. 287; Topliff
v. Vail, Harring. Ch. 340; Tuno v. Trezevant, 2 Dessaus. 270; Woddrop v.
Price, 3 Id. 203; Deveau v. Fowler, 2 Paige 400; Innes v. Lansing, 7 Id.
583; Payne v. Matthews, 6 Id. 19; Rodiguez v. Heffernan, 5 Johns. Ch.
417; Simmons v. Tongue, 3 Bland 356; Kirby v. Schoonmaker, 3 Barb.
Ch. 46; Brewster v. Hammet, 4 Conn. 540; Witter v. Richards, 10 Id. 37;
Wilder v. Keeler, 3 Paige 167; Murray v. Murray, 5 Johns. Ch. 60; Gil-
more v. N. A. Land Co., 1 Pet. C. C. 460; Morgan v. Skidmore, 55 Barb.
(N. Y.) 263.

The general rule was also expressly recognised in Murrill v. Neill, 8
How. U. S. 414; Muir v. Leitch, 7 Barb. S. C. 341; Jarvis v. Brooks, 3
Foster, (N. H.) 136; Crockett v. Crain, 33 N. H. 542; Fall River Whaling
Co. v. Borden, 10 Cush. 458; Converse v. McKee, 14 Texas 20; Talbot v.
Pierce, 14 B. Monr. 195; Inbusch v. Farwell, 1 Black (U. S.) 566; Hill v.
Beach, 1 Beas. 31; Linford v. Linford, 4 Dutch. 113; Crooker v. Crooker,
46 Maine 250; 52 Id. 267; Treadwell v. Brown, 41 N. H. 12; Matlack v.
James, 2 Beas. 126. But so far as it extends to give an actual preference
to the separate creditors over the separate estate, it has been repudiated in
several decisions, and has met the disapprobation of some of the ablest
judges in this country. It has been held, in these cases, contrary to the
English doctrine, adopted in several of the states (see above), that the joint
creditors are always entitled to come upon the separate estate, whether by
execution at law, or where a fund is created for creditors by death or insolvency, and that equity would do no more than marshal the debts, so that
the joint creditors should be compelled to proceed against the partnership
assets in the first instance: Tucker v. Oxley, 5 Cranch 35; Grosvenor v.
Austin, 6 Ohio 103; Sperry's Est., 1 Ashmead 347; Cleghorn v. Ins. Bank
of Columbus, 9 Ga. 320; Emanuel v. Bird, 19 Ala. 596; Wardlaw v. Gray,
Hill's Ch. 644-653; Gadsden v. Carson, 9 Rich. Eq. 266; Reed v. Shepardson, 2 Verm. 120; Allen v. Wells, 22 Pick. 450; White v. Dougherty, 1
Mart. & Yerg. 309; Morrison v. Kurtz, 15 Ill. 193; Pahlman v. Graves,
26 Id. 407; Black's Appeal, 44 Penn. St. 503 (modifying the rule in Bell
v. Newman, 5 S. & R. 78); Houseal & Smith's Appeal, 45 Penn. St. 484;
though see Weyer v. Thornburgh, 15 Ind. 126. In Camp v. Grant, 21 Conn.
41, the court went even further, and held, that as partnership debts are, in
equity, joint and several, joint creditors might claim against the estate of

ceiver may be appointed to conduct it.   But the Court
cannot permanently carry on the business, and will not,

---

a deceased partner, though there were a solvent partner living. As joint
creditors, however, have no recourse at law against the separate assets, in
such case, so long as there is a surviving partner, it would seem to be going
very far to interfere with the legal rights of the separate creditors, by
admitting a class of equitable debts to come in *pari passu* with, and, so
far, in derogation of them.   Equity, in the administration of legal assets,
never disregards legal preferences, though it may, in some cases, by marshalling, obviate their effect upon other creditors, as to the equitable assets,
if there be any.   As, however, all assets are now legal, the doctrine of
marshalling, so far, cannot arise.   What special equity then, have the joint
creditors?   None, it is now universally admitted, but such as they can
claim through that of the partners, which is clearly to have the partnership
assets applied to the exoneration of the separate estate.   The case of insolvency or death of a surviving partner, stands on a different footing, because there, the joint creditors have as much a legal right to recourse
against the separate estate, as the separate creditors; no analogy can,
therefore, be drawn between them.   It is submitted, indeed, that in all
cases, the true principle seems to be, that the separate creditors ought to
be as much entitled to avail themselves of the equities between the partners
as the joint creditors ; and that, without attributing any inherent equity to
either class, the assets should be so marshalled, if at all, as to throw the
burden of the debts, where, as between the partners, it ought to fall.

The preference of the joint creditors over the partnership assets, is undoubted.   See in Pennsylvania, Doner *v.* Stauffer, 1 Penna. R. 198 ; Overholt's App., 12 Penn. St. 222 ; Deal *v.* Bogue, 20 Id. 233 ; Baker's App.,
21 Id. 77 ; Snodgrass's App., 13 Id. 474.   And, indeed, the case of Andress *v.* Miller, 15 Penn. St. 316, would seem to show a return to the eu-
tire English doctrine.

This subject will be found discussed very fully in 3 Kent's Com. 65 ;
and in the note to Silk *v.* Prime, 2 Lead. Cas. Eq. 83, 3d Am. ed.

Partnership property cannot be subjected to the separate debts of partners, until all partnership debts are paid, including debts due from the
firm to the partners individually : Christian *v.* Ellis, 1 Gratt. 396 ; Buchan
v. Sumner, 2 Barb. Ch. 165 ; Conwell *v.* Sandidge, 8 Dana 279 ; Pierce *v.*
Tiernan, 10 Gill & J. 252.   But the rule does not apply in the case of a
silent partner ; in such case the partnership property may be taken for the
private debts of the ostensible partner, although there be partnership debts
unpaid : Cammack *v.* Johnson, 1 Green's Ch. 163.   The partnership creditors, as such, have no lien on the joint effects for their debts ; their right
is wholly dependent on the lien which the individual partners have upon
the joint funds for indemnity against joint debts, and for their several pro-

therefore, appoint a receiver, except with a view to getting in the effects and finally winding up the concern. (n)[1]

(n) Waters v. Taylor, 15 Ves. 10 ; 2 Ves. & B. 299; Goodman v. Whitcombe, 1 J. & W. 589 ; Const v. Harris. T. & R. 496 : Hare v. Hale, 4 Beav.

portions of the surplus, including moneys advanced by either of them beyond their share for the use of the partnership. See Snodgrass's App., 13 Penn. St. 474 ; Potts v. Blackwell, 4 Jones Eq. 58. Hence this preference of the joint stock creditors does not exist when the partnership is such that the partners, as between themselves, can enforce no such right: Rice v. Bernard, 20 Verm. 479. Or it may be terminated at any time by the acts of the parties, as, e. g., by the sale of the stock in trade by one partner to another : Parish v. Lewis, 1 Freem. Ch. 299 ; Robb v. Stevens, 1 Clarke Ch. 191; Waterman v. Hunt, 2 Rhode Island 298 ; Doner v. Stauffer, 1 Penn. St. 198. And this, if bonâ fide, whether the partnership be solvent or not: Allen v. Centre Valley R. R., 21 Conn. 130 ; or even if the partner to whom the transfer is made undertakes to pay the debts of the partnership : Baker's App., 21 Penn. St. 775 ; Robb v. Mudge, 14 Grey 534; Sigler v. The Bank, 8 Ohio (N. S.) 511; White v. Parrish, 20 Tex. 688; McNutt v. Strayhorn. 39 Penn. St. 269. And this right does not exist under a fieri facias levied after a dissolution : Cope's Appeal, 39 Penn. St. 287. But see Burtus v. Tisdall, 4 Barb. S. C. 571, where it was held, that the members of an insolvent partnership cannot by agreement divide the assets between themselves, so as to apply them to their separate creditors. See, also, Kirby v. Schoonmaker, 3 Barb. Ch. 46 ; Hoxie v. Carr, 1 Sum. 173 ; Story v. Moon, 3 Dana 334; Black v. Bush, 7 B. Monr. 210.

As a further consequence of the doctrine just stated, it must affirmatively appear, that the debts were created on partnership account; it is not sufficient to show a joint liability of the partners : Snodgrass's App.ꞌ 13 Penn. St. 474. So, too, a sale upon separate execution of each partner's interest, to the same purchaser, passes the whole interest in the partnership property discharged of the joint debts, for the equities of the partners have then ceased : Doner v. Stauffer, 1 Penna. R. 198. As joint creditors have no independent equities of their own, they have no right to come into chancery, to question or prevent any disposition by the partners of the firm assets, until, as in ordinary cases, they have exhausted their legal remedies : Greenwood v. Brodhead, 8 Barb. S. C. 593.

The equity of the partners inter se, gives them no greater right as to the separate estate of each other, than separate creditors : Mann v. Higgins, 7 Gill 265. Nor does it extend after dissolution and division of the assets : Holmes v. Hawes, 8 Ired. Eq. 21.

[1] The Court, generally, will not appoint a receiver on motion, unless it a tisfactorily appears that the plaintiff is entitled to have the partnership

If, after applying the assets, there are still outstanding liabilities, the partners must contribute in proportion to their shares ; if, on the other hand, a surplus remains, it will be distributed among them in like proportion.

369; Smith v. Jeyes, 4 Id. 503 ; infra, Receiver.⁻ [See Wolbert v. Harris, 3 Halst. Ch. 605.]

dissolved, and its affairs closed up: Garretson v. Weaver, 3 Ed. Ch. 385; Law v. Ford, 2 Paige 310; Martin v. Van Schaick, 4 Id. 479; Smith v. Lowe, 1 Ed. Ch. 33; Walker v. House, 4 Md. Ch. 40; Renton v. Chaplain, 1 Stock. 62 ; Cox v. Peters, 2 Beas. 39 ; see, also, Sloan v. Moore, 37 Penn. St. 222; a case in which a receiver was appointed. Nor without notice to those interested ; but there are exceptions, as where irreparable injury would arise from delay : Williamson v. Wilson, 1 Bland Ch. 418 ; Gowan v. Jeffries, 2 Ashm. 296; Holden v. McMakin, 1 Pars. Sel. Eq. Cas. 284; Hall v. Hall, 3 Macn. & G. 79. So where irreparable injury might ensue from the defendant's acts, a receiver may be appointed even on a bill not praying a dissolution, but restraint from breaches of partnership articles: Hall v Hall, 3 Macn. & G. 79. And the Court will not refuse a receiver, in a proper case, because questions are raised between the partners on the motion, as where the defendant in possession of the assets alleges that they are not sufficient to discharge the debts due him ; the only object of the appointment of the receiver being to protect the assets till the determination of the respective rights : Blakeny v. Dufau, 15 Beav. 40. A receiver is always granted in a clear case of exclusion : Blakeney v. Dufau, ut sup.; Wolbert v. Harris, 3 Halst. Ch. 605; especially after dissolution, or where dissolution is intended: Drury v. Roberts, 2 Md. Ch. 157; Speights v. Peters, 9 Gill 472. So where, after dissolution, one partner carries on business with the partnership effects on his own account: Speights v. Peters, ut sup.; Walker v. House, 4 Md. Ch. 40. But where, on dissolution, it is agreed that one or more of the number shall have charge of the affairs and wind up the partnership, the Court will not lightly interfere, as on mere apprehension of loss. There must be some palpable breach of duty, or an act amounting to fraud, or real endangerment of property, to justify the appointment of a receiver: Walker v. Trott, 4 Edw. Ch. 38. A receiver will not be appointed on the application of the representatives of a deceased against a surviving partner, except in a case of mismanagement or improper conduct; but where all the partners are dead, and there is no provision for winding up the concern, a receiver is of course, as between the representatives: Walker v. House, 4 Md. Ch. 40. Where one partner is bankrupt, the continuing partner is entitled to a receiver: Freeland v. Stansfield, 16 Jur. 792; Randall v. Morrell, 2 Green (N. J.) 343.

The proportions in which the partners are respectively entitled or liable are determined by the original terms of their contract; or in the absence of any express declaration on the point, by a reasonable presumption from the circumstances of the case.(o)1 If, subsequently to the [*244] *commencement of the business, advances had been made to the firm, or moneys drawn out by any partner, beyond his due proportion, their shares in the distribution will be modified accordingly. If such sums have been advanced or received by way of increase or diminution of capital, they will introduce a new element in the division of profits ; if by way of loan to or from the partnership, they will not affect the division of profits, but will be dealt with on the footing of loans in the final settlement of the account. The distinction, however, is confined to the account as between the partners themselves, and does not affect the creditors. The creditors are entitled to assume that a partner, dealing with the firm, has dealt with it in his character as a member, so that his advance shall be treated as an increase of the partnership fund, and not as an independent debt.[2] The consequence of this doctrine is, that no partner can, either by making advances to the firm or by any other course of dealing, entitle himself to a lien on the partner-

(o) Thompson v. Williamson, 7 Bli. 432.

---

[1] In the absence of any stipulation as to the division of the profits of a partnership, the law divides them equally : Jones v. Jones, 1 Ired. Eq. 332; see also Honore v. Colmesnil, 1 J. J. Marsh. 506 ; Towner v. Lane, 9 Leigh 262.

[2] See Logan v. Bond, 13 Ga. 196. A co-partner having taken money out of the hands of the partnership and carried it into a new concern which became bankrupt, it was held that the fund could not be followed specifically, so as to give the former co-partnership a priority over the other creditors of the bankrupt house : McCauly v. McFarlane, 2 Dessaus. 239.

ship assets, or on the shares of his copartners therein, except in subordination to the partnership creditors. And *e converso,* money drawn out by a partner without fraud, for his separate use, will not be considered a mere advance by the firm, recoverable as such in the character of a debt, but as having been entirely separated from the joint stock, and become the private property of the individual. If it has been fraudulently abstracted, the case is different, and the other partners, or in the event of bankruptcy, the joint creditors may reclaim it for the partnership.(*p*)

In order to effectuate the realization of assets, the payment of debts, and the distribution of surplus, the Court has an authority over partnership estate which does not exist in other cases of common ownership, that of directing its sale and conversion into money.[1] And this jurisdiction may be exercised either by the same decree which directs a dissolution, or, if dissolution has already taken place, by *an interlocutory order.(*q*) The effect [*245] of the equity to insist on such a sale, where real estate is held by the partnership, and a dissolution has been caused by death, is to raise a question of equitable conversion between the real and personal representatives of the deceased partner. The legal ownership will of

(*p*) Richardson *v.* Bank of England, 4 M. & C. 165; Pinkett *v.* Wright, 2 Hare 129; Ex parte Ruffin, 6 Ves. 119: Ex parte Yonge, 3 Ves. & B. 31.

(*q*) Crawshay *v.* Maule, 1 Sw. 495. 523; Featherstonhaugh *v.* Fenwick, 17 Ves. 298; Cook *v.* Collingridge, Jac. 607; Simmons *v.* Leonard, 3 Hare 581.

---

[1] In winding up the concerns of a partnership, after a dissolution, one partner cannot take the partnership stock at a valuation, but its value must be ascertained by the conversion of it into money: Sigourney *v.* Munn, 7 Conn. 11; Dickinson *v.* Dickinson, 29 Id. 600. See also, to this point, Evans *v.* Evans, 9 Paige 178; Dougherty *v.* Van Nostrand, 1 Hoff. Ch. 68; Conwell *v.* Sandidge, 8 Dana 278; Mayer *v.* Clark, 40 Ala. 259.

course devolve according to the limitations in the conveyance; but the equitable interest of the deceased partner in the surplus, so far as it is referable to the real portion of the assets, will devolve on his heir or his executor, according as the equity for sale is confined to satisfaction of the liabilities, or extends to distribution among the partners. The doctrines on this point appear to be as follows: first, that if there be any express contract or declaration by the partners, the question will be determined by it; (r) secondly, that if real estate be purchased with partnership funds for partnership purposes, the conversion into personal estate is absolute; (s) thirdly, that if it be not purchased with partnership funds, but being the property of one or more partners, be devoted, either partially or entirely, to the partnership business, the extent of conversion depends on the intention. And it must be determined from the circumstances of the particular case whether that intention was to convert it *in toto,* both as to the liability for debts, and also as to the destination of the surplus, or to confine it to subservience to the business during its continuance, and to a liability for the debts after dissolution; (t) fourthly, that if though purchased out of the partnership fund, it has not been purchased for partnership purposes, but has been intended as an investment of surplus profits, it is in fact taken out of the business, [*246] *and belongs to the individual partners as their separate property, according to its unconverted character; (u) and lastly, that the conversion, when it

(r) Ripley v. Waterworth, 7 Ves. 425.

(s) Phillips v. Phillips, 1 M. & K. 649; Broom v. Broom, 3 M. & K. 443; Bligh v. Brent, 2 Y. & C. 268; Houghton v. Houghton, 11 Sim. 491; [Darby v. Darby, 25 L. J. Ch. 371.]

(t) Balmain v. Shore, 9 Ves. 500; Randall v. Randall, 7 Sim. 271; Cookson v. Cookson, 3 Sim. 529.

(u) Bell v. Phyn, 7 Ves. 453.

operates at all, operates in favor of the personal representative alone, and does not create a liability to probate duty
in favor of the Crown, which is a stranger to the converting equity. (v)[1]

(v) Custance v. Bradshaw, 4 Hare 315.

---

[1] The current of American decisions in respect to real estate purchased
with partnership funds, or for the use of the firm, seems to establish : 1st.
That such real estate is in equity chargeable with the debts of the co-
partnership, and with any balance due from one partner to another, upon
the winding up of the affairs of the firm. 2d. That as between the personal representatives and the heirs at law of a deceased partner, his share
of the surplus of the real estate which remains after paying the debts of
the partnership, and adjusting the claims of the different members of the
firm, as between themselves, is to be considered and treated as real estate :
Buchan v. Sumner, 2 Barb. Ch. 165; Sigourney v. Munn, 7 Conn. 11 ;
Winslow v. Chiffelle, I Harp. Eq. 25 ; Thayer v. Lane, Walker's Eq. 200 ;
Dyer v. Clark, 5 Metc. 562; Greene v. Greene, 1 Ham. 535; Marvin v.
Trumbull, Wright 386 ; Burnside v. Merrick, 4 Metc. 541 ; Summer v.
Hampson, 8 Ohio 364; Rice v. Barnard, 20 Verm. 479 ; Smith v. Tarlton,
2 Barb. Ch. 336 ; Baird v. Baird, 1 Dev. & Batt. Eq. 524 ; Hoxie v. Carr,
1 Sumn. 173; Overholt's Appeal, 12 Penn. St. 222 ; Smith v. Jones, 12
Maine 337 ; Baldwin v. Johnson, Saxton 441 ; Richardson v. Wyatt, 2 Des-
saus. 471; Woolridge v. Wilkins, 3 How. (Miss.) 360; Peck v. Fisher, 7 Cush.
390 ; Boyce v. Coster, 4 Strob. Eq. 30 ; Buckley v. Buckley, 11 Barb. S. C. 44;
Deming v. Colt. 3 Sand. S. C. 284 ; Talbot v. Pierce, 14 B. Monr. 195 ; see
Lang v. Waring. 17 Ala. 145 ; Andrew's Heir v. Brown's Adm., 21 Ala. 437 ;
Wilcox v. Wilcox, 13 Allen (Mass.) 252; Bryant v. Hunter, 6 Bush (Ky.) 75 ;
Cornwall v. Cornwall, Id. 369 ; Nat. Bank of Metropolis v. Sprague, 20 N. J.
Eq. 13 ; Uhler v. Simple, 20 N. J. Eq. 288. But a purchaser without notice,
of partnership real estate, takes discharged of the debts : Buck v. Winn, 11
B. Monr. 320; Boyce v. Coster, 4 Strob. Eq. 30. In Peck v. Fisher, 7 Cush. 390,
it was held that a levy and sale of such real estate on a separate execution
passed a good title to the purchaser, yet subject in equity to the debts.
Ch. J. Gibson, however, in Kramer v. Arthurs, 7 Penn. St. 172, was of
opinion that as a separate creditor could sell only the contingent interest
of a partner in the profits, that being personalty, would not be bound by
a judgment. Sed qu., for the judgment would bind the legal estate ; and
unless partnership real estate is to be treated as converted out and out,
which is against the current of authorities in this country, the conversion
for the special purposes of satisfying the equities of the partnership, would

If after a partnership has been dissolved by death or bankruptcy, the assets are used by the surviving or solvent partner for the purposes of profit, he is in the same position as any other fiduciary holder of property using it for his own benefit, and is liable at the option of the executors or assignees to account for the profit which he has made.[1] It does not, however, follow, that in taking

eave it, *ultra* those purposes, unconverted. Though on the death of a partner his moiety of the legal estate in partnership land descends to his heir, yet a sale of the whole by the survivor, for the purpose of paying partnership deaths, will pass the equitable estate to the purchaser, and he may compel a conveyance by the heir: Andrews *v.* Brown, 21 Ala. 437. A lease of partnership land is to be considered a partnership transaction: Moderwell *v.* Mullison, 21 Penn. St. 259. And if the title to the real estate is in one partner only, and he dies, his heirs will be considered as trustees for the survivor: Pugh *v.* Currie, 5 Ala. 446. See also Smith *v.* Ramsey, 1 Gilm. 373. And a sale thereof, in a suit to settle the partnership affairs, binds the heirs of a deceased partner, though not parties to the suit: Waugh *v.* Mitchell, 1 Dev. & Batt. 510. See, on the other hand, Yeatman *v.* Wood, 6 Yerg. 20; Deloney *v.* Hutcheson, 2 Rand. '183 ; Smith *v.* Jackson, 2 Ed. Ch. 28 ; Hart *v.* Hawkins, 3 Bibb 502. When partners intend to bring real estate into the partnership stock, the intention ought to be manifest by deed or writing, placed on record, that purchasers and creditors may not be deceived: Hale *v.* Henrie, 2 Watts 143 ; Forde *v.* Herrón, 4 Munf. 316; Ridgway's App., 15 Penn. St. 477. See also, Ware *v.* Owens, 42 Ala. 212; Pecot *v.* Armelin, 21 La. Ann. 667.

[1] If a partnership business, after its termination by death or otherwise, is continued by any portion of the associates with the capital or appliances of the firm, all profits derived from such continued business are part of the joint estate, and are to be accounted for to the other ,partners or their representatives: Waring *v.* Cram, 1 Pars. Sel. Eq. Cas. 522. And see Washburn *v.* Goodman, 17 Pick. 519. A surviving partner is treated in the light of a trustee, and is bound to furnish a full and accurate statement of all the transactions of the partnership, and to dispose of the property at the best advantage. He cannot take the property at an estimated value, without the consent of the representatives of the deceased partner, and if he does, he will be accountable to them for the profits made thereby: Ogden *v.* Astor, 4 Sandf. S. C. 311. A partnership may be continued in equity after the death of one of the partners, for the benefit of his infant children, with the consent of the surviving partners: Powell *v.*

the subsequent account, the division of the profits is to be the same as if the partner had not died or become bankrupt, or is to be determined by any other specific rule; but the decision will be guided by the circumstances of the business, to be ascertained by inquiry under the direction of the Court, such, for instance, as the source from which the profits are derived, whether originating in mere profitable traffic or in the personal skill and activity of individual partners.(*w*) There is a doubt as to the liability of a surviving partner with respect to the mere good-will of a commercial partnership, where such good-will is unconnected with any particular premises, and consists only in the probability that the customers of the old firm will continue their connection with any new firm professedly carried on in continuance of the old. It has been considered on the one hand that such good-will belongs exclusively to the survivor, and on the other, that it must

(*w*) Crawshay *v.* Collins, 15 Ves. 218; Brown *v.* De Tastet, Jac. 284; Cook *v.* Collingride, Jac. 607; Wedderburn *v.* Wedderburn, 2 K. 772; 4 M. & C. 41; Willet *v.* Blanford, 1 Hare 253.

North, 3 Indiana (Porter) 392. An express agreement in the articles, that the widow of one of the partners should, if she elected so to do, carry on the business with the survivor, and be entitled to her husband's share of the profits and capital, creates a trust which can be enforced in equity: Page *v.* Cox, 10 Hare 163.

It may be remarked here that in a recent case in England, Buckley *v.* Barber, 6 Exch. 164, it has been held, that partnership chattels, on the death of one, do not survive to the remaining partners; and that they have no power to dispose of them by sale or mortgage in satisfaction of debts. But this is not in accordance with the doctrines on the subject as understood in this country: see Story, Partnership, § 344; 3 Kent. 37; Am. note to Buckley *v.* Barber, ut supr.: and would be likely to produce no little difficulty in the winding up of partnerships in such cases. It would rather seem, that as the exception of *jus accrescendi inter mercatores locum non habet*, was introduced for the benefit of trade, its operation should be controlled for the same reason.

be treated as a portion of the partnership assets, so as to entitle the executors of a deceased partner to a share of profits. (x)[1]

[*247]   *In addition to the general jurisdiction over partnership, there is also a jurisdiction over mines and collieries held by several persons as co-owners, on the ground of what may be termed a *quasi* partnership. It often happens that such co-owners have, by an agreement expressly made or deduced by implication from their acts, formed themselves into a trading partnership, holding the mines as a portion of its assets. When this is the case the ordinary jurisdiction over partnership will be incidental to their agreement. But it may also happen that no partnership has been formed, and that the parties have merely concurred in working their mines as tenants in common. In this case the jurisdiction over partnerships will not attach; and if it were an ordinary instance of

---

(x) Crawshay v. Collins, 15 Ves. 218, 227; Cruttwell v. Lye, 17 Id. 336; Farr v. Pearce, 3 Mad. 74; Lewis v. Langdon, 7 Sim. 421; Willet v. Blantford, 1 Hare 253, 271.

---

[1] The good-will of a business built up by a copartnership is an important and valuable interest, which the law recognises and will protect: Williams v. Wilson, 4 Sandf. Ch. 379. And upon a dissolution it must be sold; it does not survive: Dougherty v. Van Nostrand, 1 Hoff. Ch. 68. The good-will (consisting of the subscription list, &c.) of a newspaper is partnership property, and when one of the partners dies, it does not survive to the surviving partner, but is to be sold, with the presses, types and mechanical appliances of the establishment. Case of the Saturday Courier, Holden's Admr. v. McMakin, 1 Parsons' Sel. Eq. Cas. 270.

The good-will is distinct from the profits of a business; although in determining its value, the profits are necessarily taken into account, and it is usually estimated at so many years' purchase upon the amount of these profits: Austen v. Boys, 27 L. J. Ch. 714. In this case it was considered that there could be no such thing as the good-will of a business such as that of a solicitor, which is dependent principally on a confidence in the professional skill and integrity of a particular person.

tenancy in common, there would be no jurisdiction to interfere with any one of the co-owners with respect to his own share, whatever ground there might be to restrain him from excluding the rest. The rule, however, is different with respect to mines;[1] for the working of them has always been considered as a species of trade; and if each owner were to deal separately with his separate share, and to have a separate set of miners going down the shaft, it would be practically impossible to work the mine at all.

---

[1] In Roberts v. Eberhart, 1 Kay 148, however, the distinction taken in the text between mines and collieries, seems to be somewhat affected. It was said there by the Vice-Chancellor, that there were two modes of viewing a mining concern. It might be one really held as property by parties who never acquired it for purposes of trade, as where an estate containing mines, has descended from the owner to two co-heirs, and such joint owners agree to work the mines together with their joint property, and buy steam engines, and pay workmen during that working. That would be a partnership in the working, though not in the land; and either of the joint owners might at any time change his mind, and put an end to the joint working. One might then continue to work, but could not compel the other to go on; and he who continued to work might have to render an account. The other case would be where the circumstances afforded evidence that the whole property was intended to be used as a partnership concern; and, therefore, where any disagreement arose, any of the partners might come into the Court to determine the partnership and have the property divided. In either case it would be proper to ask for a dissolution and winding up of the concern, and for receiver if the partners could not agree.

In this case two tenants in common of a mine had been working it jointly, when a disagreement arose, and then one continued to work it, but the other refused to coöperate with him in doing so, or in providing some necessary expenses, though he did not interfere in the management. The managing partner filed a bill for an account and receiver, but did not pray a dissolution. The Court held that it could not, at the instance of the managing partner, and where there had been no interference by the other, and no dissolution was prayed, appoint a receiver. Where persons are engaged in working a mining claim, and share the profit and loss, they are partners, although there is no express stipulation for such communion of loss and profit: Duryea v. Burt, 28 Cal. 569. See also, as to this subject, Grubb's Appeal, 66 Penn. St. 117.

For this reason it is held upon general principle
reference to the particular circumstances of any
where tenants in common of a mine or collie
agree in its management, the Court will appoint
over the whole, notwithstanding some of the
may dissent. In accordance with the same
Court grants an injunction against trespass, a
suits for the mesne profits of a mine or coll
appears from the peculiar character of the
coupled with the general circumstances of the
the remedy would be impracticable at law.(y)

(y) Crawshay v. Maule, 1 Sw. 495, 518, 523; Jeffreys $v.$
W. 298; Fereday v. Wightwick, 1 R. & M. 45; Bentley v. Bat
182; V,ice v. Thomas, Id. 538.

*CHAPTER IV. [*248]

OF ADMINISTRATION OF TESTAMENTARY ASSETS.

THE equity for administering the assets of a testator or intestate does not authorize the Court of Chancery to try the validity of a will. The jurisdiction for that purpose in regard to wills of personal estate belongs to the Ecclesiastical Courts, and in regard to wills of real estate to the Courts of common law.[1]

---

[1] In cases of fraud, equity has a concurrent jurisdiction with a Court of law, except in the case of a will charged to have been obtained through fraud. If it be a devise of real estate, it is referred to a Court of law to decide, upon an issue of *devisavit vel non;* if a testament of personal property, to the Court of Probate. Yet, even in this instance, the bill may be retained to abide the decision of the proper Court, and relief be decreed according to the event: Gaines et ux. *v.* Chew et al., 2 How. U. S. 619, 645; Colton *v.* Ross, 2 Paige 396; Hamberlin *v.* Terry, 7 How. (Miss.) 143; Cowden *v.* Cowden, 2 Id. 806; Ewell *v.* Tidwell, 20 Ark. 136; Blue *v.* Patterson, 1 Dev. & Batt. Ch. 457; Lyne *v.* Guardian, 1 Miss. 410; Van Alst *v.* Hunter, 5 Johns. Ch. 148; Hunt *v.* Hamilton, 9 Dana 90; Muir *v.* Trustees, 3 Barb. Ch. 477; McDowall *v.* Peyton, 2 Dessaus. 313; Burrow *v.* Ragland, 6 Humph. 481; Hunter's Will, 6 Ohio 499; Gould *v.* Gould, 3 Story 516; Watson *v.* Bothwell, 11 Ala. 653; Adams *v.* Adams, 22 Verm. 50. It has been generally held, however, that equity has jurisdiction in the case of a lost, suppressed or spoliated will, to establish the same, and to decree payment of a legacy by the executor, or that the heir shall stand as trustee for the disappointed devisee: Allison *v.* Allison, 7 Dana 94; Bailey *v.* Stiles, 1 Green Ch. 220; Buchanan *v.* Matlock, 8 Humph. 390; Meads *v.* Langdon's Heirs, cited 22 Verm. 59; see Story Eq., § 254; Hill on Trustees 151; Legare *v.* Ashe, 1 Bay (S. C.) 464. *Contra*, Morningstar *v.* Selby, 15 Ohio 345, and Slade *v.* Street, 27 Ga. 17, where the jurisdiction was held to be exclusively in the Probate Courts. In Gaines *v.* Chew,

32

The validity of a will of personal estate is triable only by the Ecclesiastical Courts; and a probate copy under their seal, unless lost or destroyed, is the only admissible evidence of such validity, and of the consequent title of the executor. In like manner, if there be no executor, an administrator can only be appointed by the Ecclesiastical Court. And even fraud, if practised on a testator in obtaining a will, is insufficient to create a jurisdiction in equity. If, indeed, the fraud be not practised on the testator himself, but on an intended legatee; e. g., if the drawer of a will were to substitute his own name for that of the legatee, or were to promise the testator to stand as trustee for another, so that the question raised does not affect either the validity of the will or the propriety of the grant of probate, equity may decree a trust.[1]   Or

2 How. U. S. 645, the question was raised, but not decided, the Court holding the complainant entitled at least to discovery.

[1] In Allen v. McPherson, 1 H. Lords Cas. 101, L. Ch. Cottenham took a distinction between fraud in obtaining particular provisions in a will, and fraud in obtaining a will generally, and argued with great force that equity had jurisdiction in the former, though not in the latter case. The. majority of the Lords, however, did not sustain the distinction. That was a`case, in which the complainant alleged that the defendant, who was a residuary legatee, had fraudulently induced the testator to revoke legacies of a large amount in his (the complainant's) favor, substituting others of a trifling amount, and it was held that the matter was exclusively within the jurisdiction of the Ecclesiastical Courts. In a recent case, Hindson v. Weatherill, 1 Sm. & G. 604, Vice-Chancellor Stuart sustained a bill to decree a solicitor, who had obtained a devise by undue influence, as was alleged, a trustee for the heir; and considered the jurisdiction of equity in such cases unquestionable, notwithstanding the decision in Allen v. McPherson. See also the remarks in Dimes v. Steinberg, 2 Sm. & Giff. 75; Morgan v. Annis, 3 De G. & Sm. 461. On appeal, the case of Hindson v. Weatherill, was reversed on another point (5 De G., M. & G. 301); but L. J. Turner took occasion to express very strong doubts, whether such a bill were within the jurisdiction of equity at all. The question, however, of the validity of the execution of a power of appointment over personalty by will, has been held to stand on a different footing from that of ordinary

if it be practised, not in reference to the will itself, but to its subsequent establishment by the Ecclesiastical Court, *e. g.*, by fraudulently obtaining the consent of the next of kin, the executor *may be decreed ‚to consent to a revocation of the probate. But if the fraud were practised on the testator in obtaining the will, so that the contest really is whether the will ought to be proved, the proper course is to oppose the grant of probate, and there appears to be no jurisdiction in equity to relieve.(*a*) [*249]

The validity of a will of real estate, and of the consequent title of the devisee, is triable only by the Courts of common law. If the devisee, being out of possession, seeks to enforce the will, or if the heir, being out of possession, seeks to set it aside, their respective modes of

(*a*) Gingell *v.* Horne, 9 Sim. 539 ; Walsh *v.* Gladstone, 1 Ph. 294 ; Allen *v.* McPherson, 1 Ph. 133 ; 1 House of Lords Cases 191.

testamentary dispositions, and the jurisdiction of chancery to inquire into the state of mind of the testator, and the influences brought to bear upon it, so far as they affect that validity, asserted : Morgan *v.* Annis, 3 De G. & Sm. 461. It appears to be settled in England, that pending a suit in the Ecclesiastical Court, to recall probate of a will, alleged to have been fraudulently obtained from the testator, by the executor and one of the legatees, a bill for an account and receiver may be sustained against the latter : Dimes *v.* Steinberg, 2 Sm. & Giff. 75. Without some such qualification, indeed, the broad doctrine of Allen *v.* McPherson, and that held in this country, might be productive of very great hardship and injustice. Relief by discovery, injunction and account, is peculiarly necessary in the case of a will obtained by fraud ; while it is generally beyond the scope of the procedure of the Ecclesiastical or Probate Courts. See also, Gaines *v.* Chew, 2 How. U. S. 619, and Story's Eq., § 184, note. Whatever be the true principle upon the general question, however, there is no doubt that where a devise is fraudulently obtained on a promise to hold the land in trust for another, the trust may be enforced in equity : Jones *v.* McKee, 3 Penn. St. 496 ; s. c. 6 Id. 428 ; Jenkins *v.* Eldredge, 3 Story 181 ; Howell *v.* Baker, 4 Johns. Ch. 118 ; Hoge *v.* Hoge, 1 Watts 213 ; Miller *v.* Pearce, 6 W. & S. 97 ; Gaither *v.* Gaither, 3 Md. Ch. 158.

doing so are by ejectment at law. If there be outstanding terms or other legal impediment, they may respectively come into equity to have them removed.[1] If either party, being in possession, fears that his possession may be subsequently disturbed, he may perpetuate the testimony on a proper bill; or if, after a satisfactory verdict and judgment, he is harassed by repeated ejectments, he may have an injunction to restrain them on a bill of peace. But neither party can resort to the Court of Chancery as a tribunal for the trial of the will. If, however, there be a trust to perform or assets to administer, so that the will is drawn within the cognisance of equity, there is an incidental jurisdiction to declare the will is established, after first directing an issue *devisavit vel non*, to try its validity at law.[2] By the old practice it was

---

[1] Where the heir out of possession seeks to set aside a will, and an impediment exists as to part, as, in the case of land, an outstanding trust term, he may come into equity on account of the inadequacy of the remedy at law; and the jurisdiction having attached as to part, may be retained as to all: Brady v. McCosker, 1 Comstock 214.

[2] The law, as stated in the text, if it ever had a solid foundation, has been entirely overthrown in England, by the recent decision in Boyse v. Rossborough, 3 De G., M. & G. 817; 18 Jur. 205; affirming s. v. 1 Kay 71; and affirmed in the House of Lords, in Colclough v. Boyse, 6 H. Lds. Cas. 1; in which it was held that the Court has jurisdiction to establish a will of lands, as against the heir at law out of possession, at the suit of a legal devisee; though the estate of the latter be unaffected by a trust, and, though there be no other ground for the intervention of equity, than for the speedy determination of the question. It was shown that such had been the uniform doctrine of chancery, from the earliest times. The object of such a bill is to compel the heir to try the validity of the will at once, and it is recommended by obvious motives of convenience and justice. If no such remedy existed, a devisee might be subject to serious difficulty in making title, by adverse claims of the heir, though the latter, nevertheless, did not choose to subject them, at the time, to the test of an ejectment. It is to be understood, of course, that on a bill of this nature, the principal question is to be tried by an issue of *devisavit vel non*, or by an action directed by the court.

As the title to land can only be settled in the *forum rei sitæ*, a bill to

necessary to establish a will against the heir, whenever the Court was called upon to execute its trusts, but the rule is now abolished. The issue of *devisavit vel non* when a declaration of establishment is asked, is demandable as of right by the heir; for he can be disinherited only by the verdict of a jury. But he may waive this right by his conduct. He is also entitled to demand, that on trial of the issue, the devisee shall not confine the proof of execution to a single witness, but shall give all possible information *as to the validity of the will by examining every attesting witness who [*250] is capable of being produced.(*b*)

Assuming the right of a personal or real representative to be established, whether that of an executor or devisee, or that of an administrator or heir, there is an equity for administering the assets of the testator or intestate, originating in the inefficacy of the ordinary tribunals.[1]

(*b*) Kerrich *v.* Bransby, 7 B. P. C. 437 ; Pemberton *v.* Pemberton, 13 Ves. 290, 297 ; Bootle *v.* Blundell, 19 Id. 494 ; 31 Order of Aug. 1841 ; Tatham *v.* Wright, 2 R. & M. 1 ; Man *v.* Ricketts, 7 Beav. 93.

---

establish a will, will not affect real estate beyond the jurisdiction of the Court in which it is brought. Accordingly, in Boyse *v.* Colclough, 24 L. J. Ch. 7 ; 1 Kay & John. 124, another branch of the case just mentioned, it was held to be no answer to a bill of this character as to land in England, that such a bill had been filed by the same devisee in Ireland, and that an issue of *devisavit vel non* had been determined, and a decree made, establishing the validity of the will.

[1] In most of the United States the jurisdiction over the administration of the estates of decedents is placed in the hands of special tribunals, entitled Courts of Probate, Surrogate, or Orphans' Courts, which, in general, possess the combined powers of the Court of Chancery, and the Ecclesiastical Courts in England upon the subject. Proper means are provided to compel the executors and administrators to collect the assets, to settle proper accounts, and to satisfy the claims of creditors, legatees, and distributees. But it sometimes happens, that in order to the relief required, other remedies than those which are incident to the procedure in these tribunals, are necessary, in which case a resort to Chancery becomes unavoidable. See

The first difficulty which calls for equitable aid is that of compelling the executor or administrator to get in the assets. With respect to any assets which he has actually received, there are means, though not effectual ones, for making him account. But if he neglects or refuses to get in the assets, the Court of Chancery alone can enforce collection. (c)

With respect to assets actually received, the executor or administrator may be sued by any creditor in a Court of law; and if he does not by his plea deny the receipt, or if the plaintiff is able to falsify his denial, judgment will be obtained against him. But there are no means at law for obtaining discovery of the assets on oath, nor for distributing them ratably among all the creditors. The remedy of a legatee at law is still more limited; for a general legacy, whether pecuniary or residuary, cannot be there recovered; and even a specific legacy, which is more favorably treated, cannot be recovered unless the executor has assented to the bequest. (d)[1]

(c) Pearse v. Hewitt, 7 Sim. 471.

(d) Deeks v. Strutt, 5 T. 690; Jones v. Tanner, 9 B. & C. 542.

Pharis v. Leachman, 20 Ala. 662. Thus a bill may be filed by a creditor, to subject real or personal property, fraudulently disposed of by the decedent in his lifetime, to his debts: Hagan v. Walker, 14 How. U. S. 29; Pharis v. Leachman, ut supr. Or to follow assets which have passed into the hands of legatees or distributees, where the remedies against the executor have been exhausted: Ledyard v. Johnston, 16 Ala. 548. Or where the executor is insolvent or irresponsible: Ragsdale v. Holmes, 1 S. C. 91. In many of the states, indeed, the ordinary creditors' bills are still entertained. See Story Eq. § 543. In Gould v. Hayes, 19 Ala. 438, it was held, that the original jurisdiction of equity, is not affected by the statutory jurisdiction conferred on the Orphans' Court and similar tribunals, except where there are prohibitory or restrictive words. See also Freeland v. Dazey, 25 Ill. 294.

[1] A legacy cannot be legally reduced into possession by the legatee, without the consent of the executor; but that need not be expressly proved;

In the Ecclesiastical Court any creditor or legatee, or other person having an interest may compel the executor or administrator to deliver an inventory on oath. A creditor, however, has no power in that Court to dispute the truth of the inventory, or to enforce the payment of his *debt, but is remitted for that purpose to the Courts of law. A legatee or next of kin may dis- [*251] prove or object to the inventory, and may also, after assent, recover his legacy or distributive share; but there are no means by which assent can be compelled, or the clear residue ascertained.

It has been somtimes said that an executor holds the assets in the character of a trustee, and that the jurisdiction attaches on the existence of a trust. This, however, does not seem to be strictly accurate. It is true that in one sense an executor may be called a trustee, as any man may be so called who is bound to apply property for the benefit of others; but he is not a trustee in the technical sense. It is his duty to pay the creditors and legatees out of the assets, and he is personally liable if he neglects to do so. But there is no trust affecting the assets themselves. He may dispose of them to a purchaser in the absence of actual fraud, without affecting him with a trust by notice;[1] he may sustain or defend a suit in

---

it may be inferred from circumstances, though the legatee is himself the executor : Chester v. Greer, 5 Humph. 26: Cook v. Burton, 5 Bush (Ky.) 64. Where the estate of a testator is not indebted, the executor is bound to assent to a specific legacy. See Price v. Nesbit, 1 Hill. Ch. 445.

[1] See, to the same effect, Field v. Schieffelin, 7 Johns. Ch. 155 ; Hertell v. Bogert, 9 Paige 57 ; Tyrrell v. Morris, 1 Dev. & Batt. Eq. 559 ; Bond v. Ziegler, 1 Kelly 324 ; Miles v. Durnford, 1 De G., M. & G. 64 ; Haynes v. Forshaw, 17 Jur. 930 ; though in some of the United States, an administrator being required to sell at public sale, it is held that a private sale passes no title : Fambro v. Gantt, 12 Ala. 305 ; Baines v. McGee, 1 Sm. & M. 208 ; Saxon v. Barksdale, 4 Dessaus. 526 ; but see Bond v. Ziegler, ut

equity without joining the creditors or legatees as parties; if he neglect to invest a legacy he will not, like an ordinary trustee, be liable for loss occasioned by the delay, or for any increased value, which if sooner invested, the legacy would have borne. And it is not until the debts and legacies are paid, and the residue ascertained and appropriated, or until some legacy has been set apart from the general fund, that his representative character ceases, and he becomes a trustee of such residue or appropriated legacy, and is subject, in respect of it, to the ordinary rules respecting trust property.(e)   The position of the heir or devisee is very similar to that of the executor or administrator.   He is not technically a trustee for cred-

(e) Byrchall v. Bradford, 6 Mad. 13, 235; Phillipo v. Munnings, 2 M. & C. 309; Willmott v. Jenkins, 1 Beav. 401; Say v. Creed, 3 Hare 455.

---

supr. But if the purchaser has notice that the transaction amounts to a *devastavit*, he is liable to legatees and distributees, and the property may be pursued: Field v. Schieffelin, ut supr.; Colt v. Lasnier, 9 Cowen 320; Williamson v. Branch Bank, 7 Ala. 906; Parker v. Gilliam, 10 Yerg. 394 · Garnet v. Macon, 6 Call 361; Petrie v. Clark, 11 S. & R. 388; Graff v. Castleman, 6 Rand. 204; Lowry v. Farmers' Bank, 3 Am. L. J. N. S. 111; Williamson v. Morton, 2 Md. Ch. 94; Patterson v. Patterson, 63 N. C. 322. At law, actual collusion is necessary, but equity regards the whole transaction: Williamson v. Morton. A transfer by way of security for, or in extinguishment of a private debt of the executor, is sufficient notice: Petrie v. Clark; Field v. Schieffelin; Williams v. Branch Bank; Williamson v. Morton; Dodson v. Simpson, 2 Rand. 294. But a pledge for a contemporaneous advance in good faith has been held within the general rule: Tyrrell v. Morris, 1 Dev. & Bat. Eq. 559; see Petrie v. Clark; Miles v. Durnford; Ashton v. The Atlantic Bank, 3 Allen 217.

A distinction has been taken in England, in this respect, between particular and general or residuary legatees,—the latter not being permitted, as against the purchaser, to question a disposition of the assets by the executors: McLeod v. Drummond, 14 Ves. 361; *acc.* McNair's App. 4 Rawle 155: *contra,* Johnson v. Johnson. 2 Hill Eq. 277; and see Lord Eldon's remarks, 17 Ves. 169, 170.

The doctrine just considered, it is almost unnecessary to state, applies only to personal estate: Brush v. Ware, 15 Pet. 93.

itors, but is bound to pay them so far as the assets will go. He is accountable in equity on the same principle, and if he refuses to get in the outstanding *estate, the [*252] creditors may enforce its collection in the same way.(*f*)

In exercising the jurisdiction to administer assets, all such assets as would be recognised at law are termed legal assets, and are administered in conformity with legal rules, by giving priority to debts in order of degree;[1] so that debts of a higher degree are discharged before those of a lower; and debts of equal degree are discharged *pari passu*, subject to the executor's right of retaining any debt due to himself in preference to other creditors of the same degree. The priority of debts is according to the following order, viz. : 1. Debts due to the Crown by record or specialty, which have priority over all other debts, as well of a prior as of a subsequent date; 2. Certain specific debts which are by particular statutes to be preferred;(*g*) 3. Debts by judgment or decree, and immediately after them debts by recognisance of statute; 4. Debts by specialty, as on bonds, covenants, and other instruments under seal; but if the bond or covenant be merely voluntary, it will have priority over legacies only, and will be postponed to simple contract debts, *bonâ fide* owing for valuable consideration ;(*h*)[2] 5. Debts on simple contract, as 'on bills or

(*f*) Burroughs *v.* Elton, 11 Ves. 29.

(*g*) 2 Wms. on Ex'rs. 723.   (*h*) Lady Cox's Case, 3 P. Wms. 339.

---

[1] When the assets are legal, Chancery follows the rules of law, in order to prevent confusion in the administration of the estate: Moses *v.* Murgatroyd, 1 Johns. Ch. 119; Atkinson *v.* Gray, 18 Jur. 283. Especially will priorities of liens be regarded; judgment creditors are entitled in equi.y to their legal priority in payment out of the legal assets. See Purdy *v.* Doyle, 1 Paige Ch. 558; Pascalis *v.* Canfield, 1 Ed. Ch. 201; also Thompson *v.* Brown, 4 Johns. Ch. 619; and the remarks upon it in Wilder *v.* Keeler, 3 Paige 167; Averill *v.* Loucks, 6 Barb. S. C. 470.

[2] The rule which entitles a specialty creditor to preferences over legal as-

notes and agreements not under seal, on verbal promises
and on promises implied by law.

There are also other assets, recognised in equity alone,
which are termed Equitable Assets, and are distributed
among the creditors *pari passu*, without regard to the
quality of their debts.

Legal assets may be defined as "those portions of the
property of a deceased person of which his executor or
heir may gain possession, and in respect whereof he may
be made chargeable, by the process of the ordinary tribunals, and without the necessity of equitable interference "[1] They consist first of the personal estate, to which
the executor *or administrator is entitled by vir-
[*253]
tue of his office; and secondly, of the real estate
descended or devised, except where the devise is for payment of debts ; a devise of this latter kind rendering the
estate, as we shall hereafter see, equitable instead of legal
assets.

---

sets, applies equally where the debt is not yet due, and the executor is
bound to set aside a fund for its payment when the time arrives, to the exclusion of simple contract creditors, if necessary : Atkinson *v.* Grey, 18
Jur. 283.

[1] Assets, however, actually realized, from whatever source, and in the
hands of the executor as money, are legal assets. So the proceeds of real
estate, directed by the court to be sold for the payment of debts, and paid
by the purchaser into court, are legal assets : Lovegrove *v.* Cooper, 2 Sm.
& G. 271 ; see Story Eq., s. 551 ; see also, Southwestern R. R. *v.* Thomason,
40 Ga. 408 ; Vaughan *v.* Deloatch, 65 N. C. 378.

The distinction between legal and equitable assets was well stated by
Vice-Chancellor Kindersley in Cook *v.* Gregson, 3 Drew. 549, in the following terms : "The general proposition is clear enough that where assets
may be made available in a court of law, they are legal assets, and where
they can only be made available through a court of equity, they are equitable assets. The proposition, however, does not refer to the question
whether the assets can be recovered by the executor in a court of law or in
a court of equity. The distinction refers to the remedies of the creditor,
and not to the nature of the property." See also, Shee *v.* French, 3 Drew.
716, and Mutlow *v.* Mutlow, 4 De G. & J. 539.

The common law rule as to the liability of real estate, restricted such liability within a narrow compass. The leasehold estates of the debtor were included in his personalty, and were of course liable for all the debts. But his freeholds were only liable for debts by specialty expressly naming the heirs; and if the descent were broken by a devise, or if the heir aliened before action brought, there was no proceeding at law or in equity by which that realty could be affected. In 1691 it was enacted, that "devises, unless for payments of debts, should be treated as fraudulent and void as against specialty creditors; that the devisee should be liable jointly with the heir on a specialty recoverable by action of debt, and that if descended real estate were aliened by the heir, he should be liable to the extent of its value."(i) In 1807 a bill was introduced and carried by Sir Samuel Romilly, making the real estate of persons who at the time of their decease were subject to the Bankrupt Laws liable to all their debts, but reserving to creditors by specialty their privilege of precedence.(k) The provisions of the acts of 1691 and 1807 were at a later period consolidated and enlarged, and powers were conferred on the Court of Chancery to render effectual any sales or mortgages which might be required for satisfaction of debts, notwithstanding the infancy or other incapacity of the heir or devisee.(l) By the last statute on the subject, the injustice which so long existed has been abolished; and the land of every debtor, whether trader or not, and as well copyhold as freehold, which he shall not by will

(i) 3 & 4 Wm. & Mary, c. 14, made perpetual by 6 & 7 Wm. 3, c. 14.
(k) 47 Geo. 3, c. 74.
(l) 11 Geo. 4 & 1 Wm. 4, c. 47; 2 & 3 Vict. c. 60; Price v. Carver, 3 M. & C. 157; Scholefield v. Heafield, 7 Sim. 669; s. c. 8 Id. 470.

[*254] have *charged with or devised, subject to the payment of his debts, is made assets, to be administered in equity, for payment of both simple contract and specialty debts, reserving, however, to creditors by specialty in which the heirs are bound, the same priority which they originally possessed.(m)[1] The case of a charge for payment of debts, or of a devise subject to such payment is expressly excepted from the operation of the act, and retains its original effect of exempting the property as legal assets, and converting it into equitable assets.

In addition to the two kinds of legal assets, the personal and the real, which have been already mentioned, there is also a third kind, which though not obtainable without the intervention of equity, and therefore not in strictness legal assets, is yet, when obtained, to be administered as such, viz., property held by a trustee for the testator. For although the benefit of the trust, if resisted, cannot be enforced without equitable aid, yet the analogy of law will regulate the application of the fund. In one instance, that of a fee simple estate held on trust for the testator, the trust is made legal assets by the Statute of Frauds, so as to charge the heir in a Court of Law.(n)

Equitable assets may be defined as those portions of the property which by the ordinary rules of law, are exempt from debts, but which the testator has voluntarily charged as assets, or which, being non-existent at law, have been created in equity.[2]

(m) 3 & 4 Wm. 4, c. 104.
(n) 29 Car. 2, c. 3, s. 10; Case of Cox's Creditors, 3 P. Wms. 341.

---

[1] See under this statute, Foster v. Handley, 1 Sim. N. S. 200.
[2] In the most of the states of the Union, the doctrine of *equitable* assets

Equitable assets of the first class consist of real estate devised for or charged with the payment of debts. We have already seen that under the old law, if the descent were broken by a devise, the liability as assets was destroyed; and that the statutes for the abolition of that law

has been rendered of very limited application, by legislative enactments, on the one hand destroying preferences among the creditors of a decedent, and on the other, subjecting every species of property of the decedent, equally, to liability for his debts. And, even in those states where statutory preferences are given, as all assets are now in effect legal, equity cannot disregard the established order. See on this subject the notes to Silk v. Prime, 2 Lead. Cas. Eq., 3d Am. ed. 82; Sperry's Est., 1 Ashm. 347; Bloodgood v. Bruen, 2 Bradf. Surr. 8; Stagg v. Jackson, 1 Comst. 206. Where no such enactments have existed, it has prevailed in full effect. See Torr's Est., 2 Rawle 250. Thus, formerly in New York it was decided that the devise of an estate in trust to pay debts, and distribute the residue, made the proceeds of the estate equitable assets, out of which creditors were to be paid *pari passu.* Benson v. Le Roy, 4 Johns. Ch. 651; see Cornish v. Wilson, 6 Gill 303. So in Virginia, moneys arising from the sale of real property are equitable assets, and to be applied equally to all the creditors, in proportion to their claims: Backhouse v. Patton, 5 Peters 160; Black v. Scott, 2 Brock. 325. So in Kentucky, refer to Hilar v. Darby's Adm'rs., 3 Dana 18; Cloudas's Ex'r. v. Adams, 4 Id. 603; Speed's Ex'r. v. Nelson's Ex'r., 8 Monr. 499. See also on the doctrine, Henderson v. Burton, 3 Ired. Ch. 259. Devises of real estate in trust for the payment of debts, or charges on land for that purpose, are also recognised, and given very much the same effect, as in England, except so far as they would interfere with statutory preferences or regulations: Carrington v. Manning, 13 Ala. 628; Hines v. Spruill, 2 Dev. & Batt. 93; McHardy v. McHardy, 7 Flor. 301; Agnew v. Fetterman, 4 Penn. St. 62; Hoover v. Hoover, 5 Id. 357; Walker's Est., 3 Rawle 229. A sale by the trustees under such circumstances, will discharge the statutory lien of debts: Cadbury v. Duval, 10 Penn. St. 267; and such a trust will prevent the lien of judgments from expiring from want of revival: Baldy v. Brady, 15 Penn. St. 111. These trusts and charges, however, as they are no longer necessary to enable creditors to reach the land, are not regarded with as great favor, nor is the same forced construction resorted to in order to their establishment, as formerly: Agnew v. Fetterman, 4 Penn. St. 62; Carringotn v. Manning, 13 Ala. 628; Hines v. Spruill, 2 Dev. & Batt. Eq. 93. Where the statute directs equal distribution amongst creditors, a trust by will creating preferences, is so far void: Bull v. Bull, 8 B. Monr. 332.

contain an exemption of devises for payment of debts. With respect therefore to such devises, the old rule continues; and if a testator devises land for payment [*255] of his debts, or subject to *a charge for such payment, the devise operates to destroy the original liability, and to subject the land to a new liability by way of trust.(o)   The same rule does not apply to a bequest of personalty, for such a bequest is a mere nullity as against creditors, and does not affect the common law liability.(p)[1] Assets of this kind may be created in three ways: viz., 1. By a devise to trustees, either in fee or for a term, accompanied by a trust to sell or mortgage, or by a general direction to raise money out of the profits; 2. By a devise that the estate shall be sold, which, if the person to sell be specified, will confer on him a power of sale; or if no person be specified, but the produce is distributable by the executors, will confer on them by implication a similar power,(q) or, if no person be pointed out, either expressly or by implication, will create a charge on the estate; and, 3. By a direction that the estate shall be charged; which will authorize a sale by the person on whom the legal estate has devolved.(r)

Equitable assets of the second class consist of interests either in personal or real estate being which. non-existent at law, have been created in equity; and the principal assets of this class are equities of redemption. So long

(o) Shiphard v. Lutwidge, 8 Ves. 26.

(p) Scott v. Jones, 4 Cl. & F. 382; Lyon v. Colville, 1 Coll. 449.

(q) 1 Sug. on Powers 134; Gosling v. Carter, 1 Coll. 644.

(r) Shaw v. Borrer, 1 Keen 559; Ball v. Harris, 8 Sim. 485; 4 M. & C. 264.

---

[1] See to the same effect, Carrington v. Manning, 13 Ala. 628; Lewis v. Bacon, 3 Hen. & Munf. 106; Hines v. Spruill, 2 Dev. & Bat. Eq. 93; Agnew v. Fetterman, 4 Penn. St. 62; Cornish v. Wilson, 6 Gill 318.

as the right of redemption exists at law, it is not divested of the character of legal assets. And therefore, if the heir or executor redeem, he is chargeable at law with the surplus value; and the administration will be conducted on the legal principle.(s) If, after forfeiture, a reversion remains, to which the equity of redemption is incident, such equity will follow the character of the reversion, and will still constitute legal assets; e. g., where a fee simple is mortgaged for a term, or a *leasehold is mort- [*256] gaged by underlease.(t) If, after forfeiture, there is no reversion, as, for example, when a fee simple is mortgaged in fee, or a leasehold by assignment of the term, a different rule prevails; for there is nothing left in the mortgagor which can be assets at law, and the new interest is a mere creation of equity.[1] It has therefore been determined, notwithstanding some doubts on the point, that such interests shall be equitable assets.[2] The rule of distribution *pari passu*, however, which has been noticed as incidental to equitable assets, is modified in its application to equities of redemption, in respect both to judgment debts and to debts by specialty. It is modified in favor of judgment debts by permitting them to retain their priority over other claims, because, if such priority were not allowed, the judgment creditor might acquire it by redeeming the mortgage. And it is modified in favor of the debts by specialty, where the mortgage is of a free-

(s) Hawkins v. Lawse, 1 Leon. 155; 2 Wms. on Ex'rs. 1179.
(t) Plunket v. Penson, 2 Atk. 290.

---

[1] In this country, generally, an equity of redemption of mortgaged real estate, can be sold on execution upon a judgment at law. Until foreclosure, the mortgagor remains seised of the freehold, and the mortgagee has in effect but a chattel interest. See Clark v. Beach, 6 Conn. 142, 159, 160, and cases there cited. See also, Kent's Com., vol. iv., p. 160.

[2] But see Lovegrove v. Cooper, 2 Sm. & Giff. 273, in note.

hold estate, by permitting them to retain their priority over simple contract debts; because the claim of simple contract creditors on the freehold estate originates in the statute alone, and is postponed by the same statute to the right of creditors by specialty. But so far as those debts are concerned, to which, independently of the statute, the property can be applied, the distribution is *pari passu*. In the case of leaseholds, which are chattel interests, the modification does not apply.(*u*)

The distinction made between legal and equitable assets, by applying the former in payment according to priority, and the latter in payment *pari passu*, appears to be founded on sound principles. So far as legal assets are concerned, there is no interference with the legal priorities. The creditors have advanced their funds in reliance on those assets, and in reliance on their being applied in the order settled by law. And whether the law [*257] be just or *unjust, the Court of Chancery cannot alter it. But it was no part of their original contract that other funds, if available for their debt at all, should be available in the same order; and therefore if other assets are brought in, either by the voluntary gift of the testator, or by the special interposition of equity, they may be fairly applied on the principle, that equality is equity, and that all honest debts are equally entitled to be paid.

Where an estate consists of both legal and equitable assets, the rule is, that if any creditor has obtained part payment out of the legal assets by insisting on his preference, he shall receive no payment out of the equitable

(*u*) Case of Cox's Creditors, 3 P. Wms. 341 ; Hartwell *v.* Chitters, Amb. 308 ; Sharpe *v.* Scarborough, 4 Ves. 538; Clay *v.* Willis, 1 B. & C. 364, 372; 1 Wms. on Ex'rs. 1197 ; Coote on Mortgages 60.

assets, until the creditors, not entitled to such preference, have first received an equal proportion of their debts.[1] The manner of administration in equity is on a bill filed, either by creditors or by legatees, praying to have the accounts taken and the property administered; or if no creditor or legatee is willing to sue, then by the executor himself, who can only obtain complete exoneration by having his accounts passed in Chancery, and is therefore entitled to insist on its being done.(v)[2] The most usual practice, however, is, that the bill should not be filed by the executor, but by one or more of the creditors or legatees.

A single creditor may, if he pleases, file such a bill, praying payment of his own debt, and a discovery and

(v) Knatchbull v. Fearnhead, 3 M. & C. 122; Low v. Carter, 1 Beav. 426.

---

[1] See Chapman v. Esgar, 23 Eng. L. & Eq. 597; 1 Sm. & Giff. 575; Cornish v. Wilson, 6 Gill 303; Purdy v. Doyle, 1 Paige 558; Wilder v. Keeler, 3 Id. 165. This doctrine is not of very great importance in this country, as the distinction between legal and equitable assets no longer exists. An analogous question, however, whether a creditor holding collateral security from the debtor is entitled, notwithstanding, to claim on the estate for the full amount of his debt, has given rise to some conflict of decision. The better opinion is in the affirmative, and that equity will not interfere with his legal right: West v. Bank of Rutland, 18 Verm. 403; Shunk's App., 2 Penn. St. 304; Cornish v. Willson, 6 Gill 303; Mason v. Begg, 2 Mylne & Cr. 448; Evans v. Duncan, 4 Watts 24; Kittera's Est., 17 Penn. St. 416; though the rule is otherwise in bankruptcy. See on this subject the notes to Aldrich v. Cooper, 2 Lead. Cas Eq. 56: and to Silk v. Prime, Id. 82, &c. But the other creditors have, in such case, the right to be subrogated to the securities, where they have not been realized. See post, Marshalling.

[2] If an executor or administrator finds the affairs of the estate so complicated as to render the administration difficult and unsafe, he may institute proceedings in equity against all the creditors, to have their claims adjusted by the Court, and to obtain its judgment for his guide: Brown v. McDonald, 1 Hill Ch. 300, 301; Adams v. Dixon, 19 Ga. 513; McNeill's Adm'r. v. McNeill's Creditors, 36 Ala. 109.

33

account of assets for that purpose only. The decree on
such a bill is not for a general account of debts, but for an
account of the personal estate and of the particular debt
claimed, and for payment out of the personal estate in a
course of administration. But no decree can be made
against the real estate, unless the account is asked on
behalf of all the creditors. (w)

The more usual course is that of a bill by one or more
creditors on behalf *of all.[1] The decree on such
[*258] a bill is for a general account of the debts and

(w) Johnson v. Compton, 4 Sim. 47.

---

[1] A creditor can sue an executor or administrator in Chancery for an
account and discovery of assets, on the ground of a trust in the executor
or administrator: McKay v. Green, 3 Johns. Ch. 56. And he may come
into this Court, not only for discovery, but for distribution of assets:
Thompson v. Brown, 4 Johns. Ch. 619, 631.

A decree to account, whether in a suit by a single creditor for himself,
or for himself and all the creditors, being deemed for the benefit of all,
all the creditors should have notice to come in and prove their debts before
the Master: Id. The account cannot be taken for his benefit alone, but for
all the creditors who choose to come in: Hazen v. Durling, 1 Green Ch.
133; see also Martin v. Densford, 3 Blackf. 295; Judah v. Brandon, 5 Id.
506; Cram v. Green, 6 Ham. 429.

A bill to marshal assets, and for administration, should be on behalf of
the complainant and all other creditors, and the heirs and devisees should
be made parties. If, however, proper parties are not made, the bill should
not be dismissed, but the complainant may have leave to amend, unless a
decree for an account has been made in some other creditor's suit. If several
suits are pending, the Court may order the proceedings in all but one to
be stayed, and require the parties to the others to come in under the decree. A creditor who, with knowledge of a decree in another suit, brings
a separate suit, will be condemned in costs. In such cases the decree will
be made in the case first ready for a hearing, though not the first brought:
Stephenson v. Taverners, 9 Gratt. 398.

Creditors of a deceased debtor may proceed in equity against his heirs
residing abroad, as absent defendants, to marshal the assets, and thus subject the land descended, or its proceeds: Carrington v. Didier, 8 Gratt. 260.
And see Farrar v. Haselden, 9 Rich. Eq. 336. When creditors, being non-
residents, could not obtain letters of administration, and were unable to

for an account and application of the personal assets. If the personal estate should prove insufficient, a decree will be made against the realty.[1] By this means inconvenient preference of creditors is avoided, as well as the burden which separate actions or suits would bring on the fund. The bill is treated as a demand on behalf of all the creditors who may come in and prove their debts under it, so as to prevent the Statute of Limitations from running against them; but in other respects it continues, until decree, to be the suit of the actual plaintiff alone. He has a right either to dismiss, or compromise it; he may, if assets are admitted and his debt proved at the hearing, demand an immediate decree for payment; or, if the executor offers payment. may be compelled to accept it. When a decree has been made, the case is different. The fund has been taken into the hands of the Court; the original plaintiff, though he has still the conduct of the suit, ceases to have the absolute control; the general body of creditors, for whose benefit the decree is made, become entitled to intervene; and as a necessary result from this right of intervention, the proof of the plaintiff's debt, given at the hearing, though good against the executor, is not good against them, but it must be again proved in the Master's office.(x)

(x) Sterndale s. Hankinson, 1 Sim. 393; Owens v. Dickinson, Cr. & P.

procure any other person to administer, they were allowed to file a bill: Garner v. Lyles, 35 Miss. 184.

The title of a creditor is paramount to the heir-at-law; and on bills by creditors against the devisees and the heir, the latter is not entitled to have the bill dismissed against him, or to an issue of *devisavit vel non:* Spickernell v. Hotham, 9 Hare 73. See further, on the subject of creditor's bills, Postlewait v. Howes, 3 Clarke (Iowa) 365.

[1] A sale of real estate may be decreed, though some of the heirs are infauts; but the claims of the creditors must first be fully adjusted, so that their amount, and the necessity of a sale, may be ascertained: Cralle v. Meen, 8 Gratt. 496.

A legatee may file a bill for his single legacy, or on behalf of all the legatees for payment of all. But he cannot in either case have a preference over the rest; and therefore, even in a suit for his single legacy, the decree will not be for payment of that legacy alone, unless the executor has admitted assets, and thus subjected himself to a personal decree, but will be for a general account of legacies, and ratable payment of all.$(y)^1$

[*259]   *Immediately on the executor's answer being obtained, the balance which he admits to be in his hands is secured by payment into Court. A receiver of the outstanding personalty, and of the rents and profits of the real estate, is appointed if the circumstances render it necessary. And as soon as the cause

48, 56; Woodgate v. Field, 2 Hare 211; Whitaker v. Wright, Id. 310, 314; Tatam v. Williams, 3 Id. 347.

(y) Mitf. 168.

---

[1] As a general rule, a legatee may sue the executor for his own particular legacy, without making the residuary legatees parties to the suit. *Aliter*, where one of the *residuary* legatees sues for his share of the residue; an account of the estate being necessary in that case : Cromer v. Pinckney, 3 Barb. Ch. 466; Pritchard v. Hicks, 1 Paige Ch. 270. And see Brown v. Ricketts, 3 Johns. Ch. 553. But it has been held that one residuary legatee may file a bill on behalf of himself, and all others standing in the same situation, and it is not necessary to make them all parties to the suit. Where a bill is for the payment of a particular legacy, if the defendant admits a sufficiency of assets, a decree for the payment may be made without any general account of the estate. But if it appears by the answer that there is a deficiency of assets, the decree must be for a general account, and distribution among all who may come in, and establish their claims under the decree : Hallett v. Hallett, 2 Paige Ch. 15. And see Marsh v. Hague, 1 Ed. Ch. 174.

Legatees and annuitants are bound by the proceedings in a suit for administration between the executors and residuary legatees and devisees, although there may be a question as to the debts being primarily charged upon real estate, which may incidentally affect them ; they cannot, therefore, after decree in such suit, sustain an administration suit against the executors : Jennings v. Patterson, 15 Beav. 28.

can be brought to a hearing, a decree is made for taking the accounts.

After the decree has been made, the assets will be protected from foreign interference. It has been already stated, that until decree, the plaintiff has an absolute control over the suit, and may at his-pleasure dismiss or compromise it. There is, therefore, no ground for restraining other creditors from proceeding to enforce their claims. And it is not unfrequent that up to the decree several actions and suits should subsist together, which on a decree being made, will be stopped or consolidated. After a decree the case is different. The decree is not confined to the payment by the plaintiff, but directs a general account and administration, under which all creditors and legatees may claim. And, therefore, if separate proceedings be afterwards carried on, the assets will be protected by the Court from that needless expense. In order to obtain this protection, it is the duty of the executor to put in his answer as speedily as possible, with the view to an immediate decree, and on the decree being made, to apply for the necessary interference. The answer must contain a correct account, in order that the balance may be paid into Court, and that the executor may be under no temptation to create delay. If the answer does not state what the assets are, or if the executor be plaintiff, so that he cannot put in an answer, the application should be accompanied by an affidavit, stating the balance in his hands.(z) If the executor neglects to apply, the protection will be granted on the application of any other party interested.(a)[1]

(z) Paxton v. Douglas, 8 Ves. 520 ; Gilpin v. Southampton, 18 Id. 469.
(a) Clarke v. Earl of Ormonde, Jac. 108, 122.

[1] After a final decree has been made for the administration of a fund in

If the separate proceedings be at law, the protection

[*260] will *be given by injunction. By the old practice this could only be done on a bill filed against
the particular creditor, but such a bill is now unnecessary; and on motion in the administration suit after decree, an order will be made restraining any creditor who
is seeking, but has not yet obtained, satisfaction at law,
from proceeding further in this action. If a judgment
has been obtained before decree, there may be special
grounds to prohibit him from taking out execution; but
such is not the ordinary rule. If the executor, by misconduct, or by a slip in his defence at law, has rendered
himself personally liable for the debt, it seems doubtful
whether any equity exists for relieving him, and whether
the injunction will not be limited to protect the assets
alone.(b)

If the separate proceedings are in equity, and in the
same Court as the original suit, the protection is obtained

(b) Lee v. Park, 1 Keen 714; Burles v. Popplewell, 10 Sim. 383; Kirby
v. Barton, 8 Beav. 45; Vernon v. Thellusson, 1 Ph. 466; Ranken v. Harwood, 5 Hare 215; 2 Ph. 22.

---

the hands of executors, &c., for the benefit of all creditors who have a
claim, the Court may restrain the creditor from proceeding at law. In re
Receiver of the City Bank of Buffalo, 10 Paige Ch. 378. But an injunction will not be granted to restrain creditors from proceedings at law, until
after an account is decreed: Mactier v. Lawrence, 7 Johns. C. C. 206.

And a creditor cannot, in a bill against an executor for his own benefit,
make another creditor a party defendant, and compel him to desist from
prosecuting his suit at law against the executor: Simmons v. Whitaker, 2
Ired. Eq. 129: and see Benson v. Le Roy, 4 Johns. Ch. 651; Helm v.
Darby, 3 Dana 186.

Where lands have been sold under a decree in a suit by heirs, and the
proceeds are in the hands of a commissioner of the Court, he may be made
a party to a bill by creditors to marshal assets, and be restrained by injunction from paying over the proceeds to the heirs: Carrington v. Didier,
8 Gratt. 260.

by an order to stay the proceedings in the second suit, aud that the plaintiff may go before the Master in the first.[1] But if additional relief be asked in the second suit, or a specific right be contested in it, the second suit will go into a hearing, and a properly modified decree will be made. If the second bill be filed in a different Court of equity, there appears to be no jurisdiction in the Court of Chancery to restrain it, unless the person filing it has already proved his debt under the existing decree. But the Court in which he is unnecessarily suing, on being satisfied of the efficacy of the prior decree, will itself stay his proceedings.(c)

When the assets have been secured and their administration has been undertaken by the Court, the next step is their distribution.

The method adopted for this purpose is, to refer it to *the Master to take an account of the personal estate not specifically bequeathed, either got in [*261] by the executor or still outstanding, and of the funeral and testamentary expenses, debts and legacies; and to direct payment of the expenses and debts in a course of administration, and afterwards of the legacies. Under the head of testamentary expenses are included the executor's costs of suit, and those of the plaintiff in a creditor's suit, as being necessarily incurred in administering the estate.(d) If any further directions are required, either for administering the real estate, or for arranging

(c) Pott v. Gallini, 1 S. & S. 206; Jackson v. Leaf, 1 J. & W. 229, 232; Beauchamp v. Marquis of Huntley, Jac. 546; Moore v. Prior, 2 Y. & C. 375; [see Ostell v. Lepage, 16 Jurist 1164.]

(d) Larkins v. Paxton, 2 M. & K. 320; Barker v. Wardle, 2 Id. 818; Tipping v. Power, 1 Hare 405.

_____

[1] See Stephenson v. Taverners, 9 Gratt. 398.

the order in which the assets shall be applied, they will be given by a subsequent decree. The account of debts will be insisted on by the Court before proceeding to distribute a residue, even though the parties to the suit may be willing to waive it. For it is essential that it should be ascertained whether creditors exist, before the fund in which they have a claim is disposed of by the Court.(e) A legacy, however, may be paid on an admission of assets, although the accounts of the estate have not been taken; for the decree is personal against the executor, and the creditors, if there are any, are left untouched.[1]

If a debt is secured by mortgage, the mortgagee may, nevertheless, claim payment out of the general assets, retaining his mortgage to make good a deficiency;[2] or he

(e) Say v. Creed, 3 Hare 455 ; Penny v. Watts, 2 Ph. 149.

---

[1] See note, p. 258, supra.

[2] The personal estate of a decedent is the "natural" fund for the payment of debts and legacies, and, as a general rule, is first to be exhausted, even to the payment of debts with which the real estate is charged by mortgage, the mortgage being considered but a collateral security for the personal obligation. See Gould v. Winthrop, 5 R. I. 319 ; Bradford v. Forbes, 9 Allen 365 ; Plimpton v. Fuller, 11 Allen (Mass.) 139 ; Thomas v. Thomas, 2 Green 356. In England, by statute, the law is now otherwise ; post, p. 264, note. If, however, a mortgage debt was not contracted by the decedent but by another, as e. g., a prior owner, the land is considered as the debtor ; and, even if there has been an express contract or covenant by the decedent with the mortgagor to pay the mortgagee, this will only make the personal assets an auxiliary fund ; though, if the contract were with the mortgagee, it would be otherwise : Cumberland v. Codrington, 3 Johns. Ch. 257 ; Case of Keyzey, 9 S. & R. 73 ; Garnett v. Macon, 6 Call 308 ; Dandridge v. Minge, 4 Rand. 397 ; Stevens v. Gregg, 10 Gill & J. 143 ; Kelsey v. Western, 2 Comst. 500 ; Gibson v. McCormick, 10 Gill & J. 65 ; Bank of U. S. v. Beverly, 1 How. U. S. 134 ; Hoye v. Brewer, 3 Gill & J. 153 ; Wyse v. Smith, 4 Id. 296 ; Matter of Hemiup, 3 Paige Ch. 305 ; Stuart v. Carson, 1 Dessaus. 500 ; McDowell v. Lawless, 6 Monr. 141 ; Haleyburton v. Kershaw, 3 Dessaus. 105, 115 ; Dunlap v. Dunlap, 4 Id. 305 ; Hoes v. Van Hoesen, 1 Comst. 120 ; Walker's Estate, 3 Rawle 229 ; Mansell's Estate, 1 Pars. Eq. 369 ; Mason's Estate, Id. 129 ; Mitchell

may consent to have the mortgaged estate sold, the produce applied in payment of his debt and costs, and the surplus administered by the Court. If he refuse to give his consent, the Court must either sell the estate subject to his charge, or must pay him off and deal with the redeemed estate as assets.(ƒ) If a debt is due on judgment, the judgment creditor will be paid off, for the Court will not *sell subject to the judgment, and it can- [*262] not otherwise make a title to the estate.(g)

In order to ascertain who the creditors are, a direction is given for publishing advertisements in those quarters where they are most likely to be found. The same course is pursued where a distribution is to be made among next of kin, or where a legacy is given to a class of persons, so that it is necessary to ascertain of whom the class consists. A time is fixed by these advertisements, within which the parties are to make their claims. After the expiration of that time the Master reports the claims which have been established; and the Court, by the decree on further di-

(ƒ) Mason v. Bogg, 2 M. & C. 443 ; Hepworth v. Heslop, 3 Hare 485.
(g) Neate v. Duke of Marlborough, 3 M. & C. 407, 416.

v. Mitchell, 3 Md. Ch. 73 ; McLenahan v. McLenahan, 3 Green (N. J.) 101. When, however, the purchaser pays the full price of the land by including the encumbrances which he assumed to pay as the entire consideration of the premises, he makes the debt his own; and it must be paid out of the personalty not specifically bequeathed : Hoff's Appeal, 12 Harris 200; Lennig's Estate, 52 Penn. St. 139. See note to Duke of Ancaster v. Mayer, 1 Lead. Cas. Eq., 3d Am. ed. 505, where this subject is discussed.

In New York, by statute, the mortgage debt has been made to fall primarily on the real estate. See Rogers v. Rogers, 1 Paige Ch. 188 ; Cogswell v. Cogswell, 2 Ed. Ch. 231 ; but the statute does not apply to the lien for purchase-money : Wright v. Holbrook, 32 N. Y. 587. And see also, Kent Com., vol. iv., p. 422.

The general rule, also, is confined to mortgages and charges of that nature, and does not apply to the legatee of leasehold property liable for dilapidations during the testator's lifetime, and the former has no right to throw them upon the general residuary legatee, but must discharge them himself : Hickling v. Boyer, 3 Macn. & G. 635.

rections authorizes a distribution of the fund among them, and protects the personal representative against any future claim.[1] If, however, a claimant should subsequently appear, who was *bonâ fide* ignorant of the proceedings, he will not be barred of his right, but may be let in to partake, so long as the fund remains undistributed, or after distribution may file a bill against the other distributees and compel them to refund his share.(*h*) If the legatees are named in the will, no advertisement is requisite. But if any of them neglects to claim, an adequate portion of the assets will be set apart to pay them.(*i*)

The order in which the assets will be successively applied is the only question which remains for notice.

The *primâ facie* order of application is as follows : 1. Personal estate not specifically bequeathed; 2. Real es tate devised for payment of debts; 3. Real estate de scended;(*k*) 4· Personal and real estate specifically bequeathed or devised, subject to a charge of debts by will;(*l*) 5. Personal and real estate subject to a charge of [*263] debts by *mortgage, to the extent of such mortgage; 6. Personal and real estate specifically given, and not charged with debts. If the personalty and the *corpus* of the real estate are inadequate, the heir or devisee may be charged with bygone rents.(*m*)[2]

(*h*) David *v.* Frowd, 1 M. & K. 200; Gillespie *v.* Alexander, 3 Russ. 130; [see Davies *v.* Nicolson, 2 De G. & J. 693;] Sawyer *v.* Birchmore, 2 M. & C. 611; Brown *v.* Lake, 1 De G. & S. 144.

(*i*) Seton on Decrees 65.　　(*k*) Biederman *v.* Seymour, 3 Beav. 368.

(*l*) Harmood *v.* Oglander, 8 Ves. 106, 125.

(*m*) Curtis *v.* Curtis, 2 B. C. C. 620, 628, 633; Seton on Decrees 86; Clarendon *v.* Barham, 1 N. C. C. 668, 704.

---

[1] Where the fund is small, a reference back to the Master, when the cause comes on for farther directions, in order to apportion it among the creditors, may be dispensed with, and the apportionment made on affidavit: Bear *v.* Smith, 5 De G. & Sm. 92.

[2] Though the cases in this country, on this branch of the subject of mar-

In order that this arrangement may be clearly understood, it is requisite that certain points should be more
fully explained.

---

shalling, are not by any means reducible to one harmonious system, still
t may be more convenient to group them together, so as to show how far
hey follow or depart from the order established in England and stated in
the text.

(1.) There is, in general, no doubt that the general personal estate, as it
is the primary fund for the payment of debts, so must first bear their burden, unless expressly exonerated: Hays v. Jackson, 6 Mass. 149; Hoover
v. Hoover, 5 Penn. St. 351; Livingstone v. Newkirk, 3 Johns. Ch. 312; Kelsey v. Western, 2 Comst. 500; Miller v. Harwell, 3 Murph. 195; McLoud
v. Roberts, 4 Hen. & Munf. 443; Chase v. Lockerman, 11 Gill & J. 186;
Cornish v. Wilson, 6 Gill 301; Elliott v. Carter, 9 Gratt. 549; Hull v. Hull,
3 Rich. Eq. 65; Breden v. Gilliland, 67 Penn. St. 34; Knight v. Knight, 6
Jones Eq. (N. C.) 134; Clarke v. Henshaw, 30 Ind. 144; Newcomer v.
Wallace, Id. 216. The only departure from this rule is in South Carolina,
where it is held that where any property, real or personal, is specifically
set apart by the will for the payment of debts, it must be first applied:
Dunlap v. Dunlap, 4 Dessaus. 305; Pinckney v. Pinckney, 2 Rich. Eq. 235.
Pecuniary legacies are placed on the same footing, with or else next in
order to specific legacies, and though they cannot be actually set apart as
can the latter, yet if the personalty be exhausted before they are satisfied,
they will be entitled to exoneration out of the other assets: Hoover v.
Hoover, 5 Penn. St. 351; Post v. Mackall, 3 Bland 486; Robards v. Wortham, 2 Dev. Eq. 173; Brown v. James, 3 Strob. Eq. 24; Wilcox v. Wilcox, 13 Allen 252. In Hays v. Jackson, 6 Mass. 149, however, they appear
to have been held to follow the fate of the general personal estate in every
respect. On the other hand, a general or residuary bequest of personalty,
is not equivalent to a specific legacy, so as to be preferred to descended
lands: Walker's Est., 3 Rawle 229; Hoes v. Van Hoesen, 1 Barb. Ch. 380;
but in South Carolina, this distinction is not recognised, except as to a residuary bequest, subject to payment of debts: Warley v. Warley, 1 Bail.
Eq. 397; and in New York it has been held that a general gift of personalty exonerated it, as regards other legacies, and threw them on the land:
Hoes v. Van Hoesen, 1 Barb. Ch. 380; 1 Comst. 120; see Lewis v. Darling, 16 How. U. S. 1. It appears also that in the last state, under the
Revised Statutes, the whole personal estate is to be applied before lands
descended: Skidmore v. Romaine, 2 Bradf. Surr. 132; see Stuart v. Kissam, 11 Barb. s. c. 271.

(2) Real estate devised for the payment of debts: Robards v. Wortham,

1. It has been stated that the fund first liable is the personal estate not specifically bequeathed. The propo-

2 Dev. Eq. 173 ; Hoover v. Hoover, 5 Penn. St. 351 ; Hays v. Jackson, 6 Mass. 149.

(3) Real estate descended : Id.; Warley v. Warley, 1 Bail. Eq. 397 ; Brooks v. Dent, 1 Md. Ch. 523 ; Elliott v. Carter, 9 Gratt. 549. After-acquired land is also comprehended in this class : Livingston v. Newkirk, 3 Johns. Ch. 312 ; Comm. v. Shelby, 13 S. & R. 348. So of land devised to the heir, where, according to construction of law, he is in by descent: Ellis v. Paige, 7 Cush. 161. From some of the decisions it would appear that lands descended would not be marshalled in favor of legacies, as regards simple contract debts, though they are an implied charge upon land in this country : Robards v. Wortham, 2 Dev. Eq. 173 ; Chase v. Lockerman, 11 Gill & John. 186 ; though a doubt seems to be cast on this case, in this respect, by the language of the Court in Alexander v. Worthington, 5 Md. 471. See Mitchell v. Mitchell, 31 Md. 254. And see Alston v. Munford, 1 Brock. 266. But under the recent English statute, which assimilates the law in respect to the liability of lands for debts to that in the United States generally, the opposite doctrine is now established: Tombs v. Roch, 2 Coll. 490 ; Fleming v. Buchanan, 3 De G., M. & G. 976 ; Patterson v. Scott, 1 De G., M. & G. 531. And it would appear to be that which is followed in Pennsylvania. It is also supported by Judge Hare in his notes to Aldrich v. Cooper, 2 Lead. Cas. Eq. 56 (3d Am. ed.), and is clearly the more reasonable.

(4) Real and personal property specifically devised or bequeathed, but charged with the payment of debts: Hoover v. Hoover, 5 Penn. St. 351 ; Robards v. Wortham, ut supr.; Elliott v. Carter, 9 Gratt. 549 ; Mitchell v. Mitchell, 3 Md. Ch. 73 ; Kirkpatrick v. Rogers, 7 Ired. Eq. 44. But it is to be remembered, that such a charge on real estate, unless an intention otherwise clearly appears, will not exonerate the personalty : Patterson v. Scott, 2 De G., M. & G. 531 ; Collis v. Robins, 1 De G. & S. 131 ; Kirk-patrick v. Rogers, 7 Ired. Eq. 44 ; Buckley v. Buckley, 11 Barb. S. C. 77 ; Mitchell v. Mitchell, 3 Md. Ch. 73 ; McCampbell v. McCampbell, 5 Litt. 98 ; Leavitt v. Wooster, 14 N. H. 550 ; Hasenclever v. Tucker, 2 Binn. 525 ; though disappointed legatees will be entitled to stand in the place of the creditors as against the land charged: Paterson v. Scott, 1 De G., M. & G. 531 ; Lockwood v. Stockholm, 11 Paige 87 ; Cryder's App., 11 Penn. St. 72.

Where the realty and personalty are blended together in one disposition, and made subject expressly to a joint charge of debts or legacies, or there is a power of sale over realty, and the proceeds, together with the personalty, are constituted a joint fund for that purpose, both contribute

sitiou would perhaps be more accurately worded by confining it to the general residue after deduction of all par-

---

ratably: Elliott v. Carter, 9 Gratt. 541 ; Cradock v. Owens, 2 Sm. & Giff.
241 ; Robinson v. Governors, &c., 10 Hare 29 ; Adams v. Brackett, 5 Metcalf, 282 ; see McCampbell v. McCampbell, 5 Litt. 99 ; Ford v. Gaithur, 2
Rich. Eq. 270 ; Cox v. Corkendall, 2 Beas. 138 ; Brant's Will, 40 Mo. 266 ;
but contra, Hoye v. Brewer, 3 Gill & John. 153. In Boughton v. Boughton,
1 H. Lds. Cas. 406, overruling s. c., 1 Coll. 26, however, where a testator
gave real and personal estates to his executors in trust to receive the rents,
issues, profits and dividends thereof, to retain thereout yearly £10 for their
trouble, and then to pay certain legacies and annuities, it was held that
there was to be no apportionment, and that the personal estate was the
primary fund. This decision did not meet with the approbation of Sir
Edward Sugden (Property, H. L. 436), but it was followed by Lord Cranworth in Tidd v. Lister, 3 De G., M. & G. 857, a very similar case. In Robinson v. The Governors, ut sup., however, Boughton v. Boughton was said
not to have been intended to interfere with the general rule just stated as
to cases where the realty and personalty are thrown into one mass, but
that the decision proceeded on the ground that the construction of the will
in the particular case showed no intention to create a common mass. On
the other hand, in Lewis v. Darling, 16 How. U. S. 10, it was held, in
effect, that where legacies are given, and no fund is expressly provided
for their payment, but a general residuary disposition of realty and personalty is made to the same person, it is unnecessary, on a bill to charge
the real estate, to show that the personalty is exhausted ; and the language
of the Court goes to the length of authorizing a resort to the realty, in such
case, in the first instance. This would seem to be against the current of
authorities in England and this country, and is hardly warranted by those
cited in the opinion, which only show that, where legacies are not expressly provided for, a residuary disposition of realty and personalty makes
them a charge on land, about which there can be no doubt. But, before
Lewis v. Darling, it seemed equally clear that such a construction did not
the less make the personalty the primary fund : Hasenclever v. Tucker, 2
Binn. 525 ; Buckley v. Buckley, 11 Barb. S. C. 43 ; Leavitt v. Wooster, 14
N. H. 550. See Clery's Appeal, 35 Penn. St. 54.

The general rule that a residuary disposition of realty and personalty
will render legacies otherwise unprovided for a charge upon the realty, is
thoroughly established : see Greville v. Browne, 7 H. L. Cas. 697 ; Gallagher's Appeal, 48 Penn. St. 122 ; Shulters v. Johnson, 38 Barb. 80. And
see the remarks, in this last case, on Lewis v. Darling (supra). An exception to this rule is said to obtain where there are previous specific devises

ticular legacies.   For although pecuniary legacies
be conveniently set apart in the outset, and the d

---

of portions of the real estate: see Lupton *v.* Lupton, 2 **Johns.** C
Shulters *v.* Johnson, ut supra; Robinson *v.* McIvor, 63 **N. C.** 645.

(5.) The right of a specific legatee disappointed by the recou
mortgagee to the personal assets, to be subrogated to his remedy
the land, as against a devisee, was recognised in Mollan *v.* Gr
Paige 402.   Where the mortgage was not originally created by
tator, there could be no doubt of this right.   See note, ante, p. 261.
several estates are devised subject to debts, and the testator subse
mortgages one, the devisee of the mortgaged estate is entitled to c
tion from the others: Middleton *v.* Middleton, 15 Beav. 450.   **But**
son *v.* McCormick, 10 Gill & J. 65, where there was no express ch
debts, the devisee of the mortgaged estate in such case, was held no
titled : *Accord* Mason's Estate, 1 Pars. Eq. 129; s. c. 4 Penn. St. 4

(6.) The English rule that devisees and specific legatees are to con
ratably after the exhaustion of the previous classes, was followed i
v. Lockerman, 11 Gill & J. 185; Teas's App., 23 Penn. St. 223; Arms
Appeal, 63 Id. 312; see Alexander *v.* Worthington, 5 Md. 49.
Skidmore *v.* Romaine, 2 Bradf. Surr. 132; though it was confined ir
v. Lockerman, with not much consistency, to cases where the asset
in order had been exhausted by specialty creditors. This distinctior
to be doubted in Alexander *v.* Worthington, ut supr., and in Englar
that simple contract creditors have a remedy against the land, no
exists. See above (3). But it has been held in several cases in the
States, that the specific legacies were to abate without contributior
devises: Livingston *v.* Livingston, 3 Johns. Ch. 148; Miller *v.* Har
Murph. 194; Warley *v.* Warley. 1 Bail. Eq. 397; Rogers *v.* Rogers, 1
183; Hull *v.* Hull, 3 Rich. Eq. 65; Elliott *v.* Carter, 9 Gratt. 549; 1
v. Hoover, 5 Penn. St. 351; but *contra* Teas's App., 23 Id. 22
some of these cases, however, the English rule was plainly mistaker
there can be no possible reason, upon principle, for making a dist
between specific legatees and devisees. Where a legacy is charged o
the legatee is entitled to contribution from the other devisees: Lc
Estate, 10 Penn. St. 387; Cryder's App., 11 Id. 72; Teas's App.,
229.   In New York, under the Revised Statutes, the personal estate
applied before real estate descended and devised, and therefore, Ir
are not entitled to contribution: Skidmore *v.* Romaine, 2 Bradf.
132.

Where, therefore, the English rule is not followed, the order ir
real estate charged with debts, the pecuniary legacies ratably, ε

therefore, exempts the specific legacies alone, yet if the effect of discharging the debts is to exhaust the personalty, the pecuniary legacies will be made good out of the other assets.

2. The primary liability of the personal estate may be transferred to any portion of it specified by the testator, as between the several objects of his bounty, though not as against the creditors' right over the whole. Or it may be, to the same extent, transferred from the personal to the real estate, if the intention to exonerate the personal estate be expressed in the will, or be manifestly implied therein. But the presumption is against the intention to exonerate, and in favor of considering the real estate as an auxiliary fund.(*n*)

3. A doubt has arisen whether assets of the third class are confined to lands descended to the heir, or whether the late act, declaring that the lands of which a debtor shall die seised, shall be assets for payment of his debts, has the effect of including lands escheated to the lord; and a further doubt whether, if the escheated lands are liable, *their liability is prior or subsequent to that of lands specifically devised. The first of [*264] these points has been determined against the lord; the second appears to be undecided.(*nn*)

(*n*) 2 Jarm. on Wills 564–600; Collis *v.* Robins, 1 De G. & S. 131.

(*nn*) 3 & 4 Wm. 4, c. 104; Evans *v.* Brown, 5 Beav. 114; 11 Law J. 349.

legacies ratably, and lastly, devises: Hoover *v.* Hoover, 5 Penn. St. 351; Elliott *v.* Carter, 9 Gratt. 549.

(7.) Last in order, is real estate, over which the testator has had a general power of appointment, which he has exercised, and thus made assets for creditors: Fleming *v.* Buchanan, 22 L. J. Ch. 886; 3 De G., M. & G. 976. See ante, 99, note.

See, on this subject generally, notes to Duke of Ancaster *v.* Mayer, 1 Lead. Cas. Eq. 447; and to Aldrich *v.* Cooper, 2 Id. 56, 3d Am. ed.

4. The liability of assets of the fifth class, viz., mo
gaged property, has been the subject of much discussi
But the rule, as here stated, appears to be consistent w
all the decisions, and to be founded on a correct princip
viz., that mortgaged estates, whether devised or descend
shall be liable for payment of the mortgage debts, as ·
sets which the testator has expressly charged, but t
their liability shall be subordinate to that of ass
charged by will; because the fact of such a charge bei
made by the testator denotes his intention to exoner⟨
the estate.[1] They are accordingly liable in the hands
a devisee, as a fund for payment of the particular de]
immediately after property charged with debts and spe
fically given subject to the charge. Nor will the order
their liability be altered although the devise be in ter]
"subject to the mortgage;" for these words mean no mo
than a gift of the estate would imply. · On the oth
hand, the liability is prior to that of property given wit
out a charge, including general pecuniary legacies, but e
clusive of a mere residuary gift; because a residuary g]
denotes no intention of bounty, except as subject to
legal charges. If a mortgaged estate descend to the he
it will be liable as assets by descent after land devis
for payment of debts.(o)

In order, however, to charge any other assets in pric
ity to the mortgaged estate, it is essential that the mo

(o) Halliwell v. Tanner, 1 R. & N. 633; Wythe v. Henniker, 2 M. &
935; Johnson v. Child, 4 Hare 87; Lockhart v. Hardy, 9 Beav. 349.

---

[1] But now by Stat. 17 & 18 Vict. ch. 118, a mortgage debt is primari
a charge upon the mortgage estate. There has been some conflict
authority upon the construction of this act. See Woolstencroft v. Woolste
croft, 2 De G., F. & J. 347; Moore v. Moore, 1 De G., J. & S. 602; Ma
well v. Hyslop, L. R. 4 Eq. 407. See, also, Hill on Trustees 357, no
(4th Am. ed.).

gage debt be originally a personal one, and that it be so in reference to the testator himself, so that the land is merely liable as a collateral security. If the land were originally the primary fund, *e. g.*, if a jointure or portion be charged on land, with a collateral covenant to make it good; or if it *has become the primary fund in reference to the testator, *e. g.*, if he acquired it [*265] subject to the charge, and has not assumed the charge as his personal debt, the devisee or heir is clearly liable.(*p*)[1]

The doctrine respecting mortgaged estates applies also to legacies of chattels pledged by the testator, or which at the time of his death were subject to a charge; and has been held to include the future calls on railway shares, where the testator was an original subscriber to the undertaking.(*q*)

5. In regard to assets of the fourth and sixth classes, where both personal and real estate are included, a question has arisen, whether the personal and real estate should contribute *pro rata*, or whether the personalty is first liable. It has been determined that in both cases there is a liability *pro rata*, and that, accordingly, if land be devised, and the testator die indebted by bond, a spe-

(*p*) Scott *v.* Beecher, 5 Mad. 96 ; Oxford *v.* Rodney, 14 Ves. 417 ; Evelyn *v.* Evelyn, 2 P. Wms. 664, Cox's note ; Ancester *v.* Mayer, 1 B. C. C. 453 ; Ibbetson *v.* Ibbetson, 12 Sim. 206.

(*q*) Knight *v.* Davis, 3 M. & K. 358 ; Blount *v.* Hipkins, 7 Sim. 51 ; Jacques *v.* Chambers, 2 Coll. 435.

---

[1] This distinction has been generally recognised. See Cumberland *v.* Codrington, 3 Johns. Ch. 227, wherein it was held, that if a person purchases an estate subject to a mortgage, and dies, his *personal* estate, as against his personal representatives, shall not be applied to exonerate the land, unless there be strong and decided proof that in taking the encumbered estate, he meant to make the mortgage debt a personal debt of his own. See, also, cases, note 2, p. 261, supra.

34

cific legatee may compel the devisee to contribute
question may also arise under the present law
possible right of a specific legatee of personal
exonerated by a general or residuary devise
Under the old law every devise of real estate
specific, because the testator only could devise t
which he held at the date of his will. By th
Wills Act this rule is altered, and a general or r
devise is made to extend to all the real estate b
to the testator at the time of his death. A gift t
of land in general terms has now ceased to be a
devise.(*s*)

The order of liability which has been above ex
[*266] *subject to any variations directed by the
that in accordance with which the seve
tions of the assets will be successively applied.
however, occur, that in the course of adminis
some portion of the estate has paid more than it
or that claims, for which several funds were liab
been so paid as to exhaust a fund, which alone ꞌ
plicable for another claim. If irregularities of th
occur, they will be rectified by the equities next
ered, of contribution, of exoneration, and marshall

(*r*) Roberts *v.* Walker, 1 R. & M. 752; Attorney-General *v.* S
12 Sim. 77; Boughton *v.* James, 1 Coll. 26; [see, on this case, n
263]; Tombs *v.* Roch, 2 Coll. 490: Gervis *v.* Gervis, 14 Sim. 654.

(*s*) 1 Vict. c. 26; 2 Jarm. on Wills 547, n.

*CHAPTER V   [*267]

OF CONTRIBUTION, EXONERATION, AND MARSHALLING.

THE equity for adjusting liabilities under a common charge arises where a charge or claim affecting several persons, is or may be enforced in the matter, not unjust in the person enforcing it, but unjust or irregular with regard to their liabilities *inter se.* And it is exercised under the three forms of contribution, exoneration, and marshalling.

The equities of contribution and exoneration arise where several persons are bound by a common charge not arising *ex delicto,* and their order of liability has been accidentally deranged. If the liabilities be joint, he who has paid more than his share is entitled to contribution from the rest.[1] If some are liable in priority to the rest,

---

[1] The doctrine of contribution is not so much founded on contracts, as on the principle of equity and justice, that where the interest is common, the burden also shall be common. *Qui sentit commodum, sentire debut et onus* Campbell *v.* Mesier, 4 Johns. Ch. 334; s. c. 6 Id. 21; Russell *v.* Failer, 1 Ohio St. N. S. 327; White *v.* Banks, 21 Ala. 705. See the remarks in Yonge *v.* Reynell, 9 Hare 809. Where, therefore, land subject to a lien is held by tenants in common, and one is compelled to pay the lien creditor more than his proportion, he, or his lien creditors may be subrogated to the lien for the excess: Gearhart *v.* Jordan. 11 Penn. St. 325. Though if the debt be a personal one of the tenant in common paying, or of his own grantor, no right of contribution of course exists: Wager *v.* Chew, 15 Penn. St. 323; Cook *v.* Hinsdale, 4 Cush. 134.

the parties secondarily liable, if compelled to discharge the claim, are entitled to exoneration.

In order that either of these equities may arise, it is essential that the charge be binding, and that it do not arise *ex delicto.*

The voluntary act of one party, in expending money for the benefit of all, will not create a right to contribution. A co-owner of land, for instance, though bound to pay a mortgage on the estate, is not bound to make repairs or meliorations, and therefore, cannot be compelled to contribute to their costs, unless they have been done by his consent, or under a special custom. But there is an exception in favor of houses and mills, and of the ne-
[*268]   cessary *repairs which they require.(*a*)[1]   A similar exception has, by many foreign jurists, been thought applicable to ships, on general grounds of maritime policy; but the rule of the common law is different; and, in the absence of any express or implied

(*a*) Co. Litt. 200 b.

---

[1] See 4 Kent Com. 370; Anderson *v.* Greble, 1 Ashm. 136. A tenant in common is not entitled to charge his co-tenant with a proportion of the expenses incurred for the benefit of the common property : Carver *v.* Miller, 4 Mass. 559; Cheeseborough *v.* Green, 10 Conn. 318; 4 Kent Com. 370; Norris *v.* Hill, 1 Mann. (Mich.) 202 ; Crest *v.* Jack, 3 Watts 238 ; Volentine *v.* Johnson, 1 Hill Ch. 46 ; Hancock *v.* Day, 1 McMullan Eq. 69 ; Thompson *v.* Bostwick, Id. 75 ; Holt *v.* Robertson, Id. 475 ; though see Payton *v.* Smith, 2 Dev. & Batt. Eq. 325, 349 ; and, *e converso,* where land belonging to tenants in common or joint tenants yields no profit, and one of the owners enters and renders the estate productive, the others cannot claim a share of the profits : Id. ; Nelson *v.* Clay, 7 J. J. Marsh. 138. See, under special statutes in Maine and New Hampshire : Bellows *v.* Dewy, 9 N. H. 278 ; Buck *v.* Spofford, 31 Maine 34. Where co-tenants make partition of land subject to a mortgage, the share of the premises set off to each is primarily chargeable with half of the mortgaged debt: Rathbone *v.* Clark, 9 Paige 648. And see preceding note.

agreement, throws the costs of any repairs on the party directing them.(*b*)[1]

If the liability arise *ex delicto* there is no right to con-

(*b*) Story on Partnership, ss. 421–6 ; Smith's Merc. Law 175.

---

[1] Hardy *v.* Sproule, 31 Maine 71 ; Schooner William Thomas *v.* Ellis, 4 Harring. 309 ; Brooks *v.* Harris, 12 Ala. 555 ; Turner *v.* Burrows, 8 Wend. 144 ; Reed *v.* Bachelder, 34 Maine 205. Though part-owners are liable to contribute for repairs and necessary expenses incurred by one, with the consent of all, and for the common benefit : Story Partn., s. 419 ; see Hopkins *v.* Forsyth, 14 Penn. St. 34. But a part-owner is not, though ship's husband, authorized to borrow money, or to insure the ship, and hence is not entitled to contribution therefor : Turner *v.* Burrows, ut supr. ; Patterson *v.* Chalmers, 7 B. Monr. 598 ; Flanders on Shipping, s. 385. Whether one part-owner has a lien upon the shares of the rest for his advances, is an unsettled question in this country. Of course, no such lien can be claimed where no right of contribution exists : McDonald *v.* Black, 20 Ohio 198. And in England, it is now held, on the authority of the decision of Lord Eldon, in Ex parte Young, 2 Ves. & Beames 242, overruling Lord Hardwicke in Doddington *v.* Hallet, 1 Ves. Sr. 497, that no such lien exists in any case. Lord Eldon's opinion was followed in Patton *v.* The Schooner Randolph, 1 Gilp. 457 ; Merrill *v.* Bartless, 6 Pick. 46 ; and by Chancellor Kent in Nicoll *v.* Mumford, 4 Johns. Ch. 522. The latter decision, however, was overruled on appeal, by a majority of the Court of Errors : Mumford *v.* Nicoll, 20 Johns. 611 ; and the earlier doctrine followed ; as it was, also, in Hewitt *v.* Sturdevant, 4 B. Monr. 453 ; Pragoff *v.* Heslep, 1 Am. L. Reg. 747 ; by Ch. Dessaussure in Seabrook *v.* Rose, 2 Hill Eq. 553 ; and it was approved in McDonald *v.* Black, 20 Ohio 198. In Missouri, part-owners of steamboats have a lien by statute : Langstaff *v.* Rock, 13 Mo. 579. See also, on this subject, Gallatin *v.* The Pilot, 2 Wall. Jr. 592 ; Knox *v.* Campbell, 1 Penn. St. 366 ; and Hopkins *v.* Forsyth, 14 Id. 34; where it seems to have been held, that a purchaser of the interest of a part-owner, at sheriff's sale, was not subject to such a lien ; and yet, that it could not be claimed upon the proceeds.

There may be, indeed, a partnership in a ship, either generally, or on a particular adventure, as in any other chattel : Hewitt *v.* Sturdevant, 4 B. Monr. 459 ; Knox *v.* Campbell, 1 Penn. St. 366 ; Story Partn., s. 408 ; Mumford *v.* Nicoll, 20 Johns. 611. And in such case, the part-owners will be entitled to all the equities and liens which arise from that relationship. But, on the other hand, they cannot claim contribution or subrogation, until the whole partnership affairs are settled : Story Partn., ss. 219, 419, &c., 260 ; see Bailey *v.* Brownfield, 20 Penn. St. 45.

tribution; for there is no equity between wrongdoers
But it is otherwise with respect to mere breaches of trus
not involving any actual fraud. In such cases each d
faulting trustee is severally liable to the *cestui que tru*
for the whole loss; but contribution may be enforced
between the trustees themselves; and if any third pers
has knowingly reaped the benefit of the breach of trus
the loss may be eventually cast on him.(c)

The rights now under consideration are acknowledg
both at law and in equity, and so far as the machinery
the common law will allow, may be enforced in an actio
But the means of enforcement at law are very limite
for, in addition to the impossibility, common to all class
of account, of obtaining discovery on oath or satisfactori
investigating the items, there are other special difficulti
originating in the necessity of suing each party liable
a separate action, which renders it difficult to insure v
dicts for the true ratable shares, and disables the Cou
where one of several contributors proves insolvent, fr
distributing the consequent loss ratably among the rest.(

(c) Merryweather v. Nixan, 8 T. 186; Lingard v. Bromley, 1 Ves. &
114; Seddon v. Connell, 10 Sim. 79, 86; Attorney-General v. Wilson,
& P. 1; [see Hill on Trustees (4th Am. ed.) 814, and notes.]

(d) Cowell v. Edwards, 2 Bos. & P. 268; Deering v. Earl of Winchels
Id. 270; Browne v. Lee, 6 B. & C. 689.

---

[1] Contribution will not be enforced in equity between wrongdoers; es
cially when the party who seeks it does not stand *in æquali jure* w
the other: Peck v. Ellis, 2 Johns. Ch. 131. Courts of justice will not l
their aid to equalize burdens in such cases, but will leave the parties wh
they find them: Bartle v. Nutt, 4 Peters 184; see, also, Miller v. Fent
11 Paige 18; Dupuy v. Johnson, 1 Bibb 562; Rhea v. White, 3 H
(Tenn.) 121; Anderson v. Saylors, Id. 551. But this rule is not of
versal application. It only applies to cases where the parties, who cl
contribution, have engaged together in doing, knowingly or wantonl
wrong: Acheson v. Miller, 2 Ohio (N. S.) 203; Moore v. Appleton, 26
633.

[2] The jurisdiction of equity in cases of contribution is not affected,

The two equities of contribution and exoneration are both exemplified in the case of suretyship :[1] the one by

cause a remedy now exists at common law : Veile v. Hoag, 24 Verm. 46 ; Wayland v Tucker, 4 Gratt. 268 ; Couch v. Terry, 12 Ala. 225 ; Hickman v. McCurdy, 7 J. J. Marsh 559.

[1] The doctrines which are applied in equity to the relation of creditor and surety will be found discussed with great ability and clearness in the notes to Rees v. Berrington, 2 Lead. Cas. Eq. 814. The following is, for the most part, a summary of the conclusions drawn by the learned editor from the American cases :

As it is of the essence of the contract of the surety, that he shall see to the performance of the obligation himself, the creditor is not bound in any way towards him, to diligence in the enforcement of his remedies, against the principal. The neglect or omission to take proper measures, by which all opportunity of collecting the debt is lost, unless, perhaps, when amounting to fraud (Dawson v. Lawes, 23 L. J. Ch. 434) will not affect the liability of the surety. The only exception to this doctrine is in Pennsylvania, in the case of a guarantee, which, in that state, whether under seal or not, imports on the part of the guarantor merely an obligation to pay if the principal debtor cannot, while that of the surety arises if the principal does not pay. In such case, therefore, it is held to be the duty of the creditor to pursue the principal at once to insolvency, or at least that actual insolvency shall exist, before he can turn round on the guarantor : Parker v. Culvertson, 1 Wall. Jr. 149, and cases cited ; McClurg v. Fryer, 15 Penn. St. 293 ; Marberger v. Pott, 16 Id. 13 ; Reigart v. White, 52 Id. 438. Unless, however the guarantee is special, as to pay a note, "when due ;" in which case the principal need not be pushed to insolvency : Campbell v. Baker, 46 Penn. St. 243.

Apart from this special case, it is well established, therefore, that indulgence to the principal, even by an express promise to give time, unless the promise be upon consideration, or otherwise legally binding ; or delay in proceeding against the debtor, whether before or after suit commenced, will not discharge the surety, of itself, whatever may be its effects to his injury. See also Marberger v. Pott, 16 Penn. St. 13 ; Pittsburgh, &c., R. R. v. Shaeffer, 59 Id. 350 ; Hunter v. Clark, 28 Texas 159 ; Rucker v. Robinson, 38 Mo. 154 ; Black River Bank v. Page, 44 N. Y. 453. And, though both in England, and the United States generally, collaterals held by the creditor, are considered as constituting a trust fund for the benefit of th sureties, yet contrary to the doctrine in the former country, the creditors seem to be held, here, to no greater diligence with respect to them, than to his direct remedies.

Where, however, the creditor acts in such a way as directly to impair or

the rights of sureties as between themselves; the other by their rights as against the principal.

---

destroy the relations of the principal to the surety, or the right of the latter to recourse or indemnity, it will operate as a discharge of the surety to the extent of the injury actually suffered by him. Thus, in the case of a binding promise to give time to the principal, for however short a period, or *à fortiori*, of his release: Paulin *v.* Kaign, 3 Dutch. 503; Pierce *v.* Goldsberry, 31 Ind. 52. See also Wakefield Bank *v.* Truesdall, 55 Barb. (N. Y.) 602; Preston *v.* Hennig, 6 Bush (Ky.) 556; Calvin *v.* Wiggam, 27 Ind. 489; Adams *v.* Way, 32 Conn. 160. Of the abandonment or relinquishment of collateral securities; of the relinquishment of any lien obtained by suit on the debtor's property, or of any similar act on the part of the creditor, he loses thereby his right of recourse to the surety. But this, as has been stated, only takes place when such conduct results in actual injury to the surety, and simply to that extent. See also N. H. Savings Bank *v.* Colcord, 15 N. H. 123; Everly *v.* Rice, 20 Penn. St. 297; Armistead *v.* Ward, 2 Patt. & H. 504; The People's Bank *v.* Pearsons, 30 Verm. 715; Phares *v.* Barbour, 49 Ill. 370; Mount *v.* Tappey, 7 Bush 617. The remedy against a surety may be expressly reserved: Boaler *v.* Mayor, 19 C. B. N. S. 76; Union Bank *v.* Buck, 3 Hurl. & Colt. 672; Barkyat *v.* Ellis, 45 N. Y. 107. Where the creditor has gone farther, and varied the terms of the original contract in any essential matter, the surety is absolutely discharged, though the alteration may be shown to be actually for his benefit, when he does not assent to the change. See Smith *v.* United States, 2 Wall. S. C. 233. In all cases, however, where he insists on a discharge, the surety is bound to surrender to the creditor any indemnity or collateral which he has obtained from the principal, before he can avail himself of his right.

By consequence of the principles before stated, a creditor, as a general rule, cannot be compelled in equity to resort in the first instance to the principal or his property before he can enforce his remedy against the surety. See Hayes *v.* Ward, 4 Johns. Ch. 123; Abercrombie *v.* Knox, 3 Ala. 728; *sed vide* West *v.* Belches, 5 Munf. 187; Wright *v.* Crump, 25 Ind. 339. It would seem, however, that there may be cases where such a bill would lie, though the surety would probably be required to indemnify the creditor against the risk, delay and expense: Whitridge *v.* Durkee, 2 Md. Ch. 442; Hayes *v.* Ward, ut supr.; Stephenson *v.* Taverner, 9 Gratt. 398; Thigpen *v.* Price, Phill. (N. C.) Eq. 146; Wright *v.* Austin, 56 Barb. (N. Y.) 13. The surety, indeed, is, without doubt, in this country, entitled to the use of the creditor's remedies against the principal and his property, and is entitled, therefore, on bill against the principal, to make the creditor

*The right of contribution arises between sure- [*269]
ties where one has been called on to make good

---

a party for that purpose. See post, note ; Stephenson v. Taverner, ut supr.;
note to Reese v. Berrington, ut supr.

In some of the states, nevertheless, the same end is obtained by what is
now well settled, that although mere forbearance, however prejudicial, will
not discharge him, yet, if the surety requests the creditor to proceed
against the principal, and the creditor refuses or delays to sue until the
principal becomes insolvent, the surety is discharged : King v. Baldwin,
17 Johns. 384 ; Valentine v. Farrington, 2 Ed. Ch. 53 ; Rutledge v. Greenwood, 2 Dessaus. 389 ; Pain v. Packard, 13 Johns. 174 ; Bruce v. Edwards,
1 Stew. 11 ; see also Matter of Babcock, 3 Story 393 ; Spottswood v. Dandridge, 4 Munf. 289 ; Singer v. Troutman, 49 Barb. (N. Y.) 182. So, in
Pennsylvania, if the creditor be requested in pais, by the surety, to sue
the debtor, and neglect or refuse so to do, the surety will be discharged ;
provided such request be positive, and accompanied with a declaration
that, unless it be complied with, the surety will consider himself discharged : Cope v. Smith, 8 S. & R. 112 ; Greenawalt v. Kreider, 3 Penn.
St. 264 ; and provided, also, the debt is due: Hellen v. Crawford,
44 Id. 105. The request may be made by an agent, and to the agent
or attorney of the creditor. The request is binding, without a tender
of expenses, or offer to sue upon the obligation, unless the creditor makes
objection on that ground at the time : Wetzel v. Sponsler's Ex'rs., 18 Penn.
St. 462 ; Conrad v. Foy, 68 Id. 381. Under the Mississippi Code such
notice must be in writing : Bridges v. Winters, 42 Miss. 135.

In other states, however, this rule has not been followed. In several,
where not adopted by decision, it has been embodied in the statute law.
See note to Rees v. Berrington, ut supr.

Another consequence flowing from the relation of creditor and surety
may be mentioned here, which is the right of the former to be subrogated
to, and to avail himself of all the securities held by the surety : note to
Dering v. Earl of Winchelsea, 1 Lead. Cas. Eq. 87 ; Kramer & Rahm's
Appeal, 37 Penn. St. 76 ; Havey v. Foley, 4 Benn. (Mo.) 136 ; Vail v.
Foster, 4 Comst. 312 ; Houston v. The Branch Bank, 25 Ala. 250 ; Dozier
v. Lewis, 27 Miss. 677 ; see the remarks in Yonge v. Reynell, 9 Hare 809 ;
Irick v. Black, 2 Green 189 ; Owens v. Miller, 29 Md. 144 ; Van Orden v.
Durham, 35 Cal. 136. The right is one recognised by Courts of law: Boyd
v. McDonough, 39 How. (N. Y.) 389. This right, however, is entirely
subordinate to that of the surety, and, when he is in fact not liable on the
original contract, cannot be enforced : Bibb v. Martin, 14 Sm. & M. 88 ;
Bush v. Stamps, 26 Miss. 463.

A surety cannot compel a creditor to resort to a *collateral security* in the

the principal's default, and has paid more than his share
of the entire liability.(e)[1]   If all the sureties have joined

(e) Smith's Merc. Law 427-8 ; Davies v. Humphreys, 6 M. & W. 153, 169.

---

first instance, unless such security be as available in all respects as a proceeding against the surety : Gary v. Cannon, 3 Ired. Ch. 64 ; Kirkman v.
Bank of America, 2 Cold. (Tenn.) 397.

[1] First. It is a general principle that a surety who has paid the debt may
compel his co-surety to make contribution : Waters v. Riley, 2 Har. & G.
305 ; Pinkston v. Taliaferro, 9 Ala. 547 ; Mitchell v. Sproul, 5 J. J. Marsh.
264 ; Robertson v. Maxcey, 6 Dana 103 ; Yates v. Donaldson, 5 Md. 389.
See, on this subject, notes to Dering v. Earl Winchelsea, 1 Lead. Cas. Eq.
78. But he can only call for contribution when he has paid more than his
proportion of the debt, and then for no more than the excess : Lytle v.
Pope, 11 B. Monr. 309 ; Rutherford v. Branch Bank, 14 Ala. 92. And
he must show also that the principal is insolvent, or at least that he has
used due diligence against him. Where one of the sureties is insolvent, his
share is proportioned among the rest, in favor of the surety asking contribution : note to Dering v. Winchelsea, ut supr. ; Young v. Lyons, 8 Gill
166. A judgment against a surety, paid by a co-surety, stands against the
estate of the former for the amount claimed for contribution : Rutherford
v. Branch Bank, 14 Ala. 92. And it has been held that where, on a judgment against co-sureties, the land of one has been sold, the judgment creditors of the latter are entitled to be subrogated to the judgment, by way of
a claim for contribution, against the land of the other : Moore v. Bray, 10
Penn. St. 519. But the general doctrine is founded on the maxim, "Equality is equity," and hence where one of two sureties, without the knowledge of his co-surety, and by previous arrangement with the principal
debtor, received a share of the sum borrowed, he was held not entitled to
contribution from such co-surety, when obliged to pay the debts : McPherson v. Talbot, 10 Gill & J. 499 ; see, also, Kerns v. Chambers, 3 Ired. Ch.
576. And the rule is, that where one of several co-sureties is indemnified
or receives a fund to be applied towards the debt, he will be considered as
holding for the benefit of all the sureties : Agnew v. Bell, 4 Watts 31 ;
Moore v. Moore, 4 Hawks. 358 ; Gregory v. Murrell, 2 Ired. Eq. 233 ;
Hinsdale v. Murray, 6 Verm. 136 ; Miller v. Sawyer, 30 Id. 412 ; Ramsey
v. Lewis, 30 Barb. 403 ; Butler v. Birkey, 13 Ohio N. S. 514 ; McMahon v.
Fawcett, 2 Rand. 514 ; Bobbitt v. Flowers, 1 Swan (Tenn.) 511 ; Aldrich's
Admr's. v. Hapgood, 39 Verm. 617 ; Clapp v. Rice, 15 Gray (Mass.) 557 ;
Brown v. Ray, 18 N. H. 102 ; but so far as he has a security for indi-
vidual claims he is entitled to hold it : McCunn v. Belt, 45 Mo. 194. One
surety has, however, an unquestionable right to stipulate for a separate
indemnity, and in the absence of fraud or deceit to apply it in extinguish-

in a single bond, the general rule, in the absence of any
express or implied contract, is that of equality; if their

ment of his portion of the liability: Thompson *v.* Adams, 1 Freem. Ch.
225; Moore *v.* Moore, ubi supra; see, also, Moore *v.* Isley, 2 Dev. & Bat.
Ch. 372; Himes *v.* Keller, 3 W. & S. 401; Bowditch *v.* Green, 3 Metc.
360; Com. Bank *v.* Western Bank., 11 Ohio 444.

But a surety, who is indemnified by the principal, cannot recover for
contribution, except so far as that indemnity does not extend: John *v.*
Jones, 16 Ala. 455; Morrison *v.* Taylor, 21 Id. 779. Where a surety obtains indemnity for a consideration paid by him, a co-surety cannot claim
the benefit of it, without paying his proportion of the consideration: White
v. Banks, 21 Ala. 705. And so where one surety buys in the principal's
land, on the judgment against him, with his own money, the others cannot claim to participate in the benefit of the purchase: Crompton *v.* Vasser, 19 Ala. 259.

A surety who has neglected to interpose a legal defence, as of the
Statute of Limitations, cannot claim contribution from the rest: Fordham
v. Wallis, 17 Jurist 228. And, on the other hand, one is not entitled to
charge the rest with fees expended in defending himself in a suit brought
against him as such surety: Comegys *v.* State Bank, 6 Ind. 357.

Although the surety's right of indemnification against his principal
was provable under the Bankrupt Act of 1841, though before he was
called upon to pay, and therefore discharged by the discharge of the principal: Fulwood *v.* Bashfield, 14 Penn. St. 90; yet it is otherwise with regard to his right of contribution against a co-surety: Dunn *v.* Sparks, 1
Cart. (Ind.) 397.

One of two sureties is entitled to take out execution on a joint judgment
against them, to compel contribution by his co-surety: Cuyler *v.* Ensworth,
6 Paige Ch. 32; Croft *v.* Moore, 9 Watts 451; yet see Bank *v.* Adger, 2
Hill·Ch. 262.

Second. Equity will distinguish between principal and surety, though
the nature of the security be such as to make them all principals in a
court of law: Davis *v.* Mikell, 1 Freem. Ch. 548; McDowell *v.* Bank, 1
Harrington 369.

Third. If one becomes surety merely at the request of a co-surety, he is
not liable to the latter for contribution. See Byers *v.* McClanahan, 6 Gill
& J. 250; Taylor *v.* Savage, 12 Mass. 98, 102.

The result of the cases on these points, is thus stated, in substance, in
the notes to Dering *v.* Winchelsea, ut sup. Where several persons, or
sets of persons, enter into engagements of suretyship, which are the same
in legal operation and effect, though at different times and by different instruments, for the same debt, and to and for the same persons, the right
of contribution exists among all; and parol evidence is admissible to contradict the legal result. See, also, Norton *v.* Coons, 2 Selden (N. Y.) 33;

liabilities have been created by distinct bonds, the contribution is in proportion to the respective penalties. But
in either case the principle is the same; and provided the
transaction to which the suretyship applies, be single, the
mode in which the parties are bound, whether by the same
or by different instruments, is, with respect to the right
of contribution, immaterial.(ƒ) The equity for contribution between sureties is also applicable to underwriters or
insurers, where the owner of property has made two or
more insurances on the same risk and the same interest.
In this case, the law will not allow him to receive a double
satisfaction for a loss; but if he recover the entire loss
from one set of underwriters, they may have a ratable
contribution from the rest.(g)

(ƒ) Deering v. Earl of Winchelsea, 2 Bos. & P. 270; Coope v. Twynam,
T. & R. 426; Craythorne v. Swinburne, 14 Ves. 160.

(g) Newby v. Reed, 1 W. Bl. 416.

Bell v. Jasper, 2 Ired. Eq. 597. If, however, the obligations be for distinct things, with no relation to or operation on each other, though they
may be all founded on the same original indebtedness, there is no contribution between the sureties. One who becomes surety in the course of
legal proceedings against the principal has no right of contribution against
the original surety for the debt itself; on the contrary, the latter is entitled to be subrogated to the creditor's right against him, as in the case of
bail. Thus the sureties of a sheriff, having been compelled to pay for a
default of his deputy, may recover the amount paid from the sureties of
the deputy: Brinson v. Thomas, 2 Jones Eq. 414. Finally, one who becomes surety by a supplemental instrument, on the understanding that he
is to be liable only in default of the principal and original sureties, cannot
be called upon to contribute; and on the other hand may be subrogated
to the creditor's rights against the original sureties.

Fourth. A surety who has paid the whole debt must show the insol-
vency of the principal, to entitle him to contribution against his co-surety:
Pearson v. Duckham, 3 Litt. 385; Daniel v. Ballard, 2 Dana 296; Allen v.
Wood, 3 Ired. Ch. 386; Burrows v. McWhann, 1 Dessaus. 409; or show
that he has used due diligence, without effect, to obtain reimbursements:
McCormack v. Obannon, 3 Munf. 484.

Fifth. Hence, to a bill by a surety for contribution, the principal debtor
ought to be made a party: Rainey v. Yarborough, 2 Ired. Ch. 249.

The right of exoneration arises between surety and principal, so soon as the surety has paid any part of the debt. Immediately on making such payment, he may bring assumpsit at law against his principal for indemnity.(*h*) And he may also sue the creditor in equity for an assignment of any mortgage or collateral security for the debt, so that he may, as far as possible, be substituted in his place. But he cannot have an assignment of the debt, itself, for that is determined by his own payment, and a new debt is due from his principal to himself.(*i*)[1]

(*h*) Toussaint *v.* Martinnant, 2 T. R. 100; Pownal *v.* Ferrand, 6 B. & C. 439.

(*i*) Copis *v.* Middleton, T. & R. 224; Caulfield *v.* Maguire, 2 Jones & Lat. 141, 164; Hodgson *v.* Shaw, 3 M. & K. 183.

---

[1] In support of the doctrine that a surety, on paying the debt, is entitled to stand in the place of the creditor, and to be subrogated to all his rights against the principal debtor, see Clason *v.* Morris, 10 Johns. 524; Lewis *v.* Palmer, 28 N. Y. 276; Erb's Appeal, 2 Penna. R. 296; McDowell *v.* Bank, 1 Harring. 369; Tatum *v.* Tatum, 1 Ired. Ch. 113; Lownds *v.* Chisholm, 2 McCord's Ch. 455; Perkins *v.* Kershaw, 1 Hill Ch. 344; Foster *v.* Trustees, 3 Ala. 302; Rhodes *v.* Crockett, 2 Yerg. 346; Wade *v.* Green, 3 Humph. 547; Neimcewicz *v.* Gahn, 3 Paige 614; Salmon *v.* Clagett, 3 Bland. Ch. 173; Hampton *v.* Levy, 1 McCord Ch. 116; Burk *v.* Chrisman, 3 B. Monr. 50; Yard *v.* Patton, 13 Penn. St. 287; Brewer *v.* Franklin Mills, 42 N. H. 292; York *v.* Landis, 65 N. C. 535. Actual assignment is not necessary in this country to subrogation, in the case of a surety. Note to Deering *v.* Winchelsea, ut supr.; Lloyd *v.* Barr, 11 Penn. St. 48; Gossin *v.* Brown, Id. 531; Bailey *v.* Brownfield, 20 Id. 45; Cottrell's App., 23 Id. 294. Though it is so, in the case of a stranger, who pays the debt voluntarily: Sandford *v.* McLean, 3 Paige 117; Bank U. S. *v.* Winston, 2 Brock. 252. But subrogation does not go on the ground of contract; and, in general, when any one is compelled to pay, where another is primarily liable, subrogation takes place by operation of law; as in the case of a vendee who pays a judgment against his vendor: Kyner *v.* Kyner, 6 Watts 221. See the remarks of Strong, J., on the nature of subrogation, in McCormick's Admr. *v.* Irwin, 35 Penn. St. 117. If he is surety in a bond, he is to be considered a bond creditor of the obligor: Eppes *v.* Randolph, 2 Call 103; see also Thomson *v.* Palmer, 3 Rich. Eq. 139; note to Deering *v.* Winchelsea. And, moreover, in many of the states, it is settled in liberal advance of the doctrine stated in the text, that the surety, on paying

[*270] The same equity *which enables a surety, after payment by himself, to recover the amount from his principal, warrants him in filing a bill to compel payment by the principal, when he has been brought under liability by the debt falling due, though he may not have been actually sued. (k)[1]

(k) Mitf. 148; Antrobus v. Davidson, 3 Meriv. 569, 578.

---

the bond or judgment debt of the principal, may even become entitled to an assignment and use of the instrument or judgment for his own exoneration; the payment being regarded as a purchase, and not as an extinguishment: see Burns v. Huntingdon Bk., 1 Penna. R. 395; Fleming v. Beaver, 2 Rawle 132; Schnitzel's Appeal, 49 Penn. St. 23; Perkins v. Kershaw, 1 Hill Ch. 344; Matthews v. Aiken, 1 Comst. 595; Creager v. Brengle, 5 Har. & J. 234; Gadsden v. Lord, 1 Dessaus. 214; Cuyler v. Ensworth, 6 Paige 32; Lathrop's Appeal, 1 Penn. St. 512; Gossin v. Brown, 11 Id. 531; Baily v. Brownfield, 20 Id. 45; Storms v. Storms, 3 Bush (Ky.) 77; Arnot v. Woodburn, 35 Mo. 99; Sears v. Laforce, 17 Iowa 473. Even an entry of satisfaction on the judgment against the principal, if without the consent of the surety, will not affect the right of subrogation: Baily v. Brownfield. But see Elwood v. Diedendorf, 5 Barb. S. C. 398. This rule appears to be general in the United States, except in Alabama and North Carolina: Sanders v. Watson, 14 Ala. 198; Brailey v. Sugg, 1 Dev. & Bat. Eq. 366; the debt being considered there as extinguished at law, and the only right of the surety, as that of a simple contract creditor. See note to Deering v. Winchelsea, ut sup.

The surety is entitled, by the operation of the doctrine of subrogation, to stand in all respects in the place of the creditor, and therefore, where the latter holds a mortgage for the debt, the right of the surety to enforce the mortgage against the principal is not affected by the fact of the debt being barred by the statute: Ohio Life Ins. Co. v. Winn, 4 Md. Ch. 254. And so a surety in a bond to the United States, is entitled to avail himself of their prerogative preference against the other creditors: U. S. v. Hunter, 5 Mason 62; 5 Peters 174. The surety, however, taking the rights of the creditor, cannot claim to stand in any better position than he: Calvin v. Owen, 22 Ala. 782.

[1] As a general rule, the surety is not entitled to be subrogated, or to claim contribution, until he has actually paid the debt: Rice v. Downing, 12 B. Monr. 44; Morrison's Adm. v. Tenn. Ins. Co., 3 Benn. (Mo.) 262; Bennett v. Buchanan, 3 Porter (Ind.) 47; and see Barnett v. Reed, 51 Penn. St. 194; Hoover v. Epler, 52 Id. 522; yet when his land is extended

Another instance of contribution occurs where mortgages, renewed fines, or other encumbrances, require discharge, and the property bound by them is not absolutely vested in a single person; e. g., where different parcels of land are included in the same mortgage, and are afterwards sold to different owners, or where a mortgage estate, or a renewable leasehold, is held for life or in tail, with remainders over, or has devolved upon a dowress and the heir. In these cases the burden is to be borne by the parties interested according to the value of their respective interests, and the benefit which they actually derive from its discharge.(l)[1] And although the

---

(l) White v. White, 9 Ves. 554; Bulwer v. Astley, 1 Ph. 422; Jones v. Jones, 5 Hare 440; Averell v. Wade, Ll. & G. 252; 3 Sug. V. & P. 435–6.

---

on execution, it is sufficient, though without payment: Lord v. Staples, 3 Foster (N. H.) 448. Partial payments give no right of subrogation: Grove v. Brien, 1 Md. 439; Neptune Ins. Co. v. Dorsey, 3 Md. Ch. 334; Kyner v. Kyner, 6 Watts 221; Gannett v. Blodgett, 39 N. H. 150; though the surety acquires an interest in the securities to that extent: Grove v. Brien, ut sup. Where the principal debtor is insolvent, however, his surety may proceed, before paying the debt, against the principal for indemnity, or to subject particular assets to the payment of the debt: Polk v. Gallant, 2 Dev. & Bat. Ch. 395; Pride v. Boyce, Rice Eq. 275; Washington v. Tait, 3 Humph. 543; Stump v. Rogers, 1 Ham. (Ohio) 533; Ross v. Clore, 3 Dana 193; Bishop v. Day, 13 Verm. 81; Hatcher v. Hatcher, 1 Rand. 53; Daniel v. Joyner, 3 Ired. Eq. 513; Taylor v. Heriot, 4 Dessaus. 227; Williams v. Helme, 1 Dev. Ch. 151; Tankersley v. Anderson, 4 Dessaus. 44; McConnell v. Scott, 15 Ohio 401; Laughlin v. Ferguson, 6 Dana 111. See Henry v. Compton, 2 Head 549. So, on the same principle, where the principal is dead, the surety may file a bill quia timet against the executor and the creditor, to compel the former to pay the debt, and exonerate him. He may enforce against the estate any lien of the creditor, and as a part of the creditor's rights, may file a bill for the administration of the estate. The creditor, however, must be made a party: Stephenson v. Taverners, 9 Gratt. 398.

[1] See Thomas v. Hearn, 2 Porter 262; Chamberlayne v. Temple, 2 Rand 384; Hays v. Wood, 4 Id. 272; Dupuy v. Johnson, 1 Bibb 562; Poston v. Eubank, 3 J. J. Marsh. 34; Morrison v. Beckwith, 4 Monr. 76; Williams

creditor himself is not bound by this equity, but may proceed against whom he will, yet if he wilfully render its

---

v. Craig, 2 Ed. Ch. 279; Aiken v. Gale, 37 N. H. 501. But where there are several purchasers in succession at *different times*, of parcels of a lot bound by a judgment or mortgage, there is no equality, and no case for contribution between the purchasers. "If, for instance, there be a judgment against a person owning, at the time, three acres of land, and he sells one acre to A., the remaining two acres are first chargeable in equity with the payment of the judgment debt; and that, too, whether the land be in the hands of the debtor himself, or his heirs. If he sells another acre to B., the *remaining* acre is then chargeable, in the first instance, with the debt, as against B., as well as against A.; and, if *it* should prove insufficient, then the acre sold to B., ought to supply the deficiency in preference to the acre sold to A." Chancellor Kent, in Clowes v. Dickenson, 5 Johns. Ch. 235. In that case A. purchased a lot of land, which with several others, was subject to a judgment. B. *afterwards* purchased the residue of the lots so encumbered, and having purchased the prior judgment in the name of another, caused A.'s lot to be sold, and became the purchaser. It was held that A. was entitled to have the judgment satisfied out of the lots sold to B.; and that, on application to the court, the sale under the judgment would have been stayed. But the plaintiff's application being made as much as four year after the sale, the title was not disturbed, but B. was compelled to pay to A. the amount for which A.'s lot was sold. The same equity holds not only as between several *purchasers*, but applies where the owner of the land thus bound gives thereon several mortgages of different date: Schryver v. Teller, 9 Paige 173. The doctrine here stated has been approved and maintained by a train of decisions in the several states: James v. Hubbard, 1 Paige 228; Gouverneur v. Lynch, 2 Id. 300; Patty v. Pease, 8 Id. 277; Gill v. Lyon et al., 1 Johns. Ch. 447; Mevey's Appeal, 4 Barr 80; Rathbone v. Clarke, 9 Paige 648; Shannon v. Marselis, Saxton 413; Woodruff v. Depue, 1 McCart. 168; Britton v. Upkyke, 2 Green Ch. 125; Wikoff v. Davis, 3 Id. 224; Stanley v. Stocks, 1 Dev. Ch. 314, and note to p. 317; Stoney v. Shultz, 1 Hill Ch. 464, 500; Thompson v. Murray, 2 Id. 204; Conrad v. Harrison, 3 Leigh 532; McClung v. Beirne, 10 Id. 394; Nailer v. Stanley, 10 S. & R. 450; Zeigler v. Long, 2 Watts 205; Pallen v. Bank, 1 Freem. Ch. 419; Agric. Bk. v. Pallen, 8 Sm. & Mar. 357; Com. Bank v. Western R. Bank, 11 Ohio 444; Cary v. Folsom, 14 Ohio 365; Holden v. Pike, 24 Maine 427; Cushing v. Ayer, 25 Id. 383; Brown v. Simons, 44 N. H. 475; Cowden's Estate, 1 Penn. St. 267; Becker v. Kehr, 49 Id. 223; Gate v. Adams, 24 Verm. 70; Lyman v. Lyman, 32 Id. 79; Sheperd v. Adams, 32 Maine 65; Jones v. Myrick, 8 Gratt. 180; Winters v. Henderson, 2 Halst.

enforcement impossible, as by discharging one of several coparceners, he cannot proceed for the whole debt against the others, but at the most can only require from them

---

Ch. 31 ; Johnson *v.* Williams, 4 Minn. 268 ; Mobile Ins. Co. *v.* Iluder, 35 Ala. 717 ; Ogden *v.* Glidden, 9 Wis. 46 ; Hunt *v.* Mansfield, 31 Conn. 488 ; Cooper *v.* Bigly, 13 Mich. 463 ; Hoy *v.* Bramhall, 4 Green (N. J.) 74, 563 ; State *v.* Titus, 17 Wis. 241 ; Meng *v.* Houser, 13 Rich. (S. C.) Eq. 210 ; Iglehart *r.* Crane, 42 Ill. 261 ; McKinney *v.* Miller, 19 Mich. 142. This doctrine seems to have originated with the New York cases above cited, it not having previously been acted upon in cases susceptible of its application. See Stevens *v.* Cooper, 1 Johns. Ch. 425 ; Cheesebrough *v.* Millard, 1 Id. 409. Nor formerly in Virginia : Beverly *v.* Brooke, 2 Leigh 425. And in one or two states the rule is repudiated. See Jobe *v.* O'Brien, 2 Humph. 34 ; Dickey *v.* Thompson, 8 B. Monr. 312. And see Parkman *v.* Welch, 19 Pick. 231, 238 ; Green *v.* Ramage, 18 Ohio 428 ; Barney *v.* Myers, 28 Iowa 472. The rule that purchasers are liable to contribute in the inverse order of their purchases, to the discharge of a paramount encumbrance, is not applicable, however, where they take expressly subject to the eucumbrance, and it forms a part of the purchase-money : see Briscoe *v.* Power, 47 Ill. 447. Therefore, in Pennsylvania, where by statute, a mortgage is not discharged at sheriff's sale, except under certain circumstances, successive sheriff's vendees of different tracts bound by the same mortgage, are bound to contribute in proportion to the value of their interests without regard to priority : Carpenter *v.* Koons, 20 Penn. St. 222.

Nor is the doctrine applicable to one who has only paid part of the purchase-money, for he is liable to contribute to the extent of the unpaid balance : Beddow *v.* Dewitt, 43 Penn. St. 326.

In Sheperd *v.* Adams, 32 Maine 65, it was held that the only remedy, of the subsequent purchaser, was in equity, and that no action of assumpsit could be brought in such case.

The rule will not be so applied as to affect the statutory priority of the United States : U. S. *v.* Duncan, 12 Ill. 523.

Justice Story, in his Coms. Eq. Jurisp., s. 1233 A, refers to English authorities in support of the position, that even in the case of *successive* purchasers or encumbrancers, the original encumbrance ought to be apportioned ratably among them. But see the error of his reference pointed out by the late Judge Kennedy in Cowden's Estate, ubi supra. The learned American editor of the Leading Cases in Equity, in his note to Aldrich *v.* Cooper, 2 Lead. Cas. Eq. 56, agrees with Judge Story in his strictures on the rule. See that note, for a discussion of the subject.

35

their respective shares.(m)[1] If the burden has been already discharged by one of the parties liable, he will be entitled to contribution from the rest, unless he has shown an intention to exonerate the estate. But if his interest is that of tenant·in tail in possession, and consequently convertible at his option into an absolute estate, a presumption arises that he so intended.(n)

The doctrine of general average is another illustration of the equity for contribution, and is the last which will be here noticed. The circumstances under which this

(m) Stirling v. Forrester, 3 Bligh. O. S. 575, 590.

(n) Wigsell v. Wigsell, 2 S. & S. 364 ; Burrell v. Egremont, 7 Beav. 205; Faulkner v. Daniel, 3 Hare 199, 217.

---

[1] When a judgment or a mortgage is a lien on several lots of land owned by different persons, and the judgment creditor or mortgagee releases one of the subsequent purchasers, his lien upon the remaining lots will be diminished by the value of the lot released : Stevens v. Cooper, 1 Johns. Ch. 425; James v. Hubbard, 1 Paige 228 ; Paxton v. Harner, 11 Penn. St. 312; Guion v. Knapp, 6 Paige 35 ; Jones v. Myrick, 8 Gratt. 180; George v. Wood, 9 Allen 83 ; Stillman v. Stillman, 21 N. J. Eq. 126. So, if after a bill filed for subrogation against a creditor of two funds by the creditors of the doubly charged estate, the former releases the other fund to the debtor, though in pursuance of a previous agreement, he will be compelled to account for its value, and will be considered as paid to that extent: Fassett v. Traber, 20 Ohio 540. See James v. Brown, 11 Mich. 25. But in order to make the general rule applicable, the creditor must have actual notice of the prior conveyances : Cheesebrough v. Millard, 1 Johns. Ch. 409; Guion v. Knapp, 6 Paige 35. See too, Lock v. Fulford, 52 Ill. 166. Their registration is not notice, because it cannot appear in the line of title ; along which the creditor is bound to look : Stuyvesant v. Hone, 1 Sandf. Ch. 419; Taylor v. Maris, 5 Rawle 51. In Lloyd v. Galbraith, 32 Penn. St. 103, a creditor had a lien upon several tracts of land, some of which were sold by the debtor. The creditor then levied upon and sold the balance. It was held that a junior encumbrancer whose lien extended only to the unsold tracts was not entitled to be subrogated to the paramount creditor's lien against the tracts which had been aliened. As between the original parties, the rule, of course, does not hold : any part of the mortgaged premises is bound for the payment of the whole debt: Coutant v. Servoss, 3 Barb. S. C. 128. See Patty v. Pease, 8 Paige 277.

equity *arises are where a ship and cargo are in [*271] imminent peril, and a portion is intentionally sac- rificed for the security of the rest, *e. g.*, where goods are thrown overboard, or a portion of the ship's rigging cut away, to lighten and save the ship, or the ship itself is intentionally stranded, to save her cargo from a tempest or an enemy, or a part of the cargo is delivered up by way of ransom, or is sold for the necessity of the ship. In all these cases the impending danger is common to all, and the means by which it is averted, ought to be a common burden. If, therefore, the ship and the residue of the cargo are preserved by the sacrifice, the parties interested in the ship, her freight, and the merchandise on board, must make good ratable shares of the loss, proportioned to the value which their own goods and the goods sacri- ficed would have borne, after deducting freight, had they safely reached the port of discharge. If, on the contrary, the sacrifice is not intentionally made, but is damage in- curred by violence or stress of weather, or if it prove un- availing, or be made not to save the cargo, but to save the lives and liberty of the crew, the principle of contribution does not apply, and the loss must remain where it origi- nally falls. The rates of contribution are generally settled by arbitration, but the parties are not compellable to refer, and may have recourse to an action at law or a suit in equity.(o)[1]

The equity of marshalling arises where the owner of property subject to a charge, has subjected it, together

(o) Birkley *v.* Presgrave, 1 East 220; Plummer *v.* Wildman, 3 M. & S. 482; Power *v.* Whitmore, 4 Id. 141; Simonds *v.* White, 2 B. & C. 805; Hallett *v.* Bousfield, 18 Ves. 187; 2 Steph. Bl. 179; Smith's Merc. Law 292.

[1] Sturgess *v.* Cary, 2 Curtis C. C. 59.

with another estate, to a paramount charge, and the estate thus doubly charged is inadequate to satisfy both the claims. In this case, if the paramount charge be by way of mortgage, the only resource for the puisne mortgagee is to redeem it, and then to tack it to his own debt; but if it is only a charge payable out of the produce of the estate, and not conferring on the paramount creditor a [*272] right to *foreclose, an equity arises for marshalling the security so that both creditors may, if possible, be paid in full.$(p)^1$ The equity is a personal

(p) Aldrich v. Cooper, 8 Ves. 382; Titley v. Davies, 2 B. C. C. 393, 399.

---

[1] The rule of equity, that where one has a lien upon two funds, and another a posterior lien upon only one of them, the former will be compelled first to exhaust the subject of his exclusive lien, and will be permitted to resort to the other only for the deficiency, is well established in this country: Piatt v. St. Clair, 6 Ham. (Ohio) 233; Russell v. Howard, 2 McLean 489; Findlay's Ex'r. v. U. S. Bank, 2 Id. 44; N. Y. Steamboat Co. v. New Jersey Co., 1 Hopkins 460; Evertson v. Booth, 19 Johns. 486; Pallen v. Agric. Bank, 1 Freem. Ch. 419, 424; Kendall v. The N. England Co., 13 Conn. 394–5; Lodwick v. Johnson, Wright (Ohio) 498; Thompson v. Murray, 2 Hill Ch. 210; Miami Co. v. U. S. Bank, Wright (Ohio) 249; Williams v. Washington, 1 Dev. Ch. 137; Dorr v. Shaw, 4 Johns. Ch. 17; Trowbridge v. Harleston, Walk. Ch. 185; Goss v. Lester, 1 Wis. 43; House v. Thompson, 3 Head (Tenn.) 512. But it ought to appear that the fund which is not affected by the junior lien is fully adequate to satisfy the prior lien, and the remedy for realizing it is prompt and efficient: Briggs v. The Planter's Bank, Freem. Ch. 574; Dorr v. Shaw, 5 Johns. Ch. 17. The rule will not be applied to defeat an equity of the former on either fund, attaching prior to the existence of the latter's claim: McCormick's Appeal, 57 Penn. St. 54; Jarvis v. Smith, 7 Abb. (N. Y.) Pr., N. S. 217. See also cases cited, note 2, p. 270, supra, the distinction there illustrated being but a corollary of this doctrine.

Though the proposition that a creditor of two funds will be restrained from proceeding against the doubly charged fund till he has exhausted the other, is often repeated in the decisions, it has been acted on, in general, only where both funds were actually within the control of the Court; and the usual course is merely to compel him, while proceeding against the doubly charged fund, to place his remedies against the other at the disposal of the disappointed creditors. The equity of the latter is not, indeed, one against the debtor, and does not bind the paramount creditor, nor the debtor's alienee for value. The equity is not binding on the paramount creditor, for no equity can be created against him by the fact that some one else has taken an imperfect security. But it is an equity against the debtor himself, that the accidental resort of the paramount creditor to the doubly charged

---

against the double creditor at all, but only against the common debtor, that he should not be permitted to get back the fund not resorted to, freed from its liabilities, on account of the accident of the creditor's recourse to the other. This end can be obtained quite as well by subrogation as through marshalling by actual restraint; and it is, therefore, very difficult to understand how equity can interfere with the legal rights of the double creditor, on an equity which is no greater than his own, and which can be equally protected in another way. In several cases such interference has consequently been refused: Ramsay's App., 2 Watts 228; Evans v. Duncan, 4 Id. 24; Neff's App., 9 W. & S. 36; Shunk's App., 2 Penn. St. 304; Cornish v. Wilson, 6 Gill 299; Post v. Mackall, 3 Bland 486; U. S. v. Duncan,'12 Ill. 523; Chapman v. Hamilton, 19 Ala. 121; Knowles v. Lawton, 18 Ga. 476. See also Lafarge Ins. Co. v. Bell, 22 Barb. 34; Building Association v. Conover, 1 McCart. 219; Lloyd v. Galbraith, 32 Penn. St. 103, stated ante, note to page 270; and Warren v. Warren, 30 Verm. 530. In others the right of restraint has been confined to cases where to compel a resort to the singly charged fund would not be productive of any additional risk, injury or delay to the double creditor: Brinkerhoff v. Marvin, 5 Johns. Ch. 320; Evertson v. Booth, 19 Johns. 486; see James v. Hubbard, 1 Paige 228; Morrison v. Kurtz, 15 Ill. 193. A creditor holding security upon different kinds of property cannot be compelled to select that which is least convenient and available to himself, in order to aid other creditors not secured in the collection of their demands: Emmons v. Bradley, 56 Me. 333. In N. Y. Steamboat Co. v. The N. J. Co., 1 Hopkins 460; Thompson v. Murray, 2 Hill Eq. 204; Pallen v. Agricultural Bank, 1 Freeman Ch. 419; 8 Sm. & Marsh. 357, however, the doctrine has been carried to even a greater length. It has also been applied in New York, without hesitation, and perhaps with more propriety, to the case of a creditor, with collateral security, claiming upon a fund assigned for the benefit of creditors: Besley v. Lawrence, 11 Paige 581; though the contrary is now established in Pennsylvania: Morris v. Olwine, 22 Penn. St. 441; Kittera's Est., 17 Id. 413. This subject is discussed in the note to Aldrich v. Cooper, 2 Lead. Cas. Eq. 56.

estate, and the consequent exhaustion of that sect
shall not enable him to get back the second estate
charged of both debts. If, therefore, the paral
creditor resorts to the doubly charged estate, the p
creditor will be substituted to his rights, and will be
fied out of the other fund, to the extent to which his
may be exhausted.[1] And it seems that he may, on
posing just terms, require the paramount creditor t
ceed against the estate on which he has himself no c
His right, however, to do this is not an indeper
equity against the creditor, but a mere ,incident o
equity against their common debtor; and, therefo
the paramount claim is not chargeable on two funds,
belonging to the same debtor, but is merely due fro
persons, one of whom is also indebted to separate
itors, there is no equity to compel a resort to one r
than to the other, or to alter the consequences of the
tion which may be made.$(q)^2$

(q) Greenwood v. Taylor, 1 R. & M. 185; Mason v. Bogg, M. & C
Ex parte Kendal, 17 Ves. 514; Ex parte Field, 3 M., D. & D. 95.

[1] Bank of Kentucky v. Vance, 4 Litt. 168; see also Eddy v. Tri
Paige 521; Hawley v. Mancius, 7 Johns. Ch. 174; Hunt v. Towns
Sandf. Ch. 510; Ramsay's Appeal, 2 Watts 228; Cheesebrough v. M
1 Johns. Ch. 409; Hastings' Case, 10 Watts 303; Averill v. Lou
Barb. S. C. 470; Besley v. Lawrence, 11 Paige 581; Hunt v. Tow
4 Sandf. Ch. 510; Fassett v. Traber, 20 Ohio 540; Dunn v. Olney, 14
St. 220; U. S. Ins. Co. v. Shriver, 3 Md. Ch. 382; Nelson v. Dunn, 1
517. But this rule will not be applied where it will work injustice
creditors of the other estate: McGinnis's App., 16 Penn. St. 445
U. S. v. Duncan, 12 Ill. 523.

[2] See Ayres v. Husted, 15 Conn. 504; Sterling v. Brightbill, 5
229; Ebenhardt's App., 8 W. & S. 327. See remarks on this case, in
v. Olney, 14 Penn. St. 219. But if, in such case, one of the debti
his estate, on general equity principles, or by agreement of the par
primarily liable, the separate creditors of the other, disappointed
joint creditors, have a right to subrogation: Gearhart v. Jordan, 11
St. 331 Dunn v. Olney, 14 Id. 219; Neff v. Miller, 8 Id. 347.

The principle which refuses interference as against the creditor was strongly tested in a case arising out of the rebellion of the American Colonies. Subsequently to the Declaration of Independence, an act was passed by the legislature of Georgia confiscating the estates of all who had retained their allegiance, but providing that debts owing by them to persons who had favored the rebellion *should be paid out of the confiscated estates; [*273] so that any creditor coming within the tenor of the act had two sources of payment to which he might resort, viz., first, the American estates; and second, the personal liability of his debtor. A bill was filed by the executors of a banished loyalist, praying that certain of his creditors might be compelled to seek satisfaction in the first instance out of the confiscated property. And it is obvious that if any equity could exist for controlling the creditor, it might have been well exercised in a case where under such circumstances as these he had acquired a claim on an independent fund, from which, if rejected by him, his debtor could reap no advantage. The claim was disallowed, on the ground that it was not proved that the particular creditor could avail himself of the fund; but Lord Eldon, in reviewing the cases, expressed considerable doubt whether, even if that difficulty had not occurred, the supposed equity as between the debtor and the creditor could exist.(r)

The equity is apparently not binding on the debtor's alienee for value, notwithstanding that he may have taken with notice of the facts, unless his interest were acquired after the institution of a suit. For although the ordinary rule is, that an alienee with notice is bound by all the equities which bound his alienor, yet there is a

(r) Wright v. Simpson, 6 Ves. 714.

distinction in regard to this particular equity; because·
the omission of the creditor to take an express collateral
charge raises a presumption that he meant to leave the
equity defeasible, and to continue the owner's power of
dealing with the second estate for value, unfettered by
his claim. It is otherwise if the debtor, on creating the
single claim, covenants to satisfy the paramount charge
out of the other estate, or fraudulently conceals its existence. For then a purchaser taking with notice of the
covenant or concealment will be bound by the same equity
as the debtor himself.(*s*)

[*274] *The equities of contribution, exoneration, and
marshalling, are applied, as already noticed, in
the administration of assets, to rectify disorders which
may incidentally occur.

The two former equities are applied when debts or
legacies are charged on several kinds of assets, either
pari passu or successively; as, for example, where estates
subject to a charge descend to several heirs in different
lines of descent, or are given to several devisees, all the
heirs in the one case, and all the devisees in the other,
must contribute to the charge;[1] but if there be both heirs
and devisees, the heirs can have no contribution from

(*s*) Averall *v.* Wade, Ll. & G. 252; Hamilton *v.* Royse, 2 Sch. & L. 315,
commented on in Ll. & G. 263; Barnes *v.* Racster, 1 N. C. C. 401; Bugden
v. Bignold, 2 Id. 377.

---

[1] When lands held by several devisees in the same will, are charged in
equity to satisfy a bond debt of the devisor, the decree should be against
the lands of all the devisees, or the money received or claimed in lieu thereof, in ratable proportions, and not against the land of one only, with liberty
to that one to sue the others for contribution : Forster *v.* Crenshaw's Ex'rs.,
3 Munf. 514; See also Livingston *v.* Livingston, 3 Johns. Ch. 148. As to
contribution among co-heirs, see Schermerhorn *v.* Barhydt, 9 Paige 28.
See, on the subject of contribution between legatees : Peeples *v.* Horton,
39 Miss. 406, where it was held under the circumstances, not to exist.

the devisees, because their own estate is first liable.[1] If, on the other hand, a charge is levied on a fund out of its regular order, as, for instance, on a devised instead of a descended estate, or on a descended estate instead of the general personalty, the devisee in the one case, or the heir in the other, may claim exoneration. The necessity, however, for such a claim can only exist where the regular order of liability has been infringed; and in ordinary administration suits it is not likely to occur, except in the particular instance of a mortgaged estate. In this case the mortgage, like any other specialty debt, will, if claimed by the creditor, be discharged out of the personalty, and the question will subsequently arise, whether as between the respective owners of the several funds, the devisee or heir can claim the benefit of its discharge, or whether he must restore its amount to the personalty.(t)[2]

(t) Supra, Administration of Assets.

---

[1] See in agreement with the text, Livingston v. Newkirk, 3 Johns. Ch. 312, 320 ; Stires v. Stires, 1 Halsted's Ch. 224 ; Adams v. Brackett, 5 Metc. 280. But the right of the devisee as against the heir is different when the fund for payment of debts is by the will of blended real and personal property. Thus, when a testator devised his estate *real and personal*, to be divided among his next of kin " as soon as his debts and legacies are paid, and not until then ;" it charges the estate with payment of the debts and legacies ; and after-acquired real estate, as to which the testator died intestate, is exonerated until the other is exhausted : Hall v. Hall, 2 McCord's Ch. 269, 302. See also Hassanclever v. Tucker, 2 Binn. 525 ; Knight v. Knight, 6 Jones Eq. (N. C.) 134. See, ante, 263, note.

[2] The devisee or heir of a mortgaged estate, has, as a general rule, the right to throw the burden of the mortgage upon the personal estate, except as against specific and pecuniary legatees. See Torr's Estate, 2 Rawle 250, 254 ; Mansell's Estate, 1 Parsons's Sel. Eq. Cas. 367. But see note to page 264, ante. See also cited cases, note p. 261, supra ; and Townshend v. Mostyn, 26 Beav. 72. But not so, where the encumbrance was not the primary personal debt of the decedent ; then the land is first chargeable, and the heir or devisee cannot claim exoneration, even though there were a personal covenant by the decedent with the mortgagor to pay the debt :

The equity of marshalling is applied in administ
suits, where debts or legacies are charged, some on
ral kinds of assets, and some on one kind only, ai
doubly charged assets have been applied in discha
the doubly secured claims.

Under the old law this equity was often exerci
*favor of simple contract creditors, wher
personalty, which then constituted the only
had been wholly or partially exhausted by superior
itors, who might have resorted to the real estate·
by specialty creditors, by mortgagees, or by ve
claiming a lien for unpaid purchase-money$(u)^1$ Bι

[*275]

(u) Aldrich v. Cooper, 8 Ves. 382, 389 ; Selby v. Selby, 4 Russ.

Cumberland v. Codrington, 3 Johns. Ch. 229 ; Mitchell v. Mitchell
Ch. 73. See also note, p. 264-5, supra.

The right of exoneration by the holder of an equity of redemp
against the personal estate, accrues only on the administration
assets, and need not be asserted till there are assets to be admini
Lapse of time, therefore, where for any reason the administratioι
estate has been impossible, will not affect the right: Mellersh v. B
17 Jurist 908.

Where a testator devises several estates, charged generally w
payment of debts, to different persons, and afterwards mortgag
the devisee of the mortgaged estate is entitled to contribution frι
others: Middleton v. Middleton, 15 Beav. 450. But, in general, t
is, that a devisee subject to a mortgage, must bear the whole bur
regards other devisees: Mason's Est., 1 Pars. Eq. 129 ; s. c. 4 Pe
497.

¹ See Alston v. Munford, 1 Brock. 266 ; Haydon v. Goode, 4 1
Munf. 460; Cralle v. Meem, 8 Gratt. 496. Where specialty debts ι
ceased person have been paid out of his personal estate, which at tl
was sufficient also to pay his simple contract debts, and the executoι
quently commits a devastavit, which renders the personal estate insu
to pay the simple contract creditors, they are entitled to be paid ouι
real estate of the debtor, to the extent to which the personal estate hι
exonerated by the specialty creditors: Ellard v. Cooper, 1 Irish L. &
S. 376 (Chancellor). In the same case it was held that simple c
creditors, who have, in consequence of the payment of specialty cι

necessity for this course has ceased under the late statute, making real estate, whether freehold or copyhold, directly liable as assets for simple contract debts.(*v*) The equity, however, is still applicable in favor of devisees or legatees, though it is seldom required by devisees or by specific legatees, because their funds are seldom applied before their turn. The case of general pecuniary legacies is different; for they are not gifts of any specific thing, which may be set apart until its turn arrives, but they are gifts of money out of the general personalty after satisfaction of the debts; and, therefore, if they have not been protected by a charge on the realty, the fund may be exhausted before their turn arrives. This exhaustion is remedied by marshalling; but subject to the restriction that it must not operate against any one, who is equally an object of the testator's bounty, and whose interest is by law not liable in priority to the legatee's.

In accordance with this rule, an entire or partial exhaustion of the personal estate will warrant marshalling in favor of legatees; but such marshalling can only be directed against real assets descended, land devised for or charged with payment of debts, and land devised subject to a mortgage.[1] It cannot be directed as against other

(*v*) 3 & 4 Wm. 4, c. 104.

out of the personal estate of the deceased debtor, acquired a right of marshalling his real estate, are not barred under the Statute of Limitations by less than twenty years.

In Fordham *v.* Wallis, 17 Jurist 228, however, it was held that as simple contract creditors have now a right to the real assets in England, the doctrine of marshalling, for whatever other purpose now kept alive as to them, would not be applied merely for the purpose of giving them a longer period of limitation, by substituting them in the place of specialty creditors.

[1] Or subject to the vendor's lien for purchase-money which the person-

land devised or as against specific legatees. $(w)^1$ The manner in which the exhaustion is caused is generally by
[*276] payment *of creditors, but it may be also caused
by payment of legacies, where some legacies are
charged on both real and personal estate, and others on

(w) Wythe v. Henniker, 2 M. & K. 635; Mirehouse v. Scaife, 2 M. & C.
695; Sproule v. Prior, 8 Sim. 189; Strickland v. Strickland, 10 Id. 374;
3 Sug. V. & P. c. xviii., s. 2. [See Patterson v. Scott, 1 De G. Macn. & G.
531.]

---

alty is taken to pay: Birds v. Askey, 24 Beav. 618; Lilford v. Powys
Keck, L. R. 1 Eq. 347; where Wythe v. Henniker (infra note w), was not
followed. Real assets descended will not be marshalled in aid of either a
general or residuary legacy: Walker's Estate, 3 Rawle 229. See also Hays
v. Jackson, 6 Mass. 149; Leigh v. Savidge, 1 McCarter (N. J.) 124. *Aliter*,
if the legacy is pecuniary or specific: Mollan v. Griffith, 3 Paige 402; Wilcox v. Wilcox, 13 Allen (Mass.) 252; but see Gerken's Estate, 1 Tucker
(N. Y. Surr.) 49. But in some cases, lands taken by descent seem to have
been charged even before what are, properly, *general* legacies. See Robards
v. Wortham, 2 Dev. Eq. 173, wherein it was said that "descended lands
must pay all debts for which the real estate is liable, in exoneration of all
but *residuary* legacies, or of other land devised for the payment of debts."
To the same effect are Brown v. James, 3 Strob. Eq. 24–26, and Warley
v. Warley, 1 Bailey Eq. 397. See on this subject note, ante, p. 263;
Verdier v. Verdier, 12 Rich. (S. C.) Eq. 138.

[1] Livingston v. Livingston, 3 Johns. Ch. 148, 158; McCampbell v. Mc-
Campbell, 5 Litt. 92; Hoover v. Hoover, 5 Penn. St. 351. Respecting the
relative rights of specific legatees and devisees, there is a diversity of decision. The English rule, that if specific legacies have been applied to
pay specialty debts, the specific legatees are entitled to *contribution* against
the devisees of the realty, was upheld in Chase v. Lockerman, 11 Gill. & J.
185. But other decisions exempt the devisees altogether, and render the
specific legatees first liable. See Miller v. Harwell, 3 Murphey 194;
Warley v. Warley, 1 Bailey Eq. 397; Okeson's Appeal, 59 Penn. St. 99.
See on this subject note, ante, p. 263. Since by the English Wills Act
a residuary devise comprises all the real estate the testator may be seised
of at the time of his death, and also all devises which lapse or fail, a general
pecuniary legatee has a right of marshalling against the residuary
devisee: Hensman v. Fryer, L. R. 2 Eq. 627. Though there appears
to be some conflict of authority on the point: Robinson v. McIver, 63 N
C. 645.

the personal estate alone.[1] It will not, however, arise unless the legacy which requires its aid was originally chargeable on the personalty alone. If i originally affected both real and personal estate, but has failed as a charge on the realty by an event subsequent to the testator's death, e. g., by the death of the legatee before the time of payment, there is no case for marshalling.(x)

If the exhaustion be caused by payment of simple contract creditors under the statute, it may be questioned whether the legatees can insist on marshalling. For the statute merely declares the land assets to be administered in equity, and does not, therefore, give the creditors an election between the funds, but compels them to exhaust the personalty, before they can have recourse to the land.(y)[2]

An attempt has been made to apply the equity of marshalling to remedy the avoidance of charitable bequests, where such bequests have been made payable out of the general assets, instead of being exclusively charged on the pure personalty, such as money or stock. A charita-

(x) Hanby v. Roberts, Amb. 127 ; Prowse v. Abingdon, 1 Atk. 482 · Pearce v. Loman, 3 Ves. 135 ; 2 Jarm. on Wills 607.

(y) 3 & 4 Wm. 4, c. 104.

---

[1] Where there are two classes of legatees, one having a charge on real estate, and the other having no such charge, and the personal estate is not sufficient to pay both, equity will marshal the assets so as to throw the former class upon the real estate. The rule is the same where there is only one legacy charged upon land ; and it is not material that the charge is made only in case the personal estate shall be insufficient : Scales v. Collins, 9 Hare 656.

[2] The correctness of this view is questioned. See White and Tudor's Lead. Cas. Eq., vol. ii., part 1, p. 76, and it is now settled that legatees are entitled to marshalling, as well where the exhaustion is caused by the simple contract, as by the specialty creditors : Tombs v. Roch, 2 Coll. 499 ; Fleming v. Buchanan. 3 De G., M. & G. 976 ; Patterson v. Scott, 1 Id. 531.

ble legacy, thus given, is void by law so far as i
ble out of the mixed personalty, such for ex
mortgages and leaseholds ; and attempts have
been made to throw the other legacies on that
the estate, in order that the charitable legacy m͞
in full out of the rest.   The principle, howevei
shalling does not here apply ; for the reason of t
is not that some prior claimant has appropriated
mate fund, but that the fund given is in part ill
Court, therefore, will not, either directly or indii
[*277]   the gift, but *will appropriate the estat
legal objection existed, by charging the
both funds in proportion to their values ; and w
so much of the charitable legacy to fail, as wou
way be payable out of the prohibited fund.(z)[1]

(z) Hobson v. Blackburn, 1 K. 273 ; Philanthropic Societ
Beav. 581 ; Sturge v. Dimsdale, 6 Id. 462.

[1] See, accord, Wright v. Trustees of the M. E. Church, 1 H
But where it is clear that the testator intended that charity leg
be paid out of the pure personalty, the assets will be marshal
throw the other legacies on the personalty savoring of realty :
Geldard, 3 Macn. & Gord. 735.

*CHAPTER VI. [*278]

OF INFANCY, IDIOCY, AND LUNACY.

THE last equity which remains for notice is the equity for administering the estates and protecting the persons of infants, idiots, and lunatics.

The protection of an infant's person and estate, is, to some extent, provided for in the ordinary course of law; viz., by right of guardianship, extending sometimes to the person alone, and sometimes to both the person and estate; and the superintendence of this right is effected by writ of *habeas corpus* in respect of the person, and by writ of account at law or bill for account in equity in respect of the estate. The estate is also in many instances protected by being vested in trustees with express powers of management and application; in which case their conduct will be regulated under the ordinary jurisdiction over trusts. And if property be vested in a trustee, the right of the guardian to the general custody of the estate does not extend to the property so vested, so as to exonerate the trustee from seeing to its safety.

The guardianship of the person, during the father's lifetime, resides in him; and he is entitled in his parental right to the custody and education of the infant, but not to the custody of his estate.

The guardianship of the estate during the father's life-

time, and of both person and estate after his death,
[*279] *belonged, at common law, to the guardian in
socage, where such a guardian existed; and in
default of a statutory guardian, still belongs to him.
But guardianship of this class exists only as an incident
of tenure, and is confined to cases where the legal estate
in hereditaments of socage tenure descends on the infant.
It is vested in the nearest of kin, whether the father or
a more remote relation, who cannot by descent have the
socage estate; and determines at the age of fourteen, or
according to another opinion, so soon after that age as
there is another guardian, either by election of the infant
or otherwise, prepared to succeed. With respect to the
property of the ward, the right of guardian in socage extends to all descended hereditaments, whether lying in
tenure or not; and he is said to have, not barely an authority, but an actual estate, enabling him to demise for
the duration of his guardianship, or to occupy personally
for the ward's benefit. The extent of his authority over
the personal estate is doubtful; but Mr. Hargrave thinks
that the custody of the person must draw after it the
custody of every species of property for which the law
has not otherwise provided.[1]

The guardianship in socage is the most important of the
common law guardianships; but not the only one. There
are five other guardianships, of more limited operation;
viz., 1. By nature; which, like that in socage, is an in-

---

[1] "The guardianship in socage may be considered as gone into disuse;
and it can hardly be said to exist in this country, for the guardian must
be some relation by blood, who cannot possibly inherit, and such a case
can rarely exist:" Kent's Com., vol. ii., p. 223. "And as all the children,
male and female, equally inherit, with us; the guardianship by *nature*,
would seem to extend to all the children, and guardianship by *nurture*, is
merged in the more durable title of guardian by nature:" Id. pp. 220, 221.

cident of tenure. This guardianship is of an heir apparent only, and is vested in the ancestor whose heir the infant is. It continues till twenty-one, and is confined to the person. 2. For nurture; which is of all the children, and not only of the heir apparent. It belongs exclusively to the father, or at his decease to the mother; continues till fourteen, and is confined to the person. 3. By the custom of London; which is where a parent, free of the city, leaves an unmarried orphan. This guardianship is vested in the mayor and aldermen; continues till twenty-one as to males, and till eighteen or marriage as to females; and was originally of the person only, but subsequently extended by Richard II. *to the lands and goods. [*280] 4. By custom of other boroughs and manors. 5. By election of the infant; which is on the termination of guardianship in socage by the infant's attaining fourteen, and confers on the guardian by election the same office and employment which was previously in the guardian in socage. And it is said by Lord Coke, that in certain cases the same thing may be done by an infant under fourteen.

The guardianship by statute, which is now the most important of all the guardianships, originates in the statute for abolishing tenures *in capite.* (a) Before that statute a father, tenant in socage, could not have disposed of the custody of his heir, for it belonged to the legal guardian. But by the 8th section of that statute, the father of an unmarried infant is enabled (without prejudice, however, to the custom of London) to appoint a guardian by deed or will, whose appointment will be good against all persons claiming as guardians in socage or

(a) 12 Car. 2, c. 24, s. 8.

36

otherwise.[1] The authority of the statute guardian continues till twenty-one, and he is entitled to the custody
of the person and of the real and personal estate, including hereditaments acquired by purchase, with the same
authorities and remedies as guardian in socage.(b)

The superintendence of the guardianship in respect of
the person, so as to discharge from illegal custody, or to
protect from cruelty or ill-usage by the legal guardian. is
exercised by the Court of Queen's Bench on writ of *habeas
corpus*. The same writ is issuable out of the Court of

(b) See generally as to guardianship, Hargr. on Co. Litt.,87 b.. n. 59 to
73 ; 2 Steph. Bl. 331–345 ; Chambers on Infancy 54–74, 509–522.

---

[1] The statute 12 Car. 2, c. 24, has been very generally adopted, or re-
enacted, in the United States. See Elmer's N. Jersey Digest, title Wills ;
Act of Virginia, 1798, V. R. C., vol. i., 240; Purdon's Penn. Dig., title
Wills ; Chase's Stat. Ohio, vol. iii., 1788. A father *only*, can appoint a
testamentary guardian of his children. The power does not extend to a
grandfather : Hoyt v. Hilton, 2 Ed. Ch. 202. Nor to a mother : Matter of
Pierce, 12 How. Pr. 532. The desire of the mother expressed in a will in
regard to the appointment of a guardian will be followed, where the father
died without appointing : In the matter of Turner, 4 Green (N. J.) 433.
When a testamentary guardian is appointed by the father, the natural
right of the mother must yield to the will of the father : Van Houten's
Case, 2 Green Ch. 220. But the father's intention to appoint ought to be
very manifest : Id. ; and see Peyton v. Smith, 2 Dev. & Batt. Ch. 325 ;
Gaines v. Spann, 2 Brock. 81. The testamentary guardian has the same
right to direct the religious education of the ward, as the father : Re
Browne, 2 Irish Ch. 151. In Pennsylvania, under the Act of 1833, a devise of the guardianship of a minor by any other than the father is void.
But a devise by a grandfather, or other person, to a child, on condition
that a person named in the will shall be guardian, is good ; and a refusal
by the father to permit such guardianship, is a forfeiture of the estate. An
acceptance, however, by the father, of a benefit, under the will, estops him
from objecting afterwards. In all such cases, such a construction must be
put upon the will, as may be most beneficial to the children, without exposing the estate to forfeiture, or interfering with the intention of the testator ; and therefore where a stranger is thus appointed guardian, but the
guardianship is not expressly extended to the person, it will be confined to
the estate : Vanartsdalen v. Vanartsdalen, 14 Penn. St. 384.

Chancery ; but the jurisdiction under it is the same as at common law, and the Court can attend to nothing except illegal custody, cruelty and ill-usage.(c)[1]

The superintendent of the guardianship in respect of the estate, so as to secure a due accounting by the person *in possession, is by action of account at law, or suit for account in equity. As against the guar- [*281] dian in socage or the statute guardian, either of these remedies may be pursued; and also as against any person who not being a guardian, has occupied or taken the profits of the land of an infant tenant in socage.[2] If the infant be not tenant in the socage, the intruder is not liable to account at law, but will be compelled to account in equity.(d)

The means of protection already enumerated, although

(c) Rex v. Greenhill, 4 A. & E. 624 ; Lyons v. Blenkin, Jac. 245, 254.

(d) Chamb. 518, 521 ; Blomfield v. Eyre, 8 Beav. 250.

---

[1] When an infant is brought up on a *habeas corpus*, the Chancellor will not, in such a summary proceeding, try the question of guardianship, or deliver the infant into the custody of another ; he will only deliver the infant from illegal restraint, and if competent to form and declare an election, will allow it to make such election : Matter of Wollstonecraft, 4 Johns. Ch. 82 ; Foster v. Alston, 16 How. (Miss.) 406 ; see, also, The People v. Mercein, 8 Paige 47, 55 ; U. S. v. Green, 3 Mason 482, 485 ; Armstrong v. Stone, 9 Gratt. 102 ; see People v. Wilcox, 22 Barb. 178.

[2] Any stranger or wrongdoer who interferes with the property of a minor, and receives the rents and profits thereof, may be considered by the minor as his guardian, and held accountable as such to him for the property so received : Goodhue v. Barnwell, 1 Rice Eq. 198 ; Davis v. Harkness, 1 Gilman 173 ; Hanna v. Spotts, 5 B. Monr. 362 ; Drury v. Conner 1 Harris & Gill, 220 ; Van Epps v. Van Deusen, 4 Paige 64 ; Chaney v. Smallweed, 1 Gill 367 ; Wyllie v. Ellice, 6 Hare 505 ; Lennox v. Notrebe, 1 Hempst. 225 ; Blomfield v. Eyre, 8 Beav. 250 ; and as a fiduciary, cannot set up the Statute of Limitations : Goodhue v. Barnwell, ut sup. ; Thomas v. Thomas, 25 L. J. Ch. 159. But an executor, having rightful possession of the property of the infant, cannot be treated as a guardian without his consent : Bibb v. McKinley, 9 Porter 636.

available for the prevention of positive. misconduct, are inadequate to secure a proper education of the infant, or a prudent management of his estate. And for these purposes there is a prerogative in the Crown, as *parens patriæ*, to be exercised by the Court of Chancery, for protection of any infant residing either temporarily or permanently within its jurisdiction.[1] The possession of property is not essential to the existence of this authority, though the want of it may create a practical difficulty in its exercise, by incapacitating the Court from providing for the infant's maintenance.(e)

The mode of calling the jurisdiction into operation is by filing a bill, to which the infant is a party. This constitutes him a ward of Court; and, after he is once a ward,

(e) De Manneville v. De Manneville, 10 Ves. 52-63; Wellesley v. Wellesley, 2 Bl. N. S. 124; Johnstone v. Beattie, 10 Cl. & F. 42; Re Spence, 2 Ph. 247.

---

[1] The several kinds of guardian have, in this country, become essentially superseded in practice by the chancery guardians, and guardians appointed by the Surrogates, Ordinary, or Orphans' Courts, Courts of Probate, or other courts of similar character, having jurisdiction of testamentary matters, in the various states. And still, where there exists a Court of Chancery, the general jurisdiction over every guardian resides there. A testamentary or statute guardian is as much under the superintendence of the Court of Chancery, as the guardian in socage: Matter of Andrews, 1 Johns. Ch. 99; Ex parte Crumb, 2 Id. 439; and see Matter of Nicoll, 1 Id. 25; Preston v. Dunn, 25 Ala. 507. Such court has a general supervisory power over the persons and estates of infants; and when any part of an infant's estate is in litigation there, it is under the immediate guardianship and protection of the Court: Westbrook v. Comstock, Walk. Ch. 314; People v. Wilcox, 22 Barb. 178. Where an infant under twelve years of age was married, and immediately thereafter declared her dissent to the marriage, upon application to chancery by her next friend, she was declared a ward of the court, and all conversation, intercourse, or correspondence between her and the defendant to whom she had been married, was forbidden under pain of contempt: Aymer v. Roff, 3 Johns. Ch. 49.

See, on the subject of the jurisdiction of Chancery over Infants, notes to Eyre v. Countess of Shaftesbury, 2 Lead. Cas. Eq. 538.

any subsequent matter may be determined on petition or motion. If the infant is in illegal custody, an order for his delivery to the proper guardian may be made on petition without bill ;(*f*) and if the father is dead, the appointment of a guardian and an allowance for maintenance may be obtained in the same way. But if the receiver of the estate is wanted, or a compulsory order on trustees, or if there be complicated accounts, a bill is necessary.(*g*)

The principal incidents of wardship are three in number; *viz.: The ward must be educated under the Court's superintendence; his estate must be [*282] managed and applied under the like superintendence; and his marriage must be with the sanction of the Court.

1. The ward must be educated under the superintendence of the Court.

The right of superintendence exists in every case of wardship; and therefore, when an infant has been made a ward, he cannot be taken out of the jurisdiction of the Court without its leave.[1] But leave will not be refused, if shown to be for his benefit, provided due security be given for his return. and for acquainting the Court with his situation and progress.(*h*)

The manner in which the superintendence is exercised differs according as there is or is not a subsisting guardian.

(*f*) Re Spence, 2 Ph. 247.

(*g*) 2 Dan. C. P. ch. 39.

(*h*) Campbell *v*. Mackay, 2 M. & C. 31 ; Johnstone *v*. Beattie, 10 Cl. & F. 42 ; [see remarks on this case in Stuart *v*. Bute, 9 H. L. Cas. 440] ; Stephens *v*. James, 1 M. & K. 627 ; [see Dawson *v*. Jay, 3 De G., M. & G. 764.]

---

[1] In Rochford *v*. Hackman, 1 Kay 308, a ward of court who had enlisted in the East India service, was ordered to be discharged on application of his guardian, and notice to the East India Company. See also Dawson *v*. Jay, 3 De G., M. & G. 764.

If the father is dead, and there is no legal or statutory guardian, or none who is able or willing to act, a guardian will be appointed, and a scheme of education settled by the Court. In settling such scheme the Court will regard, as far as possible, the wishes of the deceased father. And it will more especially do so in regard to religion, by bringing up the infant in the creed of his family, if not contrary to law, and if he has not been already educated in another (i)[1] If the guardian is resident beyond the jurisdiction, he will not for that reason be displaced from his office; but it will be an inducement to join some other person in the guardianship, who may be responsible to the Court. (k)[2]

(i) Talbot v. Shrewsbury, 4 M. & C. 673; Witty v. Marshall, 1 N. C. C. 68.

(k) Johnstone v. Beattie, 10 Cl. & F. 42; Wellesley v. Beaufort, 2 Russ. 1, 18. [See Lockwood v. Fenton, 1 Sm. & Giff. 73.]

---

[1] In the appointment of a guardian for an infant, the court will regard the expressed desire of the deceased parents in reference to the religious education of the infant: Underhill v. Dennis, 9 Paige 202; Graham's Appeal, 1 Dall. 136. See In re Newberry, L. R. 1 Eq. 431.

[2] It is generally held in the United States that the rights, powers, and duties of a guardian, like those of an administrator, are entirely local, and cannot be exercised in other states: Morrell v. Dickey, 1 Johns. Ch. 169; Sabin v. Gilman, 1 N. H. 193; Armstrong v. Lear, 12 Wheat. 156; 2 Kent's Comm. 227, n.; see also, Cox v. Williamson, 11 Ala. 343; but see, in South Carolina, Ex parte Smith, 1 Hill Eq. 140; Ex parte Heard, 2 Id. 54; and see Townsend v. Kendall, 4 Minn. 412; Boyd v. Glass, 34 Ga. 253; Earl v. Dresser, 30 Ind. 11. In some of the states, however, there are statutory provisions which place foreign and domestic guardians, to a greater or less degree, on the same footing. In the case of Re Dawson, 2 Sm. & Giff. 199, it was held in England that the order of a Surrogate's Court in New York, appointing a guardian to an infant, the child of a British subject, would be recognised in the Court of Chancery with the respect due by the comity of nations; but that it did not confer on the appointee the character of guardian there. This was the case of a child whose father had been a native of Great Britain, but naturalized in the United States, where he was also domiciled. The maternal aunt had been appointed guardian, in New

If there is a father or legal guardian within the juris diction able and willing to act, the matter will be left to his direction, subject to the general control of the Court.[1] But if there be a difference of opinion among several guardians, a scheme will be directed.(*l*)

*If the father or legal guardian has volun- [*283] tarily relinquished his right,[2] or has forfeited it

(*l*) Campbell *v.* Mackay, 2 M. & C. 31, 36.

York, where the infant's property was situated. The child was brought to England by a paternal aunt, with whom it resided; and the desire of the guardian to compel its return gave rise to the question. In a subsequent branch of the case, Dawson *v.* Jay, 3 De G., M. & G. 764, the Lord Chancellor held, that the court could not compel the removal of an infant ward out of the jurisdiction, and therefore refused an application by the guardian to obtain custody of the child for that purpose. See, also, Lockwood *v.* Fenton, 1 Sm. & Giff. 73. The subject under consideration was examined in Stuart *v.* Bute, 9 H. L. Cas. 440. In that case the infant was a young marquis who was a subject of the United Kingdom, and who had a very large property both in England and Scotland; and the question was between the English and Scotch guardians, as to which class the Crown, as *parens patriæ*, having full power to deal with the matter, should assign him. It was held that the Scotch Court of Session had not displayed sufficient consideration for the disposition which had been previously made by the English Court of Chancery, and the authority of the latter tribunal was accordingly upheld. The change of domicil after the jurisdiction had attached, was considered to make no difference. See, also, in this case, the remarks on Dawson *v.* Jay, supra. See, moreover, Nugent *v.* Vetzera, L. R. 2 Eq. 703.

Although a guardian resides out of the state and has no property within it, equity has jurisdiction to hold him to account, and compel him and his sureties to pay such balance as may be found against him: Pratt *v.* Wright, 13 Grattan 175.

[1] The Court will not discharge a guardian from his trust, on his petition, unless for good reasons shown. Ex parte Crumb, 2 Johns. Ch. 439. See, also, Ex parte De Graffenreid, 1 Harp. Eq. 107.

[2] See, however, Reg *v.* Smith, 1 Bail Ct. Cas. 132; 16 Eng. L. & Eq. 221, and note; People *v.* Mercein, 3 Hill, 399; Mayne *v.* Baldwin, 1 Halst. Ch. 454. An agreement for a separation deed in which the father was to divest himself of authority over his children will not be enforced: Vansittart *v.* Vansittart, 2 De G. & J. 249. But to this rule there may be some exceptions; see Swift *v.* Swift, 34 Beav. 266.

by misconduct tending to the infant's corruption, the Court will restrain him from interfering, and will appoint some other person to act as guardian in his place. Instances of voluntary relinquishment occur where a third party has given a benefit to the infant, on condition of being allowed to appoint a guardian, and the father or legal guardian has expressly or impliedly assented to that condition, either by originally conforming to its terms, so as to alter the infant's condition in life, or by accepting a benefit under it. But there is no power in third parties, independently of such assent, to deprive the parent or guardian of his right, by making a gift to the infant on condition of its relinquishment. If, however, a gift is *de facto* made which will ultimately change the infant's condition in life, the necessity of educating him suitably to his expectations may induce some degree of interference by the Court.(*m*)[1] Instances of forfeiture by misconduct occur where the father or guardian inculcates vicious and irreligious principles, or conduct, inconsistent with the well-being of society; or where he manifests such principles in his own conduct, and brings the infant so in contact with them, that corruption is likely to ensue.(*n*)[2]

(*m*) Lyons *v.* Blenkin, Jac. 245, 255; Hill *v.* Gomme, 1 Beav. 540; 5 M. & C. 250; De Manneville *v.* De Manneville, 10 Ves. 52, 64.

(*n*) Shelley *v.* Westbrooke, Jac. 266, n.; Wellesley *v.* Beaufort, 2 Russ. 1; 2 Bl. N. S. 124; Ball *v.* Ball, 2 Sim. 35; Re Spence, 2 Ph. 247.

---

[1] See note, ante, p. 280.

[2] These principles were acted on in Cowls *v.* Cowls, 3 Gilm. 435; Comm. *v.* Addicks, 2 S. & R. 174. See Swift *v.* Swift, 34 Beav. 266.

The Court will refuse to give possession of children to their father, if he has so conducted himself as that it will not be for their benefit, or if it will affect their happiness, or if they cannot associate with him without moral contamination, or if, because they associate with him, others will shun their society. In a case where the Court entertained a strong belief that a charge of an unnatural crime, brought against a father, was true, though he had

It is enacted by a late statute, entitled "An Act to
amend the law relating to the Custody of Infants," that
the Court of Chancery, upon the petition of the mother of
any infant, may make order for the access of the petitioner
to her infant children at such times and under such regulations as the Court shall deem convenient and just; and
if such children shall be within the age of seven years,
may order them to be delivered into the custody of the
petitioner until such age. · But no mother against whom
adultery *has been established, by a judgment in [*284]
an action for criminal conversation at a suit of
her husband, or by the sentence of an Ecclesiastical Court,
is entitled to the benefit of the act.(o)   It is also enacted

(o) 2 & 3 Vict. c. 54; Re Taylor, 10 Sim 291; 11 Id. 178; [see Re Halliday's Est., 17 Jur. 56.]

been in fact acquitted thereof upon an indictment, the Court refused to permit any sort of intercourse between him and them: Anon., 2 Sim. N. S.
54; Swift v. Swift, 34 Beav. 266.

In Thomas v. Roberts, 3 De G. & Sm. 758, the Agapemone Case, a father
who had deserted his wife, and who was a member of an absurd religious
sect, whose tenets the Court considered of an injurious tendency, was
refused the custody of his child.

Infants of tender years, however, have been left *ex necessitate* with a
mother, though her principles were of an immoral tendency, and she was
living in adultery: Comm. v. Addicks, 5 Binn. 520; they were afterwards
removed, however, on arriving at a more advanced age: s. c. 2 S. & R.
174.   Mere peculiarities in religious belief will not justify the removal of
children from their father's custody: Curtis v. Curtis, 5 Jur. N. S. 1147.
Nor harsh treatment, unless it is such as will injure the children's
health: Id.

Fixed habits of intemperance constitute a sufficient reason for the removal
of a guardian: Kettletas v. Gardner, 1 Paige 488.   So, speculation by the
guardian with the husband of his female ward, in relation to her estate, or
even the insolvency of the guardian and one of his sureties, may be sufficient
cause: In re Cooper, 2 Paige 34.   On the other hand, it is no ground for
the removal of a guardian, that he has retained the funds of his ward,
instead of investing them, admitting his liability for interest: Sweet v.
Sweet, Speer's Ch. 309.   See also on the subject, Disbrow v. Henshaw, 8
Cowen 349; In re Kennedy, 5 Paige 244.

by another statute, entitled "An Act for the c⟨
education of Infants who may be convicted of F
that the Court of Chancery, on the application
person who may be willing to take charge of an
so convicted, and to provide for his maintenan
education, may assign the custody of such infant
minority, or during any part thereof to the applic⟨
such terms and subject to such regulations as the
may prescribe. And an order for that purpose, s
as it shall remain in force, is to be binding on the
and on every testamentary guardian. But it is in
case to be one of the terms imposed, that the infan
not be sent beyond the seas, or out of the jurisdic
the Court.(p)

2. The ward's estate must be managed and a
under the superintendence of the Court.

The manner of management, like that of educ
differs according to the circumstances of the cas
there are no trustees within the jurisdiction abl
willing to act, the Court will appoint a receive
there are such trustees, they will not be supersede
cept for misconduct; but a guardian is in this r
different from a trustee, and his power of manag
will not exclude a receiver.(q)

In cases where a trust exists, the degree of aut
as well as the manner of its exercise, will depend ⟨
terms of the instrument creating it. In other cas
Court is thrown on its inherent jurisdiction; an
authority to manage the estate during minority ⟨
apply its proceeds for the infant's benefit; but tl
no inherent power to dispose of or alter the estate

(p) 3 & 4 Vict. c. 90.
(q) Gardner v. Blane, 1 Hare 381.

except in cases of election or partition, where the disposition is demandable *as of right by other parties, (r)[1] and of the devolution on an infant of a [*285]

(r) Garmstone v. Gaunt, 1 Coll. 577; note to Gretton v. Hayward, 1 Sw. 413; Simson v. Jones, 2 R. & M. 356, 374; Calvert v. Godfrey, 6 Beav. 97, 109; supra, Partition.

---

[1] Rogers v. Dill, 6 Hill 415; but contra, Matter of Salisbury, 3 Johns. Ch. 347; Williams v. Harrington, 11 Ired. 616; Ex parte Jewett, 16 Ala. 409; Huger v. Huger, 3 Dessaus. 18; Stapleton v. Langstaff, Id. 22. See William's Case, 3 Bland 186. In most of the states there are now statutes which authorize the sale of the infant's estate on application by the guardian to the proper court, where it is necessary or proper for the infant's benefit. See Garland v. Loving, 1 Rand. 396; Matter of Wilson, 2 Paige 412; Pope v. Jackson, 11 Pick. 113; Talley v. Starke, 6 Gratt. 339; Duckett v. Skinner, 11 Ired. 431; Brown's Case, 8 Humph. 200; Peyton v. Alcorn, 7 J. J. Marsh. 502; Dow's Pet., Walker's Ch. 145; Young v. Keogh, 11 Ill. 642; Ex parte Jewett, 16 Ala. 409; Morris v. Morris, 2 McCarter (N. J.) 239. In New York, the jurisdiction of the court on the sale of an infant's real estate is considered to be wholly derived from the statute of that state, and not to extend to cases not there provided for: Baker v. Lorillard, 4 Comst. 257. The sale of an infant's real estate is frequently directed by act of the legislature, in this country; and there is no doubt now, of the constitutionality of such acts: Snowhill v. Snowhill, 2 Green Ch. 20; Norris v. Clymer, 2 Penn. St. 277; Davis v. Johonnot, 7 Metc. 388; Spotswood v. Pendleton, 4 Call. 514; Dorsey v. Gilbert, 11 Gill & J. 87; Nelson v. Lee, 10 B. Monr. 495; Powers v. Bergen, 2 Seld. 358; even though the infants be non-residents: Nelson v. Lee, ut supra.

A guardian or trustee for infants, has. in general, no power to convert realty into personalty, or vice versa. Royer's App., 11 Penn. St. 36; Bonsall's App., 1 Rawle 273; Kaufman v. Crawford, 9 W. & S. 131; Eckford v. De Kay, 8 Paige 89; Sherry v. Sansberry, 3 Ind. 320; Ex parte Crutchfield, 3 Yerg. 336; White v. Parker, 8 Barb. S. C. 48; Hassard v. Rowe, 11 Id. 22. But it has been held that in case of imminent necessity the guardian might purchase land with his ward's money: Bonsall's App., ut sup.; Billington's App., 3 Rawle 55; Royer's App., 11 Penn. St. 36; Bowman's App., 3 Watts 369; though see Moore v. Moore, 12 B. Monroe, 651. Permanent improvements are equivalent to a conversion: Bellinger v. Shafer, 2 Sandf. Ch. 297; Hassard v. Rowe, 11 Barb. S. C. 22; Miller's Estate, 1 Penn. St. 326. In Jackson v. Jackson, 1 Gratt. 143, however, an allowance for permanent improvements was made, it being obviously for the infant's benefit.

mortgaged estate, where a sale is the only pro
against foreclosure.(s)   If it be for an infant's bei
invest money in land, and thus to change person
real estate, the order authorizing the investment ₁
coupled with a declaration that the land shall
sidered, during minority, as constructively person₍

The statutory powers of directing conveyances
estates held on trust or mortgage, or subject to an
for specific performance, or liable as assets for pa
of debts, have devolved on an infant, have been a
noticed.(u)   There are other statutory powers
apply to the beneficial property of infants, and wh
conferred by a statute, not confined to infancy alo
providing for other cases of incapacity, and entitle
Act for amending the Laws relating to property bel

(s) Mondey v. Mondey, 1 Ves. & B. 223; Brookfield v. Bradl
634; Davis v. Dowding, 2 K. 245.

(t) Ashburton v. Ashburton, 6 Ves. 6 ; Ware v. Polhill, 11 Id. 2.
Webb v. Lord Shaftesbury, 6 Madd. 100 ; Ex parte Phillips, 19 V
122.

(u) Supra, Trust; Specific Performance ; Mortgage ; Administr
Assets.

In Sweezy v. Thayer, 1 Duer (N. Y.) 286, where there was a sa.
infant's real estate under a decree of foreclosure on a mortgage, it v
that the surplus remained real estate, and would descend as such
death; that he might elect, on coming of age, whether to take it a
or personalty; and that such surplus, though invested in person₂
rities, could not be further converted into personalty.   And see, al
where an infant's realty is converted by order of court or act of th
lature, its proceeds remain realty as regards him and his heirs,
minority: Snowhill v. Snowhill, 2 Green Ch. 20; Lloyd v. Hart, 2
St. 473 ; March v. Berrier, 6 Ired. Eq. 524.

¹ See, to this point, Huger v. Huger, 3 Dessaus. 18 ; Stapleton v
staff, Id. 22; Dorsey v. Gilbert, 11 Gill & J. 87. See also, Hedges v
5 Johns. Ch. 163 ; Mills v. Dennis, 3 Id. 370; Davison v. De F
Sandf. Ch. 456; Snowhill v. Snowhill, 2 Green's Ch. 20; sed vide :
v. Jackson, 3 Yerg. 77.

to Infants, *Femes Covert*, Lunatics, and Persons of Unsound Mind."(*v*)

By the early clauses of this statute, provision is made for the admittance of infants, *femes covert*, and lunatics, to copyhold property, and for raising the fines payable on such admittance, without requiring the sanction of a judicial order. The powers conferred by the subsequent clauses in the case of infants and *femes covert*, are to be exercised under the sanction of the Court of Chancery; and those which are conferred in the case of lunatics are to be exercised, as we shall hereafter see, by the Lord Chancellor, intrusted under the sign manual with the custody of lunatics. The acts which the Court of Chancery is thus *empowered to correct, are the sur- [*286] render of renewable leases belonging to an infant or *feme covert*, and the acceptance of renewed ones in their stead; the renewal of leases which the infant or *feme covert*, if not under disability, might be compelled to renew; the leasing of property belonging to an infant in fee or in tail, or for an absolute leasehold interest; the entering into agreements on behalf of an infant under the Act for augmenting the Maintenance of the Poor Clergy;(*w*) and the application for an infant's maintenance, of the dividends on his stock, under which name is included every fund, annuity, or security transferable in the books of any company. The clauses which relate to lunatics will be hereafter considered.(*x*)

In exercising its superintendence over a ward's estate, the Court will make a reasonable allowance for maintenance, provided the ward be entitled absolutely to a present income, and the allowance be for his benefit. The

(*v*) 11 Geo. 4 & 1 Wm. 4, c. 65 ; 1 & 2 Vict. c. 62.
(*w*) 1 Geo. 1, c. 10.   (*x*) Infra, Lunatics.

expenditure for this purpose is generally confined to income; and is rarely permittted to break in upon capital. But the capital may be applied for the advancement of the child in life, *e. g.*, for binding him apprentice, or purchasing him a commission in the army.(y)[1]

(*y*) Walker *v.* Wetherell, 6 Ves. 473; [Re Welch, 23 L. J. Ch. 344 · Nunn *v.* Harvey, 2 De G. & Sm. 301; Re Clarke, 17 Jur. 362; Re Lane, Id. 219; William's Case, 3 Bland. 186; see Ex parte Hays, 3 De G. & Sm. 485]

[1] In general, a guardian must keep his expenses on account of his ward, within the income of his ward's estate, and he cannot encroach upon the principal for this purpose, except upon the order of the Court, in such case, upon his application: Davis *v.* Harkness, 1 Gilm. 173; Davis *v.* Roberts, 1 Sm. & Marsh. Ch. 543; Anderson *v.* Thompson, 11 Leigh 439; Prince *v.* Logan, Speer's Ch. 29; McDowell *v.* Caldwell, 2 McCord Ch. 43; Myers *v.* Wade, 6 Rand. 444; Villard *v.* Chovin, 2 Strob. Eq. 40; Holmes *v.* Logan, 3 Id. 31; Hester *v.* Wilkinson, 6 Humph. 219; Bybee *v.* Tharp, 4 B. Mon. 313; Carter *v.* Rolland, 11 Humph. 339; Cornwise *v.* Bourgum, 2 Ga. Dec. 15; Frelick *v.* Turner, 26 Miss. (4 Cushm.) 393; Shaw *v.* Coble, 63 N. C. 377; Beeler *v.* Dunn, 3 Head (Tenn.) 87; Gilbert *v.* McEachen, 38 Miss. 469. It seems that increase in the value of the property of the infant may be deemed income, and be appropriated by the guardian to his support: Long *v.* Norcom, 2 Ired. Ch. 354. So a guardian will be allowed for disbursements, although they exceed the income of the ward's estate in his hands, if they do not exceed the income of the whole of the ward's estate: Forman *v.* Murray, 7 Leigh 412. And where the health, or schooling, or other circumstances, render an increased expenditure necessary, the guardian will be allowed such expenses out of the principal of the ward's estate: see Hooper *v.* Royster, 1 Munf. 119; Long *v.* Norcom, supra; Ex parte Potts, 1 Ash. 340; Ex parte Bostwick, 4 Johns. Ch. 100; Haigood *v.* Wells, 1 Hill's Eq. 59; Maclin *v.* Smith, 2 Ired. Eq. 371; Carter *v.* Rolland, 11 Humph. 339; Caffey *v.* McMichael, 64 N. C. 507. Even the principal of a vested legacy will be broken into for the purpose of educating an infant legatee: Newport *v.* Cook, 2 Ash. 332. And the rule does not operate to prevent an allowance for permanent improvements of the real estate of the ward by the guardian out of the principal of the personal estate: Jackson *v.* Jackson, 1 Gratt. 143; see ante, p. 284, and note.

Moreover, although a guardian has no right to expend the principal, yet if he purchases goods on account of the ward, the person of whom he purchases is not bound to see that they are paid for out of the *profits* of the estate: Broadus *v.* Rosson, 3 Leigh 12.

The authority of the Court to allow maintenance is distinct from its authority where maintenance is already given, whether the gift be made as an express benefit to the child's parent, or as a benefit to the child out of a stranger's estate, or as one of the trusts under a contract of settlement. In these cases, the authority of the Court is to effectuate the gift, and to allow maintenance, if directed, because it is given by the donor. In the cases which we are now considering, it is an authority to allow maintenance out of the income merely because it belongs to the infant, and because such an application is for his benefit; and it will accordingly be exerted though no maintenance *or a less maintenance be directed [*287] by the gift, or even though there be an express direction to accumulate.(z)

In order to obtain an allowance for maintenance, it must be shown that there is a present income belonging absolutely to the infant, and that the allowance will be for his benefit.

There must be a present income belonging absolutely to the infant. It is not, however, essential to a compliance with this rule that the income should belong absolutely to the individual infant. It is sufficient if it belongs absolutely to a class, all of whom can be collected before the Court, and may be equally benefited by the application. But if persons, not *in esse*, may become entitled, it is not sufficient that the parties before the Court are presumptively entitled at the time; for none of them may be eventually entitled; and the effect, therefore, of an order for maintenance out of the fund, may be to maintain one person out of the property of another.(a)

(z) Stretch v. Watkins, 1 Mad. 253.
(a) Ex parte Keble, 11 Ves. 606; Turner v. Turner, 4 Sim. 430; Cannings v. Flower, 7 Id. 523; Marshall v. Holloway, 2 Sw. 432, 436.

The allowance must be for the infant's benefit. If, therefore, there be two funds, out of either of which maintenance might be given, it will be directed out of the one which is most beneficial to him.(b)   And, on the same principle, where the infant is living with his father, or, after the father's decease, with the mother, remaining unmarried, maintenance will not be allowed, if such father or mother be of ability to maintain him, e. g., to maintain him suitably to his expectations, and according to the parent's condition in life, without injury to his other children.(c)[1]

(b) Bruin v. Knott, 1 Ph. 572.

(c) Andrews v. Partington, 3 B. C. C. 60; Hoste v. Pratt, 3 Ves. 730; Buckworth v. Buckworth, 1 Cox 80; Jervoise v. Silk, Coop. 52; Stocken v. Stocken, 4 M. & C. 95; Thompson v. Griffin, Cr. & P. 317.

---

[1] In England, by statute 23 & 24 Vict., c. 145, § 26, trustees for infants may apply the whole of the income of the trust fund for maintenance, although there is another fund provided for the purpose, or another person bound to provide. For a recognition and support of the English doctrine in respect of a father-guardian's exclusive personal liability for maintenance, see Walker v. Crowder, 2 Ired. Ch. 478; Booth v. Sineath, 2 Strob. Eq. 31; Chapline v. Moore, 7 Monr. 173; Myers v. Myers, 2 McCord's Ch. 255; Ellerbe v. The Heirs and Legatees of Ellerbe, 1 Speer's Ch. 328; Dupont v. Johnson, 1 Bailey's Eq. 279; Van Valkinburgh v. Watson, 13 Johns. 480; Addison v. Bowie, 2 Bland Ch. 606; Jones v. Stockett, Id. 409, 431; Cruger v. Heyward, 2 Dessaus. 94; Harland's Accounts, 5 Rawle 323; Matter of Kane, 2 Barb. Ch. 375; Beathea v. McColl, 5 Ala. 312; Sparhawk v. Buell, 9 Verm. 41; Walker v. Crowder, 2 Ired. Eq. 478; Morris v. Morris, 2 McCarter (N. J.) 239; though this would not apply, it seems, to a step-father: Gay v. Ballou, 4 Wend. 403; Freto v. Brown, 4 Mass. 675; see Booth v. Sineath, 2 Strob. Eq. 31. For cases of a mother's obligation, see Matter of Bostwick, 4 Johns. Ch. 100; Wilkes v. Rogers, 6 Johns. 566; Heyward v. Cuthbert, 4 Dessaus. 445; Thompson v. Brown, 4 Johns. Ch. 645. Indeed, it would seem that the obligation to maintain does not extend to the mother when the children have an ample estate: see Hughes v. Hughes, 1 Brown's Ch. C. 387; Whipple v. Dow, 2 Mass. 415; Dawes v. Howard, 4 Mass. 97; Matter of Bostwick, 4 Johns. Ch. 100; Heyward v. Cuthbert, 4 Dessaus. 445; Douglas v. Andrews, 12 Beav. 310; Bruin v. Knott, 1 Phillips 573; Anderton v. Yates, 5 De G. & Sm. 202.

The manner of maintenance is by allowing a gross annual sum proportioned to the age and rank, and to the fortune *of the infant, without inquiring, unless on special grounds, into the details of expendi- [*288] ture. And in making such allowance, the principle of looking to the infant's benefit may authorize an extension beyond what is necessary for his personal maintenance ; e. g., if he be an eldest child, and have brothers or sisters unprovided for, because it is more for his benefit that they should be brought up respectably, than that money should be accumulated for himself.(d)

If moneys have been already expended on his maintenance by a stranger, an allowance may be made for such past maintenance proportioned to the amount expended, and commencing from the period when the property first vested. But an allowance for past maintenance will not be made to the father, unless special grounds be shown.(e)[1]

(d) Wellesley v. Beaufort, 2 Russ. 1, 28.

(e) Re Mary England, 1 R. & M. 499; Ex parte Bond, 2 M. & K. 439 ; Chaplin v. Chaplin, 3 P. Wms. 368 ; Bruin v. Knott, 1 Ph. 572.

And the rule is being relaxed in this country as to the father: see Newport v. Cook, 2 Ashm. 332; Matter of Kane, 2 Barb. Ch. 375.

When the father is unable to support the infant, the court will make an allowance for its maintenance : Rice v. Tonnele, 4 Sand. Ch. 571 ; Matter of Burke, Id. 617 ; Corbin v. Wilson, 2 Ashm. 178 ; Newport v. Cook, Id. 337 ; Beathea v. McColl, 5 Ala. 312 ; Watts v. Steele, 19 Id. 656 ; Carmichael v. Hughes, 6 Eng. L. & Eq. 71. In some cases, allowances for past maintenance have been made to the father : Corbin v. Wilson ; Newport v. Cook ; Carmichael v. Hughes, ut sup. So of the mother : Matter of Bostwick, 4 Johns. Ch. 100 ; Bruin v. Knott, 1 Phill. 573. But in England, it is said that the father cannot have past maintenance, except in very special circumstances : Carmichael v. Hugh, ut supr. A direct benefit to the father, not maintaining the child, will not be allowed : Re Stables, 21 L. J. Ch. 620.

[1] As to allowance for past maintenance, see Matter of Kane, 2 Barb. Ch. 375.

37

3. The ward's marriage must be with the sanction of the Court.

In order to obtain such sanction, the Court must be satisfied that the marriage is a proper one; and, if the ward be a female, that a proper settlement is made.(f)[1] The marriage of an infant ward, without permission of the Court, is a criminal contempt in all parties except the infant, and is punishable by commitment during pleasure. If the infant be a female, the husband will be compelled, by imprisonment, to make a proper settlement of her property; and will be excluded, either wholly or in proportion to his criminality, from deriving any personal benefit out of his wife's fortune, so far as can be done without injury to her.(g)[2] If the ward has attained twenty-one, the marriage is not a contempt; but so long as her property continues under the control of the Court, [*289] she will retain an *equity for a settlement, dischargeable only by her personal consent in Court.(gg)

The jurisdiction to settle the estate of a female infant

(f) Halsey v. Halsey, 9 Ves. 471; Long v. Long, 2 S. & S. 119.

(g) Ball v. Coutts, 1 Ves. & B. 292; Re Walker, Ll. & G. 299; Hodgens v. Hodgens, 4 Cl. & F. 323; Birkett v. Hibbert, 3 M. & K. 227; Kent v. Burgess, 11 Sim. 361.

(gg) Ball v. Coutts, 1 Ves. & B. 292, 300; Long v. Long, 2 S. & S. 119; Auston v. Halsey, 2 Id. 123 n.; Hobson v. Ferraby, 2 Coll. 412.

---

[1] It is, perhaps, the duty of a guardian to apply to the court to authorize the marriage of his female ward, if she be "a ward of the court:" Shutt v. Carloss, 1 Ired. Ch. 232, 241. In Tabb v. Archer, 3 Hen. & Munf. 399, it was held, that the marriage of infants or wards is entrusted by law to the father or guardian; and, consequently, settlements made by infants through the father or guardian are binding.

[2] This rule will not be applied with strictness where the husband was ignorant of the fact that his wife was a ward: Richardson v. Merrifield, 4 De G. & Sm. 161.

is not an infringement of the rule against disposing of an infant's property; for it is confined to her personal estate in possession, which if no settlement were made, would belong absolutely to the husband; and, therefore, the settlement made is in truth his settlement, and not her own. There is no jurisdiction to settle her real estate, or personal estate to which she is entitled for her separate use.(h)

In addition to the general jurisdiction over the marriage of wards, the Court of Chancery has a special authority under the Marriage Act to appoint a guardian to give consent to an infant's marriage, when the father is dead, and there is no guardian and no mother unmarried; and also an authority to give such consent, when the father is *non compos,* or the guardian or mother is *non compos* or beyond seas, or unreasonably or from undue motives withholds consent.(i)   And by the same act it is enacted, that where the marriage of an infant by license has been procured by a party to the marriage by a wilfully false oath, or the like marriage by banns has been procured by such party, knowing that it was without consent of the parent or guardian, and having knowingly procured the undue publication of banns, the Court of Chancery, on information of the Attorney-General, at the relation of the parent or guardian, may declare a forfeiture of any interest which the offending party has obtained by the marriage, and may secure such interest for the innocent party, and the issue of the marriage; or if both parties are guilty, may secure it for the issue, with a

(h) Milner v. Harewood, 18 Ves. 259 ; Simson v. Jones, 2 R. & M. 365 ; Saville v. Saville, 2 Coll. 721 ; [Field v. Moore, 25 L. J. Ch. 66.]

(i) 4 Geo. 4 c. 76, s. 16 and 17 ; Ex parte J. C., 3 M. & C. 471.

[*290] discretionary provision for *the offending p
having regard to the benefit of the issue o
or of any future marriage.(k)

The jurisdiction to protect persons under mental
pacity is of an analogous origin with that for prot
of infants ;(l) and extends in like manner to all pe
whether subjects of the Crown or not, whose pers
property are within the local limits of the jurisdictio
The persons for whose benefit it exists are divide
two classes, viz. : idiots who have had no glimmeri
reason from their birth, and are, therefore, by lav
sumed never likely to attain any;[2] and lunatics, or p
of unsound mind, who have had understanding but
lost the use of it, either with or without occasional

(k) 4 Geo. 4, c. 76, s. 23, 24, 25 ; Attorney-General v. Mullay,
319 ; s. c. 7 Beav. 451 ; Attorney-General v. Sever, 1 Coll. 313.

(l) Sherwood v. Sanderson, 19 Ves. 280 ; Nelson v. Duncomb, {
211.

(m) Re Bariatinski, 1 Ph. 375.

---

[1] The care and custody of the persons and estates of lunatics are p
for in many of the states by local statutes. And the decisions cite
subsequent notes upon this branch must be taken, in part, as subjec
remark, and introduced merely as instances of analogy to the doct
the text. See on the subject of Chancery jurisdiction under thi
L'Amoureux v. Crosby, 2 Paige 423 ; Matter of Wendell, 1 Joh
600 ; Gorham v. Gorham, 3 Barb. Ch. 24 ; Naylor v. Naylor, 4 Da
Coleman's Case, 4 Hen. & Munf. 506 ; Warden v. Eichbaum, 14 P
127 ; Hinchman v. Richie, Bright. N. P. 143 ; Dowell v. Jacks, 5 J
417.

[2] A person deaf and dumb from his birth, is not, on that accoun
deemed non compos : though such, perhaps, may be the legal presu
until his mental capacity is proved on examination for that purpose :
v. Fisher, 4 Johns. Ch. 441 ; see, also, Christmas v. Mitchell, 3 Ir
535, the question need not be submitted to a jury : Sproyer v. Ric
16 Ohio St. 455. So of a person deaf, dumb, and blind, withou
proof of mental incapacity : Re Biddulph's and Poole's Trust, 5
Sm. 469.

intervals, and by reason of its loss have become incapable of managing their affairs.(*n*)¹ The jurisdiction in idiocy is of little practical importance, as it rarely happens that any one is found to be an idiot *a nativitate*. But the jurisdiction in lunacy is in constant exercise.

The similarity of principle between the jurisdictions in infancy and lunacy, would lead us to anticipate their exercise through the same channel and in the same form of procedure; viz., through the Court of Chancery in a regular suit. In this respect, however, a material distinction exists. The jurisdiction in lunacy is exercised, not by the Court of Chancery in a regular suit, but by the Lord Chancellor personally on petition; and the appeal, if his order be erroneous, is to the King in council, and not to the House of Lords. The origin of this distinction seems referable to the fact that the Crown, in the event of idiocy or lunacy, has not a mere authority to protect, but an actual interest in the land of the idiot or lunatic, determinable on his *recovery or death. [*291] If the owner is an idiot, the profits are applied as a branch of the revenue, subject merely to his requisite maintenance ; if he is a lunatic, they are applied on trust

· (*n*) 2 Steph. Bl. 529–531.

---

¹ It is not every case of mental weakness which will authorize the Court of Chancery to exercise the power of appointing a committee of the person and estate. To justify its exercise, the mind of the individual must be so far impaired as to be reduced to a state, which as an original incapacity, would have constituted a case of idiocy : Matter of Morgan, 7 Paige 236. Upon an inquest of lunacy, the finding of the jury that the party "is incapable of managing his affairs, or of governing himself, in consequence of mental imbecility or weakness," is not sufficient. They should find him to be of *unsound mind :* Id. ; see also, Matter of Mason, 3 Edw. Ch. 380 ; Matter of Arnhout, 1 Paige 497. The only legal test of insanity is delusion, and this consists in a belief of facts which no rational person would believe : Matter of Forman, 54 Barb. (N. Y.) 274.

for his support, and the surplus is to be accounted for to himself or his representatives.(o)   In either case there is an interest vested in the Crown, and requiring for its administration a special grant.   The duty of such administration is committed by special warrant to an officer of the Crown, who is usually, though not necessarily, the person holding the Great Seal.   By virtue of this warrant the custody of the estate and person is afterwards granted to committees, whose conduct is superintended by the Chancellor.   But it is said that the subsequent superintendence depends on the authority of the Great Seal, and not on the special warrant, and that if the warrant were to any other officer, his authority would cease with the appointment of committees.(p)[1]

The existence of a vested interest in the Crown, introduces also the additional distinction that the mere lunacy does not originate the jurisdiction; but that it must be first inquired of by a jury, and found of record, in accordance with the rule of law wherever a right of entry is alleged in the Crown.[2]

In cases where the estate has been very small, and the lunatic has been subject to the jurisdiction as party to a suit, directions have been given for the management of his property and for a fit allowance for his maintenance

(o) Steph. Bl. 529–531.

(p) 2 Story on Eq., s. 1336, and notes; Id. s. 1362–1365; Oxenden v. Lord Compton, 2 Ves. Jr. 69, 71; 4 B. C. C. 231; Ex parte Grimstone, Amb. 706; Re Fitzgerald, 2 Sch. & L. 431; Johnstone v. Beattie, 10 Cl. & F. 42, 120; [Dowell v. Jacks, 5 Jones Eq. 417.]

---

[1] But where persons of unsound mind, not found lunatics by inquisition, are entitled to property which is in or under the administration of the Court of Chancery, applications relating thereto may be entertained by the Court in its ordinary jurisdiction.

[2] See Matter of Runey Dey, 1 Stockt. 181.

without requiring an inquisition.(q)[1] And by a recent statute it is enacted, th'at where any person not found lunatic by inquisition has been detained under the provisions of the *Lunacy Acts, the Lord Chancellor [*292] may direct an inquiry into his case, and on a report that he is a lunatic may appoint guardians of his person and estate, and direct an application of the income.(r) The regular course, however, is to issue a commission under the Great Seal in the nature of a writ *de lunatico inquirendo*, to ascertain whether the party is of unsound mind. The granting of such commission is discretionary with the Chancellor, who in exercising his discretion will look solely to the lunatic's benefit; and will not on the one hand grant a commission merely because lunacy is shown to exist, nor refuse it on the other because the motives of the applicant are suspicious.(s)

The proceedings under the commission are regulated by statute.(t)[2] Their general outline is, that a jury is empannelled and sworn; the witnesses and the supposed

(q) Gillbee *v.* Gillbee, 1 Ph. 121; Nelson *v.* Duncombe, 9 Beav. 211; Sherwood *v.* Sanderson. 19 Ves. 280.

(r) 8 & 9 Vict. c. 100, s. 95, 98; Orders of Dec. 1845.

(s) Ex parte Tomlinson, 1 Ves. & B. 57; Re J. B., 1 M. & C. 538; Re Whittaker, 4 Id. 441; Re Webb, 2 Ph. 10; Re Nesbitt, Id. 245.

(t) 3 & 4 Wm. 4, c. 36; 5 & 6 Vict. c. 84, and 8 & 9 Vict. c. 100, s. 2. [See also, 16 & 17 Vict. c. 70; 25 & 26 Vict. c. 36; and c. 111.]

1 So the Court may always, in a proper case, extend its protection to the property of the lunatic *before inquest:* Owing's Case, 1 Bland Ch. 370, 373; Post *v.* Mackall, 3 Id. 486; Matter of Wendell, 1 Johns. Ch. 600; Matter of Runey Dey, 1 Stockt. 181.

2 In New York. the Court of Chancery has the entire jurisdiction over cases of idiocy and lunacy, and the manner in which the question of lunacy shall be tried is discretionary with the Court. The most satisfactory mode, is said to be by issue made up and prepared for trial under the direction of that Court: Matter of Wendell, 1 Johns. Ch. 600.

lunatic, if he thinks fit to be present, are examined;[1] and the inquisition is engrossed, and after signature by the commissioners and jury, is returned into Chancery. If there be misbehavior in executing the inquisition, or if the return be insufficient at law, the inquisition may be quashed and a new commission issued. If the return untruly finds the party lunatic, it may be traversed by himself or by any one claiming under a contract with him; if it untruly finds him of sound mind, a writ of *melius inquirendum* may be issued by the Crown.(*u*) If the lunatic subsequently recover, the commission may be superseded; but for this purpose the lunatic must in general be personally examined, and his sanity fully established.(*v*)[2]

(*u*) Ex parte Roberts, 3 Atk. 6 ; Ex parte Hall, 7 Ves. 261 ; Re Holmes, 4 Russ. 182 ; Re Bruges, 1 M. & C. 278.

(*v*) Ex parte Holyland, 11 Ves. 10; Re Gordon, 2 Ph. 242.

[1] It is the privilege of a party against whom a commission of lunacy is issued to be present at, and to have notice of its execution : Matter of Tracy, 1 Paige Ch. 580; Matter of Whitenack, 2 Green Ch. 253 ; Hinchman *v.* Ritchie, Bright. N. P. 144 ; Case of Covenhoven, Saxton 19. But see Medlock *v.* Cogburn, 1 Rich Ch. 477. Though the fact of notice does not appear on the face of the proceedings, yet they cannot for that reason be treated as a nullity in a collateral proceeding after confirmation : Willis *v.* Willis, 12 Penn. St. 159.

In Ex parte Richards, 16 Jur. 508, parties interested under a settlement executed ten years previously, were allowed to attend a commission, the object of which was to carry back the finding thirty years.

[2] On proof that the lunatic had recovered his senses, a commission of lunacy was superseded: Ex parte Drayton, 1 Dessaus. 144. On petition by a lunatic to supersede a commission, the Court will direct an inquiry, and report by a Master, as to the recovery, or direct the lunatic to be brought into Court, to be examined by the Chancellor : Matter of Hanks, 3 Johns. Ch. 567. Or he may traverse the inquisition, or have the question tried on a feigned issue : Matter of McClean, 6 Johns. Ch. 440. And where the Chancellor is satisfied that one found to be a lunatic has so far recovered his reason, as to be capable to dispose of his estate by will, he has power to suspend proceedings against him *partially*, so as to enable him to make a

The right of traversing the inquisition is conferred by *statute.(w)¹ By the common law, where a direct title of freehold appeared in the Crown by [*293] matter of record, the subject was put to his petition of right, and could not interplead with the King, either by traversing the King's title, or by setting up in avoidance a title of his own; but he is now enabled to traverse the inquisition and return, on obtaining leave by petition to the Great Seal.(x) The proviso requiring leave from the Great Seal, has occasioned doubts whether such leave is not discretionary with the Court. But it is determined

(w) 34 Edw. 3; 36 Edw. 3, c. 13; 8 Hen. 6, c. 16; 18 Hen. c. 6; 1 Hen. 8, c. 8; 2 & 3 Edw. 6, c. 8; 6 Geo. 4, c. 53.

(x) 2 Madd. C. P. 854; Eq parte Lord Gwydir, 4 Mad. 281.

---

will: Matter of Burr, 2 Barb. Ch. 208. Where a dissolution of a partnership had been decreed in consequence of the lunacy of one of the partners, and large sums had been paid into Court on the separate account of the lunatic in respect of his share of the capital and profits of the business, the Lord Chancellor, being satisfied subsequently of the complete recovery of the lunatic, ordered the whole fund to be paid out to him: Leaf v. Coles, 1 De G., M. & G. 417.

¹ It is a matter of right that a person found a lunatic under an inquisition, shall, if desirous, have a traverse of the inquisition: Ex parte Loveday, 1 De G., M. & G. 275; Re Cumming, Id. 537; and so, it seems, as to any party interested: Re Cummings, ut supr. The Lord Chancellor has, nevertheless, a discretion to exercise, upon the application for the writ being made to him, as to whether it ought to issue in the particular case. But the court will not, in exercising the discretion, enter into the question whether the lunacy was or was not proved before the jury, but will merely ascertain by a personal examination of the lunatic, whether he is capable of volition in the matter, and really desires a traverse. The court would not, for instance, permit a traverse in a case of raving madness. If the court, upon the examination, entertains a doubt as to the existence of such a desire on the part of the lunatic, it will, perhaps, look to other matters in forming its determination; such as the persons applying for the commission; and by whom the lunatic was surrounded, and what were the views and objects of the parties applying: Re Cumming, 16 Jur. 483; 1 De G., M. & G. 537.

that, if the applicant show a sufficient interest, the traverse is matter of right, and may be claimed as such either
by the alleged lunatic himself, if capable of volition and
attending personally to express his wish, or by any one
interested under a contract with him. If there be a reasonable ground of traverse, the Court may in its discretion allow funds out of the estate for trying it, and may
in the meantime suspend any further interference. (g)

On a return of *non compos* being made, and either submitted to, or established on trial of a traverse, the custody
of the estate and person is granted to committees with a
proper allowance for maintenance.[1]   And even though a
traverse be pending, the Chancellor may at his discretion
take the same course. (z)   If no one is willing to become
committee of the estate, a receiver may be appointed, with
the usual allowance; and under special circumstances
remuneration may be given to a committee. But the
general rule is, that a committee, like any other trustee,
is not entitled to remuneration, but to reimbursement
alone. (a)[2]   The duty of the committee or receiver of the
estate is to manage the lunatic's property with care,
[*294] *to bring in and pass his accounts, and to pay
and invest the balances at such times as the super-

(y) Ex parte Hall, 7 Ves. 261; Sherwood *v.* Sanderson, 19 Id. 280; Re
Bridge, Cr. & P. 338; Re Watts, 1 Ph. 512.
(z) Re Bridge, Cr. & P. 338.
(a) Ex parte Radcliffe, 1 J. & W. 619; Ex parte Fermor, Jac. 404.

---

[1] Where the lunatic has lands or other property in the state of his so-
journ, although he is domiciled abroad, a commission must be issued in
such state to authorise control over the property : matter of Pettit, 2 Paige
174; Matter of Perkins, 2 Johns. Ch. 124; Matter of Ganse, 9 Paige 416;
Matter of Fowler, 2 Barb. Ch. 305.
[2] See Matter of Roberts, 3 Johns. Ch. 43; Matter of Livingston, 9 Paige
440.

intending officer (called the Master in Lunacy) shall direct. And he is required to give security by a bond with sureties, and to satisfy the Master, on each occasion of passing his accounts, that his sureties are living, and not bankrupt or insolvent.(b)[1]

In cases requiring the exercise of discretion, it is not usual to act without previous investigation by the Court. The mode of investigation was, until recently, by referring the matter for inquiry to a Master in Chancery. But by the recent statutes and orders, all such inquiries, except in cases under the Lunatic Trustee Act,(c) or when the Lord Chancellor shall specially direct otherwise, are transferred to the Commissioners, now termed the Masters, in Lunacy. By the same orders the necessity of a previous reference is in many instances dispensed with, and an application to the Chancellor is only requisite to confirm the report.(d) The inquiries which may be thus made without a previous reference, are inquiries as to the presumptive heir and next of kin; as to the situation of the lunatic, and the nature of his lunacy; and as to his committees, his fortune, and his maintenance. There is a similar authority to inquire and report as to provisional management and maintenance, until the appointment of committees; to enlarge the time within which the committee of the estate must complete his security, to receive proposals or conduct inquiries as to

(b) Orders of April, 1844.
(c) 11 Geo. 4 & 1 Wm. 4, c. 60.
(d) 5 & 6 Vict. c. 84 ; 8 & 9 Vict. c. 100, s. 2 ; Orders of October, 1842.

---

[1] In the Matter of Elias, 3 Macn. & Gord, 234, an order was made, on the application by a curator of a lunatic resident in Holland, for the transfer to him of the *corpus* of funds in England, to which the lunatic was entitled; though it did not appear either that the lunatic was a Dutch subject, or that the curator had given security.

managing, settling, or letting the estate, or otherwise respecting the person and property; to take from time to
time the committee's account; and to determine whether
any and which of the presumptive heirs or next of kin
shall attend at the cost of the estate on any proceedings
in lunacy.(e)   The principle on which the attendance of
[*295]   the heir and next of *kin is allowed, is not that
they have any recognised interest in the lunatic's
property, but that they are most likely to possess information respecting it, and to assist in its proper administration.(f)

The power of the committee to deal with the estate
was at common law very limited; for the interest of the
Crown was determinable on recovery or death; and any
lease or other disposition by the committee was necessarily subject to the same contingency.(g)   The statutory
powers applying to the beneficial interests of a lunatic
are conferred by the statute, which has been already
noticed, "for amending the laws relating to property belonging to infants, *femes covert*, lunatics, and persons of
unsound mind."(h)

By the early clauses of this statute provision is made,
as already noticed, for admittance of lunatics as well as
of infants and *femes covert* to copyhold property, and for
raising the fine payable on admittance, without requiring
the sanction of a judicial order.   The powers conferred by
the subsequent clauses in the case of infants and *femes
covert* have been already stated.(i)   The powers conferred
in the case of lunatics are to be exercised under the sanc-

(e) Orders of October, 1842, 10 to 15.
(f) Ex parte Whitbread, 2 Meriv. 99 ; Re Pearson, 1 Coop. Ch. Ca. 314.
(g) Supra, Trust ; Mortgage.
(h) 11 Geo. 4 & 1 Wm. 4, c. 65.
(i) Supra, Infants.

tion of the Lord Chancellor, intrusted under the sign manual with the custody of lunatics. The acts which the Lord Chancellor is thus empowered to direct, are the surrender of renewable leaseholds belonging to a lunatic, and the acceptance of renewed ones in their stead; the renewal of leases which the lunatic, if not under disability, might be compelled to renew, or which it shall be for his benefit to renew; the exercise of leasing powers vested in a lunatic over property in which he has a limited estate; the leasing of property belonging to a lunatic in fee or in tail, or for an absolute leasehold interest; the entering into agreements on behalf of the lunatic under the Act for augmenting *the Maintenance of the [*296] Poor Clergy;(k) the making conveyances under a decree for specific performance, where the contracting party has become lunatic after his contract was made; the selling or charging a lunatic's estate for the purpose of raising money to pay debts, encumbrances, and costs; the transfer and payment of a lunatic's stock and dividends, under which name is included every fund, annuity, or security transferable in the books of any company; and the like transfer of stock vested in any person residing out of England, when such person has been declared lunatic, and his personal estate has been vested in a curator according to the law of his place or residence. The same act provides, that transcripts of inquisitions on commissions under the Great Seal of Great Britain may be entered of record in Ireland, and acted on there; and *vice versa*, with respect to commissions under the Great Seal of Ireland.

The principle on which the lunatic's estate is managed is that of looking to the lunatic's interest alone, and act-

(k) 1 Geo. 1, c. 10.

ing as an owner of competent understanding would do, without regard to his eventual successors. The effect of such management may, in some instances, be to alter the property from real to personal, or *vice versa ;* e. *g.*, by cutting timber on the real estate, or by paying out of the personalty for repairs or improvements.[1] And if such alteration be made, the property will devolve, on the lunatic's death, in accordance with its altered character, and not in accordance with that which it previously bore. It is otherwise, as we have seen, in the case of an infant; for an infant has different powers over real and personal estate; and is entitled, for his own sake, independently of any supposed equity between his real and personal representatives, to be protected from any conversion of the one into the other. The Court, therefore, in ordering the conversion to be made, will add a declaration that, while [*297] *the minority lasts, the converted property shall retain in equity its original character. A lunatic stands on a different footing; for at the instant of a lucid interval he has precisely the same power of disposition over either species of estate; and therefore, if in the ordinary course of management it is for his benefit to make the change, there is no equity to interfere with its result. But the rule must be understood with this guard, that nothing extraordinary is to be attempted; e. *g.*,

---

[1] Accordingly, in the Matter of Salisbury, 3 Johns. Ch. 347, it was held that in the management of a lunatic's estate the interest of the lunatic is more regarded than the contingent interest of those who may be entitled to the succession; and the court, if it be for the interest of the lunatic, may direct real estate to be converted into personal, or personal into real. Thus it may direct timber standing to be sold. As to its power to order an exchange of any portion of the estate, see Matter of Heller, 3 Paige 199; In re Livingston, 9 Id. 440; Matter of Drayton, 1 Dessaus. 136.

estates to be bought, or interests disposed of. Alteration of property is to be avoided, so far as is consistent with the proprietor's interest.(*l*)

The same principle of looking to the lunatic's advantage alone is pursued in fixing the amount of the maintenance; and provision therefore may be made for modes of expenditure which are substantially for the lunatic's benefit, though they may not be such as he is legally bound to incur; *e. g.*, if the father of a family be lunatic the Court will not consider the mere legal right of his wife and children, but will make an allowance suitable to their station in life. And so if property descend on a lunatic, and his brothers and sisters are slenderly provided for, his allowance may be increased to give assistance to them.(*m*)[1]

If after due allowance for the lunatic's maintenance, there is still a disposable surplus of his estate, such surplus may be applied in payment of his debts; and on a petition by a creditor, a reference will be made to inquire what debts there are, and how they should be discharged; but there is no instance of paying the debts without re-

(*l*) Oxenden *v.* Lord Compton, 2 Ves. J. 69; Ex parte Phillips, 19 Id. 118; Ex parte Digby, 1 J. & W. 620; Re Badcock, 4 M. & C. 440.

(*m*) Ex parte Whitbread, 2 Mer. 99; Re Blair, 1 M. & C. 300; Re Drummond, Id. 627; Re Carysfoot, Cr. & P. 76; Edwards *v.* Abrey, 2 Ph. 37; Re Thomas, Id. 169; Re Clarke, Id. 282; [In re Frost, 5 Ch. Law R. 699.]

---

[1] The court has power out of the surplus income of the estate of a lunatic, to provide for the support of persons not his next of kin, and whom the lunatic is under no legal obligation to support, as *e. g.*, persons whom he had adopted as children: Matter of Heeney, 2 Barb. Ch. 326. See on the subject of the maintenance to be allowed, Davies *v.* Davies, 2 De G., M. & G. 51; Re Burbridge, 3 M. & G. 1; Eckstein's Estate, 1 Pars. Eq. 67; Guthrie's App., 16 Penn. St. 321.

serving a sufficient maintenance, although the creditors
cannot be restrained from proceeding at law. $(n)^1$

[*298]   *On the death of the lunatic, the power of administration is at an end, except as to orders
which have been already made, or which are consequential on reports or petitions already made or presented. (o)
But the committee continues under the control of the
Court, and will be ordered on the application of the lu-
natie's heir to deliver up possession of the estate.[2]   In
the case of an idiot, where the Crown has a beneficial
interest, an *ouster le main* must be sued; and it has been

(n) Ex parte Dikes, 8 Ves. 79 ; Ex parte Hastings, 14 Id. 182.

(o) Ex parte McDougal, 12 Ves. 384 ; Rock *v.* Cooke, 1 Coll. 477.

---

[1] In New York, the real estate of a lunatic may be sold for the payment
of his debts on a creditor's bill or on petition : Brasher *v.* Van Cortlandt, 2
Johns. Ch. 242, 400.   But not till the personal estate is exhausted : In re
Pettit, 2 Paige 596.   See also, Kennedy *v.* Johnson, 65 Penn. St. 451.

In Kentucky, it would seem, the Chancellor has no right to decree a sale
of a lunatic's estate for the payment of his debts : Berry *v.* Rogers, 2 B.
Monr. 308.   Moreover, in New York, a suit at law cannot be brought
against a lunatic, under the care of a committee, without permission of the
court first obtained : Matter of Hopper, 5 Paige 489.

[2] The death of the lunatic determines the office of the committee, and
the only power which Chancery retains over the committee, as such, is to
compel him to account and deliver possession of the property as the court
shall direct.   But the committee is to retain possession, and preserve the
property until some person shall appear properly authorized to receive it
from him ; and in the meantime, if there is reason to apprehend delay in
ascertaining who are entitled to the possession, a receiver may be appointed,
upon application of the parties in interest.   The jurisdiction of Chancery
in lunacy remains, after the death of the lunatic, only to the extent and for
the purpose of having the necessary account taken, and directing the fund
or estate to be paid over to the party or parties entitled.   After the death
of the lunatic, the court will not administer the fund even for the benefit
of creditors ; they must pursue their remedies before the ordinary jurisdictions; nor will it adjudicate questions of right between opposing claimants :
Matter of Colvin, 3 Md. Ch. 278 ; Guerard *v.* Gaillard, 15 Rich. (S. C.)
L. 22.

d whether, on the death or recovery of a lunatic,
.me course should not in strictness be followed.
ractice, however, is to restore possession by an
of the Court.(p)

x parte Fitzgerald, 2 Sch. & L. 439; Re Pearson, 1 Coop. Ch. Ca.

38

*BOOK IV.

OF THE FORMS OF PLEADING AND PROCEDURE BY ꓪ
THE JURISDICTION OF THE COURTS OF EQUITY IS
CISED.

CHAPTER I.

OF THE BILL.

WE have now exhausted the consideration of th
rogative jurisdiction of the Court of Chancery.
inquiry still remains as to the forms of pleading an
cedure, in accordance with which that jurisdicti
exercised.[1]

It is obvious that in every Court some forms
exist; but the character of those forms is different
and in equity, in conformity with the different o
which the two tribunals respectively contemplate.

The object of the common law Courts in their oɪ
structure was to reduce the litigation to a single
and to obtain from the appropriate tribunal a decis
that issue; from the Court on an issue of law, f

---

[1] See some remarks upon the changes introduced into Chancery
and Procedure, in England and the United States, in the Preface.

jury on an issue of fact. By statutory enactment several distinct issues, both of law and fact, may now indeed be raised in the same action, but each issue must be kept separate, and cannot be prayed in aid of the others. In accordance with this principle the pleadings are framed, first, for the production of single or separate issues; secondly, for keeping separate the law and the fact.

*The pleadings begin with the declaration or statement by the plaintiff of his cause of action. [*300] This is followed by the defence, either by demurrer, if the declaration be insufficient in law, or by one or more pleas, if it be untrue or incomplete in fact. If the declaration be untrue, the form of pleading is by denial, disputing some material averment. If it be incomplete, by confession and avoidance, admitting the declaration to be correct, but averring some new fact to avoid or vitiate the cause of action. On demurrers, or pleas in denial, issues of law or fact are necessarily raised; on pleas in confession and avoidance, the litigation is made dependent on the new averments. These new averments, therefore, must in turn be replied to by the plaintiff, and the pleadings are continued on the same principle, each in turn superseding the rest, until all matter of confession and avoidance is exhausted, and direct issues are arrived at.

If the issues thus arrived at are issues of law, they are determined by the Court on argument. If they be issues of fact, a jury is empannelled to try them. The manner of trial by jury is that the evidence is given *viva voce* and publicly, subject to cross-examination by the opposite party; it is then summed up and the law explained by the judge, and a separate verdict is given upon each separate issue, and the verdict, when given, is without appeal. There is, however, a discretionary power in the

Court, if the Judge has misstated the law, or if the verdict given is contrary to the evidence, or there has been
a surprise upon the party failing, or for other sufficient
cause, to direct a new trial by another jury.

After the issues have been decided and the judgment
entered, it is still open to the unsuccessful party by motion to show that the case, as made on the record, is not
such as to a warrant such judgment, and to have the same
arrested; otherwise execution follows, as of course, upon
the judgment, and a writ issues to the sheriff, directing
him to levy the amount recovered out of the property of
the unsuccessful party, or to take his body in execution.

If there be error, and that error be apparent on the
[*301] face *of the record, there is an appeal by writ of
error from the decision of the Court below to
the Exchequer Chamber or the House of Lords, as the
case may be; but if the error is not an error of law on
the record, but a wrong verdict on matter of fact, there
is, as we have seen, no right of appeal, but a mere discretion in the Court to grant a new trial.

In the Court of Chancery the system is different.
The object there aimed at is a complete decree on the
general merits, and not that the litigation should be reduced to a single issue: and as all issues, whether of law
or fact, are decided, or adjusted for decision, by the
Court, it is not essential to keep them strictly distinct.
The rules, therefore, of pleading are less stringent than
at law; but they are equally regulated by principle; and
in order to secure adherence to such principle, every
pleading, except the formal replication, must be sanctioned by the signature of counsel.

The commencement of a suit in equity on behalf of a
subject is by preferring a bill, in nature of a petition, to

the Lord Chancellor or other holder of the Great Seal, or if the Seal be in the King's hands, or the holder of it be a party, to the King himself in his Court of Chancery. This is termed an original bill, to distinguish it from other bills, filed in the course of a suit to remedy defects and errors. If the party injured be an infant, or a married woman suing separately from her husband (unless the husband be banished or has abjured the realm), it is preferred by a person styled the next friend, and named in the record as such.[1] If he be a lunatic or idiot, it is

---

[1] A married woman who has instituted a suit in the ordinary way may afterwards apply for an order to sue *in forma pauperis*: Wellesley *v.* Wellesley, 16 Sim. 1; but cannot institute a suit *in forma pauperis* without a next friend: Re Page, 17 Jur. 336; 16 Beav. 588. In subsequent cases, however, before the Lords Justices of Appeal, a married woman living apart from her husband was allowed to sue *in forma pauperis*, on an affidavit of poverty, and that she could procure no person to act as next friend, and this upon an ex parte application: Re Lancaster, 18 Jur. 229.

A person of color, held in slavery, can sue in Chancery for his freedom only by a next friend: Doran *v.* Brazleton, 2 Swan 149

The executor or administrator of a decedent's estate is in general the only proper party complainant in suits against third persons touching the estate: Stainton *v.* Carron Co., 18 Beav. 146; Davidson *v.* Potts, 7 Ired. Eq. 272. Parties interested, not being the legal personal representatives, will not be allowed to sue persons possessed of assets belonging to the estate, unless they satisfy the Court that such assets would probably be lost if the suit had not been instituted. Special circumstances must always be made out. Such a bill would be supported in case of a deceased partner, where the relation between the executor and the surviving partners was such as to present a substantial impediment to the prosecution, by the executor, of the rights of the parties interested in the estate against the surviving partners. There is a distinction, however, between a general administration suit and one for the recovery of particular outstanding assets. In the former a residuary legatee, or other person interested, may, on instituting suit against the executor for the settlement of the general accounts, join the surviving partner, even though no collusion be alleged or proved. This, however, does not apply to a joint stock company, unless there be additional circumstances: Stainton *v.* Carron Co., 18 Jur. 137; Travis *v.* Milne, 9 Hare 141. In Stainton *v.* Carron Co. the Court declined to sustain a bill filed by parties interested in an estate against a joint stock

by the committee of his estate, or sometimes by the
torney-General on behalf of the Crown as the ge
protector of lunatics.(*a*)

If the suit be on behalf of the Crown, of those who
take of its prerogative, or of those whose rights are u
its particular protection, as, for example, the objects
public charity, the complaint is preferred by the Atto
or Solicitor-General, and the bill is not one of pet
[*302] or *complaint, but of information to the Col
the wrong committed.[1] If the suit does no
mediately concern the rights of the Crown, its o
generally depend on the relation of some person, te
the relator, who is named on the record as such, a
answerable for the costs; and if such relator has a
sonal ground of complaint, it is incorporated with the i
mation, and they form together an information and
An information differs from a bill in little more
name and form, and will therefore be considered u
the general head of bills.(*aa*)

(*a*) Mitf. on Plead. 24–30; 1 Dan. C. P. 72–132.
(*aa*) Mitf. on Plead. 21–24.

company of which the testator was a member, and against which b
had claims, the ground of the bill being that the executors wer
managers in the concern, and a conflict of duties and interests
feared, but no collusion or intended neglect being alleged. One p
of a set of next of kin cannot sue another portion without an ad
trator as party, and it makes no difference that those who wish
reside out of the state, and cannot procure letters of administr
Davidson *v.* Potts, 7 Ired. Eq. 272.

So to a suit by a creditor of an intestate, against an executor,
tort, for an account and payment, it is necessary that a personal rep
tative duly constituted should be a party : Creaser *v.* Robinson, 14
589.

[1] It is no longer necessary that the Attorney-General shall be a pa
proceedings in equity, in cases of public nuisance. A municipal co
tion is a proper party in such case, where the nuisance is within its l
Com. of Moyamensing *v.* Long, 1 Pars. Eq. 146.

An original bill or information consists of five principal parts, viz., 1. The statement; 2. The charges; 3. The interrogatories; 4. The prayer of relief; and 5. The prayer of process.[1]

The statement of a bill is prefaced by the heading, addressing it to the holder of the Great Seal, the terms of which are from time to time prescribed by the Court.(b) It then commences with the words, "Humbly complaining showeth unto your Lordship, your orator," &c., giving the name, description, and place of abode of the plaintiff,[2] and if necessary, of the next friend, committee, or relator,(c) and then narrating the case for relief. Its object is to show the right to relief; it must state a consistent case on behalf of all the plaintiffs, and must state it in direct terms, and with reasonable certainty.

It must state a consistent case on behalf of all the plaintiffs; for if their claims are inconsistent, or any of them have no claim, the misjoinder will be fatal to the

(b) 1 Dan. 339.   (c) Id. 340.

---

[1] The form of the bill is now much simplified in England (see the Preface); and in Pennsylvania by the Rules of Equity Practice, adopted May 27, 1865.

[2] The residence of the complainant should be stated in his bill; and if it is not stated therein, the defendant may apply to the Court and obtain an order that the complainant give security for costs: Howe v. Harvey, 8 Paige 73. Whether the defendant can demur for this cause, quære? Ibid. The description of the plaintiff is a material portion of the bill; if it is absent, the objection may be taken by demurrer; if untrue, the objection may be taken by plea. But in the latter case the plea must sufficiently aver that the description was false at the time of filing the bill: Smith v. Smith. 1 Kay, App. 23; Winnipiseogee Lake Co. v. Worster, 9 Foster 433. In New York, however, the omission to state the complainant's addition or occupation is no longer a ground for demurrer: Gove v. Pettis, 4 Sand. Ch. 403. By the 20th rule in Equity of the United States Courts, every bill must contain in the introductory part, the names, places of abode, and citizenship of all the parties, plaintiffs, and defendants. And see Dodge v. Perkins, 4 Mason 435.

suit; or, at all events, the Court will only make such a decree as will leave their claims in respect to each other wholly undecided. (d)[1]

[*303]   *It must state the case in direct terms (e) and with reasonable certainty;[2] not necessarily with

(d) Cholmondeley v. Clinton, T. & R. 117; 2 J. & W. 134; King of Spain v. Machado, 4 Russ. 2:5; Bill v. Cureton, 2 M. & K. 503; Lambert v. Hutchinson, 1 Beav. 277; Jacob v. Lucas, Id. 436; Davies v. Quarterman, 4 Y. & C. 257; Anderson v. Wallis, 1 Ph. 202; 1 Dan. C. P. 290-292.

(e) Stansbury v. Arkwright, 6 Sim. 481; Hammond v. Messenger, 9 Sim. 327, 355; [Champneys v. Buchan, 4 Drew. 123.]

---

[1] See Richardson v. McKinson, Litt. Sel. Cas. 320; Terrill v. Craig, Halst. Dig. 223; Thurman v. Shelton, 10 Yerger 383; Mix v. Hotchkiss, 14 Conn. 32; Swayze v. Swayze, 1 Stockt. 273. Parties having conflicting interests, each claiming the title in the property in dispute to be in himself, cannot unite as plaintiffs; and a bill containing an averment that one of such plaintiffs is entitled, and if he is not the other is, cannot be supported: Ellicott v. Ellicott, 2 Md. Ch. 468. But where plaintiffs properly join in a bill for relief to which all are entitled, a claim by one of them for further relief, peculiar to himself, is not ground for demurrer to the whole bill: Clarkson v. De Peyster, 3 Paige 320. And unconnected parties, having a common interest centering in the point in issue in the cause, may unite in the same bill. Thus, where two non-residents, having distinct claims against another non-resident, filed their bill in Mississippi to subject funds of the non-resident defendant, in the hands of a resident of that state, who was also made defendant, it was held, on demurrer, that the bill was sustainable: Comstock v. Rayford, 1 Sm. & M. 423; see also, Armstrong v. Athens Co., 10 Ohio 235; Ohio v. Ellis, 10 Id. 456; Dawson v. Lawrence, 13 Id. 543; Tilford v. Emerson, 1 A. K. Marsh. 483; Scrimeger v. Buckhannon, 3 Id. 219; Tilman v. Searcy, 5 Humph. 487; Morris v. Dillard, 4 Sm. & M. 636; Wood v. Barringer, 1 Dev. Eq. 67.

[2] A rigid and technical construction of bills is exploded: Roane, J., in Mayo v. Murchie, 3 Munf. 384. But every material allegation should be put in issue by the pleadings, so that the parties may be duly apprised of the essential inquiry, and be enabled to collect testimony to meet it: Kent, J., in James v. McKarnon, 6 Johns. 564. See Wilcox v. Davis, 4 Minn. 200. Every averment, therefore, necessary to entitle a plaintiff in equity to the relief prayed for, must be contained in the stating part of the bill; and if every necessary fact be not distinctly and expressly averred in that part, the defect cannot be supplied by inference, or by reference to averments in other parts: Wright v. Dame, 22 Pick 55. Nor can the plaintiff

the same technical precision as at law, but with sufficient
precision to show that there is a definite equity. And if

rely upon the interrogatories to supply defects in the stating part of his
bill: Cowles v. Buchanan, 3 Ired. Eq. 374. The allegations must be
positive, and not by way of recital: McIntyre v. Trustees of Union College, 6 Paige 239, 251. When a judgment creditor seeks the aid of a Court
of equity to enforce the payment of his judgment, he must aver in his bill
that an execution has been issued, and has been returned unproductive.
A mere averment of insolvency will not be sufficient: Suydam v. The
North Western Ins. Co., 51 Penn. St. 398 ; Hendricks v. Robinson, 2 Johns.
Ch. 283 ; Brinkerhoff v. Brown, 4 Id. 671 ; McElwain v. Willis, 9 Wend.
548. The best test of what are proper averments of facts in a bill or
answer is whether they are such matters as a witness may be called upon
to prove, or the truth of which must be established by *evidence*, to enable
a Court to act ; if they are not, then such averments are merely principles
of equity, or some of those public facts of which the Court is bound to
take judicial notice without proof: Canal Co. v. Railroad Co., 4 Gill & J.
1 ; see also, Shepard v. Shepard, 6 Conn. 37 ; Lingan v. Henderson, 1 Bland
249, 255 ; Russ v. Hawes, 5 Ired. Eq. 18 ; Caton v. Willis, Id. 355 ; Salmon
v. Clagett, 3 Bland 134 ; Townshend v. Duncan, 2 Id. 45 ; Fowler v. Saunders, 4 Call 361 ; Yancy v. Fenwick, 4 Hen. & Munf. 423 ; Cruger v. Halliday, 11 Paige 314 ; Hobart v. Frisbie, 5 Conn. 592; Davis v. Harrison,
4 Litt. 262; Harding v. Handy, 11 Wheat. 103 ; Knox v. Smith, 4 How.
U. S. 298; Spence v. Duren, 3 Ala. 251. The bill should state a case
upon which, if admitted by the answer, a decree can be made: Perry v.
Carr, 41 N. H. 371. General allegations of fraud, in a bill where the
facts stated do not make out a case of fraud, will not avail on demurrer:
Magniac v. Thompson, 2 Wall. Jr. 209 ; Hamilton v. Lockhart, 41 Miss.
460; Hanson v. Field, Id. 712. Fraud must be expressly alleged, however, in order to enable the complainant to rely on it as a part of his
case: Gouverneur v. Elmendorf, 5 Johns. Ch. 79 ; Thompson v. Jackson,
3 Rand. 504; Booth v. Booth, 3 Litt. 57 ; Miller v. Cotten, 5 Ga. 346 ;
Sawyer v. Mills, 20 L. J. Ch. 80 ; Hayward v. Purssey, 3 De G. & Sm.
399 ; Small v. Boudinot, 1 Stockt. 273 ; Moore v. Greene, 19 How. 69 ;
Bailey v. Ryder, 10 N. Y. 363. Though where the bill states with distinctness
and precision facts and circumstances which in themselves amount to fraud,
such an allegation *totidem verbis* is not absolutely necessary: McCalmont
v. Rankin, 8 Hare 1 ; Skrine v. Simmons, 11 Ga. 401 ; Kennedy v. Kennedy,
2 Ala. 571. See Smith v. Kay, 7 H. L. Cas. 750-763. Unfounded allegations
of fraud are discouraged, and where the complainant introduces them into
his bill, and fails to establish them, he will debar himself, in general
from other relief, to which the facts stated might otherwise have entitled

the equity depends on a title to property in the pla
the statement must show a sufficient title in point of
e. g., the statement of a devise must allege a w]
writing,[1] the statement of a grant must allege a deec
statement of a title by heirship must show the man]
descent. But if the title, as stated, would have
valid at common law, and regulations have been s

---

him: Price *v.* Berrington, 3 M. & G. 496 ; Eyre *v.* Potter, 15 How
56 ; Fisher *v.* Boody, 1 Curtis 211. It seems, however, that an un
statement of circumstances which would amount to fraud, without
press charge of fraud, is not sufficient to deprive him of relief: W
Mynn, 14 Jur. 341. Allegations that a complainant is informed and b
that material facts exist, are not sufficient: McDowell *v.* Graham,
73 ; Jones *v.* Cowles, 26 Ala. 612. But if the facts essential to the
mination of the plaintiff's cause, are charged in the bill to rest
knowledge of the defendant only, or must of necessity be with
knowledge only, the precise allegation is not required: Aikin *v.* B
1 Rice Eq. 13 ; as *e. g.*, a bill in equity by a partner against his cop
for an account, &c., wherein it is averred that the defendant has
partnership books and papers in his possession, or under his contr
refuses to permit the plaintiff to examine them, need not contain
certainty and particularity of statement as would be held necessar
plaintiff had access to those books and papers: Towle *v.* Pierce,]
329 ; see also, Many *v.* Beekman Iron Co., 9 Paige 188. So, in a]
dower, the widow is not presumed to know the precise nature of t]
band's title, and defective allegations in regard thereto may be a]
the answer: Garton's Heirs *v.* Bates, 4 B. Monr. 366 ; Wall et al.
7 Dana 172. It need not be stated in the bill that there is not an ad
remedy at law; it is sufficient if it appear from the facts disclosed
bill that such remedy does not exist: Botsford *v.* Beers et al., 1]
369 ; see also, Boston Co. *v.* Worcester R. R.Corp., 16 Pick. 512 ;
ner *v.* Allen, 12 Minn. 148.

[1] Where a bill is filed by persons in the character of legatees,
neither sets out in its body the contents of the will, nor has a cop
annexed, a demurrer by the defendant will be sustained, for the Cot
not see that the plaintiffs are legatees: Martin *v.* McBryde, 3 Ir
531 ; see also, Belloat *v.* Morse, 2 Haywood 157 ; Van Cortlandt t
man, 6 Paige 492.

[2] See King *v.* Trice, 3 Ired. Eq. 568.

added by statute, it is not essential, though usual to state compliance with them.(f)[1]

It is not, however, requisite to state matters of which the Court takes judicial notice, such as public acts of Parliament, the general customs of the realm, and so forth; although, for the sake of convenience, they are often introduced.[2]

The charges of a bill ought not to include, and generally do not include, any narrative of the case for relief, but are generally used for collateral objects; e. g., for

(f) Wormald v. De Lisle, 3 Beav. 18; Edwards v. Edwards, Jac. 335; Seddon v. Connell, 10 Sim. 79; Williams v Earl of Jersey, C. & P. 91; 1 Dan. C. P. 303–310, 346–9; Steph. on Pleading 341, 364, 383–6, 411; Walburn v. Ingilby, 1 M. & K. 61.

[1] Thus in England, and most of the United States, it is not necessary in a case within the Statute of Frauds, for the complainant to allege in his bill that the contract or trust, with regard to which relief is asked, was in writing; though in Georgia, the rule is otherwise: Logan v. Bond, 13 Ga. 192. But if the objection appears on the face of the bill, a demurrer will lie: Story Eq. Plead. § 503. So it is now settled, that lapse of time, in cases directly within, or by analogy to the Statute of Limitations, where it appears on the face of the bill, may be taken advantage of by demurrer; and it is incumbent on the complainant to state, by way of anticipation, the facts and circumstances which he relies on to take the case out of the operation of the general rules: Wisner v. Barnet, 4 Wash. C. C. 631; Dunlap v. Gibbs, Yerg. 94; Humbert v. Rector of Trin. Ch., 7 Paige 197, 24 Wend. 595; Maxwell v. Kennedy, 8 How. U. S. 210; Field v. Wilson, 6 B. Monr. 479; Ingraham v. Regan, 23 Miss. 213; Bank U. S. v. Biddle, 2 Pars. Eq. 31; Pratt v. Northam, 5 Mason 95; Williams v. Presb. Soc., 1 Ohio St. N. S. 478; Nimmo v. Stewart, 21 Ala. 682; Mayne v. Griswold, 3 Sandf. S. C. 464; Story Eq. Pl. § 484; contr. Bulkley v. Bulkley, 2 Day 363; Hickman v. Stout, 2 Leigh 6. But the laches must appear distinctly by the bill itself: Muir v. Trustees, 3 Barb. Ch. 477; Battle v. Durham, 11 Ga. 17. And a general demurrer, where all the grounds of relief stated in the bill are not barred by lapse of time will be overruled: Radcliff v. Rowley, 2 Barb. Ch. 23.

[2] See Story Eq. Plead. § 24. The Federal Courts of the United States take judicial notice of the laws and jurisprudence of all the states and territories: Ibid.: Owings v. Hull, 9 Peters 607.

meeting the defence by matter in avoidance, or by inquiries to sift its truth; for giving notice of evidence which might otherwise operate as a surprise; and for obtaining discovery as to matters of detail which could not be conveniently introduced in the statement.

1. For meeting the defence by matter in avoidance.[1]

The form adopted for this purpose is that of pretence and charge; viz., an allegation that the defendant pretends, &c., stating the defence, and then proceeding thus: " Whereas your orator charges the contrary to be true; and your orator charges that even if the said pretence be true, yet that," &c., stating the new matter in avoidance.

[*304] By this means the *plaintiff is enabled to state the avoidance on the record, without admitting the truth of the defence. Charges of this class are sometimes made in anticipation of an expected defence, but they are also introduced by amendment to meet a defence set up by the answer; and the latter is generally the safer course; because by attempting to anticipate the defence, a risk is incurred of misunderstanding its purport, and sometimes of suggesting an objection, which the defendant would otherwise have overlooked.

2. For sifting the truth of the defence.

---

[1] As a general rule, it seems a bill in equity should combine the qualities of a declaration and replication, by anticipating the defence, and charging the matter relied upon in avoidance: McCrea v. Purmont, 16 Wend. 460. The complainant should state, in the charging part, the anticipated defence as a pretence of the defendant, and then charge the real facts to lay a foundation for the discovery which is sought: Stafford v. Brown, 4 Paige 88. And in a sworn bill, it is equally perjury for the complainant knowingly to make a false charge in the charging part, as to make a false statement in the stating part: Smith v. Clark, 4 Paige 368.

The charging part of the bill is made unnecessary by the Equity rules in the U. S. Courts (xxi.). In Pennsylvania all merely formal parts must be omitted: New Equity Rules xvii.

Charges of this class are similar in principle to 'those of the preceding one, and only differ from it in so far, that instead of charging new matter in avoidance, they charge merely that the pretended facts are untrue, and • that so it would appear if the defendant would set forth the time, place, and other circumstances, under which he alleges them to have happened.

3. For giving notice of evidence which might otherwise operate as a surprise.

It is not requisite as matter of pleading that the evidence should be set out in detail, for the facts proved, and not the evidence, constitute the case for relief.[1] The system, however, of taking evidence secretly, the grounds of which will be hereafter considered, would render it possible to prove facts under a general statement, which though strictly admissible as evidence of its truth, would be practically a surprise on the opposite party. And the Court, therefore, will generally refuse to act on such evidence, and will refer the subject to a Master for re-investigation. In order to prevent this result, it is frequently advisable to give an outline of the evidence; and if the case is one in which the introduction of such an outline would cause an inconvenient complexity of narration, the statement may be confined to a bare allegation of the

---

[1] To this point see Russ v. Hawes, 5 Ired. Eq. 18 ; Dilly v. Heckrotte, 8 Gill & J. 171; Jackson's Assignees v. Cutright, 5 Munf. 314; Boone v. Chiles, 10 Peters 177 ; White v. Yaw, 7 Verm. 357 ; Crocker v. Higgins, 7 Conn. 342; Skinner v. Bailey, Id. 496; Hayward v. Carroll, 4 Har. & J. 518 ; Parker v. Carter, 4 Munf. 273; Miller v. Furse, 1 Bailey Eq. 187 ; Lingan v. Henderson, 1 Bland. 236; Townsend v. Duncan, 2 Id. 45 ; Anthony v. Leftwich, 3 Rand. 263; Morrison v. Hart, 2 Bibb 4 ; Lemaster v. Burckhart, Id. 26; Bank U. S. v. Schultz, 3 Hamm. 62 ; Lovell v. Farrington, 50 Maine 239 ; Camden, &c., R. R. v. Stewart, 4 Green (N. J.) 343.

equity, and may be followed by a charge of the specific details. If the evidence be not of the fact, but of an admission by the defendant, and especially if it be of a
• mere verbal admission, it is still more important to charge
[*305] it in the bill. But the mere fact that the *admission has not been specifically stated or charged does not render it inadmissible as evidence.($\textit{ff}$)[1]

4. For obtaining discovery as to matter of detail, which could not be conveniently introduced in the statement.

Charges of this class, like those of the preceding one, originate in the plaintiff's right to confine his statement to' the fact constituting the equity, and to omit the evidence by which it is proved; $e.\ g.$, to allege that the defendant had notice of his title, or encouraged him in his conduct, without stating the manner of notice, or of encouragement. And it may, as already observed, be in some cases convenient so to frame the statement.

A statement, however, of this general kind, although it would let in evidence in its support, and would warrant an interrogatory in general terms, $e.\ g.$, whether the defendant had not notice, or whether he did not encourage the plaintiff, would not warrant minute interrogatories tending to prove the fact, $e.\ g.$, whether he had not seen a particular deed, or had not employed a particular person. In order to render such interrogatories admissible, the plaintiff must insert specific allegations, by which their relevancy may be shown, and their propriety tested.[2]

($\textit{ff}$) Earle $v.$ Pickin, 1 R. & M. 547; McMahon $v.$ Burchell, 2 Ph. 127.

[1] Where a fact is put in issue in a bill, evidence of confessions, conversations, or admissions of the defendant, is receivable to prove the fact, although such confessions are not expressly charged in the bill as evidence of the fact: Smith $v.$ Burnham, 2 Sumner 612; Jenkins $v.$ Eldredge, 3 Story 183. See also, Trapnall $v.$ Byrd's Adm'r., 22 Ark. 10.

[2] A defect in the charging part of a bill cannot be supplied by a subse-

And it is not unusual to make such allegation by way of charge, so as to avoid encumbering the statement.

In bills where a discovery by the defendant is of importance, it is also usual to conclude by a charge that the defendant has or formerly had documents in his possession, which, if, produced, would show the truth of the plaintiff's case, and that he ought to give a schedule of them, and to produce them for inspection and proof.

From what has been said on the charges of a bill it will be obvious that they are in reality supplemental to the statement, and might have been included in the statement itself, but that for convenience sake they are subsequently *introduced, and are distinguished [*306] by a peculiar form of commencement. In fact, in many bills, where the circumstances of the case present no danger of intricacy, the whole of the allegations are comprised in the statement, and the charges are omitted.

The statement and charges of a bill include all its allegations, and no allegations ought in strictness to be inserted in them which are not material for some of the purposes pointed out, viz., either as establishing the plaintiff's case, rebutting that of the defendant, or obtaining discovery for one of these purposes. If any matter be alleged which is not material, whether as irrelevant in *toto* or as being matter of which the Court will take judicial notice, it is in strictness impertinent, and may be

---

quent interrogatory; and the interrogatories are to be construed by the charging part of the bill: Mechanics' Bank *v.* Levy, 3 Paige 606 ; Parker v. Carter, 4 Munf. 273 ; James *v.* McKernon, 6 Johns. 543 ; Woodcock *v.* Bennet, 1 Cowen 734. It is sufficient, however, if the interrogatory is founded upon a statement in the bill which is inserted therein as evidence merely, in support of the main charges : Mechanics' Bank *v.* Levy, supra

struck out of the bill on application to the Court.[1] And
if it be criminatory of the defendant or of any other
person, it is also objectionable on the ground of scandal.
But provided it be material, however harsh the charge
may be, it cannot be treated as scandalous. It should
also be observed that, even if the statement be material,
yet excessive prolixity will be impertinent; as, for instance, if instead of giving the effect of a document, a
plaintiff, without any sufficient motive, were to copy it at
length. But if he has a sufficient motive, as, if the precise language of the document be a matter of dispute, or
if it be desirable to elicit from the defendant an admission
of its contents, the objection will not apply.(g)[2]

In many of the older precedents we find an allegation

(g) Byde *v.* Masterman, 1 Cr. & Ph. 272; 1 Dan. C. P. 331–338; Orders
of 1845, 38–42.

---

[1] The court ought not at the commencement of the suit to treat as impertinent matter, that which at the hearing may be found to be relevant :
Reeves *v.* Baker, 13 Beav. 436.

[2] In determining whether an allegation or statement in a bill is relevant or pertinent, the bill must not only be regarded as a pleading to
bring before the court and put in issue the material allegations and charges
upon which the complainant's right to relief rests, but also as an examination of the defendant for the purpose of obtaining evidence to establish
the complainant's case, or to counter-prove or destroy the defence which
the defendant may attempt to set-up : Hawley *v.* Wolverton, 5 Paige 522.
A few unnecessary words in a bill do not render the pleading impertinent.
And the Master should not allow an exception on account of a few unnecessary words, except where they will lead to the introduction of improper
evidence, by putting in issue matters which are foreign to the cause : Ibid.
The bill should not set forth deeds or other documents *in hæc verba,* but
only so much thereof as is material to the point in question; and matter
of inference or argument is impertinent: Hood *v.* Inman, 4 Johns. Ch.
437. See also Woods *v.* Morrell, 1 Id. 103. Disparaging or abusive
words are not "scandalous" unless they are also impertinent: Henry *v.*
Henry, Phill. (N. C.) Eq. 334.

The proper remedy for verboseness is by motion to strike out: Williams
v. Sexton, 19 Wis. 42.

intervening between the statements and the charges, called the charge of confederacy. This is an allegation that the defendants are confederating with certain unknown parties to refuse justice to the plaintiff. And we find also another allegation following the charging part, called the averment of jurisdiction, which alleges that the plaintiff can only obtain his remedy in the Court of Chancery. The probability is *that these forms [*307] originated in the once doubtful state of the jurisdiction; at the present time they are unnecessary, and are fast falling into disuse.(h)[1]

The interrogatories are a series of questions intended to obtain discovery in aid of the plaintiff's case, and must be directed to facts previously stated or charged. They are prefaced by a prayer that the defendants may, if they can, show why the plaintiff should not be relieved, and may answer on oath such of the interrogatories afterwards numbered and set forth, as by a note at the end of the bill they are respectively required to answer. The numbered interrogatories follow, and at the foot of the bill a note is added, informing each defendant which of them he must answer.

The old bills in Chancery contained no special interrogatories, but merely required that the defendant should answer the bill, and he was bound without further questioning to answer the whole. The interrogatories were

(h) Mitf. on Plead. 40–41.

---

[1] By the rules in Chancery in many of the states, the confederacy and jurisdiction clauses are expressly made unnecessary : Rules U. S. Courts, No. xxi ; Penn. xvii. The confederacy clause is insufficient, even on demurrer, to avoid the effect of lapse of time ; as an allegation of fraud it is entirely inoperative and useless : Williams v. Presb. Soc., 1 Ohio St. N. S. 505.

39

afterwards added to prevent misapprehension or evasion, by inquiring not only as to the facts specifically alleged, but as to circumstances of possible variation, *e. g.*, not only whether the defendant had received a specified sum, which might perhaps be evaded by a bare denial, but "whether he or any, and what person by his order or for his use had received that sum, or any and what part thereof, or any and what sum." They were therefore at first merely supplemental, framed to prevent an evasive answer, but not exempting the defendant from answering the bill itself, and they were accordingly prefaced by the words " that the said defendant may answer the bill, and more especially that he may answer the interrogatories." This, however, was inconvenient in two respects: first, because it compelled trustees, and other persons who were affected by a portion of the bill only, to put in a long and expensive answer to the whole, or to select the material parts on their own responsibility; and secondly, because [*308] when special interrogatories had become *universal, defendants frequently did not look beyond them, and occasionally got into difficulty by leaving unanswered some statement or charge to which either accidentally or intentionally, the plaintiff had omitted to interrogate.[1]

---

[1] Where a defendant submits to answer at all, he is bound to admit or deny all the facts stated in the bill, with all material circumstances, though not specially interrogated for that purpose ; the general interrogatory in the bill " that the defendant may full answer make," &c., being sufficient: Methodist Church *v.* Jacques, 1 Johns. Ch. 65 ; Neale *v.* Hagthorp, 3 Bland 551 ; Hagthorp *v.* Hook, 1 Gill & J. 270 ; Tucker *v.* Cheshire R. R., 1 Fost. (N. II.) 29 ; Wootten *v.* Burch, 2 Md. Ch. 190 ; Ames *v.* King, 9 Allen (Mass.) 258. He is bound to answer as to his knowledge, or if he has no knowledge of the facts, then as to his information and belief: Bailey *v.* Wilson, 1 Dev. & Bat. Ch. 182, 187 ; Devereaux *v.* Cooper, 11 Verm. 103. But a defendant is not bound to answer an inter-

These objections are remedied by the present regulation, which exempts a defendant from answering any statement or charge unless specially interrogated thereto.$(i)^1$

The fourth part of the bill is the prayer for relief, or as it would be more correctly termed, the statement of relief required   The only portion of a bill which can be accurately called a prayer, is the concluding part or prayer of process, calling on the Court to issue the *subpœna.* After the statements and charges are completed, the bill does not go on to say, " your orator therefore prays that

(i) Woodroffe v. Daniel. 10 Sim. 243 ; 1 Dan. C. P. 347–360.

---

rogatory not warranted by some matter contained in a former part of the bill: Mechanics' Bank v. Lynn, 1 Peters 376 ; see also on this subject McDonald v. McDonald, 16 Verm. 630 ; Morris v. Parker, 3 Johns. Ch. 297 ; Smith v. Lasher, 5 Id. 247 ; Pettit v. Candler, 3 Wend. 618 ; Phillips v. Prevost, 4 Johns. Ch. 205 ; Cuyler v. Bogert, 3 Paige 186 ; Utica Insurance Co. v. Lynch, Id. 210 ; Davis v. Mapes, 2 Id. 105. Where suspicious circumstances, fraud, and collusion are charged in a bill, the defendant must expose not only his motives, but his secret designs, his "unuttered thoughts:" Mechanics' Bank v. Levy, 1 Edw. Ch. 316. Where a bill charges generally that certain deeds were fraudulent and void, and also propounds special interrogatories based upon some of the allegations only, the defendants have the right to answer all the allegations, whether specially interrogated or not : Glenn v. Grover, 3 Md. 212.

^{1} A similar rule exists in the United States Courts (xl.) : see Wilson v. Stolley, 4 McLean 272 ; and probably in some of the states ; though see *contra*, 7 Foster 440 ; Pitts v. Hooper, 16 Ga. 442. And the general rule that a defendant who submits to answer, must answer fully, is now so far modified, that he may protect himself by answer to to the same extent as he might by plea of discovery : Rule, xxxix. U. S. In Pennsylvania (Rule xxxix.) specific interrogatories are not included in the bill, but are filed separately.

Interrogatories for the examination of a plaintiff are on a different footing from those for the examination of a defendant in this respect, that a plaintiff is not entitled to discovery of the defendant's case, but a defendant may ask any questions tending to destroy the plaintiff's claim : Hoffman v. Postill, 4 Ch. App. L. R. 673. In other respects, the general rule applies, that he who is bound to answer must answer fully.

he may have such and such relief," but it says, " to the
end therefore that the defendant may answer the interrogatories, and that your orator may have the specified
relief, may it please your lordship to grant a writ of *subpœna,* requiring the defendant to appear by a certain day,
and to answer the bill, and abide the decree of the Court."
The only thing which the Court is asked to do, or which
can be called a prayer is, " to grant the writ." The obtaining an answer and subsequent relief are the reasons
why the writ is asked, but are not themselves the thing
asked for; and this view exactly coincides with the statement made in the outset of the present treatise, that the
writ of *subpœna* was that which from the first gave efficiency to the Court, and which, in all the opposing petitions, was the uniform subject of complaint. When the
writ of *subpœna* has issued, the defendant is obliged to
answer the interrogatories and to abide by any decree
which the Court may make; and the statement in the bill
as to the particular relief required is a mere guide in
framing the decree.

The old bills in Chancery did not contain any special
[*309] statement of relief, but only what is called the
*prayer for general relief, viz., " that your orator
may have such relief in the premises as the nature of
the case may require, and to your lordship shall seem
fit." It is said that such a prayer would still be sufficient; but the uniform practice is to insert a special
prayer, and to conclude with the prayer for general relief.

This latter prayer can never be safely omitted, because
if the plaintiff should in his special prayer mistake the
due relief, it may be given under the general prayer, if
consistent with that which is actually prayed.[1] If it be

---

[1] See Colton *v.* Ross, 2 Paige 396 ; Wilkin *v.* Wilkin, 1 Johns. Ch. 111 ;
Allen *v.* Coffman, 1 Bibb 469 ; Brown *v.* McDonald, 1 Hill's Ch. 302 ; Barr

inconsistent it cannot be obtained ;[1] and, therefore, if the
plaintiff doubt as to the proper relief, he may frame his

---

v. Haseldon, 10 Rich. Eq. 53; Kelly *v*. Paine, 18 Ala. 371; Thomas *v*. Ellmaker, 1 Pars. Eq. 99; Stone *v*. Anderson, 6 Foster 506. But the relief
to be given under a general prayer in a bill must be agreeable to the case
made by the bill, and not different from, or inconsistent with it : Chalmers
v. Chambers, 6 Har. & J. 29; Wilkin *v*. Wilkin, sup.; Franklin *v*. Osgood,
14 Johns. 527; English *v*. Foxall, 2 Peters 595; McCosker *v*. Brady, 1
Barb. Ch. 329; Smith *v*. Trenton Falls Co., 3 Green Ch. 505; Danforth *v*.
Smith, 23 Verm. 247; Hilleary *v*. Hurdle, 6 Gill 105; Dunnock *v*. Dunnock, 3 Md. Ch. 140; Hitch *v*. Davis. Id. 266; Land *v*. Cowan, 19 Ala.
297; Cawley *v*. Poole, 1 Hem. & M. 50. But under the general prayer,
any relief warranted by the case as set forth in the bill may be granted,
though not orally asked for : Lingan *v*. Henderson, 1 Bland 251; Mc-
Glothlin *v*. Hemery, 44 Mo. 350; Kirksey *v*. Means, 42 Ala. 426; Milten-
berger *v*. Morrison, 39 Mo. 71; Slemmer's Appeal, 58 Penn. St. 155
although such relief could be had at law : Bullock *v*. Adams, 20 N. J. Eq.
367.

[1] No relief can be granted under the general prayer, entirely distinct
from and independent of the special relief prayed : Thomason *v*. Smithson,
7 Porter 144; Foster *v*. Cook, 1 Hawks 509; Chalmers *v*. Chambers, 6 Har.
& J. 29; Sheppard *v*. Starke, 3 Munf. 29; Butler *v*. Durham, 2 Kelley 414;
Chapman *v*. Chapman, 13 Beav. 308; Dunnock *v*. Dunnock, 3 Md. Ch.
140; Thomas *v*. Ellmaker, 1 Pars. Eq. 99; Howell *v*. Sebring, 1 McCart.
84. Nor will the bill be amended so as to introduce a prayer for relief inconsistent with the original prayer : Thomas *v*. Ellmaker, ut supr.; Pen-
sacola R. R. *v*. Spratt, 12 Florida 26; sed vide Bailey *v*. Burton, 8 Wend.
339; wherein it is held that under the general prayer, the complainant
is entitled to any relief consistent with the case made, though inconsistent
with the specific relief prayed for. See Kelley *v*. Payne, 18 Ala. 371.

In bills of equity seeking relief, if any part of the relief sought be of an
equitable nature, the court will retain the bill for complete relief : Traip
v. Gould, 15 Maine 82. Relief can only be granted upon the facts alleged
in the bill : Maher *v*. Bull, 44 Ill. 97; Carmichael *v*. Reed, 45 Id. 108.

If a bill contains no prayer, either for specific or general relief, it is considered as a bill of discovery merely, although the word "decree" is erroneously inserted in the prayer for process of subpœna; but if the bill prays
any relief whatever against a defendant, who is made a party for the purpose of discovery only, such prayer makes it a bill for relief as well as discovery, as to such defendant, and authorizes him to put in an answer containing a full defence : McIntyre *v*. Union College, 6 Paige 239; see Smith

prayer in the alternative, to have either one relief or the other, as the Court shall decide.[1] In the case of charities and infants the proper directions will be given, without regarding the language of the prayer.(k)

The principal rules as to this portion of the bill, are that it should point out with reasonable clearness what relief is asked, that it should not combine distinct claims against the same defendant, and that it should not unite in the same suit several defendants, some of whom are unconnected with a great portion of the case. If the prayer is objectionable on either of the two latter grounds, the bill is termed multifarious.(l)

Multifariousness of the first kind, sometimes called a misjoinder of claim, is where the plaintiff has several

(k) Mitf. on Pleading 38, 39; 1 Dan. C. P. 360–366; Cruikshank v. McVicar, 8 Beav. 106, 110.

(l) 1 Dan. C. P. 320–331; [Story's Equity Pleading §§ 271–286.]

---

v. Smith, 4 Randolph 95. A bill for discovery which concludes with a prayer that such other order might be made upon the said defendant, as the nature of the case might require, is, nevertheless, a simple bill of discovery: Southeastern R. R. Co. v. Submarine Telegraph Co., 17 Jur. 1044.

[1] Upon the subject of bills framed with a double aspect, where the complainant is in doubt whether he is legally entitled to one kind of relief or another, upon the facts of the case as stated in the bill, see Strange v. Watson, 11 Ala. 324; Colton v. Ross, 2 Paige 396; Foster v. Cook, 1 Hawks 509; Lingan v. Henderson, 1 Bland Ch. 252; McConnell v. McConnell, 11 Verm. 290; Pensenneau v. Pensenneau, 22 Mo. 27. So also, where the complainant is entitled to relief of some kind against the defendants, upon the facts stated in his bill, if the nature or kind of relief to which he is entitled depends upon the existence of a fact of which he is ignorant, he may allege his ignorance of such fact, and may frame his prayer for relief in the alternative, so as to obtain the appropriate relief, according as the fact shall appear at the hearing of the cause: Lloyd v. Brewster, 4 Paige 537; McCosker v. Brady, 1 Barb. Ch. 329; see also, Durling v. Hammar, 20 N. J. (Eq.) 220.

distinct claims against the same defendant, and prays
relief in a single suit in respect to all,[1] *e. g.*, if a corpora-

---

[1] It is extremely difficult, if not impracticable, to lay down any géneral
rule on the subject of multifariousness. The Court will be governed by
considerations of convenience in particular circumstances : Dunn *v.* Cooper,
3 Md. Ch. 46. The objection is discouraged where it might defeat the ends
of justice : Marshal *v.* Means, 12 Ga. 61. A Court of Chancery allows
distinct and separate causes of complaint between the same parties to be
joined in one suit, unless it is apparent that the defence will be seriously
embarrassed by confounding different issues and proofs in the litigation :
Nourse *v.* Allen, 4 Blatchf. C. C. 376. A bill is multifarious, as the term
is generally understood, where there is a misjoinder of distinct and independent causes of action : Gardiner, J., in Brady *v.* McCosker, 1 Comst.
221 ; Carmichael *v.* Browder, 3 How. (Miss.) 252 ; Savage *v.* Benham, 17
Ala. 119 ; McIntosh *v.* Alexander, 16 Ala. 87 ; Boyd *v.* Hoyt, 5 Paige 65 ;
Marshal *v.* Means, 12 Ga. 61 ; and see Cauley *v.* Lawson, 5 Jones Eq. 132 ;
Allen *v.* Miller, 4 Id. 146 ; Tomlinson *v.* Claywell, Id. 317 ; Hughes *v.*
Cook, 34 Beav. 407 ; Bent *v.* Yardley, 2 Hem. & M. 602 ; Bouck *v.* Bouck,
L. R. 2 Eq. 19. Charging two *sources* of right by a plaintiff renders a bill
multifarious : Cumberland Valley R. R. Appeal, 62 Penn. St. 218. Unconnected demands against different estates cannot be united in the same
bill, though the defendant is the executor in both : Daniel et al. *v.* Morrison's Ex'r., 6 Dana 186. So a bill for an account against two distinct partnerships, though one of the defendants is a partner in both, is
multifarious : Griffin *v.* Morrell, 10 Md. 364. So a bill combining individual claims with claims in a representative capacity : Carter *v.* Treadwell,
3 Story 25 ; Bryan *v.* Blythe et al., 4 Blackf. 249 ; Davoue *v.* Fanning, 4
Johns. Ch. 199 ; Latting *v.* Latting, 4 Sandf. Ch. 31 ; May *v.* Smith, 1
Busbee Eq. 196. But a bill filed by one executor of two estates for directions, &c., where the affairs of the estates are so blended that it is necessary
to proceed under both bills at once, will not be multifarious : Carter *v.*
Balfour, 19 Ala. 814.

Where, in addition to the charge of adultery, a bill charges the husband
with cruel treatment, which renders it unsafe for the complainant, the wife,
to cohabit with him, and the bill is so framed as to entitle her to a decree
of separation, if she fails to establish the adultery charged in the bill, such
bill is multifarious : Rose *v.* Rose, 11 Paige 166 ; Johnson *v.* Johnson, 6
Johns. Ch. 163 ; Mulock *v.* Mulock, 1 Edw. Ch. 14 ; Pomeroy *v.* Pomeroy,
1 Johns. Ch. 606. But where a wife files a bill for divorce against her
husband, on the ground of adultery, containing a prayer for relief which
is adapted only to a charge of adultery, the bill is not rendered multifarious by the insertion therein of charges of unkind treatment or cruel

tion were to hold one estate for public purposes, and another for private charity, and a bill were filed on account of both.   In this case the objection is that the defendant would be compellable to unite unconnected matters in his answer and defence, and thus the proofs applicable to each would be liable to confusion; delays might be occasioned by waiting *for the one when the other was ripe [*310] for hearing, and different decrees and proceedings might ultimately be required.   The Court, therefore, on the ground of convenience, will not permit such a joinder. But the rule, being one of convenience, only, is not absolutely binding, and may be dispensed with if the claims

---

usage: Beach v. Beach, 11 Paige 161. A petition, containing in the same count a prayer for equitable relief and also a prayer for rents and profits and for possession of the premises, is bad for misjoinder: Young v. Coleman, 43 Mo. 179. A bill in equity, alleging that the defendant obtained a policy of insurance from the company by fraud, and praying that a commission may issue for the examination of witnesses, and that the policy may be surrendered to be cancelled, and for other relief, is not multifarious: Commercial Ins. Co. v. McLoon, 14 Allen (Mass.) 351

A bill is not multifarious where it sets up one substantial ground of relief, and also another on which no relief can be had or is asked: Pleasants v. Glasscock, 1 Sm. & M. Ch. 17; Varick v. Smith, 5 Paige 137; Mayne v. Griswold, 3 Sandf. S. C. 4 ¼4; Carpenter v. Hall, 18 Ala. 439; McCabe v. Bellows, 1 Allen 269; Richards v. Pierce, 52 Maine 562. So of a bill brought by several persons claiming under a common title, but in different shares and proportions: Shields v. Thomas, 18 How. (U. S.) 253.

Where there is a joinder of a legal and an equitable claim, and a prayer for relief as to both, the bill is not multifarious: Varick v. Smith, 5 Paige 137; Carpenter v. Hall, 18 Ala. 439.

To authorize the dismissal of a bill on final hearing on account of a misjoinder of complaints, it must be of such whose interests are so diverse that they cannot be included in one decree, or at least must differ so widely as to affect the propriety of the decree: Michan v. Wyatt, 21 Ala. 813. In a bill the various matters charged are like counts in a declaration, which, if all good, although variant in their contents, but not misjoinders, a judgment on either will be sustained: Cumberland Valley R. R. Appeal, 62 Penn. St. 218.

be so far connected that a single suit is more convenient. (m)[1]
A converse principle restrains the plaintiff from unduly
splitting up a cause of suit, *e. g.*, by filing a bill for part
of an account without seeking to have the whole taken, or
to have the present profits of a partnership ascertained
and distributed whilst contemplating the continuance of
the partnership business. (n)

Multifariousness of the second kind is where a plaintiff, having a valid claim against one defendant, joins
another person as defendant in the same suit, with a
large part of which he is unconnected,[2] *e. g.*, if a bill

(m) Shackell *v.* Macaulay, 2 S. & S. 79 ; Attorney-General *v.* Goldsmiths'
Company, 5 Sim. 670 ; Attorney-General *v.* Merchant Tailors' Company, 1
M. & K. 189 ; Campbell *v.* Mackay, 1 M. & C. 603, 618 ; 1 Dan. C. P.
326–329.

(n) Mitf. on Pleading 183 ; 1 Dan. C. P. 316–319.

---

[1] See Hinton *v.* Cole, 3 Humph. 656 ; Whitney *v.* Whitney, 5 Dana 327 ;
Lynch *v.* Johnson, 2 Litt. 98 ; Halbert *v.* Grant, 4 Monr. 580 ; Hart *v.*
McKeen, Walk. Ch. 417 ; Carroll *v.* Roosevelt, 4 Edw. Ch. 211 ; Dunn *v.*
Cooper, 3 Md. Ch. 46 ; Nourse *v.* A len, 4 Blatch. C. C. 376. A bill framed
with a twofold aspect, either for a specific delivery of the property, or an
enforcement of a supposed lien, is not multifarious : Murphy *v.* Clark, 1
Sm. & M. 221 ; Baines *v.* McGee, Id. 208.

[2] There is no general rule by which to determine whether a bill is, in
this second sense, multifarious or not ; but it must be left to the discretion
of the court under the circumstances of the case : Oliver *v.* Piatt, 3 How.
U. S. 333, 411 ; Gaines *v.* Chew, 2 Id. 619 ; Marshall *v.* Means, 12 Ga. 61 ;
Butler *v.* Spann, 27 Miss. 234 ; Fleming *v.* Gilmer, 35 Ala. 62 ; Bowers *v.*
Keesecher, 9 Iowa 422 ; Fogg *v.* Rogers, 2 Cold. (Tenn.) 290.

Multifariousness, properly speaking, is where different matters, having
no connection with each other, are joined in a bill against several defendants, a part of whom have no interest in, or connection with, some of the
distinct matters for which the suit is brought ; so that such defendants are
put to the unnecessary trouble and expense of answering and litigating
matters stated in the bill, in which they are not interested, and with which
they have no connection : Newland *v.* Rogers, 3 Barb. Ch. 432 ; Ryan *v.*
Shawneytown, 14 Ill. 20.

See in illustration of this statement, Stuart's Heirs *v.* Coalter, 4 Rand.
74 ; Coe *v.* Turner, 5 Conn. 86 ; Boyd *v.* Hoyt, 5 Paige 65 ; Swift *v.* Eck_

were to be brought by one tenant in common against another for a partition, and also against a third person to set aside a lease from the plaintiff. It is obvious that the second tenant in common is only concerned with the partition, and ought not to be involved in ligitation about the lease; and he might object to the two matters being united, as putting him to unnecessary expense. But in this case, as in the preceding one, if the nature of the transactions make a single suit convenient, the objection will not be sustained.(o)[1]

(o) Whaley v. Dawson, 2 Sch. & L. 367; Salvidge v. Hyde, Jac. 151; Attorney-General v. Merchant Tailors' Company, 1 M. & K. 189; Campbell v. Mackey, 1 M. & C. 603, 620; Sheehy v. Muskerry, 7 Cl. & F. 1; Mitf. 181; Attorney-General v. Cradock, 3 M. & C. 85; Attorney-General v. Corporation of Poole, 4 Id. 17–31; Parr v. Attorney-General, 8 Cl. & F. 409; 1 Dan. C. P. 320–326.

---

ford, 6 Id. 22; Jackson v. Forrest, 2 Barb. Ch. 566; Morton v. Weil, 33 Id. 30; Silcox v. Nelson, 1 Geo. Decis. 24; Johnson v. Brown, 2 Humph. 327; Bruton v. Rutland, 3 Id. 435; Hickman v. Cooke, Id. 640; Clamorgan v. Guisse, 1 Miss. 141; Ingersoll v. Kirby, Walk. Ch. 65; Nail v. Mobley, 9 Ga. 278; Felder v. Davis, 17 Ala. 418; Ayers v. Wright, 8 Ired. Eq. 229; Hammond v. Michigan State Bank, Walk. Ch. 214; New England Bank v. The Newport Steam Factory Co., 6 R. I. 154; Williams v. Neel, 10 Rich. Eq. 338; Hunton v. Platt, 11 Mich. 264; Brinkerhoff v. Brown, 6 Johns. Ch. 139; Metcalf v. Cady, 8 Allen 587; Waller v. Taylor, 42 Ala. 297; Kennebec, &c., R. R. v. Portland, &c., R. R., 54 Maine 173; Wilson v. Castro, 31 Cal. 420.

[1] Where the interests of different parties are so complicated in different transactions, that entire justice could not be conveniently done without uniting the whole, the bill is not multifarious: Oliver v. Piatt, 3 How. U. S. 411. The objection of multifariousness is confined to cases where the cause of each defendant is entirely distinct and separate in its subject-matter from that of his co-defendants: Kennedy v. Kennedy, 2 Ala. 571. A bill against the executors of an estate, and all those who purchased from them, is not upon that account alone multifarious: Gaines v. Chew, 2 How. U. S. 619; Patterson v. Gaines, 6 Id. 582; so a bill against the personal representatives and heirs of a party to a contract, for an account by the former under it, and specific execution of it by the latter, is not demurrable: Cocke v. Evans, 9 Yerg. 287. A bill is not multifarious, where one general

The fifth and last part of a bill is the prayer of process, which asks that a writ of subpœna may issue, di-

---

right is claimed by the plaintiff, although the defendants may have separate and distinct rights : Dimmock v. Bixby, 20 Pick. 368 ; Bugbee v. Sargent, 23 Maine 269 ; Curtis v. Tyler, 9 Paige 432 ; Bell v. Woodward, 42 N. H. 190 ; Chase v. Searles, 45 Id. 511 ; Tucker v. Tucker, 29 Mo. 355 ; and see Walsham v. Stainton, 1 De G., J. & Sm. 678 ; Kunkell v. Markell, 26 Md. 390. Nor because the bill states more than one ground in support of the same claim : Barnett v. Woods, 2 Jones. Eq. 198. A bill is not multifarious which avers that the complainants are several owners of different parcels of goods which have been obtained from them by fraud through distinct and separate transactions, by a person who has pledged them to secure an advance, if the bill offers to restore the advance : Coleman v. Barnes, 5 Allen 374. To render a bill multifarious, it must contain not only separate and distinct matters, but such that each entitles the complainant to separate equitable relief. It is not so, if it be single as to the subject-matter and object thereof, and the relief sought, if all the defendants are connected, though differently, with the whole subject of dispute : Watson v. Cox, 1 Ired. Eq. 389 ; Wheeler v. Clinton Can. Bank, Harring. Ch. 449 ; Cornwell v. Lee, 14 Conn. 524 ; Robertson v. Stevens 1 Ired. Eq. 247 ; Parish v. Sloan, 3 Id. 607 ; Wilcox v. Mills, 1 S. & M. Ch. 85 ; Donelson's Adm'rs. v. Posey, 13 Ala. 752 ; Heirs of Holman v. Bank of Norfolk, 12 Id. 369 ; Worthy v. Johnson, 8 Ga. 238 ; Larkins v. Biddle, 11 Ala. 252 ; Martin v. Martin, 13 Mo. 36 ; Booth v. Stamper, 10 Ga. 109 ; Foss v. Haynes, 31 Maine 81 ; Doub v. Barnes, 1 Md. Ch. 127 ; White v. Hall, 27 Miss. 419.

Praying relief against some of the defendants in a suit, as to whom the complainant is not entitled to relief, but to a discovery merely, does not render a bill multifarious : Many v. Beekman Iron Co., 9 Paige 188. Where a bill is filed against the representatives of a deceased partner, to obtain satisfaction of a copartnership debt out of the estate of the decedent, the joining of the surviving partner, who is insolvent, with them, as a defendant, does not render the bill multifarious : Butts v. Genung, 5 Paige 254 ; see also, Wells v. Strange, 5 Ga. 22.

The proper form in which to object to a bill for multifariousness is by demurrer ; the filing an answer and going into the testimony as to the merits, is a waiver of the objection, and it cannot be made on appeal, after a decree *pro confesso* below : Gibbs v. Çlagett, 2 Gill & J. 14 ; Grove v. Fresh, 9 Id. 280 ; Bryan v. Blythe et al., 4 Blackf. 249 ; Avery v. Kellogg, 11 Conn. 562 ; Wellborn v. Tiller, 10 Ala. 305 ; Luckett v. White, 10 Gill & J. 480 ; Abraham v. Plestoro, 3 Wend. 538, 547 ; Thurman v. Shelton, 10 Yerg. 383 ; Buffalow v. Buffalow, 2 Ired. Eq. 113 ; Betts v. Betts, 18

rected to the parties named as defendants, and req
[*311] them to *appear and answer the bill, a
abide by the decree when made. If a w
wanted besides the subpœna, *e. g.*, a writ of injunct
ne exeat regno, such additional writ is asked in the p
of process. In bills for discovery, or to perpetuate
mony, the words "to abide by the decree" are om
as well as the prayer for relief; but if the bill be fc
covery in aid of a defence at law, it asks an inju
against proceeding at law until the discovery sh
made. If a peer or lord of Parliament is a defend
is customary, as a mark of courtesy, that instead
subpœna being issued, he should be informed of t
by a letter missive from the Lord Chancellor, and s
be requested to appear and answer. The same cou
is extended to a peeress, and to a Scotch or Irish
though not a lord of Parliament. And it is the
usual, in the prayer of process, to ask a letter m
and on neglect thereof, a writ of subpœna. If th
torney-General is a defendant in his official capacit
bill prays no subpœna, but simply that he being att
with a copy may appear and answer.(*p*)   In certain

(*p*) I Dan. C. P. 368–371.

Ala. 787; Mobile, &c., R. R. *v.* Talman, 15 Id. 472; Swayze *v.* Sw
Stockt. 273. The objection of multifariousness, however, is one
may be taken on the hearing; and, indeed, may then be made
jure by the court; but see Persch *v.* Quiggle, 57 Penn. St. 247. B
not necessarily fatal, when thus interposed, and its allowance rest
discretion of the court: Story Eq. Plead., s. 284, a; Sims. *v.* Aug
Strob. Eq. 104; Felder *v.* Davis, 17 Ala. 425; Oliver *v.* Piatt, 3 H
S. 333.

A demurrer for multifariousness goes to the whole suit, and if su
the bill should be dismissed, and not retained for partial relief: M
v. Alexander, 16 Ala. 87; Boyd *v.* Hoyt, 5 Paige 65; Gibbs *v.* Cla
Gill & J. 14; Dunn *v.* Cooper, 3 Md. Ch. 46.

also, where parties are joined as nominal defendants, against whom no direct relief is prayed, so that their appearance in the suit would be a needless expense, the prayer of process may be modified by omitting to sue a writ against them, and by asking instead, that they, being served with a copy of the bill, may be bound by the proceeding in the cause.(q) The prayer of process is generally expressed in drafts by the words, "May it please," &c., and a direction is added, in the margin, as to the parties to be included in it. The prayer itself is added in engrossing the bill; and it is followed by a note, specifying the interrogatories which each defendant is respectively required to answer.[1] '

(q) 1 Dan. C. P. 405–408.

---

[1] In Wright v. Wright, 4 Halst. Ch. 143, a bill which contained no prayer of process, and was not signed by counsel, was held demurrable. In Grove v. Potter, 4 Sandf. Ch. 403, however, the want of signature of counsel, was held to be ground for a motion to take a bill off of file, but not for demurrer.

The illegibility of a bill is not ground for demurrer: Downer v. Staine, 4 Wisc. 372.

[*312]   *CHAPTER II.

OF PARTIES.

THE persons against whom process is asked are t
fendants to the bill, and should consist of all pers⟨
terested in the relief sought, who are not already
as plaintiffs[1] If no relief be sought, viz., if the
for discovery alone, it cannot be objected to for w
parties;[2] but if relief be asked, the prayer of p
must be so framed as to bring all persons interest
that relief before the Court, either as plaintiffs
defendants.[3]

---

[1] They are only parties defendant in a bill of Chancery, against
process is prayed, or who are specifically named and described as ⟨
ants: Verplanck v. Merc. Ins. Co. of N. Y., 2 Paige 438; Elmen
Delancy, Hopkins 555; Lucas v. Bank of Darien, 2 Stew. 280; G
McKinney, 6 J. J. Marsh. 193; Carey v. Hillhouse, 5 Ga. 251. P
that the "heirs" may be made defendants, without taking out]
against them or naming them in the bill, is not making them defen
Huston v. McClarty's Heirs, 3 Litt. 274; Moore v. Anderson, 1 Ir⟨
411. The process alone, and the return upon it, govern the ques
who are parties, if there is not a special entry showing the appear⟨
some one not served with process: De Wolf v. Mallett, 3 Dana 21
to making absent parties defendants by publication, see Young v.
Dana 306; Letcher v. Schroder, 5 J. J. Marsh. 513. There must
vice of process, actual or constructive: Estill v. Clay, 2 A. K. Mars
[2] Trescott v. Smyth, 1 McCord's Ch. 301, 303.
[3] See, on the general subject, Mechanics' Bank v. Seton, 1 Peter
Story v. Livingstone, 13 Id. 359; Hussey v. Dole, 24 Maine 20; McC
v. McConnell, 11 Verm. 290; Noyes v. Sawyer, 3 Id. 160; Crooker

In both these points the rule of equity differs from the rule of law, both in the necessity of joining all interested parties in the suit, and in the option of joining them as plaintiffs or defendants. At law, a disputed issue is alone contested; the immediate disputants alone are bound by the decision; and they alone are the proper parties to the action. In equity, a decree is asked, and not a decision only; and it is therefore requisite that all persons should be before the Court, whose interest may be affected by the proposed decree, or whose concurrence is necessary to a complete arrangement. The same reason which requires that the immediate disputants be the only parties at law, also requires their arrangement as parties plaintiff and defendant, so that all the plaintiffs shall support one side, and all the defendants the other side of the question in *issue. In equity, it is only requisite that the [*313] interests of the plaintiffs be consistent, and it is immaterial that the defendants are in conflict with each

gins, 7 Conn. 342; New London Bk. *v.* Lee, 11 Id. 112; Hawley *v.* Cramer, 4 Cowen 717; Oliver *v.* Palmer, 11 Gill & J. 426; Clark *v.* Long, 4 Rand. 451; Vann *v.* Hargett, 2 Dev. & Bat. Ch. 31; Frazer *v.* Legare, 1 Bailey Ch. 389; Lucas *v.* Bank of Darien, 2 Stew. 280; Park *v.* Ballentine, 6 Blackf. 223; De La Vergne *v.* Evertson, 1 Paige 181; West *v.* Randall, 2 Mass. 181; Caldwell *v.* Taggart, 4 Peters 190; Duncan *v.* Mizner, 4 J. J. Marsh. 447; Wendell *v.* Van Rensselaer, 1 Johns. Ch. 340; Wilson *v.* Hamilton, 9 Johns. 442; Key *v.* Lambert, 1 Hen. & Munf. 330; Burhans *v.* Burhans, 2 Barb. Ch. 398; Boughton *v.* Allen, 11 Paige 321; Carey *v.* Hoxey, 11 Ga. 645; Bailey *v.* Myrick, 36 Maine 50; Whitney *v.* Mayo, 15 Ill. 251; Society for Propagation of the Gospel *v.* Hartland, 2 Paine C. C. 536; Hall *v.* Hall, 11 Texas 526; Geisse *v.* Beall, 3 Wis. 367; Batchelder *v.* Wendell, 36 N. H. 204; Burnham *v.* Kempton, 37 Id. 485; Pence *v.* Pence, 2 Beas. 257; Daily *v.* Litchfield, 10 Mich. 29; Lovejoy *v.* Irelan, 17 Md. 525. All persons having the same interest should stand on the same side of the suit; but if any such refuse to appear as plaintiffs, they may be made defendants, their refusal being stated in the bill: Contee *v.* Dawson, 2 Bland. 264, 292; Whitney *v.* Mayo, 15 Ill. 251.

other, or that some of their claims are identical with those of the plaintiffs. It should, however, be observed, that although a conflict of interests among the defendants is no objection to a bill, yet it does not follow that the Court will adjudicate on their conflicting claims. It will do so if the decision be necessary to the plaintiff's right, *e. g.*, if a bill be filed by a second mortgagee against the mortgagor and a prior mortgagee, praying to redeem the first mortgage, and that the mortgagor may then redeem both or stand foreclosed. In this case, it is obvious, that before relief can be given, the validity and amount of the first mortgage must be determined, not only as between the plaintiff and the defendants, but as between the co-defendants themselves. If there be no necessity arising out of the plaintiff's claim, the Court will not adjudicate between co-defendants.(*a*)

If the suit be against a married woman, her husband must be joined as a party, unless he is an exile or has adjured the realm.[1] If it be against an idiot or lunatic,

(*a*) Farquharson *v.* Seton, 5 Russ. 45; Cottingham *v.* Shrewsbury, 3 Hare 627; Sandford *v.* Morrice, 11 Cl. & F. 667; Mitf. 81.

---

[1] And although he is a certified bankrupt, he should be joined as a party: Hamlin *v.* Bridge, 24 Maine 145; Smith *v.* Etches, 1 Hem. & M. 558. So, in a suit by a husband upon an interest in right of the wife, the wife must be a party: Schuyler *v.* Hoyle, 5 Johns. Ch. 196; Griffith *v.* Coleman, 5 J. J. Marsh. 600; Ringo *v.* Warder, 6 B. Monr. 514; Booth *v.* Albertson, 2 Barb. Ch. 313; Johns *v.* Reardon, 3 Md. Ch. 57; Flowerton *v.* Wimbish, 2 Jones Eq. 328. See Smith *v.* Pincombe, 3 Macn. & G. 653.

Where a bill is in the name of husband and wife, yet only concerns her separate estate, and no relief is asked for or against the husband, but is only to establish her rights and protect her interests, he will be regarded by the court as her next friend or trustee: Michan *v.* Wyatt, 21 Ala. 813; Boykin *v.* Ciples, 2 Hill Eq. 200; Stuart *v.* Kissam, 2 Barb. S. C. 492; Berry *v.* Williamson, 11 B. Monr. 245; Bein *v.* Heath, 6 How. U. S. 228. "In practice where the suit is brought by the wife for her separate property, the husband is sometimes made co-plaintiff. But this practice is

the committee of his estate must be joined.(*b*) If the superintendence of a public trust is involved, the Attorney-General must be a party on behalf of the Crown. And it is generally considered that the same course may be pursued where the rights of the Crown are incidentally concerned.[1] If, however, the Crown is in possession, or if a title is vested in it which the suit seeks to divest or affect, or if its rights are the immediate and sole object of the suit, the application must be to the Crown by petition of right. A Queen consort has the same prerogative. A foreign Sovereign also, whether residing within the Brish dominions or not, is ordinarily exempt from the jurisdiction. But he is competent to sue as plaintiff; and if he does so, he submits himself to the jurisdiction in re-

(*b*) Mitf. on Plead. 30; 1 Dan. Ch. P. 160–170. [See Sturge *v.* Longworth, 1 Ohio N. S. 544.]

---

incorrect; and in all such cases she ought to sue as sole plaintiff by her next friend, and the husband should be made a party defendant; for he may contest that it is her separate property, and the claim may be incompatible with his marital rights:" Story's Equity Pleading, ¿ 63 ; Johnson *v.* Vail, 1 McCart. 423 ; Daniel's Ch. Prac. 105 ; see also Michan *v.* Wyatt, 21 Ala. 823 ; Barham *v.* Gregory, Phill. (N. C.) Eq. 243. But in Smith *v.* Etches, 1 Hem. & M. 558, it is said that the husband ought to be joined as *co-plaintiff;* and see Hope *v.* Fox, 1 John. & H. 456. A person cannot be made a defendant in the action upon his own application : Drake *v.* Goodridge, 6 Blatchf. 151.

[1] In a suit to enforce a contract made by the agent of the Auburn State Prison for the labor of the convicts, it seems that the Attorney-General should be made a party : Jones *v.* Lynds, 7 Paige 305 ; see, also, Garr *v.* Bright, 1 Barb. Ch. 157, 164 ; Harvard College *v.* Society for Promoting Theological Education, 3 Gray 280. The interest of a tax payer, where money is to be raised by taxation, or expended from the treasury, is sufficient to enable him to proceed in equity to test the validity of the law which proposes the assessment or expenditure : Page *v.* Allen, 58 Penn. St. 338.

40

[*314] spect of the *matter sued for, and must ans on oath to a cross-bill. $(c)^1$

If a bill be filed either by or against uninteres parties, their joinder is sometimes spoken of as a f in pleading, but it seems more correct to say that, to extent of such misjoinder, there is a failure on the mei and the suit will be dismissed accordingly.[2] The o exception to this rule is in suits against a corporation

(c) Mitf. on Plead. 30; 1 Dan. Ch. P. 138–140; Duke of Brunswi‹ King of Hanover, 6 Beav. 1.

---

[1] See United States v. Wagner, L. R. 2 Ch. Ap. 582; Prioleau v. United States, L. R. 2 Eq. 659; ante, page 2, note 1.

[2] The general rule is that an objection for nonjoinder or misjoind parties ought to be made by demurrer: Bartlett v. Boyd, 34 Verm. but see Case v. Carroll, 35 N. Y. 385, plea or answer. If taken on hearing, it is discretionary with the Court to allow it. After hearing decree, it is too late to object: Bunnell v. Read, 21 Conn. 586; Hunl‹ Hunley, 15 Ala. 91; McMaken v. McMaken, 18 Id. 576; Woodwai Wood, 19 Id. 213; Gilbert v. Sutliff, 3 Ohio (N. S.) 129. In the case,] ever, of the omission of indispensable parties, or when a complete valid decree cannot be made, or the rights of absent parties woul‹ affected, the objection may be taken on the hearing by the Court itse‹ mero motu, or for the first time, on appeal: McMaken v. McMakeɪ Ala. 576; Gould v. Hayes, 19 Id. 438; Woodward v. Wood, Id. 213; C man v. Hamilton, Id. 121. A demurrer for want of parties should ɪ out the proper parties: Chapman v. Hamilton, 19 Ala. 121; Caldwe Blackwood, 1 Jones Eq. 274; Hightower v. Mustian, 8 Ga. 506. On murrer, the bill is not dismissed, but the complainant is at libert amend, except where proper parties cannot be made; Hightower v.] tian, ut supra; Smith v. Kornegay, 1 Jones Eq. 40. See, as to the n of proceeding, where objection is taken by answer, Rules in Equity, l Courts, No. lii.; Penna., No. xxvii.

Where a complainant amends according to the suggestions of the swer, by the addition of parties, he cannot afterwards allege them t unnecessary, in order to dispense with a want of service on them : Mo v. Bannister, 1 Drew. 514. But he will not be justified in making a pe a party merely, because the defendants insist that he ought to be ma party ; and as to the person so joined the bill will be dismissed with cc Williams v. Page, 24 Beav. 654.

'which their clerk or other officer may be made a defendant, though unaffected by the relief sought, in order that he may give discovery on oath, which the corporate body cannot do. (d)[1] If the bill be for discovery alone, in aid of proceedings at law, no person can be made a defendant who is not a party to the record at law. (e)

With respect to the nature of the interest which requires a person to be joined in a suit, there is, of course, no difficulty as to persons against whom relief is expressly asked. But with respect to those who are incidentally connected with the relief asked against others, the line of demarcation is less easy to draw. The interests, however, which require such joinder, seem generally referable to one of the three following heads: first, interests in the subject-matter which the decree may affect, and for the protection of which the owners are joined; secondly, concurrent claims with the plaintiff, which if not bound by the decree, may be afterwards litigated; and thirdly, liability to exonerate the defendant or to contribute with him to the plaintiff's claim.

(d) Glasscott v. Copperminers' Company, 11 Sim. 305.
(e) Kerr v. Rew, 5 M. & C. 154.

[1] The case of officers or agents of a corporation, is an exception to the rule that a person who has no interest in the subject-matter, and who is a mere witness, cannot be made a defendant in a bill in Chancery. See Ayers v. Wright, 8 Ired. Eq. 229; Yates v. Monroe, 13 Ill. 212. But they can only be made parties for discovery, where relief is sought against the corporation, and not where the whole relief claimed is against persons other than the corporation: Many v. Beekman Iron Co., 9 Paige 188. The United States of America can sue in that name in the English Chancery, without putting forward any public officer who could be called on to give discovery on a cross-bill: U. S. of A. v. Wagner, L. R. 2 Ch. 582; but the Court may stay proceedings till this is done: Id.

Where there is charge of fraud in a transaction, in which an agent participated, and it is so charged in the bill, he may be made a party, and subjected to the costs of suit, even if no other decree be made against him: Gartland v. Nunn, 6 Eng. (Ark.) 721.

The nature of the interest comprised under each of these definitions will be best explained and illustrated by examples; but the question, whether the interest which in each particular case an individual may possess is or is not within the scope of the suit, is one of law rather than of pleading, and cannot properly be here considered. (f)

[*315]   *1. The joinder of parties for protection of their own interests may be illustrated by the case of suits for dealing with property, to which several persons are entitled as co-owners,[1] or as tenants for life and in remainder, or as having charges on the estate. In all these cases, if the object proposed is not confined to any particular interest, but affects the *corpus* of the estate, all such persons ought to be parties. (g)   But if their interests be prior or paramount to the objects of the bill, so that they will not be affected by the decree, such interests will make their joinder requisite; *e. g.*, the interest of a mortgagee on a bill respecting the equity of redemption, or the interest of an encumbrancer or other prior and adverse claimant not privy to the contract, on a bill for specific performance. (h)[2]

(f) 1 Dan. Ch. P. ch. 5.

(g) Brookes *v.* Burt, 1 Beav. 106; [Townend *v.* Toker, L. R. 1 Ch. 446.]

(h) Devonsher *v.* Newenham, 2 Sch. & L. 199, 210; Lewis *v.* Zouche, 2 Sim. 388; Tasker *v.* Small, 3 M. & C. 63; [De Hoghton *v.* Money, L. R. 2 Ch. Ap. 164; West Midland R. R. Co. *v.* Nixon, 1 Hem. & M. 176;] Nelthorpe *v.* Holgate, 1 Coll. 203.

---

[1] Every party interested in land belonging to co-tenants is a necessary party to a bill for partition: Borah *v.* Archers, 7 Dana 176; Newman *v.* Kendall, 2 A. K. Marsh. 234; Pope *v.* Melone, Id. 239. So of tenants in common of chattels: Ramey *v.* Green, 18 Ala. 771.

To a bill filed by an heir to avoid the deed of the ancestor, all the heirs should be made parties: Young *v.* Bilderback, 2 Green Ch. 206. A bill in equity to enforce the specific performance of a contract, made by a deceased person, for the sale of land, must include his heirs as parties defendant: Moore *v.* Murrah, 40 Ala. 573

[2] To a bill for foreclosure and sale of mortgaged premises, all encum-

The joinder of parties for protection of their own interests is usually brought in question where such interests are concurrent with that of the plaintiff, for if they are concurrent with that of the defendant, the necessity of joining their owners is generally made apparent by the introduction of a prayer for direct relief.

brancers, or persons having an interest existing at the commencement of the suit, subsequent as well as prior in date to the plaintiff's mortgage, must be made parties, otherwise they will not be bound by the decree: Haines v. Beach, 3 Johns. Ch. 459; Ensworth v. Lambert, 4 Id. 605; Porter v. Clements, 3 Ark. 364; Huggins v. Hall, 10 Ala. 283. Those becoming encumbrancers *pendente lite* on a mortgage are not necessary parties to a bill to foreclose: Youngman v. Elmira & W. R. R., 65 Penn. St. 278. Though a junior mortgagee may be a necessary party, if known to the senior mortgagee, in his suit for a foreclosure and sale, it does not follow, it is said, that if he be not known, and a decree of foreclosure and sale be made, that an innocent purchaser should be deprived of the benefit of his purchase: Bank of the U. S. v. Carroll, 4 B. Monr. 40.

The mortgagees who are vested with the legal title are necessary parties to a bill to redeem. So, if a special authority be vested in one or more of the mortgagees for the benefit of the whole, all must be joined. If the mortgagee be only a trustee, his *cestui que trust* must be joined: Woodward v. Wood, 19 Ala. 213; but see the New Jersey Franklinite Co. v. Ames, 1 Beas. 509. In some cases it has been a question how far a prior encumbrancer is a necessary party: see Finley v. Bank U. S., 11 Wheat. 306; Post v. Mackall, 3 Bland 495; Wakeman v. Grover, 4 Paige 23; Cocron v. Middleton, 19 How. 113; Johnson v. Brown, 11 Foster 405; Miles v. Smith, 22 Mo. 502; Story Eq. Pl., § 185, 193. In Hagan v. Walker, 14 How. U. S. 29, the true rule was held to be, that where it is the object of the bill to procure the sale of land, and the prior encumbrancer holds the legal title, and his debt is payable, it is proper to make him a party, in order that a sale may be made of the whole title. But it is in the power of the court to order a sale subject to the prior encumbrance; a power which it will exercise in proper cases, as where the prior encumbrancer is not subject to, or is out of the jurisdiction. and the validity of the encumbrance is admitted; and will in such case dispense with his being made a party.

Where a state occupies the position of a prior mortgagee, it need not be made a party to a suit to foreclose a mortgage; its right being paramount: Pattison v. Shaw, 6 Ind. 377. The mortgagee is a necessary party to a suit to reform a mortgage deed, brought by a purchaser at a sale by the mortgagee: Haley v. Bagley, 37 Mo. 363.

The rule requiring the joinder of all persons whos
terests the decree may affect is subject to two modi
tions, which, at first sight, appear to be exceptions,
which are in reality mere limitations of its effect, o
nating in the same principles as the rule itself. The
of these modifications is the exclusion of remainder
after an estate tail; the second is the exclusion of l
tees or next of kin on bills for a debt or legacy ag
the personal representative.

The exclusion of remaindermen after an estate
originates in the possession by tenant in tail of an a
[*316] lute *power to destroy the remainders, so tha
alone represents the inheritance, and the su
quent remaindermen have no interest to protect. If
subsequent estates are independent of the estate tai
if that estate should determine during the suit, witl
their destruction having taken place, the remainderi
must be made parties.(*i*)[1]

The exclusion of legatees or next of kin, on a bill
a debt or legacy against the personal representative, (
inates in the assumption that such legatees or nex
kin have in reality no interest in the object of the s

(*i*) Mitf. 173–4; Lloyd *v.* Johnes, 9 Ves. 39–55; Gaskell *v.* Gask(
'Sim. 643.

---

[1] See on this subject, Sohier *v.* Williams, 1 Curtis 479 ; Lushingt
Boldero, 13 Beav. 418; Beattie *v.* Johnston, 8 Hare 169 ; Nodine *v.* G
field, 7 Paige 544.

[2] The personal estate of a testator is represented by the executor, a
residuary legatee is not a necessary party to a bill by the creditor see
to charge the general assets of the testator: Burwell *v.* Cawood, 2]
U. S. 575; Wiser *v.* Blackley, 1 Johns. Ch. 437 ; Watts *v.* Gayle, 20
824; Melick *v.* Melick, 2 Green (N. J.) 156. Nor are the general i
itors proper parties in such a suit: Dias *v.* Bouchaud, 10 Paige 445.
can a creditor filing a bill against an executor make a debtor a party
less under special circumstances : Long *v.* Magestre, 1'Johns. Ch.

For although they are in some sense concerned in it, yet it is only in the same sense in which every creditor is concerned in the management of his debtor's estate; viz., it is important to them that the ability to meet their claims should not be diminished; but the personal representative is not a trustee for them, nor have they any interest in the estate itself.(*k*) If the claimants are not mere legatees payable by the executor, but specific owners of the property itself, the ordinary rule applies; *e. g.*, where they take as appointees under a married woman's will,(*l*) or where their legacies are charged on real estate. In this latter instance, however, a modification has lately been introduced, assimilating to some extent a devisee on trust with a personal representative; and it is directed that, in all suits concerning real estate which is vested by devise in trustees, who are competent to sell and to give discharges for the purchase-money and for the rents and profits of the estate, such trustees shall represent the persons beneficially interested in the same manner, and to the same extent, as the executors or administrators in suits concerning personal estate; and it

(*k*) Hertford *v.* De Zichi, 9 Beav. 11 ; Mitf. 168.
(*l*) Court *v.* Jeffery, 1 S. & S. 105.

As to when heirs should be parties to such suit, see Kennedy *v.* Kennedy, 2 Ala. 571; Telfair *v.* Stead, 2 Cranch 407; Galphin *v.* McKinney, 1 McCord's Ch. 280. In a suit for final settlement of a partnership, it is not necessary to join those beneficially entitled to the share of a deceased partner, their rights being sufficiently protected by the personal representative: Coster *v.* Clarke, 3 Edw. Ch. 428.

Though ordinarily a bill may be sustained by one legatee alone: Pritchard *v.* Hicks, 1 Paige 270 ; Brown *v.* Ricketts, 3 Johns. Ch. 553 ; Ramey *v.* Green, 18 Ala. 776; yet it is different as to a residuary legatee, who must join all parties interested: Pritchard *v.* Hicks, ut sup.; West *v.* Randall, 2 Mason 181 ; Gould *v.* Hays, 19 Ala. 438 ; see Sellings *v.* Baumgardner, 9 Gratt. 273.

shall not be necessary to make the persons benefic
interested parties to the suit. But the Court ma
[*317] *the hearing require them to be joined, if it ,
think fit.(*ll*)

2. The joinder of parties who have concurrent cl
with the plaintiff, which, if not bound by the de
might be afterwards litigated, is most directly illustr
by cases in which a plaintiff sues on an equitable
and the legal title is vested in a trustee for him.
these cases the trustee must be made party, either
co-plaintiff or a defendant,[1] for although the trustee
no interest to protect, yet he has a legal right agains
defendant which would not otherwise be bound ; *e. g.*,
heir or devisee of a deceased mortgagee in fee must
party to any bill of foreclosure by the executor ;(*m*)'
assignor of a debt or other *chose in action*, not transfer

(*ll*) 30th Order of August, 1841. [See Rules in Eq. U. S. Courts
xlix. ; Penn., xxiii.]
(*m*) Scott *v.* Nicoll, 3 Russ. 476.

---

[1] Malin *v.* Malin, 2 Johns. Ch. 238 ; Fish *v.* Howland, 1 Paige 20 ;
of America *v.* Pollock, 4 Edw. Ch. 215 ; Cassiday *v.* McDaniel, 8 B. ,
519 ; Carter *v.* Jones, 5 Ired. Eq. 196 ; Everett *v.* Winn, 1 Sm. & N
67 ; McKinley *v.* Irwine, 13 Ala. 681 ; Swan *v.* Dent, 2 Md. Ch. 111 ;
v. Simons, 1 Curtis 122 ; Sayre *v.* Sayre, 2 Green (N. J.) 349. The h
of the legal title, as well as those from whom the complainant deriv
equity, should be made parties : Johnson *v.* Rankin, 2 Bibb 184 ; U
v. Brooks, 2 Story 623. Where it becomes necessary to file a bill in e
to enforce the payment of a bill of exchange, he who holds the naked
title may sue alone, as at law, though he who is entitled to the pro
may come in, and be made a party, if he wishes it : Hopkirk *v.* Pa
Brock. 20, 42.

[2] It is not necessary to make the personal representatives of the
gagor a party to a bill to foreclose or sell ; but upon the death of the
gagee, it is necessary to make both his heirs and personal represent:
parties : Worthington *v.* Lee, 2 Bland 684.

at law, must be a party to any suit by the assignee respecting it.(n)[1]

(n) Cathcart $v.$ Lewis, 1 Ves. Jr. 463; Walburn $v.$ Ingilby, 1 M. & K. 61.

---

[1] If there remain any interest, right, or liability, in the assignor, which can be affected by the decree, a *scintilla juris* even, the assignor is a necessary party: Thompson $v.$ McDonald, 2 Dev. & Batt. Eq. 463; Hopkins $v.$ Hopkins, 4 Strob. Eq. 207; Montague $v.$ Lobdell, 11 Cush. 111. The assignor of a bond or note, the payment of which is secured by a mortgage, should be made a party to a suit by the assignee to foreclose the mortgage: Bell $v.$ Schrock, 2 B. Monr. 29. See Beals $v.$ Cobb, 51 Maine 348.

To a bill on a bond by an assignee, the assignor is a necessary party, where the bond is not assignable at law: Gatewood $v.$ Rucker, 1 Monr. 21; Forman $v.$ Rodgers, 1 A. K. Marsh. 426.

To a bill by the assignee of a debt, to obtain certain securities given by the debtor to the attorney of the assignor, where the attorney had assigned the same against the attorney and his assignee, the assignor of the complainant is a necessary party: Elderkin $v.$ Shultz, 2 Blackf. 345.

Whether the assignee of the exclusive right to use a patented machine may join his assignor as a co-plaintiff in a suit for a violation of the patent, Quære? See Woodworth $v.$ Wilson, 4 How. U. S. 712.

In some cases, the heirs of the assignor are necessary parties to a bill by the assignee. See Edwards $v.$ Bohannon, 2 Dana 98.

To a bill by the assignee of a judgment, the assignor should be a party: McKinnie $v.$ Rutherford, 1 Dev. & Batt. Eq. 14; Elliott $v.$ Waring, 5 Monr. 338; Pemberton $v.$ Riddle, 5 Monr. 401; Cooper $v.$ Gunn, 4 B. Monr. 594. See, as to the joinder of the assignor in a judgment creditor's bill filed by the assignee: Morey $v.$ Forsyth, Walk. Ch. 465; Beach $v.$ White, Id. 495.

Where the assignment is absolute and unconditional, and leaves no remaining right or liability in the assignor which can be affected by the decree, the assignee need not make the assignor a party. Thus, assignors are not necessary parties to suits by assignees on bonds, where there are statutes authorizing the assignment of bonds. See Snelling $v.$ Boyd, 2 Monr. 132. So, the assignor of a note in controversy, who has no interest in it, and against whom no relief is prayed, is not a necessary party to the bill: Everett $v.$ Winn, 1 S. & M. Ch. 67. See also on this subject, Polk $v.$ Gallant, 2 Dev. & Batt. Eq. 395; Thompson $v.$ McDonald, Id. 463; Snelling $v.$ Boyd, 5 Monr. 172; Kennedy $v.$ Davis, 7 Id. 372; James River Co. $v.$ Littlejohn, 18 Gratt. (Va.) 53.

The assignor of an entry need not be made a party in a suit by the assignee to obtain a title: Oldham $v.$ Rowan, 3 Bibb 534. And in Bruen $v.$

The same principle of requiring that all con(
claims shall be bound, is applicable to many cases
fall under the first head of interest. For where
rest exists which requires protection, it is possibl
claim exists in respect of that interest, and the de
is entitled to have all such claims settled together,
the matter may be completely and effectually di
of.(o)   Its operation, however, is excluded where
son possessing a partial interest is seeking redress
injury, or enforcement of a contract, which affects l
and his partial interest alone, although in some s
relates to the entire subject-matter; e. g., where a
pier complains of an injury to his possessory right
out seeking to establish any claim respecting the
itance, or where a partner or co-owner complains o
practised on himself, although other parties hav
[*318] similarly defrauded.(p)   *And, in like m
one of several *cestuis que trust* may procee(
rately for his share of the fund, where the resp
shares have been already ascertained.[1]   But it is
wise if an account be necessary to ascertain the s

(o) Munch v. Cockerell, 8 Sim. 219, 231.
(p) Tooth v. Dean of Canterbury, 3 Sim. 61; Semple v. Birn
Railway, 9 Id. 209; Blain v. Agar, 2 Id. 289; Mare v. Malachy,
C. 559; Turney v. Borlase, 11 Sim. 17; Bridget v. Hames, 1 Coll.

Crane, 1 Green Ch. 347, it was decided that where a judgment, w
lien on land mortgaged, is assigned absolutely and uncondition
assignor is not a necessary party to a bill for foreclosure.

When a plaintiff parts with all his interest in the subject-matt
suit, the case can be no longer prosecuted in his name; but the
must make himself a party by an original bill in the nature of s
mental bill: Mason v. York R. R. Co., 52 Maine 82.

[1] Hares v. Stringer, 15 Beav. 206; Piatt v. Oliver, 2 McLean :
Chapman v. Hamilton, 19 Ala. 121.   See now, in England, 15 &
c. 86, s. 42; Macleod v. Annesley, 17 Jur. 612.

if the fund itself has been lost and its replacement is required, or if the entirety is in any way to be dealt with. And it is doubtful whether a trustee can ordinarily be compelled to divest himself of any part of his trust, unless all the *cestuis que trust* are before the Court. so that he can get rid of the whole.(*q*)

The operation of the rules requiring that all persons should be parties to a suit who had any interest which the decree might affect, or any concurrent claim which it ought to bind, was often productive of serious inconvenience, by compelling the joinder of claimants in small amounts, who would willingly have left their rights in the hands of the Court rather than to incur the expense of appearing to litigate them. This evil is now remedied by orders of the Court, declaring that where no direct relief is sought against a party, such party, on being served with a copy of the bill, may be bound by the proceeding without the necessity of appearing to the bill; subject however, to the discretion of the plaintiff as to whether he will compel such an appearance, and to that of the defendant as to whether he will submit to be bound without it.[1] The person possessing the interest must still be a party, but by the operation of these orders he may be so without serious expense.(*r*)

3. The joinder of parties who are liable to exonerate the defendant, or to contribute with him to the plaintiff's claim, is in many cases dispensed with under the present practice. The principle was that of requiring a complete decree, and a final ascertainment of the amount of lia-

(*q*) Munch *v.* Cockerell, 8 Sim. 219, 231; Henley *v.* Stone, 3 Beav. 355; Goodson *v.* Ellison, 3 Russ. 583; [Lenaghan *v.* Smith, 2 Phillips 302.]
(*r*) Supra, Prayer of Process.

[1] See Rules in Eq. U. S. Courts, No. liv.; Penn., No. xviii.

[*319] bility, *so that any one of the parties 1 satisfying the plaintiff, might obtain cont from the rest.[1]

On this principle, it was held, that if several were co-obligors in a joint and several bond, th all necessary parties to a suit for payment, with ception of such as were mere sureties, and, there liable. to contribution.(s)[2] So, if several trust committed a breach of trust, they must have beei ties to a suit for redress; but if the act compl: were an actual fraud, no right of contribution ar any one might be sued alone.(t)[3] It was in like unnecessary to join an insolvent in the suit, 1 whether liable or not, he was unable to contribute. course, if the absent parties were primarily liable the defendant was entitled, not only to a cont from them, but to an actual indemnity, it was a tional reason for insisting on their presence.   Th

(s) Bland v. Winter, 1 S. & S. 246.

(t) Seddon v. Connel, 10 Sim. 79; Attorney-General v. Wilson Ph. 1; [Oliver v. Piatt, 3 How. U. S. 333; Cunningham v. Pell, 612.]

(u) Seddon v. Connell, 10 Sim. 79.

---

[1] See Purcell v. Maddox, 3 Munf. 79. Where a judgment is different parcels of land, in a suit by one of the several owners a; judgment creditors, he must, in order to a decree for contributi all the persons interested parties: Avery v. Petten, 7 Johns. See, also, Campbell v. Mesier, 6 Johns. Ch. 21; Hooper v. 1 Munf. 119; Venable v. Beauchamp, 3 Dana 321.

[2] So all.the obligors in a bond should be made parties to a bil to obtain relief against it, unless in a special case of collusion:] Collier, 8 Ham. 43.

[3] In White v. Turner, 1 B. Monr. 130, it was held, that all th concerned in suppressing a will, by which slaves who were emanci thereby retained in slavery, are jointly liable to a decree for dama if one of the parties has died, his representatives should be ma(to the suit for freedom.

a bill could not be filed against a surety without the principal, (v)[1] nor against an heir-at-law for payment of debts, without the executor; (w) but an order has now been made, directing that if the plaintiff's demand be several as well as joint, and whether the defendants be liable as principals or sureties, he may proceed against all or any at his own option. (x)

It sometimes happens, that compliance with the rule requiring the joinder of all interested parties is rendered practically impossible in a particular case, because the persons interested are too indefinite or numerous to be individually joined in the suit. In this case, the rule admits of modification so that one or more members of a class may sue or be sued on behalf of the whole, provided *the interest of every absent member in [*320] the claim made or resisted is identical with that of the members who are personally before the Court.[2]

(v) Brooks v. Stuart, 1 Beav. 512.

(w) Knight v. Knight, 3 P. Wms. 333.

(x) 32d Order of August, 1841. [See Rule li., U. S. Courts in Eq.; Penn. xxv.]

---

[1] Roane v. Pickett, 2 English (Ark.) 510; Hart v. Coffee, 4 Jones Eq. 322. So the principal debtor must be a party in a bill by a surety against the creditor for relief: Vilas v. Jones, 1 Comst. 284: Bronson, J. So also he must be in a bill by a co-surety to make another contribute: Trescot v. Smyth, 1 McCord's Ch. 301. Where a party liable to contribute is insolvent, he need not be joined in the bill: Watts v. Gayle, 20 Ala. 817; Montague v. Turpin, 8 Gratt. 453. But the insolvency must be at the time of bill filed: Young v. Lyons, 8 Gill 162. See, in addition, as to these points, note, p. 269, supra. Where a surety has paid the debt of his principal, he may proceed against him, or may subject a fund which he has provided, without making the creditor a party; but where the debt is unpaid and the surety seeks for exoneration, there, as a matter of course, the creditor must be made a party; for the relief is not to have the amount paid to the surety, but paid to the creditor who is decreed to accept it in discharge of his liability: Murphy v. Jackson, 5 Jones Eq. 14.

[2] See upon this subject, Clements v. Bowes, 1 Drewr. 684; 16 Jur. 96;

The most ordinary instances of this dispensation
suits by creditors or legatees. For as a single cred
legatee may sue for his demand out of the personal ɛ
without bringing the others before the Court, it is
matter of convenience than of indulgence to permi
a suit by a few on behalf of all; and it tends to pɪ
several suits by several creditors or legatees, which
be inconvenient in the administration and burde
on the fund administered.$(y)^1$ The rule, however,

(y) Mitf. 166.

Macbride v. Lindsay, 9 Hare 574 ; Long v. Storie, 22 L. J. Ch. 20(
mons v. Laing, 12 Beav. 377 ; Duke of Devon v. Eglin, 14 Id. 53
lock v. Jenkins, Id. 628 ; Harmer v. Gooding, 3 De G. & Sm. 407
v. Hoxey, 11 Ga. 645 ; Putnam v. Sweet, 1 Chand. (Wis.) 287 ;
Commissioners, 1 Pars. Eq. 501 ; Smith v. Swormstedt, 16 How. U
Whitney v. Mayo, 15 Ill. 251 ; Thornton v. Hightower, 17 Ga. 1 ;
v. Lewis, 36 Verm. 91 ; Hendrix v. Money, 1 Bush (Ky.) 306 ;
Bartholemew, 42 Verm. 356 ; Davis v. Clabaugh, 30 Md. 508.   Nu
ness does not always and necessarily constitute an exception to the
rule, that all parties interested must be joined : it is only where
so very numerous that to join them would be impracticable; wit
most interminable delays and other inconveniences, which would
and probably defeat the ends of justice : Carey v. Hoxey, 11
Whether a case is within the exception is a matter of discretion ᴠ
Chancellor, and he must be fully advised by allegation and proc
extent of the litigation : Id. ; Society for Propagation of Gospel
land, 2 Paine C. C. 536. Thus, on a bill filed by some next of ki
half of themselves and all others, the court will direct that some
be produced to show that the others were inconveniently numerou
the decree is drawn up : Leathart v. Thorne, 15 Jur. 162, 762.
by some shareholders of a company on behalf of the rest, the dire
far as no relief is sought against them, do not constitute a distin
from the rest, so as to be necessary parties : Clements v. Bowes,
96 ; 1 Drewr. 684. But a bill on behalf of all shareholders, com
of transactions in which some have concurred, cannot be maintaine
v. Jackson, 14 Beav. 369 ; 2 De G., M. & G. 49.

See also, Rule No. xlviii., U. S. Courts in Equity ; No. xxii., Pe
which it is provided that where the parties are very numerous, tɩ
may, in its discretion, dispense with the joinder of all.

¹ One legatee may file a bill in behalf of himself and the other

confined to cases of this class, but has been extended to other cases where several persons have distinct rights on a common fund, as creditors under a trust deed, residuary legatees, or next of kin; and in such cases, if the parties are very numerous, one has been allowed to sue on behalf of all, although he could not have sued for his separate share without bringing the others before the Court. The ground for this indulgence is, that if all were made actual parties the suit would be liable to frequent abatements, and it would be practically impossible to bring it to a hearing. The Court, however, in such cases will not proceed to a decree until it is satisfied that the interest of all is fairly represented, and that there would be a preponderating inconvenience in bringing them individually before it.(z)

The same principle applies where there is a common

(z) Mitf. 167; Harvey v. Harvey, 4 Beav. 215; Hawkins v. Hawkins, 1 Hare 543.

who may choose to come in, against the executors for an account and payment; but where the bill is for the residue, all the residuary legatees must be made parties: Brown v. Ricketts, 3 Johns. Ch. 553; Davoue v. Fanning, 4 Id. 199. But see Hallett v. Hallett, 2 Paige Ch. 15, in which it was held that one residuary legatee may file a bill on behalf of himself and all others standing in the same situation, and it is not necessary to make them all parties to the suit.

In a suit against the personal representatives of a deceased debtor to recover a debt due from his estate, it is only necessary for the complainant to file the bill in behalf of himself and of all other creditors in the same situation, when it appears upon the face of the bill that there will be a deficiency in the fund, and that there are other creditors entitled to a ratable proportion with the complainants: Dias v. Bouchard, 10 Paige 445.

As to the right of one distributee of an estate to file a bill on behalf of himself and other distributees, and whether to a bill by one distributee, the others must be made parties, see Messervey v. Barelli, Riley's Ch. 138; Cherry v. Belcher, 5 Stew. & Port. 133; Turley v. Young, 5 J. J. Marsh. 133; Richardson v. Hunt, 2 Munf. 148.

right against the defendants, *e. g.*, where relief is sought on behalf of a partnership or other˙ numerous body against strangers, or on behalf of all the members of such body except the defendants, against members who have committed .a wrong. Such a bill has accordingly been sustained on behalf of a company against the direc-
[*321] tors to redress or *prevent a misapplication of the˙ funds,(*a*) on behalf of the inhabitants of a parish against the commissioners under an act of Parliament to restrain an injury to their common right,(*b*) and on behalf of a company against third parties to enforce or rescind a contract, or to obtain an injunction against proceedings at law.(*c*)¹   And *e converso* it has been held that

(*a*) Chancery *v.* May, Pr. in Ch. 592 ; Hichens *v.* Congreve, 4 Russ. 562 ; Preston *v.* Grand Collier Dock Company, 11 Sim. 327 ; Mozley *v.* Alston, 1 Ph. 790.

(*b*) Attorney-General *v.* Heelis, 2 S. & S. 67 ; Bromley *v.* Smith, 1 Sim. 8.

(*c*) Taylor *v.* Salmon, 4 M. & C. 134 ; Small *v.* Attwood, Younge 407 ; Fenne *v.* Craig, 3 Y. & C. 216 ; Lund *v.* Blanshard, 4 Hare 9 and 290.

---

¹ Where the associates or shareholders of a private association are numerous, a bill may be filed by one of such associates, on behalf of himself and all the others, against the trustees of such association, to compel the execution of the trust, and for an account and distribution of the funds and property of the association among the shareholders. And it is not necessary that all of the associates should unite in a bill for that purpose : Mann *v.* Butler, 2 Barb. Ch. 362 ; Beatty *v.* Kurtz, 2 Peters 566 ; The New London Bank *v.* Lee, 11 Conn. 112. But the others must either be made parties defendant, or the suit must profess to be as well in their behalf as that of the complainants : Whitney *v.* Mayo, 17 Ill. 252 ; New England Bank *v.* Stockholders, &c., 6 R. I. 191. Where a large number of persons are associated for the purposes of trade, the legal title to all their property being in a part of them for the benefit of the whole, it is sufficient if those having the legal title be made parties defendant or complainant in a bill in equity : Martin *v.* Dryden, 1 Gilm. 187.

But a bill will not lie by a freeholder or inhabitant of a town, in behalf of the town, respecting its common property without the consent of the town duly declared : Denton *v.* Jackson, 2 Johns. Ch. 320. Nor can indi-

where a person has a right against several individuals who are liable to common obligations, a bill may be filed against some on behalf of all, provided such a number be brought before the Court as will fairly represent their interests.[1] And on a bill so framed the Court will make a decree binding all, although so far as the absent parties are concerned it cannot make them do any specific act.(d)

In order, however, that the principle of the exception may apply, it is essential that the parties represented and those who profess to represent them should have strictly identical interests. If that be not the case, but the suit be one which will bring into controversy their mutual rights, they must all be personally before the Court. As, for example, where the real object of a suit is to obtain a decision, whether consistently with the articles of a company there can be a dissolution and divi-

(d) Meux v. Maltby, 2 Sw. 277; Adair v. New River Company, 11 Ves. 429; Lanchester v. Thompson, 5 Mad. 4, 13; Attwood v. Small, 9 Law J. Ch. 132; 6 Cl. & F. 232.

---

vidual stockholders of an incorporated company file a bill against the agent and treasurer of the company for misconduct and account; such a bill should emanate from and be filed in the name of the corporate body. In some cases individual stockholders can file bills, but only where the officers have the control, and are guilty of breach of duty as trustees: Forbes v. Whitlock, 3 Ed. Ch. 446; Bronson v. La Crosse R. R. Co., 2 Wall. S. C. 302.

A single stockholder may file a bill on behalf of himself and others, to restrain directors of a company from acts ultra vires: Natusch v. Irving, Appendix to Gow on Partnership 576; Colman v. The Eastern Counties Railway Co., 10 Beav. 1; Simpson v. The Hotel Co., 8 H. L. Cas. 717; Gifford v. The New Jersey R. R. Co., 2 Stockton 171; Stevens v. Rutland & Burlington R. R., 29 Verm. 545; see, also, Philadelphia & Erie R. R. v. Catawissa R. R., 53 Penn. St. 20.

[1] In a bill against an unincorporated banking company, the members of which are numerous, and in part unknown, it is not necessary to bring all the stockholders before the Court, before a decree can be made: Mandeville v. Riggs, 2 Peters 482. See, also, Dana v. Brown, 1 J. J. Marsh. 304.

sion of the funds, or whether an alleged dissolution is fraudulent, or for the purpose of obtaining directions for managing the business, or having the partnership dissolved and the like, a bill would be held objectionable unless all the partners were parties, because every one of the absent partners would have a separate and substantial interest in the question of right.$(e)^1$

[*322]   *It appears to have been at one time cousidered impossible that any bill for winding up a partnership should be sustained unless a dissolution were also sought, and every partner were personally joined. In the case of unincorporated joint stock companies, and of other numerous partnerships, this rule operated practically as a denial of relief, but it has been relaxed, as we have already seen, in their favor, and bills have been sustained which asked more limited relief, viz., that the assets of such partnership, on its abandonment or insolvency, might be collected and applied in discharge of the debts, leaving questions of distribution and contribution as between the partners entirely open for future settlement. A bill of this latter kind does not bring into controversy the rights of individual partners, and may therefore be sustained by a few partners, on behalf of all, against the directors of the company. And it has been suggested that, even on a bill praying a dissolution, the presence of all might, perhaps, be dispensed with, pro-

(e) Beaumont v. Meredith, 3 V. & B. 180; Evans v. Stokes, 1 K. 24; Van Sandau v. Moore, 1 Russ. 441; Long v. Yonge, 2 Sim. 369.

---

[1] If a bill in equity be brought by one of several partners, founded on partnership transactions, and some of the partners are insolvent, still they must be made parties; and, if bankrupts, their assignees should be made parties in their place: Fuller v. Benjamin, 23 Maine 255. See also, Hoy v. McMurry, 1 Litt. 364; Dozier v. Edwards, 3 Litt. 67; Noyes v. Sawyer, 3 Verm. 160. Yet see Townsend v. Auger, 3 Conn. 354.

vided there were a strong necessity shown, and sufficient parties were before the Court to represent each conflicting interest, and to discuss the questions freely and without restraint.(f)

In cases where persons interested are out of the jurisdiction of the Court, it is sufficient to state that fact in the bill, and to pray that process may issue on their return; and if the statement be substantiated by proof at the hearing, their appearance in the suit will be dispensed with.(g)[1] The power of the Court to proceed to a decree in their absence will depend on the nature of their interest, and the mode in which it will be affected by the decree. If they are only passive objects of the judgment of the Court, or their rights are incidental to those of parties before the Court, a complete determination may be obtained. *But if they are to be active in performing the decree, or if they have [*323] rights wholly distinct from those of the other parties, the Court, in their absence, can not proceed to a determination against them.(h)[2] The powers conferred by

(f) Supra, Partnership; Wallworth v. Holt, 4 M. & C. 619; Richardson v. Larpent, 2 N. C. C. 507; Richardson v. Hastings, 7 Beav. 301, 323; Clough v. Radcliffe, 1 De G. & Sm. 164; Apperly v. Paige, 1 Ph. 779; Wilson v. Stanhope, 2 Coll. 629.

(g) Burton v. Egginton, 1 Hare 488; Munoz v. De Mastet, 1 Beav. 109.

(h) Mitf. on Pleading 32; Fell v. Brown, 2 B. C. C. 276; Brown v. Blount, 2 Russ. & M. 83; Willats v. Busby, 5 Beav. 193; 1 Dan. Ch. P. 199, 200.

---

[1] See Spivey v. Jenkins, 1 Ired. Eq. 126; Milligan v. Milledge, 3 Cranch 220; Lainhart v. Reilly, 3 Dessaus. 590; Rule No. xlvii., U. S. Courts in Eq.; No. xx., Penna.

[2] See Joy v. Wirtz, 1 Wash. C. C. 517; Mallow v. Hinde, 12 Wheat. 193; Corron v. Mellaudon, 19 How. 113. In a suit to recover a debt against the estate of a deceased partner, the other partners are proper and necessary parties; and, although when they are out of the jurisdiction of the Court they may be dispensed with, yet this exception does not apply

statute of serving such parties with process a
thus bringing them before the Court, will be
considered.

---

to cases involving important rights of the absent partners,
not to cases where the facts are mainly in their knowledge,
circumstances occurred in the place where they are: Vose *v*
Story 336. See Burwell *v.* Cawood, 2 How. (U. S.) 575; 1
Bank, 3 Sumner 422.

The Supreme Court of the United States will not make.
upon the merits of a case, unless all persons essentially i
parties, although some of those persons are not within the j
the Court: Russell *v.* Clark, 7 Cranch 69; but see now the R
No. xlvii.

*CHAPTER III. [*324]

OF PROCESS AND APPEARANCE.

AFTER the bill has been filed it is next requisite that the *subpœna*[1] should be served; that the defendant should enter his appearance; and that after appearance he should put in his defence. The defence may, as we shall hereafter see, be of four kinds, Disclaimer, Demurrer, Plea, and Answer. But the most usual form, and the only one to which compulsory process applies, is that of answer.

The ordinary service of *subpœna* is by delivering a copy to the defendant personally, or leaving one at his place of actual residence. And in special cases, where an absconding or absent defendant has a recognised agent in the matter litigated, substituted service on such agent has been allowed.(*a*)[2] But as a general principle the Court has no inherent authority to dispense with service on the defendant himself, or to authorize any service beyond the limits of its own jurisdiction.(*b*)[3]

(*a*) Hobhouse *v.* Courtney, 12 Sim. 140; Murray *v.* Vipart, 1 Ph. 521.
(*b*) Whitmore *v.* Ryan, 4 Hare 612.

---

[1] The writ of subpœna is now abolished in England, and instead thereof a printed bill is served on the defendants. In some of the United States the subpœna is still in use; in others, as in Pennsylvania, service by copy of the bill is substituted. See Daniel's Chan. Prac. 428.

[2] See on this subject, Eckert *v.* Baeert, 4 Wash. C. C. 370; Ward *v.* Seabry, Id. 426, 472.

[3] The Court of Chancery has power, under the recent General Orders, to direct service of its process abroad: Drummond *v.* Drummond, L. R. 2 Eq.

Assuming the *subpœna* to be duly served, the defendant must next appear. If he be contumacious and refuse, his disobedience may be punished as a contempt.

The processes of contempt were originally five, viz. :—

1. A writ of attachment directed to the sheriff of the defendant's county, commanding that the defendant's person should be attached. To this writ the sheriff might return, 1. That he had the defendant in custody ; 2. That he had taken him, but had accepted bail; 3. That he [*325] could not *find him within his bailiwick. On the first of these returns being made, the defendant was brought up by *habeas corpus*, on the second by the messenger of the Court, or the serjeant-at-arms, and in either case was committed to the Fleet, now altered to the Queen's Prison. On the third return, that of *non est inventus*, the next process of contempt issued.

2. A writ of attachment with proclamations; on which the same returns might be made, and the same results would follow.

3. A writ of rebellion directed to commissioners appointed by the Court, and extending into all the counties of England. On this process no bail could be taken, but the commissioners either brought the defendant up in custody, on which he was committed to the Fleet; or made a return of *non est inventus*, upon which followed,

An order that the serjeant-at-arms, as the immediate officer of the Court, should effect the arrest. If an arrest were made under this process, it was followed, like other arrests, by committal to the Fleet. But if the return

335; affirmed in L. R. 2 Ch. Ap. 32. In some of the states, publication is authorized by statute, in the case of non-resident defendants. See Haring *v.* Kauffman, 2 Beas. 297. Such provisions have been held to include lunatics in their effect: Sturges *v.* Longworth, 1 Ohio St. N. S. 550.

were *non est inventus*, there was no further process against the person.

5. A writ of sequestration, issuable only on the return *non est inventus* of the serjeant-at-arms, or on a defendant in custody being committed to the Fleet. This writ was issued, not against the person, but against the property of the defendant, and authorized the sequestrators to take his goods and personal estate, and to enter on his real estate, and to sequester the rents and profits. If the sequestration proved ineffectual, there was no further process. And in the reign of Elizabeth, even the right to sequester was disputed, and it was said by the judges that the Court had no authority beyond personal commitment, and that if a sequestrator were killed in the execution of process, it was not murder.(c)

*In the case of a person having privilege of [*326] peerage or Parliament, and exempt, therefore, from committal for civil contempt,(d) a sequestration *nisi* was substituted for an attachment, which if no cause were shown was afterwards made absolute. In the case of a corporation, which cannot be attached, the first process was by *distringas*, and the second by sequestration.

Assuming an appearance to be entered, an answer was next required. And if this were refused, the process of contempt was again enforced; but if resisted to a sequestration, the plaintiff was not restricted to that remedy, but on issuing the writ, might apply to the Court to take his bill *pro confesso*, and to decree against the defendant on the assumption of its truth.

If a decree were ultimately made against the defendant, its performance was enforced by a like process of con-

(c) 1 Smith C. P. 571.
(d) Wellesley's Case, 2 R. & M. 639.

tempt, with the exception that the attachment was not bailable.

In addition to other inconveniences of being in contempt, it has the effect of preventing a party from making any application to.the Court in the same cause, except for the purpose of clearing such contempt.(e)

It is obvious, from the nature of the process of contempt, that if a defendant absconded so as to avoid its operation, or if, when arrested under it, he perversely refused to submit, there were no means of compelling obedience.   And on the other hand, if a defendant in custody under process were incapable of doing the required act, his committal was practically imprisonment for life.

Several attempts have been made by the Legislature to remedy these evils.   But the earliest of those which need here be noticed is that made by 1 Wm. 4, c. 36, afterwards amended by 2 Wm. 4, c. 58, and generally known as Sir Edward Sugden's Act.

The provisions of this act, besides abridging under certain circumstances the general process of contempt, [*327] applied *especially to three classes of persons; viz., absconding defendants, privileged defendants, and defendants in custody under process. , In respect to the former class, it authorized the Court to make an order for the defendant's appearance, and on due publication of such order to dispense with both service and appearance, and proceed at once to take the bill *pro confesso*.   In respect to the other two classes, it authorized an appearance to be entered for them ; shortened the steps for taking the bill *pro confesso*, and conferred on bills taken *pro confesso* under it additional efficacy, by directing that ˙ they should not only warrant a decree, but should be evi-

(e) 1 Dan. Ch. P. 450.

dence in any other proceeding as equivalent to an admission by answer. It, at the same time, provided for the protection of a defendant in custody, by requiring that he should, within a limited time, be brought by the plaintiff to the bar of the Court, to be there dealt with as pointed out by the act; and that within a further limited time, the plaintiff should proceed according to the nature of the contempt to enter an appearance for him, or to have his bill taken *pro confesso*, and that in default of his so doing, the defendant should be discharged.

The case of absent defendants, not having absconded to avoid process, was provided for to a limited extent by 2 Wm. 4, c. 33, and 5 Wm. 4, c. 82, authorizing service abroad. But those acts applied to such suits only as had reference to hereditaments in England, Wales, or Ireland, or to encumbrances thereon, or to stock or shares, or the dividends thereof.

The partial remedies afforded by these acts have been extended by the statutes of the present reign, for "facilitating the Administration of Justice in the Court of Chancery," and by the general orders made under them.(*f*)

The present process of the Court for enforcing obedience is chiefly regulated by those orders, and it is therefore *necessary to point out in what respects they have modified the previous system. [*328]

1. They have remedied some of the difficulties respecting service of process, by directing that where a defendant, having been in this country within two years before the *subpœna* issued, appears to have absconded to avoid process, an order for his appearance duly published may be substituted for such service; and that when a defend-

(*f*) 3 & 4 Vict. c. 94; 4 & 5 Vict. c. 52; 8 & 9 Vict. c. 105; General Orders of August, 1841; April, 1842; and May, 1845.

ant in any suit is out of the jurisdiction, an order may be made, on satisfactory evidence of his probable abode, authorizing service abroad. (*g*)

2. They have shortened the process of contempt by abolishing the writ of attachment with proclamations, and the writ of rebellion in all cases; and by abolishing the use of the messenger and serjeant-at-arms, in the case of contempts for non-appearance. (*h*)

3. They have provided for defaults in appearance, by distinct regulations for the several cases of an adult and capable defendant served within the jurisdiction, of an absconding defendant on whom an order to appear has been made, of an infant or person of unsound mind, and of a defendant served out of the jurisdiction; authorizing in each case under certain restrictions an appearance to be entered for such defendant. (*i*) And their effect appears to be that on neglect by a defendant to appear, the plaintiff may waive all process of contempt and enter an appearance for him; or may, at his option, issue an attachment. But on the return of this writ, whether it be "in prison," "*cepi corpus*," or "*non est inventus*," he can issue no further process, but must proceed to enter an appearance; for in the first case he is expressly bound to do so by 1 Wm. 4, c. 36, s. 13; in the second he cannot have a messenger, and has, therefore, no means of reaching the [*329] defendant; and in *the third he cannot have a serjeant-at-arms, and a sequestration cannot issue on an inferior process.

4. They have provided for default in answering after an appearance, whether entered by or for the defendant.

In this case there are three modes of procedure open to the plaintiff, viz., by process of contempt, by taking the

(*g*) 1845, xxxi., xxxiii.   (*h*) 1841, vi., vii.   (*i*) 1845, xxix., xxxvi.

bill *pro confesso*, or by going into evidence without an answer.

If he adopt the first course, by process of contempt he may issue an attachment, either immediately on default, or if the defendant is likely to abscond, at an earlier period.(*k*) If the defendant is not taken on the attachment, the plaintiff, on a return of *non est inventus*, may dispense with intermediate process, and obtain an immediate sequestration.(*l*) If he is taken, the plaintiff must proceed within a further period to bring him to the bar of the Court, to answer his contempt there.

The second course open to the plaintiff is that of taking his bill *pro confesso*.[1] And he is entitled under the present practice to adopt this course immediately on the execution of an attachment for want of answer, or at any time within three weeks afterwards, or whenever he is unable, with due diligence, to procure an attachment or subsequent process for want of answer to be executed.(*m*)

The third course is that of going into evidence without an answer, which, where the plaintiff can rely on the strength of his evidence, is occasionally advisable. For this purpose a power was given by the 11th and 12th rules of Sir E. Sugden's Act to file a formal answer in the defendant's name. By the present rules a simpler plan is adopted; and the plaintiff is authorized to file a traversing note, expressing his intention to proceed as if an answer had been filed traversing the bill.(*n*)

| (*k*) 1845, lxxxii. | (*l*) 1841, ix. |
| (*m*) 1845, lxxvi., lxxix. | (*n*) 1845, lii., lviii. |

[1] See on this subject, Rules of U. S. Courts in Equity, No. xviii., &c.; in Penna., No. xiii. and xxix; Guerry *v.* Durham, 11 Ga. 9; Carradine *v.* O'Connor, 21 Ala. 573. A decree *pro confesso* cannot be made against one not served: Hurter *v.* Robbins, 21 Ala. 585.

[*330]   *The outline which has been just g
process of the Court is sufficient to
general character.   Its precise details would
to the purpose of the present Treatise.(o)   A
now proceed, on the assumption of a regular
and defence, to consider in what manner su
should be made.

(o) 1 Dan. Chap. 7, 8, 9, 10, 12.

*CHAPTER IV [*331]

OF THE DEFENCE.

THE grounds of defence in equity may be divided into six classes, viz. :—

1. Want of jurisdiction in the Court, where the equity alleged is exclusively cognisable in some other Court of equity, and not in Chancery; as if the suit be for land in a county palatine, or the defendant claim the privilege of a University.(*a*)

2. Disability in the plaintiff to sue, as if he be an outlaw, or an alien enemy; or in the defendant to be sued, as if he be an uncertificated bankrupt; or if an infant, married woman, or lunatic, attempt to sue in his or her own name.(*b*)

3. A decision already made, or still pending, on the same matter in the Court itself, or in some other Court of competent jurisdiction.[1]

4. Want of equity,[2] where no case is established on

(*a*) 1 Dan. Ch. P. 509, 595.   (*b*) 1 Dan. Chap. 3.

---

[1] See Pearse *v*. Dobinson, L. R. 1 Eq. 241.

[2] A defendant need not demur to a bill that is wanting in equity, but may, at any time, reach the defect by motion to dismiss: Lockard *v*. Lockard, 16 Ala. 423 ; but see, Brill *v*. Stiles, 35 Ill. 305. But, if not demurred to, evidence will be received in support of its allegations: Groves *v*. Fulsome, 16 Mo. 543. A special reservation by a defendant, in his answer of exceptions to the sufficiency of a bill for want of equity, has the defect of a demurrer: Lovett *v*. Longmire, 14 Ark. 339.

the merits. This includes not only cases where there is no right in the plaintiff, but also those where his right, though in fact existing, is not alleged with sufficient certainty in his bill, or where it is a right at law and not in equity; and also cases of lost deeds, interpleader, &c., where the affidavit required for transferring the jurisdiction into equity, has not been annexed to the bill.[1]

5. Multifariousness and unduly splitting up a cause of suit.

6. Want of parties.

[*332]   *The doctrines which affect the validity of each of these defences are not material to be here considered. Our present inquiry assumes a defence to exist, and is directed to the form in which it should be made.

The forms of defence are four in number, viz., Disclaimer, Demurrer, Plea, and Answer. A disclaimer denies that the defendant has any interest in the matter. A demurrer submits that on the plaintiff's own showing his claim is bad. A plea avers some one matter of avoidance or denies some one allegation in the bill, and rests the defence on that issue. An answer puts on the record the whole case of the defendant, whether by way of demurrer, of avoidance, or of denial, and whether raising one or more issues.

A defendant, however, is not necessarily confined to one of these forms of defence, but may use two or more of them against the same bill, provided he applies them to different parts, and distinctly points out the application of each.[2] Such, for example, would be the case if

---

[1] An objection to the jurisdiction of the court on the ground that the plaintiff has an adequate remedy at law, must be taken by answer, or it is waived: Tenney v. State Bank, 20 Wis. 152. See also, Pella v. Scholte, 21 Iowa 463.

[2] By the Equity Rules of the United States Courts, No. xxxii., it is pro

the bill prayed a conveyance of land, as to part of which the defendant was a purchaser for value without notice, and as to the residue was affected by notice. In this case the bill would in effect be combining two claims to be met by the defendant in different ways; and accordingly he might put in as to one part of the land a plea "that he had purchased for value without notice," and as to the other part a disclaimer of all interest.(c) A class of cases also exists, in which the claim made by the bill is strictly single, and cannot therefore be met by several defences, in the sense in which the expression has just been used, but in which the bill itself is so constructed as to give rise to a peculiar defence, compounded of plea and answer, and technically termed "a plea supported by an answer." The nature of the defence will be considered under the head of Pleas.

We will now direct our attention separately to each of the four forms of defence.

1. A disclaimer. If the plaintiff, demanding certain *property, untruly state that the defendant has an interest therein, the defendant may put in a disclaimer of any right in the matter. If this be done, all controversy between himself and the plaintiff is at an [*333]

(c) Mitf. 106, 319; Wigr. on Discovery, s. 12.

---

vided that the defendant may, at any time before the bill is taken for confessed, or afterwards, with the leave of the court, demur or plead to the whole bill, or to part of it, and he may demur to part, plead to part, and answer as to the residue; but in every case in which the bill specially charges fraud or combination, a plea to such part must be accompanied with an answer fortifying the plea, and explicitly denying the fraud and combination, and the facts on which the charge is founded. In Pennsylvania (Rule xxxii.) no demurrer or plea is allowed to be filed unless supported by affidavit that it is not interposed for delay; and, if a plea, that it is true in point of fact.

end, and he may be either dismissed from the suit, or a decree made against him, according as the nature of the disclaimed interest and the plaintiff's security require. It seldom, however, happens that a disclaimer can be put in alone; for as it is possible that the defendant may have had an interest which he has parted with, or may have set up an unfounded claim, which may make him liable for costs, the plaintiff is entitled to an answer on those points.[1] Of course, if the plaintiff is not merely seeking property which he believes the defendant to claim, but is actually charging the defendant as accountable for a wrong committed, a disclaimer cannot apply. (d)

2. The principle of a defence by demurrer is that o the plaintiff's own showing, his claim is bad.[2] It i applicable to any defence which can be made out from th allegations in the bill, but the most ordinary grounds o demurrer are, want of jurisdiction, want of equity, multi fariousness, and want of parties. The frame of a demur rer is very simple, and, after the formal commencement runs thus: "This defendant doth demur in law to th said bill, and for cause of demurrer showeth that it ap

(d) Mitf. on Pleading 318 ; Perkin v. Stafford, 10 Sim. 562; Graham v Coape, 3 M. & C. 638 ; Glassington v. Thwaites, 2 Russ. 458.

---

[1] A disclaimer must be full and explicit in all respects, and be accompa nied by an answer, denying the facts deemed necessary to be denied Worthington v. Lee, 2 Bland 678. The defendant must renounce all clai to the subject of the demand made by the plaintiff's bill, in any capacity and to any extent: Bentley v. Cowman, 6 Gill & J. 152. A defendan cannot, by a disclaimer, deprive the plaintiff of the right to require a ful answer from him, unless it is evident that the defendant should not, afte the disclaimer, be continued a party to the suit: Ellsworth v. Curtis, 1 Paige 105; see also, Spofford v. Manning, 2 Edw. Ch. 358.

[2] A demurrer does not lie to an *answer*. If an answer is irregular, i may be treated as no answer and taken off the file ; if it is merely defect ive, it must be excepted to: Travers v. Ross, 1 McCart. 254 ; Stone v Moore, 26 Ill. 165. And a demurrer does not lie to a plea or to a replica tion ; they should be set down for hearing : Beck v. Beck, 36 Miss. 72.

pears by the said bill that," &c., stating in the regular
form on what class of objection the defendant relies, or if
there be more than one ground of objection, stating each
ground successively with the prefatory words, "and for
further cause of demurrer, this defendant showeth," &c.,
and concluding with the words, "wherefore and for divers
other good causes of demurrer appearing in the said bill
this defendant doth demur to the said bill, and prays the
judgment of this honorable Court whether he shall be compelled to make any other answer thereto; and he humbly
prays to be hence dismissed, with his reasonable costs
in this behalf sustained." The formal *statement, however, of the causes of demurrer, though [*334]
usual, is not absolutely necessary;[1] nor does the statement
of one cause preclude the defendant from relying in argument on any others extending to the same part of the bill;
for the assertion of a demurrer is, that the plaintiff has
not, on his own showing, made out a case, and if that
position can be established on any ground, the demurrer
is good. In such a case, however, the defendant will not
be entitled to his costs.(e)

The form of demurrer just given is that of a demurrer
to the whole bill. But although a demurrer may be to
the whole bill, it is not necessarily of that extent; nor,
if less extensively framed, is it confined to any particular
portion of the bill. It may be to the relief sought, it may
be to the discovery, or it may be to both, or to only a part
of one or of both.[2]

(e) Mitf. 217; Wellesley v. Wellesley, 4 M. & C. 554; 1 Dan. Ch. P. 539
545.

---

[1] See Nash v. Smith, 6 Conn. 421; Vanhorn v. Duckworth, 7 Ired. Eq
261.

[2] Where the demurrer does not go to the whole bill, it must clearly ex-

42

If it be to the whole relief, it will necessarily extend to the discovery, and should be framed accordingly; for, if the relief cannot be given, it would be idle to require a discovery; and if the discovery be required for any other purpose, it should be sought by a separate and independent bill.(*f*)¹ If the demurrer be to a part only of the relief, it will not necessarily extend to the discovery, because discovery may be necessary for obtaining the rest of the prayer. It may also happen that the demurrer will leave the relief untouched, and will extend only to the discovery or part of the discovery, on the special ground that the subject-matter is one in which the defendant is not obliged to answer, *e. g.*, where it would expose him to a penalty or forfeiture, or would be a disclosure of professional confidence.² But, unless such special ground

(*f*) Morris *v.* Morgan, 10 Sim. 341.

---

press the particular part which it is designed to 'cover, so that upon a reference of the answer to the residue of the bill upon exceptions for insufficiency, the master may be able to ascertain precisely how far the demurrer goes, and how much of the bill remains to be answered: Jarvis *v.* Palmer, 11 Paige 650 ; Clancy *v.* Craine, 2 Dev. Eq. 363; Gray *v.* Regan, 23 Miss. (1 Cushm.) 304 ; Burch *v.* Coney, 14 Jur. 1009.

A defendant cannot answer a bill and demur to the interrogatories: Kisor *v.* Stancifer, Wright 323.

¹ See Souza *v.* Belcher, 3 Edw. Ch. 117; Miller *v.* Ford, Saxton 358; Welles *v.* River Raisin R. R. Co., Walk. Ch. 35 ; Pool *v.* Lloyd, 5 Met. 525.

² Livingston *v.* Harris, 3 Paige 528 ; Brownell *v.* Curtis et al., 10 Paige 210.

But in such case the demurrer should be confined to such parts of the bill as tend to implicate him in the supposed crime: Burpee *v.* Smith, Walk. Ch. 327.

To a bill for a discovery against a surviving partner, and for an account, a demurrer to the discovery, alleging that it might subject him to penalties under the laws of the United States, is bad; it should state why and wherefore a forfeiture would be the consequence of discovery: Sharp *v.* Sharp, 3 Johns. Ch. 407. A demurrer to a bill because it prayed a discovery of that which would subject the defendants to the penalties of the act against

exist, the general rule is that the defendant cannot admit the right to relief, and at the same time demur to the discovery by which the relief is to be obtained.(*g*)　In all cases alike the rule *prevails, that the extent to which the demurrer is meant to be a defence should be distinctly pointed out.[1]　And if the protection claimed be too extensive, the defence will fail.　For a demurrer cannot be good in part and bad in part; but if it be general to the whole bill, and there be any part, either as to relief or discovery, to which an answer is requisite, the demurrer being entire, must be overruled.(*gg*)[2]

[*335]

(*g*) 1 Dan. Ch. P. 502.　　　　　(*gg*) 1 Dan. Ch. P. 538–540.

---

buying pretended titles, cannot be supported, if the answer need not necessarily show a *scienter* of the vendor's being out of possession, and a subsisting adverse possession: Le Roy *v.* Servis, 1 Cai. Cas. Eq. 3; s. c. 1 Johns. Cas. 417.　See also, on the point, Patterson *v.* Patterson, 1 Hayw. 167; Wolf *v.* Wolf, 2 Har. & Gill 282; Livingston *v.* Tompkins, 4 Johns. Ch. 415; Northrop *v.* Hatch, 6 Conn. 361. See, in addition, supra, Book I., chap. i., on Discovery.

[1] See Atwill *v.* Ferrett, 2 Blatchf. C. C. 39.

[2] Livingston *v.* Story, 9 Pet. 632 ; Brockway *v.* Copp, 3 Paige 539; Le Roy *v.* Veeder, 1 Johns. Cases 417 ; Laight *v.* Morgan, Id. 429; Verplank *v.* Gaines, 1 Johns. Ch. 57 ; Le Fort *v.* Delafield, 3 Edw. Ch. 32; Thompson *v.* Newlin, 3 Ired. Eq. 338 ; Russell *v.* Lanier, 4 Hey. 289 ; Kimberly *v.* Sells, 3 Johns. Ch. 467 ; Livingston *v.* Livingston, 4 Id. 294; Higinbotham *v.* Burnet, 5 Id. 184 ; Parsons *v.* Bowne, 7 Paige 354 ; Castleman *v.* Veitch, 3 Rand. 598 ; Griggs *v.* Thompson, 1 Ga. Decis. 146; Hollsclaw *v.* Johnson, 2 Id. 146 ; Blount *v.* Garen, 3 Hey. 88; Fancher *v.* Ingraham, 6 Blackf. 139 ; Carter *v.* Longworth, 4 Ham. 384; Western Ins. Co. *v.* Eagle Fire Ins. Co., 1 Paige 284 ; Parish *v.* Sloan, 3 Ired. Eq. 607 ; Harden *v.* Miller, Dudley 120 ; Williams *v.* Hubbard, Walk. Ch. 28; Thayer *v.* Lane, Harring. Ch. 247; Shed *v.* Garfield, 5 Verm. 39 ; Clark *v.* Davis, Harring. Ch. 227 ; Bank U. S. *v.* Biddle, 2 Pars. Eq. 32; Gray *v.* Regan, 23 Miss. (1 Cushm.) 304 ; Vanderveer *v.* Stryker, 4 Halst. Ch. 175; Conant *v.* Warren, 6 Gray 562 ; Atwill *v.* Ferrett, 2 Blatchf. C. C. 39. See also, Rowe *v.* Tonkin, L. R. 1 Eq. 9 ; Banta *v.* Moore, 2 McCarter (N. J.) 87; Metler *v.* Metler, 4 Green (N. J.) 457 ; Bonney *v.* Bonney, 29 Iowa, 448 ; Reilly *v.* Cavanaugh, 32 Ind. 214; O'Harra *v.* Cox, 42 Miss. 496 ; see also, Hawkins *v.* Clermont, 15 Mich. 511 ; State *v.* Young, 65 N. C. 579.

A demurrer might also have been overruled under the old practice, on the ground that it did not cover so much of the bill as it might by law have extended to, or that it was coupled with an answer extending to some part of the matter which was covered by the demurrer; but a different rule now prevails.(h)[1]

The principle on which a demurrer in equity is decided is the same which applies to a demurrer at law, viz., that, assuming the plaintiff's allegation to be true, he has not made out a sufficient case. And as it is therefore an invariable rule that on argument of a demurrer, all allegations of fact contained in the bill, except as to matters of which the Court takes judicial notice, must for the purposes of the argument be deemed conclusive,[2] a demurrer introducing contrary or additional averments, is termed a

(h) Orders of 1841, xxxvi., xxxvii.

But the demurrer will not be overruled if the bill is multifarious. See Dimmock v. Bixby, 20 Pick. 368. When a demurrer to a bill, on the ground of multifariousness, is sustained as to part of the bill, all that part of the bill not objectionable on that ground remains in court, and the complainant may proceed upon it as if no demurrer had been interposed : Durling v. Hammar, 20 N. J. Eq. 220.

[1] See Spofford v. Manning, 6 Paige 383; Kuypers v. Reformed Dutch Church, Id. 570 ; Clark v. Phelps, 6 Johns. Ch. 214 ; Chase's Case, 1 Bland. Ch. 206 ; McDermott v. Blois, R. M. Charl. 281 ; Robertson v. Bingley, 1 McCord's Ch. 352; Jarvis v. Palmer, 11 Paige 650. Where a bill is demurred to in part, and answered in part, the captions should be distinct, and specify the nature of the pleadings ; and if they do not so specify them, they will be had in form. The parts demurred to should be pointed out, for if left indefinite, the answer will overrule the demurrer: Bruen v. Bruen, 4 Edw. Ch. 640. A similar change to that stated in the text, however, has been introduced into the practice of the U. S Courts, Rules in Equity, No. xxxvi.; vii.; and in Pennsylvania, Rules in Eq. No. xxxv.

[2] But facts charged on the complainant's information merely, are not admitted by demurrer: Williams v. Presbyt. Soc., 1 Ohio St. N. S. 478. So where a fact is charged as a conclusion from other circumstances stated in the bill, but which do not in fact support the allegation : Redmond v. Dickerson, 1 Stockt. 507.

speaking demurrer, and can not be sustained.[1] But if the allegations are inconsistent or uncertain, or if any material allegation be omitted, the construction on demurrer will be against the bill.(i)[2]

The course of procedure on demurrer depends upon the plaintiff's opinion of its validity. If he thinks that, as the bill stands, the objection is good, but that he can remove it by restating his case, he may submit to the demurrer and amend his bill. If he thinks the demurrer bad, he may set it down for argument. If the demurrer is allowed on argument, the suit is at an end, unless the demurrer is confined to a part of the bill, *or the Court give permission to the plaintiff to [*336] amend. If it is overruled, the defendant must make a fresh defence by answer, unless he obtain permission to avail himself of a plea.(k)[3]

It is not compulsory on a defendant to demur. The principal motives for doing so are, to avoid a prejudicial discovery, and to prevent unnecessary expense. And where the only matter in dispute is a point of law, this

(i) Mortimer v. Frazer, 1 Dan. Ch. P. 500; Taylor v. Barclay, 2 Sim. 213 : Edsell v. Buchanan, 4 B. C. C. 254; Campbell v. Mackay, 1 M. & C. 603; Foss v. Harbottle, 2 Hare 461, 503.

(k) 1 Dan. Ch. P. 545–560; Orders of 1845, xliv.–xlvii.

---

[1] A demurrer can be objected to as a speaking demurrer, only when it introduces some new fact or averment which is necessary to support the demurrer, and which does not distinctly appear on the face of the bill: Brooks v. Gibbons, 4 Paige 374. See also on the subject, Tallmadge v. Lovett, 3 Edw. Ch. 563; Saxon v. Barksdale, 4 Dessaus. 522; Redd v. Wood, 2 Ga. Decis. 174; Gray v. Regan, 23 Miss. 304; Black v. Shreeve, 3 Halst. Ch. 440.

[2] See Simpson v. Fogo, 1 Johns. & H. 18.

[3] Story Eq. Plead. § 460; Cole Co. v. Anghey, 12 Mo. 132; Henderson v. Dennison, 1 Cart. (Ind.) 152. See, on this subject, Rules Eq. U. S. Cts., No. xxxiv.; Penna., No. xxxii. As to amendment of a demurrer, see Holliday v. Riordon, 12 Ga. 417.

latter object may often be attained by a bill intentionally
so framed, as to be open to demurrer upon that point.
If these motives do not exist, it is generally an inexpe-
dient and often an objectionable course, as involving a
premature discussion of the case, of which the plaintiff
will probably take advantage. If fraud or misconduct
be alleged in the bill, it affords an additional reason
against demurring, as it may expose the defendant to unfavorable comments.[1]   And even when he wishes to avoid
discovery, he may now, to some extent, if the bill be demurrable, protect himself by answer.(*l*)

3. The principle of a defence by plea is, that the defendant avers some one matter of avoidance, or denies
some one allegation of the bill, and contends that assuming the truth of all the allegations in the bill, or of all
except that which is the subject of denial, there is sufficient to defeat the plaintiff's claim.[2]   It is applicable, like
a demurrer, to any class of objections; but the most usual
grounds of plea are, 1. Want of jurisdiction; 2. Personal
disability in the plaintiff; 3. A decision already made by
the Court of Chancery, or by some other Court of competent jurisdiction, or a suit already pending in a Court
of equity respecting the same subject.   But the suit must

(*l*) Mitf. 108 ; Wigr. on Discovery, 2d ed., p. 95 ; 38th Order of August,
1841.

---

[1] If a bill contain an allegation of fraud, it is a general rule that such
allegation must be answered, and a general demurrer cannot be allowed :
Stovall *v.* N. Bank of Miss., 5 S. & M. 17 ; Anderson *v.* Lewis, Freem.
206 ; Rambo *v.* Rambo, 4 Dessaus. 251 ; Niles *v.* Anderson, 5 How. (Miss.)
365 ; Carter *v.* Longworth, 4 Ham. 384 ; Miller *v.* Saunders, 17 Ga. 92. See
ante, 332, note.

[2] The office of a plea is not to " deny the equity (of a bill) but to bring
forward some fact which, if true, displaces it :" New Brunswick Co. *v.*
Muggeridge, 4 Drew. 696.

be pending in a Court of equity. If there be a pending action at law, the proper course is to put the plaintiff to his election by motion, which Court he will proceed in.(*m*)   4. Want of equity, where the equity depends on a single point.

*Pleas of the first class, or those in which new matter is alleged in avoidance, are termed affirm- [*337] ative. They do not require any special comment, and it will be sufficient to mention a few of the most ordinary occurence, viz., the Statute of Limitations, the Statute of Frauds, a release under seal, an account settled or stated account, an award, and a purchase for valuable considera- tion without notice.(*n*)¹

Pleas of the second class, or those in which an allega- tion of the bill is denied, are termed Negative Pleas, and are applicable when the plaintiff, by false allegation on one point, has created an apparent equity, and asks dis- covery as consequent thereon, *e. g.*, where he alleges

(*m*) Orders of May, 1845, 16, 20, 21, 15 ; 1 Dan. Ch. P. 599, 604, 79 1 795.

(*n*) 1 Dan. Ch. P. 606–643.

---

¹ A plea of the Statute of Limitations is bad, unless accompanied by an answer supporting it, by a particular and precise denial of all the facts and circumstances charged in the bill, and which in equity may avoid the statute: Goodrich *v.* Pendleton, 3 Johns. Ch. 384 ; Bloodgood *v.* Kane, 8 Cowen 360. But it is not necessary to refer, in terms, to the statute which creates the bar: Van Hook *v.* Whitlock, 7 Paige 373. See Stearns *v.* Page, 1 Story 204.

A plea of stated account must aver that the accounts settled all dealings between the parties, and were just, and fair, and due ; and these averments must be supported by an answer to the same effect: Schwarz *v.* Wendell, Harring. Ch. 395. If the complainant does not, in his bill, allege that there has been any statement of accounts between the parties, the defendant may plead an account stated, without annexing a copy of the account to his plea : Weed *v.* Smull, 7 Paige 573. See Danels *v.* Taggart, 1 Gill & J. 311.

himself to be a partner or heir-at-law, and asks for an account of the business, or particulars of the estate. In this case a denial by answer would exclude the relief, but it would not protect the defendant from giving the required discovery, because on a principle which has been already explained, a defendant who answers at all must answer fully. (o)   In order, therefore, to avoid such discovery, he must resort to a negative plea, denying the allegation of partnership or heirship; and until the validity of his plea is determined, he will be protected from giving discovery consequent on the allegation.[1]

It is, however, very seldom that a pure negative plea can be made available. For although it protects against discovery consequent on the alleged equity, it does not protect against discovery required to prove it. If, therefore, there be any statements in the bill tending to prove the disputed allegation, distinct from such allegation itself, the discovery asked on those points must be excepted from the plea, and must be given by an answer in support. Thus, if the equity alleged were that a testator was indebted to the plaintiff, and the bill asked discovery consequent on the debt, e. g., payment of interest, a plea [*338] of "no debt" would cover *all the discovery and relief sought, including the allegation of debt, but excepting the discovery in evidence of the debt. (p)[2]

The same principle has been held applicable where the plea was negative in substance though not in terms ; e. g.,

(o) Supra, Discovery.

(p) Thring v. Edgar, 2 S. & S. 274 ; Denys v. Locock, 3 M. & C. 205.

---

[1] A plea simply denying a fact alleged in the bill, as e. g., a partnership is bad : Innes v. Evans, 3 Edw. Ch. 454 ; Bailey v. Le Roy, 2 Edw. Ch. 514 ; Black v. Black, 15 Ga. 445.

[2] See Everitt v. Watts, 3 Edw. Ch. 486.

where the bill alleged that a deceased person had left no heirs *ex parte paternâ*, and that the plaintiff was heir *ex parte maternâ*, and alleged further, that the defendants by correspondence had admitted the plaintiff's title, a plea that a specified person was heir *ex parte paternâ* was over-ruled, because it was not coupled with an answer as to the alleged correspondence.(*q*)

There is a third class of plea, which may be termed the anomalous plea, which is applicable when the plaintiff has anticipated a legitimate plea, and has charged an equity in avoidance of it; *e. g.*, when having stated his original equity, he states that a subsequent release was given, or is pretended by the defendant to have been given, and charges fraud in obtaining such release. In this case the release or other original defence may be pleaded with averments denying the fraud, or other equity charged in avoidance. The term anomalous is applicable to such plea, because it does not tender an independent issue, but sets up anew the impeached defence, with averments in denial of the impeaching equity.

It is obvious from the nature of the anomalous plea, that it is only good against the original equity, and is in-effectual against the equity charged in avoidance; and therefore, the allegations which constitute that equity must not only be denied by averments in the plea, in order to render the defence complete, but must in respect of the plaintiff's right of discovery be the subject of a full answer in support.(*r*)[1]

(*q*) Wig. on Disc. ss. 115, 120; Emerson *v.* Harland, 3 Sim. 490; 8 Bli. 62; Clayton *v.* Winchelsea, 3 Y. & C. 426.

(*r*) Foley *v.* Hill, 3 M. & C. 475.

---

[1] A defendant is bound to support his plea by an answer, as to those circumstances stated in the bill, which, if admitted to be true, would be

Where an answer in support is not required, a plea to
[*339] all *the relief is a bar to all the discovery; for
the discovery is only material in order to obtain
the relief.(s)   It has been doubted whether this rule applies, where the relief is at law, *i. e.*, whether the defendant to a bill seeking discovery in aid of an action at law,
can plead his legal defence in bar to the discovery, so as
to preclude the plaintiff from proving thereby his case at
law, and to transfer the trial of the legal defence into a
Court of equity.   There may, perhaps, be inconvenience
in this course, but the principle on which the rule is based
seems to include both cases alike, and to render the plea
a protection against all discovery, except such as would
disprove or avoid it.(t)[1]

If an answer in support is requisite, the part to which
the plea applies must be distinctly shown, for the answer

(s) Sutton *v.* Scarborough, 9 Ves. 71.

(t) Hindman *v.* Taylor, 2 B. C. C. 7 ; Wigr. on Discovery, s. 66 ; Hare
on Discovery, p. 47–62.

---

evidence to counter-prove the plea : Bogardus *v.* Trinity Church, 4 Paige
178 ; Tompkins *v.* Ward, 4 Sandf. Ch. 594 ; Cox *v.* Mayor of Griffin, 17
Ga. 249 ; or would tend in any way to discredit it : Hunt *v.* Penrice, 18
Jur. 4.   And the averments are as necessary as the answer ; for where a
bill charged misrepresentation, coercion, and fraud, in procuring a release
of a debt, and the defendant put in a plea and answer, and in his plea insisted on the release in bar, without noticing the allegation of fraud,
though in the answer it was fully met and denied, the plea was held bad :
Allen *v.* Randolph, 4 Johns. Ch. 693.   See also on this point, Fish *v.*
Miller, 5 Paige 26 ; Bolton *v.* Gardner, 3 Id. 273 ; Bellows *v.* Stone, 8 N.
H. 280 ; French *v.* Shottwell, 5 Johns. Ch. 555 ; Ferguson *v.* O'Harra, 1
Peters C. C. 493.   See as to rules in the United States and Pennsylvania,
ante, 332, note.

[1] See Lane *v.* Stevens, 3 Edw. Ch. 480 ; 9 Paige 622 ; in which it was
decided, that a defendant in a suit at law can be compelled, through a discovery bill, to answer, even though the discovery may be fatal to the defence he sets up.

is necessary in determining the validity of the plea.[1] If, therefore, the plea cover too much, and so prevent an answer on any material point, or if the answer, though in terms applying to all the requisite discovery, be substantially insufficient, the plea will be disallowed.(u) For on argument of the plea, every fact stated in the bill which ought to be, but is not denied by the answer, will be taken to be true as against the plea. And by the old practice, if the plea covered too little, e. g., if it did not cover so much of the bill as it might by law have extended to; or if the answer covered too much, and extended to some part overruled by the plea, in both cases the plea was bad.[2] If an answer is not required in support, the plea is not vitiated by applying it to too large a portion of the bill, but may be allowed as to that part only to which it would properly extend. And in this respect

(u) 1 Dan. Ch. P. 591; Foley v. Hill, 3 M. & C. 475; Harris v. Harris, 3 Hare 450.

---

[1] See Jarvis v. Palmer, 11 Paige 650.

[2] An answer can overrule a plea only where it relates to matters which the defendant by his plea declines to answer : Bogardus v. Trinity Church, 4 Paige 178; Souzer v. De Meyer, 2 Id. 574; Ferguson v. O'Harra, 1 Pet. C. C. 493.

A general answer, and not merely in support of the plea, overrules the plea: Taylor v. Luther, 2 Sumner 228; Clark v. Saginaw Bank, Harring. Ch. 240. So, an answer containing more than is strictly applicable to the support of the plea: Stearns v. Page, 1 Story 204.

If an answer commences as an answer to the whole bill, it overrules a plea or demurrer to any particular part of the bill, although such part is not in fact answered: Leacraft v. Demprey, 4 Paige 124. Now, however, by Equity Rule xxxvii. of the United States Courts, and Equity Rule xxxv.. in Pennsylvania, it is provided that no demurrer or plea shall be held bad and overruled on argument, only because the answer of the defendant may extend to some part of the same matter, as may be covered by such demurrer or plea.

it differs from a demurrer, which can not, as we have already seen, be good in part and bad in part. (v)[1]

[*340] *The form of a pure plea, whether affirmative or negative, is that " This defendant doth plead to the said bill, and for plea saith," &c., stating the matter of avoidance or denial on which he relies; and then concluding, "All which this defendant doth aver to be the truth, and pleads the same to the said bill."

The form of a plea supported by an answer, whether negative or anomalous, is that " This defendant as to all the discovery and relief, other than and except so much of the bill as seeks a discovery, whether," &c. (setting out at length the excepted interrogatories), " doth plead thereto, and for plea saith, &c., all which this defendant doth aver to be the truth, and doth plead the same to the said bill, except such parts thereof as aforesaid; and this defendant, not waiving his said plea, but relying thereon, doth for answer to so much of the said complainant's said

(v) Mitf. 295.

---

[1] A plea may be good in part or bad in part: French v. Shotwell, 20 Johns. 668; Kirkpatrick v. White, 4 Wash. C. C. 595.

Where a plea is overruled, the Court may either order it to stand for an answer, with liberty to the plaintiff to except, or it may be overruled altogether, and the defendant ordered to answer: Goodrich v. Pendleton, 3 Johns. Ch. 394. The Court may permit a plea to stand for an answer, if it contains matter which, if put in the form of an answer, would have constituted a valid defence to some material part of the matter to which it is pleaded in bar: Orcutt v. Orms, 5 Paige 459. By allowing a plea to stand for an answer, the Court decides that it contains matters of defence; but that it is not a full defence to all which it professes to cover, or that it is informally pleaded; or that the defence cannot be properly made by way of plea; or that the plea is not properly supported by answer: Id. See also Souzer v. De Meyer, 2 Paige 574; Leacroft v. Demprey, 4 Id. 124. When a plea is adjudged a good defence in part, and ordered to stand for an answer, it is a sufficient answer to so much of the bill as it covers, unless by the order the complainant is given leave to except: Beall v. Blake, 10 Ga. 449.

bill as this defendant hath not pleaded to, answer and say," &c., following the ordinary form of answers.(w)

The rules of pleading applicable to a plea are, that it must raise a single issue, and that its averments must have the same certainty as those of a plea at law.

It must be confined to a single issue.[1] It is not necessary that it should consist of a single fact; for the defence offered by way of plea may in equity, as at law, consist of many facts, provided they all tend to one point constituting the defence. But it cannot include several defences, or as it is technically termed, a defendant cannot, without special leave, put in a double plea to the whole bill, or to the same part of it. He cannot, for example, plead to a charge of infringing a patent, first, that it is not a new invention; and secondly, that it is not a useful one; because either of these facts, if true, would be a separate defence.(x) Of course this rule does not apply where the bill makes a double claim, so as to prohibit different pleas to the different *parts of such a bill; for such pleas [*341] are not, in fact, a double defence to the same claim, but distinct defences to distinct claims.

Its averments must have the same certainty as those

(w) Denys v. Locock, 3 M. & C. 205.

(x) Whitbread v. Brockhurst, 1 B. C. C. 404; Kay v. Marshall, 1 Keen 190; Strickland v. Strickland, 12 Sim. 253.

---

[1] Saltus v. Tobias, 7 Johns. Ch. 214; Van Hook v. Whitlock, 3 Paige 409; Goodrich v. Pendleton, 3 Johns. Ch. 386; Driver v. Driver, 6 Ind. 286.

The cases in which the court allows the defendant to make several defences by pleas to the bill, are those in which the making the defences by answer would render it necessary for the defendant to set out long accounts, or where the discovery sought by the bill would be productive of injury to the defendant in his business, or otherwise: Didier v. Davison, 10 Paige 615; see Moreton v. Harrison, 1 Bland Ch. 491; Ridgley v. Warfield, 1 Id. 494, in notis.

of a plea at law. It has been already stated,
the bill and answer in equity, there is not requii
same certainty of averment as at law; partly bec
is not necessary to reduce the litigation to a singl
and partly because all issues, whether of law or f.
decided or adjusted for decision by the Court.   It
therefore, essential that they should be kept stric
tinct.   On a plea, however, there can be but on
raised; and we shall presently see that the issues
and fact, though both decided by the Court, are
cided at the same time, but the law is first settled
argument, and the fact afterwards at the hearing
plea.   For this reason, the laxity of averment i
and answer is not permitted in a plea; but it is r
that every essential fact be expressly* averred, so
the validity of the plea be questioned, it may be
the argument whether the alleged facts constitut
fence; and if its truth be impugned, no doubt ma
as to the specific facts to which the evidence n
directed.

It is also necessary to the validity of a plea, th.
verified by the defendant's oath.[1]   This rule is in
ance with the general principle of equity that l
shall set up a defence which he does not believe
true.   The exceptions to it are where the matter]
is provable, not by evidence of witnesses, but by
of record, *i. e.*, by the enrolled proceedings of a C
record.   In this case, the mere inspection of the
is conclusive, and no oath is required.(*y*)

The course of procedure on a plea will depend

(*y*) 1 Dan. Ch. P. 651–656.

---

[1] Wild *v.* Gladstone, 15 Jur. 713.   It seems the proper course is
to take the plea off file, if it be unsworn : Ibid.

view taken by the plaintiff as to the sufficiency in law, or the truth in fact, of the defence. If he thinks the plea *valid, but that he can meet it by amendment, he may do so. If he thinks it invalid, he may [*342] set it down for argument. If he thinks it untrue, he may file a replication, and go to a hearing on the issue of its truth.[1] If the plea be overruled on argument, the defendant must answer. Or the Court may pursue an intermediate course by reserving the benefit of it till the hearing, or by directing it to stand for an answer with liberty for the plaintiff to except to its sufficiency.[2] If it is allowed on argument, its validity is established, but the plaintiff may still file a replication, and go to a hearing on the question of its truth. He may sometimes, too, obtain permission to amend his bill, but this is not a matter of course after the allowance of a plea, and will only be granted on a special application. If the plea be replied to, either originally or after its allowance on argument, the cause will be brought to a hearing on the single question of its truth. If it is sustained by the evidence, there will be a decree for the defendant. If it is disproved, he can set up no further defence, but a decree will be made against him.(z)

A plea, like a demurrer, is not compulsory on the defendant. And if he has no strong motive for resisting discovery, an answer is generally the safer defence.

4. ˙ The defence by answer is the most usual, and generally the most advisable course. It puts. on the record the whole case of the defendant, enabling him to

(z) 1 Dan. Ch. P. 656–668, 1845–48–50.

---

[1] See, as to the practice in this point, Wilkes v. Henry, 4 Edw. Ch. 672.
[2] See cases cited, supra, note, p. 339.

use all or any of his grounds of defence, subject onl
the necessity of verifying them on oath;[1] and an ol
tion which might have been made by demurrer or]
will, in most cases, be equally a bar to relief when insi
on by answer, although it will not, as we have alre
seen, excuse the defendant from giving the discovery
quired by the bill.

In the case of an objection for want of parties,
taken by demurrer or plea, the rule formerly was 1
whether pointed out in the answer or not, such. objec
[*343]   *was valid at the hearing, but that the
          might stand over for the plaintiff to amend,
ject, however, if notice had been given by the answe
payment of the defendant's costs of the day.   This
has been recently modified in two respects; viz.
Where an objection for want of parties is suggeste(
the answer, by enabling the plaintiff to set it down
immediate argument, and if he neglect to do so by de
ring him, at the discretion of the Court, from libert
amend at the hearing; and, 2. When the objectioi
not so suggested, by enabling the Court to reject it at
hearing, and to make a decree saving the rights of
absent parties.(a)

The answer sustains a double character.   It is fir
narrative of the defendant's case, and secondly a disco\
in aid of the plaintiff.   It commences, "This defi
ant, reserving to himself all benefit of exception to
said complainant's said bill of complaint, for ans
thereto saith."[1]   It then goes on to answer the plaint

(a) 39th and 40th Orders of August, 1841. [And see Rules in Eq.
Courts, No. lii., liii.; Penn. xxv., xxvii.]

---

[1] See Daniels' Ch. Prac. 748.

[2] The general reservation of exceptions in the commencement (

interrogatories, and to introduce such new matter as may be required; and concludes with what is termed the general traverse or denial of all matters in the bill. This is usually expressed in drafts by the words, "Without this, that," &c., and is filled up in the engrossment.

It is said to have obtained, when the practice was for the defendant to set forth his case, without answering, every clause in the bill. And, though now unnecessary, it is still continued in practice.(b)

The averments of an answer, so far as it is a narrative of the defendant's case, are governed by the same rules as those of a bill; viz., they must state the defence with reasonable certainty and without scandal or impertinence.[1]

In so far as the answer consists of discovery, it is regulated by the principles already discussed under that head of jurisdiction; viz., no defendant need discover matters tending to criminate himself, or to expose him to penalty or forfeiture; no defendant need discover legal advice *which has been given him by his professional advisers, or statements of facts which have passed   [*344]

(b) Mitf. on Plead. 314.

---

answer cannot be relied on as raising exceptions to the jurisdiction; neither can it perform the office of a general demurrer, or of exceptions to the averments of the bill: O'Neill v. Cole, 4 Md. 107; Oldham v. Trimble, 15 Mo. 225.

Where an answer is regularly entitled in the cause, the absence of the preliminary words, "to the said complainant's bill of complaint," is not objectionable: Rabbett v. Squire, 1 Eq. Rep. 56.

[1] Repetition of a material statement in an answer to an amended bill is impertinent. It is no defence to an application to strike out impertinent matter, that it will make the pleading inconsistent, unreasoning, and incongruous: Allfrey v. Allfrey, 14 Beav. 235; 15 Jur. 831; Gier v. Gregg, 4 McLean 202. Where parts of an answer are *primâ facie* scandalous, the court will order a reference to a master without examining whether they are or are not responsive: Mathewson v. Mathewson, 1 R. I. 397.

43

between himself and them in reference to the dispute
in litigation, and official persons must not disclose any
matter of state, the publication of which may be prejudicial to the community; but subject to these restrictions,
every competent defendant must answer on oath as to all
facts material to the plaintiff's case. He must answer
fully, if he answer at all; *i. e.*, he must either protect
himself by demurrer or plea, or must answer every legitimate interrogatory, and he must answer distinctly, completely, without needless prolixity, and to the best of his
information and belief.(*c*)[1]   He is not, however, bound to

(*c*) Supra, Discovery.

_____

[1] See Story's Equity Pldg. §§ 846–848 ; Brooks *v.* Byam, 1 Story 296;
Taylor *v.* Luther, 1 Sumner 228 ; Bradford *v.* Geiss, 4 Wash. C. C. R. 513 ;
Devereaux *v.* Cooper, 11 Verm. 103 ; Woods *v.* Morrell, 1 Johns. Ch. 103 ;
Robertson *v.* Bingley, 1 McCord's Ch. 333 ; Hagthorp *v.* Hook, 1 Gill & J.
270 ; Bailey *v.* Wilson, 1 Dev. & Batt. Eq. 182 ; Carneal *v.* Wilson, 3 Litt.
80 ; Dinsmoor *v.* Hazleton, 2 Foster 535 ; Warren *v.* Warren, 30 Verm.
530 ; McKim *v.* White Hall Co., 2 Md. Ch. 510.; Wootten *v.* Burch, Id.
190 ; Kinnaman *v.* Henry, 2 Halst. Ch. 90. It is a general rule that a defendant cannot, by answer, excuse himself from answering: Bank of Utica
v. Messereau, 7 Paige 517.

On the other hand, a defendant may answer in part, and by his answer
state reasons why he should not be compelled to make further answer:
Hunt *v.* Gookin, 6 Verm. 426. That an answer is insufficient in some particulars, does not destroy its effect upon the points upon which it answers
directly : Whitney *v.* Robbins, 2 Green (N. J.) 360.

A defendant need not answer any allegations in the bill which are not
material to be answered : Utica Insurance Co. *v.* Lynch, 3 Paige 210;
Butler *v.* Catling, 1 Root 310; West *v.* Williams, 1 Md. Ch. 358. Yet in
such case it should appear that an answer would, in no aspect of the complainant's case as made by the bill, be of service to him: Gilkey *v.* Paige,
Walker's Ch. 520. Nor need a defendant answer any interrogatory not
founded on some allegation in the bill: Miller *v.* Saunders, 17 Ga. 92; nor
respond to an allegation as to his own insolvency : Mayer *v.* Galluchat, 6
Rich. Eq. (S. C.) 1. Where a defendant denies all knowledge of a fact
charged in the bill, it is not necessary for him to state his belief in relation
to it: Morris *v.* Parker, 3 Johns. Ch. 297. Where a fact is charged in a
bill, which is within the defendant's knowledge as an act done by him, he

answer as to conclusions of law, nor as to conclusions of fact, when the evidence only is within his knowledge, and not the fact which it tends to prove. And in such cases it is generally advisable to detail exactly the facts or evidence,

---

must answer positively, and not according to his remembrance and belief; but where the fact charged did not occur within six years, it is an exception to the rule : Carey v. Jones, 8 Ga. 516. A defendant cannot be compelled to answer interrogatories based upon a hypothetical statement in the bill: Grim v. Wheeler, 3 Edw. Ch. 334. Nor a mere recital in the bill: Mechanics' Bank v. Levy, 3 Paige 606. Nor a mere arithmetical proposition : McIntyre v. Union College, 6 Id. 239. And where there is a general denial in the defendant's answer, which is clear and distinct, any ambiguity in a particular part will not vitiate or destroy other parts. The whole answer is to be taken together. See Smith v. Fisher, 2 Dessaus. 275; and, in addition, upon the requisites of the answer, note, page 307, **ante.**

By the Equity Rules of the U. S. Courts, No. xxxix., and of Penna., No. xxxviii., it is provided, that the rule that if a defendant submits to answer, he shall answer fully to all the matters of the bill, shall no longer apply in cases where he might, by plea, protect himself from such answer and discovery. And it is also provided, that the defendant shall be entitled in all cases, by answer, to insist upon all matters of defence (not being matters of abatement, or to the character of the parties, or of matters of form) in bar of, or to the merits of the bill of which he may be entitled to avail himself by a plea in bar; and in such answer he shall not be compellable to answer any other matters than he would be compellable to answer and discover upon filing a plea in bar, and an answer in support of such plea, touching the matters set forth in the bill to avoid or repel the bar or defence. Thus, for example, a *bonâ fide* purchaser, for a valuable consideration, without notice, may set up the defence by way of answer instead of plea, and will be entitled to the same protection, and will not be compellable to make any further answer or discovery of his title than he would be in any answer in support of such a plea.

A bill wanting in equity can derive no aid from the answer, and is liable to be dismissed on motion, though the answer disclose a case that would entitle the complainant to relief: Lockard v. Lockard, 16 Ala. 423.

The defendant may state in his answer and take issue on matters which have happened after bill filed, but the Court will not deal with the subject of the suits by interlocutory order, which occur after the answer has been filed, and are not brought forward by amendment, by supplemental bill, or by supplemental answer: Stamps v. Birmingham, &c., R. R., 7 Hare 258 ; 2 Ph. 673.

and to submit to the Court whether they warrant the plaintiff's conclusion, and then to conclude with a special traverse in the words of the interrogatory that " save as aforesaid the defendant cannot state as to his belief or otherwise whether," &c.

In framing an answer it is seldom possible to keep the narrative and discovery separate, nor is it generally advisable to do so, beyond what may be requisite for bringing out distinctly the defence itself. For by intermingling the two, and embodying in the discovery a running connection with the defence, it is rendered less available to the plaintiff, who can scarcely read any portion of it in evidence, without at the same time reading the defensive statement.

The answer is generally, though not always, followed by schedules, containing accounts, lists of documents, and other matters of a similar kind, which have been asked for by the bill, or which the defendant considers necessary to his defence. And such schedules are referred to in the [*345] *body of the answer, by stating that they are annexed thereto, and praying that they may be taken as part thereof.

After the answer is put in, the next step in procedure regards the question of its sufficiency, viz., whether the defendant has given all due discovery. If he has not, the plaintiff may except.[1] The exceptions are signed by

---

[1] Exceptions are applicable, however, only where matters alleged in the bill are not sufficiently answered, and not because the answer does not state matters set forth in avoidance or defence, with fullness and explicitness: Lanum v. Steel, 10 Humph. 280 ; or for mere matters of irregularity of form, for which the remedy is to move to take the answer off file : Vermilye v. Christie, 4 Sandf. Ch. 376. Where an answer is responsive to any one material allegation, it cannot be stricken from the file as frivolous, but the remedy is by exception : May v. Williams, 17 Ala. 23.

counsel, and are delivered within a limited time to the proper officer.[1] They are headed with the name of the cause, and are entitled "Exceptions taken by the said complainant to the insufficient answer of the said defendant." They then go on successively, "First, for that the said defendant has not, to the best of his knowledge, remembrance, information, and belief, answered and set forth whether," &c., following the words of the interrogatory which has been insufficiently answered; "Secondly, for that the said defendant has not in manner aforesaid answered and set forth whether," &c., following the words of the next interrogatory which has been insufficiently answered; and so on throughout; and they then conclude, "In all which particulars the said complainant excepts to the answer of the said defendant, and humbly prays that the said defendant may be compelled to put in a sufficient answer thereto." If the defendant does not submit to the exceptions, they are referred to one of the Masters for consideration; and if he reports the answer insufficient, a further answer must be filed on the points excepted to. If either party is dissatisfied with the Master's decision, he may bring the question before the Court by exceptions to the report, and it will then be finally decided. If the defendant puts in a second or third insufficient answer, the plaintiff does not deliver new exceptions, but must refer it for insufficiency on the old ones, pointing out in the order which he obtains, the particular exception or exceptions to which he requires a further answer.[2] If a third answer is reported insufficient, the defendant is

---

[1] Improperly or carelessly drawn exceptions will be overruled : Duke of Brunswick v. Duke of Cambridge, 12 Beav. 279; McKeen v. Field, 4 Edw. Ch. 379.

[2] See Rider v. Riely, 2 Md. Ch. 16.

examined personally on interrogatories; and is committed
to prison until he shall have perfectly answered them.[1]

[*346]   *The next step, after the sufficiency of the answer is determined, is the amendment of the
plaintiff's bill.[2] Before the answer is filed, the plaintiff

---

[1] See, on the practice as to exceptions to answers, Rules in Equity of U.
S. Courts, No. lxi., &c.; Penn., xl., xliii., &c.

[2] See, as instances of amendment, Noyes *v.* Sawyer, 3 Verm. 160; Aren-
dell *v.* Blackwell, 1 Dev. Eq. 354; Stephens *v.* Terrel, 3 Monr. 131; Gayle
v. Singleton, 1 Stew. 566; Ontario Bank *v.* Schermerhorn, 10 Paige 109;
Ayres *v.* Valentine, 2 Edw. Ch. 451; Buckley *v.* Corse, Saxton 504; West
v. Hall, 3 Har. & J. 221; Walker *v.* Hallett, 1 Ala. N. S. 379; Jennings
v. Springs, 1 Bailey Eq. 181; Baynton *v.* Barstow, 38 Maine 577. But an
amendment will not be permitted, unless it appears that the plaintiff will
be entitled to relief upon the case made by the bill, after the amendment
made: Mitchell *v.* Lenox, 1 Edw. Ch. 428. Nor where the court is satisfied
that the proposed allegation cannot be substantiated : Prescott *v.* Hubbell,
1 Hill. Ch. 210.   Nor where the matter of the proposed amendment might,
with reasonable diligence, have been inserted in the original bill : North
American Coal Co. *v.* Dyett, 2 Edw. Ch. 115.   Nor when, on demurrer, a
bill has been dismissed on the merits of the case as stated, for want of
equity : Lyon *v.* Tallmadge, 1 Johns. Ch. 184. See Farmers' and Mechanics'
Bank *v.* Griffith, 2 Wis. 443.

Amendments to a bill can only be granted where the bill is defective in
parties, or in the prayer for relief, or in the omission or mistake of a fact
or circumstance connected with the substance, but not forming the substance itself, nor repugnant thereto; and not so as to create a different case
or a new bill, or it will be demurrable : Carey *v.* Smith, 11 Ga. 539; Larkins *v.* Biddle, 21 Ala. 252; Lyon *v.* Tallmadge, 1 Johns. Ch. 184; Garner
v. Keaton, 13 Ga. 431; Rumbly *v.* Stainton, 24 Ala. 712; Shields *v.* Barrow, 17 How. U. S. 130; School Dist. *v.* Macloon, 4 Wis. 79. So they are
permissible only as respects matters occurring prior to the filing of the
original bill : Burke *v.* Smith, 15 Ill. 158. On demurrer, however, the court
cannot inquire into the competency or regularity of an amendment previously allowed by the order of the court: McGehee *v.* Jones, 10 Ga. 127.
An injunction or other sworn bill cannot be amended by *striking out* material and substantial allegations and charges; but only by addition of explanatory or supplemental statements: Carey *v.* Smith, 11 Ga. 539; and
in such case the amendment must also be verified under oath. The complainant also must show a sufficient excuse, and the application must be
made as soon as the necessity is discovered: Id.; McDougald *v.* Dougherty,

may amend as often as he thinks fit; but after an answer, he is precluded from doing so, until its sufficiency or insufficiency is admitted or determined. If the answer be insufficient, he is remitted to his former right of amending at discretion. If it be sufficient, he is entitled as of course to one order for amendment, but any subsequent order must be obtained on special grounds. The object of amendment may be either to vary or add to the case originally made, or to meet the defence by new matter. The old method of doing this was by a special replication followed up, if necessary, by rejoinder, surrejoinder, &c. according to the forms of pleading at law. But the

---

11 Ga. 570. Where the new matter would affect the opposite party prejudicially, it should not have relation back to the time of filing the original bill, but the suit should be considered as pending only from the time of amendment: McDougald v. Dougherty, 11 Ga. 570. On an amendment, however trifling, at any time before answer, the general rule is, though its reasonableness has been doubted, that the defendant may demur de novo to the whole bill. But where the amendment is made after a demurrer made and decided and answer filed, the defendant cannot demur again to the whole bill, unless the amendment is so far material as to vary the case made by the original bill, and change the complainant's equity : Booth v. Stamper, 10 Ga. 109. After the pleadings are made up, and the cause set down for trial, the bill is not amendable, except within the discretion of the court upon special cause shown ; and this whether it be a sworn bill or not. If an amendment be made after issue joined, without order and verification in a sworn bill, it will be struck out on motion: Molyneaux v. Collier, 13 Ga. 406 ; see Michan v. Wyatt, 21 Ala. 813. An amended bill is to be considered in many respects as an original bill: Carey v. Smith, 11 Ga. 539 ; and when a new defendant is added, it is entirely original as to him, and he is entitled to the same time to plead, answer, and demur, as to an original suit : Hoxey v. Carey, 12 Ga. 534.

See, on the subject of amendments, Rules in Equity in the U. S. Courts, Nos. xxviii., xxxv., xlvi.; in Pennsylvania, Nos. xlviii. to liv. Under these rules it is held that an amendment to a bill in equity, which would so change its character as to make it substantially a new case, will not be allowed after the cause has been argued ; especially when no evidence is offered to show that the amendment could not have been made part of the original bill: Snead v. McCoull, 12 How. U. S. 407.

modern practice is to amend the bill. If the amendments make further discovery requisite, the plaintiff may call for a further answer. And if he has successfully excepted to the answer, and the exceptions have not been answered, he may require the amendments to be answered at the same time. If the plaintiff does not require a further answer, the defendant may nevertheless file one if he considers it material to do so. (d)

The right of thus amending, by introducing altered or additional statements, is not absolutely confined to the plaintiff. The defendant may also under special circumstances obtain a similar indulgence ;[1] but as an answer is

(d) Orders of May, 1845, lxix., lxx., lxxi.; 1 Dan. C. P. 376, 400.

---

[1] In mere matters of form, or mistakes of dates, or verbal inaccuracies, Courts of Equity are very indulgent in allowing amendments of answers; but reluctant to allow amendments in material facts, or such as essentially change the ground taken in the original answer: Smith v. Babcock, 3 Sumu. 583; see also Jackson v. Cutright, 5 Munf. 308; McWilliams v. Herndon, 3 Dana 568; Stephens v. Terrel, 3 Monr. 131; Carey v. Ector, 7 Ga. 99; Thomas v. Doub, 1 Md. 252; Mounce v. Byars, 11 Ga. 180. As a general rule, a special case must be shown, before the court will allow a defendant to amend his answer. Amendments, however, will be allowed where new matter has come to the knowledge of the defendant since his answer was filed, or in case of surprise or mistake, or where an addition has been made to the draft of the answer after the defendant has perused it; and in some other special cases. The unwillingness of the court to permit a defendant to change or add to the grounds of defence set up in the first answer, is increased, where the application is made after the opinion of the court and the testimony have indicated how it may be modified to accomplish his purposes : Williams v. Savage Manufact. Co., 1 Md. Ch. 106; and see Campion v. Killey, 1 McCart. 229. A motion for leave to file a supplementary answer must be accompanied with an affidavit· Thomas v. Doub, 1 Md. 252.

A defendant cannot evade the rule as to amending his answer, by means of his answer to a supplemental bill, which must be restricted entirely to the matters alleged in the latter : Swan v. Dent, 2 Md. Ch. 111.

See further, on this subject, Phelps v. Prothero, 2 De G. & Sm. 274.

put in on oath, the Court, for obvious reasons, will not readily suffer alterations to be made.

Such permission, however, may be obtained on a full and satisfactory affidavit showing the cause of the omission and the new matter intended to be introduced, in cases where, at the time of the original answer being put in, the defendant was ignorant of particular facts, and could not by reasonable diligence have known them. And the like indulgence has been given, where the defendant had been *induced to leave out a fact in the original answer by the mistaken advice of his [*347] solicitor.[1] But the Court is always unwilling to give this permission, where the new matter would be prejudicial to the plaintiff, though it will be inclined to yield if it is intended for his benefit.[2] If the error to be corrected is a mere matter of form, it may be done by amending and re-swearing the answer. But when the object is to correct a mistaken statement, or to introduce new matter, it must be done by a supplemental answer, leaving the former answer on the record.(e) If the defendant cannot obtain permission to file a supplemental answer, he has no other way of correcting his original answer. He cannot do so by filing a cross bill.(f)

(e) Curling v. Townshend, 19 Ves. 628; Greenwood v. Atkinson, 4 Sim. 54; Fulton v. Gilmore, 1 Ph. 522; Bell v. Dunmore, 7 Beav. 283; 1 Dan. Ch. P. 752, 757.

(f) Berkley v. Rider, 2 Ves. 533, 537.

---

[1] A defendant may, for good cause shown, be permitted to amend his answer, and plead the Statutes of Frauds and Limitations, after the issue joined, and it is sufficient ground that the defendant's counsel advised him that he could take advantage of such defence without pleading: Jackson v. Cutright, 5 Munf. 308.

[2] See Western Reserve Bank v. Stryker, 1 Clarke Ch. 380, 383; Mounce v. Byars, 11 Ga. 180.

The final results of the pleadings is that the ultimat
amended bill, and the answer or successive answer:
the defendant, constitute the whole record.

It then becomes the plaintiff's duty to consider
nature of the allegations in the answer, and their bear
on his own case. If the answer admits his claim, anc
is content that it shall be taken as true throughout,
cause may be heard on bill and answer. If he inte
to controvert any part of the answer, or requires
ditional proof of his case. he must join issue with the
fendant, in which case he is required to file a replieati
stating the course he intends to pursue;[1] and it is
quired to be as nearly as possible in the following foi
"The plaintiff in this cause hereby joins issue with
defendant."(g)

On the filing of a replication the cause is at issue, ‹
the parties proceed to the proof of their respect
cases.(h)   If the plaintiff omit to file a replication
time, the defendant may dismiss the bill for want
prosecution.(i)[2]

(g) Orders of May, 1845, xciii.
(h) Orders of May, 1845, 16, 37–41, 93; 1 Dan. Ch. P. c. 19.
(i) Orders of 1845, xciv.; 1 Dan. Ch. P. 767, 784.

---

[1] Special replications are now disused: White v. Morrison, 11 Ill. ‹
Duponti v. Mussy, 4 Wash. C. C. 128; and are expressly prohibited by
rules in equity of the U. S. Courts, No. xlv., and of Penn., xlviii.
general replication, however, puts in issue only the allegations of bill
answer.   The proper course is for the complainant, if he is aware of ar
tended defence, to anticipate it in his bill by suitable charges and all
tions; or he may have leave to amend on motion, where necessary : W
v. Morrison; Duponti v. Mussy.   Joining issue on an answer is a waive
any mere technical objections to the form in which the defences in ε
answer are represented: McKim v. White Hall Co., 2 Md. Ch. 510.
general replication waives all objection to the sufficiency of the ansv
Slater c. Maxwell, 6 Wall. (U. S.) 268.

[2] See equity rules U. S. Courts, No. lxvi.; of Pennsylvania, No. xlv
Where a suit becomes nugatory by matters subsequent, as where filec

*CHAPTER V. [*348]

OF INTERLOCUTORY ORDERS.

THE answer of the defendant is the chief foundation of interlocutory orders, that is, orders not made at the hearing of the cause, but obtained during its progress for incidental objects. And such orders, therefore, will naturally fall under our notice at this stage of our inquiry.

The mode of obtaining interlocutory orders is either by a *viva voce* application, called a motion, or by a written one called a petition. The statements made in the answer have generally a considerable influence on the application, and in some instances they are the only admissible evidence; where other evidence is admissible it is brought forward, not by the regular examination of witnesses, but by the affidavits of voluntary deponents.(*a*)

It is not necessary for the purpose of this Treatise to discuss the practice on motions and petitions. But it will be sufficient to observe that they are divided into two classes, viz., 1. Motions and petitions of course, or such

(*a*) 2 Dan. Ch. P. c. 30, of Affidavits.

---

the authority of a reported case, afterwards reversed, the Court has jurisdiction, ou motion to dismiss it without costs: Sutton, &c., Co. *v.* Hitchens, 15 Beav. 161.

A plaintiff in Chancery has a right to dismiss his bill at any time before final hearing upon payment of costs, if he be not in contempt: Elderkin *v.* Fitch, 2 Carter (Ind.) 90. But to this there may be some exceptions. See Saylor's Appeal, 39 Penn. St. 495.

as seek an order which by the practice of the Court
be granted on asking, without hearing both sides ; ai
Special motions or petitions, or those which can onl
granted for cause shown.   Where the application is o
latter kind, it will not be granted *ex parte*, except in (
of emergency, but notice of the motion, or a cop
[*349] *the petition, must be previously served oi
parties interested.(*b*)

The procedure by petition is also resorted to
variety of objects not arising· in the progress of a
but dealt with under the summary jurisdiction by sta
already noticed as existing in the Court,(*c*) *e. g.*, for
veyance by incapacitated trustees.   And in one cla
cases, where the appointment of a guardian and allow
of maintenance for an infant is required, the same cc
is sanctioned, as already observed, by the inheren
thority of the Court.(*d*)   The jurisdiction over solici
and in lunacy and bankruptcy, is also exercised by oi
on petition.

The objects of interlocutory orders are numerous.
include, for instance, the issuing of attachments or
process of the Court, the taking of bills *pro confesso*
compelling of plaintiff to elect whether he will sue a
or in equity, the dismissal of bills for want of prosecu
and the taking of any other steps to remedy dela
irregularity in the cause.   But an inquiry into orde
this class would turn principally on technical rul
practice, and would be unsuited to our present pur
The only objects of interlocutory orders which seem
rial to be here noticed are five in number, viz., 1.

(*b*) 2 Dan. Ch. P. c. 31 ; Interlocutory Application.
(*c*) Supra, Introduction, 2 Dan. Ch. P. c. 40.
(*d*) Supra, Infants, 2 Dan. Ch. P. 29.

production of documents ; 2. The payment of money into Court; 3. The appointment of a receiver; 4. The grant of an injunction ; and 5. A writ of *ne exeat regno.*

I. The production of documents is ordered for completion of the discovery in the defendant's answer.(e)[1]

The discovery obtained from the answer itself is not the whole to which the plaintiff is entitled. It gives him a statement by the defendant on oath as to all facts to which he was interrogated, and also a schedule of all documents in the defendant's power relating to the subject-matter of the suit. But the documents still remain to be examined, and *the information which they con- [*350] tain is frequently the most important part of the discovery. For the purpose of obtaining such examination, the plaintiff is entitled, either before or after the sufficiency of the answer has been determined, and without prejudicing any question on that point, or at any subsequent period in the cause, to move that "the defendant may produce, and that the plaintiff may have liberty to inspect, and take copies of all the documents so scheduled, and that the same may be produced before the examiner and at the hearing of the cause."(f) Upon this application an order will be made that they shall be deposited with the clerk of records and writs, or, if a special reason be shown, e. g., their being in constant use in the defendant's business, then in the defendant's own office.(g)

The doctrines by which production is regulated have been already discussed in reference to discovery, viz., 1. The right of requiring it is for the purpose of discovery

(e) 2 Dan. Ch. P. c. 38.
(f) Lane v. Paul, 3 Beav. 66 ; Fencott v. Clarke, 6 Sim. 8.
(g) Prentice v. Phillips, 2 Hare 152.

---

[1] See on this subject, ante, B. i.. Ch. 1.

alone, and does not depend on nor will be aided b
to possess the documents themselves. 2. The e
of the right must be shown from admissions in the
that the documents are in the defendant's posse
power, and that they are of such a character as t
tute proper matter of discovery within the ordinaɪ
3. It is a right belonging to a plaintiff only, alt
defendant may occasionally be permitted on
grounds to delay his answer until some doeum
terial for making out his defence has been prod
the plaintiff.

II. Payment of money into Court is directe
the defendant admits money to be in his hands v
does not claim as his own, and in which he adm
the applicant is interested.(h)[1]

In a case of obvious and gross misconduct, wl
plaintiff has made affidavit of the facts, and the d
[*351]   *has attempted to explain them by a coɪ
fidavit, this order has been made before
on the admissions in the defendant's affidavit.(i)
general rule is, that it shall not be made until the
is put in, and that it must be sustained entirel
admissions made. The reason of this requiremen
the motion is made before witnesses can be regul
amined, and therefore the defendant may fairly cl
either his answer shall be taken as true, or that t
dication shall be delayed till he has an opport

(h) 2 Dan. Ch. P. c. 36.
(i) Jervis v. White, 6 Ves. 738.

---

[1] See on this subject, Hosack v. Rogers, 9 Paige 468; Clagett
Gill & John. 81; Contee v. Dawson, 2 Bland. 293; Nokes v. S
Phillips 19; Maddox v. Dent, 4 Md. Ch. 543; Daniels' Chan.
xli.; Hagill v. Currie, 2 Ch. L. R. 449.

proof.(*k*) The admissions necessary to warrant the order are, first, that the defendant has the fund in his hands, or at all events that he once had it, and has not legitimately disposed of it; secondly, that he does not claim it as his own; and thirdly, that the applicant is interested in it.(*l*)[1] If the admissions in the answer do not warrant the application, it may be made at the hearing on the evidence in the cause, or may be made between the original hearing and the hearing on further directions, either on admission in the examination of an acting party, or on the Master's report.(*m*)[2]

The order thus made is strictly one of precaution. The fund is brought into Court, that it may be preserved until the decree, and not that an earlier decision of the cause may be made. The Court will not therefore, indirectly adjudicate on the right, as, for example, by directing pay-

(*k*) Richardson *v.* Bank of England, 4 M. & C. 165, 176; Boschetti *v.* Power, 8 Beav. 98.

(*l*) Freeman *v.* Fairlie, 3 Meriv. 29, 39; Meyer *v.* Montriou, 4 Beav. 343; Dubless *v.* Flint, 4 M. & C. 502.

(*m*) Hatch *v.* ——, 19 Ves. 116; Creak *v.* Capell, 6 Mad. 114.

[1] Those who make the motion to have money brought into court, must show that they have an interest in the sum proposed to be called in, and that he who holds it in his possession, has no equitable right to it whatever; and the facts on which these positions are based, must be found in the case as it then stands, either admitted or so established as to be open to no further controversy at any subsequent stage of the proceedings: Hopkins *v.* McEldery, 4 Md. Ch. 23. A contingent interest, however, is sufficient to entitle a party to move: Ross *v.* Ross, 12 Beav. 89; Bartlett *v.* Bartlett, 4 Hare 631. A final order upon a petition asking the defendant to bring money into court for the purpose of investment, cannot be passed without notice to, or hearing of, the opposite party, who has answered the petition and objected to the application: Brooks *v.* Dent, 4 Md. Ch. 473.

[2] The order cannot be made on motion after decree, and before hearing on further directions, merely on admissions in the answers: Binns *v.* Parr, 7 Hare 288; Wright *v.* Lukes, 13 Beav. 107.

ment of interest to one of the litigants, but will retain
fund untouched until the hearing of the cause.(n)

The principle on which the order is based is that
fund, of which payment into Court is asked, is a fu
held by the defendant in trust; and it therefore does 1
apply to suits for a mere payment of a debt claimed
due from the defendant to the plaintiff. But to this r
[*352] there are *two apparent exceptions: the one
the case of an executor who owes money to
testator, the other in that of a purchaser, sued for spec
performance, who is in possession of the land, and 1
not paid his purchase-money. The reason of the fi
exception is that the executor, being himself both deb
and creditor, is presumed in equity to have discharg
himself of the debt, and to have retained the money
part of the assets.(o) That of the second is, that thou
the purchaser may be ultimately entitled, according
the result of the suit, either to the estate or to t
purchase-money, yet he cannot be entitled to both; a
therefore his election to keep possession of the estate
in substance an election to be a trustee of the purchas
money.(p)

The mode of obtaining the order is by a motion ma
on notice, that the defendant may be ordered on or befo
a specific day to pay the amount into the name, and wi
the privity of the Accountant-General, in trust in t
cause; and that the same, when paid in, with all accum
lations thereon, may be laid out in the purchase of thr
per cent. consols.

(n) Nedby v. Nedby, 4 M. & C. 367.
(o) Richardson v. Bank of England, 4 M. & C. 165.
(p) Morgan v. Shaw, 2 Meriv. 138; Tindal v. Cobham 2 M. & K. 38
Cutler v. Simons, 2 Meriv. 103.

If the object is to obtain a transfer of stock, the terms of notice are varied accordingly.

III. A receiver is appointed where an estate or fund is in existence, but there is no competent person entitled to hold it, or the person so entitled is in the nature of a trustee, and is misusing or misapplying the property.(q)[1]

The former of these grounds applies where the owner of property is dead, and probate or administration has not been granted, but is *bonâ fide* litigated in the Ecclesiastical Courts. In this case a receiver will be appointed of the personal assets, not on the ground that the contest exists, but because there would otherwise be no proper person to receive them. If, on the contrary, probate or administration has *been granted, there is a proper person, and the pendency of litigation to re- [*353]

(q) 2 Dan. Ch. P. c. 35 ; [Chap. xxviii., 3d Amer. ed.]

---

[1] A Court of Equity will appoint a receiver, whenever it can be made to appear that the property in regard to which the controversy exists, is in danger: Ladd *v.* Harvey, 1 Foster (N. H.) 514; Reid *v.* Reid, 38 Ga. 24. But it must be a strong case that will justify such appointment, which is the ultimate resort of a Court of Equity. It is a high power, never exercised where there exists any other safe or expedient remedy : Speights *v.* Peters, 9 Gill 472 ; Dougherty *v.* McDougal, 10 Ga. 121 ; Furlong *v.* Edwards, 3 Md. 99 ; Blondheim *v.* Moore, 11 Id. 374 ; Haight *v.* Burr, 19 Id. 134; and a Court of Chancery will never appoint a receiver pending a plea to its jurisdiction, but to guard against abuse of dilatory pleas will order an immediate hearing or trial of the plea: Ewing *v.* Blight, 3 Wall. Jr. 139.

The granting of a receiver is a matter of discretion, to be governed by a view of the whole circumstances of the case, one of such circumstances being the probability of the plaintiff being ultimately entitled to a decree : Nichols *v.* The Perry Patent Arm Co., 3 Stockton 126. Thus a receiver was refused in a case where important points arose upon the construction of deeds, that construction being attended with considerable doubt and difficulty : Owen *v.* Homan, 3 M. & G. 378 ; s. c. 4 House Lds. Cas. 997 ; see Lenox *v.* Notrebe, 1 Hempstead 225; see also Baker *v.* Backers, 32 Ill. 80. A receiver has no powers except those conferred upon him by the order for his appointment: Grant *v.* Davenport, 18 Iowa 179.

44

call the grant will not warrant a receiver.$(r)^1$ On the same principle a receiver will be appointed of an infant's estate, if it be not vested in a trustee, for he is himself incompetent to take charge of it.

The most obvious instance of the second ground ˈof appointment is in the case of actual trustees, who are abusing their trust, and bringing the property into danger. But unless there be misconduct on their part, the Court will not interpose to take the property from them for the mere purpose of confiding it to an officer of its own.(s)

If, again, the legal owner, though not an actual trustee, holds the property subject to clear equities in other parties, but is using it in a manner inconsistent with them, a receiver may be obtained against him.   On this principle an equitable mortgagee may have a receiver against his mortgagor.   If there be a prior mortgagee not in possession, the receiver may be appointed, without prejudice to his taking possession; but, if he be in possession, a receiver cannot be ordered against him unless the applicant will pay off his demand, as he states it himself.   A legal mortgagee cannot have a receiver, but must take possession under his legal title.(t)

(r) Atkinson v. Henshaw, 2 Ves. & B. 85 ; Rendall v. Rendall, 1 Hare 152; Reed v. Harris, 7 Sim. 639.

(s) Middleton v. Dodswell, 13 Ves. 266 ; Browell v. Reed, 1 Hare 434; Bainbridge v. Blair, 3 Beav. 421 ; Skinners' Company v. Irish Society, 1 M. & C. 162.

(t) Berney v. Sewall, 1 Jac. & W. 627.

---

[1] Although there is no rule of practice that, in cases where the will is in contest in the Ecclesiastical Court, the Court of Chancery will not grant a receiver where the property is in the hands of the executor, yet it must be clearly shown that the nature and position of the Court are such as to warrant the interference of the Court: Whitworth v. Whyddon, 2 M. & G. 56 ; s. v. 2 H. & Tw. 445; 15 Jur. 152;   In Dimes v. Steinberg, 2 Sm. & Giff. 75, however, an injunction and receiver were granted pending a suit to recall probate of a will alleged to have been fraudulently obtained by the executor and a legatee.

If there are several equitable encumbrancers the Court will put the property in the possession of a receiver, to apply the profits for their benefit according to their respective priorities, permitting legal encumbrancers to proceed at law; and the appointment will not prevent their so doing, though it will make it necessary for them to obtain leave from the Court.(u)

*A receiver has also been appointed as between vendor and purchaser during a suit for specific [*354] performance; but the order was made under special circumstances, the purchaser not having been in exclusive possession, but having had a sort of mixed possession with the vendor.(v)

A receiver may also be appointed in cases of partnership, where one of the partners, having got the business into his hands, is destroying the partnership property, or is claiming to exclude his copartners from the concern.[1] In this case, as all the partners have an equal right to the management, and no one of them has an exclusive right, the Court must exclude all for the protection of all, and will appoint a receiver to get in the assets. It cannot, however, undertake to carry on the trade, and will therefore only interpose with a view to dissolution.(w)[2] On the same principle, a receiver may be appointed of a mine

(u) Davis v. Marlborough, 2 Sw. 138; Angel v. Smith, 9 Ves. 335; Brooks v. Greathed, 1 J. & W. 178; Smith v. Effingham, 2 Beav. 235; Pritchard v. Fleetwood, 1 Meriv. 54. [See Cortleyeu v. Hathaway, 3 Stockt. 39.]

(v) Hall v Jenkinson, 2 Ves. & B. 125; Boehm v. Wood, 2 J. & W. 236; Shakel v. Marlborough, 4 Mad. 463.

(w) Waters v. Taylor, 15 Ves. 10; Goodman v. Whitcomb, 1 J. & W. 589; Hale v. Hale, 4 Beav. 369; Const v. Harris, T. & R. 496; Smith v. Jeyes, 4 Beav. 503.

---

[1] See Whitman v. Robinson, 21 Md. 30.

[2] See note 1, p. 241, supra. See also Sieghortner v. Weissenborn, 20 N. J. Eq. 172.

or colliery, which is regarded rather as a trade or partnership than as a mere tenancy in common.(x)   In the case
of a mere tenancy in common, where the title is legal, it
is doubtful whether the Court would interfere.[1]   It might
compel the tenant in possession to account to his co-
tenant, but would probably not act against his legal possession.(y)

There is also jurisdiction to make the order, though
the defendant does not sustain a fiduciary character, but
insists on a distinct adverse title, which title is contested
in the suit.   But the Court will be reluctant to interfere,
and will only do it if gross fraud or imminent danger be
shown.(z)[2]

The appointment of a receiver, like payment of money
[*355]   *into Court, may be ordered on affidavit before
answer, or even before the defendant has ap-
peared, if any urgent necessity exist.[3]   But the application
must generally be made after answer, and must be supported by the admissions of the defendant.(a)

The appointment, when made, is for the benefit of all

(x) Jefferys v. Smith, 1 J. & W. 298.

(y) Tyson v. Fairclough, 2 S. & S. ¡42.

(z) Stilwell v. Wilkins, Jac. 280; Huguenin v. Basely, 13 Ves. 105;
Jones v. Goodrich, 10 Sim. 327; Clark v. Dew, 1 R. & M. 103; Toldervy
v. Colt, 1 Y. & C. 621.

(a) Lloyd v. Passingham, 3 Meriv. 697; Ramsbottom v. Freeman, 4
Beav. 145.

---

[1] See, however, Williams v. Jenkins, 11 Ga. 595.

[2] And the Court will not, in general, interfere at the instance of a person
alleging a legal title in himself against other persons who are in possession of the estates, to grant him a receiver, or put them out of possession:
Talbot v. Scott, 27 L. J. Ch. 278; 4 K. & J. 96.

[3] A temporary or ad interim receiver may not only be appointed before
answer, but even before the subpœna to appear and answer has been
served, when it is shown that extraordinary danger would ensue unless
the property were taken under the care of the Court: Jones v. Dougherty,
10 Ga. 274; Williams v..Jenkins, 11 Ld. 595.

parties interested, and not for that of the applicant alone. If there be only one party interested, as where a receiver is appointed of an infant's estate, the possession of the receiver is considered as his possession. If there are adverse claims in different parties, the possession of the receiver is treated as the possession of the party who ultimately establishes his right.(b)[1]

IV. An injunction is granted to restrain a defendant,[2] so long as the litigation continues, from doing acts productive of permanent injury, or from proceeding in an action at law, where an equity is alleged against his legal right.(c)

The principle of injunctive relief by decree has already

(b) Bainbrigge v. Blair, 3 Beav. 421 ; Sharp v. Carter, 3 P. Wms. 379.

(c) 2 Dan. Ch. P. ch. 32.

---

[1] The appointment of a receiver does not determine any right, or affect the title of either party in any manner whatever ; he is the officer of the Court, and his holding is the holding of the Court for him from whom the possession was taken. He is appointed on behalf of all parties, and his appointment is not to oust any party of his right to the possession, but merely to retain it for the benefit of the party ultimately entitled ; and when he is ascertained, the receiver will be considered as his receiver : Ellicott v. Warford, 4 Md. 80 ; Matter of Colvin, 3 Md. Ch. 280. See further, as to the power and authorities of receivers, Porter v. Williams, 5 Selden 142 ; Receivers v. Patterson Gaslight Co., 3 Zabrisk. 283.

Where a receiver is appointed, but the bill is afterwards dismissed for want of equity, the functions of the receiver cease, *inter partes*, but his accountability as an officer of the Court continues. The fund remains subject to the order of the Court, and will be returned thereby to the party as whose fund it was taken, unless retained upon a claim properly made and presented to the chancellor. A party having a claim on a fund so situated will be allowed to intervene, *pro interesse suo*, upon a proper application. But the receiver, as such, is not subject to the process of garnishment : Field v. Jones, 11 Ga. 413.

It is not necessary to bring to a hearing a suit for the appointment of a receiver *pendente lite* : Anderson v. Guichard, 9 Hare 275.

[2] An injunction cannot be granted against one who is not a party to the suit : Schalk v. Schmidt, 1 McCart. 268.

been considered as an independent subject.(d)   We are
now only concerned with the interlocutory writ issued for
the protection of the subject-matter until litigation is decided.

The ordinary mode of obtaining this injunction is by
moving after notice to the defendant; but in particular
cases, where giving notice might accelerate the mischief,
it will be granted *ex parte* and without notice; *e. g.*, in
cases of waste, or of negotiating a bill of exchange, and,
even where that special ground does not exist, yet if the
act to be prohibited is such, that delay is productive of
serious damage, as in piracies of copyright and patent,
an *ex parte* injunction may be obtained.   In order to'
obtain an injunction *ex parte*, the application must be
[*356]   made at the *first possible moment, and all the
facts must be fully and honestly stated; if any
concealment or misrepresentation be detected, the injunction will be dissolved, although the facts, if truly
stated, would have been sufficient to sustain it.(e)[1]

(d) Supra, Injunction.
(e) Hilton v. Granville, 4 Beav. 130.

---

[1] It is an almost universal practice to dissolve the injunction, where the
answer fully denies all the circumstances upon which the equity of the
bill is founded; and likewise to refuse the writ, if application is made after
the coming in of such answer: Hoffman v. Livingston, 1 Johns. Ch. 211;
McFarland v. McDowell, 1 Car. L. R. 110; Cowles v. Carter, 4 Ired. Eq.
105; Livingston v. Livingston, 4 Paige Ch. 111; Gibson v. Tilton, 1 Bland
Ch. 355; Perkins v. Hallowell, 5 Ired. Eq. 24; Williams v. Berry, 3 Stew.
& Port. 284; Green v. Phillips, 6 Ired. Eq. 223; Wakeman v. Gillespy, 5
Paige 112; Stoutenburgh v. Peck, 3 Green Ch. 446; Hollister v. Barkley,
9 N. H. 230; Eldred v. Camp, Harring. Ch. 163; Freeman v. Elmendorf,
3 Halst. Ch. 655; Adams v. Whiteford, 9 Gill 501; Furlong v. Edwards,
3 Md. 99; Dennis v. Green, 8 Ga. 197; Wood v. Patterson, 4 Md. Ch. 335;
Harris v. Sangston, Id. 394; Woodworth v. Rogers, 3 Wood. & M. 135;
Wright v. Grist, 1 Bush. Eq. 203; Mahon v. Central Bank, 17 Ga. 111;
Greenon v. Hoey, 1 Stockt. 137; Van Kuren v. Trenton Manufact. Co., 2

If the injunction be applied for before the answer, it must necessarily be sustained on affidavit; and the de-

---

Beas. 302; Winslow *v.* Hudson, 21 N. J. Eq. 172; Yonge *v.* Sheppard, 44 Ala. 315. On motion to dissolve an injunction upon answer, exceptions filed are no objection to the motion, unless they affect the answer in points relating to the grounds of the injunction: Lewis *v.* Leak, 9 Ga. 95.

An answer made and sworn to before defendant's death, though filed subsequently, may be used on a motion to dissolve the injunction: Dennis *v.* Green, 8 Ga. 197.

Where the bill shows no equity on its face, the injunction will of course be dissolved: Stark *v.* Wood, 9 Gratt. 40.

It is a general rule, that an injunction will not be dissolved, on answer, until the answers of all the defendants are put in. See Money *v.* Jordan, 13 Beav. 229. But there are many exceptions; *e. g.*, it will be considered unnecessary, if those who have not answered are merely formal parties: Higgins *v.* Woodward, Hopkins' Ch. 342. Or parties who cannot be compelled to answer, as a foreign corporation: Balt. & Ohio R. R. *v.* Wheeling, 13 Gratt. 40. So it may be dissolved upon the answer of one or more defendants within whose knowledge the facts charged especially or exclusively lie, although other defendants have not answered: Dunlap *v.* Clements, 7 Ala 539; Coleman *v.* Gage, 1 Clarke 295; Ashe *v.* Hale, 5 Ired. Eq. 55. So also where that defendant against whom the *gravamen* of the charge rests, has fully answered: Depeyster *v.* Graves, 2 Johns. Ch. 148; Noble *v.* Wilson, 1 Paige 164; Stoutenburgh *v.* Peck, 3 Green Ch. 446; Vliet *v.* Lowmason, 1 Id. 404; Price *v.* Clevenger, 2 Id. 207. See also Goodwyn *v.* State Bank, 4 Dessaus. 389. And this, too, where all the defendants are implicated in the same charge, and the answer of all can and ought to come in, but the plaintiff has not taken the requisite steps, with reasonable diligence, to speed his cause: Depeyster *v.* Graves, *ubi supra*. See also Bond *v.* Hendricks, 1 A. K. Marsh. 594.

Upon an application to dissolve an injunction on bill and answer, the defendant's answer is entitled to the same credit as the complainant's bill. It therefore makes no difference on such an application that the bill is supported by the oaths of several complainants: Manchester *v.* Dey, 6 Paige 295.

There is, however, no inflexible rule with regard to dissolving an injunction, on answer denying the allegations of the bill; the granting and continuing an injunction must always rest in the sound discretion of the court, to be governed by the nature of the case: Roberts *v.* Anderson, 2 Johns. Ch. 204; Poor *v.* Carleton, 3 Sumn. 70; Bank of Monroe *v.* Schermerhorn, 1 Clarke 303; Holt *v.* Bank of Augusta, 9 Ga. 552; Nelson *v.* Robinson, 1 Hempst. 474; Crutchfield *v.* Donelly, 16 Ga. 432; Dent *v.* Summerlin, 12 Id. 5; Hoagland *v.* Titus, 1 McCart. 81; Morris Coal Co. *v.*

fendant may resist it on counter affidavits; or if it has
been obtained *ex parte*, he may move to dissolve it on

Jersey City, 3 Stockt. 13; Conally v. Cruger, 40 Ga. 259; De Godey v.
Godey, 39 Cal. 157. Thus in some special cases, as where fraud is
the *gravamen* of the bill, the injunction will be continued, though the defendant has fully answered the equity charged: Dent v. Summerlin, ut
supr.; Nelson v. Robinson, 1 Hempst. 464; Semmes v. Mayor of Columbus, 19 Ga. 471.

Where the defendant in his answer admits, or does not deny the equity
of the bill, but sets up new matter of defence, on which he relies, the in-
junction will be continued to the hearing: Minturn v. Seymour, 4 Johns.
Ch. 497; Lindsay v. Etheridge, 1 Dev. & Bat. Eq. 38; Hutchins v. Hope,
12 Gill & J. 244; Lyrely v. Wheeler, 3 Ired. Eq. 170; Nelson v. Owen, Id.
175; Drury v. Roberts, 2 Md. Ch. 157; Rembert v. Brown, 17 Ala. 667;
Deaver v. Irwin, 7 Ired. Eq. 250; Lewis v. Leak, 9 Ga. 95; Hutchins v.
Hope, 7 Gill 119; Wilson v. Mace, 2 Jones Eq. 5, 149. See Carson v.
Coleman, 3 Stockt. 109; Brewster v. The City of Newark, Id. 114; West
Jersey R. R. v. Thomas, 21 N. J. Eq. 205. Thus, for example, where
the bill charges the receipt of money, and a general accountability,
and the answer admits the receipt, and seeks to account for the money
by alleging its application to some particular purpose, then the injunction will not be dissolved on the answer. But when the bill charges
payment on a particular account, and the answer denies that any payment
was made on that account, and accompanies the denial with an admission
that a certain sum was received, as a payment on some other account, then
the injunction will be dissolved; for there is no confession and avoidance
by new matter, but a positive denial of the allegation, together with
an explanation of a circumstance relied on to give color to an allegation:
Deaver v. Erwin, 7 Ired. Eq. 250.

So upon motion to dissolve, credit can only be given to the answer in so
far as it speaks of responsive matters, within the personal knowledge of the
defendant, and unless, so speaking, the equity of the bill is sworn away, the
injunction cannot be dissolved. And, on the other hand, so much of the
bill as is not denied by the answer is taken as true, and if any one of its
material allegations remains unanswered, the injunction will be continued:
Brown v. Stewart, 1 Md. Ch. 87; Doub v. Barnes, Id. 127; Cronise v.
Clark, 4 Id. 403; Rembert v. Brown, 17 Ala. 667; Horn v. Thomas, 19
Ga. 270; Wheat v. Moss, 16 Ark. 243. So where a supplemental bill has
been filed: Rogers v. Solomons, 17 Ga. 598.

So the injunction cannot be dissolved, if the answer be evasive and apparently deficient in frankness, candor, or precision: Little v. Marsh, 2
Ired. Eq. 18; Williams v. Hall, 1 Bland Ch. 194; Swift v. Swift, 13 Ga.
140; Deaver v. Eller, 7 Ired. Eq. 24. Nor if it be contradictory: Tong

counter affidavits, or may wait until he has filed his
answer, and then move to dissolve.

---

v. Oliver, 1 Bland Ch. 199. Nor if there be extreme improbability in its
allegations: Moore *v.* Hylton, 1 Dev. Eq. 429. Nor if it be merely upon
information and belief: Ward *v.* Van Bokkelen, 1 Paige 100; Apthorpe *v.*
Comstock, Hopkins 143; Poor *v.* Carleton, 3 Sumner 70; Doub *v.* Barnes,
1 Md. Ch. 127; Nelson *v.* Robinson, 1 Hempst: 464; Calloway *v.* Jones,
19 Ga. 277. See, however, Ashe *v.* Johnson, 2 Jones Eq. 49. And, moreover, where the equity of an injunction is not charged to be in the knowledge of the defendant, and the defendant merely denies all knowledge and
belief of the facts alleged therein, the injunction will not be dissolved on
the bill and answer alone: Rodgers *v.* Rodgers, 1 Paige 426; Quackenbush
v. Van Riper, Saxton 476; Everly *v.* Rice, 3 Green Ch. 553; Coffee *v.*
Newsom, 8 Ga. 444.

An injunction may be partially dissolved in accordance with the case
made out by the answer: Edwards *v.* Perryman, 18 Ga. 374; or it may be
revived after a dissolution on the merits, or awarded afresh on special motion, or new facts stated in an amended or supplemental bill, or on proof
taken: Tucker *v.* Carpenter, 1 Hemp. 440; Rogers *v.* Solomons, 17 Ga.
598; but see France *v.* France, 4 Halst. Ch. 619.

In general, no affidavits can be read in contradiction of the answer denying the equity of the bill; Brown *v.* Winans, 3 Stockt. 267; but in certain excepted cases, as nuisance, waste, and trespass, where irreparable
damage might ensue upon the refusal or dissolution of the injunction, such
affidavits will be allowed, and the continuance of the injunction will be
within the discretion of the Court, whether, upon the whole evidence, more
injury will be done to the complainant by withholding, or to the defendant
by granting the injunction: Waring *v.* Cram, 1 Pars. Eq. 523; Smith *v.*
Cummings, 2 Id. 92; Poor *v.* Carleton, 3 Sumu. 70; Village of Sen. Falls
v. Matthews, 9 Paige 504; Lessig *v.* Langton, Bright. N. P. 191; see Shrewsbury, &c., R. R. *v.* London, &c., R. R., 3 M. & G. 70.

In cases of imminent danger of injury to the complainant, a temporary
injunction will be granted on filing amendments to a bill after appearance,
but the injunction will be accompanied with an order to show cause why
the bill should not be amended, and why the injunction should not be continued: Hayes *v.* Heyer, 4 Sandf. Ch. 485. So a preliminary injunction
will not be refused, for error in a bill which is amendable, though the
amendment has not been actually made, as in the case of a bill by parties
in their own instead of in a corporate capacity: Packer *v.* Sunbury, &c.,
R. R., 19 Penn. St. 211.

The common injunction having been dissolved in an original bill, cannot be obtained as of course on an amended bill, for default before appear-

If the motion, either to grant or dissolve the injunction, is heard after answer, the admissibility of affidavits is a questionable point. If the answer denies the plaintiff's title, affidavits are not admissible to support such title; or in other words, the title will not be tried before the hearing.(*f*) If, however, documents of title are stated in the bill, and the answer merely professes ignorance respecting them, they may be verified by affidavit; but this liberty does not

(*f*) Manser *v.* Jenner, 2 H. 603 ; Clapham *v.* White, 8 Ves. 36.

---

ance : Zuleuta *v.* Vinent, 14 Beav. 209 ; *contra,* Eyton *v.* Mostyn, 3 De G. & Sm. 518.

In general, in this country, no injunction can be obtained without notice. The Rule in U. S. Courts, in Equity, No. lv., is as follows :—

Whenever an injunction is asked for by the bill to stay proceedings at law, if the defendant does not enter his appearance and plead, demur, or answer to the same within the time prescribed therefor, by those rules, the plaintiff shall be entitled as of course, upon motion and notice, to such injunction. But special injunctions shall be grantable only upon due notice to the other party by the Court in term, or by a judge thereof in vacation, after a hearing, which may be *ex parte*, if the adverse party does not appear at the time and place ordered.

But in Pennsylvania, see Rule lxxv.

In most of the states, the complainant is also obliged to give bond before an injunction can issue ; and in Pennsylvania the Commonwealth itself has been held to be comprehended within a statutory provision to that effect: Comm. *v.* Franklin Canal Co., 21 Penn. St. 117. But an omission to give bond is not a ground for dismissing an injunction bill: Gueray *v.* Durham, 11 Ga. 9. An injunction directed to a corporate body, is binding not only on the corporation, but every individual member : Davis *v.* Mayor, &c., of N. Y., 1 Duer 451. Where it forbids performance of any corporate act, it is violated by every member of the corporate body, by whose assent or coöperation the act so forbidden is performed ; and, every such member is guilty of a contempt, for which he may be punished. An injunction which forbids a corporation to make a particular grant is violated by the passage of an ordinance or resolution, as a corporate act, which by its terms is meant to operate as the grant which is prohibited. Every member, therefore, who votes for the adoption of such an ordinance, commits a breach of the injunction, and is guilty of a contempt: Id. See too, Rorke *v.* Russell, 2 Lans. (N. Y.) 242.

extend to matters of fact.(*g*) If the answer does not deny the title, the question arises, whether affidavits can be read against it in proof of waste, or of acts analogous to waste, *e. g.*, mismanagement and exclusion. On this point the rule is, that if affidavits have been filed before the answer, the Court will read them, and also read any further affidavits filed after the answer, whether the injunction was obtained or not; that is, it will try the question of waste, though not that of title, on affidavit against the answer. But if no affidavit has been filed before the answer so as to give a *locus standi* for a hearing on affidavit, affidavits filed after the answer cannot be read.(*h*)[1]

*The grant of the interlocutory injunction is discretionary with the Court; and depends on [*357] the circumstances of each case, and on the degree in which the defendant or the plaintiff would respectively be prejudiced by the grant or refusal.

If the mischief done to the plaintiff, assuming him to have a right, by a continued infringement, is a mere matter of profit and loss, and, therefore, susceptible of compensation, the Court will also consider what may be the consequences to the defendant, assuming him to be right, of granting an injunction; and even if the anticipated act would destroy the property, and affords, therefore, *primâ facie* a fair reason to interfere, yet the Court will not act as a mere matter of course, but will consider

(*g*) Barrett *v.* Tickell, Jac. 156 ; Morgan *v.* Goode, 3 Meriv. 10; Ord *v.* White, 3 Beav. 357; Castellain *v.* Blumenthal, 12 Sim. 47; Edwards *v.* Jones, 1 Ph. 501.

(*h*) Jefferys *v.* Smith, 1 J. & W. 300 ; Smythe *v.* Smythe, 1 Sw. 252; Lloyd *v.* Jenkins, 4 Beav. 230 ; Gardner *v.* McCutcheon, Id. 534 ; Manser *v.* Jenner, 2 Hare 600.

---

[1] See Kinsler *v.* Clarke, 2 Hill Ch. 620.

whether it is not possible that still greater damage w
be caused to the defendant by an injunction.(*i*)   If,
ever, an injunction is for such cause refused, and
subject-matter of the suit is one of profit and loss, a
termediate course is often adopted, and the defendar
directed to keep an account, that so, if the plaintiff sh
establish his right, he may ascertain at once the com
sation due for its infringement.(*k*)

The injunction, if granted, is for intermediate pro
tion only, and will be cautiously excluded ·from
further effect. If, therefore, the subject-matter of
suit be not of equitable jurisdiction, the legal right n
be tried as speedily as possible; and the Court is bo
even though not requested by the parties, to aecomp
its order by a provision to that effect.(*l*)

In the case of stock which may be transferred w
great facility, a more speedy protection existed under
old practice, by writ of *distringas* out of the Excheqt
[*358] and *service of it on the bank.   The *distrin*
was not in strictness binding on the bank,
the practice was to give notice to the party serving il
any application were made for transfer, and to delay
transfer for a limited time, during which an injunct
might be obtained.   On the transfer of the Excheq
jurisdiction to the Court of Chancery, a similar reme
was given by *distringas* issuable out of that Court.   A
a further remedy was also given by a restraining ordei
the Court, to be summarily made on petition or mot
without bill filed, and to continue in force until (

(*i*) Hilton *v.* Granville, 1 Cr. & P. 283.
(*k*) Bacon *v.* Jones, 4 M. & C. 436.
(*l*) Harman *v.* Jones, 1 Cr. & P. 299; Ansdell *v.* Ansdell, 4 M. &
449; Bacon *v.* Jones, Id. 436 ; Few *v.* Guppy, 1 Id. 507.

charged, imperatively restraining the bank, or any public company, from permitting a transfer or paying a dividend.(m)

The interlocutory writ against proceeding at law, technically termed the common injunction, is obtainable by the plaintiff on a motion of course, if the defendant fail to appear within four days after the subpœna has been served, or to answer the bill within eight days after his appearance.

If the common injunction is obtained before a declaration is delivered, it stays all the proceedings at law. If afterwards, it only restrains execution, and the plaintiff at law is at liberty to proceed to judgment. But the plaintiff in equity, on a second motion supported by an affidavit, that he believes the answer will afford discovery material to his defence, may obtain a further order extending it to stay trial. And it would seem, though not free from doubt, that, on the answer coming in, this further order may be discharged independently of the original injunction.(n)

If the defendant is diligent enough to prevent the common injunction from issuing by filing a sufficient answer within the time allowed, the plaintiff must move specially on the merits confessed in the answer. If, on the other hand, the proceedings at law are such as to afford no opportunity of *obtaining the common injunction, a special injunction may be obtained on affidavit [*359] before answer; but, except under very special circumstances, the Court is unwilling to grant it.(o)

(m) 5 Vict. c. 5, s. 4 & 5; Orders of November, 1841; Re Hertford, 1 Hare 584; 1 Ph. 129; Id. 203; 2 Dan. Ch. P., c. 33.

(n) Earnshaw v. Thornhill, 18 Ves. 485; Rawson v. Samuel, 1 Cr. & P. 167.

(o) Drummond v. Pigou, 2 M. & K. 168; Bailey v. Weston, 7 Sim. 666.

As soon as the defendant has put in a full answe
may move to dissolve the injunction. And it is tl
question for the discretion of the Court whether, on
facts disclosed by the answer, or as it is techni
termed, on the equity confessed, the injunction sha
at once dissolved, or whether it shall be continued t
hearing.

The general principle of decision is, that if the an
shows the existence of an equitable question, such (
tion shall be preserved intact until the hearing. Bu
particular mode of doing this is discretionary witl
Court.

If the plaintiff is willing to admit the demand at
and to give judgment in the action, but is unwillii
pay money which it might be difficult to recover bacl
may protect himself by paying it into Court, to be t
taken care of, until the suit is decided. If he desire
try his liability at law, the injunction will be disso
with liberty to apply again after verdict. But, unless
defendant's right at law be admitted, he will not b
strained from trying it, except where it is obvious on
own answer that the relief sought will be decreed at
hearing. If he has already tried his right at law,
obtained judgment, he will be restrained from issuing
cution, if it appear that there is an equitable questic
be decided, before the Court can safely allow the m
to be disposed of elsewhere.(p)

If the injunction be against a proceeding before s
other tribunal, and not before the Courts of common
it is not in the first instance obtained as of course.
must be the subject of a special application.(q)

(p) Playfair v. Thames Junction Railway Company, 1 R. C. 640 ·
nard v. Wallis, Cr. & P. 85; Bentinck v. Willink, 2 Hare 11.

(q) Anon., 1 P. Wms. 301; Macnamara v. Macquire, 1 Dick. 223.

*V. The writ of *ne exeat*(*r*) is a writ to restrain a person from quitting the kingdom without the [*360] King's license, or the leave of the Court. It is a high prerogative writ, and was originally applicable to purposes of state only, but is now extended to private transactions, and operates in the nature of equitable bail.[1] It is grantable wherever a present equitable debt is owing, which if due at law would warrant an arrest, and also to enforce arrears of alimony in aid of the Spiritual Court, in respect of the inability of that Court to require bail.(*s*)[2] It may

(*r*) 2 Dan. Ch. P., c. 34.

(*s*) Jackson *v.* Petrie, 10 Ves. 164 ; Gardner *v.* ——, 15 Ves. 444 ; Blaydes *v.* Calvert, 2 Jac. & W. 211 ; Whitehouse *v.* Patridge, 3 Sw. 365 ; Sealy *v.* Laird, Id. 368 ; Pearne *v.* Lisle, Amb. 75.

---

[1] See, in accordance, Dunham *v.* Jackson, 1 Paige 629 ; Mitchell *v.* Bunch, 2 Id. 606 ; Johnson *v.* Clendenin, 5 Gill & J. 463. The district judges of the courts of the United States have no authority to issue writs of *ne exeat :* Gernon *v.* Boecaline, 2 Wash. C. C. 130.

[2] A writ of *ne exeat* cannot be granted, unless, 1st, there be a precise amount of debt due ; 2d, it be on an equitable demand, on which the plaintiff cannot sue at law, except in cases of account, and a few others of concurrent jurisdiction ; and third, the defendant be about to quit the country, proved by affidavits as positive as those required to hold to bail at law : Rhodes *v.* Cousins, 6 Randolph 188 ; Wallace *v.* Duncan, 13 Ga. 41. In Alabama and New York, a certain sum need not be sworn to : Lucas *v.* Hickman, 2 Stewart 111 ; Thorn *v.* Halsey, 7 Johns. Ch. 189.

If the party against whom a final decree is made, intends to remove beyond the jurisdiction of the court, before the decree can be enforced by execution, a *ne exeat* will be granted : Dunham *v.* Jackson, 1 Paige 629.

Where a wife had filed a bill for alimony against her husband, and it appeared that he had abandoned her, without any support, and threatened to leave the state, the court, on the petition of the wife, granted a writ of *ne exeat republica* against the husband : Denton *v.* Denton, 1 Johns. Ch. 364.

A suit in Chancery, by a judgment and execution' creditor, to reach equitable interests, things in action, and effects, is an equitable and not a legal demand, and the defendant may be arrested on a *ne exeat* therein Ellingwood *v.* Stevenson, 4 Sandf. Ch. 366 ; see also Buford *v.* Francisco, 3 Dana 68.

But the demand must be an equitable one, or within one of the excep-

be granted where there is a concurrent jurisdiction at law, *e. g.*, on bills for an account, or for specific performance;[1] but not where the claim is of legal cognisance alone.(*t*) The writ is issuable if the defendant is within the jurisdiction, although his domicile may be abroad,(*u*) but not if the plaintiff be himself resident abroad.(*v*)[2] In general it can only be granted after a bill is filed, and it is usual, though not indispensable, to ask it by the prayer.(*w*) It is applied for *ex parte* by petition or motion;[3] and the application must be supported by affidavit, stating the amount of the debt, and stating that the defendant intends to go abroad, or his threats or declarations to that effect, or facts evincing his intention, and stating also that the debt will be endangered by his so doing.(*x*)

(*t*) Boehm *v.* Wood, T. & R. 332; Raynes *v.* Wyse, 2 Meriv. 472; Morris *v.* McNeil, 2 Russ. 604; Jenkins *v.* Parkinson, 2 M. & K. 5.

(*u*) Howden *v.* Rogers, 1 Ves. & B. 129; Flack *v.* Holm, 1 J. & W. 415.

(*v*) Smith *v.* Nethersole, 2 R. & M. 450.

(*w*) Collinson *v.* ——, 18 Ves. 353; Barned *v.* Laing, 13 Sim. 255.

(*x*) Rico *v.* Gualtier, 3 Atk. 501; Hyde *v.* Whitfield, 19 Ves. 342; Còl-

tional cases of concurrent jurisdiction. The writ cannot be granted for a debt founded on a promissory note not due: Cox *v.* Scott, 5 Har. & J. 384. Nor where the defendant is an executor or administrator, and there is no affidavit that assets have come to his hands: Smedburg *v.* Mark, 6 Johns. Ch. 138; see also, Seymour *v.* Hazard, 1 Id. 1; Brown *v.* Haff, 5 Paige 235; Williams *v.* Williams, 2 Green's Ch. 130; Hannahan *v.* Nichols, 17 Ga. 77.

[1] See Mitchell *v.* Bunch, 2 Paige 605; Porter *v.* Spencer, 2 Johns. Ch. 169; Brown *v.* Haff, 5 Paige 235.

[2] In New York it is held that citizens of other states and foreigners are, while sojourning there, liable to a writ of *ne exeat*. The Court determines the amount in which the defendants shall be held to bail, and the sheriff must take the bond in the amount directed as the penal sum: Gilbert *v.* Colt, 1 Hopkins 496. And it may issue on demands arising abroad: Woodward *v.* Schatzell, 3 Johns. Ch. 412; Mitchell *v.* Bunch, 2 Paige 606.

[3] It seems that a writ of *ne exeat* will not be granted on petition and motion only, without a bill previously filed: Mattocks *v.* Tremain, 3 Johns. Ch. 75.

The writ is directed to the sheriff, and requires him to take security from the defendant in a specified amount that he will not go beyond seas, or into Scotland, without leave *of the Court, and in case he refuse to give such security, to commit him to safe custody.$(y)^1$ [*361] If a capture be made under the writ, the defendant cannot obtain his discharge without giving such security, either by bond with sureties, or by deposit or otherwise, as shall satisfy the sheriff.(z) An application to discharge the writ, if grounded on an irregularity or impropriety in the grant, may be made on affidavit.(a) But if it be on the merits, viz., because the defendant is not going out of the jurisdiction, or because the plaintiff has no case, the answer must be first put in.$(b)^1$

linson v. ——, 18 Id. 353; Tomlinson v. Harrison, 8 Id. 33; Stewart v. Graham, 19 Id. 313.

(y) Bernal v. Donegal, 11 Ves. 43.

(z) Boehm v. Wood, T. & R. 340.

(a) Grant v. Grant, 3 Russ. 598.

(b) Russell v. Ashby, 5 Ves. 98; Jones v. Alephsin, 16 Id. 470; Leo v. Lambert, 3 Russ. 417.

---

[1] See, on the nature of the security and the conditions of the defendant's discharge, McNamara v. Dwyer, 7 Paige 239; Mitchell v. Bunch, 2 Id. 606; Ancrum v. Dawson, McMullan's Eq. 405; O'Connor v. Debraine, 3 Edw. Ch. 230; Cowdin v. Cram, 3 Edw. Ch. 231; and, as to the damages recoverable, see Burnap v. Wight, 14 Ill. 301.

[2] See Nixon v. Richardson, 4 Dessaus. 108.

[*362]   *CHAPTER VI.

OF EVIDENCE.[1]

THE next regular step after replication is, that t]
should prove their case by evidence.

The rules of evidence are the same in equity ‹
Each litigant must prove by legitimate evidence
of the facts alleged in his pleadings as are mater
decree asked or resisted, and are not admitted 1
by his opponent.

I. They must be facts material to the decree.

In reference to this doctrine, it is important t
that the decree asked or resisted, in the sense
the expression is here used, is not necessarily o1
whole relief sought, but is merely that decree ›
cording to the practice of the Court, can be ma
first instance.(a)   If, for example, a bill be file
administration of assets, or for the specific perfo
an agreement for sale, the decree in the first cas
first instance for an account of assets, or for an i
to the parties interested therein; and, in the se

(a) Infra, Decree.

---

[1] See upon this subject, generally, Greenleaf's Evidence, v
vi., " Of Evidence in Proceedings in Equity;" Daniel's Ch
xxi. And also a valuable collection of American cases on the la
Evidence, in the Appendix to the 13th vol. of McKinley and L‹
Library.

for an inquiry as to the validity of the vendor's title. The plaintiff is not bound, therefore, before the hearing, to prove every allegation in such bills, but should confine himself in the one case to establish his *primâ facie* right by proof of his debtor relationship, and in the other by proof of the agreement, or of such other facts as will lay a foundation *for the inquiry.(*b*) And in like manner, the defendant's evidence should be confined to disproving those facts. [*363]

II. They must be facts not admitted in the suit by his opponent.

If any facts are made the subject of express admission in the suit, or are admitted by the pleadings as true, and the party making the admission is competent to do so, it is, of course, unnecessary to prove them by evidence. But admissions by an infant, however made, whether by express agreement, or by his bill as plaintiff, or his answer as defendant, or by his omission as plaintiff to reply to an answer, are unavailing, and the facts must be proved by evidence.[1] And admissions by husband and wife cannot bind the wife's inheritance.(*c*)

The rules with respect to admissions by answer have been already explained under the head of Discovery,[2]

(*b*) Law *v.* Hunter, 1 Russ. 100; Tomlin *v.* Tomlin, 1 Hare 240.
(*c*) Evans *v.* Cogan, 2 P. Wms. 449.

---

[1] See 3 Greenleaf's Evidence, s. 278. An infant, however, on coming of age, may be permitted to file another answer; and if he unreasonably delays to apply for leave to do this, he will be taken to have confirmed his former answer, and it may be read against him: Id. s. 279; see Watson *v.* Godwin, 4 Md. Ch. 25.

[2] A direct admission contained in the answer of a defendant, is, of course, always evidence against him: 3 Greenl. Ev., s. 277; even in a subsequent suit: Royal *v.* McKenzie, 25 Ala. 363. Though it is otherwise where it is made upon information merely, and not upon information and belief: Id. s. 282. Where an answer admits a fact charged, but sets up

viz., that the answer of the defendant is evidence against
himself but not against a co-defendant; that the answer,

---

another fact in avoidance, the fact admitted is established; but the fact in
avoidance must be proved: Clements *v.* Moore, 6 Wallace (U. S.) 299.
Silence alone will not be construed to be an admission, as to matters
not charged to be within the knowledge of the defendant: Lynn *v.* Bolling,
14 Ala. 753. And a complainant cannot, in general, rely merely upon
admissions in the answer as the ground for relief, without having by his
bill made them an integral part of his case: Small *v.* Owings, 1 Md. Ch.
363.

The admissions in the answer of one defendant cannot usually be made
evidence to affect his co-defendants: 3 Greenl. Ev., ¿ 283; ante 20, note;
Briesch *v.* McCauley, 7 Gill 189; Hitt *v.* Ormsbee, 12 Ill. 166; Whiting *v.*
Beebe, 7 Eng. (Ark.) 421; Glenn *v.* Grover, 3 Md. 212; Farley *v.* Bryant,
32 Maine 474; Gilmore *v.* Patterson, 36 Id. 544; Blakeney *v.* Ferguson,
14 Ark. 641; Lenox *v.* Notrebe, 1 Hempst. 251; but see Miles *v.* Miles, 32
N. H. 147. Where, however, partnership or privity is established between
the defendants, or the answer of one is referred to or relied on by the rest,
it becomes evidence against all: Greenl. Ev., ut supr.; Clayton *v.* Thompson, 13 Ga. 206; Van Reimsdyk *v.* Kane, 1 Gallis. 630; Chase *v.* Manhardt,
1 Bland 336; Whiting *v.* Beebe, 7 Eng. (Ark.) 421; Osborn *v.* U. S. Bank,
9 Wheat. 738; Judd *v.* Seaver, 8 Paige 548; Dexter *v.* Arnold, 3 Sumn.
152; though see Winn *v.* Albert, 2 Md. Ch. 169; Gilmore *v.* Patterson, 36
Maine 544; Blakeney *v.* Ferguson, 14 Arkansas 641. So, where the right
of the complainant to a decree against one defendant is only prevented
from being complete by some questions between a second defendant and
the former, he may read the answer of the second defendant for that purpose: Whiting *v.* Beebe, 7 Eng. (Ark.) 421. The joint answer of a husband and wife may be read against the wife as to her separate estate:
Clive *v.* Carew, 1 John. & H. 207.

On the other hand, the answer of a defendant, so far as it is responsive
to the bill, is evidence for him, and is conclusive in general, unless contradicted by two witnesses, or one witness corroborated more or less strongly
by circumstances, according to the nature of the case: ante 21, note;
Horton's App., 13 Penn. St. 67; Ringgold *v.* Bryan, 3 Md. Ch. 488; Bank
U. S. *v.* Beverly, 1 How. (U. S.) 134; Carpenter *v.* Prov., &c., Ins. Co., 4
Id. 185; West *v.* Flanagan, 4 Md. 36; Brooks *v.* Thomas, 8 Id. 367; Miles
v. Miles, 32 N. H. 147; Busbee *v.* Littlefield, 33 Id. 76; Williams *v.* Philpot,
19 Ga. 567; Stouffer *v.* Machen, 16 Ill. 553; Dyer *v.* Bean, 15 Ark. 519;
Autrey *v.* Cannon, 11 Texas 110; Calkins *v.* Evans, 5 Ind. 441; Turner *v.*
Knell, 24 Md. 55; Clark *v.* Hackett, 1 Cliff. C. C. 269; Delano *v.* Winsor,
Id. 501; Bird *v.* Styles, 3 Green (N. J.) 297; Willdey *v.* Webster, 42 Ill.

if replied to, cannot be evidence in favor of the defendant, unless where a positive denial is opposed to the

---

108: Blow v. Gage, 44 Id. 208; De Hart v. Baird, 4 Green (N. J.) 423;
Bent v. Smith, 20 N. J. Eq. 199. But this must be taken with some
qualifications. Circumstances alone, independent of any direct proof, it
is said, may often justify and require a decree against the answer: White
v. Crew, 16 Ga. 416. It is not material in respect to the conclusiveness of
the answer, that the equity of the complainant's bill is grounded on allegations of fraud: McDonald v. McLeod, 1 Ired. 226; Murray v. Blatchford,
1 Wend. 583; Dilly v. Bernard, 8 Gill & John. 171; Eberly v. Groff, 21
Penn. St. 251; Morris & Essex R. R. Co. v. Blair, 1 Stockt. 635; or that
proof upon the denial of the allegations of the bill is in the reach of the
defendant, but is inaccessible to the complainant: Thompson v. Diffen-
derfer, 1 Md. Ch. 487. So an answer responsive to the charging part of
the bill, or to allegations as to the motives and views under which acts
have been done, must be overborne by the same testimony as in other
cases: Smith v. Clark, 4 Paige 368; Glenn v. Grover, 3 Md. 212; but see
Lea's Ex'rs. v. Eidson, 9 Gratt. 277. If the bill is supported by the testimony of a single witness only, and the defendant by his answer positively,
clearly and precisely denies the allegations it contains, the Court will not
make a decree, but will dismiss the bill. But if there is anything to corroborate the testimony of the witness, as, for example, letters of the defendant, it will be sufficient to turn the scale. See Jordan v. Money, 5
H. L. Cas. 185, 217–218; Smith v. Kay, 7 Id. 760; Brittin v. Crabtree, 20
Ark. 309; Pusey v. Wright, 31 Penn. St. 287.

This general rule, however, is open to some exceptions. Thus it is the
prevailing doctrine in the United States that it is not applicable to an unsworn answer, though an answer under oath is not required by bill, the
rule being otherwise in England. See 3 Greenl. 286, note; Union Bank
v. Geary, 5 Peters 99; Patterson v. Gaines, 6 How. (U. S.) 586; Bartlett
v. Gale, 4 Paige 503; Willis v. Henderson, 4 Scamm. 13; Tomlinson v.
Lindley, 2 Carter (Ind.) 569; McLard v. Linnville, 10 Humph. 163; Taggert v. Bolden, 10 Md. 104; Wilson v. Towle, 36 N. H. 129; Wallwork v.
Derby, 40 Ill. 527; Hyer v. Little, 20 N. J. Eq. 443; Willenborg v. Murphy,
36 Ill. 344; but see Clements v. Moore, 6 Wall. (U. S.) 299; Story Eq. Pl.,
§ 875, &c.; and it is so expressly provided by statutory and judicial regulation in some states: Greenleaf, ut sup. See Bingham v. Yeomans, 10
Cush. 58. By statute, in Iowa, a sworn answer does not make other or
greater proof necessary than if the answer was not verified by oath:
Mitchell v. Moore, 24 Iowa 394. It has, therefore, been held that the
answer of a corporation under seal only cannot be relied on as evidence
in its favor, as though it were on oath: Lovett v. Steam, &c., Ass., 6 Paige

testimony of a single witness, or where the question i
to costs alone ; and that the plaintiff does not, by reac

54; McLard *v.* Linnville, 10 Humph. 163 ; Maryl., &c., Co. *v.* **Winge**
Gill 170 ; State Bank *v.* Edwards, 20 Ala. 512 ; *contra*, **Bayard** *v.* **Ch**
Del. Co., cited 3 Bland 165' In Haight *v.* Morris Aqueduct, 4 Wash.
601, however, such an answer was held sufficient to prevent the gran
of an injunction ; and see Carpenter *v.* Prov., &c., Insurance Co., 4 I
(U. S.) 218 ; and in general it will put in issue allegations to which
responsive, and throw on the complainant the burden of proving th
Balt. & Ohio R. R. Co. *v.* Wheeling, 13 Gratt. 40 ; Taggert *v.* Bolder
Md. 104. The effect of an answer under oath to an original bill cal
for an answer under oath, cannot be avoided by the filing of an amended
waiving the oath : Wylder *v.* Crane, 53 Ill. 490. In order to enable
defendant to claim the protection of the general rule, moreover, the
stated in the answer must be responsive to the allegations and interrogat
of the bill, and the denial made must be positive and distinct, not evasiv
illusory : Wakeman *v.* Grover, 4 Paige 23 ; Lucas *v.* Bank of Darie
Stew. (Ala.) 280 ; N. E. Bank *v.* Lewis, 8 Pick. 113 ; Philips *v.* Rich
on, 4 J. J. Marsh. 213 ; Cocke *v.* Trotter, 10 Yerg. 213 ; O'Brien *v.* Ell
15 Maine 125 ; Buck *v.* Swazey, 35 Id. 42 ; Smith *v.* Kincaid, 10 Hun
73 ; Jacks *v.* Nichols, 1 Seld. (N. Y.) 178 ; Stevens *v.* Post, 1 Beas. 4
Coleman *v.* Rose, 46 Penn. St. 184 ; Wells *v.* Houston, 37 Verm. 247; see a
356, note. So the defendant cannot rely upon his statements of matter
defence, though in form responsive, but must prove them in the ordin
way : Hagthorp *v.* Hook, 1 Gill & John. 272 ; Paynes *v.* Coles, 1 M
373 ; Walton *v.* Walton, 2 Benn. (Mo.) 376 ; ante, 356, note ; Gilber
Mosier, 11 Iowa 326. A further qualification is, that where the f
stated or denied in the answer could not be by possibility within the
sonal knowledge of the defendant, as in the case of an executor or heir
where stated or denied only upon information and belief, or by way of
ference from facts not particularly stated, the same amount of counterv
ing proof is not required : Combs *v.* Boswell, 1 Dana 474 ; Lawrenc
Lawrence, 4 Bibb 358 ; Harlan *v.* Wingate's Adm., 2 J. J. Marsh. 1
Carneal's Heirs *v.* Day, Litt. Sel. Cas. 492 ; Knickerbacker *v.* Harri
Paige 209 ; Drury *v.* Conner, 6 Har. & Johns. 288 ; Pennington *v.* .
tings, 2 Gill & John. 208 ; Clark's Adm. *v.* Van Reimsdyk, 9 Cranch 1
Paulding *v.* Watson, 21 Ala. 279 ; Copeland *v.* Crane, 9 Pick. 73. A
on the other hand, where a bill was filed to set aside a deed as fraudul
against creditors, and it was charged in the bill that the consideration
not paid, it is not satisfactory that the defendant relies upon his answe
there are suspicious circumstances attending the transaction. The evide
of the payment must have been in the defendant's possession, and it sho
have been produced : Callan *v.* Statham, 23 How. 477. So upon the p

extracted passages, make other passages evidence, except so far as they are explanatory of the passages read.

---

ciple that the answer of an infant by his guardian is not binding on him, *e converso*, it cannot be used as evidence in his favor : Bulkley *v.* Van Wyck, 5 Paige 536. And it may be further stated here, that the general rule in some of the states is subjected to certain modifications by statutory provisions. See 3 Greenl. Ev. ¿ 289, note.

Most of these exceptions, it is to be remembered, are only applicable where the complainant has put in a replication, and taken issue upon the allegations of the answer. Where he does not do so, however, or where, after putting in a replication, he sets the case down for hearing on bill and answer, he so far waives his rights, and the answer is to be taken as true whether responsive or not : Cherry *v.* Belcher, 5 Stew. & Port. 134 ; Pierce *v.* West's Ex'rs., 1 Peters C. C. 351 ; Dale *v.* McEvers, 2 Cow. 118 ; Jones *v.* Mason, 5 Rand. 577 ; Scott *v.* Clarkson, 1 Bibb 277 ; Moore *v.* Hylton, 1 Dev. Eq. 429 ; Carman *v.* Watson, 1 How. (Miss.) 333 ; 3 Greenl. ¿ 288; Lanning *v.* Smith, 1 Pars. Eq. 17 ; Ware *v.* Richardson, 3 Md. 505 ; Mason *v.* Martin, 4 Id. 124 ; Perkins *v.* Nichols, 11 Allen 542 ; Farrell *v.* McKee, 36 Ill. 225.

The answer of one defendant, on the other hand, is not, in general, evidence in behalf of another defendant : Morris *v.* Nixon, 1 How. U. S. 119 ; Larkin's Appeal, 38 Penn. St. 457 ; 3 Greenl. ¿ 283 ; see Farley *v.* Bryant, 32 Maine 474 ; Gilmore *v.* Patterson, 36 Id. 544. Though where it is directly responsive and furnishes a disclosure of the facts required unfavorable to the complainant, and especially where the title of such other defendant is merely derivative, it has been held otherwise : Greenl. ut sup. ; Mills *v.* Gore, 20 Pick. 28. The answer of one defendant cannot be read in evidence against a co-defendant when there is no privity between the two : Adkins *v.* Paul, 32 Ga. 219 ; Alden *v.* Holden, Id. 418 ; see also, Hoff *v.* Burd, 2 Green (N. J.) 201 ; Eckman *v.* Eckman, 55 Penn. St. 269.

In equity, a complainant is entitled to read so much of the answer only in evidence, as contains the admissions on which he desires to rely, subject, however, to this exception, that he must also read all the explanations and qualifications, by which the admissions may be accompanied, though contained in a distinct part of the answer, but incorporated by reference in the admissions : Parrish *v.* Koons, 1 Pars Eq. 97 ; Gleen *v.* Randall, 2 Md. Ch. 220 ; ante, 21 ; 3 Greenl., ¿ 281. This, however, does not apply to what is really matter of discharge or defence, relied upon by the defendant in connection with an admission of the liability charged in the bill, which, as has been stated above, must be proved by him at the hearing, if the answer has been replied to ; and if the matter in avoidance has been so skilfully interwoven into the grammatical construction of the passages containing the admissions, that both must be read together, the complainant will be enti-

III. The proof must be by legitimate evidence.
The only doctrine under this head which can b
sidered peculiar to Courts of Equity regards the ad
bility as witnesses of parties to the suit.(d)
ordinary rules of evidence, until altered by a late statu
a person interested in the result of the suit was in
sible as a witness, and it is obvious that this gro
objection applied more forcibly to the immediate]
on the record than to any other person. The g
incapacity in respect of interest has been abrogat
[*364] that statute, but the case *of the immediat
ties to the record is expressly excepted fro
effect.

If, however, the person tendered for examin
though nominally a party on the record, had in tru
interest in the event, he was even at law a com]

(d) 1 Dan. Ch. P. 845.   (e) 6 & 7 Vict. c. 85

---

tled to have the matter of avoidance considered as struck out: 3
§ 281 ; McCoy v. Rhodes, 11 How. U. S. 131; Whiting v. Beebe,
(Ark.) 421 ; Baker v. Williamson, 4 Penn. St. 467.

Where, nevertheless, a decree is sought upon grounds disclosed
answer variant from those assumed in the bill, the whole answer]
taken together, the matter of charge as well as discharge, and mus
so taken, make out a proper case for relief: Mulloy v. Young, 10 I
298.

It is equally settled, however, that at law, a party relying on an
to a bill of discovery, must read the whole or none ; ante 21 ; and tl
has been also held to apply in cases where the Court, having obtai
risdiction of discovery, goes on to give the necessary relief, to avoid
tiplicity of suits, though there be a full and adequate remedy at law
is generally done in the United States : Lyons v. Miller, 6 Gratt. 43
answer cannot be attacked by evidence tending to impeach the defe
credibility; and such evidence is inadmissible: Brown v. Bul
McCart. 294. In this case, Butler v. Catlin, 1 Root 310, and Sal
Clagett, 3 Bland 165, were followed; and Miller v. Tolleson, 1 Ha
145, where a contrary doctrine had been held, was disapproved.

witness. (*f*)   But it rarely happens that at law any person is joined on the record who is not interested either
in the issue or in the costs.   In equity, on the contrary, it often happens that parties
are joined as trustees,[1] or otherwise, without possessing or
claiming a beneficial interest, or that, even if they have a
beneficial interest, it extends only to some of the points
at issue.   The principle, therefore, which before the
alteration of the law established the admissibility of such
persons as witnesses was one of frequent operation, and
seems to be correctly embodied in the following rule :
that where any person was made a defendant for form's
sake, and no decree could be had which he had any beneficial interest in resisting,[2] or where he had by his answer

(*f*) Phillips on Evidence, 51 ; Worrall *v.* Jones, 7 Bing. 398.

---

[1] A trustee defendant, having a legal interest altogether nominal, is a
competent witness as to the merits or design of the trust deed : Hawkins
v. Hawkins, 2 Car. Law Rep. 627.

In equity, a mere trustee may in general be a witness : Neville *v.* De-
meritt, 1 Green Ch. 321 ; Harvey *v.* Alexander, 1 Rand. 219 ; Taylor *v.*
Moore, 2 Id. 563 ; Trustees of Watertown *v.* Cowen, 4 Paige 510 ; Hodges
v. Mullikin, 1 Bland 503 ; Hardwick *v.* Hook, 8 Ga. 354. See Southard *v.*
Cushing, 11 B. Monr. 344. This rule has been adopted at law in Pennsylvania : Drum *v.* Simpson, 6 Binn. 481 ; King *v.* Cloud, 7 Penn. St. 467 ;
Keim *v.* Taylor, 11 Id. 163 ; Sorg *v.* First German, &c., 63 Id. 156. But it
is to be remembered that where, as is the case now in most of the United
States, a trustee is entitled to commissions, he is so far interested in the trust
estate ; and must release that interest, before he can be permitted to testify
in a cause in which it may be in any way affected. See Anderson *v.* Neff,
11 S. & R. 208 ; Patton *v.* Ash, 7 Id. 116 ; King *v.* Cloud, 7 Penn. St. 467.

[2] A defendant made a party *pro forma* only, or where, in general, no
decree could properly be passed against him, may be made a witness for
his co-defendant : Kirk *v.* Hodgson, 2 Johns. Ch. 550 ; Ragan *v.* Echols, 5
Ga. 71 ; Sharp *v.* Morrow, 6 Monr. 305 ; Warren *v.* Sproule, 2 A. K. Marsh.
539 ; Wright *v.* Wright, 2 McCord Ch. 185 ; Butler *v.* Elliott, 15 Conn.
187 ; see also, Caphart *v.* Huey, 1 Hill Ch. 405 ; Jones *v.* Bullock, 2 Dev.
Ch. 368 ; Bell *v.* Jasper, 2 Ired. Eq. 597 ; Wilson *v.* Allen, 1 Jones Eq. 24.
And he may be a witness against a co-defendant, where he is necessarily

submitted to a decree, and had therefore ceased t
such interest,[1] or where, though having an inter
had it in respect of a part only of the matters in
he might be examined as a witness either generally
respect to those matters in which he had no int

---

a party, but will not be affected by the decree against his co-de
and does not swear in favor of his own interest: Williams v. Beard
158 ; Miller v. McCan, 7 Paige 457. A party charged as combini
others in a fraud against which relief is sought, and therefore me
fendant, no particular relief being prayed against him, may be a
for his co-defendant, though liable for costs : Neilson v. McD
Johns. Ch. 201 ; 2 Cowen 139. But not so where he is affected by the
and may be liable for more than the costs : Ormsby v. Bakewell,
98, 1st part; Pope v. Andrews, 1 S. & M. Ch. 135; see Whippl
Rensselaer, 3 Johns. Ch. 612 ; Farley v. Bryant, 32 Maine 474.

[1] A defendant who suffers the bill to be taken as confessed, and
enables the complainant to obtain a decree against him individua
competent witness for his co-defendant : Holgate v. Palmer, 8 Pa
Post v. Dart, Id. 639 ; Lupton v. Lupton, 2 Johns. Ch. 625.

[2] Lingen v. Henderson, 1 Bland 268. The mere fact that a p
made a defendant to a bill in chancery does not render him an i
tent witness in the suit as to matters in which he has no interest.
a decree, one defendant may have an order for the examination o
defendant as to matters in which the latter is not interested, savio
plaintiff all just exceptions. And it is not a good exception that h
interest in any other matters embraced in the cause, unless these
will be affected by his examination : Williams v. Maitland, 1 Ired.
Sproule v. Samuel, 4 Scammon 135; Dyer v. Martin, Id. 146 ; A
Allison, 7 Dana 92; Armsby v. Wood, Hopk. 229 ; Second Cong.
v. First Cong. Soc., &c., 14 N. H. 315; Tolson v. Tolson, 4 Md.
But an order must be first obtained : Hewett v. Crane, 2 Halst.
Second Cong. Soc. v. First Cong. Soc., ut supr. ; Hoyt v. Hamm
How. U. S. 350.

But it has been held, that the omission to procure the previous
the court for the examination of a defendant as a witness, is a me
ularity, and when it is apparent that no substantial injustice has
flicted upon the opposite party by denying him the benefit of a cro.
ination, and that delay and injury will be visited upon the party
upon the proof, an objection thereto on this ground ought not to
Tolson v. Tolson, 4 Md. Ch. 119. See, on this subject, 8 Gree
§ 314, &c.

And liberty so to examine him might be obtained as of course by either the plaintiff or a co-defendant, saving just exceptions. The application to examine him was accompanied by a suggestion that he had no interest.(g) If that suggestion were untrue, the deposition was disallowed at the hearing; and if the examination had been by the plaintiff, he could not pray an adverse decree against the defendant examined, nor against others who might be secondarily liable.(h)[1] The act above referred to abolished the suggestion of "no interest," and provides that in Courts of equity any defendant may be *examined as a witness, saving just exceptions, and [*365] that any interest which he may have, shall not be deemed a just exception to his testimony, but shall only be considered as affecting or tending to affect his credit.(i)

The plaintiff is in all cases incompetent as a witness. If a co-plaintiff be desirous of his evidence, and the defendant will not consent to the examination, he must move for leave to strike out his name as plaintiff on payment of the costs already incurred and to make him a defendant

(g) Murray v. Shadwell, 2 Ves. & B. 401.
(h) Massy v. Massy, 1 Beatty 353; Champion v. Champion, 15 Sim. 101.
(i) 6 & 7 Vict. c. 85, s. 1.

---

[1] Where a defendant has been used by the complainant as a witness, no decree can in general be made against him or against others who may be secondarily liable with him as to the matters upon which he has been examined; and if he has been examined upon the whole case made by the bill, it must be dismissed as to him and them: Lingan v. Henderson, 1 Bland 268; Bradley v. Root, 5 Paige 633; Palmer v. Van Doren, 2 Edw. Ch. 192. But this rule does not apply to the case of a mere formal defendant, as an executor or trustee, against whom no personal decree is sought, and who has no personal interest in the question as to which he is examined as a witness against his co-defendants; nor to the case of a defendant who, by his answer, admits his own liability, or who suffers the bill to be taken as confessed against him : Bradley v. Root, 5 Paige 633.

by amendment.[1] If the examination is required on behalf of a defendant, it can only be had by the plaintiff's
consent.(*k*)

The manner of taking evidence is different in equity
and at law. It is taken at law *vivâ voca,* and publicly; in
equity it is written and secret. The origin of this distinction is the difference of the objects which the two
tribunals have in view.[2]

The object at law is to enable the jury to give their
verdict on the issue joined between the parties. They

(*k*) Fisher *v.* Fisher, 2 Ph. 236.

---

[1] Leavitt *v.* Steenbergen, 3 Barb. S. C. 155; Helms *v.* Franciscus, 2
Bland 544; Eckford *v.* De Kay, 6 Paige 565; 3 Greenl. Ev., ? 314. See
Pusey c. Wright, 31 Penn. St. 287. So, an application by a defendant
having a common interest with the plaintiffs, adverse to that of the other
defendants, for leave to examine a plaintiff against the other defendants,
is treated as if made by the plaintiffs themselves, and such permission will
not be granted: Eckford *v.* De Kay. 6 Paige 565 ; see, also, Ross c. Carter,
4 Hen. & Munf. 488.

[2] Very considerable changes have been introduced in many of the United
States, in the manner of the trial of disputed issues in Chancery, in the
method of examination of witnesses, and the like. Mr. Greenleaf (3 Evidence, s. 267) thus sums up the diversities existing among the different
states in these respects: " In some, the parties may examine each other as
witnesses; in others, this is not permitted. In some, the witnesses may be
examined in court *vivâ voce,* as at law ; in others, the testimony is always
taken in writing, either in open court, by the clerk, the judge, or in depositions, after the former method. In the latter case, however, there is this
further diversity of practice, that, in some states, the parties may examine
and cross-examine the witness, *ore tenus,* before the magistrate or commissioner ; in others, they may only propound questions in writing, through
the commissioner; and in others, they may only be present during the examination and take notes of the testimony, but without speaking; while in
others, the parties are still excluded from the examination. In some of the
states, also, it is required that all matters of fact, in all cases, shall be tried
by the jury ; in others, it is at the option of the parties ; in others, it is
apparently left in the direction of the court; but with plain intimations
that it ought not to be refused, unless for good cause." In the previous
sections, these distinctions are more elaborately dwelt upon.

are not required to decide on the merits of the case generally, or to elicit a legal conclusion from a series of facts, but are to give their verdict on the balance of testimony, affirmative and negative, direct and indirect, submitted to them on the issues joined. In order, therefore, that this object may be best attained, it is necessary, not that the evidence should be correctly recorded, but that at the time of its being given it should be thoroughly compared and sifted; and this is done by an examination *vivâ voce* and in public. The jury are thus aided by the tone and manner of the witnesses, as well as by his actual assertions. They have, in a comparatively short time, the witnesses on both sides brought under their notice, their inaccuracies or obscurities corrected or explained, and the entire mass of evidence commented on by counsel, and summed up by the judge, and the danger of mistake or misapprehension in the witnesses, as well as that of a deliberate perjury, is partly remedied by the solemnity *of a public [*366] trial, and in a still greater degree by the searching ordeal of cross-examination. The verdict, when given, is added to the record, but there is no judicial record of the evidence. If the verdict is complained of as being against the evidence, the private notes of the judge, or the admissions of counsel, are the only materials furnished to the Court; and if the Court in its discretion grants a new trial, such new trial must take place as on a new issue, before a new and independent jury, who will decide according to the evidence laid before themselves. If the verdict is undisturbed, but its legal effect on the question in dispute is doubted, that, as a question of law, must be decided by the Court; but for the purpose of such decision, as well as of any subsequent appeal, the verdict only, and not the evidence, appears upon the record.

In a Court of law, therefore, a *vivâ voce* examin
in public is the regular mode of proof. In equity
object of the evidence is different, and so also is the
of taking it.

The trial and determination of disputed issues ar
the principal objects of evidence in equity; for the n
of the questions there litigated does not generally
rise to such issues; and those which do occur, if
present any serious difficulty of trial, are generall
ferred to the verdict of a jury.(*l*)   The power, ther
of sifting and comparing testimony, which is the pri
requisite at law, becomes comparatively unimporta
equity; and the principal objects there contemplate
first, to elicit a sworn detail of facts, on which the
may adjudge the equities; and secondly, to preserve
an accurate record, for the use, if needed, of the App
Court.

For this reason it is required in equity that all
nesses shall be examined before the hearing, and
answers taken down in writing, so that, when the
comes on for decision, the judge may not be distr
[*367] by the trial *of separate issues on evidence
brought forward for the first time, but may
his undivided attention to the decree, which the
admitted or proved will warrant; and that, if his d
be appealed from, the Court of Appeal may hav
an authorized record, all the materials on which
founded.

The protracted nature of a written examination n
sarily involves the risk that defects of evidence mig
discovered in the course of taking it, and false testi
procured to remedy them.   In order to avoid this

(*l*) Infra, Issue.

the witnesses are examined privately by an officer of the Court; and it is an imperative rule, that until the examination has been completed and the entire depositions given out, which is technically termed passing publication, neither party shall be made acquainted with his adversary's interrogatories, nor with any part of the answers on either side; and that after publication, no further witnesses can be examined without special leave.(m)

The secrecy thus observed must to some extent involve the possibility, not only of false evidence being given, but of true evidence being given in an imperfect form, where a party, in the absence of his opponent, so frames his interrogatories as to elicit testimony respecting part only of a transaction. This is an evil which cannot altogether be avoided; but it is in a great degree remedied by the rule, that in order to give weight to evidence, the facts which it is intended to support must have been previously detailed in the pleadings. Should this security prove insufficient, so that a doubt exists at the hearing whether all material facts are before the Court, further inquiries may be directed, and the decision in the meantime delayed.

The mode of examination is by written interrogatories, which, in the cases of witnesses resident within twenty *miles of London, are administered by an officer called the examiner; or if they are resident beyond that distance, and the parties are unwilling to incur the expense of bringing them to town, by commissioners specially appointed for the purpose.(n)[1]   [*368]

The interrogatories, as well as the bill and answer,

(m) 1 Dan. Ch. P. 948.

(n) Mostyn v. Spencer, 6 Beav. 135; Orders of 1845, xciv.–cx.; 1 Dan. Ch. P. 860.

---

[1] See, on this subject, 3 Green. Evid., s. 319, et seq.

must be signed by counsel, as a security to the Co
no irrelevant or improper matter is inserted.

They are framed as a series of questions, direc
cessively to the several facts in issue, and nu
First Interrogatory, Second Interrogatory, and s
and a marginal note is usually affixed to each,
out the witness for whom it is intended.

In framing interrogatories the same rule mus
served as in putting questions to a witness at la\
they must not be leading or suggestive on material
and they must not be so framed as to embody i
facts admitting of an answer by a simple neg;
affirmative, and thus presenting to the Court the e
not as it would be stated by the witness himself, 1
the coloring prompted by professional skill and a
knowledge of the case to be proved.   In guarding
the latter of these objections, a risk is necessarily i
of framing the question in so general a form, tha
ness may unawares, or through misapprehension,
important fact; and, if such omission should oc
framer of the interrogatories has not, like an ex
counsel at *nisi prius* the opportunity of adding
varying his question, so as to suit the apprehe
the witness.   Great care is therefore requisite in
ing the interrogatories, that the witness's mind
led into the right channel of thought; and the d
[*369]   of effecting this is materially diminished
         .fore the interrogatories are settled, an ‹
statement is prepared of each witness's evidence
same manner as at *nisi prius*.   Beyond these gene
ciples it is impossible to lay down any uniform sy.
interrogatories, which must necessarily vary in e
stance, according to the circumstances of the in‹
case.

At the conclusion of each interrogatory the following words, denoted in the draft by the words "Declare," &c. are inserted in the engrossment: "Declare the truth of the several matters in this interrogatory inquired after, according to the best of your knowledge, remembrance, and belief, with your reasons fully and at large;" and at the end of the set the draftsman may, if he please, add what is called the general Concluding Interrogatory, "Do you know or can you set forth any other matter or thing which may be of benefit or advantage to the parties at issue in this cause, or either of them, or that may be material to the subject of this your examination, or to the matters in question in this cause? If yea, set forth the same," &c.(o) The addition, however, is not compulsory · and it is generally more prudent to omit it; for, if due care has been taken in preparing the evidence, all matters beneficial to the examining party will have been already elicited by the special interrogatories; so that any evidence elicited by the general one is likely to benefit his adversary rather than himself.

Before the witnesses are examined, the examining officer is generally instructed as to the interrogatories applying to each witness. During the actual examination, the examining officer and the witness are the only persons present, all third persons being strictly excluded. The witness is then examined on each interrogatory in order, his answers being taken down on paper, and is not permitted to read, or hear read, any other interrogatory, until that in hand be fully answered.

*When all the interrogatories have been gone [*370] through, the deposition is read over to the witness, who, after correcting any error or omission, signs it.

(o) 1 Dan. Ch. P. 858.

46

The affixing of his signature completes his examin
and he cannot be again examined on behalf of the
party.(*p*)

If any of the interrogatories are such as the witr
not bound to answer, *e. g.*, if they intend to expose l
a penalty or forfeiture, or involve a breach of profes
confidence, he may decline to answer them,[1] stating
same time on oath his reasons for so doing; a proc
which is somewhat inaccurately called a Demurrer
terrogatories. The examiner or commissioner takes
the statement in writing, and the objection is hear
decided by the Court.(*q*)   If the witness himself do
object to the question, and its impropriety depe
general grounds, and not on such as are personal t
self, as where it involves a breach of professional
dence, or where the interrogatories are leading, or t
positions scandalous, or where any serious irregulari
occurred in taking them, the Court, on motion wit
reasonable time will suppress the depositions.(*r*)

The witnesses examined in chief by either part
be cross-examined by his opponent; and the inte
tories filed for this purpose, which are termed Cro
terrogatories, are in all respects similar to the inte
tories in chief, except that they are not subject to
tion on the ground of leading the witness. It is, ho
very seldom that any good result is effected by a

(*p*) Cockerell *v.* Cholmeley, 3 Sim. 313; Whitaker *v.* Wrigh
412.

(*q*) Parkhurst *v.* Lowten, 2 Swanst. 206; Langley *v.* Fisher,
443; Carpmael *v.* Powis, 1 Ph. 687.

(*r*) Shaw *v.* Lindsey, 15 Ves. 381; Healey *v.* Jagger, 3 Sim. 494
ton *v.* Spedcer, 6 Beav. 135.

[1] The witness cannot refuse to be sworn, however: Ex parte B
L. J. Ch. 614.

examination in equity; for it is conducted in ignorance of the question in chief, and therefore, as applied to the adversary's case, is uncertain and often dangerous; and it cannot be applied, as at *nisi prius*, to the proof of an independent *case. If the evidence of the witness is required for that purpose, he may be examined [*371] on original interrogatories; but his cross-examination must be confined to those points on which he has been already examined in chief.(*s*)

The time for publishing the depositions is fixed by the general orders of the Court.(*t*) If either party wishes to delay this step, in order to complete the examination of his witnesses, he must apply to the Master to whom the cause stands referred, to enlarge the publication for a further time. And, even after publication has nominally passed, yet if the depositions have continued secret, and through surprise or accident, without blamable negligence, either party has failed to examine his witnesses, a similar indulgence may be obtained. An order, however, for this latter purpose, although in form for enlarging publication, is in reality for leave to examine, notwithstanding publication passed, and must be obtained by application to the Court.(*u*)

After the depositions have been published and read, no further evidence is admissible without special leave, except evidence to discredit a witness, either by impeaching his general credibility, or by showing him to have sworn falsely in a part of his evidence not material to the issue in the cause. With respect to the material parts of his evidence, such discretionary evidence is not admissible,

(*s*) 1 Dan. Ch. P. 856.
(*t*) Orders of 1845, cxi., cxiii.
(*u*) Carr *v.* Appleyard, 2 M. & C. 476.]

lest, under the pretence of impeaching his credibility, new evidence should be introduced.$(v)^1$

The rule excluding evidence after publication passed, is subject to the discretion of the Court.[2] And the infirmity of written testimony taken in the absence of both judge and counsel, and without any means of rectifying slips while the examination proceeds, renders it sometimes necessary to apply for a relaxation. Permission has accordingly been granted to examine witnesses after [*372] publication, *where the interrogatories originally exhibited have failed of effect, either by a suppressal of the depositions on the ground of leading, or by reason of the questions being improperly framed, or where, being misunderstood by the witness, errors occur which at law, where both judge and counsel are present, would have been remedied by putting the question in a better form.(w) The same indulgence has been given where the plaintiff had relied on admissions in the answer, which were held insufficient or ineffectual at the hearing; and where, through the inadvertence of counsel, the plaintiff had omitted to give evidence on a point which, though material to the relief sought, was not really contested in the cause. But the Court must be satisfied by affidavit, or otherwise, that the slip has been wholly accidental, and has not been purposely made in order to have an opportunity of re-examining. And there does not appear to be any instance where liberty has been given to supply evidence on the actual question in dispute.(x) The regular

(v) 1 Dan. Ch. P. 948.   (w) 1 Dan. Ch. P. 942.
(x) Cox v. Allingham, Jac. 337 ; Hood v. Pimm, 4 Sim. 101 ; Stanney

---

[1] See on this point, Gass v. Stinson, 2 Sumner 605 ; Troup v. Sherwood, 3 Johns. Ch. 558 ; Evans v. Bolling, 5 Ala. 550.

[2] See 3 Greenl. Ev., s. 340, et seq. ; Ridgeway v. Toram, 2 Md. Ch. 303, as to where evidence will be allowed to be taken after publication.

mode of obtaining permission to examine witnesses after
publication is by a distinct motion before the hearing;
but if the necessity is not sooner discovered, the cause
may be directed at the hearing to stand over, with liberty
to exhibit interrogatories to supply the defect. Orders
have occasionally been made for a reference to the Master
where such course has not been resisted, but such a reference is in truth a substitution of the Master for the Court
to decide on the evidence in the cause, and the more regular course is by leave to exhibit interrogatories.(*y*)

The only exceptions to the system of taking evidence
on written interrogatories and before publication, are in
the case of documents in the custody of a public officer,
which are proved by the officer's testimony to that fact,
and of *documents, the authenticity of which is [*373]
not impeached, and which only require the proof
of handwriting, or the evidence of an attesting witness.
In these cases interrogatories may be dispensed with, and
the evidence given by affidavit at the hearing, a method
recently substituted for the former one, of a *vivâ voce* examination of the witness. This exception does not apply
where the authenticity of the document is impeached, or
where more than the mere handwriting or execution must
be proved, *e. g.*, in proving a will of real estate, where not
only the execution but the sanity of the testator must
necessarily be shown, or in proving the execution of a
deed where a particular form of execution is requisite
In such cases proof by affidavit is not available, but the

v. Walmsley, 1 M. & C. 361 ; Hughes *v.* Eades, 1 Hare 486 ; Woodgate *v.*
Field, 2 Id. 211 ; Attorney-General *v.* Severne, 1 Coll. 313 ; Cass *v.* Cass,
4 Hare 278.

(*y*) Hughes *v.* Eades, 1 Hare 486 ; Lechmere *v.* Brasier, 2 Jac. & W.
288.

evidence must be taken on interrogatories with the
lar opportunity to cross-examine.(z)[1]

After publication has passed, it is the plaintiff's
to set down the cause for hearing, and to serve a *sul*
to hear judgment.(a)   If he fails to do so in proper
the defendant may move to dismiss the bill for wa
prosecution, or he may set the cause down at his ow
quest, and serve a *subpœna* to hear judgment on the
tiff. Formerly the plaintiff might, at any time befoi
decree, dismiss the bill upon payment of costs, as a n
·of course, without prejudicing his right to file a ne
for the same matter.[2] But now, if after the cause
down, the bill is dismissed, either on the plaintiff'
application or by reason of his default when the cai
called on to be heard in Court, such dismissal is equiv
to a dismissal on the merits, and may be pleaded in
another suit for the same matter.(b)

(z) 43d Order of August, 1841 ; Maber *v.* Hobbs, 1 Y. & C. 585 ·
ney-General *v.* Pearson, 7 Sim. 309 ; Brace *v.* Blick, Id. 619 ; Lake
ner, 1 Jac. & W. 9.

(a) 2 Dan. Ch. P. 955, 960.   (b) Ord. May, 1845,

---

[1] See, on this subject, 3 Greenl. Ev., s. 340 ; Gafney *v.* Reeves,
71. In New York, if a document intended to be produced in a d
quiring proof by a witness, or a certified copy of a record which i
the examination of a witness to prove it genuine, the party must
in the usual way before the examiner, or must obtain an order fo
to prove it at the hearing, although it is set out or referred to in th
ings : Pardee *v.* De Cala, 7 Paige 135.

Where an exhibit in a bill was alleged to be well known to the
ant, and to be genuine, and this allegation was not denied, the exh·
taken at the hearing to be genuine : Armitage *v.* Wickliffe, 12 B.
488.

[2] The propriety of permitting a complainant to dismiss his bill
prejudice, rests in the sound discretion of the court ; and is to be e
with reference to the rights of both parties : Conner *v.* Drake, 1
N. S. 166. See also, ante, 347, and notes.

*CHAPTER VII. [*374]

OF THE HEARING AND DECREE.

AT the hearing of the cause the pleadings and evidence are stated, and the Court makes its decree. If the defendant appears, it is an ordinary decree; if he does not appear at the hearing, it is a decree by default; (a) and if he has never appeared in the suit, or if after appearance, he has neglected to answer, it is a decree *pro confesso*. (b) The minutes of the decree are then prepared by the registrar, and delivered by him to the parties. If it be doubted whether they correctly express the judgment of the Court, they may be discussed either on a motion to vary them, or by obtaining leave to have the cause spoken to on minutes. After the minutes have been finally settled the decree is drawn up, passed, and entered. The only remaining step is the enrolment of the decree, which renders it conclusive in the Court of Chancery, and precludes any subsequent variation in its terms except by an appeal to the House of Lords. (c)

The practical details of procedure in preparing a decree are not the subjects of our present consideration, which will be devoted rather to the nature of decrees themselves.

(a) With respect to decrees by default, see 44th Order of August, 1841, and 1 Smith Ch. P. 254; 2 Dan. Ch. P. 990.

(b) With respect to decrees *pro confesso*, see 11 Geo. 4 & 1 Wm. 4, c. 36; 3 & 4 Vict. c. 94; 4 & 5 Vict. c. 52; 9th, Order of August, 1841; Orders of May, 1845, lxxvi.–xcii.; 1 Smith Ch. P. 231; 1 Dan. Ch. P. 479.

(c) 2 Dan. Ch. P. c. xxiv.

[*375]   *Decrees, considered in this light, will be
vided into Preliminary and Final. The preli
nary decree provides for the investigation of questi
which are material either in determining on subsequ
steps, or in deciding the issue between the parties.[1]
final decree, called the Decree on Further Directions
on the equity reserved,(d) disposes ultimately of the s
The causes which create a necessity for a prelimin
decree are four in number; viz., 1. That in the cours
the suit a dispute has arisen on a matter of law, wh
the Court is unwilling to decide ; 2. That a similar disp
has arisen on a matter of fact ; 3. That the equity clain
is founded on an alleged legal right, the decision of wh
the Court of Chancery declines to assume ; and 4. T
there are matters to be investigated, which although wi
in the province of the Court, are such as the presid
judge cannot at the hearing effectually deal with.
obviate these impediments the preliminary decree direc
1. A case for a Court of law ; 2. An issue for a jury ;
An action at law, to be determined in the ordinary cour:
or 4. A reference to one of the Masters of the Court,
acquire and impart to it the necessary information.   E&
of these methods of inquiry may be also adopted on
terlocutory applications by motion or petition,(e) but, a

(d) Bruin v. Knott, 12 Sim. 453.

(e) Ansdell v. Ansdell, 4 M. & C. 449 ; Lancashire v. Lancashire
Beav. 259.

---

[1] A decree in Chancery which leaves the equity of the case, or some :
terial question connected with the merits, for future determination, is
interlocutory, and not a final decree: Teaff v. Hewitt, 1 Ohio St. N. S. &
See also, Dabbs v. Dabbs, 27 Ala. 646 ; Humphrey v. Foster, 13 Gr
653 ; Re Colom, 3 Md. Ch. 278 ; Hudson v. Kline, 9 Gratt. 379 ; Harri
v. Rush, 15 Mo. 175 ; Verden v. Coleman, 18 How. U. S. 86 ; Ayres
Carver, 17 Id. 391 ; Craighead v. Wilson, 18 Id. 199 ; Wilhelm v. Cay
32 Md. 151.

part of the regular proceedings of the Court, they properly occur under the preliminary decree, and will be now most fitly considered.

1. A case for the opinion of a Court of law is directed, where a question of law arises incidentally in a suit. The direction is not made necessary by any want of jurisdiction; for, subject to any restraint which its own discretion may impose, the Court has jurisdiction to decide every question, whether of law or fact, incidentally brought before it. If, however, a doubtful question of law arises, which can be *effectually separated [*376] from the equitable matter, its ordinary practice is to direct, on the application of either party,(f) that a case may be made for the opinion of the common law Court, reserving its decision on the consequent equities until after the judges shall have given their certificate.

The certificate of the judges is usually adopted by the Court, and a decree made in conformity with it. But it is not absolutely binding; and if the judge in equity be still in doubt, he may return the matter for reconsideration to the same, or to another Court of law; or may, if he think fit, decide in opposition to the certificate.(g)[1]

2. An issue is directed where an incidental question of facts is so involved in doubt by conflicting or insufficient evidence that the Court, considering the inefficacy of written testimony, is desirous of referring it to the verdict

(f) Morrice v. Langham, 11 Sim. 280.

(g) Lansdowne v. Lansdowne, 2 Bligh. O. S. 86 ; Spry v. Bromfield, 12 Sim. 75 ; Muddle v. Fry, Mad. & G. 270 ; Northam Bridge Company v. Southampton Railway Company, 11 Sim. 42.

---

[1] The practice of stating cases for the opinion of a court of law is now abolished: Stat. 15 & 16 Vict. c. 86, s. 61 ; 25 & 26 Vict. c. 42, s. 1 ; Daniell's Chan. Prac. 1121.

of a jury.(*h*) It can, however, only be adopted ℩
the evidence creates a doubt, and not as a substitut
omitted evidence; and, therefore, the party claiminℊ
issue must first prove his case by regular depositiøn

(*h*) Moons *v.* De Bernales, 1 Russ. 301 ; Lloyd *v.* Wait, 1 Ph. 61.
(*i*) Clayton *v.* Meadows, 2 H. 29 ; Whitaker *v.* Newman, 2 Id. 30'

---

[1] See, on this subject, Daniell's Chan. Prac., ch. xxvi., s. 1. Whe
suit in equity there is no conflict of testimony, but a simple faili
prove material facts, it is improper to direct an issue: Kearney t
rell, 5 Jones Eq. 199 ; and if in such case there is a verdict on the is
favor of the complainant, the decree should nevertheless be for th
missal of the bill : Reed *v.* Cline, 9 Gratt. 136 ; Wise *v.* Lamb, Ic
An issue should not, moreover, be directed where the truth of the
can be sufficiently and satisfactorily ascertained by the court itself:
v. Williamson, 2 Penn. St. 116 ; Johns *v.* Erb, 5 Id. 237. A chan
may decide every question of fact himself ; but any question he con
very doubtful, he may and should refer to a jury. But the verdic
satisfy the conscience of the chancellor, and if he is not satisfied w
he should disregard it ; on the other hand, if he concurs with the ju
if his mind still oscillates, he should allow the verdict to be decisive
v. Beatty, 8 Dana 207. The practice of referring doubtful question
jury is not confined to those cases where witnesses are to be introd
but when the chancellor is perplexed with doubtful questions of fa
may have the aid of a jury, as well where the decision must be upo
written evidence in the record, as where oral testimony is to be
duced : Id. 212. The submission of the entire case to a jury is con
to practice : Milk *v.* Moore, 39 Ill. 584.

In many of the United States, and in the Federal judicature, how
the trial by jury is secured to suitors, by constitutional or statutorʝ
visions, in such a manner that even where it is not an express righ
discretion of a Court of equity in granting an issue in a case prope
a jury, has become merely nominal. And in nearly all the states, il
least very doubtful whether a verdict on an issue is not equally bi₁
with that in a suit at law, and subject only to the same revisory ₁
which is exercised in granting new trials in other cases. See, on thi;
ject, 3 Greenl. Ev., part vi., ch. 1, § 261, *et seq* , § 339 ; Hoffman *v.* S
1 Md. 475 ; Thomason *v.* Kennedy, 3 Rich. Eq. 440 ; Harrison *v.* Rく
4 Wash. C. C. 32 ; Pleasants *v.* Ross, 1 Wash. (Va.) 156 ; Marsく
Brackett, 9 N. H. 336 ; Charles R. Bridge *v.* Warren Bridge, 7 Pick.
Parsons *v.* Bedford, 3 Peters 433 ; Ward *v.* Hill, 4 Gray 593 ; Dro
Miller, 1 Hempst. 49 ; Lapreese *v.* Fall, 7 Ind. 692 ; see, however, 1

The form of an issue was formerly that of an action on a wager, assumed to have been made respecting the fact in dispute; but this fiction is now dispensed with, and the question may be referred to the jury in a direct form.(*k*)

The result of an issue is not necessarily a mere general verdict, but liberty may be given to take a special verdict, or a special case.(*l*) And a direction is frequently given, that if the substance of the issue is found, but with special circumstances, which may be material in measuring the relief, the special matter shall be endorsed on the *postea*.(*m*)

*The Court will also provide that the issue shall effectually raise the real question, cleared [*377] of all extrinsic matter, by directing all requisite admissions to be made; and will secure its satisfactory investigation, by compelling the parties to produce at the trial all material documents in their possession or power.[1]

The privileges of an heir-at-law and of a rector or vicar, in suits for establishing a will or modus, to demand an issue as a matter of right, have already been considered in treating of the jurisdiction for such establishment.(*n*) With these exceptions, the granting of an issue is discretionary with the Court, and the attendant expense and delay will only be incurred when, in the exercise of a sound discretion, it is deemed necessary.(*o*)[2]

(*k*) 8 & 9 Vict. c. 109, 19. (*l*) Clayton *v*. Nugent, 1 Coll. 362.
(*m*) White *v*. Lisle, 3 Sw. 345.
(*n*) Supra, Tithes; Testamentary Assets.
(*o*) Short *v*. Lee, 2 J. & W. 495; Hampson *v*. Hampson, 3 Ves. & B. 43.

v. Williamson, 2 Penn. St. 116; Johns *v*. Erb, 5 Id. 237; and in New York, before the Rev. Code, Patterson *v*. Ackerson, 1 Edw. Ch. 96.

[1] See, on this subject, 3 Greenl. Ev., ₹ 377, &c.; Apthorp *v*. Comstock, 2 Paige 482; Baker *v*. Williamson, 2 Penn. St. 116; Johns *v*. Erb, 5 Id. 237.

[2] Scheetz's Appeal, 35 Penn. St. 94; Blake *v*. Shreve, 2 Beas. 456; Black *v*. Lamb, 1 Id. 108; Kirkpatrick *v*. Atkinson, 11 Rich. Eq. 27.

The same discretion is exercised after a verdict has been returned. The object of an issue, like that of a case, is not to bind the Court, but to satisfy its conscience. If, therefore, the verdict, coupled with the information of the judge's notes, does not afford satisfaction, a new trial will be directed, although there be no surprise or fraud, nor manifest miscarriage, and the verdict be one which at common law would be undisturbed.(p) And even though no new trial is sought, yet when the cause is brought on for further directions, the Court, if it thinks that the issue as tried does not answer the purpose intended, may direct a new one to be framed; or may, on reconsideration of the evidence, decide at once against the verdict.(q)[1] In suits relating to land, and seeking to bind the inheritance, a direction for a new trial is not unfrequent, though the original verdict may be free from objection, but it is not a matter of right.(r)

[*378] *3. An action at law is directed where the equity is based on a disputed legal right, but the trial of such right at law is prevented either by equitable impediments, which the Court is asked to remove, or by the mere pendency of the suit itself; e. g., where an heir-at-law is unable to bring an ejectment, by reason of an outstanding mortgage or term, or where the bill seeks an injunction against the infringement of a disputed patent.[2]

(p) Bootle v. Blundell, 19 Ves. 500; Northam Bridge Company v. Southampton Railway Company, 11 Sim. 42; East India Company v. Bazett, Jac. 81.

(q) Armstrong v. Armstrong, 3 M. & K. 45.

(r) Locke v. Colman, 2 M. & C. 42; White v. Wilson, 13 Ves. 88; Baker v. Hart, 3 Atk. 542; Wilson v. Beddard, 12 Sim. 28.

---

[1] But see ante, note to p. 376. See also Austin v. Baintor, 50 Ill. 308; Lowe v. Traynor, 6 Cold. (Tenn.) 633.

[2] See Daniell's Chan. Prac., ch. xxvi., section 2.

In this class of cases there is not a mere point of law or fact incidentally in dispute, as to which the Court, for its own satisfaction, seeks the aid of another tribunal; but there is a general question of right, determinable as such by the ordinary Courts, and requiring a decision, according to the course of those Courts, both of disputed facts and of the law as applicable thereto. The general rule, therefore, is that where the foundation of a suit is a legal demand, on which the judgment of a Court of law, whether obtained on a verdict or in any other shape, ought to be conclusive, the Court of Chancery will not direct a case or issue, but will either order an action to be brought, providing that the term or other like impediment shall not be set up as a defence at law, or will retain the bill for a limited period, with liberty for the plaintiff to proceed at law.(s) The Court will not in general retain the bill unless it thinks that, if the action succeeds, a valid equity will exist; but the retainer is not conclusive on the point, and the decree, on further directions, may be against the plaintiff.(t)[1] If there are any persons equitably interested, and who cannot therefore be parties at law, they will have liberty given them to attend the trial, and to make such defence as they may be advised. Provision will also be made for a satisfactory trial, by directing admissions by the parties, and produc-

(s) Pemberton v. Pemberton, 13 Ves. 298; Bootle v. Blundell, 19 Id. 500; Waterford v. Knight, 11 Clarke & F. 662; Butlin v. Masters, 2 Ph. 290.   (t) Harmood v. Oglander, 6 Ves. 225.

[1] See, on this point, Ches. & Ohio Canal v. Young, 3 Md. 480.

Where a bill has been ordered to be retained for a twelvemonth, with liberty for the plaintiff to bring an action, the Court will extend the time, if satisfied that there is a bonâ fide intention to proceed with the action, and there has been promptness in bringing the matter to an adjudication: Farina v. Silverlock, 26 L. J. Ch. 790.

tion of documents, as in the case of issues. Bι
Court of Chancery assumes no jurisdiction over the ‹
[*379] and if *either party be dissatisfied with 1
sult, a new trial must be moved for in the
of law.

4. A reference to the Master is generally made
of the three following purposes, viz., the protecl
absent parties against the possible neglect or malfe
of the litigants; the more effectual working out
tails, which the judge sitting in Court is unable to
tigate ; and the supplying defects or failures in eviι
And it differs materially from a case, an issue,
action, because these steps, when directed, are
transfers to another tribunal than steps of proced
the Court itself. But a reference to a Master
ordinary step in the cause, and comparatively few
of importance are decided without one or mor
references.

1. The reference for the protection of absent paι

---

¹ The Master's office is a branch of the Court: Stewart v. T
Edw. Ch. 458. The master, in his ministerial character, is bound
to follow the instructions of the Court: Fenwicke v. Gibbes, 2
629. A reference will not be ordered to inquire relative to a fac
tuting the gist of the controversy, and put in issue by the pl
Lunsford v. Bostion, 1 Dev. Eq. 483; see Gilmore v. Gilmore, 40 M
Where the evidence in a case is all written, and a decree thereon
rendered without difficulty, a reference to a master is unnecessary
v. Redwood, 9 Porter 79. As to the practice in taking testimon
order of reference to a master, see Remsen v. Remsen, 2 Johns.
Gass v. Stinson, 2 Sumn. 605; Jenkins v. Eldredge, 3 Story 299;]
v. Barkley, 11 N. H. 501; Benson v. Le Roy, 1 Paige 122; McDo
Dougherty, 11 Ga. 570; Dougherty v. Jones, Id. 432; Gilmore v.
40 Maine 50.

See, on the subject of references to and proceedings before maste
U. S. Courts in equity, No. lxxiii. et seq.; Penna. No. lxii. et
Greenl. Evid., ₹ 332, et seq.

made where a claim, or the possibility of a claim, to the property in suit belongs to creditors or next of kin, or other persons entitled as a class, so that it is uncertain at the hearing whether they are all before the Court. In order to remove this uncertainty, a reference is made to the Master to ascertain the fact before any step is taken for ascertaining or distributing the fund.(*u*) And, on the same principle, if a proposal of compromise or of arrangement by consent is made where any of the parties are infants or *femes covert*, and therefore unable to exercise a discretion, the Court, before sanctioning the proposal, will ascertain by a reference, whether it is for their benefit.[1]

2. A reference for the working out of details is prinpally made in matters of account, when the Court declares that the account must be taken, and refers it to the Master to investigate the items.[2] The same principle applies to the investigation of a vendor's title; for the Court cannot undertake to peruse the abstract, and that duly devolves on the Master.[3] In like manner it will be referred to the Master to settle conveyances or other

(*u*) Dan. Ch. P. 683 ; Fisk *v.* Norton, 2 Hare 381.

---

[1] Where a suit is instituted on behalf of an infant by a *prochein ami*, the Court, on a suggestion of its being improperly instituted, will refer it to a master, to inquire into the circumstances, and to report whether the suit is for the benefit of the infant: Garr *v.* Drake, 2 Johns. Ch. 542.

[2] See Hart *v.* Ten Eyck, 2 Johns. Ch. 513; Consequa *v.* Fanning, 3 Id. 591 ; Barrow *v.* Rhinelander, Id. 614; Maury *v.* Lewis, 10 Yerg. 115.

[3] And where the plaintiff, in a bill for specific performance, shows his right to a conveyance, but the defendant has, by sale or otherwise, put it out of his power to convey, it may be referred to a Master to ascertain the damages: Woodcock *v.* Bennet, 1 Cowen 711. Upon a bill for specific performance, the title will not be referred, where the nature of it is distinctly seen: Wilbanks *v.* Duncan, 4 Dessaus. 536; Dominick *v.* Michael, 4 Sandf. S. C. 394 ; see ante 84, notes.

[*380] deeds, to superintend *sales, to appoint trus
receivers, and guardians, and so forth.

For the same reason, the Masters are deputed to j
of impertinence or insufficiency in pleadings, the dec
of which must depend on a minute examination of
details. And it is now ordered by statute that they ,
determine all applications for time to plead, answe
demur, for leave to amend bills, for enlarging publica
and all such other matters relating to the conduct of s
as the Lord Chancellor, with the advice and assistanc
the Master of the Rolls and Vice-Chancellor, or o
them, shall by any general order or orders direct, sul
to an appeal, by motion to the Lord Chancellor, Ma
of the Rolls, or Vice-Chancellor, but without any fur
appeal.(v)

On bills for a partition, for settling boundaries, an
assignment of dower, the appointment is not made
reference to a Master, but, in analogy to the proces
law, to commissioners specially appointed, reserving
further directions until after their return.

Formerly the mode of directing these accounts anc
quiries was by a preliminary decree at the hearing of
cause, reserving the ultimate decision until after a rej
In the case of a bill for specific performance, when
title only is in dispute, it has long been the practic
refer it on motion, either before or after answer.(w)
in the generality of cases the direction was delayed
the hearing, and the consequent necessity of two suc
sive decrees was frequently productive of needless d
and expense.

(v) 3 & 4 Wm. 4, c. 94, s. 13.
(w) Balmanno v. Lumley, 1 Ves. & B. 224 ; Matthews v. Dana, 3
470.

In order to remedy this evil, it has been ordered that "in all cases in which it shall appear that certain preliminary accounts and inquiries must be taken and made, before the rights and interest of the parties to the cause can be ascertained, or the questions therein arising can be determined, the plaintiff shall be at liberty, at any time. *after the defendants shall have appeared to the [*381] bill, to move the Court, on notice, that such inquiries and accounts shall be made and taken, and that an order referring it to the Master to make such inquiries, and take such accounts, shall thereupon be made, without prejudice to any question in the cause, if it shall appear to the Court that the same will be beneficial to such (if any) of the parties to the cause as may not be competent to consent thereto, and that the same is consented to by such (if any) of the defendants, as, being competent to consent, have not put in their answers, and that the same is consented to by, or is proper to be made upon, the statements, contained in the answers of such (if any) of the defendants as have answered the bill."(x)

The order, however, only applies where it is obvious that the accounts and inquiries must be directed at the hearing, as incidental to the admitted allegations, of the bill. If, in order to warrant them, it is necessary that parts of the bill should be established by evidence, the order does not apply, e. g., where a person alleging himself to be next of kin, files his bill against the administrator, who does not admit that he sustains the character. In this case an inquiry as to the other next of kin, and an account of the estate, cannot be directed on motion. The same principle was followed in a suit for specific

(x) 5th Order of May, 1839.

47

performance, where the purchaser alleged that the contract had been rescinded through the vendor's failure in
showing title by a specified day. The vendor moved for
the ordinary inquiry, whether he could make a good title,
and when first such title was made, without prejudice to
any question in the cause. But it was refused, because
such an inquiry assumed that a title shown after the specified time would be available, and therefore if the purchaser's objection succeeded at the hearing, the inquiry
might be useless. The plaintiff then offered to take an
[*382] inquiry whether, on the day of the alleged *rescission, or on an earlier day, a good title had been
shown. But that inquiry was also refused, because, although in any view of the case an affirmative answer
would decide the case, yet, if the purchaser's objection
were overruled, a negative one would lead to no result.(*y*)

In cases not falling within the scope of that order the
former practice still continues.

3. The third class of cases in which a reference to the
Master is made, is where it becomes necessary to supply
defects or failures in evidence. It has been already mentioned that such a reference is occasionally made for ascertaining the truth of an allegation, with respect to which
there has been an accidental omission of evidence, but
that such course is not strictly regular. The circumstances under which the reference would, in regular
course, be made, are where the evidence already given
has induced a belief in the Court that new matter might
be elicited by inquiry, or where allegations have been

(*y*) Topham *v.* Lightbody, 1 Hare 289; Curd *v.* Curd, 2 Id. 116; Breeze
v. English, Id. 118; Clifford *v.* Turrell, 1 N. C. C. 138.

made in the answer, though not established by proof, which, if true, would be material to the cause.(z)

Iu directing a reference to the Master, the Court provides for a full investigation of the matter referred, by a direction that the parties shall produce, on oath, all documents in their power, and shall be examined on interrogatories as the Master shall direct.(a)[1] And he has a similar power of examining, either on interrogatories or *vivâ voce,* any creditors or other persons who, by coming in to claim before him, may render themselves *quasi* parties to the suit.(b)

The method in which the Master proceeds is by issuing warrants from time to time, directing all parties concerned to attend before him at the time and for the purposes *therein mentioned.   The proceedings [*383] under a warrant may be attended by all persons beneficially interested, whether actual parties to the suit, or such as have become *quasi* parties by having come in and established a claim, whenever the object is such as may affect their interests, or increase or diminish their proportion in the fund.   And, on the same principle, all such persons are entitled to take copies of any written proceeding brought into the office, or of any part thereof which affects their interest.

On the proceedings being thus commenced, all the parties who take an active part in the inquiry lay before the Master written narratives, called States of Facts, of the circumstances on which they respectively rely ; and

(z) Broadhurst v. Balguy, 1 N. C. C. 16 ; Connop v. Hayward, Id. 33 ; Miller v. Gow, Id. 56 ; McMahon v. Burchell, 2 Phill. 127.

(a) 9th Order of 1828.   (b) 72d Order of 1828.

---

[1] As to the Master's power of examining a complainant, see McCrackan v. Valentine, 5 Selden (N. Y.) 42.

as the report is ultimately formed on the basis of these states of facts, it is material they should be carefully drawn. The parties then proceed to support them by proof, consisting, first, of the depositions, affidavits, and other evidence already used in the cause; (c) and, secondly, of any additional evidence which may be produced in the office, subject, however, to the restriction that a witness who has been already examined in the cause cannot be re-examined before the Master by the same party without leave of the Court. (d)[1] The additional evidence thus brought forward ought in strictness to be given on inter-rogatories or *vivâ voce*, (e) but it is usual to substitute affidavits by express or tacit consent.[2] During the pro-gress of the inquiry, the several states of facts may, from time to time, be amended, or new ones brought in and supported by further evidence, until either publication has passed, where the evidence has been taken on inter-rogatories, or the warrant has been issued for preparing the report. (f)

[*384]   *After the warrant for preparing the report no further evidence can be received, but the Master

― (c) 65th Order of 1828.

(d) Willan v. Willan, 19 Ves. 590; Rowley v. Adams, 1 M. & K. 545; Whitaker v. Wright, 3 Hare 412; England v. Downs, 6 Beav. 281.

(e) 69th Order of 1828; [Dougherty v. Jones, 11 Ga. 432.]

(f) Trotter v. Trotter, 5 Sim. 483; Nelson v. Bridport, 6 Beav. 295; 67th Order of 1828.

---

[1] See Remsen v. Remsen, 2 Johns. Ch. 501. If the defendant wishes to controvert any allegations in the bill he should put them in issue by plea or answer; and neglecting this he is precluded from introducing evidence for that purpose before the Master on reference: Ward v. Jewett, Walk. Ch. 45.

[2] See Story v. Livingston, 13 Peters 359. A party examined before a Master has a right to demand the questions in writing; but not so a witness: McDougald v. Dougherty, 11 Ga. 570.

will proceed to settle and sign his report on the evidence as it then stands. At this stage of the proceedings, and whilst the report is still in draft, it is the duty of any dissatisfied party to lay before him written objections, specifying the point in which he considers it erroneous. If that be not done, exceptions, which, as we shall presently see, are the mode of contesting it before the Court, will not be entertained. The exceptions, when taken, though not necessarily identical in words, must in substance agree with the objections, and the practice generally is to prepare the objections in the form of the intended exceptions, and, on their disallowance, to convert them into exceptions. If the objections are allowed by the Master, he will alter his draft accordingly; and it will then be the business of the other side to object, as they may be advised.

When the Master has disposed of all objections, and come to a conclusion on the matters referred, he settles and signs his report, and such report is then filed. The ordinary mode of framing a report is to refer separately to each of the directions in the decree, and then, with respect to each direction, first to mention on what evidence the Master has proceeded, (g) and then to state the conclusion at which he has arrived. In stating his conclusion, he should so far detail the facts which warrant it as may enable the Court to judge of its correctness; and it is frequently advantageous, though not necessary, that he should also state the reasons which have induced his decision. But he must not omit the conclusion itself, or state evidence, or circumstances which are presumptive evidence, without finding whether they amount to a sat-

(g) 48th Order of August, 1841; In re Grant, 10 Sim. 573; Meux v. Bell, 1 Hare 93.

isfactory proof.(*h*)   And if liberty be given, as it fre-
[*385] quently is, *to state special circumstances, he
should state, not the evidence, but the facts
proved, as on a special verdict at law.(*i*)[1]

If any of the inquiries directed by the decree are such
as cannot conveniently be delayed until the general report, the Master may make a separate report,(*k*) which
is prepared, disputed, and confirmed in the same manner
as a general one; the only difference being that when it
is intended to act on such a report, the cause is not set
down for further directions, but a petition is presented
praying such directions as are consequent on the separate
report.

Subject to this right of making separate reports, the
rule is, that a Master's report must dispose of all matters
referred, either by actual findings on each section of the
decree, or by pointing out what matters of reference have
been waived, and what have been disposed of by separate
reports; and the omission of any such matters, or the introduction of any matter not referred to him, will render
his report erroneous.(*l*)

As soon as the Master's report has been filed, the next
step is its confirmation by the Court.

(*h*) Lee *v.* Willock, 6 Ves. 605 ; Meux *v.* Bell, 1 Hare 91 ; Champernowne *v.* Scott, 4 Mad. 209.

(*i*) Marlborough *v.* Wheat, 1 Atk. 454.

(*k*) 70th Order of 1831.

(*l*) Winter *v.* Innes, 4 M. & C. 101 ; Jenkins *v.* Briant, 6 Sim. 605 ; Gaylor
v. Fitzjohn, 1 Keen 469.

---

[1] Where certain facts are referred to the decision of a Master, it is his
duty to report his conclusions; and it is irregular and improper for him to
report the evidence, without the special direction of the Court: Matter of
Hemiup, 3 Paige 305; Bailey *v.* Myreck, 52 Maine 132.   See, in Indiana,
McKinney *v.* Pierce, 5 Ind. 422.

In the case of reports under orders made on petition, a petition is the usual mode of objection and confirmation. (*m*) But with respect to reports under a decree or decretal order, the regular mode of confirmation is by an order nisi, made on a motion, of course, or petition at the Rolls, and directing that the report shall stand confirmed, "unless the defendant shall, within eight days after notice, show good cause to the contrary." If no cause is shown within the eight days, a further order is made on motion, confirming the report absolutely. (*n*)[1]

If any of the persons interested, whether actual or quasi *parties, are dissatisfied with the report, [*386] they may file exceptions after service of the order nisi, and show them as cause against its being made absolute.

The exceptions, which, like the pleadings and interrogatories, require the signature of counsel, are a written enumeration of the alleged errors, and of the corrections proposed; and they should be so framed as not merely to allege error in general terms, but to enable the Court to decide distinctly on each point in dispute. (*o*)[2] If, how-

(*m*) Empringham *v.* Short, 11 Sim. 78; Ottey *v.* Pensam, 1 Hare 322; Beavan *v.* Gibert, 8 Beav. 308.

(*n*) 2 Dan. Ch. P. 1227.

(*o*) Purcell *v.* McNamara, 12 Ves. 166; Ballard *v.* White, 2 Hare 158; Flower *v.* Hartopp, 6 Beav. 485; Stocken *v.* Dawson, 2 Phill. 141.

---

[1] See Hulbert *v.* McKay, 8 Paige 652.

[2] Story *v.* Livingston, 13 Peters 359; Dexter *v.* Arnold, 2 Sumn. 108. The proceedings before a master are in the nature of an informal bill in equity, and the supervisory Court will not interfere to correct any but substantial defects: McDougald *v.* Dougherty, 11 Ga. 570. An error mus be clearly made to appear, in the report, before the Court will interfere, where a question of fact was submitted to the master, which depended upon the credibility of witnesses: Sinnickson *v.* Bruere, 1 Stockt. (N. J.) 659; Izard *v.* Bodine, Id. 309; Howe *v.* Russell, 36 Maine 115; Miller *v.*

ever, there be error apparent on the report, as, for exa
ple, if the facts stated contradict the conclusion, it
unnecessary to except.[1]   And even if the facts stat
though not contradicting the conclusion, are insufficient
support it, the Court may, of its own motion, decline
act, leaving the parties to get rid of the finding in si
way as they may be advised.(p)   On the same princip
the introduction of matter merely irrelevant, is no
ground of exception, for its irrelevancy must be appar
from the report itself.

The next step after filing exceptions, is that they shou
be heard and determined by the Court, and in doing t
there are three courses open for adoption.

1. They may be disallowed, or allowed absolutel
which has the effect of at once confirming the rep
either as it stands, or with such changes as the allowa
of the exceptions may make.

2. If the facts are imperfectly stated in the report,
that no judgment can be formed as to the proper conc
sion; or if the existing evidence is unsatisfactory, bu
is possible that other evidence exists, which in con
quence of a favorable finding has not been adduced;
if the nature of the matter contested, or the frame
the exceptions, is such, that their allowance shows a

(p) Adams v. Claxton, 6 Ves. 226; Ottey v. Pensam, 1 Hare 3
Gregory v. West, 2 Beav. 541.

Whittier, Id. 577; McKinney v. Pierce, 5 Indiana 422; Foster v. Godd
1 Black S. C. 509.

See, as to practice on exceptions to Masters' reports, in the United Sta
Courts, Rule in Eq. No. lxxxiii. et seq.; Penna. No. lxix., &c.

[1] Where the Master disregards the instructions and directions of
Court, or where he does not furnish the facts necessary to enable
Court to make a decree, the report will be set aside, though no excepti
have been filed: Lang v. Brown, 21 Ala. 179.

cessity for *further investigation : it may be re- [*387]
ferred back to the Master to review his report,
continuing in the meantime the reservation of further
directions, and either allowing the exceptions, or making
no order thereon. On a reference back to review, the
Master may receive additional evidence; but if it be accompanied by an allowance of the exception, he can come
to no conclusion inconsistent with the terms of the exception. If no order is made on the exception, his finding
on reviewal is unfettered.(q)

3. If the suit has taken such a course, that at the time
of hearing the exceptions, it is apparent, that whatever
order be made, the same decree will follow, the Court may
decline to adjudicate on them, and may proceed to decree on further directions, as if no exceptions had been
filed.(r)[1]

The plaintiff may, at his discretion, set down exceptions for hearing at the same time that he sets down the
cause on further directions. But the propriety of so
doing will depend on the probability of the exceptions

(q) Egerton v. Jones, 1 Russ. & M. 694; Twyford v. Trail, 3 M. & C.
645; Livesey v. Livesey, 10 Sim. 331; Ex parte Grant, Id. 573; Ballard v.
White, 2 Hare 158; Stocken v. Dawson, 3 Phil. 141.

(r) Hall v. Laver, 1 Hare 571; Robinson v. Milner, Id. 578; Courtenay
v. Williams, 3 Id. 554, 639.

---

[1] The bill may be dismissed on the hearing of exceptions to the Master's
report, where the court changes its opinion as to the title of the complainant to recover. The previous interlocutory orders are then open to revision: Fourniquet v. Perkins, 16 How. U. S. 82. In Lang v. Brown, 21
Ala. 179, however, it was held that where, from the improper frame of the
decree of reference, the justice of the case cannot be got at without an alteration of the decree, the report of the Master must be directed to stand
over, and that portion of the decree containing the erroneous direction be
reheard; but that the court cannot on exceptions make an order inconsistent with the decree. The decree of reference may also be reheard on
appeal, though no exceptions have been taken : Id.

requiring or not requiring a reviewal of the report. For if there be a reference back to review, the cause cannot be heard on further directions, and the expense of setting it down will have been uselessly incurred.

When the exceptions have been disposed of and the report confirmed, the cause is heard on further directions and this is repeated from time to time, as often as any further directions are reserved.(s)

The decree on further directions is confined to carrying out the equities appearing on the report, consistently with the original decree. If circumstances have occurred since the original decree which vary the form of relief required, but leave the substantial equity the same, they [*388] may be *stated in a petition to be heard with the cause.(ss) But no order can be made on further directions which will vary or impugn the original decree, whether on a point which it had expressly decided, or one which, being raised by the pleadings, and not depending on the questions referred, has been left unnoticed, and thus by implication disallowed.(t) If the original decree is erroneous, the proper mode of correction is by a re-hearing or appeal.

A decree thus made, without any reservation of further directions, constitutes a final decree; and after it has been pronounced, the cause is at an end, and no further hearing can be had. It often happens, however, that although the decree requires no reservation of further directions, yet there is a possibility of future interests arising, which having a potential existence only, cannot be then the subject of judicial decision, and which, there-

(s) 2 Dau. Ch. P. c. 26.
(ss) Pinkus v. Peters, 5 Beav. 253 ; Tanner v. Dancey, 9 Id. 339.
(t) Le Grand v. Whitehead, 1 Russ. 309 ; East India Company v. Keighley, 4 Madd. 38; Camp v. Moody, 2 Ves. 470; Creuze v. Hunter, 2 Ves. Jun. 164.

fore prevent the cause from being altogether disposed of; *e. g.*, where a fund is given to a tenant for life, living at the time of the decree, with remainder to a class of individuals who cannot be ascertained till his death. In this case the Court will not declare the future interests, because it cannot know what alterations may be produced by time; but it will order payment of the income to the tenant for life, or make such other decree as the immediate circumstances warrant, with liberty for all parties to apply, as their respective interests arise. The effect of this liberty is to enable them to apply summarily by petition or motion, without the necessity of again hearing the cause. If a similar difficulty exist with respect to part only of the property in litigation, and such property be in the hands of the Court, it will be met by carrying it over to a separate account, distinguished by an explanatory title. with a like liberty to apply. In this way the share of an infant, or of a married woman, will be carried over to a separate account, entitled in the *one case the infant's account, and in the other, the account of the husband and wife, with liberty [*389] for the infant to apply on attaining twenty-one, and for a husband and wife to apply generally, so that the consent of the wife to relinquish her equity for a settlement may be ascertained.(*u*)

On the same principle, if a sum of money appears at the hearing to belong *primâ facie* to one person, subject to claims by others which cannot then be discussed, it will be carried to the account of the *primâ facie* owner, with a direction that it shall not be paid to him without notice to the adverse claimants, and such claimants may then present a petition to have the fund out of Court,

(*u*) 2 Dan. 1251.

and may serve it on the party in whose n stands.(v)

The hearing of the cause on further directions i rally the occasion for deciding on the "costs of the The precise nature of the costs included under t pression, as distinguished from incidental costs, are disposed of as they arise, need not be here dis but it will be important to consider briefly th which determine by whom the "costs of the caus be borne.

In considering this subject it must be borne i that the jurisdiction in equity is not like that at c law, purely litigious, but in many instances pro and administrative; and it is obvious that under these heads the rule as to costs may properly b different.

In suits under the protective and administrative diction of the Court, the general principle is, tl party requiring aid shall be liable for the costs.[1]

(v) 2 Dan. Ch. P. 1342.

---

[1] The subject of costs is now very much governed by statute, a rules of Court, in the different states. Subject to such provi general principles stated in the text appear to govern.

Thus it is established that the costs of a bill of discovery are t by the complainant, unless the defendant, on application made b filed, has unreasonably refused to make disclosure: Burnett v. Sa Johns. Ch. 503; King v. Clarke, 3 Paige 76; Boughton v. Phili 334; Harris v. Williams, 10 Id. 108; Price v. Tyson, 3 Bls McElwee v. Sutton, 1 Hill Eq. 32; Dennis v. Riley, 1 Foster (N If, however, the bill also pray general or special relief, the costs other cases: McDougall v. Miln, 2 Paige 325; Ross v. Adams, 5 And the costs on successful exceptions to an answer, are of cou paid by the defendant: Price v. Tyson, 3 Bland 392.

So, a mortgagor is obliged to pay the costs, on bill to redeem, u mortgagee has set up an unconscientious defence, or has claimed perty as owner: Slee v. Manhattan Co., 1 Paige 48; Turner v.

for instance, are suits for discovery and for perpetuating
testimony, in which the costs are paid by the plaintiff;
suits for partition, in which, by analogy to a partition at
law, the costs of the commission and of making out the
title are paid in proportion to the respective interests,
and *no other costs either precedent or subse- [*390]
quent are allowed; and suits for assignment of
dower, in which by the same analogy, no costs are
given;(vv) suits for redemption, or in the nature of redemption, as for setting aside a purchase on repayment of
the money advanced, in which the party redeemed is, in
the absence of gross misconduct, entitled to his costs;(w)
suits against an heir to establish a will, or against a vicar
or rector to establish a modus, in which the heir, unless he

(vv) 2 Dan. 1103; Bamford v. Bamford, 5 Hare 203.
(w) 2 Dan. Ch. P. 1260–1267.

Munf. 66; Saunders v. Frost, 5 Pick. 259; May v. Eastin, 2 Porter 414;
Bridgen v. Carhartt, Hopkins 234; Phillips v. Hulzizer, 20 N. J. Eq. 308.
On the other hand, the complainant in an interpleader suit, where his bill
is necessarily and properly filed as against both defendants, is entitled to
his costs out of the fund: Richards v. Salter, 6 Johns. Ch. 445; Badeau v.
Rogers, 2 Paige 209; Atkinson v. Manks, 1 Cowen 691; Canfield v. Sterling, Hopkins 224; Spring v. So. Car. Ins. Co., 8 Wheat. 268; or from the
unsuccessful defendant: Beers v. Spooner, 9 Leigh 155. So a mere stakeholder who submits to the judgment of the Court, is entitled to his costs,
or at least is not subjected to them: Dowdall v. Lenox, 2 Edw. Ch. 267;
Stafford v. Mott, 3 Paige 100; Buck v. Swazey, 35 Maine 42. Though he
is not entitled to counsel fees: Ohio Life Ins. Co. v. Winn, 4 Md. Ch.
253.
In partition, the costs generally come out of the estate, or are divided
between all the parties: Coles v. Coles, 2 Beas. 365. But where the complainant causes additional litigation by setting up an unfounded claim, he
will be charged with the additional costs occasioned thereby: Crandall v.
Hoysradt, 1 Sandf. Ch. 40.
Where heirs are necessary parties, and make no resistance to the decree,
they will be entitled to their costs: Dyer v. Potter, 2 Johns. Ch. 152.
See, on the subject of costs, Daniell's Ch. Prac. ch. xxx.

vexatiously litigate the will, and the vicar or rector, unless
he dispute the *modus*, are entitled to costs;(*x*) suits for
the performance of trusts, in which the trustees are entitled to their reasonable costs out of the fund, except in so
far as their own misconduct has occasioned the suit;(*y*)
and suits for the administration of assets, in which the
costs are treated as expenses of administration, and are
payable, first, to the personal representative, and next, if
the bill be a creditor's bill, to the plaintiff, as the primary
charge on the personal estate.(*z*)[1]   The same principle is
applied where a legal mortgagee, instead of foreclosing,
resorts for his own benefit to a decree for sale; in which
case the costs of suit become costs of administering the
estate, and are discharged in the first instance.(*a*)   If the
costs have been incurred in administering several funds,
of which the ultimate destinations are different, an apportionment may be made.(*b*)   A claim has also been made
on behalf of the Attorney-General to have his costs from
the plaintiff in suits where a claim by the Crown is involved, on the ground that they are incurred in performance of a public duty; and a similar claim has been set
up on behalf of provisional assignees in suits for foreclosure of a bankrupt's or insolvent's estate.   *But
[*391] both these claims have been disallowed; for whatever be the hardship on the parties making them, it is
not to be remedied at the plaintiff's expense.(*c*)

(*x*) 2 Dan. Ch. P. 1257–1260.   (*y*) Id. 1286.

(*z*) Shuttlewerth *v.* Howarth, Cr. & P. 228; Larkins *v.* Paxton, 2 M. &
K. 320; Tipping *v.* Power, 1 Hare 409; Tanner *v.* Dancey, 9 Beav. 339.

(*a*) Tipping *v.* Power, 1 Hare 409; Hepworth *v.* Heslop, 3 Id. 485.

(*b*) Christian *v.* Foster, 2 Ph. 161.

(*c*) Perkins *v.* Bradley, 1 Hare 233; Appleby *v.* Duke, 1 Phill. 272.

[1] See, on this subject, Decker *v.* Miller, 2 Paige 149; Hunn *v.* Norton,
Hopkins 344.

The amount of costs payable in a suit, whether given out of a fund or payable by a party, is ascertained by taxation, which, if conducted by the strict rule of the Court, is termed a taxation as between "party and party." But there is in some cases a more liberal allowance called "costs as between solicitor and client." In suits of a litigious class, the taxation is always "as between party and party," but in those of a protective or administrative kind, its adoption though general is subject to exceptions. The suits in which an exception is made are those for performance of trusts and administration of assets, in which the trustee or personal representative has always his costs as between solicitor and client; and if payments have been made by him not coming strictly under the name of costs, he may obtain them also by a direction for "charges and expenses, not strictly costs in the cause."(d)[1] In suits to establish or administer a charity, if the fund be of adequate amount, and the parties have conducted themselves with propriety, the taxation "as between solicitor and client," is extended to the costs of all; and a privilege of a like character is conferred on the plaintiff in a creditor's suit, if the estate to be administered prove insolvent; for in this case the creditors, whom he represents, are entitled to the whole fund. But if there be any surplus, so that other persons become interested, he can claim only his costs, as between party and party.(e)

In suits under the litigious jurisdiction of the Court, the general principle is that the costs shall follow the result.

(d) 2 Smith, Ch. P. 461.   (e) Stanton v. Hatfield, 1 Keen 358.

[1] See, on this subject, Hill on Trustees 856, et seq., and notes, 4th Am. ed. ; McKim v. Handy, 4 Md. Ch. 228.

In the particular case of a bill against a vendor for specific performance, and a subsequent dismissal through his want of title, a doubt has existed whether, notwith-

[*392] standing *such dismissal, he may not be charged with costs. But the rule seems to be established that the bill in such case will be dismissed without costs ; and in all other cases the rule is so far strictly adhered to that a successful party never pays costs. (*f*) If a decree for specific performance is obtained by a vendor, who has not shown a good title before the suit commenced but who has made out a title afterwards, he will be liable for all the costs incurred previously to the making out of such title

With respect, however, to the right of the successful party to receive costs, the practice is less uniform, and decrees are frequently made, and bills dismissed without costs, on the ground that the failing party has been misled by his adversary's conduct, or that the question in dispute was one of very doubtful character, or even in some instances merely in consideration of the hardship of his case. (*g*)

The propriety of making exceptions to the rule, on the ground of doubt or hardship, appears to be very questionable, because, however doubtful the title may be, or however reasonable the litigation, it is but fair that the party ultimately found entitled should be reimbursed the ex-

(*f*) 3 Sug. V. & P. 137 ; Westcott v. Culliford, 3 Hare 275 ; Malden v. Fyson, 9 Beav. 347. [See Brooks v. Byam, 2 Story 553.]

(*g*) Fenton v. Brown, 14 Ves. 144 ; Robinson v. Rosher, 1 N. C. C. 7 ; Cogan v. Stephens, Lewin on Trustees 730 ; 2 Dan. Ch. P. 1279.

---

¹ See Bradley v. Chase, 22 Maine 511; Pinnock v. Clough, 16 Verm. 500; Clark v. Reed, 11 Pick. 446 ; Hammersley v. Barker, 2 Paige 372 ; Pattison v. Hull, 9 Cowen 747 ; Jones v. Mason, 5 Rand. 577 ; Blakeney v. Ferguson, 14 Ark. 460 ; Tatham v. Lewis, 65 Penn. St. 65.

pense of defending his right.(*h*)   There is, however, no doubt that a limited discretion is exercised by the Court; but, subject to such discretion, the general rule is that the costs will follow the event, and more especially so if the plaintiff's claim be either made or resisted on the ground of fraud.(*i*)¹   If several claims or defences are set up, of which some only succeed, the costs˜ of suits may be apportioned accordingly, or, instead of such apportionment, each party may be left to the payment of his own.(*k*)²

*If a specific tender of the amount due be made before the commencement of the suit, or after its [*393] commencement of the amount and costs already incurred, a proof of such tender, and of its refusal by the plaintiff, will throw on him the burden of subsequent costs; and

(*h*) Millington *v.* Fox, 3 M. & C. 352.

(*i*) Scott *v.* Dunbar, 1 Moll. 442 ; Wright *v.* Howard, 1 S. & S. 190.

(*k*) 3 Dan. Ch. P. 40 ; 2 Smith 463 ; Strickland *v.* Strickland, 3 Beav. 242.

---

¹ As a general rule, the prevailing party is entitled to costs. This, however, is a matter to a certain extent within the discretion of the court, though that discretion is limited by fixed rules : Nicoll *v.* Trustees, 1 Johns. Ch. 166 ; Eastburn *v.* Kirk, 2 Id. 317 ; Matter of Hemiup, 3 Paige 305; Woodson *v.* Palmer, 1 Bail. Eq. 95; Lee *v.* Pindle, 12 Gill & J. 288 ; Clark *v.* Reed, 11 Pick. 446 ; Tomlinson *v.* Ward, 2 Conn. 396 ; Stone *v.* Locke, 48 Maine 425 ; Brooks *v.* Byam, 2 Story 553 ; Gray *v.* Gray, 15 Ala. 779. Partial relief usually entitles the complainant to costs : Rough *v.* Marshall, 4 Bibb 567; Hightower *v.* Smith, 5 J. J. Marsh. 542. Where there has been an oppressive accumulation of costs, occasioned by the errors and imperfections of the complainant's proceedings, the court will relieve the defendants from their payment : Blakeney *v.* Ferguson, 14 Ark. 460.

² Though there is no rule that in every instance in which a defendant takes several grounds of defence, one feasible and successful, the rest doubtful or invalid, that circumstance ought to avail the plaintiff on the subject of costs ; yet, where, upon the evidence, the plaintiff's case fails absolutely and wholly as a case for equitable relief, but the defendant has in the suit endeavored to support claims without any just foundation, and vexatiously disputed the legal title of the plaintiff, the bill ought to be dismissed without costs : Clowes *v.* Beck, 2 De G., M. & G. 731.

48

even where no tender can in strictness be made, yet if a
defendant has offered terms which would have rendered
the suit unnecessary, the plaintiff, though in strictness
entitled to a decree, may be refused his costs.(*l*)

The manner of compelling obedience to a decree still
remains for consideration.(*m*)   The power of the Court
for this purpose, like that for compelling appearance or
answer, was originally confined to process of contempt.
If the order disobeyed was for appearance and answer,
disobedience was a contempt of the *subpœna*, if for performance of a decree, it was a contempt of another writ
also issued under the Great Seal, termed the writ of execution.   In either case, the process of contempt was by
the five successive steps of attachment, attachment with
proclamations, writ of rebellion, serjeant-at-arms, and
sequestration; or in the case of a privileged person, by
sequestrations *nisi* and absolute, and in that of a corporation by *distringas* and sequestration.   The only differences
were, that an attachment for non-performance of a decree
was not, like an attachment on *mesne* process, a bailable
writ;(*n*) that in the particular instance of a decree for delivering up an estate, the Court might effectuate its own
order by issuing a writ of assistance to the sheriff, commanding him to put the plaintiff in possession; and that
on a decree for payment of money, the receipts under a
sequestration, though intended as a means of punishment,
might indirectly operate as a performance.

We have already seen that by the present orders of the
Court the two steps of attachment with proclamations and
writ of rebellion are abolished, and the process of con-

(*l*) Millington *v.* Fox, 3 M. & C. 352; Kelly *v.* Hooper, 1 N. C. C. 197.
[See Rucker *v.* Howard, 2 Bibb 166.]

(*m*) 2 Dan. 1020.   (*n*) Id. 1326.

tempt *reduced to attachment, serjeant-at-arms, [*394] and sequestration.(o)

The same orders which effected this reduction have also abolished the writ of execution, and have substituted service of a copy of the decree. With this view, it is directed that every order or decree requiring an act to be done, shall state the time, or time after service, within which it is to be done; and that if a decree directing an act within a limited time be disobeyed after due service, · the party prosecuting it shall be entitled to an attachment, and on default after arrest to sequestration, or if the sheriff return "*non est inventus*" to an order at his option, for an immediate sequestration or a serjeant-at-arms, and if the decree is for delivering up possession, shall also be entitled to a writ of assistance. And it is further declared that the same process shall be available, although the person in favor of, or against whom the order is made, be not a party to the record.(p)

If the decree or order direct the payment of costs alone, it is enforced by a *subpœna* for costs and a non-bailable attachment. But if the payment of other moneys be also directed, the ordinary process will extend to the whole, and a *subpœna* is unnecessary. If payment be directed out of a fund or an estate, a *subpœna* does not lie, but a sufficient proportion will be ordered to be sold.(q)[1]

The inefficacy of the process of contempt for compel-

(o) Supra, Appearance; Answer.   (p) Aug. 1841, x., xiii., xv.
(q) 2 Dan. Ch. P. 1328.

---

[1] The costs of a suit instituted to obtain the opinion of the Court upon a specific devise of real estate, in which infants were interested, were directed to be raised by sale or mortgage of a sufficient part of the estate.: Mandeno v. Mandeno, 23 L. J. Ch. 511.

ling a perverse defendant to obey has been already commented on, as well as the remedies which have been provided in respect to appearance and answer. In respect to contempts by non-performance of a decree, remedies have been also provided; first, by 1 Wm. 4, c. 36, in regard to the execution of instruments, and the delivery up of documents; and, secondly, by 1 & 2 Vict. c. 110, in regard to the payment of sums of money.

[*395]   *By the fifteenth rule of 1 Wm. 4, c. 36, it is directed that when the execution of any instrument, or the making of any transfer or surrender is decreed, the Court shall have authority, on default by the defendant after committal, to direct a Master to execute, surrender, or transfer in his stead;(r) and by the sixteenth rule of the same act, it is directed that where a party is in contempt for non-production of documents, the sequestrators may seize such documents and dispose of them as the Court shall direct.

By the 1 & 2 Vict. c. 110, s. 18, it is directed that all decrees and orders of Courts of equity, by which any sum of money or costs shall be payable to any person, shall have the effect of judgments at law. And by sect 20 of the same act, and the General Orders of May, 1839, a party to whom payment of any sum of money or costs has been ordered may enforce it, not only indirectly by sequestration, but by direct writs of *fieri facias* or *elegit ;* and if it appears on a return of a *fieri facias* that the sheriff has seized, but not sold the goods, then by a further writ of *venditioni exponas.*(s)[1]

(r) 2 Dan. 1050.   (s) Ibid. 1020.

---

[1] It seems now settled, after some doubts, that an action may be maintained upon a decree in equity for the payment of a specific sum: Pennington v. Gibson, 16 How. U. S. 65. See Evans v. Tatem, 9 S. & R. 252.

Where none of these remedies can be adopted, as when the act ordered requires the personal agency of the defendant, the Court is remitted to the process of contempt, and can only enforce its decree by imprisonment and sequestration.[1]

By the eighty-third of the new Equity Rules in Pennsylvania, it is provided that final process for the execution of any decree may, if the decree be solely for the payment of money, be by a writ of execution in the form used in the same Court in suits at common law in actions of debt or assumpsit.

[1] By the 8th Rule in Equity of the United States Courts, it is provided that final process to execute a decree may, if the decree be solely for the payment of money, be by a writ of execution in the form used in the Circuit Court in suits at common law in actions of *assumpsit.* If the decree be for the performance of any specific act, as for example, for the execution of a conveyance of land, or the delivering up of deeds, or other documents, the decree shall, in all cases, prescribe the time within which the act shall be done, of which the defendant shall be bound without further service to take notice ; and upon affidavit filed in the Clerk's office, that the same has not been complied with within the prescribed time, the clerk shall issue a writ of attachment against the delinquent party, from which, if attached thereon, he shall not be discharged, unless upon full compliance with the decree, and the payment of all costs, or upon a special order of the Court, or of a judge thereof, upon motion and affidavit enlarging the time for the performance thereof. If the delinquent party cannot be found, a writ of sequestration is to issue against his estate. In Pennsylvania, see Rule lxxxiii.

[*396]   *CHAPTER VIII.

OF THE REHEARING AND APPEAL.

THE next subject for consideration, after the r
conclusion of a suit by decree is the jurisdiction fo
ration or reversal.(a)   And, it should be observec
the authority for this purpose is not confined as at]
the final judgment, but extends to interlocutory pr
ings in the cause.

The first step after judgment is, as we have see
giving out and settlement of the minutes.   If the m
do not correspond with the judgment, the requisite ,
tions are effected in the manner already pointed out.
in order that the judgment itself may be impeache
decree must no longer remain in minutes, but mus
been regularly drawn up, passed and entered, so
constitute a record, though not a conclusive one,
Court of Chancery.

After an entry and before enrolment, the decre
some sense still *in fieri*, and may be altered by a r
ing before the same jurisdiction, viz., either befo
judge who originally made it, or before the Lord
cellor as the head of the Court.   If it be reheard
the same judge, it may be again reheard by the
cellor.(b)   But after it has been reheard by the Ch

(a) 2 Dan. 1331.
(b) Brown v. Higgs, 8 Ves. 567.

lor, it cannot, without special cause shown, be again reheard.(c)

If the error complained of be a mere clerical slip, it
may *be rectified before enrolment on a common [*397]
petition, without the expense of a rehearing.(cc)
And if the order' itself has been made on motion, or on
ex parte petition irregularly presented, it is not the subject of rehearing, but may be discharged on an independent motion.(d)¹ In all other cases, a revisal or variation
before enrolment must be effected by a petition or re-
hearing.² So long as the decree is capable of rehearing
it is not capable of appeal; but as soon as enrolment
has taken place it becomes a conclusive decree in Chancery, and can only be altered by an appellate jurisdic-

(c) Moss v. Baldock, 1 Phill. 118.
(cc) 45th Order of 1828 ; 2 Smith Ch. P. 14 ; Whitehead v. North, Cr. &
P. 78.
(d) West v. Smith, 3 Beav. 306.

¹ Gardiner, J., Gracie v. Freeland, 1 Comstock 236.
² A rehearing is not a matter of right, but rests in the sound discretion
of the court: Daniel v. Mitchell, 1 Story 198 ; Hodges v. N. E. Screw Co.,
5 Rhode Island 9 ; Zinc Co. v. The Franklinite Co., 1 McCart. 309 ; Bru-
magim v. Chew, 4 Green 337. It is only allowed where some plain error.
omission or mistake, has been made, or where something material to the
decree is brought to the notice of the court which had been before overlooked : Jenkins v. Eldredge, 3 Story 299. It is not sufficient to show that
injustice has been done ; but it must appear that it occurred under circumstances authorizing the court to interfere ; that the petitioner has not been
guilty of laches ; and that the matter on which he relies could not have
been obtained by reasonable diligence at the former hearing : Walsh v.
Smyth, 3 Bland 9 ; see also, Burn v. Poaug, 3 Dessaus. 596 ; Wilcox v.
Wilkinson, Cam. & Nor. 528 (538) ; s. c. 1 Murph. 11 ; Townshend v.
Smith, 1 Beas. 350. A rehearing may be granted even after the lapse of
thirty years, for an obvious error in the decree, where a fund, which was
the subject or the original suit, has remained undistributed : Brandon v.
Brandon, 25 L. J. Ch. 896. See, further, post, note to page 399.

tion.(e)[1]   If, therefore, either party desire a rehearing, he should enter a *caveat* against enrolment, which will stay it for twenty-eight days, and give him an opportunity to apply for the purpose. But if he neglect this, and the enrolment takes place before an order to rehear has been served, it cannot afterwards be vacated except on special grounds of fraud, surprise, or irregularity.(f)

The appellate jurisdiction in equity is twofold; viz., 1. In the King, whose conscience is ill-administered, and who may issue a special commission *pro re natâ* to reconsider his Chancellor's decree;(g) and 2. In the House of Lords, on petition to them as the supreme judicature of the realm.

The latter of these courses, a petition to the Lords, has now altogether superseded the former; but in the latter part of the seventeenth century a vehement dispute respecting its validity arose between the Houses of Lords and Commons, and it was contended that the appellate jurisdiction in equity, like that on writs of error at common law, could only be exercised under a reference from the [*398] Crown, *and not on a mere petition to the Lords. The dispute on this point had been preceded by a similar one, arising out of a cause of Skinner v. The East India Company, as to the Lords' claim to an original jurisdiction, and the result of that contest, though in terms

---

(e) McDermott v. Kealy, 1 Phill. 267 ; Sheehy v. Muskerry, 7 Cl. & F. 1 ; Andrews v. Walton, 8 Id. 457.

(f) Hughes v. Garner, 2 Y. & C. 335 ; Sheehy v. Muskerrry, 7 Cl. & F. 22 ; Dearman v. Wych, 4 M. & C. 550.

(g) Hale's Jurisdiction of the House of Lords, Pref. xxxix., and p. 186.

---

[1] Ducker v. Belt, 3 Md. Ch. 13 ; Hitch v. Fenby, 4 Id. 190 ; Simpson v. Downs, 5 Rich. Eq. 421 ; Robinson v. Lewis, 2 Jones Eq. 25. See also Hurlburd v. Freelove, 3 Wisc. 537.

a compromise, has been practically an abandonment of the
claim.(*gg*)

The contest on the appellate jurisdiction arose in the
session of 1675, on three petitions of appeal in the causes
of Shirley *v.* Fagg, Stouton *v.* Onslow, and Crispe *v.* Dal-
mahoy. In each of these suits the respondent in the
appeal was a member of the House of Commons; and their
alleged privilege of not being summoned to attend the
Lords was in the onset the principal matter in dispute.
The contest speedily assumed a different aspect, and was
put by both Houses on the express issue, whether the
House of Lords was, as asserted by its members, the Assembly where the King is highest in the royal estate, and
where the last resort of judging on writs of error and
appeals in equity is fixed. It was for a time quieted by
a prorogation; but at the re-assembling of Parliament it
was resumed, and a resolution was passed by the Commons, "that whosoever shall solicit, plead, or prosecute
any appeal against any commoner from any Court of
equity before the House of Lords, shall be deemed and
taken a betrayer of the rights and liberties of the people
of England." The resolution, however, thus passed, was
their last effort of resistance. And at the meeting of Parliament, after the next prorogation in February, 1677, the
Commons appear to have tacitly abandoned the contest;
and although their previous resolution was not in terms
rescinded, the jurisdiction has been since exercised without dispute.(*h*) The jurisdiction is confined to appeals
in equity, and does not extend either to the administra-

(*gg*) Hargrave's Pref. to Hale's Jurisdiction, p. xcix.–cxxiv.
(*h*) Hale's Jurisdiction of Lords; Hargrave's Preface, cxxxv.–clxvii.,
Macqueen's Practice 70–92.

[*399] tive power in lunacy, or to *the jurisdictions conferred by statute, unless where such appeal is expressly given, or where the statutory jurisdiction is a mere
extention of a previous equity.(*i*)

There exists a marked distinction in principle between
rehearing and appeal in regard to the evidence which may
be used on each. On a rehearing which is strictly what
its name expresses, a second hearing before the original
jurisdiction, any evidence may be used, which might have
been used originally, whether it were in fact so used or
not.(*k*)[1] But on an appeal, which is a resort to a superior

(*i*) Bignold *v.* Springfield, 7 Cl. & F. 71.
(*k*) Wright *v.* Pilling, Prec. Cha. 496 ; Lovell *v.* Hicks, 2 Y. & C. 472 ;
Herring *v.* Clobery, Cr. & P. 251 ; Roberts *v.* Marchant, 1 Phill. 371.

---

[1] There are but two grounds upon which a petition for a rehearing will
be entertained: first, for error of law apparent on the face of the decree,
and any part of the record may be resorted to for the purpose of making
such error manifest ; second, for newly discovered testimony ; and this testimony must be important, and must materially vary the case made ; it
must not be cumulative as to the evidence which was before the Court upon
the trial ; and it must be such as the party petitioning for a rehearing was
not aware of before the trial, and could not by proper diligence and inquiry
have discovered: Hunt *v.* Smith, 3 Rich. Eq. 465 ; Thompson *v.* Edwards,
3 W. Va. 659 ; Hill *v.* Bowyer, 18 Gratt. (Va.) 364 ; Kemp *v.* Mitchell, 29
Ind. 163. Upon a rehearing no evidence can be gone into which was in
the case at the original hearing and capable of being then produced: Story,
J., in Jenkins *v.* Eldredge, 3 Story 299. But where evidence in the case
was omitted to be read at the original hearing, such, for example, as a
document, or where the proof of an exhibit in the original cause was
omitted, the Court will make an order allowing them to be read or proved,
saving just exceptions : Ibid.

Rehearings, when asked for on the ground of newly-discovered evidence,
are mainly governed by the same considerations that apply to cases where
leave is asked, after publication of testimony, and before the hearing, to
file a supplemental bill, to bring forward such new evidence ; or where,
after a decree, leave is asked to file a bill of review on like ground: Daniel
v. Mitchell, 1 Story 198. See, also, Baker *v.* Whiting, Id. 218.

Where a party has had it in his power to ascertain the importance of

jurisdiction to determine whether the Court below was right, no evidence can be tendered except that which is entered as read in the decree, or the rejection of which is a ground of appeal.$(l)^1$

(*l*) Eden *v.* Lord Bute, 1 B. P. C. 465.

testimony before the hearing of his case, and has neglected to do so, and to obtain the testimony, a rehearing will not be granted on the ground that the importance of the evidence had been ascertained after the decision, although the justice of the case might be promoted by it : Prevost *v.* Gratz, Peters C. C. 365 ; see, also, Cock *v.* Evans, 9 Yerg. 287 ; Cleland *v.* Gray, 1 Bibb 38 ; Bentley *v.* Phelps, 3 Wood. & M. 403.

If the court will at all grant a rehearing, where the newly-discovered evidence consists wholly of confessions made by the plaintiff since the decree, it will be only when the confessions are of the most full and direct character, and are proved by disinterested testimony, and not susceptible of different interpretations : Daniel *v.* Mitchell, ubi supra.

In Hinson *v.* Pickett, 2 Hill Ch. 351, it was held that a rehearing should not be granted in any case on the ground of after-discovered oral evidence. And a rehearing is never granted upon new evidence, which is merely cumulative to the litigated facts already in issue, or which is designed to contradict the witnesses examined by the adverse party : Walworth, Ch., Dunham *v.* Winans, 2 Paige 24 ; Baker *v.* Whiting, ubi supra. McDougald *v.* Dougherty, 39 Ala. 409 ; Nisbett *v.* Cautrell, 32 Ga. 294 ; Powell *v.* Batson, 4 W. Va. 610.

A rehearing, however, will sometimes be ordered on terms, though in strictness no rule of law has been violated, as where it appears that by the rejection of evidence offered, the party prevailing has obtained an unconscientious advantage : Simms *v.* Smith, 11 Ga. 195.

The Supreme Court of the United States will not allow a case, even a suit in equity, once argued before it and decided, though by an equally divided court, to be re-argued, unless one of the judges who concurred in the judgment, desires it ; in which case, the court will order a re-argument without waiting for the application of counsel: Brown *v.* Aspden, 14 How. U. S. 25. Nor will the court grant a rehearing where the case has been remitted to the court below : Peck *v.* Sanderson, 18 How. U. S. 42.

[1] An appeal from a final decree opens up the whole merits for investigation which were involved in or connected with the subject-matter of such decree: Teaff *v.* Hewitt, 1 Ohio St. N. S. 511. And so an appeal from a decree upon a cross-bill opens the whole case presented both by the original and cross-bill; though there be no appeal from the decree dismissing the original: Woodrum *v.* Kirkpatrick, 2 Swan 218.

None but parties to the decree are entitled to take an appeal: Mckim *v.*

The manner of obtaining a rehearing, or of making an appeal, is by petition stating the order or decree complained of, and the subsequent orders, if any have been made, and praying in the one case for a rehearing, in the other for a reversal or variation. (*m*)   The petition is signed by two counsel, who, in the ease of an appeal, must have been either counsel in the cause below, or must attend as counsel on the appeal; and must be accompanied by a certificate that in their opinion there is a reasonable cause for rehearing or appeal. (*n*)   It is not necessary, though sometimes convenient, that the petition should state the ground of objection. (*o*)[1]   But on an appeal to the Lords it is required, that besides the mere petition of appeal, each party should deliver a printed case, signed by counsel, (*p*) containing a narrative of facts, and a summary of the reasons on which he relies, and accompanied by an appendix of evidence.

[*400]   *In order to warrant a rehearing or appeal, it is sufficient that some litigated question has been decided, and that it is certified by counsel to be fit for reconsideration.   But it is essential that the decision be on a litigated point, and, therefore, a decree by consent is

(*m*) 50th Order or 1841; Macqueen 131.
(*n*) Wood *v.* Milner, 1 J. & W. 616.
(*o*) Giffard *v.* Hort, 1 Sch. & L. 398.
(*p*) 2 Dan. 1367.

Mason, 3 Md. Ch. 186.   And in general no appeal can be taken by a party, until all the questions in the cause, as to others as well as himself, are settled.   Where, however, the claims of the complainant against several defendants are several and distinct, and a separate decree is made as to one without interfering with the rest, the defendant thus affected may have an appeal, though the rest of the case may be undisposed of : Dougherty *v.* Walters, 1 Ohio St. N. S. 201.

[1] A petition for rehearing should state the grounds on which it is asked : Wiser *v.* Blachly, 2 Johns. Ch. 488.

excluded.(*q*)[1]   A decree made on default of appearance at the hearing, is also incapable of being appealed from or reheard, unless a special ground be shown for indulgence.(*r*)   And in cases where the bill has been taken *pro confesso*, the defendant, though he may obtain a rehearing, must waive any objection to the *pro confesso* order, and must submit to pay such costs as the Court shall direct.(*s*)   If the costs of suit are in the nature of relief, a miscarriage respecting them will be a sufficient ground of complaint; *e. g.*, where they are improperly given or refused, out of an estate or fund.   But the ordinary costs of suit are discretionary with the Court, and if the decision on the merits is admitted to be correct, the Court will not rehear it on a mere question of costs.(*t*)[2]   It is otherwise if, without going into the merits, it is apparent on the face of the decree that the order as to costs is at variance with a settled practice.(*u*)

With respect to costs of a rehearing or appeal, it is held, that whatever be its result, no costs can be given against the respondent, if he confines himself to supporting the original decree;(*v*) but that in the event of an affirmance or a trifling variation, they will generally be given to

(*q*) Wood *v.* Griffith, 1 Meriv. 35, 270; Woodmason *v.* Doyne, 10 Cl. & F. 22; 2 Dan. 1331.

(*r*) Booth *v.* Creswicke, Cr. & P. 361; 44th Order of August, 1841; Stubbs *v.* ——, 10 Ves. 30.

(*s*) 89th Order of 1845; 1 Dan. 480.

(*t*) 2 Dan. 1334.

(*u*) Attorney-General *v.* Butcher, 4 Russ. 181; Taylor *v.* Southgate, 4 M. & C. 203; Angell *v.* Davis, Id. 360; Chappell *v.* Purday, 2 Phill. 227; 2 Dan. 1334–5.

(*v*) 2 Dan. 1355.

---

[1] Coster *v.* Clarke, 3 Edw. Ch. 405.
[2] See Travis *v.* Waters, 1 Johns. Ch. 48; Eastburn *v.* Kirk, 2 Id. 317.

him.[1]   And in the ease of an appeal, which is a
beyond the ordinary procedure in a cause, they will
times be so given, though, on a rehearing belov
      *costs would have been given, or they would
[*401]
      been paid out of the estate.

The effect of a successful rehearing or appeal is
ously to render useless, either wholly or in part, an
ceedings under the original decree. It does, not, hov
follow that they will be saved during its pendency;
is presumed until reversal that the decree is right
if there are special grounds for requiring their s
distinct application must be made to the discretion
Court. If an order to stay them is made, it may
companied, in a case of rehearing, by an order to ad
the cause, or in the case of an appeal, by a requir
that a similar order be applied for in the House of Lorc

(w) Storey v. Lennox, 1 M. & C. 685; Corporation of Glouc
Wood, 3 Hare 150; 1 Ph. 493; Garcias v. Ricardo, Id. 498; D
Drake, 3 Hare 523 ; 2 Smith, C. P. 74.

---

[1] Costs on appeal are now regulated by statute in most of the
States. Where there are no special provisions on the subject, the
rule still appears to be to give the appellant no costs on the rev
the decree: Evertson v. Booth, 20 Johns. 499; Murray v. Blatch
Wend. 221 ; Burrows v. Miller, 3 Bibb 77; see The Margaret v. T
estoga, 2 Wall. Jr. 116; and to give the appellee his costs on affir
Mowatt v. Carow, 7 Paige 328; Boyd v. Brisban, 11 Wend. 529;
v. Thompson, 1 Litt. 310.

*CHAPTER IX. [*402]

OF THE CROSS-BILL; BILL OF REVIVOR, AND OF SUPPLEMENT;
AND OF THE BILL TO EXECUTE OR TO IMPEACH A DECREE.

In the observations which have been hitherto made on procedure in equity, three things have been assumed; viz., 1. That a decree on the plaintiff's bill will determine the litigation; 2. ·That the bill is properly framed at the outset for obtaining that decree; and 3. That the suit is conducted to its termination without interruption or defeat. It is obvious that these assumptions cannot always be correct; and it is therefore requisite, before quitting the subject, to consider the means of remedying any such imperfections as may occur.

The first class of imperfection is, where a decree on the plaintiff's bill will not determine the litigation.[1] This

---

[1] The Court sometimes, in its discretion, when it appears that the suit is insufficient to bring before the Court the rights of all the parties, and the matters necessary to a just determination of the cause, will at the hearing before publication, direct a cross-bill: Kent, Ch., in Field v. Schieffelin, 7 Johns. Ch. 250. But see, in general, Sterry v. Arden, 1 Id. 62; and White v. Buloid, 2 Paige 164, wherein the subject of cross-bills is discussed.

The ordinary course of the Court is not to stop the progress of a cause, unless a cross-bill is filed in due time: Eddleston v. Collins, 3 De G., M. & G. 1; 17 Jur. 331; per L. J. Turner. In England, as a general rule, a cross-bill must be filed before publication passed; but in Georgia it is held, that it must be filed before the pleadings are made up. Time for filing the cross-bill, however, may be enlarged on cause shown: Josey v. Rogers, 13 Ga. 478; Sterry v. Arden, 1 Johns. Ch. 62; Story Eq. Pl. § 395.

By the Rules in Eq. U. S., No. lxxii., it is provided that where a de-

imperfection may arise either from cross relief or discovery being required by the defendants, or from the existence of litigation between co-defendants.[1]   In either case
it is remedied by one or more cross-bills, filed by one or

---

fendant in equity files a cross-bill for discovery only against the plaintiff
in the original bill, the defendant in the original bill shall first answer
thereto, before the original plaintiff shall be compellable to answer the
cross-bill. The answer of the original plaintiff to such cross-bill may be
read and used by the party filing the cross-bill at the hearing, in the same
manner, and under the same restrictions as the answer praying relief may
now be read and used. A party filing a cross-bill must take steps to obtain an answer, make an issue and have a hearing, at the same time with
the original bill: Reed v. Kemp, 16 Ill. 445. An answer to a cross-bill is
substantially a replication to an original bill: Whyte v. Arthur, 2 Green
(N. J.) 521.

A cross-bill, formal in other respects, but which omits the prayer, that
it be allowed as such, and heard with the original bill is amendable; and
on application to the chancellor, in vacation, to dissolve an injunction obtained on the bill, should be regarded by him *pro hac vice*, as amended:
Nelson v. Dunn, 15 Ala. 501.

In Pennsylvania (Rule xli.) cross-bills for discovery only are abolished.

An original and a cross-bill make but one suit, and when the original is
dismissed, the dismissal carries with it the cross-bill: Elderkin v. Fitch, 2
Carter (Ind.) 90; Cockrell v. Warner, 14 Ark. 346; see also, Randolph's
Appeal, 66 Penn. St. 178. So when a question raised by a bill has been
adjudicated, it cannot be reheard upon cross-bill and answer: Barker v.
Belknap's Estate, 39 Verm. 168. And on the other hand, where a defendant files a cross-bill founded on matters clearly cognisable in equity, the
cross-bill will supply any defect in jurisdiction: Id. If the original bill
is without equity, or if it is inconsistent with the answer, the cross-bill
cannot be sustained: Dill v. Shanan, 25 Ala. 694. New parties cannot be
introduced by a cross-bill: Shields v. Barrow, 17 How. U. S. 130 *contra*,
in Illinois, Jones v. Smith, 14 Ill. 229.

In Arkansas, if a defendant denies in his answer the allegations of the
bill, and sets forth a complaint against the complainant, calls for an answer and prays for a decree, this is considered for all substantial purposes
as a cross-bill: Allen v. Allen, 14 Ark. 666.

See as to costs on a cross-bill dismissed on dismissal of original bill:
Derbyshire v. Home, 5 De G. & Sm. 702; affirmed 3 De G., M. & G. 80.

[1] See Talbot v. McGee, 4 Monr. 375; Anderson v. Ward, 6 Id. 419; Eddleston v. Collins, 17 Jur. 331; 3 De G., M. & G. 1.

more of the defendants against the plaintiff, and against such of their co-defendants, as the cross relief may affect.[1] If this has not been done and the difficulty appears at the hearing, the cause may be directed to stand over for the purpose. A cross-bill may also be filed to answer the purpose of a plea *puis darrein continuance*, where a new defence arises after answer; but not for the purpose of indirectly altering the answer itself.(*a*)[2] *The [*403] proper frame of a cross-bill is, that it should state the original bill and the proceedings thereon, and the rights of the party exhibiting the bill, which are necessary to be made the subject of cross litigation, on the ground on which he resists the claims of the plaintiff in the original bill, if that is the object of the new bill.[3] But

(*a*) 1 Dan. 565.

---

[1] Armstrong *v.* Pratt, 2 Wisc. 299.

[2] Miller *v.* Fenton, 11 Paige 18; Taylor *v.* Titus, 2 Edw. Ch. 135; White *v.* Bullock, 3 Id. 453; Graham *v.* Tankersley, 15 Ala. 634; Draper *v.* Gordon, 4 Sandf. Ch. 210; Andrews *v.* Hobson, 23 Ala. 219; Lambert *v.* Lambert, 52 Maine 544; Pearson *v.* Darrington, 32 Ala. 274.

[3] A cross-bill is a matter of defence. It cannot introduce new and dis tinct matter not embraced in the original suit, and, if it does so, no decree can be founded on those matters: Galatian *v.* Erwin, Hopk. 48; s. c. 8 Cowen 361; May *v.* Armstrong, 3 J. J. Marsh. 262; Daniel *v.* Morrison's Ex'rs., 6 Dana 186; Fletcher *v.* Wilson, 1 S. & M. Ch. 376; Draper *v.* Gordon, 4 Sandf. Ch. 210; Josey *v.* Rogers, 13 Ga. 478; Slason *v.* Wright, 14 Verm. 208; Rutland *v.* Paige, 24 Id. 181; Draper *v.* Gordon, 4 Sandf. Ch. 210; Cross *v.* De Valle, 1 Wall. S. C. 14; Hurd *v.* Case, 32 Ill. 45; Homer *v.* Hanks, 22 Ark. 572. But it seems that a cross-bill may set up additional facts not alleged in the original bill, where they constitute part of the same defence, relative to the same subject-matter. See Underhill *v.* Van Cortlandt, 2 Johns. Ch. 339, 355. So, though the allegations of a cross-bill must relate to the subject-matter, it is not restricted to the issues of the original bill: Nelson *v.* Dunn, 15 Ala. 501. Thus, where the plaintiff in the cross-bill seeks discovery in order to enable him to protect himself against discovery, or sets up any special matter by way of estoppel or in

49

a cross-bill being generally considered as a defence, or as
a proceeding to procure a complete determination of a
matter already in litigation in the Court, the plaintiff is
not, at least as against the plaintiff in the original bill,
obliged to show any ground of equity to support the jurisdiction of the Court.(b)[1]

The second class of imperfection arises where the bill
is framed improperly at the outset. This imperfection
ought regularly to be rectified by amendment; but if the
time for amendment has elapsed, it may be rectified by a
supplemental bill, or by a bill in the nature of supplement,
the character of which bills will be considered under the
head of imperfections of the third class.

(b) Mitf. 80–83; Farquharson v. Seton, 5 Russ. 45; Cottingham v. Lord
Shrewsbury, 3 Hare 627; Sanford v. Morrice, 11 Cl. & F. 667.

bar, it is not obnoxious to the objection of introducing new matter into the
suit: Josey v. Rogers, 13 Ga. 478.

A defendant, however, cannot file a cross-bill where his rights are fully
protected by his answer: Morgan v. Smith, 11 Ill. 194. A plaintiff in a
cross-bill is not allowed to contradict his answer to the original bill. If he
has made a mistake as to the facts in his answer, the only mode of correcting it is by application for leave to amend the answer, or file a supplemental one, and not by the exhibition of a cross-bill: Graham v. Tankersley,
15 Ala. 634; Jackson v. Grant, 3 Green (N. J.) 145.

It would seem that when a defendant is desirous of impeaching a deed
on which the complainant's case depends, he must file a cross-bill, and
cannot raïse the defence by answer: Eddleston v. Collins, 17 Jur. 331; 3
De G., M. & G. 1.

Evidence taken on the cross-bill, where it is properly brought, may be
used in the original suit; but where the cross-bill makes a new case, evidence therein cannot be used in the original suit: Draper v. Gordon, 4
Sandf. Ch. 210; Gray v. Haig, 21 L. J. Ch. 542.

[1] See Cartwright v. Clark, 4 Metcalf 104; Nelson v. Dunn, 15 Ala. 501;
Lambert v. Lambert, 52 Maine 544.

A decree upon a cross-bill, pending the original suit, is not a final decree,
from which an appeal can be taken, under the Act of Congress: Ayres v.
Carver, 17 How. 391. Demurrer will lie to a bill called a cross-bill, if it
is not really so: Moss v. Anglo Egyptian, &c., Co., L. R. 7 Chan. 108.

Imperfections of the third class are those which originate in an interruption or defect subsequent to the institution of the suit, and they are rectified, according to circumstances, by bill of revivor or in the nature of revivor, and by bill of supplement or in the nature of supplement. They occur where, by reason of some event subsequent to the institution of the suit, there is no person before the Court by or against whom it can, either in whole or in part, be prosecuted. They are technically called abatements, and are cured by a bill of revivor, or in the nature of revivor. The events which cause such abatements are, the death of any litigant whose interest or liability does not either determine on death or survive to some other litigant, and the marriage of a female plaintiff or co-plaintiff. Upon the marriage of a female defendant the suit does not abate, *but the husband must be named in the subsequent proceedings. [*404]

And if a female plaintiff marries, pending a suit, and afterwards, before revivor, her husband dies, a bill of revivor becomes unnecessary, her incapacity to prosecute the suit being removed; but the subsequent proceedings ought to be in the name, and with the description which she has acquired bv the marriage.$(c)^1$

(c) Mitf. 56–60.

---

¹ See on the subjects of Bills of Revivor, &c., Story Equity Pl., ? 354, et seq.; Boynton v. Boynton, 1 Foster 246. By the rules of the Courts of Equity of U. S., No. lvi., it is provided, that where a suit of equity shall become abated by the death of either party, the same may be revived by a bill of revivor, or in the nature of revivor, which bill may be filed at any time; and upon suggestion of the facts, a *subpœna* shall issue, requir_ ing proper representatives of the other party to show cause why the cause should not be revived; and if cause be not shown, it is thereupon revived, as of course, after a certain time has elapsed. It is also provided by Rule in Equity U. S., No. lvii., that it shall not be necessary, in a bill of revivor, to set forth any of the statements in the original suit, unless the special cir-

It will be observed, that in order to cause an abatement it is essential that the person dying be a litigant; and therefore, if he be not named a party to the suit, or if, being named, he die before appearance, the suit is not abated, but non-existent, and must be recommenced by original bill against his representative. (d)

It is also essential that his interest or liability be such as does not either determine by his death, or survive to another litigant. For if it determine on his death, there is no such abatement as can interrupt the suit against the remaining parties, although if he be the only plaintiff, or the only defendant, there will necessarily be an end o litigation. If it survive to another litigant, and the circumstances be such that no claim can be made by or against the representatives of the party dying, there is no abatement: e. g., if a bill is filed by or against trustees or executors, and one dies, not having possessed any of the property, or done any act relating to it which may be questioned in the suit; or if it be by or against husband and wife, in right of the wife, and the husband dies under circumstances which admit of no demand by or against

(d) Crowfoot v. Mander, 9 Sim. 396.

cumstances may require it. In Pennsylvania it is provided, by Rule liv., that whenever the circumstances are such as to require a bill of revivor, supplemental bill, or bill in the nature of either or both, or where additional or different parties are required to be joined, the same shall be made by way of amendment or addition to the original bill, and copies of such amendments or additions, being served on the parties to the original bill or their counsel on the record, shall entitle the plaintiff to proceed as on an original bill, after service. See, also, Foster v. Burem, 1 Heisk. (Tenn.) 783.

A bill of revivor cannot be properly brought upon a bill for discovery merely, after the answer is put in and discovery made; for the bill has answered its end: Horsburg v. Baker, 1 Peters' S. C. 236 ; Story Eq. Pl., § 371, &c.

his representatives; or again, if a bill be filed by several creditors, on behalf of themselves and all other creditors, and one of the co-plaintiffs die. For in all these cases the persons remaining before the Court either have in them the whole interest in the matter in litigation, or at least are competent to sustain the suit, and to call upon the Court for its decree. If indeed, upon the death of a husband *suing in his wife's right, the widow does [*405] not proceed in the cause, the bill is considered as abated, and she is not liable to the costs. But if she thinks proper to proceed, she may do so without revivor, for she alone has the whole interest, and therefore the whole advantage of the proceedings survives to her; so that if any judgment has been obtained, even for costs, she will be entitled to the benefit of it. But if she takes any step in the suit after her husband's death, she makes herself liable to the costs from the beginning.(e)   If the husband or wife be made defendants in respect of her inheritance, the husband's death, it seems, is an abatement of the suit, and makes a bill of revivor necessary against the wife, but if she be sued *in auter droit* a different rule appears to prevail.(f)   A decree on a bill of interpleader may terminate the suit as to the plaintiff, though the litigation may continue between the defendants by interpleader, and in that case, the cause may proceed without revivor, notwithstanding the plaintiff's death.(g)

The effect of an abatement is, that all proceedings in the suit are stayed to the extent of the abated interest, viz., on abatement by the death of a plaintiff or co-plain-

(e) Mitf. 59 ; [Story Eq. Pl., § 357, &c.]
(f) White on Supplt. 168 ; 1 Dan. Ch. P. 169 ; 2 Id. 1418.
(g) Mitf. 60.

tiff, they are stayed altogether; on the death of a defeu
ant they are stayed as to him.   And in order to set the
again in motion, the suit must be revived by order
decree.

For the purpose of obtaining such order or decree it
requisite that a new bill be filed, stating the proceedinɡ
in the suit, the abatement, and the transmission of tl
interest or liability, and praying that the suit and pr
ceedings may be revived.   If the transmission is by a
of law, viz., to the personal representative or the heir
a deceased party, or to the husband of a married plainti
the bill is termed a bill of revivor; and unless the defenɡ
ant shows cause against it by demurrer or plea, withi
[*406] a limited time, an *order to revive is made.(ℎ)
If the transmission is by act of the party, viz
to a devisee, an original bill in nature of a revivor mu
be filed, and a decree made at the hearing to revive th
suit.(i)[1]   The bill, however, though termed an origina
bill in respect of the want of privity between the origina
and new defendants, is framed like a bill of revivor, anɡ
will so far have the same effect, that if the validity of th
transmission be established, the same benefit may be haɡ
of the former proceedings.(k)

There was also anciently a practice, where a suit abateɡ
after decree signed and enrolled, to revive the decree bɡ
subpœna in the nature of a scire facias; but this practic
is now disused, and it is customary to revive, in all case
indiscriminately, by bill.(l)

(h) Pruen v. Lunn, 5 Russ. 3 ; Langley v. Fisher, 10 Sim. 349 ; Ordeɪ
of May, 1845, 61, 62; Mitf. 69, 76, 78.
(i) Folland v. Lamotte, 10 Sim. 486.
(k) Mitf. 71-97.   (l) Mitf. 69, 70.

---

[1] See Douglass v. Sherman, 2 Paige 358; Slack v. Walcott, 3 Mason 50ɡ
Story Eq. Pl., § 379 ; Ridgeley v. Bond, 18 Md. 433.

The liability to abatement, and the consequent right of revivor, are not limited to any particular stage of the suit.[1] The only requisite is, that there be some matter still in litigation, for the decision of which revivor is needed. And if the decree has been in all other respects performed, the mere non-payment of costs will not warrant a revivor, except where they have been decreed out of a fund, or where they have been taxed and certified before abatement, so as to constitute in equity a judgment debt.(m)[2]

The principle that there can be no revivor for costs, precludes any other person than the plaintiff or his representative from reviving before decree; for the plaintiff may at his pleasure, dismiss the bill with costs, and therefore a revivor by any other party would in effect be for costs alone. If the plaintiff neglect to revive, the defendant's remedy is to move that he may do so within a limited *time, or that the bill may be dismiss- [*407] ed.(n) It is otherwise after decree; for then all parties are equally entitled to its benefit; and on neglect by the plaintiffs, or those standing in their right, a defendant may revive.(o)[3]

The construction of a bill of revivor is similar in principle to that of an original bill. It states the filing of the original bill, and recapitulates so much of its statements as is requisite to show the right to revive.(p) But it

(m) Andrews v. Lockwood, 15 Sim. 153.
(n) 1 Smith C. P. 659 ; Lee v. Lee, 1 Hare 617 ; Orders of May, 1845, 63.
(o) Mitf. 79 ; Upjohn v. Upjohn, 4 Beav. 246.
(p) 49th Order of August, 1841 ; Griffith v. Ricketts, 3 Hare 476.

[1] See Peer v. Cookerow, 2 Beas. 136 ; 1 McCart. 361.
[2] See Travis v. Waters, 1 Johns. Ch. 85.
[3] Story Eq. Pl. § 372. As to revivor by one not a party, as in the case of an administration suit, see Williams v. Chard, 5 De G. & Sm. 9.

recapitulates it as the statement of the original bill.
not as matter of substantive averment; nor can s
statement be contravened by the defence further tha
done by the answers to the original bill.(q)   It then st.
the original prayer.of relief, the proceedings which h
taken place, and the event which has caused abatem
and prays that the suit may be revived.

In the case of a pure bill of revivor no answer is
quisite, but the revivor is ordered as of course, un
cause be shown by demurrer or plea.   If, therefore,
original bill has been answered, the prayer of proces
for a *subpœna* to revive, and not to answer; but if
abatement be before answer, it prays an answer to
original bill, and the *subpœna* is framed accordingly.
the case of revivor against the representatives of a p.
chargeable, an answer is generally asked as to as
But a bill praying such an answer, though generally ca
one of revivor alone, appears to be in strictness su
mental also, and if assets be not admitted, require
hearing and decree for account.

On an original bill in the nature of a revivor, a de
is as we have seen the object sought, and the *subp*
therefore requires an answer; and if the original bil
unanswered, it asks an answer to that also.

If a suit becomes abated, and the rights of the pa1
[*408]   *are affected by any event, other than that w
causes the abatement, *e. g.*, by a settlement,
not sufficient to file a mere bill of revivor, although
a bill might be adequate for merely continuing the
so as to enable the parties to prosecute it.   But the
ties must incorporate in their bill a supplemental s

(q) Devaynes v. Morris, 1 M. & C. 213 ; Langley v. Fisher, 10 Sim.
White 122.

ment of the additional matter; so that all the facts may be before the Court. The compound bill thus formed is termed a bill of revivor and supplement. And the rules relating to it, so far as its supplemental character is con-černed, are the same with those which will be presently considered under the head of pure supplemental bills.(r)

Defects in a suit subsequent to its institution may be caused, either in respect of parties by the transfer of a former interest, or the rise of a new one, or in respect of issues between the existing parties, by the occurrence of additional facts. And they are cured by a bill of supplement, or in the nature of supplement.[1]

Where a defect in respect of parties is caused by transfer of an interest already before the Court, the transferree may be joined in the suit by supplemental bill; but the necessity of so joining him depends on the character of the transfer.

If the transfer is by act of the party, e. g., on assign-

(r) Mitf. 70, 71 ; Bampton v. Birchall, 5 Beav. 330 ; 1 Ph. 568.

---

[1] See on this subject, Story Eq. Pl., ch. viii., § 333, et seq. A supplemental bill is a mere continuation of the original suit, by or against a party having or acquiring the interest of a former party, and forms, together with the original bill and the proceedings under it, but one record : Harrington v. Slade, 22 Barb. (N. Y.) 161. See also Wright v. Meek, 3 Iowa 472; O'Hara v. Shepherd, 3 Md. Ch. 306. It is provided by the Rules in Equity, U. S. Cts., No. lvii., that whenever any suit in equity shall become defective from any event happening after the filing of the bill (as, for example, by a change of interest in the parties), or for any other reason, a supplemental bill, or a bill in the nature of a supplemental bill, may be necessary to be filed in the cause, leave to file the same may be granted by any judge of the Court upon proper cause shown, and due notice to the other party, who must thereupon demur, plead, or answer thereto within a certain time limited.

It is also provided by Rules in Eq. U. S., No. lviii., that it shall not be necessary in such bill to set forth any of the statements of the original suit, unless special circumstances may require it.

ment or mortgage, the general principle is, that an al
ation *pendente lite* cannot affect the remaining litiga
And therefore, unless the alienation disable the p,
from performing the decree, *e. g.*, by conveyance
legal estate or endorsement of a negotiable securit
does not render the suit defective, nor the alienee a
cessary party.   But the alienee himself, if he clain
interest, may add himself to the cause by suppleme
bill, or may present a petition to be heard with the caus
If it is necessary to bring the alienee before the Co
[*409]   the object is effected by *a supplemental
stating the original bill and proceedings, and
subsequent transfer, and praying to have the same r
against him as was originally asked against his alie
In all cases, however, such an alienee, acquiring hi
terest *pendente lite*, is bound by the proceedings in
suit, and depositions taken after the assignment, and
fore he became a party, may be used against him, as t
might have been used against the party under whon
claims.(*t*)

If, on the other hand, the transfer be by act of law
on bankruptcy or insolvency, the rule as to aliena
pendente lite, does not apply; but the suit becomes d
tive for want of the assignees.(*u*)[1]   If, therefore,
bankrupt is a defendant, the plaintiff must either dis
his suit, and go in under the bankruptcy, or must add

(*s*) Eades *v.* Harris, 1 N. C. C. 230. But as to assignment by a
plaintiff, see Clunn *v.* Crofts, 12 Law J. Ch. 112; White on Suppl.
Booth *v.* Creswicke, 8 Sim. 352; [and see Sedgwick *v.* Cleveland, 7
287.]
(*t*) Mitf. 73, 74.
(*u*) Hitchens *v.* Congreve, 4 Sim. 420; Lee *v.* Lee, 1 Hare 621.

[1] See on these distinctions, Sedgwick *v.* Cleveland, 7 Paige 290, *acc*

assignees by supplemental bill, praying the same relief against them as might have been had against the bankrupt;(*v*) and if the relief originally asked were payment of money, he should further pray for liberty to prove against the estate.(*w*)   If the bankrupt were a party, not in respect of a liability, but in respect of an interest, the assignees must of course be joined; and if the plaintiff neglect to add them, they may themselves file a supplemental bill after notice to him of their intention.(*x*)   If the plaintiff be the party becoming bankrupt, he is placed under an incapacity (permanent or temporary as the case may be) of prosecuting the suit.   And unless his assignees file a supplemental bill, and so take proceedings to sustain the original suit, it would in strictness, after the usual time, be dismissed with costs, for want of prosecution.   But in cases where the bankrupt is the sole plaintiff, the modern practice is, to order that it be dismissed without costs, unless within a limited time a supplemental bill be filed.(*y*)

*The doctrine as to alienation by act of law is also applicable where the interest of a plaintiff [*410] suing *in auter droit* entirely determines by death or otherwise, and some other person becomes entitled in the same right; *e. g.*, where an executor or administrator becomes entitled upon the determination of an administration *durante minori ætate* or *pendente lite*, and in such cases the suit may be added to and continued by supplemental

(*v*) Monteith *v.* Taylor, 9 Ves. 615.

(*w*) Ex parte Thompson, 2 M. D. & D. 761 ; Thompson *v.* Derham, 1 Hare 358.

(*x*) Phillips *v.* Clark, 7 Sim. 231.

(*y*) Mitf. 66, 67 ; Lee *v.* Lee, 1 Hare 621 ; Kilminster *v.* Pratt, 1 Id. 632; Whitmore *v.* Oxborrow, 1 Coll. 91.

bill.(z)   The same rule was formerly applicable on
death of the assignees of a bankrupt or insolvent; b
is now enacted, that where such assignees are plai
no fresh bill shall be required, but the names of the
assignees shall be substituted in the subsequent pro
ings.(a)[1]

In the case also of a plaintiff suing as the repres
tive of a class, e. g., of creditors or legatees, a similar
ciple is applied after decree.   The plaintiff, until de
has the sole interest in the suit, and therefore on a
ment by his death, his personal representative can ⟨
revive.   But, after a decree, all the members of the
are interested, and therefore if an abatement then oc
and the personal representative declines to revive,
almost a matter of course to permit any other memb
the class to file a supplemental bill.(b)

When a defect in respect of parties is caused b
rise of a new interest, it cannot be remedied by a
plemental bill, but a bill must be filed in the nature
supplement, restating the case against the new party
praying an independent decree.   The reason of th
that the interest in respect of which he is introduc

(z) Mitf. 64.
(a) 6 Geo. 4, c. 16, s. 67 ; 7 Geo. 4, c. 57, s. 26 ; Bainbrigge v.
Younge 386 ; Man v. Ricketts, 7 Beav. 484.
(b) Houlditch v. Donegall, 1 S. & S. 491 ; Dixon v. Wyatt, 4 Mad
2 Dan. Ch. P. 1109.

[1] The propriety of the distinction as to the character of bill to l
in the case of the determination of the interest of the plaintiff su
auter droit, and of the determination of that of a plaintiff suing in h
right, which is in effect incorporated in the text, from Lord Rede
Equity Pleading, is doubted by Mr. Justice Story.   He considers 1
both cases the bill should be an original in the nature of a supple
bill, for it brings forward, in either case, new interests by new p.
Story Eq. Pl., § 340, in note.

not derived from any former litigant, and has not been previously represented in the suit, so that he cannot be bound by what has taken place, but is entitled to have the entire case proved anew, and an independent decree made. The instance most usually given of an interest of this class, is that of an ecclesiastical *person suc- [*411] ceeding to a benefice, of which the former holder was before the court. The interest which such a person holds ·is obviously independent of the prior holder; and therefore, if the claim is pursued against him, he must be added to the suit by a bill, which though in some sense supplementary, is in strictness original, and is called an original bill in nature of supplement. On such a bill a new defence may be made; the pleadings and deposi- tions cannot be used in the same manner as if filed or taken in the same cause; and the decree, if any has been made, is not otherwise of advantage, than as it may in- duce the Court to make a similar decrec.(c)

The rule, that an original bill in nature of supplement must re-open the litigation, is modified in the case of a remainder after an estate tail, where such remainder falls into possession pending the suit. We have already seen that the estate tail is held to represent the entire inherit- ance, and that, notwithstanding the general doctrine as to parties, the remainderman need not be before the Court until his estate falls into possession. When that event occurs, he must be added to the suit. The bill for this purpose is in strictness original, in the nature of supple- ment, because the remainderman makes title under no previous litigant. But in respect of the rule enabling the tenant in tail to represent the inheritance, it is so far

(c) Mitf. 73 ; Lloyd v. Johnes, 9 Ves. 54, 55 ; Attorney-General v. Fos- ter, 2 Hare 81 ; 13 Sim. 282.

treated as supplemental that the remainderman wil
bound by the previous proceedings, unless he can e
lish any special distinction between his own case anc
predecessors.(d)   A question of the like character
occur where a suit.has been commenced against a te
for life and the ultimate remainderman, and an inte
diate tenant in tail has been born pending the litiga
The bill for adding the tenant in tail as a party wil
[*412]   strictly original in the *nature of supplen
       ᱽ But it may be presumed that the Court, in
fering the suit to proceed in its previous form, im
that such tenant in tail, when brought before it, sha
bound by the previous proceedings.(e)

The frame of an original bill in nature of supplen
is similar to that of a supplemental bill; viz., it s
the original bill and proceedings, and the supplem
matter, and prays the same relief against the new de
ant, as if he had been originally a party to the
But it is subject to the distinction, that as the pro
ings in the original suit are not conclusive, an aven
that certain statements were made therein is not reg
and the facts should be again averred and put in i.
This may be done either by restating the whole ca.
its original form, and then stating that the original
was filed containing statements to that effect, or by
ing the contents of the original bill, as in an ordi
case of supplement, coupled with an averment of
correctness.(f)

Where a necessary party has been omitted at the
mencement of the suit, but the regular time for am

(d) Mitf. 63, 72; Lloyd v. Johnes, 9 Ves. 37.
(e) Giffard v. Hort, 1 Sch. & L. 408 ; Lloyd v. Johnes, 9 Ves. 59.
(f) Attorney-General v. Foster, 2 Hare 81 ; Lloyd v. Johnes, 9 V

ment has been allowed to pass, he may in like manner be added to the suit by a bill, generally termed supplemental, but which would, perhaps, be more accurately called original in the nature of supplement. (g)[1]

Where a defect in the issue between the existing parties is caused by the occurrence of new matter, it is remedied by a supplemental bill.

It should be observed, however, that in order to warrant its introduction, the new matter must be supplemental to the old.[2]   If, therefore, it is meant to show a new title in the plaintiff, it is inadmissible; *e. g.*, where a party having filed his bill as heir-at-law, afterwards, on his heirship being disproved, purchased a title from his devisee; for the *plaintiff must stand or fall by such title as he had when his bill was filed. (h)   If, again, [*413] it be merely new evidence of the original equity, it does not appear necessary to have a supplemental bill.   But it seems that the proper course would be to move specifically for leave to examine witnesses on the new matter

(g) Mitf. 61; Jenkins *v.* Cross, 15 Sim. 76; [see OHara *v.* Shepherd, 3 Md. Ch. 306.]

(h) Tonkin *v.* Lethbridge, Coop. 43; Barfield *v.* Kelly, 4 Russ. 355; Pritchard *v.* Draper, 1 R. & M. 191; Mutter *v.* Chauvel, 5 Russ. 42; Bampton *v.* Birchall, 5 Beav. 330; 1 Phill. 568; [see Wright *v.* Vernon, 1 Drewry 68.]

---

[1] So a complainant who has dismissed the bill against a defendant who had appeared, if other of the defendants object that he is a necessary party, is entitled to file a supplemental bill to bring him again before the court: Wellesley *v.* Wellesley, 17 Sim. 59.

[2] A new title, or new interest, may be set up by a supplemental bill, where the title relied upon in an original bill is sufficient to entitle the plaintiff to relief; but a confessedly bad title, thus relied upon, cannot be supported by a title subsequently acquired, which is sought to be introduced by way of supplement: Winn *v.* Albert, 2 Md. Ch. 42; Bank of Kentucky *v.* Schuylkill Bank, 1 Pars. Eq. 222.

and to have their depositions read at the hearing, (*i*) discovery is required, to file a supplemental bill for purpose alone. (*k*)

If the new matter be really supplemental, *i. e.*, if, ing the original equity untouched, it varies the for which relief must be given, or creates the necessit additional relief, the defect must be remedied by a su mental bill, stating the new matter, and praying the sequent relief; *e. g.*, where the original bill praye injunction against an action at law, but, in conseqt of the refusal of an interlocutory injunction, the pla at law recovered during the pendency of the suit. the evidence under such a bill must be confined t new matter; and if publication has passed in the ori cause, and witnesses are examined in the supplem suit as to matters previously in issue, their deposi cannot be read. (*l*)

If material facts, which existed when the suit b are discovered when the time for amendment is pa they may be introduced by supplemental bill, pro they corroborate the case already made;[1] but i object of introducing them is to vary that case, so produce two inconsistent statements, they are inadmi by way of supplement, and the plaintiff must obtain s leave to amend. (*m*)[2]

(*i*) Milner *v.* Harewood, 17 Ves. 148 ; Adams *v.* Dowding, 2 Mad
(*k*) Milner *v.* Harewood, 17 Ves. 148 ; Usborne *v.* Baker, 2 Madd.
(*l*) Pinkus *v.* Peters, 5 Beav. 253 ; Malcolm *v.* Scott, 3 Hare 39 ;
v. Bridges, 2 Beav. 239 ; Catton *v.* Carlisle, 5 Madd. 427 ; 2 Dan.
1490 ; Mitf. 326.
(*m*) Mitf. 55, 62 ; Colclough *v.* Evans, 4 Sim. 76 ; Crompton *v.* ˀ

[1] See Story Eq. Pl., ? 333 ; Barringer *v.* Burke, 21 Ala. 765 ; Gre
Valentine, 4 Edw. Ch. 282 ; Hope *v.* Brinckerhoff, Id. 348.
[2] But where the subject-matter and title remain the same, it is

*It has also been determined on an analogous [*414] principle, that where the defendant was an infant at the date of the original bill, so that no discovery could be obtained, the plaintiff might file a supplemental bill on his coming of age, requiring him to answer those interrogatories of the original bill, which were not originally answered by him.(n)

The frame of a supplemental bill, whether strictly so termed, or one which is original in the nature of supplement, is similar in principle to that of an original bill. It states the filing of the former bill, and recapitulates so much of its statement as is required to show the bearing of the supplemental matter; coupling with such recapitulation, if the bill be original in the nature of supplement, a substantive averment that the statement is correct.(o) It then states the original prayer for relief, the proceedings in the suit, and the supplemental matter; and concludes, if it be not for discovery alone, with the appropriate prayer for relief. With respect to the parties against whom process should be prayed, the principle which has been already stated in regard to original bills, applies equally to those of a supplemental kind, viz., that all persons must be parties who are interested in the relief sought. The plaintiffs in the original suit are in all cases so interested, and must be joined either as plaintiffs or as

well, Id. 628; Attorney-General v. Fishmongers' Company, 4 M. & C. 9; Walford v. Pemberton, 13 Sim. 442; Blackburn v. Staniland, 15 Id. 64.

(n) Waterford v. Knight, 9 Bligh N. S. 307; 3 Cl. & F. 270.

(o) 49th Order of May, 1841; Vigers v. Lord Audley, 9 Sim. 72; Griffith v. Ricketts, 3 Hare 476.

jection that a supplemental bill introduces matter which may vary the relief to which the complainant is entitled : Ramy v. Green, 18 Ala. 771; Bank of Kentucky v. Schuylkill Bank. 1 Pars. Eq. 222.

defendants.(*p*) But the defendants are not necessarily
in the same position, and the test with regard to them
appears to be, that if any supplemental matter is introduced, which may affect their interests, or if a new party
is introduced, with whom they may have rights to litigate,
and against whom, therefore they are entitled to state their
case on the record, they are necessary parties to the
[*415] supplemental suit; but they are not *necessary
parties, if the supplemental matter is immaterial
to them, or if the new party is added in respect of an interest in the plaintiff alone.(*q*)[1]

If the bill be not for discovery alone, the cause must

(*p*) Fallowes *v.* Williamson, 11 Ves. 306.

(*q*) Mitf. 75; Dyson *v.* Morris, 1 Hare 413; Jones *v.* Howells, 2 Id.
342; Holland *v.* Baker, 3 Id. 68.

---

[1] A supplemental suit grafts into the original suit the new parties brought
before the Court by the supplemental suit, and enables the Court to deal
with the parties to both records as if they were all parties to the same
record. A defendant to an original suit is not to be made a party to a supplemental suit, on the mere ground of right to question the representative
character of the defendant to the supplemental suit; for his character to
sustain that title cannot be tried in a Court of equity: Wilkinson *v.* Fowkes,
9 Hare 193.

The original defendants are necessary parties to a supplemental bill,
where the supplemental suit is occasioned by an alteration after the
original bill is filed, affecting the rights and interests of the original defendants as represented on the record; but they are not necessary parties
to a supplemental bill, where there may be a decree upon the supplemental
matter against the new defendants, unless the decree will affect the interests of the original defendants; nor are they necessary parties where
the supplemental bill is brought merely to introduce formal parties: Wilkinson *v.* Fowkes, 9 Hare 193.

When a supplemental bill brings new parties into Court, it is as to them
a new suit, and is to be considered as being commenced when the supplemental bill is filed in the office: Morgan *v.* Morgan, 10 Ga. 297.

A supplemental bill, however, is to be considered as part of the original
bill; and if, upon the whole record, the complainant is entitled to relief,
it will be decreed him: Cunningham *v.* Rogers, 14 Ala. 147.

be heard on the supplemental matter at the same time that it is heard on the original bill, and a decree must be taken in both suits, or if the cause has been already heard, it must be further heard on the supplemental matter, and a decree taken thereon.

If new matter occurs or is discovered after the decree it is not properly matter of supplement, but may be introduced into the cause, if necessary, by a bill expressly framed for the purpose, and called a bill to execute or to impeach a decree.

A bill to execute a decree is a bill assuming as its basis the principle of the decree, and seeking merely to carry it into effect.[1] For example, such a bill may be filed where an omission has been made in consequence of all the facts not being distintly on the record;(r) or where, owing to the neglect of parties to proceed under a decree, their rights have become embarrassed by subsequent events, and a new decree is necessary to ascertain them;(s) or where a decree has been made by an inferior Court of equity, the jurisdiction of which is not equal to enforce it.(t) And a bill of the same nature is sometimes exhibited by a person who was not a party, nor claims under a party, to the original decree, but claims in a similar interest, or is unable to obtain the determination of his own rights until the decree is carried into execution.(u)

(r) Hodson v. Ball, 1 Ph. 181.
(s) Mitf. 95. (t) Id. 96.
(u) Id. 95; 2 Dan. Ch. P. 1405; Oldham v. Ehoral, 1 Coop. Sel. Ca. 27.

[1] See on this subject, Story Eq. Pl., § 429. A supplemental bill may be filed as well after as before a decree ; and if after, may be either in aid of a decree, that it may be carried into full execution, or that proper directions may be given upon some matters omitted in the original bill, or not put in issue by it, on the defence made to it: O'Hara v. Shepherd, 3 Md. Ch. 306.

The distinguishing feature of a bill of this class is, that it must carry out the principle of the former decree. It must take that principle as its basis, and must seek [*416] merely to supply omissions in *the decree or proceedings, so as to enable the Court to give effect to its decision. If it goes beyond this, it is in truth a bill to impeach the decree, and is subject to the restrictions which will be hereafter considered as imposed on bills of that class.(v)   It appears, however, that although the plaintiff in such a bill cannot impeach the decree, yet the defendant is not under the same restriction. If the decree can be enforced by the ordinary process, it will be assumed, until reversal, to be correct   And even where a decree is required in aid, the same assumption will be generally made. But it is competent for the Court, in respect of the special application, to examine the decree, and if it be unjust, to refuse enforcement.(w)[1]

A bill to impeach a decree is either a bill of review, a supplemental bill in the nature of review, an original bill of the same nature, or an original bill on the ground of fraud. There is also another class of bills mentioned by Lord Redesdale, termed "bills to suspend or avoid the operation of decrees." They appear, however, to be adapted only to contingencies arising from public events; and as the instances of them which are to be found in the books, originated chiefly in the embarrassments occasioned

(v) Hodsón v. Ball, 11 Sim. 456; 1 Ph. 177; Toulmin v. Copland, 4 Hare 41; Davis v. Bluek, 6 Beav. 393; [O'Hara v. Shepherd, 3 Md. Ch. 306.]

(w) Mitf. 96 ; 2 Dan. Ch. P. 1407 ; Hamilton v. Houghton, Bligh O. S. 169.

[1] In certain cases a defendant has the right, after decree, to file a supplemental bill, to bring new and necessary parties before the court: Lee c. Lee, 17 Jur. 272 ; affirmed, 17 Jur. 607.

by the Great Rebellion, they are to be considered with much caution.(*x*)

A bill of review is used to procure the reversal of a decree after signature and enrolment. It may be brought upon error of law apparent on the decree, or on occurrence or discovery of new matter.[1] In the former case the bill may be filed without leave of the Court, but the error complained of must not be mere error in the decree, as on a mistaken judgement, which would in effect render a bill of review a mere substitute for an appeal, but it must be error apparent on the face of the decree, as in the case of an absolute *decree against an infant.(*y*) [*417] Errors in form only, though apparent on the face of the decree, and mere matters of abatement, seem not to have been considered sufficient ground for review.(*z*)

(*x*) Mitf. 74 ; 2 Dan. Ch. P. 1408.

(*y*) Mitf. 84 ; Perry *v.* Phelips, 17 Ves. 179 ; [Ross *v.* Prentiss, 4 McLean 106 ; Seguin *v.* Maverick, 24 Texas 534 ; Bartlett *v.* Fifield, 45 N. H. 81.]

(*z*) Mitf. 85 ; [Guerry *v.* Perryman, 12 Ga. 14 ; Dexter *v.* Arnold, 5 Mason 312.]

---

[1] See on this subject, Story Eq. Pl., ? 414; Riddle's Estate, 19 Penn. St. 433 ; Creed *v.* Lancaster Bank, 1 Ohio St. N. S. 1 ; Ducker *v.* Belt, 3 Md. Ch. 13 ; U. S. *v.* Samperyac, 1 Hempstead 118 ; Sloan *v.* Whiteman, 6 Ind. 434 ; Rush *v.* Madeira, 14 B. Monr. 212 ; Clapp *v.* Thaxton, 7 Gray 384 ; Thompson *v.* Goulding, 5 Allen 81.

In England it is held that the error in matter of law, for which a bill of review will lie, must be apparent on the face of the decree. In the United States in general, however, decrees are usually, and by the Rules in Equity in the United States Courts, No. lxxxvi., and in Pennsylvania, No. lxxviii., necessarily, drawn up without any statement of the facts upon which they are based, and without embodying even the substance of the bill, answer. and other proceedings. Under these circumstances, therefore, the rule is so far modified in this country, that upon the whole record, consisting of the bill, answer and other pleadings and decree, but not the evidence at large, a bill of review for error apparent may be founded : Whiting *v.* Bank of U. S., 13 Peters S. C. 6 ; Dexter *v.* Arnold, 5 Mason 311 ; Webb *v.* Pell, 3 Paige 368 ; Story Eq. Pl., ? 407 ; Riddle's Estate, 19 Penn. St. 433.

Where a bill of review is founded on the occurren͟c discovery of new matter, the leave of the Court mu͟s first obtained; and this will not be granted except o affidavit satisfying the Court that the new matter c not by reasonable diligence have been produced or by the applicant at the time when the decree was m and showing also that such new matter is relevant material, either as evidence of matter formerly in i͟s or as constituting a new issue, and is such as, if p ously before the Court, might probably have occasi a different decision.(*a*) If such a bill is filed wit͟ leave, it will be taken off the file, or the proceed stayed.(*b*)[1]

(*a*) Mitf. 84–87; Partridge *v.* Usborne, 5 Russ. 195; Hungate *v.* coyne, 2 Ph. 25; [Ross c. Prentiss, 4 McLean 106.]

(*b*) Hodson *v.* Ball, 11 Sim. 456; 1 Ph. 177; Toulmin *v.* Copla Hare 41; [Simpson *v.* Watts, 6 Rich. Eq. 364; Thomas *v.* Rawling Beav. 50; Winchester *v.* Winchester, 1 Head. 460.]

---

[1] See, on the subject of bills of review for newly discovered m Story Eq. Pl., § 412.

A bill of review for new facts or newly discovered facts, must aver such facts came to the knowledge of the complainant within nine m prior to the filing of his bill: Hitch *v.* Fenby, 4 Md. Ch. 190; Dex Arnold, 5 Mason 312; Ridgeway *v.* Toram, 2 Md. Ch. 303; Simps Watts, 6 Rich. Eq. 364; Stevens *v.* Dewey, 1 Williams (Verm.) 638. the parties to the original decree, or their representatives, must be pa͟ϯ Friley *v.* Hendricks, 27 Miss. 412.

So, such a bill cannot be maintained where the newly discovered dence, upon which the bill purports to be founded, goes to impeac͟l character of witnesses examined in the original suit. Nor can it be tained where the newly discovered evidence is merely cumulative, an lates to a collateral fact in the issue, not of itself, if admitted, b͟y means decisive or controlling; such as the question of adequacy of when the main question was, whether a deed was a deed of sale or a gage: Southard *v.* Russell, 16 How. U. S. 547. The new matter mu͟s be such as the party could not by the use of reasonable diligence known: Story Eq. Pl., § 414; Dexter *v.* Arnold, 5 Mass. 312; Livin *v.* Hubbs, 3 Johns. Ch. 124; Ridgeway *v.* Toram, 2 Md. Ch. 303.

A bill of review, on new matter discovered, has been permitted even after an affirmance of the decree in Parliament; but it may be doubted whether a bill of review on error apparent can be brought after such affirmance.[1] If a decree has been reversed on bill of review, another bill of review may be brought upon the decree of reversal. But when twenty years have elapsed from the time of pronouncing a decree, which has been signed and enrolled, a bill of review cannot be brought;[2] and after a demurrer to a bill of review has been allowed, a new bill of review on the same ground cannot be brought.(c)

It is a rule of the Court that the bringing of a bill of review shall not prevent the execution of the decree impeached, and that a party shall not be allowed, except under very *special circumstances, to file or prosecute such a bill, unless he performs at the proper time all that the decree commands.(d)[3]   [*418]

(c) Mitf. 88.   (d) Ibid ; Partridge v. Usborne, 5 Russ. 195.

[1] Where a case is decided by an Appellate Court, and a mandate is sent down to the Court below to carry out the decree, a bill of review will not lie in the Court below, to correct errors of law alleged on the face of the decree. Resort must be had to the Appellate Court: Southard v. Russell. 16 How. U. S. 547.

Nor will a bill of review be founded on newly discovered evidence, after the publication or decree below, where a decision has taken place on an appeal, unless the right is reserved in the decree of the Appellate Court, or permission be given on an application to that Court directly for the purpose: Southard v. Russell, ut supra.

[2] As to the time within which a bill of review must be brought, see U. S. v. Samperyac, 1 Hemp. 118; Conter v. Pratt, 9 Md. 67; Creath v. Smith, 20 Missouri 113.

[3] The objection that the general decree has not been obeyed or performed cannot be raised by a general demurrer to a bill of review, filed for the purpose of annulling or reversing it. The objection can go only to the propriety of filing the bill, and not to the equity of it when filed: Cochran v. Rison, 20 Ala. 463.

In Alabama, the chancellor has the power under the statute of that

In a bill of this nature it is necessary to state the former bill, and the proceedings thereon ; the decree and ,the point in which the party exhibiting the bill of review conceives himself aggrieved by it, and the ground of law or the new matter upon which he seeks to impeach it; and if the decree is impeached on the latter ground, it seems necessary to state in the bill the leave obtained to file it, and the fact that the new matter has been discovered since the decree was made.[1] It has been doubted whether this last statement is traversable after leave has been given to file the bill. The bill may pray simply that the decree may be reviewed and reversed in the point complained of, if it has not been carried into execution. If it has been carried into execution, the bill may also pray the further decree of the Court to put the party complaining of the former decree into the situation in which he would have been if that decree had not been executed. If the bill is brought to review the reversal of a former decree, it may pray that the original decree may stand. The bill may also, if the original suit has become abated, be at the same time a bill of revivor. A supple-

---

state to direct the decree on the original bill to be stayed in such manner as he may deem advisable; or he may allow the bill of review to be filed, and let the complainant proceed with the execution of the original decree: Cochran v Rison, ut supr.

[1] See Story's Eq. Pl., § 420.

It is not sufficient in a bill of review to refer to a record of the decree sought to be reviewed, as a paper on file in the Court, with a request that it may be made part of the bill. It must be fully set forth in the bill, or appended as an exhibit: Groce v. Field, 13 Ga. 24. All parties to the original decree must be made parties to the bill of review : Sturges v. Longworth, 1 Ohio St. N. S. 54 ; but see Bayse v. Beard, 12 B. Monr. 581.

Where a demurrer to a bill of review for error on matter of law is overruled, the decree is reversed, and the errors allowed : Guerry v. Perryman, 12 Ga. 14.

mental bill may also be added if any event has happened which requires it, and if any person not a party to the original suit becomes interested in the subject, he must be made a party to the bill of review by way of supplement. (e)

A supplemental bill, in the nature of review, is used to procure the reversal of a decree before enrolment, on the occurrence or discovery of new matter. The leave of the Court must be obtained for filing it, and the same affidavit is required for this purpose as is necessary to obtain leave for a bill of review.[1] The manner of procedure on such a bill *is to petition for a rehearing of the cause, and to have it heard at the same [*419] time on the new matter introduced. The bill itself in its frame resembles a bill of review, except that instead of praying that the former decree mav be reviewed and reversed, it prays that the cause may be heard with respect to the new matter, at the same time that it is reheard upon the original bill, and that the plaintiff may have such relief as the nature of the case made by the supplemental bill requires. (f) If the ground of complaint be error apparent, it may be corrected on a rehearing alone, and a supplemental bill is unnecessary.

An original bill, in nature of review, is applicable when the interest of the party seeking a reversal was not before the Court when the decree was made.[2] Thus, if a decree

(e) Mitf. 88–90.
(f) Perry v. Phelips, 17 Ves. 178 ; Mitf. 90, 91.

[1] O'Hara v. Shepherd, 3 Md. Ch. 306 ; Ridgeway v. Toram, 2 Id. 303 ; Cochran v. Rison, 20 Ala. 463.

[2] A person not a party to the suit, and aggrieved by a decree made in his absence, and afterwards served on him, so as to attempt to bind him in subsequent proceedings, must move, on notice, for leave to file a bill in the nature of a bill of review : Kidd v. Cheyne, 18 Jur. 348.

is made against a tenant for life, a remainderman in 1
or in fee, cannot defeat the proceedings, except by a
showing the error in the decree, the incompetency in
tenant for life to sustain the suit, and the accrual of
own interest, and thereupon praying that the proceedi
in the original cause may be reviewed, and that for t
purpose the other party may appear to and answer
new bill, and the rights of the parties may be prop
ascertained.   A bill of this nature, as it does not seel
alter a decree made against this plaintiff himself, or aga
any person under whom he claims, may be filed with
the leave of the Court.(*g*)

A bill to impeach a decree for fraud used in obtain
it sufficiently explains its own character.[1]   It may be f
without the leave of the Court, because the alleged fr.
is the principal point in issue, and must be established
proof before the propriety of the decree can be inve
gated.   And where a decree has been so obtained,
Court will restore the parties to their former situat
whatever their rights may be.   Besides cases of di
fraud in obtaining a decree, it seems to have been con
[*420]   ered that where a *decree has been made agai
a trustee, without discovering the trust, or bri
ing the *cestui que trust* before the Court, or against a
mer owner of property without discovering a subsequ
conveyance or encumbrance, or in favor of or against
heir, without discovering a devise of the subject-ma
of the suit, the concealment of the trust, of the sul
quent conveyance or encumbrance, or of the will, ou

(*g*) Mitf. 92.

---

[1] See Story Eq. Pl., ? 426; Guerry *v.* Durham, 11 Ga. 9; De Lou
Meek, 2 Greene (Ia.) 55; Hitch *v.* Fenby, 4 Md. Ch. 190; Person *v.* Ne
32 Miss. 180.

to be treated as a fraud. It has been also said, that where an improper decree has been made against an infant, without actual fraud, it ought to be impeached by original bill. When a decree has been made by consent, and the consent has been fraudulently obtained, the party grieved can only be relieved by original bill.

A bill to set aside a decree for fraud must state the decree and the proceedings which led to it, with the circumstances of fraud on which it is impeached. The prayer must necessarily be varied according to the nature of the fraud used, and the extent of its operation in obtaining an improper decree.$(h)^1$

(h) Mitf. 93, 94.

---

[1] Where a demurrer to a bill to set aside a decree which has been obtained by fraud, is overruled, this does not vacate or reverse the original decree, but the complainant must proceed to establish his case : Guerry v. Perryman, 12 Ga. 14.

INDEX.

THE PAGES REFERRED TO ARE THOSE BETWEEN BRACKETS [   ].

800 INDEX.

ASSETS—*continued.*
getting in of, 250, 251, 252
of partnership, administration of, 240, 241
interest in, 241, 242
testamentary, administration of, 248–266
answer to bill of revivor as to, 407

ASSIGNEES,
in bankruptcy, 142
grants void against, 145
suit defective for want of, 409
plaintiff, death of, 410
See *Bankrupt; Bankruptcy; Chose in Action.*

ASSIGNMENT,
of chose in action, 53, 54, 80, 142, 148
of coyyright, 215
of debt, 53, 54
of dower, 233, 234
suits for, costs of, 390
of lease, 3
of possible and contingent interests, 54
of right, 53, 54
of trust or confidence, 28, 53
fraudulent, 151
injunction against, 144
See *Conveyance; Grant; Term; Elegit.*

ASSIGNOR,
of chose in action, 317

ASSISTANCE,
writ of, 393, 394

ASSUMPSIT,
action of, 224

ATTACHMENT,
writ of, 324, 394
with proclamations, 324
abolished, 328, 393
when sequestration substituted for, 326
in default of appearance, 328
of answer, 329
for non-performance of decree, 393
non-bailable for costs, 394

ATTAINDER,
of cestui que trust, effect of, 50
of trustee or mortgagee, 50

ATTENDANCE,
before Master, 382, 383

ATTENDANT. See *Terms.*

ATTESTING,
witness, evidence of, 249, 250, 373

ATTORNEY,
communication with, 6

BANKRUPTCY—*continued.*
fiat in, not notice, 157
conveyances &c. avoided by, 145, 148
assignees in, injunction to restrain, 198
petition in, 349
set-off in, 223
of partner, 241, 246
pendente lite, 409
suit, defective by, 409
BARGAIN,
set aside in equity, 186, 187
BENEFICE,
person succeeding to, bill against, 410, 411
BENEFIT,
obtained by influence, 184
See *Consideration ; Trustees.*
BEQUEST. See *Election ; Charitable.*
BIBLE,
right to printing of, 214
BILL,
generally, 301–311
statement in, 302, 303
charges in, 302, 303
interrogatories in, 302
prayer of relief, 302
process, 302
for administration, 257
of assets, evidence in, 362
of foreclosure, 113, 119
or sale, 120
of interpleader, 202–206
of peace, 199–201, 249
in cases of election, 95, 96
for discovery in aid of other proceedings, 20, 21, 22, 197
for establishing modus, 236
for redemption, dismissal of, 120
for account, writ of ne exeat regno on, 360
for specific performance, writ of ne exeat regno on, 360
founded on the solet, 238
to make infant ward of Court, 281
to perpetuate testimony, 23-25
to revive, 406
to execute a decree, 415, 416
to impeach decree, 415, 416
for fraud, 419, 420
to suspend or avoid operation of decree, 416
of review and revivor, 418
by way of supplement, 418
and information, 73, 74, 76
by one partner against another, 240, 241

51

ε

JURISDICTION—*continued.*
  of equity, after judgment at law,
    196, 197
  of court to decide questions whether
    of law or fact, 375
  of court, in cases of cross-bill, 403
  statutory, of court of chancery, 398,
    399
  appellate, in equity, 397–399
    House of Lords, contest of, with
      House of Commons as to, 397,
      398
  averment of, in bill, 306
  want of, demurrer for, 333
      plea of, 336
  persons out of, 322
  guardian resident beyond, 282
  ward taken out of, 282
  infant taken out of, 284
    See *Discovery; Fraud; Ne Exeat
      Regno.*
JURY,
  in matters of account, 224–226
  See *Issue.*
LAND,
  sale of, contract for, 83, 85
  cultivation of, 83
  converting. See *Waste.*
LANDLORD,
  equity of, on deposit of lease, 141, 142
LAPSE,
  by death of legatee, 276
  of time in case of breach of trust, 62
    how affecting charitable trust,
      68, 69
      no bar to relief in cases of
        fraud, 176
LAW,
  questions of, 9
  mistake as to, 188, 192
  mistaken, facts known, 189
  uncertainty as to, 189
  conclusions of, answer as to, 344
  deviation from rule of, 85
  See *Action; Case.*
LEADING INTERROGATORIES, 368
LEASE,
  by tenant for life, 3, 4
      in tail, 99
  contract for granting, 82
  under power, rent reserved in, 174
  renewal of, on request, 89
      by trustee for, 55
  renewal of, by trustee or executor,
    59, 60
  of infant or feme covert, renewal of,
    285
  belonging to lunatic, renewal of,
    295

LIEN,
what it signifies, 126
possession, foundation of, 126
when at an end, 128, 129
equitable, of vendor or purchaser,
122, 126–129, 152
by judgment, equity under, 149
See *Deposit.*
LIMITATION,
of personal estate, analogous to
strict settlement, 42
of account of mortgagee, 119
of title of mortgagor to redeem, 119
See *Statute of.*
LIQUIDATED DAMAGES,
fixed sums as, 108
LIS PENDENS,
privileged communications, 6, 7
notice by, 157
not notice of unregistered encumbrance, 154
to bind purchaser, 157
LITIGATION,
matters in, communications as to,
6, 7
See *Bill of Peace.*
LITURGIES,
right of printing, 214
LIVING,
presentation to, by mortgagor, 118,
120
See *Presentation.*
LOAN
by trustee to lend, 56
LORD
of parliament, a defendant, 311
See *House of Lords; Manor.*
LOSS,
compensation for, 91
of bond, excusing profert, 167
of bill or note, 168
indemnity in case of, 168
See *Affidavit.*
LUCID INTERVAL, 297
LUNACY,
effect of, 182, 183
partner, incapacitated by, 243
jurisdiction in, how exercised, 290,
398, 399
petition in, 349
LUNATIC,
who considered, 290
lucid interval of, 297
suit by, 301, 331
suit against, parties to, 313
without committee, answer by, 8
where contracting party becomes,
81
trustee being, 37, 38

52

THE END.

Lightning Source UK Ltd.
Milton Keynes UK
UKOW01f1658150917
309248UK00006B/966/P